Praise for the second edition:

'For those who think modern or contemporary dance is dead, this book opens a window of wonder, by revealing the intriguing and novel creations happening around the world. This book is the first of its kind to explore widespread contemporary dance diversity and its resulting rich global innovations. It is a must read for all those interested in contemporary dance.'

Constance Kreemer, President of the
Mel Wong Dance Foundation, Inc

FIFTY CONTEMPORARY CHOREOGRAPHERS

Fifty Contemporary Choreographers is a unique and authoritative guide to the lives and work of prominent living contemporary choreographers; this third edition includes many new names in the field of choreography.

Representing a wide range of dance genres and styles, each entry locates the individual in the context of contemporary dance and explores their impact. Those studied include:

Kyle Abraham	Germaine Acogny
William Forsythe	Marco Goeke
Akram Khan	Wayne McGregor
Crystal Pite	Frances Rings
Hofesh Shechter	Sasha Waltz

With an updated introduction by Deborah Jowitt and further reading and references throughout, this text is an invaluable resource for all students and critics of dance and all those interested in the ever-changing world and variety of contemporary choreography.

Jo Butterworth launched BA and MA dance degrees in the UK, the Netherlands and Malta. She wrote *Dance Studies: The Basics* (2012), co-edited two editions of *Contemporary Choreography: A Critical Reader* (2009, 2018), and was awarded the DSA Distinction in Dance Award in 2018.

Lorna Sanders has lectured within higher education in the UK and Europe. She edited the second edition of *Fifty Contemporary Choreographers* and leads the Diploma in Dance Teaching and Learning at Trinity Laban Conservatoire of Music and Dance, London.

ROUTLEDGE KEY GUIDES

Fifty Key Theatre Directors
Shomit Mitter and Maria Shevtsova

Fifty Key Contemporary Thinkers
John Lechte

Art History: The Key Concepts
Jonathan Harris

Fifty Contemporary Choreographers
Jo Butterworth and Lorna Sanders

https://www.routledge.com/Routledge-Key-Guides/book-series/RKG

FIFTY CONTEMPORARY CHOREOGRAPHERS

Third edition

Edited by
Jo Butterworth and Lorna Sanders
With an updated introduction by Deborah Jowitt

Routledge
Taylor & Francis Group

LONDON AND NEW YORK

Third edition published 2021
by Routledge
2 Park Square, Milton Park, Abingdon, Oxon, OX14 4RN

and by Routledge
52 Vanderbilt Avenue, New York, NY 10017

Routledge is an imprint of the Taylor & Francis Group, an informa business

© 2021 selection and editorial matter, Jo Butterworth and Lorna Sanders;
individual chapters, the contributors

The right of Jo Butterworth and Lorna Sanders to be identified as the authors of
the editorial material, and of the authors for their individual chapters, has been
asserted in accordance with sections 77 and 78 of the Copyright, Designs and
Patents Act 1988.

First edition published by Routledge 1999
Second edition published by Routledge 2010

British Library Cataloguing-in-Publication Data
A catalogue record for this book is available from the British Library

Library of Congress Cataloging-in-Publication Data
Names: Butterworth, Jo, editor. | Sanders, Lorna, editor.
Title: Fifty contemporary choreographers / edited by Jo Butterworth and
Lorna Sanders; with an updated introduction by Deborah Jowitt.
Description: Third edition. | Abingdon, Oxon; New York, NY: Routledge, 2020. |
Series: Routledge key guides | Includes bibliographical references.
Identifiers: LCCN 2020029977 (print) | LCCN 2020029978 (ebook) |
ISBN 9780367376765 (hardback) | ISBN 9780367376789 (paperback) |
ISBN 9780429355578 (ebook)
Subjects: LCSH: Choreographers–Biography. | Choreography. | Modern dance.
Classification: LCC GV1785.A1 F54 2021 (print) | LCC GV1785.A1 (ebook) |
DDC 792.8/20922 [B]–dc23
LC record available at https://lccn.loc.gov/2020029977
LC ebook record available at https://lccn.loc.gov/2020029978

ISBN: 978-0-367-37676-5 (hbk)
ISBN: 978-0-367-37678-9 (pbk)
ISBN: 978-0-429-35557-8 (ebk)

Typeset in Bembo
by Deanta Global Publishing Services, Chennai, India

CONTENTS

ALPHABETICAL LIST
OF CONTENTS

CONTRIBUTORS

Tammy Ballantyne is Research Associate at The Ar(t)chive, a pioneering resource project for contemporary dance, at Wits School of Arts, Johannesburg. Expertise lies in research, dance writing, editing, arts activism and teaching. Collaborations on several books, including consultant editor for Adrienne Sichel's ground-breaking *Body Politics: Fingerprinting South African Contemporary Dance*.

Bertha Bermúdez has danced with Emio Greco and Pieter C. Scholten for several years, also co-directing interdisciplinary research projects; including *(Capturing) Intention, Inside Movement Knowledge* and *Pre-choreographic Elements*.

Ramsay Burt is Director of the Dance, Drama and Performance Studies Research Institute, De Montfort University. Publications include *Ungoverning Dance* (2016) and *Dance, Modernism and Modernity* (2020) with Michael Huxley. In 2013–2014, with Christy Adair, funded research into British Dance and the African Diaspora culminated in *British Dance: Black Routes* (2016).

Shane Carroll is a former dancer with Nederlands Dans Theater and Sydney Dance Company. He has taught for many of Australia's leading dance companies. He works for Bangarra Dance Theatre, with a focus on education and professional development. A former Chair of the Dance Board, Australia Council for the Arts, in 2013 he received a Services to Dance Award, Australian Dance Awards.

Ya-Ping Chen is Associate Professor, Graduate Institute of Dance, Taipei National University of the Arts. She authored the Chinese monograph *Enquiry into Subjectivity: Modernity, History, Taiwan Contemporary Dance* (2011). Chair of the Graduate Institute of Dance at TNUA, 2015–2018, currently president of the Taiwan Dance Research Society.

Lou Cope is a dance and theatre dramaturge who has worked in the UK, Europe and the Middle East. As well as working with artists such as Gary Clarke, Jose Agudo, Hagit Yakira, Sidi Larbi Cherkaoui, and companies such as English National Ballet and Birmingham Royal Ballet, she dramaturges organisations, hosts podcasts, and is founder of CoAD – The Centre of Applied Dramaturgy (thecoad.org).

Michelle Elliott is Subject Leader for Dance at Bath Spa University, UK, with interests in creativity studies, cultural memory and the pedagogy of creative dance practices. In addition to a range of conference and research presentations, she has written for *Research in Dance Education*.

Anna Furse is Artistic Director of *Athletes of the Heart* and an award-winning director of over 50 international works. Active in the New Dance movement at X6, she co-founded Chisenhale. She directs the MA in Performance Making at Goldsmiths, University of London and co-directs the research hub, The Centre of the Body. *Performing Nerves: Four Plays, Four Essays, On Hysterias* was published in 2020 by Routledge.

Paul RW Jackson trained in music and dance and has worked in both professions internationally. He has written extensively on dance and music and is the biographer of Sir Robert Cohan, and Sir Malcolm Arnold. Until his retirement he was Reader in Choreography and Dance at the University of Winchester, UK.

Chris Jones has held prominent positions in the archives of Rambert, the Royal Opera House, and the National Resource Centre for Dance at the University of Surrey, UK.

Deborah Jowitt wrote for *The Village Voice* from 1967 to 2011 and publishes criticism at artsjournal.com. Her books include *The Dance in Mind*, *Time and the Dancing Image* and *Jerome Robbins: His Life, His Theater, His Dance*. She taught at New York University until 2016 and lectures worldwide.

Einav Katan-Schmid is an independent researcher, dance maker and dramaturge, based in Berlin and working in the intersection of dance practice, technology, philosophy and cultural criticism. She is the author of *Embodied Philosophy in Dance: Gaga and Ohad Naharin's Movement Research* (Palgrave Macmillan 2016).

Pavlos Kountouriotis is a performance artist, dramaturge and performance theoretician. Head of Master Theatre Practices, ArtEZ University of the Arts (Netherlands), postdoctoral research explored training techniques in the performing arts that induce altered states of consciousness. Has worked with seminal artists including: Trisha Brown, Ron Athey, Mårten Spångberg, Jonathan Burrows, Ann Liv Young, Boris Charmatz and Mehmet Sanders.

Scott deLahunta has worked on many documentation/ digitisation projects including with Emio Greco | PC, Wayne McGregor and William Forsythe. Currently Professor of Dance, at Coventry University, UK and co-directing (with Florian Jenett) Motion Bank, Hochschule Mainz University of Applied Sciences.

Cristina de Lucas is Associate Professor at the University of Valladolid and Tutor at Bird College, London. A specialist on Kenneth MacMillan and narrative ballet, she has received awards for her research, including the runner-up prize of *Dance Chronicle*'s 2020 Founding Editors' Awards. She is the treasurer of the Society for Dance Research, UK.

Josephine Leask has written for a range of mainstream press and dance publications but currently writes for *DanceTabs* and edits *Resolution Review* each year at The Place Theatre which profiles emerging writers writing alongside critics. She lectures on the BA dance degree at London Studio Centre and the MA programme at Rambert and Central.

Francesca Magnini is currently Professor of Digital Archives and Museums for Performing Arts at Rome's Sapienza University and is also Artistic Director of Balletto di Roma Company.

Laure Malécot created *African Resonance*, a weekly sociocultural radio magazine, in Paris, from 2004–2012. She directed the 2017 documentary film *Iya tundé, the Mother returned*, about Germaine Acogny (produced by Méditatik Senegal), and authored Acogny's biography *Dance the Humanity* (Vives Voix, Senegal). She works as a journalist, director and scriptwriter in Senegal.

Hamish McIntosh is a queer Pākehā artist and dramaturge. His research draws on queer theory to explore queer populations and meanings in dance. He is a SpringBoard and Twinning Board member of Dance and the Child International. Previously a guest writer and critic for *Dance Aotearoa* New Zealand, he currently teaches ballet at the University of Melbourne, Australia.

David Mead is editor of SeeingDance.com and writes for other publications including *Dancing Times, Dance International, Hong Kong Dance Journal* and *Taipei Times*. He has contributed to several books, most recently *Ballet: The Definitive Illustrated History*. With a particular interest in East Asian dance, he divides his time between the UK and Taiwan, where he has choreographed works for full-time vocational dance schools.

Melissa Melpignano is a Lecturer and Interim Dance Director in the Department of Theatre and Dance, The University of Texas at El Paso. Her writings appear in *Dance Research Journal, The Dancer-Citizen* and the forthcoming *Oxford Handbook on Jewishness and Dance*, among others. Melissa is also a performer, dramaturge, and curator.

Dara Milovanović is Assistant Professor of Dance and Head of the Department of Music and Dance, University of Nicosia. Publications include: 'Cabaret: A Study in Choreography of Fascism, Sexuality, and Politics', in *Perspectives on American Dance: The Twentieth Century*; 'Fosse/Verdon: Gwen Runs the Show!' *Peephole Journal*; 'Popular dance on screen as an archive: the case of Bob Fosse's recycled style', *Dance Research* (upcoming).

Lucy Moelwyn-Hughes trained at London Contemporary Dance School. She performed and taught for Tardis Dance Company, V-TOL Dance Company and CandoCo Dance Company. Currently, she co-produces Hofesh Shechter Company's extensive CPD programme and writes all the resources accompanying Hofesh's work.

Ann Nugent has disseminated about 70 articles, papers, talks and broadcasts, on William Forsythe's choreography. A senior lecturer at the University of Chichester, UK, she leads the MA Dance Research programme, while also working as a writer and critic. She was founding editor of Dance Now and editor of Dance Theatre Journal. Her first career was as a dancer with London Festival Ballet and Sweden's Gothenburg Ballet.

Elizabeth Old performed with Australian Dance Theatre, Siobhan Davies and Rambert, where she was also rehearsal director. As Associate Artistic Director of Australian Dance Theatre, she initiated a significant audience engagement programme and was instrumental in programming and curating platforms for new work. Currently she is a full-time lecturer at Queensland University of Technology.

Ruth Pethybridge is a Dance Artist and Senior Lecturer at Falmouth University, UK. A practitioner in Community Dance and a dramaturge, recently assisting choreographer Rosemary Lee. Recent publications: *Dancing through the hard stuff: Repetition, Resilience and Female Solidarity in the landscape – Rosemary Lee's Passage for Par* (2019); *From Direct Action to Being There: The Ambiguous Politics of Community Dance and the Occupy movement* (2020).

Lucía Piquero is currently Head of Dance Studies, University of Malta. She researches embodied cognition and the experience of emotion in dance. She has presented research and choreographic work internationally, including conferences, commissions, and residencies: ŻfinMalta, Spanish National Dance Company, Le Performance (France). She has also directed several choreographic practice-as-research projects.

Stacey Prickett is Reader in Dance Studies, University of Roehampton, UK, investigating relationships between dance, society and politics through historical and sociological perspectives. Publications include *Shifting Corporealities in Contemporary Performance: Danger, Im/mobility and Politics* (2018), and the *Routledge Companion to Dance Studies* (2020) as co-editor.

Antonio Ramírez directs STABIVO trans-scenic art company, dedicated to performing arts and the evolution of consciousness. He is the dramaturge of company Sharon Fridman and has taught workshops around creative processes, performance art, and the rite in the arts. He is a psychologist, in Oxigeme Process, coordinated by Doctor Manuel Almendro.

Leena Rouhiainen is Professor in Artistic Research at the Theatre Academy, University of the Arts, Helsinki. She is a dancer and choreographer. Publications include co-edited books, *Dancing Research: Approaches to and methods in dance research* (2014) with Hanna Järvinen, and a special issue of *Dance Articulated* entitled *Choreography Now*, with Tone Pernille Østern (forthcoming).

Shweta Saraswat is an independent dance scholar and cultural worker based in Los Angeles. She works for the Alliance for California Traditional

Arts, California's official state partner serving the folk and traditional arts field. Shweta is also a kathak dancer, choreographer, and teacher trained in the Lucknow gharana under Guru Rachana Upadhyay.

Sue Smith is an independent dance artist, an Associate Lecturer at Falmouth University and Director of Dance in Devon, UK. Sue is inspired by landscape, cross-disciplinary research and communities. She also works extensively in health and social care. A Clore Fellow (2016) and Rayne Fellow (2006), Sue was a founding member of CandoCo Dance Company and is on the Board of Directors of Gecko Theatre Company.

Christel Stalpaert is Full Professor Performing and Media Art Studies, Ghent University; director of the research centre S:PAM; and co-founder of the dance research network CoDa. Publications include: *The Choreopolitics of Alain Platel's les ballets C de la B* (with Guy Cools and Hildegard De Vuyst, 2020); and *Performance and Posthumanism,* (with Kristof van Baarle and Laura Karreman), upcoming in 2020.

David Steele FRSA, was Dean of the School of Dance, Hong Kong Academy for the Performing Arts. Previously: Vice Principal of London Contemporary Dance School, Director of Studies at the Centre National de Danse Contemporaine, France, and founding rector of The Danish National School for Contemporary Dance. Created a Chevalier dans l'Ordre des Arts et des Lettres (2008), for significant contribution to contemporary dance.

Sigrid Øvreås Svendal is a writer and historian with a doctorate in dance history and is currently the managing director for Dance Info Norway – the national resource centre for dance in Norway. She has contributed to several anthologies and also edited books: *Bevegelser – Norsk dansekunst i 20 år* (2016) and *Mer Bevegelse – nye tekster om dansekunst* (2019).

Angela Testa has worked as a director, assistant director, organiser, producer, public relations manager and journalist. Her recent activities include: the organisation, production and direction of dance events; and the management, editing and writing of the website and web-magazine *Dance&Culture*.

Lucille Toth is Assistant Professor of French at the Ohio State University, Newark. Trained in contemporary dance, her research interests lie at the intersection of dance, medical humanities, gender and migration studies. She is also a choreographer and currently the artistic director of On Border(hers), a dance project for and with female immigrants.

Steriani Tsintziloni lectures at the University of Athens; the Dance School of the Greek National Opera; and the Greek State School of Dance. Dance curator for Athens and Epidaurus Festival (2016–2019), co-curated events for the Duncan Research Dance Centre; Performance Studies International; and European Dancehouse Network. Articles appear in journals, including *Research in Dance Education* and *Journal of Greek Media and Culture*.

Lise Uytterhoeven is Director of Dance Studies at The Place, London. She is the author of *Sidi Larbi Cherkaoui: Dramaturgy and Engaged Spectatorship* (2019) and has published in *Contemporary Theatre Review*, *Research in Dance Education*, *The Bloomsbury Companion to Dance Studies* and *The Ethics of Art*. Lise is Chair of the Society for Dance Research and part of the Associate Board of *Dance Research*.

Katja Vaghi is a Swiss dancer, choreographer, dance researcher and somatic teacher. Her areas of interest are the relation between theories developed for language and dance, with attention to the role of embodiment in understanding, and humour in dance. She currently teaches at Die Etage in Berlin, and is guest lecturer at the Rambert School of Ballet and Contemporary Dance.

Annelies Van Assche studied the working and living conditions of contemporary dance artists in Brussels and Berlin, in her FWO-funded research on *Dancing Precarity*. Currently undertaking postdoctoral research on labour and aesthetics in contemporary dance in Europe's Eastern periphery, at Ghent University. *Labor and Aesthetics in European Contemporary Dance*, Palgrave Macmillan, is upcoming in 2020.

Graham Watts OBE is a freelance dance writer and critic. He has written the biography of Daria Klimentová (*The Agony and the Ecstasy*) and contributed a chapter about the work of Akram Khan to the *Oxford Dictionary of Contemporary Ballet*. He is Chairman of the Dance Section of The Critics' Circle and of the UK National Dance Awards and regularly lectures on dance writing and criticism at The Royal Academy of Dance and The Place.

Liesbeth Wildschut has lectured in dance history, theory and dramaturgy at Utrecht University since 1995. She is currently undertaking empirical research in collaboration with the Donders Institute for Brain, Cognition and Behaviour, Radboud University. She was Chair of the Dutch Society for Dance Research, co-editor of Danswetenschap in the Netherlands, and adviser for Fonds Podiumkunsten. She co-edited *Contemporary Choreography*.

Erin Whitcroft trained at The Royal Ballet school. A post-graduate at the University of Durham, UK, she was awarded the President's Prize (British Society for Eighteenth Century Studies). Currently Honorary Research Associate at the University of Exeter, freelance dance critic, and doctoral candidate at the University of Cambridge where she organises the Drama and Performance Seminar Series and creates works for dancers.

Libby Worth, Reader in Contemporary Performance, Royal Holloway, University of London, is a Feldenkrais and Halprin trained practitioner. Publications include articles and books on Mabel Todd, Feldenkrais, Anna Halprin, Ninette de Valois, rapper short sword dancing, *Time and Performer Training* (2017), and *Jasmin Vardimon's Dance Theatre: Movement, Memory and Metaphor* (2017). She co-edits the journal *Theatre, Dance and Performance Training*.

Mario Alberto Zambrano danced for Batsheva Dance Company, Hubbard Street Dance, Nederlands Dans Theater, and Ballett Frankfurt. Received the John C. Schupes Fellowship for Excellence in Fiction. *Loteria*, his first novel (Harper Collins, 2013), was a Barnes & Noble Discover Great New Writers pick. Currently, Program Director for Orsolina28's Kylián Summer Program and Associate Director of Dance, The Juilliard School, New York City.

EDITORS' NOTE

This book was commissioned as a contribution to the 'Fifty Contemporary . . .' series intended to provide, in handbook form, introductory guides to fifty practitioners or thinkers in various fields.

In setting out to determine the scope of a book on choreographers, it was decided that the notoriously fluid description 'contemporary' would, in this case, mean living choreographers whose work, spanning the decades from the late 1940s to the present, has often exemplified post-war trends in choreography. We therefore continue in this 3rd edition, in the 21st century, not to limit ourselves to a specific definition of the genre known as 'contemporary dance'. Contemporary choreography is no longer confined to theatrical contexts but is concerned with dancemaking in an ever-expanding and diverse field of applications. The boundaries between dance genres are increasingly blurred as choreographers from every continent and culture strive to find their own voice, as did their predecessors, but now they can be influenced in many ways: by the work of their peers, for example, through increased opportunities for international touring and a myriad of online sources which are available to them as never before. Dancers and artist-practitioners also learn a wide range of techniques and approaches in training and apply these in collaborative practice with other artists, whether in a small collective or an established ballet company. As experience and ability mature, their artistry develops and creative approaches multiply, so that the principles for making dance, and such questions as who should dance, and what dance might convey, are reconsidered and repurposed.

The choreographers chosen here are not intended to form a canonical or exclusive group. Rather, the forty new entrants have been selected from hundreds shortlisted, to demonstrate a wide range of dance phenomena from five continents across the globe that have developed in the decade since the 2nd edition. The emphasis here is on foregrounding choreographic practices that have not yet been widely documented or otherwise made accessible to dance studies students, giving insights into the range of individual processes at various stages of their careers. Identifying the emergence of new styles which are boundary breaking and hybrid, we have included experimentalists in ballet, tap, kathak, bharata natyam and flamenco and those areas where dance merges with other art forms, such as opera, drama, performance art, film, site specific and site sensitive approaches and installations.

Choreographers today reflect the society in which they live, their individual artistic beliefs and often their increasing interest in political issues. Some undertake dramatic, narrative or character-based approaches, others transfer the canon of classical works to an unconventional environment; some prefer extremely abstract concepts or highly technical challenges, or find other methods of stepping beyond previous choreographic boundaries applied to the creation of dance content and its forms. The careers discussed here also highlight the significant numbers of dancemakers involved in youth and/or community work in local or national contexts, and equally the internationalism of the life of professional choreographers as they fly around the world making works for major companies.

Thus, in this third edition, while we acknowledge the recent concerns of dance studies with transnationalism, gender, hybridity and other provocations that challenge assumptions about previously accepted aesthetics, we also recognise that this dance is generated in a 21st century context, whilst still being grounded in footprints of traditional knowledge.

A NOTE ON THE ENTRIES

Each entry consists of four sections:

1 An essay on the choreographer's career by a commissioned contributor.
2 A biographical sketch, with essential details of birth, education and training, career, dance-company affiliations, and awards/ honours.
3 A list of choreographic works, as comprehensive as possible, by year of premiere. Choreographic collaborators, where relevant (and known), appear in the brackets after the titles. Where collaborators are identified in the essay, we have not always further included them in the list due to reasons of space. Any significant later version of a work is usually noted alongside the original

version: there are some exceptions here, usually involving a change of the work's title.

4   A list of Further Reading, subdivided into interviews, articles, and books. Items are listed in chronological order. We have generally not included the normal review columns from newspapers and dance periodicals, though where a review has been substantial enough to become a feature article, or where little other available written material exists, then we have retained it. For the most part we have confined ourselves to English-language material, except where the most substantial writing exists in other widely spoken languages. Where journals —usually quarterlies — designate issues by season (e.g. Winter 1988), we have preferred to list them thus; sometimes periodical series are inconsistent in this respect, and so some citations here include volume and issue numbers instead. Web addresses are not given in full, but the reference includes sufficient information to find the material when the site is accessed.

INTRODUCTION TO THE
THIRD EDITION

At least twice in the history of contemporary dance, renegade chore-ographers have rebelled against everything they have been taught, and pared dance back to a state of ardent simplicity. It was in the 1950s that Merce Cunningham, a former Graham dancer, began his controversial and thoroughly eye-opening reinvestigations of time, space, and com-positional procedures.

Redefining 'nature' has been a crucial mission in the development of contemporary dance. Cunningham's vision of nature followed the ideas of his colleague, the radical composer and theorist John Cage, who wrote in 1973, 'Art changes because changes in science give the artist a different understanding of nature'. Ideas from eastern philoso-phy and particle physics helped shape the aesthetic that Cunningham developed from the early 1950s. The apparent negation of causality in quantum mechanics, the fact that even our choices may be the result of chance or random selection – such theories found parallels in Cunningham's methods and in his vivid, disquieting stage pictures.

Viewing space as an open field, Cunningham upset the convention of central focus, a dominant feature of proscenium stage presenta-tions. His compositional strategies included such chance procedures as tossing coins on charts to determine path, sequence, personnel, even movement. His beautifully trained dancers never played roles onstage or appeared to influence one another enduringly. In keep-ing with the Zen Buddhist principles that he and Cage subscribed to, he allowed each element of a dance to reveal its own nature with a minimum of manipulation: music, décor, lighting, costumes, and choreography existed as separate strands coming together only at the final rehearsal. The process and formal practice of his dances is one of complexity and unpredictability. It made many people uncomfortable, but Cunningham possibly had more direct impact on contemporary dance-making in the latter half of the twentieth century than those of anyone else.

Certainly, his ideas, and more particularly Cage's, sparked the influential revolution of the 1960s in New York, most of which occurred under the auspices of Judson Dance Theater, a group of smart, irreverent choreographers. They wanted to understand the essence of dance, in the vastly altered political and social climate of their times.

Prominent members included Yvonne Rainer, Trisha Brown, Steve Paxton, David Gordon, Lucinda Childs, Elaine Summers, Robert Rauschenberg, Robert Morris, Deborah Hay, and Simone Forti, all included in *Terpsichore in Sneakers* by Sally Banes. In a preface to the second edition in 1987, Banes distinguished several strands, spanning three decades, of postmodernism in dance. But perhaps the term applies most neatly to choreographers of the 1980s and 1990s whose artistic strategies and interests are more in tune with postmodernism in art and architecture than were those of the Judson group and the independents who began to sprout around them (such as Meredith Monk, Kenneth King, and Twyla Tharp).

The radical dancers, composers, and painters of the 1960s have been compared to the Dadaists operating in Switzerland, Germany, and Paris around the time of World War I. True, some Judson performances echoed the witty and obstreperous playfulness of Dada performances, where, according to Tristan Tzara, the act of demanding 'the right to piss in different colors', and following it up with demonstrations, counted as a performance activity (Goldberg, 1979). However, neither the Judson dancers nor John Cage in his seminal composition courses at the New School for Social Research in New York were this nihilistic in their rowdiness. At a time when young people worldwide were questioning political and social establishments, these artists were querying the separation of the arts, the hierarchical arrangement of compositional elements, the elitism, and potential eradication of individuality inherent in much academic training. Further, if, according to Cage, any noise could be part of a musical composition, why couldn't any movement be considered dance?

Exploration of everyday movement, the use of untrained performers, dances structured like tasks or ingenious games, objects used literally, process as a possible element of performance, absence of narrative or emotion, avoidance of virtuosity and glamour to seduce an audience – these gave many dances of the 1960s a resolute purity. And the iconoclasm of the 1960s initiated another cycle of invention, development, imitation, and potential stagnation.

★★★

In American contemporary dance, the individual styles developed by such choreographers as Brown, Gordon, Tharp, Paxton, and Childs were seeded in part from ordinary behaviour, rough-and-tumble athletics, Asian martial arts forms, and the casual dislocations of rock and roll; they little resembled the dominant 'modern' dance. The loose, fumbly duets of Paxton's contact improvisation, Gordon's complicated word play, Childs's exacting rhythmic patterns of travelling steps, the liquid-bodies dancing, and brainy structures Brown built, Tharp's equally rigorous experiments with a style that, increasingly, drew on black vernacular dancing for its casual wit and complexity – however difficult these styles were to execute, they bred dancers focused on the business of doing, looking more spontaneous and more relaxed.

Following Cunningham's example, and perhaps Balanchine's too, many American choreographers of the 1970s tended to focus on movement and form, believing that these were in themselves expressive. However, radical choreographers elsewhere were not fighting to free dance of literary-dramatic trappings; they had other agendas. Butoh – a style and an artistic movement – developed in Japan during the 1960s as part of a reaction in all the arts against the rapid Westernisation of the post-war years. The impulse of the two men acknowledged as founders of butoh, Tatsumi Hijikata and Kazuo Ohno was transgressive and anti-conventional in expertise, but it took a darkly dramatic form. Like the work of radical contemporary Japanese writers, painters, and theatre directors, butoh emphasised poverty of means, bad taste, and extreme physical and spiritual states. It moved with excruciating slowness; it shattered all conventions, presenting the body with its imperfections magnified: toed in, club-footed, twitching, grimacing, knotted with tension. Images of violence, eroticism, and androgyny permeate the work, offset by irony and absurdity. The influence of butoh has extended not only to Saburo Teshigawara, but to non-Asian choreographers in Canada, the United States, and Europe.

The term *Tanztheater* is applied to the work of choreographers beside Pina Bausch, but it is she who made it world-famous. This renaissance of bold contemporary dance in the Germany of the 1970s shared with *Ausdruckstanz* its essentially dark nature and view of life as a struggle of adversarial forces. In Bausch's work, these forces were no longer located within the body as much as they were outside it; in her hours-long theatrical spectacles, performers persist in impossible or humiliating tasks, or battle one another. Involving singing, speech, and motion, her pieces are collages of small intense scenes which acquire a ritualistic fervour. With immense theatricality, they often present life as a no-win battle of the sexes in an inertly bourgeois world. Compared to the abstract images of society in struggle that the early modern dancers created, Bausch's society is without visible ideals or heroes.

★★★

Looking back over the last decades of the twentieth century, one can note the remarkably accelerated growth of innovative contemporary forms in countries such as Great Britain, France, Spain, Belgium, the Netherlands, and Canada. Martha Graham's formidable technique was already over 30 years old when Robin Howard founded the London School of Contemporary Dance (1966) and London Contemporary Dance Theatre (1967). Less than five years later, choreographers like Richard Alston were already attracted to a less emotion-laden aesthetic inspired by Cunningham. Mary Fulkerson and her fostering of release work and contact improvisation soon after its 'invention' by Steve Paxton also influenced Alston's company Strider, and the historian Stephanie Jordan (1992) saw the explosion of British 'fringe' dance beginning in the late 1970s as being triggered in part by the arrival on the scene of the first graduating class trained by Fulkerson at Dartington College of Arts in Devon. Choreographers like those associated with the X6 Collective (Fergus Early, Maedée Duprès, Jacky Lansley, Emilyn Claid, and Mary Prestidge) and those who presented work under X6's auspices (Laurie Booth, Rosemary Butcher, and others), were creating Britain's 'New Dance'.

An intriguing aspect of the postmodern scene has been the ways in which contemporary choreographers built on the radical experimental work of the 1960s, gradually reintroducing in new guises much of what was discarded. Virtuosity, once told to stay in the ballet world where it belonged, now often worked in ironic companionship with the unassuming, everyday look cultivated by dancers during the 1960s. Someone might slouch or saunter onto the stage, perhaps wearing street clothes, then offhandedly fling a leg towards the roof. The French choreographer Jérôme Bel included 'ordinary people' in his dances but presented them in frankly entertaining ways. Some choreographers, such as Belgium's Wim Vandekeybus, Britain's Lloyd Newson, Canada's Edouard Locke, or the United States's Elizabeth Streb (four highly dissimilar artists), began by reconstruing virtuosity as ordeal or as risk. Putting dancers in what looks like danger or working them to a point of visible exhaustion could induce a kinaesthetic response in spectators, different in quality but similar in effect to that caused by a ballet dancer's phenomenal leap.

During the early 1970s, the Grand Union – which included former Judson Dance Theater mavericks like David Gordon, Trisha Brown, and Steve Paxton – charmed (or alarmed) adventurous audiences with their wholly unplanned presentations. When spectators know that a performance is improvised, they're drawn into the process, aware that they're experiencing a heady kind of mind-body virtuosity involving on-the-spot decisions and instant responses. Nigel Charnock was proud to let theatregoers know that no two performances of his *Stupid Men* (2007) are alike. Berlin choreographer Felix Ruckert built on the notion of task or game structures developed in the 1960s; for instance, to create his 2005 *Messiah Game*, he devised, 'a syllabus of rules that allow for improvisation, spontaneity, and chance' (Guzzo Vacarino, 2007). Ruckert's structures also incorporated audience members into the performance, further heightening their perception of the unexpected. Some choreographers use improvisation more subtly – perhaps giving the performers a degree of freedom to choose in performance from among various composed phrases and movements or, like Susan Marshall, making it a vital part of the creative process. During the 1980s, Dana Reitz, who once likened her composition-improvisation strategies to those of jazz musicians ringing changes on a known melody (Jowitt, 1980), created solos so elegant and formally coherent that people were often unaware of the role that spontaneity played.

Contact improvisation, as Steve Paxton formulated it in the 1970s, was an 'art sport', a totally improvised duet form that featured exchanges of weight, with partners clambering over each other or levering one another off the floor. Because they so rarely use their hands to initiate moves, the action, although it can look erotic or competitive, never seems manipulative. Contact improvisation is still practised worldwide in its 'pure' form, but it also opened up new possibilities for generations of choreographers.

In the 1980s, a rekindled interest in emotion and narrative surfaced among choreographers who had been nurtured on the Cunningham aesthetic. Economic pressures, feelings of political helplessness, and the spread of AIDS may have had some influence in spawning themes of dependency, helplessness, anger. In response, a gritty physicality derived in part from contact improvisation became a metaphor for flawed human relationships and oppressive societies in countries as diverse as Canada, Croatia, and Venezuela. With the fall of communism, Eastern European countries hastened to nurture contemporary forms that had been disapproved of and suppressed by former regimes, and provocative works from South America challenged repressive ideologies. The lifts and supports are neither effortless nor attractive; they may be about a person who can hardly stand up trying to help another, about the terrible weight of a human body, about embraces that never quite work, about diving through the air and daring someone to catch you.

These contacts are not always tender. Postmodern dance and dance-theatre alike often feature a violence that is more unabashed and far less glamorous than its equivalent in classic modern dance. Thinking over the contemporary scene of the last decades, one garners images of fierce, unstopping energy (as in the work of Stephen Petronio), but also more obviously dramatic ones of boots stomping, of people hauling one another around in painful or humiliating ways, of ordeals as punishment. In Jean-Claude Gallotta's *Docteur Labus* (1988), created for his Grenoble-based Groupe Emile Dubois, a man raised a woman by sticking his fingers in her ears; another pulled his partner around by a hand jammed into her mouth.

Radical artists of the 1960s occasionally presented the nude body as a statement against both censorship and prudery. In the 1970s, a climate that fostered free love and a return to nature engendered poetic presentations of nakedness that could be equated with innocence. In the twenty-first century, stripping someone of clothes can suggest not only erotic possibilities, as in the male duet in John Jasperse's *Fort Blossom* (2000), but a stripping away of identity.

A sentence by Jasperse (undated) about *Fort Blossom* resonates with various enquiries into the body that have permeated scholarly discourse over the last two decades: 'In *Fort Blossom*, through a very personal look at the body (alternately medical, eroticised and/or aestheticised), the audience is invited to examine contemporary notions of how we experience the body as both owners and spectators'. While innovators of the 1960s and into the 1970s vaunted a natural human body over a trained and polished one, it is difficult to imagine any of them designing the movements for a quite spectacular dance on the effects of a muscular disease on the human body, as Wayne McGregor did in 2004 with *AtaXia*.

Many of the elements that characterise postmodernism in art and architecture also figure in contemporary dance forms. Eclecticism is no longer a pejorative term; choreographers feel free to borrow from ballet and street dance in the same work. Karole Armitage and Michael Clark mixed ballet-born vocabularies with pop imagery. Twyla Tharp built her phenomenal style by mingling the slouchy complexity and casual manners of jazz with ballet's linear precision.

Critics of postmodernism have deplored its addiction to making references to the past as purposeless nostalgia and pastiche, but in dance, such references often do point out ironic structural parallels, or disassemble the traditional so that new meanings may be squeezed out. One example is Pina Bausch's disconcertingly desolate and poignant update of Bluebeard (*Blaubart*, 1977). William Forsythe's *Impressing the Czar* (1988) deconstructed *fin-de-siècle* Russian art and social politics. In *Last Supper at Uncle Tom's Cabin/ The Promised Land* (1990), Bill T. Jones used fragments of text and action drawn from Harriet Beecher Stowe's anti-slavery novel (with a performer representing Stowe as reader and commentator) to enquire into religious faith and the often subtle nature of prejudice against black people, women, and homosexuals. Equally political, Matthew Bourne's all-male *Swan Lake* (1995) not only wreaked gender havoc on a nineteenth-century classic but aimed darts at monarchy's power plays in general and Britain's royal family in particular. David Gordon's *Dancing Henry V* (2004) interwove Shakespeare's words with movements and additional text to create an eloquent – though subtle and unfailingly witty – denunciation of leaders who take their nations into war claiming that God is on 'our' side.

The fascination with history takes many forms and includes revamping classics or the music associated with them. Bourne has made a career out of revisiting famous ballets, operas, and films. Angelin Preljocaj recast Shakespeare's plot as a battle between the military of an unspecified communist state and a crew of homeless rebels in *Roméo et Juliette* (2005). Javier De Frutos choreographed four works to *Le Sacre du Printemps*, Molissa Fenley danced the entire score as a solo ordeal in her 1988 *State of Darkness*, and Finnish choreographer Tero Saarinen used it to create a powerful private drama, *Hunt* (2002).

Explorations of history also extend to personal, racial, and cultural heritages. Meredith Monk's great music-theatre-dance work *Quarry* (1976) could be said to prefigure this trend. In recent years, a number of contemporary choreographers worldwide have been exploring their roots or expanding upon an inherited tradition. While Alvin Ailey built two of his most famous early pieces, *Revelations* (1960) and *Blues Suite* (1958), on African-American religious fervour and urban jazz, later generations of dance-makers investigating the black experience, like Jawole Willa Jo Zollar, David Rousseve, and Kyle Abraham have employed speaking and singing, as well as dance, to render more specific dramatic insights into cultural phenomena. In very different ways and to different degrees, Akram Khan and Shobana Jeyasingh in Britain and the late Chandralekha in India have built contemporary works on reinterpreted classical Indian techniques: kathak, bharata natyam, and kalaripayat respectively. In the United States, Rennie Harris used his expertise as a hip-hop artist to re-envision Shakespeare's *Romeo and Juliet* (as *Rome & Jewels*, 2000).

Postmodernist eclecticism fosters the incorporation or plundering of other forms – club dancing, hip-hop, burlesque, cinema, literature, closed-circuit television, digital manipulation – whether to enhance a work's visual texture as Philippe Decouflé has done with film, or to ignite ideas and visions by rubbing disparate 'texts' together. Choreographers such as Wim Vandekeybus became absorbed in the possibilities of cinema – not just to accompany dance, but as film-dance creations. Designers for Merce Cunningham and Trisha Brown utilised the process known as motion capture to create décor, and choreographers everywhere began to experiment with computer-generated imagery and techniques that juxtapose live dancers with virtual ones.

Postmodernism even embraces artists like Mark Morris, who in some ways might be considered a throwback to Balanchine because of his emphasis on music and musicality. Such practices as blending exalted feeling with down-to-earth manners, embracing culture via its music and social conventions, and downplaying or reversing traditional gender roles define Morris as undeniably contemporary. So do his references to past styles – the evocations of Balkan dance, early German modern dance, Greek friezes, scarf dancers, or down-and-dirty dancing are not simply quotations, but transformations.

Because of dance's ephemerality, styles of the past are continually being recycled in a more literal way too. Ballet choreographers have recreated late nineteenth-century Russia; Asian choreographers have paid homage to Martha Graham. In a larger sense, the 'contemporary' scene is as diverse as individual notions of contemporaneity and as subject to individual adventurousness. For Jirí Kylián, known for his lush movement style, to make a piece like *Last Touch* (2003), which suggests 'a silent Strindberg play performed at a butoh dancer's pace' (Jowitt, 2004), is as daring in its way as John Jasperse's *Prone* (2005), in which half the audience viewed the performance while lying on a gleaming installation of air mattresses.

As the twenty-first century advanced, politics and social issues began to tangle in often surreal choreographic ways; some dance-makers haven't shied away from thorny subjects. Jane Comfort pulled gender apart in her 1995 *S/he,* appearing as a gutsy male alongside a drag queen. In 2008, her *An American Rendition* juxtaposed reality shows like American Idol with the rendition of American terrorist suspects to be interrogated and tortured on foreign soil. The amount of repetition in Brian Brooks's 2006 *again again* doesn't ally him with the Minimalism of the 1970s; instead 'the sequences he choreographs are strenuous, redolent of effort and emotion, and he worries them like a dog with a bone, changing them in small, compelling ways' (Jowitt, 2006).

Contemporary choreographers often see it as their mission to challenge decades-old rules. Gideon Obarzanek's 2008 *I Like This* created the illusion that the three members of his Australia-based Chunky Moves were controlling the piece's plugs and wires, flashes of light and coloured gels – all of which appeared to illuminate and alter what the audience saw and heard. Ohad Naharin's 2006 *Telofaza* challenged the accepted boundary that exists between a proscenium stage and an audience. A performer's taped voice instructed us to copy the gestures she exhibited on a projected video and consider how they might make us feel. She got the spectators on their feet and dancing, while the performers emptied the stage.

At one point in Sasha Waltz's *Kreatur* (2018), the dancers occasionally unrolled and held up in front of themselves what appeared to be translucent window shades. Seen through one of these, a moving dancer might fluidly distort and multiply, gaining on occasion an additional head. A society perhaps out of touch with its own reality – Marco Goeke's 2018 *Walk the Demon*, required the members of Netherlands Dance Theater to use their faces to express feelings as they writhed and twisted their bodies and those of others.

The proliferation of media techniques applied to dance could reflect the dystopian nature of unsettled times worldwide. No live dancers were on view in chameckilerner's 2016 *Eskasizer*, titled after a vintage exercise machine. And those visiting a gallery never saw the faces of Roseane Chamecki and Andrea Lerner's four dancers (one in her twenties, one in her thirties, one in her forties, one in her fifties). Instead, their bodies, seen in close-up, filled the screen, creating skin-covered hills and valleys, hollows and crevices. No flesh-and-blood dancers inhabited *Tesseract Part I* (2017) by media artist Charles Atlas, Silas Riener, and Rashaun Mitchell (both members of Cunningham's last company). The audience at the Brooklyn Academy of Music, wearing 3-D viewing glasses, saw the dancers on a virtual stage projected onto the actual stage and defined by its proscenium arch.

Much of the presumed cutting-edge dance created in recent decades can be characterised by its frequent social, political, and historical concerns, its voracious strain of eclecticism, its interest in text and narrative, and its use of digital technology as an expressive force. These interests broadened and deepened dancing itself, but did not, as some feared, weaken movement invention. Although Andrea Miller's

2016 *Boat* was created in response to the Syrian Refugee Crisis, it showed how people related to others through movement and structure, and by the music that bolstered these. The following year, Pam Tanowitz, another American, created a stunning work, over an hour long, titled *New Work for Goldberg Variations*. Although some artists may simply be shaping their ideas in accord with current trends, others respond profoundly and directly to contemporary life.

To scholars and admirers of modern dance, its glory lies in its diversity. At the core of each style is the single artist's way of moving and feeling, fuelled by his or her vision of what dance means in the world and how the world reveals itself in dance. We should, perhaps, be grateful that modern dance did not become a powerful monolithic entity like ballet, that choreographers can remain utterly susceptible to the world around them, able to design the present, even sometimes the future, on moving bodies.

Deborah Jowitt

Bibliography

Banes, Sally, *Terpsichore in Sneakers (1980)*, 2nd edition with new preface, Middlebury, CT: Wesleyan University Press, 1987.

Cage, John, *Silence: Lectures and Writings*, Middletown, CT: Wesleyan University Press, 1973, p. 194.

Goldberg, RoseLee, *Performance: Live Art 1909 to the Present*, New York: Harry N. Abrams, 1979, p. 41.

Guzzo Vacarino, Elisa (ed.), *Body and Eros*, catalogue of the Festival Internationale di Danza Contemporanea, La Biennale di Venezia 2007. Venice: Marsilio Editori, 2007, p. 109.

Jasperse, John. www.johnjasperse.org/index.php?name=rep4 (undated).

Jordan, Stephanie, *Striding Out: Aspects of Contemporary and New Dance in Britain*, London: Dance Books, 1992, p. 61.

Jowitt, Deborah, 'Dana Reitz', *The Drama Review*, 24(4) (T88), December 1980, p. 36.

Jowitt, Deborah, *The Village Voice*, March 17–23, 2004, p. 75.

Jowitt, Deborah, *The Village Voice*, October 11–17, 2006.

Livet, Ann (ed.), *Contemporary Dance*, New York: Abbeville Press (in association with Fort Worth Art Museum, TX), 1978, p. 54.

FIFTY CONTEMPORARY CHOREOGRAPHERS

KYLE ABRAHAM

In multi-layered creations that come into being through collaborations with dancers, designers, and composers, performer/choreographer Kyle Abraham draws on diverse movement impulses. A body ripple is juxtaposed against a series of expansive leaps; a casual handshake or a hug contrast with taut limbs that cut through space in dynamic rhythmic patterns. Abraham interweaves ballet, modern/contemporary dance, and hip-hop with vernacular gestures to create what he described as a 'postmodern gumbo' (Abraham *et al.*, 2015/2016). His choreography is shaped by his personal history and experiences as an African-American gay man, concerns that intersect with the social and political zeitgeist, linking individual and communal histories with the present. Social justice, racial oppression, discrimination, and the search for belonging inspire many of his dances, although the negative is often balanced by the power of resilience, resistance, hope, and love. A vivid musicality encompasses Bach to Bernstein, Britten to Beyoncé, and Max Richter to Otis Redding. Many commissions from modern dance, contemporary dance, and ballet companies have led to international acclaim for Abraham and his company A.I.M.

Abraham grew up in a tight-knit middle-class family in Pittsburgh, Pennsylvania. His artistic foundations are rooted in classical music (piano and cello) and the visual arts, studying at the Creative and Performing Arts High School and the Civic Light Opera Academy. He was attracted to dance after seeing the Joffrey Ballet perform *Billboards* to music by Prince (1993). Performing in musicals in high school, his formal dance training began at the relatively late age of 17. Initially this was in José Limón technique, ballet, jazz, and tap, although late nights dancing in clubs and at raves added to a vast range of movement. Training in Martha Graham, Merce Cunningham, and release-based techniques occurred while a BFA student at the State University of New York. After graduating in 2000, Abraham toured for a year as a dancer with the Bill T. Jones/Arnie Zane Company, but realised choreography was more important to him than a performing career. He was drawn to how Jones reflected on his African-American gay identity, its connections to his choreography, and collaborative processes with the company's dancers (Abraham *et al.*, 2015/2016).

Breaks from a career in dance occurred when Abraham moved to London to explore singing, returning to Pittsburgh to work in the Andy Warhol Museum. Prioritising dance, he was awarded an MFA from the Tisch School of the Arts in 2006. Valuable performing experience was gained with the David Dorfman Company, among other small groups. A compelling solo set a high standard. In *Inventing Pookie Jenkins* (2006), Abraham was a 'bare-chested homeboy in drag – thanks to a white floor-length tulle tutu' which revealed 'a multiplicity of selves: macho man/gay man/hu-man within a tripartite dance vocabulary: ballet/modern/hip' (Straus, 2013). The creation of the mixed race A.I.M. dance company (formerly Abraham.In.Motion) in 2006 was followed by commissions from key institutions, such as The Kitchen in New York, and residencies at New York Live Arts, Jacob's Pillow, and the Joyce Theatre, whose resources helped him to develop choreographically and refine his creative processes. Attracting early critical acclaim, Abraham was selected as 1 of 25 to watch by *Dance Magazine* in 2009.

In addition to the freedom of energy and movement experienced from hip hop and dancing in raves, Abraham cites his mentor Neil Greenberg from whom he learned improvisational tools. A former Merce Cunningham dancer, Greenberg developed his own postmodern choreographic style and taught Abraham at NYU. Improvisation sessions, with dancers generating material which is recorded and reworked, fed into *The Radio Show* (2010). This brought his group choreography into line with his solos, which seamlessly combined virtuosic dance technique with multiple movement styles, including social dance and hip hop. Abraham began using a 'catch what you can' approach, in which he dances and the dancers try to replicate what they see, each focusing on different aspects of the phrase. The work was a tribute to the local black-owned radio station his family listened to when he was growing up. When WAMO FM and its partner AM radio station closed, the neighbourhood lost a source of communication which had helped to generate a sense of belonging and identity. The work also reflected on his father's inability to communicate because of Alzheimer's and aphasia. Abraham explored how to 'live in his essence as a performer' rather than imitate his father's physical actions (in Cotter, 2017). Smooth shifts between dance styles in solos, duets, and group sections emerged as structural devices that have shaped his style. *The Radio Show* received a Bessie Award and led to extensive tours which offered opportunities to engage with local communities, feeding back into Abraham's ethos.

Live: The Realest M.C. (2011) evoked the search for acceptance, updating the Pinocchio story in the pressure to conform, in this instance to heteronormative values and masculine gender representations. Abraham described the context as 'urban, Hip-Hop and gay' (2015/2016, p.13), connecting a freedom of the body from club dancing with the dynamic control and virtuosity of codified dance techniques. Moments of intimacy with a simple touch between dancers and the stillness of a long lunge contrast with luxurious arabesques and convulsive shaking, ending with Abraham standing next to a microphone, his back to the audience as a physical impulse ripples across his back. Sexuality and social dance were also foregrounded in *Ramp to Paradise* (2011), which drew on the history of the 1970s and 1980s gay club scene at the Paradise Garage in New York.

Pavement (2012) hurtled Abraham into international prominence, and its imagery remains a stark commentary on the theme of race relations and a testament to the power of stillness, gesture, and dance. Inspired by the twentieth anniversary of John Singleton's 1991 film *Boyz n the Hood* and writers on race such as W.E.B. Du Bois, Abraham questioned what had changed over time in the experience of being black in the USA. The creative period occurred when shootings of unarmed black people prompted the formation of the Black Lives Matter movement. The premiere of *Pavement* coincided with the controversial killing of Trayvon Martin. This young man's death is often associated with the dance, although Abraham began working on it in 2010. The dance's vignettes and shifting characterisations offer a commentary on race and power relationships within and outside a community. A stark urban setting is evoked by: the outline of a sports court on the floor; a neglected basketball hoop which becomes the screen for a video of a building being blown up; and Dan Scully's dramatic lighting, such as the floor divided by rectangles of blue light and the flashing red light of an emergency vehicle. Key moments among the seven dancers are an ominous 'hands-up' gesture and arms moving (or being moved) behind their backs as if being handcuffed. The accompaniment shifts from rap to classical music, opera to rhythm and blues, with snippets from the Singleton film soundtrack providing police sirens and gunfire. It evoked visceral responses: 'You feel the movements – sensuous, weighty – rippling out from deep in the dancers' bodies. Sudden steps flash out and subside. You don't think, "oh, a leap;" instead you watch an eruption' (Jowitt, 2019).

A residency at New York Live Arts (2012–2014) marked a prolific creative period, including the official premiere of *Pavement*. He was also supported by a prestigious MacArthur Foundation Fellowship in 2013. Civil rights struggles in the USA and abroad and Max Roach's 1960 jazz recording (*'We Insist!' Freedom Now Suite*) inspired a series of dances produced in a short space of time, shown across two evenings. The full-length work *The Watershed* (2014) paid tribute to anti-apartheid protesters in Soweto, South Africa, while Glenn Ligon's sets evoke moss-laden trees in the American South as the tension between black and white is played out in abstract passages and multiple tableaux. A triple bill included: *When the Wolves Came in* (2014), inspired by the 50th anniversary of the Civil Rights Act and 150 years since the Emancipation Proclamation (1863) which freed slaves in the USA; the trio *Hallowed* (2014), accompanied by Spirituals; and *The Gettin'*, which involved swing partnered steps that resonated with joy, set against threats of oppression with video and pictorial reminders of the power of apartheid. Commissions with strong social commentary for other companies generated further critical prestige. The trilogy *Untitled America* (2015–2016) for the Alvin Ailey American Dance Theater explored contemporary race relations and the impact of mass incarceration, integrating text from letters and interviews with people who were imprisoned and their families. Themes of loss, oppression, and discrimination remind us that the persecutions of the past remain dominant forces.

Dearest Home (2017), a series of solos and duets for A.I.M., is performed in silence although viewers can opt to listen to music through headsets. Highly personal, it was inspired by letters his father wrote to his mother when they were in college. Regarding the two sources of inspiration in the title, 'dearest' stems from the greeting in the letters, while 'home' reflects on his sense of feeling settled with his then-partner. Returning to themes of love and loss experienced during the creative process, Abraham spoke of how the dancers are required to 'be honest' and to 'be emotionally present', which enable the dance's resonance to extend beyond the originating impulses (in Cotter, 2017).

Collaborations have resulted in breath-taking moments of innovative virtuosity as well as intense, and at times, intimate gestural actions. For example, he exposes hidden aspects of the technical artistry of ballet. In 2013, Abraham choreographed and performed with Wendy Whelan in the duet *The Serpent and the Smoke* as part of her trilogy *Restless Creature*. Languid flowing arms and partnering work draw together the opposing strengths of classical ballet and street/contemporary dance. *Ash*, a solo created for African American ballerina Misty Copeland in 2019, broke from classical traditions as well. Solo passages within group dances, such as Taylor Stanley's opening moments in *The Runaway* (for New York City Ballet, 2018), remain memorable long after viewing. A ball of energy ripples through Stanley's body, awakening movement that travels beyond the extended limbs. Calm strength is exuded as he faces upstage, standing in plié, right leg in high extension, and torso tilted away from his centre. Stillness punctuates virtuosic fluidity, returning momentarily to a familiar crossed position, turned out leg resting on the floor in tendu. Musical juxtapositions challenge expectations, providing the soundscape for dancers to push the envelope in movement terms, with isolations from street dance and vogueing catwalk passages. Kayne West's startling hip hop rhymes and rhythms reverberate against the classical resonance of Nico Muhly's original score. Giles Deacon's black and white costumes transformed the silhouette of New York City Ballet dancers, accentuating the action or reshaping their bodies into otherworldly creatures.

Peppered between the group dances for A.I.M. and other companies are Abraham's solos, created for himself or other dancers, continuing collaborative processes involving music, design, and the visual and digital arts. *Ne Me Quitte Pas* (2012) responded to the photography of Carrie Mae Weems. Abraham's *Dance Response Videos* (2014) with Carrie Schneider are performed to songs by musicians such as James Blake and Kanye West. The solos and duets demonstrate Abraham's versatility and the artistry of his collaborators. For example, in *Show Pony* (2018), a shimmering unitard reveals the intricacies of the female body in action, and Scully's lighting enhances the dancer who moves through a sliver of blue or a golden-hued wash, her costume transformed by the shifts in colour. Abraham created *INDY* for himself in 2018 to music by Jerome Begin and designs by Abigail DeVille, whose black fringed costume adds to the sense of movement. Deacon, who dressed many of Abraham's earlier works, created a vibrant silky costume that evokes translucent butterfly wings for the solo *Cocoon* which premiered at the Joyce in 2019.

Another aspect is Abraham's ability to shift into popular culture forms, such as choreography for Beyoncé's photoshoot for US *Vogue* magazine in 2013. In 2014, he created and danced in a sensual duet for an advertising video for the fashion house Rag & Bone, directed by Wendy Morgan. *Only the Lonely* (2019), a commission for the iconic Paul Taylor Dance Company, attests to the breadth of Abraham's appeal and acclaim. In 2019, Abraham's appointment as Visiting Professor in Residence at the University of California, Los Angeles, marked the significance that teaching holds in his career. Underpinning his aesthetic is a vibrant theatricality, where movement, lighting, design, and costume humanise and individualise dancers, their collaborative efforts acknowledged in programme notes. Abraham puts technical brilliance on display, countered by gestural actions that are at times subtle and at other times glaring, evoking a gambit of emotions in the viewer that reflect back on personal and social histories that transcend their originating impetus.

Stacey Prickett

Biographical details

Born in Pittsburgh, Pennsylvania, 14 August 1977. **Studied** at Pittsburgh's Creative and Performing Arts High School and Civic Light Opera Academy; BFA, State University of New York, Purchase, 2000; MFA, Tisch School of Arts, New York, 2006. **Career:** performed with Bill T Jones/Arnie Zane Company, 2000; briefly with David Dorfman Company; The Kevin Wynn Collective; Nathan Trice/Rituals; Dance Alloy; and Attack Theatre. Established Abraham.In.Motion (now A.I.M.) dance company, 2006. Lincoln Center, Education Artist in Residence, 2012; New York Live Arts Resident Commissioned Artist, 2012–2014; appointed Visiting Professor in Residence, Department of World Arts and Culture/Dance, University of California, Los Angeles, starting 2019. **Awards and honours** include Jerome Travel Award, 2008; New York Dance and Performance Award ('Bessie'), 2010; Princess Grace Foundation Fellowship, 2010; *Out Magazine* "Best and Brightest" 2011; Jacob's Pillow Dance Award, 2012; United States Artist Ford Fellow, 2012; MacArthur Fellow 2013; Creative Capital Award, 2013; Honorary Doctorate, Washington and Jefferson College, 2014; Doris Duke Award, 2016; Joyce Residency Award, 2017–2018; Princess Grace Statue Award, 2018; *New York Times* Award, 2018.

Works

Inventing Pookie Jenkins (2006); *Fading into Something Tangible* (2006); *Op. 1* (with Carrie Schneider, 2010); *The Radio Show* (2010); *The Corner* (2010); *Live! The Realest MC* (2011); *Quiet Dance* (2011); *A Ramp to Paradise* (2012); *Ne Me Quitte Pas* (2012); *Pavement* (2012); *The Serpent and the Smoke* (with Wendy Whelan, 2013); *Watershed* (2014); *When the Wolves Came In* (2014); *Hallowed* (2014); *The Gettin'* (2014); *Dance Response Videos* (with Carrie Schneider, 2014); *Untitled America*, (2015–2016); *Drive* (2017); *Meditation: A Silent Prayer* (with Carrie Mae Weems, 2018); *Show Pony* (2018); *INDY* (2018); *The Runaway* (2018); *The Book of Henry* (feature film, dir. Colin Trevorro, 2019); *Dearest Home* (2019); *The Bystander* (2019); *Only the Lonely* (2019); *Ash* (2019); *Cocoon* (2019); *An Untitled Love* (2020); *Studies on a Farewell* (2020).

Further reading

Interviews: Jim Cotter, 'Kyle Abraham: A Life in Motion', *Articulate*, articulateshow.org, 14 November 2017; Theresa Ruth Howard, 'How Kyle Abraham Feels about Being NYCB's First Black Choreographer in a Decade', *Dance Magazine*, 2 May 2018; John Soltes, 'Kyle Abraham Revives', hollywoodsoapbox.com, 31 March 2019.

Articles: Rachel Straus, 'Kyle Abraham at Jacob's Pillow Dance Festival', rachelstraus.com, 20 August 2013; Alastair Macaulay, 'Turning in to an Earlier Time, When Moving Was Easy', *The New York Times*, 18 March

2014; Stacey Prickett, 'Constrained Bodies: Dance, Social Justice and Choreographic Agency', *Dance Research Journal*, 48(3), 2016; Siobhan Burke, 'The Choreographer Kyle Abraham Mixes Things Up at City Ballet', *The New York Times*, 21 September 2018; Deborah Jowitt, 'Anthologizing Abraham', *Dancebeat Blog*, artsjournal.com, 5 August 2019.

Books: Kyle Abraham, Fumni Adewole, Ivan Blackstock, Jreena Green, Robert Hylton, Jo Read, Nefeli Tasiouti, Tima-Monique Uzor, Orson Nava, and Danilo DJ Walde, *Blurring Boundaries: Urban Street Meets Contemporary Dance*, New York, 2015/2016; Aneta Stojnić and Marina Gržinić (eds.), *Shifting Corporealities: Danger, Im/Mobility, Politics*, London, 2018.

GERMAINE ACOGNY

According to Germaine Acogny, Senegalese choreographer, dancer and teacher, dance is a powerful philosophy and path of education. An essential dialogue with the cosmos, a universal connection between humans and their environment, combining elegance, harmony, gentleness, and revolt, it offers sensitive answers to our collective questions. Acogny's technique and her creations reflect the survival and affirmation of an Africa proud of its roots, while celebrating its ability to adapt its openness to the world and to modernity.

Acogny uses the gestural vocabulary of the technique codified in her book *African Dance* (1980), which according to South African choreographer Robyn Orlyn is a weapon, an indispensable working tool for African choreographers in search of cultural references (from the documentary film *Iya tundé, the Mother has returned*, directed by Laure Malecot, Production Médiatik/Moctar Ndhfiouga Ba, Senegal, 2017). The Acogny technique, which established African contemporary dance at a global level, is inspired by traditional African dances and everyday movements of nature. It revolves around 'the spinal column, snake, tree of life, from which all movement starts' (in *Iya Tundé*), from which the undulations start, with the bases being both anchoring to the ground and rising towards the sky, as most African dances do. Acogny has combined traditional African dances with contemporary and western classical dance since her first dance classes in Dakar (from 1968), in the aftermath of independence in Senegal, a time of affirmation of negritude advocated by President Léopold Sédar Senghor (whom she often quotes and whose poems she has danced to several times). Acogny has gradually imposed this vision of dance, whose ancestral anchoring allows her to open herself to the present in the joy of uncomplicated mutual enrichment.

Firmly rooted like the Cheesemaker tree, the symbol of her technique, Acogny knows how to take influences from elsewhere to make it her essence', as described in her speech at the World Dance Alliance Summit in Angers, July 2014. She does this by meeting new musical styles (butoh, urban dances) and choreographers from different contexts; Kota Yamazaki for *Fagaala* (2002) and Jawolé Zollar for *Les écailles de la mémoire* (2008). For her son Patrick Acogny, with whom she regularly collaborates, the Acogny technique is 'a form to be manipulated to lend itself to different dances' (in *Iya Tundé*).

One movement of the Acogny technique, the Offering (legs stretched out, chest bent towards the earth, then body stretched towards the sky) recalls the sacred dance of Aloopho, her Beninese grandmother (who was a Yoruba priestess), a founding figure of her style: 'with trembling shoulders, a wave went through her whole body. With her arms outstretched in a circle, she swung back and forth, bending her knees slightly' (Acogny, in *Dance Africaine*, 1988, prologue). This *sacred* understanding of dance is similar to that of Maurice Béjart (with whom she collaborated as Artistic Director of the Mudra African International School of Dance): for him, dance was 'a way of transcending our poor human condition in order to participate fully in the deep life of the cosmos' (Béjart in *Dance Africaine*, 1988). Acogny, as a dancer, alternates this Beninese undulating instinct and the ample gesture of the Sabar in Senegal, as she describes in *Iya Tundé*. These inspirations are found in her choreographies: movements for the fifty Senegalese majorettes of her first popular creation (1975) are derived from the distinctive hip actions of the Sabar; dancers crawl and then free themselves through undulations, contortions, subtle or spectacular in *Yewa* (1996) and *Fagaala* (2002); the jumps in *Waxtaan* (2004) are powerful.

In the Acogny-technique classes, rather than checking the technicality in a mirror, we look for harmony, looking at the other. Her choreographies are imbued with this spirit of community, of sharing, between dancers and with the public. In the solo *Songook Yaakaar* (2010), Acogny dances in front of the trainees of the Ecole des Sables (founded with Helmut Vogt in Dakar, Senegal) whose images are projected on the back of the stage, before concluding by inviting the audience to dance salsa on stage.

Rigour and discipline are the key words of Acogny, the pedagogue-educator, who as choreographer has also preferred a minimalist stage set-up: black background, empty stage, and a few everyday objects, whose use, location, and meaning evolve throughout the narrative – the red rose petals sown by Acogny in *Songook Yakaar*, reminiscent of the custom during weddings, also seem like bloodstains on the black ground, related to the themes evoked (emigration, colonisation, exile). In *A un endroit du début* (2015), the flour she throws on the ground, drawing a large circle, delimiting the space dedicated to her dance (a limit she will cross in the end), is a reference to the gestures of the priestesses of the Ndeup ceremony, who circumscribe the space of their dance by throwing curdled milk on the floor. This flour becomes sacred make-up when she covers her face with it sporadically, sitting in her father's armchair, to the rhythm of techno music (in West Africa, during certain ceremonies, people cover their faces and bodies with ashes), shouting "Stop putting flour on your face!". The video projection by Sébastien Dupouet, integrated into the scenography of *A un endroit du début*, adds landscapes of Senegal, images of waves washing on the sand, of women, children, or of Acogny visiting Disneyland, a dreamer, a reminder of her long exile in Europe. She enters the stage interacting with the video, boxing, alone, and in white projection, in a fight both against darkness, the unknown, and herself, expressing her fight as a woman and as an artist.

The music compositions, by percussionists such as Arona Ndiaye for *Femme Noire* (1972) and *Yé'ou, L'éveil* (1988), and Etienne Schwarcz for *Yewa Eau Sublime* (1996) and *Tchouraï* are original creations, particularly those of Fabrice Bouillon LaForest, with whom Acogny has been collaborating since 2004. He composed music for *Fagaala, Les écailles de la mémoire* (2004), *Songook Yaakaar, Waxtaan, Afro-dites* (2012) and *A un endroit du début* (2015). He mixes natural sounds (waves, wind, animal cries) with rhythms, traditional African songs, or techno/electro beats, underpinned by layers of synthesisers, organ, sung chants, all enhanced by acoustics (guitar, piano). The voices affirm her attachment to orality, with which the dance interacts. The main thread of the narration in *Femme Noire* is the voice of the Haitian actor Joseph Zobel, interpreting the poem *Femme nue, femme noire* (1961) by Léopold Sédar Senghor; it is punctuated in a tender interpolation by her husband Helmut Vogt for *Songook Yaakaar*, reviving the story, or a parenthesis-tribute to a tale of Aloopho told by director Mikaël Serre in the middle of *A un endroit du début*. Here Acogny evokes her birth in Benin and the spiritual heritage of Aloopho, dancing on the floor to the rhythm of her words in the spirit of African storytellers-dancers-singers. Towards the end, furious and poignant in her interpretation of an excerpt from Euripides' *Medea,* she proves to be a tragedian. The soundtrack is punctuated by silences, also rhythmic movement, as in traditional African dance. The body in tension, energetic or seized by trembling, relaxes until immobility, giving time for introspection. The dance is rhythmed by energies, emotions, and subtle bodily impulses. The silence enhances the power of the gesture, reinforcing its significance, when Germaine puts on a large costume of a fantastic bird, wearing a dinosaur's tail, a shell from which she slowly emerges.

Costumes are simple and revealing. We dance barefoot during her classes, most of the time, to mark the anchorage on the ground. If we wear shoes, it means they are meaningful – red pumps with heels in *Songook Yaakaar*. The ample outfits, the wide Senegalese 'chaya' trousers (which Acogny also frequently wears on stage) offer modesty and dignity, values that are dear to her. But when it comes to presenting the palaver between politicians, the dancers of Compagnie Jant Bi in *Waxtaan* (meaning discussion) dance in three-piece suits and ties. And to proclaim her internationality and that of dance, Acogny doesn't hesitate to wear a red cap on her legendary shaved head, visor back, before elegantly wiggling her hips to techno music *(Songook Yaakaar)*. Links between her creations are underlined by costume: her anthracite grey, long dress in *A un endroit du début*, reminds us of her outfit in *Yewa eau sublime* (1996), and thus highlights the tribute to Aloopho, to whom *Yewa* was dedicated.

Her three autobiographical solos (*Tchouraï*, *Songook Yaakaar*, and *A un endroit du début*) tell us about her journey: as a child and teenager in colonial Africa witnessing the independence of her continent while her adult life blossomed, as an artist driven into exile, and finally returning home with the formidable ambition of educating through dance. The narration, nourished by her dancer's experience (personal and artistic) and by improvisation, takes up themes such as slavery (*Les écailles de la mémoire*), the genocide in Rwanda (*Fagaala*), immigration and exile (*Songook Yaakaar*), and colonisation (*A un endroit du début*), with a certain amount of humour and self-mockery. The search for identity draws on ancestral, cultural, spiritual, and philosophical heritage, but it is by looking the past in the face that we can confront the present, hope, Acogny tells us clearly (confronting hope: the meaning in Wolof of *Songook Yaakaar*).

A un endroit du début (meaning a place from the beginning), is the fruit of a multidisciplinary collaboration, and her most intimate creation to date. She sheds light on the important points of her life, her questions, anger, and frustrations, and tackles head-on the dichotomy that underlies her general approach: education – the one her father Togoun Servais Acogny gave her, steeped in the Catholicism imposed by colonisation, a man who was a high official at the United Nations and administrator of the colonies. And the one he received, the animist heritage of his mother Aloopho, a Yoruba priestess whom he

22

disowned, and therefore did not pass on to his daughter. The quotations from her father's biography, projected and spoken by the choreographer, indicate this confrontation. In the conclusion of the dance, coming out of the magical circle drawn by herself, she affirms her identity, her unfailing link with Aloopho, and finally forgives her father for having taken her away from her cultural heritage, which she has since reconstituted through dance. This show, an intergenerational testimony, bears witness to one of the most serious consequences of colonisation: acculturation, both spiritual and philosophical. As proof of its relevance, the interest in this creation by programmers and audiences around the world has been growing since 2016. The collective wounds caused by colonial racism, loss of identity, and self-esteem are still struggling to heal.

The worldwide impact of the choreographic and pedagogical work of Germaine Acogny, the 'Mother of Contemporary African Dance', is undeniable. Introducing *A un endroit du début,* sitting on the floor facing a large open book, in front of the portrait of her father, in uniform, projected on a curtain of white threads, she reads aloud the conclusion of his biography: "Let me express one wish: that all men, whatever their origin or their religious or philosophical conception, should know that they complement each other and establish the indispensable dialogue". For Germaine Acogny, life is about establishing an essential dialogue not only between humans, but also with the cosmos, in action, in movement, through dance...

Laure Malécot

Biographical details

Born: 28 May 1944, Porto Novo, Benin; moved to Senegal aged four. **Studied** at Simons Siegel School, Paris, France, 1965, (physical and sports education; and harmonic gymnastics). **Career**: African dance teacher since 1968. After her first two solos, 1972/75, taught her own dance technique, codified in her book *African Dance,* first published in 1980 and then translated into three languages; it was the pillar of the development of dance among the arts in Senegal in the cultural policy of President L.S. Senghor. Artistic Director of Mudra Afrique, a contemporary dance school, in Dakar, 1977–1983. Moved to Europe, 1983 to 1997 (Brussels then Toulouse); in 1985, with Helmut Vogt, co-founded the Studio-Ecole-Ballet-Théâtre in Toulouse (offered African Dance training of international scope). Artistic Director, dance section of Afrique en Création in Paris (1997 to 2000); in Senegal, with Helmut Vogt, co-founded Ecole des Sables, International Centre for Traditional and Contemporary African Dances (EDS) in 1997, the company Jant Bi (men) in 1999 and Jant Bi Jigueen (women) in 2009. From 2014, artistic direction of EDS handed to her son, teacher and choreographer Patrick Acogny; gives master classes and supervises EDS with Helmut Vogt. Performed in 2015 under the direction of choreographer Olivier Dubois in *Mon Elue Noire*, which won a Bessie Award in 2019. On tour since 2015 with *A un endroit du début*, and since 2019 with Salia Sanou (Burkinabe dancer/choreographer) and Nancy Huston (Canadian writer) in *Multiples*. In 2020, EDS is collaborating with the Pina Bausch Foundation (Germany), the International Centre for Traditional and Contemporary African Dances and Sadler's Wells (UK) for the *Rite of Spring* performed by 40 African dancers, and a duet by Germaine Acogny and Malou Airaudo (Pina Bausch Company). **Awards and honours** include London Dance and Performance Award, 1991; Pioneer woman, Senegalese Ministry of Family and National Solidarity, 1999; New York Dance and Performance Awards ('Bessie'), 2004 for lifetime achievement, 2007, 2019; Knight of the Order of Merit, upgraded to Commander in the Order of Arts and Letters of the French Republic, 2009; Knight of the National Order of the Lion, Officer of the Arts and Letters, Commander of the Arts and Letters of the Senegalese Republic, 2012; Prix International Elsa Wolliaston – Festival Danses et Continents Noirs, 2018; Officier de la légion d'honneur de la République Française 2016; ECOWAS Grand Prix, 2019; Prix d'Excellence de la CEDEAO, 2019.

Works

Femme Noire (1972); *Coumba Amoul Ndaye* (1975); *Sahel* (1987); *Yé'ou, l'éveil* (1988); *Afrique, ce corps mémorable* (1989, 1991); *Yewa, eau sublime* (1994, 1995); *Z* (1995); *Tchouraï* [incense] (with Sophiatou Kossoko, 2001); *Fagaala* (with Kota Yamazaki, 2002); *Waxtaan* (with Patrick Acogny, 2004); *Bintou Wéré, l'Opéra du Sahel* (2007); *Les écailles de la mémoire* (with Jawolé Zollar, 2008); *Songook Yaakaar* (with Pierre Doussin, 2010); *Afro-dites* (with Patrick Acogny, 2012); *A un endroit du début* (dir. Mikaël Serre, 2015); *Double Je* (2016); *Multiples* (2019); *Common ground[s]* (duet with Malou Airaudo, 2020).

Further reading

Interviews: 'Traversing a Life Through Movement, Text, and Film: Germaine Acogny interviewed by Nicole Loeffler-Gladstone', bombmagazine.org, 24 September 2019.

Articles: Jennifer Dunning, 'Play and Ritual in the Village, an Unseen Terror at the Gates', *New York Times*, 13 March 2007; Michael Upchurch, 'Suits and ties Take Over from African Robes in Compagnie Jant Bi's '*Waxtaan*', *Seattle Times*, 8 October 2010; Victoria Looseleaf, 'Chosen One: The Fearless Work of Germaine Acogny', fjordreview.com, 5–7 October 2018; Gabriele Klein, 'Artistic Work as a Practice of Translation on the Global Art Market: The Example of "African" Dancer and Choreographer Germaine Acogny',

Dance Research Journal, 51, 23 April 2019; Amy Swanson, 'Codifying African Dance: the Germaine Acogny technique and antinomies of postcolonial cultural production', *Critical African Studies*, 11 (1), August 2019; Brian Seibert, 'An African Dance Matriarch Brings Out the Knives', *New York Times*, 27 September 2019.

Books: Laure Malécot, *Germaine Acogny, Danser l'Humanité*, Dakar, Senegal, 2019; Germaine Acogny, *African Dance*, Weingarten, Germany, 1980.

JOSE AGUDO

At the beginning of *Silk Road* (2017), created by Spanish-born, London-based choreographer Jose Agudo, Agudo enters the stage bare-chested and in flamenco shoes. He puts his black shirt on, makes the Catholic sign of the Cross, and performs a long flamenco solo (by guest choreographer Rafael Amargo). After a musical interlude, Agudo dances a kathak solo choreographed by Nahid Siddiqui. He is now wearing a long shirt, is bare-footed, and the introductory ritual gesture that he performs is Islamic. In part two of the show, Agudo shares the stage with another performer (bharatanatyam dancer Mavin Khoo in the original production; Kenny Wing Tao Ho in a later staging). Their movement vocabulary is neither purely flamenco nor kathak. Rather, it weaves elements of these two dance traditions with contemporary dance. It is Agudo's choreography, characterised by technical virtuosity, incessant pirouettes, interplay between stillness and speed, expansive arms, and expressivity orientated towards spirituality and human interiority. In performative terms, its base is contemporary dance while it also incorporates references to flamenco and kathak. Dance critic Ditta Rudle described it as 'fluent, soulful, accurate', radiating 'beauty and harmony' ('Impulstanz: Agudo Dance Company, *Silk Road*', *Tanzschrift*, 4 August 2019. Translation, Christina Nikolaidis-Strommer).

Silk Road is perhaps the most representative work in Agudo's repertory. He describes it as 'an exploration of the rituals and dance forms along nomadic routes' (Wilson, 2017), a journey from the West to the East that perhaps echoes Agudo's professional journey into dance. He started his career in Andalusia, training in flamenco with Antonio Vallejo and in Spanish theatre dance with Maite Galán. He had his first foray in contemporary dance when he joined Omar Deza's dance-theatre company DA.TE Danza, with which he toured Spain from 1999 to 2001. He gained formal training in contemporary dance after this, first at Centro Andaluz de Danza in Seville (then directed by

Ramón Oller) and subsequently at Centro Coreógrafico de Valencia. He resumed his performing activity in 2004, dancing in several contemporary dance companies across Europe such as Charleroi Danse (Belgium), Ballet de Marseille, T.R.A.S.H. (the Netherlands), and Shobana Jeyasingh Dance (UK). In a decisive career move, he settled in London in 2010 when he joined Akram Khan Company. He was performer, rehearsal director, and assistant choreographer there for six years. Among other creations, he participated in *Desh* (2011), *iTMOi* (2013), *Torobaka* (Khan's collaboration with flamenco dancer Israel Galván, 2014), *Chotto Desh* (2015), *Until de Lions* (2016), the London 2012 Olympic Games opening ceremony, and Sylvie Guillem's farewell tour (2015). During this period, Agudo trained intensely in kathak and witnessed first-hand Khan's creative process. This close contact with Khan completed his training in multiple movement vocabularies and his craftsmanship in choreography.

Two other events are key to understanding his aesthetic. In 2007, he joined the physical theatre company T.R.A.S.H. in the Netherlands. This encounter with an extreme physical practice that strongly emphasises the expressivity of movement radically changed his view of dance; in a personal interview he explained, "it was a very radical experience for me … it deconstructed my whole way of thinking about dance" (17 October 2019, material also used elsewhere in the article). He became consciously aware of the dramatic potential of dance, something that he was missing in his background in contemporary dance. This new awareness also connected Agudo with a major tenet of Stanislavsky's acting methodology, which states that the body is the starting point to build a character. In Agudo's creative process this principle implies that movement is the driving force of his choreography. The visual aesthetics of the body in motion also play a role in the construction of his dance sequences, but that comes after the initial corporeal impulse. The kinetic quality of movement is always his primary source for creating.

In 2009, Agudo spent two months in an ashram in Kerala, India. He undertook a Sivananda yoga teacher-training programme and became fascinated by the daily rituals and ceremonies in the temple, which he would keenly attend in his free time (Claire Cunningham, Producer of Agudo Dance Company, personal communication with author, 9 January 2020). This immersion in a spiritual community was highly significant for Agudo. It reconnected him with his own spirituality (originally formed within a Catholic society) and triggered a deeper understanding of the self and its place in society.

These two inspirational events helped shape crucial aspects of Agudo's approach. Expressive and highly dynamic physicality together with a dramatic focus on the inner aspects of human experience are fundamental traits of his choreography. These quickly emerged in his repertory. *Ki* (2013), a demanding solo for a male dancer, focuses on the inner fears and insecurities of a boy in the process of becoming a powerful man. It is inspired by Genghis Khan's life story, and its kinetic imagery includes, like *Silk Road* and later productions, gestural allusions to rituals. Spiritual growth also structures the story underpinning *Paradiso: Man's Enduring Search for Perfection* (2017). Based on the last section of Dante's *The Divine Comedy*, the male protagonist faces the obstacles of vanity, ambition, aggression, and desire before finding enlightenment at the end of his journey (*Paradiso* Programme Notes, 24 May 2017). Agudo's choreography, deeply infused with kathak elements in this production, alternates dynamic passages with unhurried, slow-paced sequences that suggest the hardships and spiritual rewards of the struggle.

Two earlier pieces, *A Thousand Shepherds* (2013) and *Selah* (2015), delve into spiritual traditions. The former stems directly from Agudo's spiritual retreat in India, stressing aspects of religious devotion such as discipline, commitment, and dedication. Among the variety of cultural references underlying it, several come from Agudo's Andalusian background, including the manifestation of faith in Easter's Catholic processions, Federico García Lorca's play *The House of Bernarda Alba* (1945), and Enrique Morente's flamenco song *1000 Pastores* (A Thousand Shepherds) (Willett, Agudo Dance Company website, 2019). *Selah* also possesses a strong Catholic component. Agudo created it for ŻfinMalta National Dance Company, before his tenure as associate artist of the company from 2016–2018. It captures the prominent role that religion plays in Maltese society. The narrative shapes a recurrent theme in Agudo's repertory – the constraints that society imposes upon individuals. The repetitive choreographic patterns, as well as the mechanical and assertive gestures, expose deeply rooted religious conventions underlying the group rejection of one of its members. *Selah* was converted into a short film in 2019, co-directed by Agudo and Matthew Beckett.

Many of the plots structuring Agudo's choreography pivot around the central theme of the journey, physical and/or emotional. *Ten* (2013) explores the idea of leaving, moving away, which anticipates the tour through nomadic routes in *Silk Road*. *SAM* (2018) reflects on migration and hopeful departures, whereas *BHAJ-to belong to*

(2019) centres on the notion of belonging, of being part of something. Agudo's interest in other cultures and practices is evident, theme-wise, in *Artic* (2014), about Inuit traditions, and in *Glansvit* (2018), a dance adaptation of a short story by Swedish author Alfhild Agrell.

While Spanish traditions and culture have inspired aspects of Agudo's choreography from the early stages of his career, his flamenco roots took time to enter his choreographic aesthetic.

He had been encouraged to reprise them early in his career, first by Jeyasingh, later by Khan, but by the time he danced in flamenco shoes in *Silk Road,* over ten years had passed since his previous flamenco performance (interview by Tomorr Kokona, *One Dance UK,* 21 May 2017). He had the opportunity to fully embrace flamenco rhythms and movements when he created his version of *Carmen* for ŻfinMalta in 2018. The explicit Spanish theme allowed for the full materialisation of a flamenco influence alongside kathak (in the spins, in the open arms, in the lower body rooted to the ground) in Agudo's personal dance language.

Collaboration is a fundamental aspect of Agudo's working methods. His most regular collaborator is dramaturge Lou Cope, who was part of the team in *Ki* and has worked with Agudo in six further works. Her input contributes to drive Agudo's expressive choreography into structural and dramatic cohesion. Costume designer Kimie Nakano is responsible for the elegant simplicity that has become the staple of Agudo's visual aesthetic. And the Austrian composer Bernhard Schimpelsberger exemplifies the symbiosis that Agudo has achieved with the musicians he has worked with. Trained, like Agudo, in both Western and Eastern practices, his specially commissioned scores incorporate contemporary sounds as well as folk rhythms and melodies. In *Silk Road*, for instance, the music progressively builds a kaleidoscopic aural atmosphere reminiscent of the sounds of the silk route while retaining contemporary resonances.

In 2017, Agudo founded his London-based company, which is presenting a new version of *Carmen* in 2020. He has an established reputation as a freelance choreographer across Europe and South Africa. His eclectic style draws 'things together [and explores] movement through an exchange of forms, traditions, rituals, religions, ideas and energies in the evolving space of contemporary dance' (Willett, 2019). His repertory explores human complexity, cultural traditions and possibilities for exchange. He is a rising choreographer who is quietly but steadily finding his place within the European contemporary dance scene.

Cristina de Lucas

Biographical details

Born in Pinos Puente, Granada, Spain, 18 September 1976. **Studied** flamenco with Antonio Vallejo, 1995; and Spanish theatre dance with Maite Galán, 1995–99; contemporary dance with Omar Meza, DA.TE Danza, 1999–2001; trained at Centro Andaluz de Danza, Seville, under the direction of Ramón Oller, 2001–02, and at Centro Coreográfico de Valencia, 2002–03; Sivananda Yoga teacher training, Kerala (India), 2009; trained in kathak with Akram Khan, London, 2011–16; postgraduate diploma in Advanced Dance Studies, London Contemporary Dance School (University of Kent), 2013. **Career:** Danced with DA.TE Danza, Spain, 1999–2001; Charleroi Danse, Belgium, 2004–05; Ballet de Marseille, 2006; T.R.A.S.H., the Netherlands, 2006–07; Shobana Jeyasingh Dance, 2007–08; performer, assistant choreographer, and rehearsal director, Akram Khan Company, 2010–16. Founded Agudo Dance Company in London, 2017. Began choreographing during his training in Spain; resident artist at Déda, 2008–09; associate artist, ŻfinMalta, 2016–18. Has also choreographed for ACE Dance and Music (Birmingham, UK), Phoenix Dance Theatre (Leeds, UK), Cape Dance Company (South Africa), ŻfinMalta National Dance Company, Norrdans (Sweden), BODHI PROJECT Dance Company (Austria), Akademi (London), Three Score Dance Company (Brighton, UK), and Davis Cup opening ceremony (Spain). Choreography for student companies and schools includes English National Ballet School, London Contemporary Dance School, London Studio Centre, Area Jeune Ballet (Switzerland), MAP Dance (University of Chichester, UK), Reina Sofia Dance Conservatory (Spain), and Northern School of Contemporary Dance (Leeds, UK). **Awards** include Third Prize, Andalusian Choreographic Contest, 2002; Best Dancer, Madrid Choreographic Contest, 2003.

Works

4m2 (with Claire Cunningham, 2008); *Time/Dropper* (2011); *Ki* (2013); *A Thousand Shepherds* (2013); *Ten* (2013); *Artic* (2014); *Korba* (2015); *Selah* (2015); *Paradiso: Man's Enduring Search for Perfection* (2017); *Silk Road* (with Mavin Khoo, additional choreography by Rafael Amargo and Nahid Siddiqui, 2017); *Regnum* (2018); *Carmen* (2018, 2020); *SAM* (2018); *Glansvit* (2018); *Inside the Animal* (2018); *Selah* (short film, co-director Matthew Beckett, 2019); *BHAJ-to belong to* (2019); *Return* (2019); *Davis Cup Opening Ceremony* (2019).

Further reading

Interviews: with HG, available at Déda website, 2015; Tomorr Kokona, *One Dance UK*, 17 March 2017; Jessica Wilson, *Dance Direct*, 8 May 2017.

Articles: Marian Kennedy, 'Agudo Dance Company – Silk Road at Sadler's Wells', londontheatre1.com, 7 May 2017; Rachel Elderkin, 'Agudo Dance

Company: Silk Road', *The Stage*, 8 May 2017; Jonathan Willett, 'A Dance Odyssey: Between Choreography and Performance on the Silk Road', joseagudo.co.uk, 2019.

JÉRÔME BEL

The problem of trying to write this entry about the French dance artist Jérôme Bel is that his performance works directly attack so many of the assumptions underlying much of the choreography discussed elsewhere in this book. Does Bel even belong in a book about contemporary choreography? He uses the term 'realiser' to describe himself. While choreography, he says, concerns setting steps and movements into sequences, what he does is concerned with ideas and concepts. The pieces his company performed in his name in some ways amount to a series of provocations that undermine the assumption that the artist's name is a sign and guarantee of authorship, authenticity, and originality. One of the things that come as a shock, when one sees a piece by Bel, is the realisation that he doesn't subscribe to the notion that contemporary dance is an open field whose practitioners embrace the freedom to invent a new and previously inconceivable aesthetic. What can make this uncomfortable for spectators is the accompanying realisation of how much one may have believed in this view of contemporary dance without knowing it.

In his twenties, Bel danced for Angelin Preljocaj, Joëlle Bouvier, and Regis Obadier, key figures in the rapid expansion of French contemporary dance during the 1980s. By 1992, he was dissatisfied with the work in which he had been performing. Finding himself with a healthy bank balance after assisting Phillipe Decouflé to create the opening ceremony for the Winter Olympics in Albertville, Bel spent two years living frugally in Paris and used this time to find an artistic direction for himself. He read books about dance history and by French philosophers whose ideas had been affected by the events in Paris in May 1968, in particular Roland Barthes and Michel Foucault.

This was a time when other dancers of his generation (including Boris Charmatz, Emmanuelle Huynh, Benoît Lechambre, Xavier Le Roy, Loïc Touzé, and Christophe Wavelet) were forming groups to discuss dance, philosophy, and politics. These groups criticised current dance practice and collectively wrote essays and manifestos, not always finished or published, for example Groupe 20 Août (Isabelle Launay, 1999) and the 2001 Manifesto for a European Performance Policy (André Lepecki, in Carter, 2004). Dance companies in France were benefiting from supportive policies and funding, but a side effect of this was institutionalisation. This, Xavier Le Roy observed, 'influenced and sometimes to a large degree also determined how a dance piece should be. Most of the time, producers and programmers have to significantly follow the rules of global economy' (in Helmut Ploebst, 2001). Bel, Le Roy and others began making works which challenged the largely tacit assumptions about what dance might be, thus engaging in a kind of institutional critique.

In the 1990s, Bel created works that used signs and images in a disruptive, deadpan, literal way, informed by philosophical critiques of representation. His 1992 work *Nom donné par l'auteur* (*Name Given By The Author* – a dictionary definition of 'title') for himself and Frédéric Seguette was initially performed only for close associates. It involved entirely logical but increasingly irrational combinations of a small group of familiar objects found in any bourgeois interior, including a hair dryer, vacuum cleaner, dictionary, ball, and a tin of table salt. The piece, which played with the meanings of signs, was entirely worked out in advance of rehearsals, and destabilised conventions about dancers' self-presentation and use of space.

Jérôme Bel (1995), which launched him on the international dance circuit, again explored representation in disruptive, provocative ways. Where Barthes (*Writing Degree Zero*, London, 1967) had written about 'writing degree zero', Bel explored what dancing degree zero might be. Four naked dancers performed on a bare stage, lit by a single light bulb held by a woman who wrote 'Thomas Edison' in chalk on a blackboard. Two dancers wrote, in chalk, their names, measurements, telephone numbers, and bank balances. A fourth wrote 'Stravinsky, Igor' and then sang the entire score of *Rite of Spring*. The piece was a series of ironic statements about the minimum of what being human means while foregrounding the materiality of bodies, their functions and social construction. They wrote on their bodies in lipstick, the woman inscribing 'Christian Dior' down her leg. At one point she pressed her hair between a male dancer's closed legs and then pulled it back out. Later they urinated and used this to wash off some of the chalk letters leaving the sentence 'Eric chante Sting' (Eric sings Sting), after which a man named Eric appeared and sang a song by the English pop star.

Le dernier spectacle (*The Last Performance*, 1998), a piece for himself and three other dancers, was made entirely of pre-existing movement. Bel approached several choreographers but only Susanne Linke gave permission, so an extract from her 1978 *Wandlungen* was one of four units of material whose repetitions made up the piece. A man who said he was Jérôme Bel, but wasn't, set an alarm on his digital watch and stood waiting for it to go off before exiting. Another, dressed for tennis, said he was André Agassi and played tennis against the back wall for a few minutes. Another, dressed in a black, renaissance costume, said he was Hamlet and recited the soliloquy 'To be or not to be'. A woman in a white silk dress said she was Susanne Linke and danced an extract from *Wandlungen*. Then one after another, the three men also in dresses, danced it. These four repetitions lasted nearly 30 minutes, their gradual familiarity increasingly making spectators aware of the endurance of watching. Later, performers returned to say they were not Bel, Agassi, Linke, or Hamlet, and performed the related material in logically developed ways. The piece ended with an empty stage; a recorded voice read out the names of all the people who had reserved tickets for that performance. Whether performers are or are not who they say they are (it was Bel who said he was not Jérôme Bel) depends on the way representations circulate within society. This, according to Foucault, is the meaning of the surrealist artist Magritte's painting of a pipe and its inscription *Ceci n'est pas une pipe* (*This Is Not A Pipe,* Los Angeles, 1982). Just as *Jérôme Bel* made audiences aware of the constructedness of bodies, *Le dernier spectacle* drew attention to the constructedness of performative signs.

Gerald Siegmund suggests that, by calling his fourth piece 'the last performance', Bel was announcing his premature retirement. When commissioned to make a new piece in 2000, he therefore asked Xavier Le Roy to make it for him, although Bel is named as the author of *Xavier Le Roy* and collects the royalties when it is performed. (Should this piece therefore be discussed in an article on Bel's work?) Le Roy says he made a piece as much like Bel's work as possible. Le Roy, wearing a long blonde wig that obscured his faces, appeared as Charlie Chaplin, Hitler, Christ on the cross, Michael Jackson, and Marilyn Monroe. These were examples of movement clichés whose over-familiarity meant that their performance created a disturbing blankness.

In the twenty-first century, Bel's works largely fall into two categories – group pieces and works where one or two dancers directly address the audience about dance. *The Show Must Go On* (2000/2001), for a group, announced his return to dance making. This was constructed around a series of 18 well-known pop songs, triggers for the layers of public and private association they have accumulated. In typical Bel fashion, each inspired a literal interpretation of a single element in its lyrics. Thus, the stage remained empty for 'Tonight'; and during 'Let The Sunshine In', performers only entered when the Beatles actually sang the words "come together", and didn't move again until

David Bowie sang the chorus of 'Let's Dance'. Commissioned by Paris's Théâtre de la Ville, it was Bel's first opportunity to explore the resources of a large conventional stage, thus 'Yellow Submarine' saw the cast descending through a trapdoor to sing along from underneath the stage. A large part of the Parisian audience demonstrated disapproval by walking out, invading the stage, or with slow handclaps.

The Paris Opéra commissioned *Véronique Doisneau* (2004) for and about a retiring 'sujet' (corps de ballet dancer who sometimes performs minor roles). Doisneau talked to the audience about her life and career, said how much she earned, and demonstrated extracts from her repertoire. Pointing out that what audiences often find most magical about the ballet can be excruciatingly boring to perform, she showed her movement during the second act adagio of *Swan Lake*. This consists of maintaining a long held pose until the musical cue to change to another. Bel adopted similar autobiographical formats in further solos: *Cédric Andrieu* (2009), for the French dancer who was a member of the Merce Cunningham Dance Company and *Lütz Forster* (2009) from Tanztheater Wuppertal. Similarly autobiographical, *Pichet Klunchun and Myself* (2004) was a duo for Bel and Pichet Klunchun, master of the Thai classical masked dance style 'khon'. In this, they talked about their careers and demonstrated their work to one another and for the audience, including different ways in which death is represented in their dance traditions. Refusing to fall into the trap of finding in movement a supposedly universal language that transcends cultural differences, the piece offered a combative series of exchanges between the two. Another duo, *3Abschied* (2010), co-created with Anne Therese de Keersmaeker, was based around the final song in Mahler's 1908 *Das Leid von der Erde*. In this Bel talks to the audience and asks the musicians in the orchestral ensemble to perform the score as if they were dying, later De Keersmaeker sings Mahler's *Lied* in her untrained, undeveloped voice.

In the 2010s, Bel's work questioned who has the right to appear on theatre stages. *Disabled Theater* (2012) was created at the invitation of the Swiss company Theater HORA. Continuing Bel's concern with autobiography, eleven neuro-diverse performers each tell the audience about themselves and dance an uplifting solo to a favourite song. Some audience members, unused to seeing dancers with disabilities, found the work disturbing. Trained dancers, amateurs, and dancers with disabilities performed together in *Gala* (2015), paired in duets that simultaneously revealed and discounted differences. In *Cour d'honneur* (2013), for the Avignon Festival whose main stage is the courtyard of the Pope's Palace, fourteen audience members, one after another, recollected past festival performances. In *Tombe* (2016), another commission from the Paris Opéra, three male soloists are paired in a duet with someone who wouldn't normally appear on this historic stage – an African dancer, a dancer with disabilities, and an elder balletomane. The title refers to Giselle's tomb in the antique backdrop used as scenery. Siegmund links this to a recurring concern with death in Bel's work.

Over the years Bel has honed an approach in which the act of performing reflects back to spectators their own desires and expectations with a directness that reminds them of their own potential for innovation and change. English-speaking writers sometimes use the word 'deconstruction' to describe this approach. In France, however, Laurent Goumarre's definition of 'deceptive' art has gained currency, which combines perception of the material body (rather than its imagined potential to evoke metaphysical ideals), conceptual art, and deception. As Bel himself wryly observes (in Etchells, 2004), "Sometimes I think people are getting more and more clever watching us be more and more stupid".

Ramsay Burt

Biographical details

Born in France, 1964. **Studied** for 1 year at the Centre Nationale de Danse Contemporaine, Angers, 1984–1985. **Career:** Danced in the 1980s for Angelin Preljocaj, Joëlle Bouviere, Regis Obadia, Daniel Larrieu, Caterina Sagna among others; assistant director to Philippe Decouflé for the ceremonies of the XVIth Winter Olympic Games, Albertville and Savoie, 1992; began creating work in 1994 with *Nom donné par l'auteur*; has created work for the Paris Opera Ballet; curated with Alain Platel, the Klapstuk Festival, Leuven, 2003; participated in 'Parallel Voices', a series of conversations between artists curated by Jonathan Burrows, at the Siobhan Davies Dance Studios, London, 2007. **Awards** include New York Dance and Performance Award ('Bessie'), 2005; Routes Princess Magriet Award, 2008; Swiss Dance Award, 2013.

Works

Nom donné par l'auteur (1993); *Jérôme Bel* (1995); *Shirtology* (1997); *Le dernier spectacle* (1998); *Xavier Le Roy* (2000); *The Show Must Go On* (2001); *The Last Performance (une conférence)* (2004); *Véronique Doisneau* (2004); *The Show Must Go On 2* (2004); *Pichet Klunchun and Myself* (2005); *Isabel Torres* (2005); *Cédric Andrieu* (2009); *Lutz Förster* (2009); *3Abschied* (2010); *Disabled Theatre* (2012); *Cour d'honneur* (2013); *Gala* (2015); *Tombe* (2016); *Posé arabesque, temps lié en arrière, marche, marche …* (2017); *Danser comme si personne ne regardait* (2018); *Conférence sur rien* (2018); *Rétrospective* (2019); *Isadora Duncan* (2019).

Further reading

Interviews: with Gia Kourlas, 'Jérôme Bel Talks about Disabled Theatre', *Time Out New York*, 29 October 2013.

Articles: Laurent Goumarre, 'Deceptive Art', *Art Press*, September 1998; Isabelle Launay, 'Les signataires du 20 Août, état du grève à Kerguéhennec: corps en suspens', *Mouvement*, January–March 1999; Tim Etchells, 'More and More Clever Watching More and More Stupid: Some Thoughts Around Rules, Games and *The Show Must Go On*', *Dance Theatre Journal*, 20(2), 2004; Una Bauer, 'The Movement of Embodied Thought the Representational Game of the Stage Zero of Signification in *Jérôme Bel*', *Performance Research*, 13(1), 2008; SanSan Kwan, 'Even as We Keep Trying: An Ethics of Interculturalism in Jérôme Bel's *Pichet Klunchun and Myself*', *Theatre Survey*, 55(2), 2014; Sarah Gorman, 'Performing Failure? Anomalous Amateurs in Jérôme Bel's Disabled Theater and The Show Must Go On 2015', *Contemporary Theatre Review*, 27(1), 2017.

Books: Helmut Ploebst, *No Wind No Word: New Choreography in the Society of the Spectacle*, Munich, 2001; André Lepecki, *Rethinking Dance History*, in Alexandra Carter (ed.), London and New York, 2004; André Lepecki, *Exhausting Dance: Performance and the Politics of Movement*, London and New York, 2006; Jérôme Bel and Boris Charmatz, *Emails 2009–2010*, Paris, 2009; Ramsay Burt, *Ungoverning Dance*, London and New York, 2016; Gerald Siegmund, *Jérôme Bel: Dance, Theatre, and the Subject*, Basingstoke, 2017.

CAMILLE A. BROWN

Camille A. Brown is the first to admit that her journey has been a struggle at times, yet today she is one of America's most prolific choreographers. One of a number of black artists redefining the African-American story, her concert dance work explores literal relationships and complex themes, but always with an eye on the past and present. Her work inhabits that space between dance and theatre. Her choreography comes from her roots and makes connections with personal experiences. It reflects on history while making connections with the contemporary world, all through the lens of the modern black female that she is.

Her movement vocabulary comes from a personal place too, a fusion of modern, hip hop, ballet, and tap. Black social dance, which she sees as rooted in the African-American experience, is especially important as an expression of community and experience. Thus, her dance is not so much about bodily technique as the entire language of the body and the history it carries. Indeed, to foster a deeper understanding of black history and culture, she offers reference guides in programmes and post-performance dialogues presented as integral to the evening, not as a post-show bolt-on. For her, dancers have voices too, and it is important they are heard.

Brown credits her myriad influences to her upbringing. She is from Jamaica in Queens, New York, and proud of it. Her mother, who loved musical theatre and took her to shows, also used to play funk in the car. Her father taught salsa. She encountered Yoruba traditions at her local community centre. She said, "I have been around so much information and it comes back around" (in Scherr, 2019). What is important is that the movement is authentic, she continued, not in the sense of absolute historical accuracy but in that it arises from individual experience, from something inherent in people and in the culture.

She studied locally before gaining a place at New York's prestigious Fiorello H. LaGuardia High School of Music & Art and the Performing Arts, simultaneously attending The Ailey School on scholarship. She later went to college at the North Carolina School of the Arts. On the concert dance pathway, she ran up against issues of body image. She didn't fit some teachers' ideals and in college struggled to get audition calls for similar reasons. Eventually, she found herself enjoying composing her own movement and gravitated towards choreography. This was put to one side after she got a job dancing with Ronald K. Brown and his Evidence: A Dance Company. Then a friend sent her a letter about a choreography competition at Hubbard Street 2. She submitted and won.

As a black female, Brown ran up against the usual issues of the male-dominated world of choreography and is on record as saying she sometimes felt she had to work twice as hard for the same opportunities. She admitted in a 2019 interview with Risa Sarachan that the problems she encountered caused her to shrink back at times. Equally, she feels it important that female choreographers, let alone black female choreographers, empower each other and recognise that they are representing something larger than themselves.

Her concert dance work ranges vastly. *The Evolution of a Secured Feminine* (2007) is a witty portrayal of a character vacillating between uncertainty and carefree expression. Full of the joy of life, it's a celebration of womanhood. Other lighter pieces include *Groove to Nobody's Business* (2007), made for Alvin Ailey Dance Theater, which imagines the meeting of strangers on a subway and glimpses humanity in everyday movements and interactions. *Been There, Done That* (2010), tells the struggle of a dancing duo from the 1950s and 1960s. More spiritual-based is *New Second Line* (2006), inspired by the events of the 2005 Hurricane Katrina and a celebration of the spirit and culture of

New Orleans. *City of Rain* (2010) is a work created in honour of a close friend and former dancer who passed away following a severe illness. She is best known for her politically-charged dances into which personal anxieties and stories are writ large. Most notable is her trilogy on culture, race, and African-American identity: the Bessie Award-winning *Mr. TOL E. RAncE* (2012), the Bessie-nominated *BLACK GIRL: Linguistic Play* (2015), and *ink* (2017).

Inspired by Mel Watkins' book *On the Real Side: From Slavery to Chris Rock*, Spike Lee's movie *Bamboozled*, and American comedian Dave Chappelle's 'dancing vs. shuffling' analogy about making art rather than playing the fool, especially the black fool for white audiences, *Mr TOL E. RAncE* addresses stereotypes of black people in entertainment, using comedy, film, and spoken dialogue alongside dance and live music. Considering the position of black performers through history, it examines the 'double-consciousness' concept introduced by W.E.B DuBois in his *The Souls of Black Folk*, which refers to a source of inward 'twoness' putatively experienced by African-Americans because of oppression and disvaluation in a white-dominated society. As the title suggests, it speaks about how much black performers had to tolerate and considers modern day forms of minstrelsy occurring today. It is not a history lesson, however, but is a work engaging in a dialogue about where the black community has been, where it is now, and where it might want to be.

Aware that black women are often portrayed in terms of their strength, resiliency, or trauma, in *BLACK GIRL: Linguistic Play*, Brown presents a nuanced narrative of black womanhood, albeit in a racially and politically-charged world. She explores the experience of childhood from a personal perspective, creating dance out of playground games and the rhythmic play of African-American dance including social dance, double dutch, steppin', tap, and Juba. Aware that black girls tend to be sexualised and seen as older, Brown shows how their identity is shaped by the environment as they journey from childhood innocence, where they are girls who play just like any other girls, through awareness to maturity.

The trilogy culminates with *ink*, inspired by the people, gestures and rituals of the African diaspora. It examines that part of black culture which is often appropriated, rewritten, or silenced. The dancers represent superheroes, a nod to the idea that black people always keep rising, showing their superhuman power to persevere, overcome, and transform, even within hostile environments. Brown, aware of the narrative existing within society that the African-American community is one of single-parent homes, dysfunctional families, and aggressive males, insists the truth is different. She highlights, instead, black love through a male-female duet inspired by the hustle and lindy-hop, and positive male relationships in a playful duet for two men emphasising brotherhood. Live music centres on percussion, this African element gaining force in a final vibrant, communal dance.

The idea of cultural continuity, that the present contains the past, is a characteristic theme in her work. It's the explicit message of Brown's 2016 TED video *A Visual History of Social Dance in 25 Moves*, a four-minute look at African-American social dances viewed more than a million times online (ted.com, June 2016).

Since 2011, when director Daniel Aukin asked her to interpret the music of the 1970s for *The Fortress of Solitude*, Brown has forged a parallel career in theatre. She created the choreography for a number of hit shows including NBC's *Jesus Christ Superstar Live in Concert* in 2018. The following year, for *Choir Boy*, she was the first black woman to be nominated for a Tony in the category for over two decades, and she created the dance for the Metropolitan Opera's new production of *Porgy and Bess*, significant in that it featured an all-black cast similar to its premiere in 1935. Whatever the subject, her instinct for movement that resonates with the story and social dance is clear. There are moments of Charleston in *Porgy and Bess* and steppin' in *Choir Boy*, for example.

Porgy and Bess had only 8 professional dancers in the cast of 90, so part of Brown's task was to redefine what it means to be a dancer for the singers. Reflecting her belief that technique can be defined in multiple ways and exists within social dance and the community, as well as forms such as ballet and modern dance, she saw her task as being about empowering everyone, awakening their spirit and making them feel confident about the movement language that they have in their bodies, as well as about the steps themselves.

Her musical theatre work and that for her dance company inform each other. The double-dutch jump-rope moves in *BLACK GIRL: Linguistic Play* had their origin in something she created for *Fortress of Solitude*, the musical version of the Jonathan Lethem novel at the Public Theater, New York in 2014, for example. 'Working in both worlds has helped me be a better choreographer because theater is all about the story, the story, the story. And as a choreographer in concert dance, I want to be a storyteller' (Brown in Siebert, 2018).

Brown and her company are involved in ongoing educational initiatives, brought together in 2018 under the community engagement platform, Every Body Move. These include: The Gathering, an annual open forum for intergenerational black female artists to advocate for greater cultural equity and acknowledgement in the contemporary dance world; Black Girl Spectrum, a community initiative seeking to amplify the cultural and creative empowerment of black girls and women through dance, dialogue, and education; and Black Men Moving.

Brown remains ambitious. In an interview with Kristen Tauer (2019), she recalled researching Jerome Robbins' career and thinking that she wanted to do all that too, although even after all her success, she still wonders if being a black woman might restrict her opportunities. She is very aware of what she represents to younger black women, telling Tauer, 'Most of the time we don't see ourselves in the front of the room, in power. I want to normalise that. I feel that when you get that door open, it is your responsibility to keep it open for others'.

David Mead

Biographical details

Born 11 December 1979 in Jamaica, Queens, New York. **Studied** at Bernice Johnson Cultural Arts Center and DeVore Dance Center, Fiorello H. LaGuardia High School of Music & Art and the Performing Arts, Ailey School. Received a BFA in Dance from The University of North Carolina School of the Arts. **Career:** Danced with Ronald K. Brown/ Evidence: A Dance Company, 2001–2007. Guest dancer with Alvin Ailey American Dance Theater, 2008 & 2011, and Rennie Harris/Puremovement (2008–present). Founded Camille A. Brown & Dancers, 2006. Has also choreographed for Reflections Dance Company, Alvin Ailey American Dance Theater, Urban Bush Women, and PHILADANCO! among others; plus universities, major Broadway shows and regional theatre, opera, and television. Alongside ongoing education initiatives, she teaches widely while on tour, for other dance companies and at universities. **Awards and honours** include Presidential Scholar of the Arts Award, 1997; The Project Next Generation Award, 2006; five Princess Grace Awards, 2006, 2019; Works in Progress Residency Award, 2013; Choreographic Mentorship Co-Commission Award, 2013; Founder's Award of the International Association of Blacks in Dance, 2013; New York Dance and Performance Award ('Bessie') 2014; appointed a TED Fellow, 2015; Guggenheim Fellow, 2016; USA Statue Award, 2016; Ford Foundation Art of Change Fellow, 2017.

Works★

Awakened in Slumber (2002); *Nahum* (2005); *Afro Blue* (2006); *New Second Line* (2006); *More Time than Anybody* (2006); *Here We Go … Again?* (2007); *The Evolution of a Secured Feminine* (2007); *The Groove to Nobody's Business* (2007); *Saverio Palatella's Line – Wholegarment 3D*, New York Fashion Week, (2008); *Un Festin Divin* (2008); *Matchstick* (2008); *The Blues on Beale* (2009); *Mary* (2009); *Those Who See Light* (2009); *Good Times, Ha!* (2009); *Our Honeymoon is Over* (2010); *Been There, Done that* (2010); *Good and Grown* (2010); *Girlz Verse 1* (2010); *City of Rain* (2010); *By Way of East* (with Kyle Abraham, 2010); *One Second Past the Future* (2012); *A Streetcar Named Desire* (musical, dir. Emily Mann, 2012); *Soul Doctor* (musical, dir. Danny Wise, 2012); *Memories* (2012); *Strum* (2012); *Bind* (2012); *Mr. TOL E. RAncE* (2013); *The Winter's Tale* (musical, dir. Rebecca Taichman, 2013); *Fortress of Solitude* (musical, dir. Daniel Aukin, 2014); *The Box: A Black Comedy* (theatre, dir. Seth Bockley, 2014); *tick, tick … BOOM!* (musical, dir. Oliver Butler, 2014); *Galois* (rock musical, dir. Victor Maog, 2014); *Stagger Lee* (musical, dir. Patricia McGregor, 2015); *BLACK GIRL: Linguistic Play* (2015); *Cabin in the Sky* (musical, 2016); *BELLA: An American Tall Tale* (musical, dir. Robert O'Hara, 2017); *Once on this Island* (musical, dir. Michael Arden, 2017); *ink* (2017); *Jesus Christ Superstar Live* (musical for television, dir. David Leveaux, 2018); *The Wiz* (musical, dir. Denis Jones, 2018); *This Ain't No Disco* (rock opera, dir. Darko Tresnjak, 2018); *Choir Boy* (dir. Trip Cullman, 2019); *Much Ado about Nothing* (musical, dir. Kenny Leon, 2019); *Toni Stone* (theatre, dir. Pam MacKinnon, 2019); *Once* (opera, dir. J. Michael Zygo, 2019); *Porgy & Bess* (opera, dir. James Robinson, 2019); *For Colored Girls …* (musical, dir. Leah Gardiner, 2019); *Dreaming Zenzile* (musical, 2020); *Disney's Aida* (musical, dir. Schele Williams, forthcoming 2021).

★Published sources vary: order of works and dates cited are compiled primarily from Camille A. Brown's website and official CV, with additional research by the author.

Further reading

Interviews: with Risa Sarachan, 'Choreographer Camille A. Brown: A Queens Girl Who Now Creates Dance Everywhere', *Forbes Magazine*, 18 January 2019; Apollinaire Scherr, 'Camille A. Brown: For Me, Authenticity is a Top Priority', *The Financial Times*, 8 November 2019; Kristen Tauer, 'The Tony-Nominated Choreographer Discusses Her Met Opera Debut – *Porgy and Bess* – and Upcoming Revival of *For Colored Girls*', *WWD Digital Daily*, 24 September 2019.

Articles: Camille A. Brown, *BLACK GIRL: Linguistic Play*, TedxBeaconStreet Talk, tedxbeaconstreet.com, (video, 2016); Brian Seibert, 'Dance – A Storytelling Choreographer Who Listens to Her Audience', *New York Times*, 27 January 2018; Theresa Ruth Howard, 'Don't Dare Underestimate Camille A. Brown', *Dance Magazine*, April 2018; Jasmine Johnson, 'A Politics of Tenderness, Camille A. Brown and Dancers, BLACK GIRL: Linguistic Play', *The Black Scholar, Journal of Black Studies and Research*, 49(4), 2019.

CHENG TSUNG-LUNG

Cheng Tsung-lung, born in 1976 in Taipei, is one of the most active choreographers in Taiwan. He joined the Cloud Gate Dance Theatre of Taiwan as a dancer in 2002. In 2006, he began choreographing for

Cloud Gate 2 and served as its artistic director from 2014 to 2019. In 2020, he succeeded Lin Hwai-min as the artistic director of the Cloud Gate Dance Theatre of Taiwan, one of the most prominent modern dance companies in the world.

Cheng demonstrated talent in choreography while still a student at Taipei National University of the Arts (TNUA). In 2002, he choreographed *Yiao*, a ten-minute solo inspired by the shamanistic ritual of the Taoist religion in Taiwan, which was invited to open the Asia-Pacific Arts Forum in Taipei in 2005. *Yiao* foretold Cheng's interest in exploring the folk elements of Taiwan's local culture in later work, including *Beckoning (Lai)* in 2015 and *13 Tongues (Shisan Sheng)* in 2016.

Trained and cultivated in Taiwan's dance education system and professional environment, Cheng is an outstanding example of his generation of Taiwanese dance artists, in his mastery of diverse dance styles and interest in seeking artistic innovation with cultural originality. Since the 1970s, various styles and techniques of contemporary dance have entered the training system in Taiwan at different times, including Graham, Limon, Cunningham, contact improvisation, release technique, *Tanztheater* methods, and so on, in both educational and professional scenarios. At the same time, ballet has been an important foundation for training since its introduction during the later years of the Japanese colonial era (1895–1945). Parallel to these styles are *tai-chi*, martial arts, Peking Opera (*jingju*), and other *xiqu* bodily training, as well as Chinese dance. In other words, international exposure and indigenous systems are equally highlighted, while openness to hybridised innovation is encouraged. At TNUA where Cheng was educated, understanding the fundamental principles of movement, rather than just learning dance steps and exterior forms, has been emphasised since Lin Hwai-min founded the dance department in 1983, with the objectives of establishing a tradition of contemporary dance in Taiwan with cultural originality and corporeal authenticity.

When Cheng started choreographing professionally for Cloud Gate 2, he devoted himself to honing his craftsmanship by challenging minimalist music and its structural complexities in works like *Change (Bian)* in 2008 and *The Wall (Qiang)* in 2009. Choreographed to Terry Riley's *Keyboard Study #2*, *Change* begins with a male solo composed of movements evolving from small gestures such as nodding the head, twitching a shoulder, a knee or a foot, to isolated limb moves, to whole body motions. These motifs are then picked up by other dancers in solos, duets, and groups, as the tempo and rhythmic complexity of the music accumulate. Later in the dance, isolated limb gestures, brisk and sharp, interlock in duets to create unusual partnering configurations or are executed in confrontational engagements with suggestive emotional overtones.

A year later in *The Wall*, spatial configurations are deployed to convey meaning: programme notes (2011) suggest that 'Wall, being a protection, can also be an enclosure. Abstract and realistic at the same time, it may be the real wall that surrounds us and the psychological wall in our minds'. Dancers, clad in black, walk in lines on the periphery of the stage or cluster tightly in rows, creating images of the 'wall' through dance steps performed in canon with accumulated intensity, coloured by the rapid and tense rhythm of the string sextet in Michael Gordon's *Weather*. Angular gestures of dancers in black are counterpointed by more fluid and holistic movements in the second part of the dance, performed by some who have changed into light-coloured costumes. The coexistence and contrasting qualities of the groups endow the abstract choreography with layers of psychological connotation, from oppressive commanding postures to sweeping flows with a breath of free expression.

After a trip to Yunnan Province in southwestern China, *On the Road (Zai Lu Shang)* was a turning point in 2011. During the journey, Cheng observed the everyday bodily gestures of the people he encountered and listened to the local sound and music. This expanded his perception about movement vocabulary and he looked anew at the world in which he grew up, its people, sounds, colours, etc. In this male trio, choreographed to music from various cultures and traditions, the gestural vocabulary is like a mental mirror of a traveller, in which is reflected glimpses of gestures and body images collected in the journey and then remembered and mixed with things at home afterwards. As the dance proceeds, invisible ink prints on the dancers' white T-shirts gradually emerge, creating shadowy patterns when the dancers' sweat soaks into the fabric: corporeal memories imprinted on the dancers' bodies. This dance of choreographic travelogue won the grand prize for choreography at the MASDANZA in Spain in 2011 and later the prestigious Taishin Performing Arts Award in Taiwan in 2012.

Growing up in the oldest district of Taipei City, where ancient temples and religious festivals were abundant and mixed with working-class populations and vendors, Cheng was familiar with vernacular culture and people from all walks of life. Hence, when he posed questions to himself, 'Who am I? Where did I come from?', as he matured as a choreographer, all the physical images, colours, stories, and sounds from his memory became important sources of inspiration.

Choreographed for Cloud Gate 2 in 2015, *Beckoning* marks a milestone in this pursuit. The grounded weight of the dancers' bodies as well as fluid spiral movements demonstrate their solid training in *taichi daoyin* and martial arts in addition to contemporary dance, a training system similar to the Cloud Gate Dance Theatre of Taiwan. Yet unlike Lin Hwai-min's more poetic and refined interpretation of these Eastern body-mind methods, Cheng addresses a more robust and sometimes even vulgarised style of expression. The dancers' squat is deeper and wider. Their pelvises swing and gyrate, propelling torsos and limbs into figure-8 spirals or holding them buoyantly with suspended attitude. These bodily gestures and postures evoke the images of demi-gods, such as *jiajang*, or spiritual mediums, *jitung*, in Taiwanese folk religious parades, an ambience reinforced by the chiming of copper bells and the sound recording of an actual folk Taoist ritual in the music score.

References to Taiwanese local cultural and folk religious elements are further developed in *13 Tongues* (2016), the nickname of a legendary storyteller with the skill of mastering the voices of multiple characters. Inspired by this mythical figure described to him by his mother, Cheng transforms the magical power of plural-tongue storytelling into the diverse narrative elements of a multi-media dance. Famous pop musician Lin Chiang created a soundtrack collage of Taoist ritual chanting, old folk tunes, and traditional Beiguan music (northern winds), while visual artist Wang Yi-sheng designed a spectacular stage projection composed of Taoist sutra scripts, fluorescent colours from temple fairs, and the image of a huge koi carp swimming in and out of the stage setting. Voices play an important role too. Drawing upon the visceral energy from yelling, groaning, singing, and chanting, the dancers' spiralling and swinging steps are accentuated by raw pulsating rhythm. In the scene "Descending", a female dancer in a multi-coloured dress, glowing eerily in semi-darkness, is carried aloft by other dancers in black. Gesturing dramatically and flexing her legs as if flying, she is like a spiritual medium or the incarnation of a deity, being hoisted on the shoulders of worshippers or swayed in an imaginary holy palanquin.

Since *Beckoning*, an emphasis on the pulsating force of the pelvis, originated in the corporeal culture of folk religious parade formations (*zhentou*), has become a trademark of Cheng's choreography. In *13 Tongues*, it creates an intriguing mixture of the images of grass-root raw energy and magical sacred power. In *Lunar Halo* (*Mao Yueliang*) (2019), the energising strength of the pelvis is further associated with primordial, reproductive vitality through the violent shaking and gyrating motions of the dancers, evoking the idea of a tribe of people in a mythical place and time, faced with looming forces of destruction. The piece is full of ritualistic images ranging from nature worshipping circular dances, to rites of submission, to the dominating presence of the 'deity of technology', symbolised by the rigid image of a gigantic nude man on a high-resolution LED screen towering over a cluster of worshippers. As though an allegory foreseeing the fate of humankind, the dance narrates a world of depleted nature, in which the dancers, playing the role of exorcists, summon all the sensuous power of their bodies to combat the numbing and disembodying threat of artificial technology.

Ya-Ping Chen

Biographical details

Born in Taipei, 28 October 1976. **Studied** at the Taipei National University of the Arts, Taiwan (earning BFA degree in Dance, 2002). **Career:** Danced with Taiwanese choreographer Henry Yu, 1993, and with Cloud Gate Dance Theatre of Taiwan, 2002 to 2003; started choreographing for Cloud Gate 2 in 2006 before serving as its artistic director, 2014 to 2019; succeeded Lin Hwai-min as artistic director of Cloud Gate Dance Theatre of Taiwan in 2020. Has also choreographed for HORSE Dance Company (Taiwan), Taipei National University of the Arts, Expressions Dance Company (Australia), Transitions Dance Company (Trinity Laban, UK), and Sydney Dance Company (Australia). **Awards** include MASDANZA, Spain, 2011; Taishin Performing Arts Award in Taiwan, 2012.

Works

Yao (2002); *White Adhesives* (2005); *Memory* (2006); *Tête-Bêche* (2006); *A Dignified Joke* (2006); *Fragments of Memory* (2007); *Change* (2008); *Radix* (2009); *The Wall* (2009); *Happiness and Music* (2009); *Crack* (2010); *On the Road* (2011); *Blue Hour* (2013); *Present* (2013); *Dorian Gray* (2014); *Beckoning* (2015); *13 Tongues* (2016); *Full Moon* (2017); *Dream Catcher* (2017); *Lunar Halo* (2019); *Multiplication* (2019).

Further reading

Interviews: with Li Chia-chi, 'Pondering on the Living World and Retrieving What We Have Forgotten: Lin Chiang & Cheng Tsung-lung', *Performance Arts Review*, February 2016; Li Chia-chi, 'Cheng Tsung-lung's *Lunar Halo* Beckoning the Primitive Energy of the Body', *Performance Arts Review*, April 2019; Fan Xiang-jun, 'Cheng Tsung-lung: Seeing the Light in Darkness, Seeing the World in the Body', *Artouch*, 11 April 2019.

Articles: Lin Yatin, 'Re-writing/Re-dancing Dorian Gray', *Sino-corporealities: Contemporary Dance from Taipei, Hong Kong, and New York*, Taipei, 2015; Gerard Davis, '13 Tongues', *Dance Europe*, April 2016; Cheng Tsung-lung and Hsieh Wang-ling, 'Dialogue through Literature' (*Wenshui xiangduilun*), *United Daily* (*Lianhe bao*), 3, 10, 17, 26, 31 December 2018; David Mead, 'The Right Time', dancing-times.co.uk, February 2020.

SIDI LARBI CHERKAOUI

The dancer and director Sidi Larbi Cherkaoui creates large-scale dance theatre and opera, commissions for ballet companies, music videos, musicals, and circus. His oeuvre is characterised by transcultural exchange, collaborating with dancers, actors, musicians, and visual artists from diverse cultural backgrounds, and by an eclectic blending of global dance styles, such as Kuchipudi, breaking, flamenco, ballet, tango, martial arts, and other bodily practices, gestures, songs, speech, music, and design. His works explore life's big questions: identity, community, culture, war, migration, religious fundamentalism, geo-politics, and environmental crisis.

Cherkaoui grew up in Belgium with a Flemish mother and a Moroccan father; hence different languages, cultural traditions, and religions influenced his sense of multifaceted identity from the start. As a young dancer, he was spotted by Alain Platel in the Best Belgian Dance Solo competition in 1995 and invited to perform with Les Ballets C de la B in *Iets op Bach* (1998). This eclectic dance theatre company supported Cherkaoui in the early development of his choreographic practice, including momentous collaborations with dramaturges Hildegard De Vuyst and Guy Cools. He was thus a part of the new dance dramaturgies that emerged from within the internationally significant Flemish contemporary dance scene. Transcultural dialogue and far-reaching collaboration, with other choreographers, dancers, musicians, composers, designers, visual artists, and film-makers, are his core artistic values.

Diverse casts, loosely episodic structures, and multi-layered and complex mise-en-scène became Cherkaoui's dominant aesthetic in the first decade of the 21st century. *Rien de Rien* (2000), the work through which he became renowned on the international dance scene, featured comical scenes incorporating lambada, tango, ballet, and voguing. In juxtaposition, Cherkaoui dances some confronting solos and duets in this work, where his body is contorted, inverted, and violently manipulated, suggesting his subjective experience as a second-generation immigrant during the rise of the Flemish populist radical right. Travel stories revealing cultural friction were recounted

45

by more than one person in unison, in different languages left untranslated. The choreographic and dramaturgic strategies worked to confound spectators, often leaving them not understanding and having to work hard to complete the process of meaning production.

This multi-layered and kaleidoscopic choreographic aesthetic, where multiple small scenes occur simultaneously away from centre stage, was developed further by Cherkaoui in large group works later in the decade. *Foi* (2003) explores belief and religion through a mismatched group of protagonists who are looking to each other for support in the moments after a catastrophe. A group of 'angels', dressed in white and beige, manipulate the protagonists into action without them being aware of their presence. In *Myth* (2007), some of those same protagonists interact with 'shadows' dressed in black, this time representing their repressed emotions and desires in a Jungian psychoanalytical sense. These early works are sometimes compared to the medieval Flemish paintings of Pieter Bruegel the Elder or Hieronymous Bosch (Micrologus, *Myth – Sidi Larbi Cherkaoui: The Music*, booklet with CD, 2007). They share the same dramaturgical blueprint of juxtaposing disparate layers of meaning – confronting choreographic images, shards of stories, songs, and religious iconography – inviting engaged spectatorship in order to weave these together into meaningful wholes. Pieces of the transcultural puzzle are always missing to any one spectator, so that dialogue with others, further thinking, and research are needed.

A key collaboration that challenged Cherkaoui's approach in terms of an overfilled mise-en-scène was with the British sculptor Antony Gormley. They first worked together on *zero degrees* (co-choreographed and co-directed with Akram Khan, 2005). There, the stage is pared back in muted colours, with the musicians located behind a gauze screen upstage. Two dummies (casts of Cherkaoui and Khan's bodies) and the multiple shadows created through Mikki Kunttu's lighting, offer potential for meanings to emerge. The two performers explore their shared and diverging experiences of identity through storytelling, song, kathak, and kung fu. *Sutra* (2008), in collaboration with the monks of the Shaolin temple, is based on Cherkaoui's visit to and ethnographic inquiry into this unique Buddhist community. Gormley designed a set of man-sized wooden boxes, open on one side and of such dimensions that they are combinable and reconfigurable like building blocks, 'mobile architecture' (Sabine Sörgel, *Dance and the Body in Western Theatre: 1948 to the Present*, London, 2015). In *Babel(words)* (co-choreographed with Damien Jalet, 2010), Gormley's set of five aluminium cuboid structures frame the performers' bodies and their activities in yet another way; these structures are manipulated by the group and illustrate that space is continuously claimed, transformed, and repurposed. The work's focus on borders, territory, and language is aligned with Cherkaoui and Jalet's interest in geopolitics; again, the dramaturgical layers invite spectators to engage in a similar questioning of the world around them.

While leading his own dance company Eastman, based in Antwerp, Cherkaoui also pursues commissions for ballet companies. *In Memoriam* (2004) and *Mea Culpa* (2006) for Les Ballets de Monte Carlo and *Boléro* (co-created with Damien Jalet and Marina Abramović, 2013) for the Opéra National de Paris are noteworthy here. Working with classically trained dancers means that Cherkaoui sometimes includes pointe work, while exploring what emerges when classical movement coordination is combined with the fluid and circular motions that are characteristic of his own practice. He choreographs operas, for example the Wagner trilogy *Der Ring des Nibelungen* (2010–2013) in collaboration with director Guy Cassiers for Teatro alla Scala in Milan and the Staatsoper in Berlin. He also increasingly directs operas, for example *Shell Shock: A Requiem of War* (2014) for La Monnaie, with music by Nicholas Lens and text by Nick Cave. Cherkaoui's opera work indicates a continuing interest in exploring different artistic practices, transcending disciplinary boundaries and reaching new audiences. In 2015, he became Artistic Director of the Royal Ballet Flanders in his hometown Antwerp. Not only does he choreograph for this company, but he also uses his international network to secure historically significant repertoire and ground-breaking new commissions for them.

Cherkaoui does not subscribe to perceived hierarchies between so-called high art and popular culture and has explored the intersections between different art forms and media throughout. He recently choreographed the music video *Apeshit* (2018) for Beyoncé Knowles and Jay-Z. Set in the Louvre in Paris, it juxtaposes images of dancers of different ethnicities with some of the many depictions of imperial conquest in the museum's permanent collection. Commentators noticed that '"Apeshit" makes some pithy [...] comments on racism, slavery and the dominance of western neoclassical aesthetic standards' (Bidisha, 'A guide to Beyoncé and Jay-Z's new video ...', *The Guardian*, 18 June 2018). The feature film *Girl* (2018) by Lukas Dhont, explores the mental and physical challenges of the 15-year-old transgender ballerina Lara, played by Victor Polster. The film uses dance to illustrate how the body and gender are closely intertwined. It received international accolades, but also significant criticism from trans and queer writers (Cathy Brennan, 'It's winning awards, but Girl is no victory for trans representation', *British Film Institute* website, October 2018). *Jagged Little Pill* (2018), by Alanis Morissette and Diablo Cody, signifies Cherkaoui's longstanding interest in musicals. The choreography challenges what Broadway audiences expect, as it combines 'highly structured improvisations [and] eerie, ghostlike "avatars", as dancers express characters' inner emotions when words alone can't do them justice' (Madeline Schrock, 'Inside Jagged Little Pill's Arresting Dance Scene That Depicts Opioid Overdose', *Dance Magazine*, December 2019).

Cherkaoui's aesthetic is deeply perfused with the effects of collaboration – across cultures, disciplines, and media – and continues to stretch a growing audience's engagement with dance in an expanding range of contexts.

Lise Uytterhoeven

Biographical details

Born in Antwerp, 10 March 1976. **Studied** at P.A.R.T.S., Brussels. **Career:** performed and choreographed with Les Ballets C de la B, Ghent, c. 1998–2004, and Toneelhuis, Antwerp, c. 2004–2009; associate artist at Sadler's Wells Theatre, London, and Théâtre National de Bretagne, Rennes; founding dancer, choreographer, and director, Eastman, Antwerp, 2010 onwards; Artistic Director of Royal Ballet Flanders since 2015. Has also choreographed and directed for other theatres, opera houses, and dance companies, including Les Ballets de Monte Carlo, Royal Danish Ballet, Teatro alla Scala, GöteborgsOperans Danskompani, Opera Ballet Vlaanderen, La Monnaie, The Royal Ballet, Paris Opéra Ballet, and Martha Graham Dance Company. Created work with and/or for artists including Akram Khan, María Pagés, Shantala Shivalingappa, Colin Dunne, Natalia Osipova, Ivan Vasiliev, Carlos Acosta, and Beyoncé. Choreographed for Cirque du Soleil, films, music videos, and musicals, including *Jagged Little Pill*. **Awards and honours** include Olivier Awards, 2010 and 2014; Ballet-Tanz awards, 2008, 2011, 2017; Kairos Prize, 2009; Flemish Culture Award, 2012; Commandeur dans l'Ordre des Arts et des Lettres, 2019.

Works

I Wanna Melt with U (1995); *Atamé (Bal Moderne)* (1997); *Afwezen (fatalidad)* (1999); *Anonymous Society* (dir. Andrew Wale, 1999); *Rien de Rien* (2000); *Tower* (film, dir. Koen Gisen, 2000); *Sherazadje* (co-directed with Michel Scohy and Abdelmalek Kadi, 2001); *It* (with Wim Vandekeybus, 2002); *Ook* (with Nienke Reehorst, 2002); *In the Mood (Bal Moderne)* (2002); *D'avant* (with Juan Kruz Diaz de Garaio Esnaola, Luc Dunberry, Damien Jalet, 2002); *Hôtel Palace* (film, dir. Jérôme Cassou, 2003); *Foi* (2003); *In Memoriam* (2004);

Tempus Fugit (2004); *Terre Battue* (film, dir. Jérôme Cassou, 2004); *Corpus Bach* (with Nicolas Vladyslav, 2005); *Zero Degrees* (with Akram Khan, 2005); *Some Girls Are Bigger than Others* (musical, dir. Andrew Wale, 2005); *Loin* (2005); *Tempus Fugit* (film, dir. Anaïs Spiro and Olivier Spiro, 2005); *Ik hou van u/Je t'aime, tu sais (Bal Moderne)* (with Damien Jalet, 2005); *End* (2006); *Mea Culpa* (2006); *Aleko* (with Damien Jalet, 2006); *L'homme De Bois* (2007); *Intermezzo* (dir. Guy Cassiers, 2007); *Myth* (2007); *La Zon-mai* (multimedia installation, with Gilles Delmas, 2007); *Apocrifu* (2007); *Hermesdanse (Bal Moderne)* (with Damien Jalet, 2007); *Sutra* (2008); *Origine* (2008); *Modern Love* (film, dir. Stéphane Kazandjian, 2008); *Le bruit des gens autour* (film, dir. Diastème, 2008); *Interconnexions* (2008); *49-jae* (2009); *Adam's Appels* (with Iris Bouche and Laura Neyskens, 2009); *House of the Sleeping Beauties* (opera; dir. Guy Cassiers, 2009); *Faun* (2009); *Orbo Novo* (2009); *Dunas* (with María Pagés, 2009); *Babel(words)* (with Damien Jalet, 2010); *Rein* (2010); *Everland* (with Dirk De Lathauwer, Natascha Pire, Mike Alvarez, Koen De Preter, Randi De Vlieghe, Christophe Lequesne, 2010); *Shoes* (with Stephen Mear, Aletta Collins, Kate Prince, Mark Smith, 2010); *Play* (with Shantala Shivalingappa, 2010); *Bound* (2010); *Das Rheingold* (opera, dir. Guy Cassiers, 2010); *Labyrinth* (2011); *It 3.0* (with Wim Vandekeybus, 2011); *TeZukA* (2011); *Constellation* (2011); *Puz/zle* (2012); *Niente Di Me* (film, co-directed with Paul Van Caudenberg, 2012); *Siegfried* (opera, dir. Guy Cassiers, 2012); *Venn* (with Damien Jalet, 2012); *Anna Karenina* (film, dir. Joe Wright, 2012); *Automaton* (with Renee Jaworski, 2012); *Valtari* (film, dir. Christian Larson, 2012); *Michael Jackson ONE* (dir. Jamie King, 2013); 生长genesis (2013); *milonga* (2013); *Boléro* (co-directed with Jalet and Marina Abramović, 2013); *4D* (with Damien Jalet, 2013); *Götterdämmerung* (opera, dir. Guy Cassiers, 2013); *A Season in the Congo* (dir. Joe Wright, 2013); *Shell Shock, a Requiem of War* (opera, 2014); *Noetic* (2014); *Icarus* (2014); *La Mano Encima* (film, with Nelida Rodriguez de Aure, dir. Hesdy Lonwijk, 2014); *KURIOS, Cabinet of Curiosities* (dir. Michel Laprise, 2014); *Mercy* (2014); *Fractus V* (2015); *Fall* (2015); *Pluto* (2015); *Frame[d]* (with Damien Jalet, 2015); *Hamlet* (dir. Lyndsey Turner, 2015); *Der Feuervogel* (2015); *Bijenkorf: Fashion Identity* (film, dir. Nadav Kander, 2015); *West Side Story* (dir. Maja Jantar, 2015); *Harbor Me* (2015); *Pan* (film, dir. Joe Wright, 2015); *Qutb* (2016); *Icon* (2016); *Babel 7.16* (with Damien Jalet, 2016); *Exhibition* (2016); *Casse-Noisette* (with Edouard Lock and Arthur Pita, 2016); *Les Indes Galantes* (opera, 2016); *Human Sanctuary* (video installation, dir. Daniel Sannwald, 2016); *Break the Routine* (film, dir. Noam Murro, 2016); *Satyagraha* (opera, 2017); *Mermaid* (2017); *Memento Mori* (2017); *Nomad* (2017); *Mosaic* (2017); *Requiem* (2017); *I Will Fall for You* (film, co-directed with Yoann Lemoine, 2017); *In Your Room* (film, dir. Anton Corbijn, 2017); *When I Am Laid in Earth* (2017); *Mononoke* (2017); *Cain and Abel* (2017); *Twilly d'Hermès* (film, with Jennifer White; dir. Arnaud Uyttenhove, 2017); *Girl* (film, dir. Lukas Dhont, 2018); *Pelléas et Mélisande* (with Damien Jalet, 2018); *Jagged Little Pill* (musical by Alanis Morissette and Diablo Cody, 2018); *Apeshit* (music video with JaQuel Knight; dir. Ricky Saiz, 2018); *Stoic* (2018); *The Kuru Field of Justice* (2018); *Universal Machine* (film, dir. Daniel Askill, 2019); *Scenes from Nomad* (2019); *Spirit* (film, dir. Jake Nava, 2019); *Autumn (Four Seasons)* (film, dir. Rahi Rezvani, 2019); *Summer (Four Seasons)* (film, dir. Rahi Rezvani, 2019); *Medusa* (2019); *Session* (with Colin Dunne, 2019); *Alceste* (2019); *Invisible Cities* (dir. Leo Warner, 2019).

Further reading

Interviews: with Lise Uytterhoeven, 'On Collaboration and Navigating between Dance Cultures', in *The Ethics of Art: Ecological Turns in the Performing Arts* (eds. Guy Cools and Pascal Gielen), Valiz, 2014; Guy Cools, *body:language #1. The Mythic Body: Guy Cools with Sidi Larbi Cherkaoui,* Sadler's Wells, 2012.

Articles: Lou Cope, 'Sidi Larbi Cherkaoui: Myth – Mapping the Multiple', in *Making Contemporary Theatre: International Rehearsal Processes* (eds. Jen Harvie and Andy Lavender), Manchester, 2010; Lise Uytterhoeven, 'Dreams, Myth, History: Sidi Larbi Cherkaoui's Dramaturgies', *Contemporary Theatre Review*, 21(3), August 2011; Sanjoy Roy, 'Polyphony, Playing and Politics: The Many Voices of Sidi Larbi Cherkaoui', *Springback Magazine*, December 2018.

Books: Lise Uytterhoeven, *Sidi Larbi Cherkaoui: Dramaturgy and Engaged Spectatorship*, London, 2019; Guy Cools, *In-between Dance Cultures: On the Migratory Artistic Identity of Sidi Larbi Cherkaoui and Akram Khan*, Amsterdam, 2015; Sabine Sörgel, *Dance and the Body in Western Theatre: 1948 to the Present*, London, 2015; Jo Butterworth and Liesbeth Wildschut (eds.), *Contemporary Choreography: A Critical Reader*, 2nd ed., London and New York, 2018; Ramsay Burt, *Ungoverning Dance: Contemporary European Theatre Dance and the Commons*, Oxford, 2016; Lise Uytterhoeven, *Oxford Handbook of Contemporary Ballet* (Kathrina Farrugia-Kriel and Jill Nunes Jensen, eds.), 2021.

DEBORAH COLKER

Deborah Colker's choreography is infused with the vibrancy and diversity of the Brazilian culture. Her theatrical and entertaining dance style engages audiences with its accessibility, but at times this is a challenging issue: 'Call them pieces of sophisticated populist fusion or smart art with plenty of heart. However you label Colker's dances, they are as authentically Brazilian as their creator. 'My work is like Brazil,' Colker agrees, 'with the mix of colours, the dynamics and rhythms'…' (Hutera, undated).

Given the varied interests in Colker's background, including music, psychology, sport, ballet, contemporary dance, and movement direction within theatre contexts, it is perhaps unsurprising that within a single piece she often mixes dance techniques, familiar everyday gestures, gymnastic, and circus skills. However, her work is best known for use of three-dimensional set designs, often colossal in size. Not only visually stylish, set design is crucial: prompting specific uses of space; ideas around motion; interaction during the initial movement exploration; and challenges to physical possibilities.

Companhia de Dança Deborah Colker, which she founded in 1994, has been funded by Petrobras (Brazil's state oil company) since 1995. This assisted her to forge a collaboration with visual artist Gringo Cardia, hence striking set designs are in her earliest works. *Mix* (1996), for example, consists of sections from *Vulcão* (1994) and *Velox* (1995). In the final section 'Mountaineering' (from *Velox*), dancers explore vertical space, challenging gravity by traversing a huge wall covered in rows of small projecting hand-holds. They use these to climb, hang off, and to balance on, performing broad gestures with limbs released from support. Groups of dancers often perform in dare devil unison, presenting abstract sculptural design and pulse-driven moving patterns. For example, dancers in close proximity bounce up and down the surface with coordinated, sure-footed aplomb. Their confidence is breath-taking (there are no soft surfaces below if they fall) but so too is the ingenuity needed in the engineering of this wall.

Even in its title, 'Mountaineering' demonstrates that influences from sport, such as energy and athleticism, are evident in these early works (Colker was a serious volleyball player). This provides reviewers with another perspective with which to address her choreographic style, as Watson (2000) indicates for *Mix*: 'The ideal of aesthetic athleticism, as embodied in her dancers, is the moving force that steers her work. It's most evident in the floor-bound sections taken from *Velox* ... directly inspired by the dynamics of sport'. In the section called 'Quotidian' for example, dancers parade back and forth, their intense focus on the body evoking the competitive qualities of elite athletes. Costuming accentuates this with sportswear references, for example there are numbers on the backs of the T-shirts. This section also has a striking set design – several large rotating blades overhead, like wind turbines, draw attention to the repetitive, rhythmical qualities of the pulse-driven dance phrases. The fusion of movement and set design in *Mix* was popular with audiences and critics alike. When it toured to London in 2001, Colker received a Laurence Olivier Award for outstanding achievement in dance.

In *Rota* (1997), an episodic approach again occurs with floor-bound and aerial sections. A backcloth, patterned with lines like grid references on a map, echoes the dance's title (route). Gestural phrases occur again, a hand brushing the hair back for example, interspersed with angular actions and energetic travel, dancers leaping, rolling and sliding across the floor. Like *Mix*, repetition and fast paced rhythmicality produce movement that is abstract in impact, 'aesthetic athleticism' to borrow Watson's apt terminology. Later, a giant metallic wheel structure dominates the stage. Dancers use their body weight to provide momentum to move this: two dancers, hanging off either side, counterbalance each other to see-saw up and down in long gliding arcs; and four travel through the top rungs producing continuous rotations, for example. Dancers soar above the stage in aerial playfulness, but their movement is also functional. It determines how far and fast the wheel will circle. Function and form are in harmony with the physical mechanism.

Colker starts with an idea which is further developed in collaboration with the designer. Cardia, now a long standing collaborator, brings a sense of visual style and an understanding of practical structures. Her ideas come from personal experience. A visit to Disneyland suggested the wheel in *Rota*. For *Casa* (1999), a visit to the Bauhaus Museum in Germany prompted an enormous set. As Colker explained to Meisner, (2002):

> "And I phoned Gringo and I said, 'Oh, I'm thinking of doing a house', and he said, 'WHAAAT?' " She also told him that she wanted a house that could mutate, so it would move along with the performers. "He said, 'OK, let's try, but it will be hard.' He had to think carefully about the construction because with 16 dancers it has to be very strong."

Cardia provided Colker with an enormous opened-out house built on multiple levels. The walls can move, so like much of the earlier set design it is not static. Again, everyday gestures are integrated with abstract actions into technically proficient, rhythmic, and energetic phrases: *Casa* foregrounds 'the acrobatics of relationships and the accommodations people sharing a space must make in order to fit into each other's lives ... movement material is derived from universally familiar activities like cooking and eating, sleeping, fighting, dressing and undressing, and having sex' (Hutera, undated). Colker references the realities of life but without presenting them literally.

Sets can contextualise the movement as in *Casa*, but also prompt inventiveness by offering restrictions. In *4 por 4* (2002), Colker responds to four visual artists. For the final section Cardia covers the stage with ninety china vases placed in multiple rows. The dancers travel along these, their sure-footed linear pathways embracing the technical challenge, audacious physicality pitted against the delicate quality of the porcelain. Colker explains: "it is very important to propose new spaces to find new movement, create new possibilities and new experiences" (in Meisner, 2002).

The use of set design to provide spatial challenges and ideas is an abiding interest. For example, in the first part of *Nó* (2005), dancers explore desire and bondage using 120 ropes. In *Cruel* (2008), three revolving mirrors with holes through the centre are large enough to hang through, producing a two-headed torso (reflection in the mirror creating symmetry) or disconnected limbs. Both works, in a non-narrative manner, again suggest the realities of living: love, isolation, cruelty, and control.

A new source for ideas materialised with *Tatyana* (2011). Based on the character in Pushkin's 19th century book *Eugene Onegin*, Colker's choreography did not retell the plot, it was an exploration of feelings. As she explained to Skinner (2016):

> It's more a life story than a love story – about choice and the moment you realise that you're in love; how love is the most important thing in life, which can transform everything.... It was then I understood how much poetry and dance are related. They're both abstract, full of metaphors and verses. It's a different kind of dramaturgy than narrative; it's about creating an atmosphere, a scene, a texture full of meaning and feeling.

Belle (2014) continues this approach. In Joseph Kessel's 1928 book, *Belle de Jour*, the protagonist Severine is trapped between her bourgeois existence and her secret life in a brothel. Colker echoes this double identity by using two dancers to indicate Severine and disrupt a narrative approach.

In 2016, Colker was the director of movement for the opening ceremony of the Olympic Games, in Rio de Janeiro. The experience of presenting something of the essence of Brazilian culture brought to the fore her interest in exploring this and the human condition further. Her latest work in 2017, *Cão Sem Plumas* [Dog Without Feathers], is based on Joao Cabral de Melo Neto's poem about the Capibaribe River in Northeast Brazil. According to Colker (in Masso, 2019):

> Day-to-day life was also the subject of many pieces: things that seem very trivial on the surface always interested me a lot. Themes such as home, sports, the streets and play were always my inspiration. But since 2005, the human condition, the enigmas of life, the inconceivable in existence have become my focus. I have found that what's under the surface has more feeling.

The choreography is structured into sections, her characteristic approach, which link around themes from the poem. The river and the indigenous people who live along its banks are known to Brazilians (the river runs dry but the rainy season replenishes it), but can also be interpreted as metaphors for ecological crisis, inequality, and survival. Colker added a new medium in her collaboration with the film-maker Claudio Assis. The dancers perform in front of a huge screen, creating an interactive dialogue between the film and the movement.

Colker also found a source of ideas in the geographical location, which she and the company visited. The dancers for example, are covered in dry mud from top to toe, faces caked with it, hair plastered down. This hides their individuality and promotes a communal identity; it also dehumanises and disguises their bodies almost as if they had crawled out of the river. Crabs are found in the mangroves of the riverbank, and she translates this into crablike movement − crouching, a low level stance, and angular arms with elbows bent upward, give the dancers a half-human appearance. Dark lighting by Jorginho De Carvalho, another of Colker's long-term collaborators, continues the disguise. It allows the real and filmed dancers to become indistinguishable as they ebb and flow, close up body parts and distanced bodies interacting, so that where the live group begins and ends is masked.

The film also shows the arid landscape when the river runs dry, and one particular interaction identifies the close relationship between the celluloid dancer and the living one: 'After a figure in the film creates puffs of dust by rubbing his feet on the dry earth, a dancer, onstage, swivels and swirls under a spotlight within a cloud of powder' (Kourlas, 2020).

Colker's dancers are trained in contemporary dance and ballet. In *Cão Sem Plumas*, she uses the latter for technical content and expressive quality. For example, in a section called 'Herons', three dancers in pointe shoes, step, balance, and preen with a birdlike aloof disdain. It is open to interpretation: natural life on the river asserting itself, a memory of what has been lost, creatures who stand apart from the human condition, or people who are careless of ecological destruction. The representations are not literal but evoke possibilities. Set design furthers this. Wooden, box-like slatted structures which thereby seem fragile, on which the dancers move, render the precariousness of the human condition in a different form.

Colker's work typically results from lengthy research and development periods. As Colker tells Wilson, (2019):

For two years Claudio and I talked and discussed what was essential in the poem. He went to most of the rehearsals. We've started this creative process in July 2014. In 2016, we did a three-week residency in the Brazilian state of Pernambuco, where we filmed in six cities, gave workshops, performed in public squares and shared experiences with the people of these cities (workers, popular artists, dancers, poets, and more). We left this residency filled with enough raw material to complete *Dog Without Feathers*, it took us a long time to bring the film and the stage performance together. The stage invades the film, and the film invades the stage.

Colker achieved rapid success with her company, and her work is popular within Brazil. For example, *Casa* was presented at a continuous nine-week run in Rio de Janeiro, unusual anywhere for a contemporary dance company. While known globally for use of stylish set design, as Hutera (undated) indicates: 'the point of Colker's dances, and the key to their enormous popularity in her native country, is accessibility, not high concepts. They're loaded with visual imagination and kinetic daring, yet at the same time thoroughly grounded in a recognisable reality'.

Lorna Sanders

Biographical details

Born in 1960, Rio de Janeiro, Brazil; Jewish Russian heritage. Father was a violinist and conductor. **Studied** piano from age eight, and later jazz, tap, ballet and then contemporary dance; was a championship volleyball player. Studied music at PROART, School of Music and a degree in Psychology at the University of Rio de Janeiro. **Career:** includes: stage-directing Domingos de Oliveira's *The Irresistible Adventure* in 1984, then movement direction for over 30 plays; choreographed music shows, video clips, Carnival parades for important schools of samba 1995–1997 and 2005–2007; danced, choreographed and taught at Grupo Coringa, 1980–1988, a contemporary dance company led by Graciela Figueiroa (dancer with Twyla Tharp in the 1960s). Founded Companhia de Dança Deborah Colker in 1994, Rio de Janeiro; tours Brazil and internationally, including North and South America, United Kingdom, Europe, New Zealand, Hong Kong, and Singapore. Director of movement for Rio de Janeiro Olympics 2016. Artist in residence, Southbank Centre, London, UK, from 2019. **Awards and honours** include Jornal O Globo Awards 1995 & 1997; Jornal Do Brasil Awards 1995, 1997, & 1999; Brazil's Prêmio Ministério da Cultura Award 1997; Laurence Olivier Award 2001; Benois de la Danse Award 2018.

Works

Vulcão (1994); *Velox* (1995); *Mix* (fusion of *Vulcão* and *Velox*, 1996); *Rota* (1997); *Casa* (1999); *4 por 4* (coll., with visual artists Cildo Meireles, Chelpa Ferro, Victor Arruda, Gringo Cardia, 2002); *Ela* (2003); *Nó* [Knot] (2005); *Dínamo* (originally *Maracanã*, 2006); *Cruel* (2008); *Ovo* (2009); *Tatyana* (2011); *Belle* (2014); *Opening Ceremony, Rio de Janeiro Olympics Games* (2016); *Vero* (fusion of *Velox* and *Rota*, 2016); *Cão Sem Plumas* (2017).

Further reading

Interviews: with Nadine Meisner, 'Deborah Colker: A Real Live Wire', *The Independent*, 7 October 2002; Althea Skinner, 'Deborah Colker, The Olympian Choreographer of Brazil', danceicons.org, August–September 2016; Glen Wilson, 'Deborah Colker on Dog Without Feathers and Returning to London', southbankcentre.co.uk/blog, 11 March 2019; Giverny Masso, 'Choreographer Deborah Colker: Dog Without Feathers is the Most Visceral Show I've Made', thestage.co.uk/features, 7 May 2019.

Articles: Donald Hutera, 'Focus on Deborah Colker', danceconsortium. com/features, undated; Donald Hutera, 'Profile of Deborah Colker', *Dance Magazine*, February 2000; Keith Watson, 'You're My Wonder Wall', *The Guardian*, 22 July 2000; Jenny Gilbert, 'A Bull in a China Shop. But No Breakages', *The Independent*, 14 December 2003; Sanjoy Roy, 'Step-by-Step Guide to Dance: Deborah Colker', *The Guardian*, 14 April 2010; Gia Kourlas, 'Film Overwhelms Dance in a Mud-Caked Trip to Brazil', *New York Times*, 5 February 2020.

Book: Giselle Ruiz, *Graciela e Grupo Coringa. A Dança Contemporânea Carioca dos Anos 1970/80* (Portuguese Brazilian), Mauad, 2013 (information about the dance company Colker performed with).

JORGE CRECIS

Jorge Crecis is one of the most unique practitioners of his generation. His work is marked by a searching mind that brings to his creations mathematical precision and a unique ensemble energy derived from the risk factors and rule-bound games he designs for his choreographies. For Crecis, group practice is the execution of an ethic: without wide-awake collaboration we simply cannot survive. This requires a certain mental attitude, trained through action. His commitment to presence, and to ensuring a heightened state of focus at each moment of performance, derives from his experience of Dervish Whirling, an ancient Sufi practice in which turning on the spot for extended periods induces states of trance. His research into how to reproduce the psycho-physical condition achieved in whirling has become his training methodology *Towards Vivencia* (towardsvivencia.com), 'vivencia' being a Spanish word for 'experience', better translated as 'lived experience'. This was crafted during a decade of PhD study at Goldsmiths University, London, in the Department of Theatre and Performance.

Crecis' interdisciplinary research is indicative of his idiosyncratic approach to dance-making. He read enthusiastically into psychology, neuroscience, anthropology, phenomenology, theatre training methodologies, and performance studies, as he heuristically forged his system for replicating altered states of consciousness. His oeuvre might be understood as an expression of Merleau-Ponty's assertion that the body, understood in phenomenological terms, is 'no longer conceived as an object of the world but as our means of communicating with it' (*The Phenomenology of Perception,* London, 2004, p.106). Merleau-Ponty's legacy has been to link experience to consciousness as corporeally constituted: perception is embodied. It is such ideas on how consciousness operates within and from proprioceptive awareness that drives Crecis' creative impetus.

The pragmatic quest is to create a space of safe danger in which the individual submits to an organised group dynamic, where reflexes are excited and concentration is at its maximum. Crecis' project is an adventure into what the body can do with others in space and time, and a social commitment in terms of collectivising 'peak performance' as a human resource. He believes that such practice has the potential to generate real change in people's lived experience.

In 2014, Crecis co-founded, with the Palestinian Samar Haddad King, *min tala,* a Pan-Arab dance company that uses contemporary dance as a peacekeeping, personal and professional development tool in areas of conflict in the Middle East. This is one example of the way he connects his politics directly with his practice. A consistent theme emerges: commitment to exploring how dance can speak about human society as a collaborative organism. A socialist spirit is practised in his work, posited thematically as task-based group movement scores, and amplified in the revealed labour of the dancer. Ensemble actions within his choreographic purpose equal social necessity: cooperation. There is no literal message, his entire scenographic oeuvre – understood as embracing everything on stage including performers – connotes meaning. His signature material elements provide compositional functionality: jeopardy against which the dancers must collaborate to ensure the safety of all.

Inspired by his involvement in the Madrid Occupy movement protests in May 2011, *Kingdom*, created for Scottish Dance Theatre in

2014, challenged ten performers to construct a six metre human shelter using eighty bamboo poles and one hundred and twenty pieces of red rope, an endeavour completed in a challenging time frame: teamwork explored as compositional substance. A three-dimensional structure evolves during the performance, alluding to the fact that many of the world's dwellings are constructed of such material, vulnerable to flood and earthquake. The fluid movement echoes the quality of bamboo itself. This pragmatic yet poetic dramaturgy aims to replicate the experience of cooperative struggle, translating the Occupy movement into a carefully designed effort at building and moving together. *Trans La Valo*, created in Beijing for Nine Dance Theatre in 2013, addresses urban motifs, exploring unpredictability and the imperative of social cohesion for group survival, for '[a] crowd will always be stronger than an individual' (jorgecrecis.com/trans-la-valo-en). Here, obstacles require the negotiation of a constantly mobile scenography: swinging perspex boxes, inside which are sculptural forms connoting cityscapes. Performers dodge these as if teaching pedestrians the necessary art of crowd flow in densely populated conditions. The choreography reminds us, typically, of a sports event.

A competitive karate practitioner, trained from the age of six, there is more than a trace of martial arts in Crecis' vocabulary, blended with dancerly somatic plasticity. His choreographies deploy patterns, systems, real actions, and high-octane riffs. Despite his love of virtuosic movement, derived from synthesising sport, martial arts, and dance principles, Crecis does not promote his performers as its hero(in)es. His works are not about showing off but showing how. There is certainly, if unconsciously, *verfremdungsteffekt* or alienation effect (Bertolt Brecht, *Brecht on Theatre*, London, 2014) at work, given his impulse to dislodge the spectators' and dancers' comfort, provoking awareness of the live situation that each is engaged with. And, just as Brecht established the ensemble as an expression of Marxist egalitarianism, there are no star turns, only imagination given form in a range of inventive strategies.

The success of Crecis' early works has led to a global career. His creations have been performed on main stages including in the UK (Scottish Dance Theatre, Sadler's Wells, the Royal Opera House) and the USA (New York City Centre). *Twelve* (2017), originally created as *36* in 2011 and commissioned in various adaptations for companies internationally, including ŻfinMalta Dance Ensemble in 2019, was awarded the Best Dance Prize in Cuba, 2017. It proved to be Carlos Acosta Danza's most successful and frequently performed work. Conceived to articulate his PhD, *Twelve* is the pièce de résistance of

Towards Vivencia. Demanding from the dancers maximum physical and mental disposition, this work plays with sport and mathematical elements. Illuminated one-and-a-half litre bottles of water are thrown and caught with great speed, flying through the air like fireflies in the night. This complicates enthrallingly as the stage constantly mutates, a shifting interplay of bottles and bodies. The dancers themselves decide the direction of the game, improvising according to a given numerical score. Like footballers realigning themselves in the field, they shift positions to send and receive the constant hail of plastic missiles. This is Crecis' genius at its height. He has created a theatrical event that is highly complex yet stems from a simple idea: the bottles themselves are non-human bodies – filled with the amount of water proportional to that in the human. *Twelve* sits somewhere between sport, dance, athletics, ritual, and circus. Thrilling, because the risk is palpably real, audiences engage enthusiastically with this intensely beautiful event. Depending on absolute presence of mind and wide-awake experience, *Twelve* is the creative expression of *Vivencia*.

Towards Vivencia is a training system rooted in uncovering how the nervous system works so that performance presence is enhanced. It involves the ritualisation of actions, from the peeling of an egg to throwing objects at speed between players. The purpose is to encourage the skill of multi-tasking, achieved through playfulness and mindfulness. Participants learn to tie knots, lash bamboos together, and perform movement sequences repetitively, whilst simultaneously obeying rules of rapidly shifting sequencing. Typical of Crecis' approach is to start simply and add more layers of intricacy. *Towards Vivencia* is designed to produce healthy peak performance. Safety is a priority at all times. There are no accidents, he will insist, only mistakes, and mistakes arise with loss of concentration. Another feature of the training is for the performer to be fully aware of when they are in this zone and when not. Cooling down, reflecting, and articulating are as important as learning how to enter the zone itself. This is its proprioceptive gift.

Towards Vivencia is highly successful. 1,500 people have participated globally to date. Crecis has trained four tutors and is now launching the methodology online. Professional and layperson can engage alike in its call for presence. Unlike mere exercise, and refusing to claim spiritual reward (he would rather leave that to the individual than claim to cultivate it), Crecis presents an urgently needed antidote to a culture in which social and physical comfort – as well as constant psychological reassurance and increased controls to avoid upset or disturbance – risks producing a generation of risk-averse, defenceless individuals. As the world gets tougher, he seems to be suggesting, so might our need to work together in peak conditions of awareness and empathy, to push ourselves into commitment to movement in every sense, and to 'Throwing the Body into the Fight' (Mary Kate Connolly, *Throwing the Body into the Fight, A Portrait of Raimund Hoghe*, Bristol, 2013).

Crecis is aware that his mission that began before dance now surpasses it. He knows that it is possible, within a relatively short period of training, to develop human potential. In this respect he is deeply connected to the paratheatrical experiments of the Polish theatre director Jerzy Grotowski, whose 'paratheatre' project in the 1970s removed the spectator-performer divide and led selected groups of international individuals into tests of endurance, ritual, reflex, and collaboration with natural environments (Jennifer Kumiega, *The Theatre of Grotowski*, London, 1985). Crecis' version of this search to release atrophied human ability contributes a specific, guided, and repeatable curriculum that enables any participant who chooses to engage and develop themselves. In this sense, he is both a dedicated teacher and an insistently democratic choreographic artist.

Crecis' creative sensibility has also touched human emotion, handled with characteristic philosophical reflection, avoiding sentimentality. *Through & Out* (2016) is a dance-skipping performance that connects with the emotional states that a marathon runner endures over 26.2 miles. Performing solo with a live musician, Crecis skips while narrating an autobiographical text. He tells that the mental stages in a runner's experience echo the stages in grief. He anchors this in the story of his own truncated father-son relationship. Intensely personal, this work applies Crecis' own athleticism to comprehend and articulate the (metaphorical as it turns out) death of a parent, who we discover has violently abused his son. In a startling coup-de-théâtre, he announces that the facts of his story have been false. His father never died, never taught him to ride a bicycle, never took him fishing. What died on the night he has described was a relationship, since it had been violated: "He died the night he slammed me into the wall and tried to kill me". This is a work about taking responsibility. Neither maudlin nor mawkish, Crecis' self-exposure urges the spectator to consider where we might also draw the line with regard to human behaviour, where our ethics lie. In performing an act of perseverance with his skipping rope, he is asking what the body is capable of, why it moves, how it stores memory and trauma, what pain means as a psycho-physical experience, and, ultimately, what it means alive and dead. Through poetic autobiography juxtaposed with the simplicity of repetitive action, life itself is declared a marathon of survival and endurance.

Anna Furse

Biographical details

Born in Madrid, Spain, 20 March 1978. **Studied** Sport Science at the Universidad Politécnica de Madrid 1999–2004; The Royal Conservatoire of Dance, Madrid 2000–2004 and created the artists' collective *somoSQuien* while studying there. Received PhD from Goldsmiths, University of London, 2018. **Career:** performed with Jovén Marta de la Vega Ballet; professional debut with Lanònima Imperial *Orfeo* in 2004; danced with Losdedae Dance Company, 2004–2005. Moved to Belgium: joined Compagnie Thor in Brussels, 2004–2007 and performed with IOTA dance company, 2005–2006. Moved to London: worked with Candoco 2007–2008. Taught full time at London Contemporary Dance School 2008–2012, then as a guest, 2012–2019. Guest Lecturer in several UK universities, including: Trinity Laban Conservatoire of Music and Dance; Derby; De Montfort; Chichester; Falmouth; and London Studio Centre. International teaching includes Beijing Dance Academy, Roger Williams University (USA), Minzu University (China), University of Malta, Balletto di Roma, Latvian Akademi of Culture, SEADs (Austria), Universidad Europea, and also Conservatorio Superior de Danza (both Madrid). Artistic Director for Aerowaves Festival in Burgos (Spain) in 2011 and wrote for *Eter* dance magazine 2007–2012. Research scholarships include: Ministerio de Exteriores 2008 and 2009; CDD professional development 2010 and 2011. In 2014, with Samar Hadad King, created the first Pan-Arab dance company *min tala*. **Awards** include the Premio Villanueva, Cuban critic circle, 2017.

Works

Res-publica (2003); *Shirt, Skin and Entrails* (2005); *Davay!* (2005); *Paradoxal* (2006); *s_in_fin* (2007); *Arenas* (with Athina Vahla, 2008); *Bf* (with Freddie Opoku Addaie (2008); *HTAP.Studio nº3* (2010); *I Love You … Not* (2010); *What Happens between Us* (2010); *Trade Fair* (2011); *36* (2011); *Tres. We Don't Know What this Piece is about Yet* (2012); *Aqui y Ahora* (2012); *Labyrinth of Hawara* (2013); *Thick and Grey* (2013); *aLL tHE nAMES* (2013); *Through & Out* (2014); *(854)/(14' 59")=57bpm [it's complicated]* (2014); *Trans la Valo* (2014); *I Was Going to Tell You My Story* (2014); *Kingdom* (2014); *Whistleblower* (2015); *Through & Out²* (2015); *Agonal* (2017); *Twelve* (2017); *9 Minutes* (2018); *Tnax* (2019); *The Constant Prince* (2019); *7:36* (2020).

Further reading

Interviews: 'with internationally acclaimed Artist Jorge Crecis, Jane Cuppage, speaks with the choreographer whose new methodology works on performers' consciousness', *Dance Magazine*, July–September 2014; 'Jorge Crecis – On the Ropes in Greenwich', LondonDance.com, June 2014; Evelyn Francourt, 'The Movement – Acosta Danza Social Mover Review', blog.sadlerswells.com, 30 September 2017; Rachel Elderkin, 'An Athlete's Mind in a Dancer's Body', dance-dialogues.simplecast.com, undated.

Articles: Luke Jennings, 'Hobson's Choice, Exposure: Dance Review', *The Observer*, 26 February 2011; Omar Khan, Jorge Crecis, Pura Presencia, *Susy Q*, March 2014; Carlos Forcada, 'Jorge Crecis', *Danza Europa y Américas*, October 2015; Philippa Newis, 'Signed, Sealed and Delivered', *Bachtrack*, 30 September 2017; Rachel Elderkin, 'Acosta Danza: Debut at Sadler's Wells', *Exeunt Magazine*, 27 September 2017; Luke Jennings, 'Carlos Acosta is Still Keeping Good Company', *The Observer*, 1 October 2017.

FLEUR DARKIN

"I make work to *research* and explore *deeply*. I want to *arrest people* somehow, affect a change of *hearts and minds*, challenge how things are" (personal communication with the author, 2019). Several of the drivers at the heart of Fleur Darkin's practice are encapsulated in this statement. Pursuing these ambitions led to a variety of positions: as an independent choreographer, as artistic director of her own Fleur Darkin Company, seven years as Artistic Director for Scottish Dance Theatre, and again as an independent choreographer and director since 2019.

Born in London, brought up by her Irish mother, a keen social dancer and political activist, and her English/German Jewish father, in childhood she was a fanatical self-taught dancer and a performer at family weddings and parties. Aged fourteen, Darkin saw London Contemporary Dance Theatre at the Bristol Hippodrome and describes how she "couldn't speak for about two days after". She discovered breakdancing in Bristol (although too shy to join in, she absorbed it all), and in 1995 headed to Northern School of Contemporary Dance in Leeds and then to Alvin Ailey/New York University, for a three-month placement.

"Hip hop and popular culture were massive influences on how I danced, and improvisation was the mother of all my invention. When I got into the conservatoire system it was a different planet. It felt dry, learning codified steps is a culture of obedience, and I sought a culture of questioning". In a characteristically bold move, she left and went to study at Bretton Hall – a progressive multi-disciplinary art college in Yorkshire. She started to cultivate her own way of moving and making, learning how to collaborate with musicians, sculptors, and film-makers and becoming as interested in ideas as in their execution.

Graduating in 1998, Darkin worked as a dancer and wrote, choreographed, and directed her first short piece, *The Sound Clash* in 2000. Though only eighteen minutes long, it was presented at The Place, London and Battersea Arts Centre. It embodies a number of forms and themes that have remained throughout her career thus far: it was semi-autobiographical, exploring complex parental and family relationships; it had a script, written by Darkin; and it played with two forms – dance and naturalistic theatre. The father, Mark Catley, sat unmoved, delivering a monologue while the children played downstage and the mother arranged things in the background. Then, the stage reversed; the father now sat facing the children playing upstage, as the mother, Darkin, thrashed on the floor.

What is not emblematic is the didactic way Darkin approached her directorial role here. She developed the premise, wrote the text, and created the movement before rehearsals began; whereas in subsequent years, she has created *with* the dancers and embraced a sense of *finding* in the rehearsal processes. She realised that "getting lost and responding to an unknown landscape is my preferred process, I'm interested in blind spots, in the transmission of intimacies and unnameable feelings; the places where I don't know the answers".

In 2001, Darkin wrote and choreographed *Stories* in collaboration with Lucy Cullingford and Ben Duke. Exploring desire and gendered ways of seeing, it presented a deepening intimacy between a young man and woman, and received multiple five star reviews at The Edinburgh Festival. *Stories* introduced some of Darkin's most enduring theatrical motifs – bodies and chairs placed on opposite sides of the stage, dancers removing items of clothing to a state of undress, thrashing women and cerebral men. She began to work with collaborators to explore un-muting dancers and telling explicit stories with dance, working with tasks to elicit and develop spatial thinking, narrative, and choreographic material.

Throughout these early years Darkin supported herself by working as a journalist and lecturer. Nevertheless, money was tight and for many months she slept on people's sofas. The passion that saw her through this period is something Darkin is known for. Driven, fiercely intelligent, and extremely well read, she describes UK contemporary dance culture as "a little light on discourse". When she speaks she is poetic, philosophical, emotional, and unflinching. In terms of how she works with dancers in the studio and the impact she aspires to have on audiences, Darkin is evangelical about the power of dance to transform performers and audiences: "The power of art is to bring out what the real values of life are, and in that sense it has more in common with god than the human establishment. Life is ephemeral and there is a lot of mystery. Discipline, purity, rigour, compassion and empathy matter more than status. We need to explore the mysteries".

Life experiences were important: "I left home early in difficult circumstances, and when I got to dance school, I started from the bottom, the humiliations were daily! I sucked it up because I needed to cultivate a discipline to transform myself. That discipline had an enormous impact; it gave me a second chance. I take that discipline wherever I go, and I expect it from others, because I know they can transform too. I've made dance projects in schools, colleges, pupil referral units, and it's always this same question of commitment to self-realise. Once when performing in a prison, a bunch of inmates started actively ridiculing the dance. I was the only one onstage. I kept going until they stopped laughing, and I even remember making eye contact with the culprits! Courage is an essential part of self-transformation".

This fiery passion can land askew. She is candid with those she works with. Though in many she inspires trust, admiration, and lasting loyalty, some less successful collaborations lie in her wake: "I have hurt dancers and lashed out, especially in the earlier days when I was so consumed with making the piece I wasn't considering how the dancers felt. It's taken me time to appreciate the responsibility and privilege of my role". With typical zeal, Darkin has written about what is fascinating in the complex negotiations of these relationships and considers the multiple collaborations that underpinned *Velvet Petal*, created 2016 (see Butterworth and Wildschut 2018).

In 2006 Darkin decided to free herself from the "shackles" of narrative and started *Augustine,* which she describes as her "first proper dance piece", relying on female bodies in lines of comparisons: men washing women, a series of games and physical tasks, tests done as live improvisations, and performers dancing to the ragged edges of exhaustion. It was also the first, and not final, time that she drew inspiration from the visual arts – namely photographs of hysterical female patients and their (male) doctors, including Dr. Charcot, Freud's teacher, at the Salpêtrière Hospital in Paris in the late 1890s. With her profile growing, this work was supported by Trinity Laban, The Place, and also P.A.R.T.S. (Anne Teresa De Keersmaeker's dance school in Brussels), where Darkin and her dancers spent a summer in residence. "This was a watershed. Until this point my training had been Anglo-American, but at Laban and PARTS, I could feel the future here in self-generated movement research and generous rehearsal periods, and dancing invented now, in the moment, I was the primary motor – not codified modernist techniques formed sixty years before I was born".

When *Augustine* was presented at Trinity Laban in 2007, a now pregnant Darkin worked with a group of students, integrating them into the show as the 'hysterics' in the psychiatric institution. This early example of merging professional and non-professional casts is something she repeats later in her career.

In 2008 Darkin was commissioned by The Place Prize to make *DisGO*, which also formed the basis of the follow-up *SisGO* which toured the UK and Europe on and off until 2014. *DisGO* and *SisGO* explored the movement of the audience, "the choreography of the mass". Spectators entered the stage from the wings to discover the safety curtain down and an enclosed space lit by a waist-high pen of light. The viewer/viewed distinction was destroyed, everybody present was a facet of the performance. *SisGo* explored frequencies of energy and the physical experience of dance. For example: how a dancer brushes past the audience, or what happens when you feel a duet occurring right behind you, or a dancer leans on you forcing you to move – experiences Darkin continues to explore.

It is not just the work that affected Darkin's trajectory. The conditions of The Place Prize had a deep and lasting impact, one that affects her still. "On the first day of rehearsals I went into The Place and all the other commissionees had covered the windows of their studios so no one could see inside. It was my first time working directly with my peers and a hope for kinship was replaced by rivalry. I couldn't produce in those conditions and came to realise my making has as much to do with context as ideas. I've since created forums where artists can work together in true kinship, through initiatives like Collaboratory which I developed at Laban and led in China, Mexico, Brazil, Argentina and the UK".

In 2011 Darkin made two sister-shows, *Experience* and *Innocence*: the former, a full-length evening show centring on the parent-child relationship, and the latter a show for families and under-fives. *Experience*, written in collaboration with Tanya Ronder and myself as dramaturge, saw Darkin return to her interest in combining text, theatre, character, and dance. She ran two rehearsal periods simultaneously, producing two works – pushing her funding to its limits.

Innocence became one of her most successful, influential pieces. Inspired by the childhood and work of William Blake, it was made during workshops with children and babies focussing on the pioneering theories of Swiss psychologist Jean Piaget. Understanding that 'construction is superior to instruction' (one of Piaget's maxims), the dancers facilitated play and physical exploration that is, crucially, led by the young audience. The performers function as leaders, listeners, and enablers, and the piece is seminal for the sophistication, respectfulness, and creativity it offered to children and adults. The dancers made strong images: crawling tigers hunting frolicking lambs, twenty blackbirds leaping across the floor. "Innocence genuinely relies on playfulness. The show is successful when the adults in the room loosen up, because children have no problem with freedom. The children's spontaneity steers the show when the dancers are trained enough to relinquish control and construct the show with the guests".

In 2012 Darkin became Artistic Director of Scottish Dance Theatre (SDT), Scotland's national company. During her six-and-a-half-year tenure, starting when her third child was three months old, Darkin commissioned dozens of choreographers and artists, including Jo Stromgren, Victor Quihada, Damien Jalet, Anton Lachky, Lia Rodrigues, Veenapani Chawla, Sharon Eyal, Botis Seva, Colette Sadler, Claire Cunningham, Felix de Assis, and Rita Aquino. *Miann* (2014), her first full-length show for the company and for which I was again dramaturge, was inspired by a desire to unite the musicians of Glasgow's One Ensemble and SDT's dancers in collaboration, as well as a personal need to articulate the loss of her much loved step-father. It toured the UK, Mexico, and Brazil, and unusually for dance at this scale was performed in the round, enabling Darkin's passion for bringing dancer and audience into closer proximity.

Velvet Petal (2016), her second full-length show for SDT, was inspired by Mapplethorpe's photographs, particularly his *Polaroids*. The show won several awards, and was described as 'fantastically edgy' and 'intensely sexual' (Teresa Guerreiro culturewhisper.com, 1 September 2018). "The breakthrough with that show was finding a physical language that felt true to an amateur feeling of dance – the feeling I've always had which is a shyness but a passion to dance my heart out. The dancers were able to wear their training lightly and be humans onstage, replacing feats of achievement with feats of style. It's the piece that comes closest to how I authentically dance and it was most popular with audiences, which amazed me. I realised dance is a feeling of freedom, it's not necessarily an act of displaying".

Darkin's next major collaboration, *Equilux*, was made with Danze Contemporanea de Cuba in 2017. Initially awe-struck by the skills of these twenty-seven dancers, Darkin realised that her own movement language, one of gravity, falling, and experiencing one's own weight, challenged them. A process of teaching technique and material, as well as working to find authentic movement signatures, led to one of her most commercially successful works to date.

Running an organisation like Scottish Dance Theatre, part of a local repertory theatre, offers complexities that are worthy of exploration not possible here. "We built a team that was collaborative, inclusive and extremely successful – international touring increased significantly and company turnover grew to its highest ever. It was a shame to leave such a trusted and dynamic team". Darkin ended her relationship with SDT at the end of 2018.

Since then a series of productions continue to explore how worlds, beyond the body, can become amplified by movement. Darkin calls this way of working, non-literal translations. "I'm not staging stories, but finding a rich collage of states that embody something meaningful for the text and multiplies possibilities. Text in the Barthesian sense. I can bring life that is independent and illuminates through the liveness of the present moment".

In 2018 she co-wrote and directed *The Lover*, an adaptation of Marguerite Duras' novel *L'Amant*, with theatre director Jemima Levick. This premiered at Edinburgh's Royal Lyceum. In 2020 she collaborates with the David Foster Wallace Trust – who for the first time gave permission for his writing to be brought to the stage. For *The Qualies*, Darkin worked with the all-male dance company 2Faced on exploding the meanings of Wallace's essay on the rigours of professional sports through a slew of images, which included lyrical dance, a language of explosive jumping, testy fights, and an unsupported handstand held, statue-like, for over two minutes.

Darkin is now beginning research into a work on gender and power. Working with a range of partners, she will be confronting inconvenient truths. "It was clear to me at an early age that the cultural space I desired was not granted so readily to females. As a choreographer interested in pattern, I see unchanging hierarchies and inequalities, the repression of new and other voices, and a repetitive systemic bias that perpetuates white male power. Those patriarchal systems are the problem we all work within; I will make anyway, and look at the shame I have felt as a female. Because I'm not the only one who experiences it. And there is crucial work to do. It's in the ways projects are put together; in the dismantling of inherited hierarchies that are tolerated throughout our industry; and ultimately, excitingly, the work to change things in the studio".

Lou Cope

Biographical details

Born in London in 1975. **Studied** at Northern School of Contemporary Dance, 1994–1995; undertook a three-month placement at Alvin Ailey NYU in 1995; graduated from Bretton Hall 1997; MA, University of Leeds, 1998.

Career: joined Union City Dance as dancer 1998–1999. Founded own company, the Darkin Ensemble in 2001, called Fleur Darkin Company from 2009 and Artistic Director/CEO until 2012. Artistic residency at P.A.R.T.S. in Belgium, 2006; Choreographer in Residence, Glastonbury Festival, 2004–2007; Choreography intensive leader Trinity Laban, 2007–2009; Associate Artist at Bristol Old Vic, 2010–2012. Founder of Collaboratory, a peer-led choreographic laboratory, 2012–ongoing. Artistic Director of Scottish Dance Theatre, 2012–2018. Collaborations include productions with National Theatre; National Theatre of Scotland; Abbey (Dublin), The Globe; Cervantino Festival (Mexico); SESC (Brazil); Adishakti (India); Danza Contemporanea de Cuba; South Bank Centre. Visiting Scholar at University of St. Andrews 2019–2021. **Awards** include Jardin D'Europe, 2011; Glasgow Cultural Olympiad 2014; Linbury Prize 2014; Lustrum Prizes, Edinburgh Festival, 2016 & 2017.

Works

(dates provided by the choreographer)

The Sound Clash (2000); *Stories* (2001); *Hotel* (2003); *Dr Tatiana*, (TV musical, Channel 4/Discovery, 2006); *Parabolic* (2006); *Virgins* (theatre, with John Retallack, 2007); *Augustine* (2007); *Helter Skelter* (Circus, 2007); *Roam* (theatre, 2008); *DisGo* (2008); *DisGo/SisGo* (2009); *Peter Pan* (aerial choreography, 2009); *The Three Musketeers* (theatre, 2010); *Innocence* (2011); *Experience* (2011); *War and Peace* (Circus, 2011); *Miann* (2014); *Velvet Petal* (2016); *Shibboleth* (theatre, 2016); *Winter's Tale* (theatre, 2016); *Equilux* (2017); *The Lover [L'Amant]* (2018); *Mr Gum* (musical, 2019); *The Qualies* (2020).

Further reading

Interviews: 'Fleur Darkin Q&A', londondance.com, 9 April 2010; Carmel Smith, 'Interview: Fleur Darkin', londondance.com, 4 March 2013; Teddie Jamieson, 'Choreographer Fleur Darkin on Patti Smith, Robert Mapplethorpe and What it Takes to Be a Dancer', *The Herald,* heraldscotland.com, 26 May 2018.

Articles: Nicholas Minns, 'Scottish Dance Theatre: Miann at Queen Elizabeth Hall', writingaboutdance.com, 22 April 2015; Lyndsey Winship, 'It's not Bob and Patti: The Ballet. New Show Celebrates Mapplethorpe and Smith's Metamorphoses', *The Guardian,* 12 October 2016; Gareth K. Vile, 'Velvet Petal Revels in Beauty and Sexual Passion', *The List,* 9 May 2017; unattributed, 'Scottish Dance Theatre's Fleur Darkin on Velvet Petal: The Disco-Punk Production Inspired by Patti Smith', creativescotland.com, 23 May 2018.

Books: Fleur Darkin, *Contemporary Choreography: A Critical Reader,* 2nd edition (Butterworth and Wildschut, eds.), London and New York, 2018.

PHILIPPE DECOUFLÉ

French choreographer Philippe Decouflé is best known for his mastery of visual imagery and unashamedly spectacular dances. His works are an extravaganza of physical tricks and surreal optical illusions. Funny and childlike, his wild ideas are drawn from his deeply imaginative explorations into human experiences. His choreography demonstrates a belief that one of the roles of art is to allow people to dream, and his ambitious creations draw audiences away from the mundane of the everyday into a more poetic, imaginative realm.

Decouflé refuses to be constrained by the boundaries of any particular form, and his work reveals the passion he has for working across theatre, dance, circus, and film. His approach has resulted in a new word being added to the French lexicon: 'decoufleries', a term used to describe the unusual blend that arises from this mixed media play. His movement vocabulary has always been open to a variety of stylistic approaches, explaining: 'everything is so interesting to explore – folk dance, hip hop, there are no limits' (Pakes, 2005). The resulting material is precise and playful in its physicality and bold in its structural form.

Decouflé has made work for both stage and film for nearly four decades, establishing himself as a distinctive, creative force. Born in Paris in 1961, he trained in drama and circus arts, studying from the age of fifteen at L'Ecole du Cirque. Decouflé explored a passion for mime with the legendary Marcel Marceau, before moving on, aged eighteen, to train in contemporary dance at the Centre National de Danse Contemporaine. A scholarship supported a year in New York with American choreographer Alwin Nikolais, and where his exposure to both modern and postmodern dance forms, and the newly emerging field of video dance, provided a catalyst that broadened his artistic sensibilities at a formative stage.

The French dance scene in the early 1980s respected US postmodern dance but was intent on seeing dance as serving broader theatrical functions, beyond the self-referential minimalism of artists such as Lucinda Childs, Yvonne Rainer, and Trisha Brown. For Europeans, the narrative ballets of John Cranko and Jiri Kylian, and the spectacular works of Maurice Bejart and Pina Bausch, revealed a preference for dance that delivered powerfully in theatrical scale and dramatic impact. Within this context, Decouflé established his company DCA in 1983, as a vehicle for his artistic ambitions. He had been working as a performer for Karole Armitage, Régine Chopinot, and Alwin Nikolais, but his choreographic potential was identified when he won the top Bagnolet prize aged 21 for his work *Vague Café* (1983). It was clear in this seven-minute quartet that Decouflé was interested in presenting material that displayed the technical prowess of the dancers, but in an inventive manner. Dancers move playfully as if free from gravity, their elastic limbs gesturing frenetically before collapsing. The baggy zoot suiting and eclectic range of headwear revealed early confidence with visual styling and reflected the growing interest in France at that time in punk radical chic.

DCA was originally a collective to allow Decouflé to work alongside a range of artists. The desire to explore the possibilities arising from collaborative processes is a continuing interest. During this early period, he also earned his living working in advertising, taking on different roles as choreographer, dancer, director, and actor. He extended his work into film, experimenting with creating choreography for music videos by UK bands, most notably New Order's 1987 *True Faith* video. Referencing the 1977 film *Light/Dark* by Marina Abramovic and Ulay, the video opens with two men, clad in Bauhaus-styled tubes, taking turns to slap each other's faces. Other fantastical, inflatable characters jump and bounce down the street in comic fashion, and the action escalates into a series of slapstick fights. Subsequent music video work for the Fine Young Cannibals international hit *She Drives Me Crazy* (1988) allowed further experimentation in this medium.

Decouflé draws inspiration from an eclectic range of influences, including the Marx Brothers, German expressionist film makers, American cartoonist Tex Avery, and French cabaret artists to name just a few. This approach is exemplified in *Contact* (2014), originally conceived as a tribute to the musical form, which draws on Faustian themes of pleasure and greed. The work features dancers, musicians, actors, and singers, in a riot of wigs and flamboyant costumes. There are references to figures in American popular culture including Fred Astaire, Busby Berkeley, Jerome Robbins, and cult film maker Brian De Palma. In a lengthy ensemble section, a dance-battle recalls the warring action of the rival gangs of *West Side Story*, the rhythmic stepping and clicking drawn from Broadway jazz. Performer boundaries are blurred, the musicians join the choreography and dancers burst into song. The dizzying visuals include a series of flamboyant digital graphics projected onto different angled surfaces. Live music by rock duo Nosfell and Pierre Le Bourgeois adds a further layer, and the subsequent collage of ideas and mediums creates a surreal world. Reviewing the London staging, dance critic Donald Hutera warned audiences not to go to *Contact* looking for profundity, because the work was primarily a tongue-in-cheek spectacle ('Contact', *The Times*, 18 June 2015). However, Decouflé always deflects criticism that his work is vacuous or empty. He describes how he continues to be inspired by his early teacher Nikolais and the belief that the medium *is* the message: 'Dance shouldn't have pretensions – it's a simple art form, and we shouldn't wrack our brains over it' (Pakes, 2005).

Whilst Decouflé's works may appear to be about surface concerns, there is nothing simple about his ambitious and often large-scale creations. His distinctive style lends itself to elaborate works, and he has taken on numerous grand scale projects that have facilitated his desire to work with new artistic collaborators. One of the first significant projects of this nature was the 1992 opening and closing ceremonies for the Winter Olympics. Decouflé received international acclaim, and critics began to take his work more seriously. He describes how the shift in response to his work was perhaps driven by a sense that people could understand the ways in which his work could 'be a bridge between the large audience and the research laboratory' (Donald Hutera, 'Ringmaster totally over the Big Top', *The Times*, 5 March 1997). Following the success of the Olympics, DCA established a permanent home in 1995 at a former power station in St Denis, a suburb north of Paris. Nicknamed La Chaufferie, rehearsal rooms, stage space, and offices provide DCA with an extraordinary creative laboratory.

Decouflé often begins the creative process by drawing and sketching his ideas. As a child his first dream was to draw comic books. He credits his time studying video dance with Merce Cunningham in the 1970s as the source of his initial understanding of the principles of optics and movement, and visual trickery has always been one of Decouflé's hallmarks. He is unafraid to allow audiences to see the mechanics behind his illusions. In the closing melancholic moments of *Solo* (2003), a screen rises to expose the technical equipment responsible for generating multiple reproductions of his body on stage. Decouflé is seen moving in singular, stark human form for one final time. This idea of exposing trade secrets was central to the interactive installation *Opticons* (2012), a collaborative project conceived as a performative game which took over five years to produce. Working with a team of longstanding collaborators, including lighting designer Patrice Besombs and video designer Olivier Simola, Decouflé allowed audiences to roam freely through twelve different spaces filled with image-generating machines. Shadow play, video effects, and mirrors allowed for mesmerising interplay between structural forms, each individual placed at the centre of the illusions.

Decouflé's resistance to being constrained by the boundaries of a particular form is demonstrated through his ability to embrace the cultural traditions of both popular and high art forms. In 2009, he worked alongside renowned fashion photographer Ali Mahdavi to direct *Désirs,* a work for the legendary Parisian cabaret Crazy Horse. The show offers a fresh take on traditional French burlesque and incorporates a series of high-tech projections, creating an erotically charged visual display. Despite the contemporary visual look of *Désirs,* the show remains unapologetically a showcase for female nude chic. Arched silhouettes draw attention to the pelvis and exposed breasts; bodies reduced to a series of erotic, geometric designs. This approach contrasts markedly with his earlier 2007 work *Coeurs Croisés* (Crossed Hearts), which offered a subversive and humorous take on strip-tease and eroticism. Premiered at the Paris Quartier D'été Festival, action centred around a small stage crawling with bodies, as desire and pleasure mixed with the absurd and grotesque. The cast of unlikely, kitsch characters come in all shapes and sizes, at times reminiscent of a Victorian curiosity cabinet. In one scene, a female dancer sneezes and finds her costume blown off from the impact. She stands awkwardly in her underpants jiggling two tassel-covered breasts; the effect is simultaneously funny and disconcerting.

The idea of popularising dance has always been a driver for Decouflé, and he appears to see little conflict in the tension that can arise in making work that allows for artistic expression whilst remaining commercially viable. In 2011 he wrote and directed *Iris,* his first work for the Cirque du Soleil. Drawing inspiration from the painter Frances Bacon and French cinema pioneers Louis and Auguste Lumiere and Georges Melies, he explored his passion for circus and film. *Iris* pays homage to the silent world of early cinema and was created in collaboration with film composer Danny Elfman. The collaborative process with Elfman was highly iterative and the final music score matched the expressive visual imagery in both pace and intention. Decouflé's work with Cirque du Soleil offered a new outlet for his passion for circus arts; the 2016 production *Paramour* helped to solidify this association further.

Decouflé is a risk-taker, who enjoys new challenges, and is resolutely determined to remain an independent artist. He works largely outside of the major French grant system because he is reluctant to take on the responsibility that is inevitably attached to high-profile roles. As he explained to Pakes in 2005, "I want to be an artist, and I think artists should have the right to be irresponsible. I want to keep that freedom". This approach enables him to retain an extraordinary amount of artistic control and engage in projects that stretch his choreographic sensibilities in different directions. Decouflé creates theatrical experiences that are both absurd and spectacular, and it can be argued that his fascination with exploring what is real and what is not plays into important philosophical questions about the human experience. His magical works connect us to the realms of dream and fantasy, inspiring us to reimagine our relationships with the self, others, and the world around us.

Michelle Elliott

Biographical details

Born in Neuilly-sur-Seine, 22 October 1961. **Studied** at L'Ecole du Cirque and Centre National de Danse Contemporaine. **Career:** Dancer for Régine Chopinot and Karole Armitage companies; founded own company, DCA, in 1983; choreographed opening and closing ceremonies for Winter Olympics, February 1992, and opening ceremony of Rugby World Cup, 2007. Associate artist, Chaillot – Théâtre National de la Danse until 2020. **Awards and honours** include Concours de Bagnolet prize, 1983; Le Prix de la Qualité, Le Centre National du Cinéma, 1986; BRIT Award, 1988; Silver Lion prize; Venice Film Festival, 1989; IMZ Dance Screen Award, 1994; Grand Prix National du Ministère de la Culture pour la Choréographie, 1995; Commandeur des Arts et des Lettres, France, 2015.

Works

La Voix des Legumes (1982); *Vague Café* (1983); *Jump* (film, dir. Decouflé and Charles Atlas, 1984); *Tranche de Cake* (1984); *Le Trio épouvantable* (1984); *Caramba* (film, dir. Decouflé, 1986); *Codex* (1986; film version, 1987; reworked as *Decodex*, 1995, and *Tricodex*, 2004); *Tutti* (1987); *True Faith* (music video, 1987); *Technicolor* (1988); *She Drives Me Crazy* (music video, 1988); *La Danse des sabots* (1989); *Triton* (1990; recreated as *Triton et le petits Tritures*, 1998); Opening and Closing Ceremonies, Winter Olympic Games, Albertville, France (1992); *Petites Pièces Montées* (1993); *Le P'tit Bal* (film, 1994); *Dora, le chat qui a vécu un million de fois* (Musical, 1996); *Micheline* (1996); Opening Ceremony, International Film Festival Cannes (1997); *Marguerite* (1997); *Shazam!* (1998); *Abracadabra* (film, dir. Decouflé, 1998); *Cyrk 13* (2001); *Iris* (2003; new version, *1Iris*, 2004, and *2Iris*, 2005); *Solo* (2003); *L'Autre defile* (2006); *Sombrero* (2006; new version, *Sombreros*, 2008/9); *Coeurs croisés* (2007); *Désirs* (revue, with Ali Mahdavi, 2009); *Face* (feature film, dir. Tsai Ming-Liang, 2009); *Octopus* (2010); *Iris* (2011); *Swimming Poules and Flying Coqs* (2011); *Panorama* (2012); *Les Opticons* (Installation, 2012); *Retrospective to the City* (Exhibition, 2012); *Fine Arts* (2013); *Contact* (2014); *Weibo* (2015); *Paramour* (2016); *Counterpoint* (2016); *My Name is Shingo* (musical, 2016); *Nouvelle Pieces Courtes* (2017); *The Three-Body Problem II: The Dark Forest* (opera, dir. Decouflé, 2019).

Further reading

Interviews: with Thomas Hahn, *Ballett International*, June 1999; Anna Pakes, 'Solo but not Alone', *Dance Theatre Journal*, 20(4), 2005; *The Magic of Dance*, Euromax Newsfilm, dw.com, 2018.

Articles: Keith Watson, 'Unnatural Histories', *Dance Now*, 1996/97; Karyn Bauer, 'France Dances Through New York', *Dance Magazine*, April 2001; Ramsay Burt, '*Solo*. Decouflé's Magic Isle', *Dance Magazine*, December 2004; Donald Hutera, 'Philippe Decouflé', *Dance Now*, 13(4), 2004; Keith Watson, 'Lyon Opera Ballet Review', *Dance Now*, 14(4), 2005; Virginie Oks, 'Philippe Decouflé: The Unclassifiable Choreographer', *France-Diplomatie*, 23 March 2007; Elisa Guzzo Vaccarino, 'The Best of Decoufle', *Ballet 2000*, 1 November 2012; Sonia Schoonejans, 'Decoufle's Enjoyable Delirium', *Ballet 2000*, March/April 2015; Katherine Holmes, 'From Big Top to Broadway', *Dance Magazine*, 1 May 2016; Linda Armstrong, 'Paramour is Thrilling Theatre', *New York Amsterdam News*, 21 July 2016; Rosita Boisseau, 'Philippe Decouflés Race for Images', *Le Monde*, 14 October 2016.

Books: Rosita Boisseau, *Philippe Decouflé: Textuel musique et danse* (FRENCH), Textual, 2003; Bonnie Rowell, *Fifty Contemporary Choreographers*, 2nd ed. (eds. Bremser and Sanders), London and New York, 2011.

MICHELLE DORRANCE

Michelle Dorrance is a force of nature. A YouTube video from the Taptastic! Festival in Germany, 2019, showcases Dorrance during the Concert of the Masters. Wearing a black stylish blazer with exposed shoulders, hair in a messy top knot and her signature hoop earrings, she displays tremendous ability to build musical phrases by layering rhythms in the manner of a virtuosic jazz drummer. With her well-worn tap shoes, Dorrance plays with dynamics, creating an aural and visual atmosphere that embodies tap ancestry but explores the grooves of the 21st century. A technical powerhouse, she performs with a defining athleticism and exuberance. Her dancing and choreography are guided by the idea that form follows function in tap, therefore she emphasises the sounds produced rather than the neatness of the physicality. Sarah Kaufman comments on her unruly upper body, describing her dancing as 'overrun with joy, arms winging and feet blurring in spasms of mad syncopations' ('Putting tap where we wouldn't expect it', *The Washington Post*, 6 September 2018).

Dorrance began tap dance and ballet at her mother's ballet school in Chapel Hill, North Carolina, aged three. She credits her parents for her fast feet and dance abilities. Her mother was a ballet dancer who performed with Eliot Feld's company; her father was a Head

Coach for University of North Carolina Women's Soccer Team. She joined the North Carolina Youth Tap Ensemble aged eight, under the leadership of Gene Medler, who exposed her to various styles and improvisatory techniques through collaborations with tap greats, such as Josh Hilberman, Barbara Duffy, Savion Glover, Margaret Morrison, Brenda Bufalino, and Lane Alexander. Moving to New York in 1997, Dorrance performed with *STOMP* as a dancer-drummer and several influential tap dance companies, such as Savion Glover's Ti Dii, Barbara Duffy & Company, Manhattan Jazz, and *Imagine Tap!*. Dorrance earned a BA at the New York University Gallatin School of Individualized Study, studying American democracy and race within the arts with a focus on tap.

Dorrance began her choreographic career while still dancing in *STOMP*, creating a work for the North Carolina Youth Tap Ensemble. She founded her New York based dance company in 2011, which aims to push the limits of tap, rhythmically, conceptually, and aesthetically, whilst honouring its heritage. She won her first Bessie that same year for *Remembering Jimmy* (2011), a tribute to tap master Jimmy Slyde, and *Three to One* (2011). In the latter, Dorrance performed between two contemporary dancers lighting only their bottom halves. She executed the same steps, highlighting the contrast between barefoot dancing and tap to expose emotions hidden in the mechanics of tap technique.

In 2013, Dorrance created the site-specific work *SOUNDspace* (2013) for the Danspace Project in St. Marks Church, later adapted for various spaces. This was the first tap choreography commissioned by Danspace, the emblem of the downtown experimental dance scene, indicating her ability to shift between various dance contexts and explode ideas regarding tap. Dancers performed in socks, bare feet, leather shoes, and wooden taps to explore the acoustic possibilities offered by St. Marks. The aural experience of textured rhythms utilised the performing space fully, including backstage areas and balcony. Using a traditional tap tactic, the lights were sometimes turned off, forcing the audience to concentrate on the sound and allowing the sonic experience to define the space.

Dorrance's dance company had their Jacob's Pillow debut in 2011, beginning a fruitful relationship with the festival with numerous choreographic, educational, and performing residencies. These provided opportunities to continue exploring her interest in merging dance styles. In 2013 she received the Jacob's Pillow award for exceptional vision for *The Blues Project*. Premiered at the Pillow and performed at the Joyce Theatre, New York, this work, which won another Bessie, explores the history of blues music. *The Blues Project* honours the tap legacy and its subversive power and marks the collaborative nature of Dorrance's work – naming Dormeshia Sumbry-Edwards and Derick K. Grant as co-creators. Using nine dancers, Dorrance demonstrates her skill to choreograph ensemble work while allowing space for dancers' individual styles. It honours tap's West African roots, set to the sounds of the zydeco fiddle, followed by Appalachian flatfooting and the 1920s Shim Sham. In the 'Blues' section, Dorrance explores the oppression experienced in the history of tap and blues music and its joyful potential, showing her interest in creating politically pertinent work.

Collaboration is central to her process (she names dancers in the choreographic credits). During her 2014 Jacob Pillow's residency, for example, she developed *ETM: The Initial Approach,* the title playing on the acronym EDM (Electronic Dance Music). It grew out of experiments with collaborator Nicholas Van Young. The stage became an instrument by incorporating electronic floorboards. Dorrance sought to explore more than technology however, concentrating on the quality of emotions. *ETM: Double Down* (2016), a continuation of this research, was performed by three musicians, a female hip-hop break-dancer and seven tap dancers. The stage floor functions as an electronic drum pad activated with the touch of a foot. Dancers produce sound or start and stop pre-recorded music samples, referring to contemporary music trends and indicating her ability to employ postmodern compositional practices. Brian Seibert describes the structure: 'the production works by addition and subtraction: building a loop upon musical loop and breaking them down, bringing on more bodies or sending them away' ('Review: Dorrance Dance, Where Tap and Computers Intersect', *The New York Times*, 27 April 2016).

In 2015, City Center commissioned *Myelination*, a work for 12 dancers including Dorrance and 4 musicians, with music by Gregory Richardson and Donovan Dorrance. This work exposed her agenda to illustrate that tap *is* music, allowing it to build atmosphere and provide rhythmic structure. The work gets its name from myelin sheath, the membrane that allows nerve impulses to move rapidly, evident in her twitchy, fast choreography. Dorrance was named New York City Center Choreography Fellow for 2016–2017, allowing her to develop *Myelination* into a larger 40-minute work, performed during the Fall for Dance City in 2017.

In 2015, the Martha Graham Dance Company commissioned her for their 'Lamentation Variations' project, asking choreographers to create new works inspired by Graham's 1930 iconic solo. Dorrance created a work for ten dancers utilising rhythmic complexity in the music, rather than tap shoes. She explores grief, the theme of the original work, with physical signifiers of mourning such as faces buried in hands and heaving chests. The work sits in the contemporary dance genre in its use of minimal and gestural movement. A complex musical sensibility emerges through interplay between bodies, shifting into various positions in unpredictable rhythmical patterns, showing Dorrance's tap-influenced approach to musicality.

During residencies at the Vail Dance Festival in Colorado, Dorrance had further opportunities to collaborate. In 2016 she created *1-2-3-4-5-6* featuring herself, Memphis Jookin' dancer Lil' Buck, New York City Ballet's Robert Fairchild, and Cunningham dancer Melissa Toogood, bringing together various dance styles to interpret the complex polyrhythms of Steve Reich's score. In 2018 she collaborated with Justin Peck, ballet dancer and choreographer, on *They Try to Tell Us*. This soft shoe duet begins with a call-and-response structure and ends with intimate close couple positions that expose a more sensitive side of the choreographer.

Dorrance was commissioned to create three works (*Praedicere; Ex Pluribus One; Dream with a Dream (deferred)*) for ABT Women's *Move*ment initiative in 2018, after Kevin McKenzie saw her work with ballet dancers at Vail. Dorrance pushes dancers out of their comfort zones, for example, asking ballet dancers to improvise during the creative process. These works explore two ideas: the acoustic possibilities of a pointe shoe and the ways classical technique adapts when emphasis is placed on rhythm rather than aesthetics. Dancers were asked to create music and movement combined, for example by accentuating their landings or adding a clap during a pirouette to complicate the rhythmical structure. The box of the pointe shoe creates a noise when struck against the floor, as well as a swishing sound when sliding against it. The dancers also wore leather loafers for variety of sound and Dorrance created polyrhythms by layering patterns for different groups. Courtney Escoyne in *Dance Magazine* asserts the power of the choreography: 'the music dancers make with their feet seems to shiver up though their bodies, lending the classical steps new vibrancy' ('Beautiful Noise', September 2018).

Dorrance is a keeper of traditions concentrated on preserving the heritage of tap dance. She credits her experience of studying with tap masters for her understanding and embodiment of the history of the form and the importance of its cultural and social history – a key element in her work. She is keenly aware of tap being an American dance form through a blending of cultures and crucial in communicating concert and popular dance forms in a way not previously seen. Gia Kourlas in *The New York Times* asserts that Dorrance has charged herself to 'put tap on the cultural map by bringing it back to the concert stage; to educate the world about it' ('Michelle Dorrance, the Tireless Ambassador of Tap', 14 April 2016), by creating works that ask audiences to appreciate tap as a complete work of art that communicates aesthetically, sonically, and emotionally.

Dorrance's ability to imbue tap as an art form with new possibilities earned her a MacArthur Genius Grant in 2015. Upon receiving this, Dorrance said 'people who have never thought about tap dance are talking about it. This is what I dream for our form. And I hope it leads to institutional and academic support of tap dance' (in Kristin Schwab, 'Michelle Dorrance Receives $625,000 – No Strings Attached', *Dance Magazine*, January 2016). Dorrance is perpetually pushing the boundaries of her technique in order to make music through her love of improvisation, particularly with other dancers. She is able to perform and create work for a multitude of spaces, including cultural monuments, such as the Guggenheim museum, some of the most iconic theatres in New York City, the open air stages of Jacob's Pillow and Vail Dance Festival, and street performances on portable pieces of wood honouring tap's roots as a social and vernacular dance form. Dorrance's choreography is experimental and ground-breaking, allowing tap dance to tell stories and stir emotions.

Dara Milovanović

Biographical details

Born in Chapel Hill, North Carolina, USA, 12 September 1979. **Studied** ballet and tap at the Ballet School at Chapel Hill; with Gene Medley, founder of North Carolina Youth Tap Ensemble, from eight years old; and with tap greats, including Clayton (Peg Leg) Bates. B.A. from New York University's Gallatin School of Individualized Study combining political science, history, and literature. **Career:** performed with STOMP, Derick Grant's *Imagine Tap!*, Jason Samuels Smith's Charlie's Angels/Chasing the Bird, Ayodele Casel's Diary of a Tap Dancer, Mable Less's Dancing Ladies, Savion Glover's Ti Dii, Manhattan Tap, Barbara Duffy and Co, JazzTap Ensemble, and Rumba Tap. Founded own company, 2011; also created work for Martha Graham Dance Company and American Ballet Theatre. **Awards and honours** include Princess Grace Award, 2012; Field Dance Fund Recipient 2012; Jacob's Pillow Dance Award, 2013; Alpert Award, 2014; MacArthur Genius Award, 2015; New York Dance and Performance Awards ('Bessie'), 2011 and 2015; Ford Foundation Art of Change, 2017; Doris Duke Artist, 2018.

Works

Bluegrass (2004); *A Suite for the City* (2005); *The Blues in "d"* (2009); *A Petite Suite* (2010–2011); *Remembering Jimmy* (2011); *Three to One* (2011); *The Twelve/Eight* (2012); *Jungle Blues* (2012); *The Blues Project* (with Derick K. Grant, Toshi Reagon, Dormeshia Sumbry-Edwards, 2013); *SOUNDspace* (2013); *ETM: The Initial Approach* (2014); *Myelination* (2015, expanded version, 2017); *ETM: Double Down* (with Nicholas Van Young, 2016); *Lessons in Tradition* (with Bill Irwin, 2016); *1-2-3-4-5-6* (2016); *Until the Real Thing Comes Along (A Letter to Ourselves)* (2017); *Works and Process Rotunda Project* (with Nicholas Van Young, 2017); *Satyric Festival Song* (original by Martha Graham, reimagined with Janet Eilber (2017); *All Good Things Come to an End* (with Hannah Heller, Melinda Sullivan, Josette Wiggan Freund, Jillian Meyers, 2018); *Praedicere* (2018); *Ex Pluribus One* (2018); *Dream with a Dream (deferred)* (2018); *Elemental* (with Nicholas Van Young, 2018); *They Try to Tell Us* (with Justin Peck, 2018); *Destination Moon* (2019); *Basses Loaded* (2019); *The Nutcracker Suite* (with Hannah Heller, Melinda Sullivan, Josette Wiggan Freund, 2019).

Further reading

Interviews: with Nicholas Van Young, *Dance Journal Hong Kong*: dancejournalhk.com/single-post/, 20 April 2017; Michelle Dorrance: 'I Just Knew I Would Never Stop Tap Dancing', National Public Radio: npr.org, 29 September 2015.

Articles: Brian Seibert, 'Michelle Dorrance: Feet Precise, Limbs Wild', *Jacob's Pillow Interactive*, danceinteractive.jacobspillow.org, undated; Emily Macel, 'Tap Out Loud', *Dance Magazine*, May 2008; Brian Seibert, 'Sounding Off: Michelle Dorrance Emerges as a Choreographer', *Dance Magazine*, June 2013; Deborah Jowitt, 'Dancing as the Leaves Fall', *Arts Journal Blog*, 15 October 2015; Joan Acocella, 'Happy Feet', *The New Yorker*, May 2016; Judith Mackrell, 'Tap-Dancing Dynamo Michelle Dorrance Stamps on a Man's World', *The Guardian*, 13 July 2017; Roslyn Sulcas, 'Michelle Dorrance to Make Dances for American Ballet Theater', *The New York Times*, 13 March 2018; Brian Seibert, 'Sliding Toward Tap, and Taking Risks, at American Ballet Theater', *The New York Times*, 12 October 2018; Susan Reiter, 'In Step with Dorrance Dance', *New York City Center Blog*, 8 March 2019.

WILLIAM FORSYTHE

William Forsythe, who has spent much of his working life in Europe, is one of today's most celebrated choreographers. His choreography grows out of an insatiable curiosity, for he is a philosopher question-ing the nature of dance. He is a mathematician devising strategies for dancing bodies to move in space. He is a reader of cultural theory, questioning the conditions necessary for performance. He is a seminal choreographer who has altered the possibilities of dance theatre.

The large body of work he has produced over nearly fifty years is multidisciplinary and kicks against convention. The choreography is conceptual, with ideas abstracted from diverse sources and delivered variously: theatre; installation; exhibition; and film. Forsythe works with skilled dancer–artists who combine articulate bodies with creative imagination. Letting go of the ingrained habits of ballet and contemporary dance, these dancers embody cognitive knowledge of improvisatory tactics, enabling them to generate movement in performance. When Forsythe creates work on other companies, or recreates work from his oeuvre, his choreography tends to relate more closely to the ballet lexicon, albeit extending its organisation into contemporary mode. Most of the world's major ballet companies have a Forsythe work in their repertoire. Or they clamour for one.

Yet it was not until university that Forsythe enrolled in formal ballet training. By then he was steeped in popular culture, with experience of dancing in clubs and musicals and a passion for everything connected with creating theatre. These wider experiences, when combined with the rigour of ballet, gave him an unusual outlook. As he points out, "the nonorthodox and the orthodox resided together *in my body*: I am the territory and I feel fine having a popular/musical sensibility and a vernacular approach to coordination, *and* being a trained classical ballet dancer" (in Louise Neri and Eva Respini, *William Forsythe: Choreographic Objects*, New York, 2018).

Forsythe's first works, made for the Stuttgart Ballet, were, in a sense, orthodox. The spatial, linear detail of *Urlicht* (1976), *Daphne* and *Flore Simplici* (both 1977) paid homage to Balanchine's neo-classicism. Indeed, Forsythe's first ballet teacher, Nolan Digman, had been a Balanchine alumnus, inculcating in him an awareness of the interconnectedness of space and time. As a student at the Joffrey Ballet School, Forsythe attended performances by New York City Ballet that gave him opportunities to analyse different aspects of Balanchine's choreography. He would never imitate Balanchine, but he could see that the choreography offered opportunities for change.

Also significant during Forsythe's developmental years was the work of Rudolf Laban. Laban's complex study of movement, published in *Choreutics* (1966), grew out of ballet's classically structured logic, centrally organised body, and kinespheric reach. The mathematical exactitude inspired Forsythe, who saw that the system was ripe for development. He envisaged movement strategies involving multiple kinespheres, changing orientations and a density of counter-pointed detail held together by coordinated rhythms.

Forsythe began his career as a dancer, first in New York with the apprentice company Joffrey Ballet 2 and then in 1973 moving to Germany and the Stuttgart Ballet, where he danced in a range of classical and contemporary ballets. Arriving in Stuttgart in the aftermath of the death of John Cranko, the company's celebrated choreographer/director, there was heightened concern to honour Cranko's legacy and nurture emerging choreographers.

In 1975 Forsythe created a short work for the Noverre Society for young choreographers. *Ürlicht*, a sculptural duet for a man and a woman to Mahler's music with moments of breath-taking stillness, was notable. A year later it was taken into the Stuttgart Ballet's repertoire and led to Forsythe's appointment as a Resident Choreographer. If orthodoxy was apparent, so too was the individuality of his creative voice.

After this, came burgeoning relationships with ballet, expressionism, and text. He was, after all, working in Germany where expressionist art was rife, and where Pina Bausch's psychological enquiries were taking choreography into a darker, angst-ridden world. *Orpheus* (1979), his first evening-long work, was a collaboration with the composer Hans Werner Henze and Marxist playwright Edward Bond, bringing the socio-political into the frame. *Orpheus* included a grim scene in hell populated by the manic dead, where Eurydice was represented as a woman who had lost all reason. In contrast, *Love Songs* (1979), to music by Aretha Franklin and Dionne Warwick, was set in a night club and featured spirited exchanges between heterosexual couples. The tone was ironic, and the movement sometimes brutal.

During his twenty-year directorship of Ballett Frankfurt (1994–2004), Forsythe gained a reputation as one of the most acclaimed (and controversial) choreographers of his time. Radical experiments with sound, light, and technology became part of an uncompromising approach to theatre that questioned everything. The work caught the attention not just of the international dance community, but also of the wider, radical arts world, with artists from all disciplines and continents flocking to see it.

Ranging from extravagant theatricality to small scale minimalism, each work established its own discrete world, drawing in wildly disparate elements. Variously the symbolic could be seen alongside the abstract; the surrealist in tandem with the futurist – often threaded through with comedy and fragmented texts delivered by dancers speaking in various languages. In *New Sleep* (1987), domains of dance, household decoration, and surrealist characters spilled into a montage of disconnected elements. *The/The* (1995), a collaboration with Dana Caspersen, focused on gesture and upper body movement, with its two dancers sitting on the floor throughout. The sound in *N.N.N.N.* (2002) was provided by the thudding feet of four men whose exertions left them panting for breath.

Forsythe danced the 1995 *Solo*, setting out something of his movement principles in a seven-minute film in which ballet's central control yielded to decentred forms and fleeting images. Here was deconstruction – or expansion – of the ballet vocabulary. Legs turned out and in, arms busied themselves around the upper body, and the torso twisted in decentred directions. Forsythe's movement principles, which grew out of his own agility and coordination, were later assembled into a CD-ROM recording, *Improvisation Technologies: A Tool for the Analytical Dance Eye.*

Evening-long works involving the full company of more than thirty dancers were a feature of Ballett Frankfurt. None offered straight narratives or made linear sense. Rather, conceptual ideas grew out of disparate texts extending from the intellectual to the popular. *Isabelle's Dance* (1986), for which Forsythe also created the music and some of the text, was a wittily ironic musical in which the dancers also sang (rather well). If their extrovert personalities and spatial amplitude sometimes felt American, so the psychological awareness of individual characters often seemed more European.

Impressing the Czar (1988), a vividly theatrical five-act work, alluded to a stretch of history reaching from the baroque to the contemporary, and released a network of symbolic and textual references into a hybrid mixture of dance. *Czar*'s second act – *In the Middle, Somewhat Elevated* – had been created the previous year as a stand-alone work for Sylvie Guillem and the Paris Opera Ballet. *Middle* is renowned for its relentless beat, whiplash spins, and razor-sharp extensions, and is one of Forsythe's most performed ballets. It typifies works categorised by him as belonging to his 'ballet ballets'. These are classically orientated, virtuoso works that parody convention. Not requiring the creative complexity of strategic improvisation, they can be danced by other companies. Yet they require fearless dancers who can cope with daring weight changes, off-kilter balances, and limb-hitting extremities so as to deliver new thoughts about the power and plasticity of the body.

Steptext is also a 'ballet ballet'. Created in 1985 for Aterballetto, it features a woman and three men who trace bold acrobatic patterns in space or remain stationary, making gestural shapes with their arms. *Steptext*'s material was drawn from *Artifact* (1984), a ballet in four contrasting acts with a large Ballett Frankfurt cast and two main characters who step between inner and outer worlds. At the start, the woman opens her arms beguilingly and announces, 'welcome to what you think you see', as if alerting viewers to expect countless ways of experiencing Forsythe's work. *Artifact* introduces a philosophical issue about where the dance 'is', for in the second act a specially weighted curtain is lowered several times while the music (Bach's Chaconne for solo violin) continues. Each time the curtain rises, the sequencing has changed, and the dancers are in different places. The question is, can the dance be said to *exist* when the audience cannot see it?

Forsythe's intricate improvisational strategies came to fruition in *Eidos: Telos* (1995), with movement assembled into symbolic word sequences collectively known as 'The Alphabet'. In act one, the dancers establish and re-organise the alphabet, diving into rapid and diverse shifts in trajectory, dynamic, and planal level. The central act is an exposition of an ancient ritual delivered in modernised tones of an urgent enigma. Then the drama slips into incongruity and a flippant song and dance routine. In the final act, a sea of surging dancers rises up arbitrarily like waves. The effect may seem chaotic but could only have been envisioned by a master of counterpoint.

The first act of *Endless House* (1999), direction by Caspersen with stage design and lighting by Forsythe, who was also one of the performers, was presented in Frankfurt's Opera House. It featured a dialogue between two crazed men, set against glowing colour changes, though with little actual dance. For act two, audiences travelled across the city to the Bockenheimer Depot (a vast, converted tram base), where, as they wandered around compartmentalised spaces, they encountered dance in abundance.

In 2005 Forsythe launched The Forsythe Company (TFC), extending ideas from the Ballett Frankfurt as he developed new and more diverse material, always expanding the scope of 'choreography'. Inevitably there were changes as works transmogrified from the larger to the smaller company, but Forsythe abhors fixity and with successive performances of his ballets, his habit is to keep injecting new ideas into them. Sometimes with TFC he reached into more democratic styles of presentation. Interdisciplinary play in *Three Atmospheric Studies* (2006) included a heart-breaking interrogatory scene about a mother's suffering for her missing son. In *Human Writes* (2005), multiple tables provide drawing boards. The dancers transcribed ideas in charcoal from the Declaration of Human Rights with different parts of their bodies, as members of the public wandered in the space.

The installation *City of Abstracts* (2000) called for a battery of cameras, lights, and technological devices through which images of people passing in the street were projected onto walls and transformed into brightly coloured shapes to flow along an ever re-forming stream. There were no humans in *Black Flags* (2014); industrial robots in a large gallery manipulated two giant flags into a changing geometry of lines and contours. Hence, the relationship between objects and space came to life as part of Forsythe's 'Choreographic Objects' series.

Now approaching his half century as a choreographer, Forsythe is without a company of his own but still mounts occasional productions with a handful of specially selected dancers. In addition, he has returned to his ballet roots to create work on selected companies, among them Boston Ballet, Paris Opera Ballet, and English National Ballet. What emerges from these roots grows, of course, in unexpected directions. Hinting at an ancient art form, it proclaims its contemporariness – in celebration of the zeitgeist.

Ann Nugent

Biographical details

Born Long Island, New York, 30 December 1949. **Studied** ballet while a student of humanities at Jacksonville University, Florida; later at Joffrey Ballet School, New York, from 1969. **Career:** Danced with Joffrey Ballet 1 & 2 (1971–73); joined Stuttgart Ballet as a dancer, 1973 and appointed Resident Choreographer 1976, created 12 works, leaving in 1980 for an independent career. In 1970s/80s also created work for ballet companies in Munich, The Hague, London, Basel, Berlin, Frankfurt am Main, Paris, New York, and San Francisco. Director of Ballett Frankfurt, 1984–2004. Founded The Forsythe Company, 2005–2015, with bases in Frankfurt and Dresden. Work is in the repertories of Mariinsky Ballet, National Ballet of Canada, England's Royal Ballet, Semperoper Ballet Dresden, and Paris Opera Ballet. Major retrospectives in Munich (2006); London (2009). Currently, Professor of Dance and Artistic Advisor for the Choreographic Institute, University of Southern California Glorya Kaufman School of Dance. Continues to work with selected ballet companies, including Boston Ballet, Paris Opera Ballet, English National Ballet; occasionally presents work on his own small ad hoc company. **Awards and honours** include New York Dance and Performance Awards ('Bessie'), 1988, 1998, 2004, 2007; Laurence Olivier Awards, 1992, 1999, 2009; Chevalier de l'Ordre des Arts et des Lettres, 1992, 1999; Hessen Arts Prize, 1995; International Theatre Institute Award, 1996; Grand Prix Carina ARI, 1996; German Distinguished Service Cross, 1997; Wexner Prize, 2002; Golden Lion, 2010; Samuel H Scripps/American Dance Festival Award for Lifetime Achievement, 2012; Grand Prix de la SACD, 2016; FEDORA Prize, 2018; Critics' Circle Award, 2020.

Works*

(*Selected titles only. Forsythe has created too many ballets, installations, exhibitions and films to list in their entirety.)

Bach Violin Concerto in A-Minor (1977); *From the Most Distant Time* (1978); *Dream of Galilei* (1978); *Folia* (1978); *Time Cycle* (1979); *Joyleen Gets Up, Gets Down, Goes Out* (1980); *'Tis a Pity She's a Whore* (1980); *Famous Mothers Club* (solo, 1980); *Say Bye Bye* (1980); *Die Nacht aus Blei* (1981); *Whisper Moon* (1981); *Event 1, 2, 3* (1981); *Gänge 1 – Ein Stück über Ballett* (1982); *Gänge* (1983); *Mental Model* (1983); *Square Deal* (1983); *France/Dance* (1983); *Berg AB* (film; 1984); *LDC* (1985); *Skinny* (1986); *Die Befragung des Robert Scott* (1986); *Big White Baby Dog* (1986); *Baby Sam* (1986); *Pizza Girl* (1986); *Same Old Story* (1987); *The Loss of Small Detail* (1987); *Behind the China Dogs* (1988); *The Vile Parody of Address* (1988); *Enemy in the Figure* (1989); *Slingerland I* (1989); *Limb's Theorem* (includes *Enemy in the Figure*, 1990); *Slingerland II and III* (1990); *Slingerland TV* (1990); *The Second Detail* (1991); *The Loss of Small Detail* (1991); *Snap, Woven Effort* (1991); *Alie/nA(c)tion* (1992); *Herman Schmerman* (1992); *Quintett* (1993), *As a Garden in this Setting* (1993); *Self Meant to Govern* (1994); *Pivot House* (1994); *Four Point Counter* (1995); *Firstext* (1995); *Invisible Film* (1995); *Of Any If And* (1995); *Six Counter Points* (includes *TheThe, Duo, Trio, Four Point Counter*, 1995); *Approximate Sonata* and *The Vertiginous Thrill of Exactitude*, (both 1996); *Tight Roaring Circle* (with Dana Caspersen, 1997); *Hypothetical Stream 11* (1997); *From a Classical Position* (film, 1997); *Workwithinwork* (1998); *Small Void* (1998); *Op. 31* (1998); *White Bouncy Castle* (1999); *One Flat Thing, Reproduced* (2000); *Kammer/Kammer* (2000); *Woolf Phrase* (2001); *The Room As It Was* (2002); *Scattered Crowd* (2002); *Decreation* (2003); *Wear* (2004); *You Made Me a Monster* (2005); *Heterotopia* (2006); *The Defenders* (2007); *Yes We Can't* (2008); *I Don't Believe in Outer Space* (2008); *Theatrical Arsenal 11* (2009); *The Returns* (2009); *Synchronous Objects* (interactive web project with Ohio State University, 2009); *Transfigurations* (exhibition, of Forsythe's installation work, 2009); *Now This When Not That* (2011); *Study # 3* (2012); *Sider* (2013); *Selon* (2013); *Stellentstellen* (2013); *Blake Works* (2016); *Alignigung* (video installation, 2017); *Playlist*; *A Quiet Evening of Dance* (2018).

Further reading*

(*for readings prior to 2000, see Genter, *Fifty Contemporary Choreographers*, 2nd ed, 2011.)

Interviews: with Senta Driver, (ed) 'William Forsythe', *Choreography and Dance*, 5 (3), 2000; Roslyn Sulcas, 'Drawing Movements', *The New York Times*, 29 March 2009; Ana Bogdan, 'William Forsythe: "No One Has any Idea What Really Works"', *The Talks*, 24 January 2018; Sarah Crompton, 'William Forsythe: "Ballet Demands Strength that Few Would Be Willing to Muster"', *The Guardian*, 11 April 2018; Roslyn Sulcas, 'William Forsythe Interview: "I Like Being Part of the Big Ballet Conversation"', *The New York Times*, 10 March 2019.

Articles: Senta Driver, (ed) 'William Forsythe', *Choreography and Dance*, (Special issue), 5 (3), 2000; Ann Nugent, 'The Forsythe Saga', *Dance Now*, Spring 2001 and 'Profile: William Forsythe', *Dance Theatre Journal*, 19 (2), 2003; Sanjoy Roy, 'The Forsythe Company', *Dance Now*, 14 (4), 2005/06; Ann Nugent, 'William Forsythe, Eidos: Telos, and Intertextual Criticism', *Dance Research Journal*, Summer 2007; Sabine Huschka, 'Media-Bodies: Choreography as Intermedial Thinking Through in the Work of William Forsythe', *Dance Research Journal*, 42 (1), 2010; Helena Hammond, '(The Royal) Ballet, Forsythe, Foucault, Brecht, and the BBC', *Dance Research*, Winter 2013; Tamara Tomic-Vajagic, 'Hidden Narratives: Dancers' Conceptualisations of Noncharacter Roles in Leotard Ballets by George Balanchine and William Forsythe', *Dance Research*, 34 (2), 2016; W. Lim, 'An Enhanced Otherworldliness: Thierry de Mey's Screendance Based on William Forsythe's One Flat Thing, Reproduced', *Dance Research Journal*, 50 (1), 2018; Marcia Siegel, 'Dance the Choreography of William Forsythe', *The Hudson Review*, 72 (1), 2019.

Books: Roslyn Sulcas in Judy Mitoma (ed), *Envisioning Dance on Film and Video*, New York/London, 2002; Gerald Seigmund (ed), *William Forsythe. Denken in Bewgung*, Berlin, 2004; Arnd Wesemann, *Forsythe – Bill's Universe*, Berlin, 2004; Rebecca Groves and William Forsythe, *Tanzplan Deutschland Jahresheft* (eds. Christiane Kühl and Barbara Schlinder), Berlin, 2007; Jo Butterworth and Liesbeth Wildschut (eds) *Contemporary Choreography: A Critical Reader*, London, 2009; William Forsythe, et al., 'Synchronous Objects, Ohio State University', williamforsythe.de/installations, 2009; Stephen Spier (ed), *William Forsythe and the Practice of Choreography*, Abingdon, 2011; Nora Zuniga Shaw in Gabriele Klein, Sandra Noeth (eds), *Emerging Bodies: The Performance of Worldmaking in Dance and Choreography*, Bielefeld, 2011; Mark Franko (ed), *Choreographing Discourses: A Mark Franko Reader*, Abingdon, 2019; Ann Nugent, *The Oxford Handbook of Contemporary Ballet* (eds. Jill Nunez Jensen and Kathrina Farrugia-Kriel), New York, 2020.

SHARON FRIDMAN

Sharon Fridman was introduced to dance as a child through Israeli folklore. Years later he joined the professional company Ido Tadmor Company and was later accepted into the prestigious Kibbutz Contemporary Dance Company and Vertigo Company in Jerusalem. In the latter he discovered contact improvisation and became aware of the importance of the relationship he had developed with his mother. She suffers from Arnold Chiari disease, a condition generating balance problems. Fridman had looked for ways to generate encounters with the falls of his mother and had begun to develop the idea of the common centre and understand how to control verticality, where to feel gravity and its manipulation.

In these beginnings, he found a dance that unites, that is aware of nature and the communion between human beings. For Fridman, this heritage is combined with the evolution of contemporary dance, expressing a passion for the constant search to resolve the obstacle, to turn it into a catapult towards harmony. His focus is on the difficulty, the acceptance of fragility, and the need for support.

Since 2008 he has worked in Madrid, as choreographer and artistic director of his own company, Compañía Sharon Fridman. Throughout this time, there has been a notable evolution in the form of his work, towards a greater awareness of the purpose of dance to create communion between people, a means to raise a difficulty and the way to engage with this. Through the concept of 'human landscapes', the participation of numerous people (anyone who is interested) in the company's projects has consolidated his social commitment, as in *Rizoma* (2012) which is discussed later.

Technology has found its place too. In later works, for example *All Ways* (2016) and *Dose of Paradise* (2020), audio-visual resources offer other planes of reality, an overflowing of time and space, which disrupt a linear, deterministic sense of time by entering into the subjectivity of the emotional. For example, in *Dose of Paradise*, a work about a love relationship, the dramaturgy of light is a fundamental approach in offering multi-layered intentions (ideas of soul landscapes, remnants of human nature, emotions that we all feel). It gives prominence to visual and imaginative universes that allow performers and spectators to delve into landscapes that simulate emotional spaces where the composition takes place: the interior of a body, the heart. From a technical point of view we are talking about video-projection onto smoke and air, synchronised with the music through a computer system. Four projectors on stage generate virtual spaces in three dimensions. A territory created and illuminated by these *four eyes* makes up a new world where heaven and earth are transposed, and the concept of gravity is questioned. These *eyes* create a type of light like a great wall of smoke, whose quality opens up a new dialogue with the bodies.

The dance that Fridman proposes is a way of engaging audiences with their own nature, so that once reconciled, they can generate an open and peaceful relationship with others, and thus access the flow of life. *Nido* (2016) for example, was developed in an open natural space for the Oerol Festival, held annually on the island of Terschelling off the coast of the Netherlands. Prior to experiencing the show, people were invited to engage in a meditative, contemplative walk towards the performance space, in single file, to achieve a heightened state of consciousness.

Works, such as *All Ways* and *Dose of Paradise*, can be conceived of as spaces of consciousness in which to perceive the drawing of emotional landscapes. It is a way of connecting with the mythical, in which symbols and archetypes of multiple traditions are displayed; for example, those present in the process of living, love, loneliness, death, suffering, and friendship, without ignoring their anchorage within daily existence and the plots we develop in it. In *Erritu* (2018), a collaboration with Kukai Danza, for example, Fridman focuses on ritual to enter into communion with other people. He had found a respect for nature in Israeli folklore and traditional Basque dances, a connection with the imperishable; these dances connect with our essential human qualities. In *Erritu*, different rituals are explored, from festive to funeral dances, in all of which are found a generous expression of the spirit, the understanding of natural cycles. The contiguity between art and life is palpable, the dance happens everywhere.

Fridman encourages audiences to connect with their own emotional matter. This makes the dance a personal experience for spectators. For example, *All Ways* delves into the archetype of the Way, one of the most ancestral aspects of the human psyche. Without a path we feel lost, we are filled with confusion, aimless, with no compass or stars to guide us. We see the dancers as walkers who never walk alone, tracing multiple paths that coexist and intertwine in the pursuit of harmony.

Witnessing a work by Fridman involves immersion into a chaos of physical and emotional instability, like entering the vortex of a hurricane and from there trying to find a state which leads to acceptance and surrender, thus being able to access meaning. The dancers often resemble autopoietic machines who, despite the changes occurring, maintain a sense of community due to the use of constant contact. In *CaídaLibre / Free Fall* (2011), winner of the Max award for best dance show, the chaotic compositional flow (based on extensive research into contact dancing) is clear. A slight event, such as the fall of a person, generates multiple and extreme trajectories. Being sensitive to that allows a rupture of symmetry, the dancers ride on instability until its culmination, where restructuring and stability are re-achieved. This work explores an essential feature of human nature: survival. It addresses how groups can be constituted to generate support, creating physical and emotional networks that allow the individual to fall and get up.

Another common feature in Fridman's choreography is the repetition of movement patterns, in which nuances of information about the development of relationships or individual processes are revealed.

In *Al menos dos caras* (2011), co-produced by Festival de Otoño en Primavera, choreography enters into cyclical repetition of movement seen from different positions in respect of the public and the scenography, revealing multiple information about the same event. It is a game of identities, which explores the many perspectives that an event can offer depending on who is watching. The intense duo *Hasta donde ...?* (2011), is an example of an energetic relation between two dancers with homeostatic yearning. Roger Salas (June 2012) wrote of this piece:

> A gem of intensity and nuances ... from the lack of love towards chaos ... Dancers slog their guts out in the speech, they know that everything that unites them, will separate them, and they transmit it in a high level tragic and torn up breath.

The pillar of Fridman's work is contact. Beyond being his fundamental language, it also constitutes an existential philosophy. The company explores contact to express the nature of human relationships and their lives in space. Contact, in their dance, is not only physical, but also emotional, mental, and energetic. In the last decade, Fridman has been developing a series of dynamics that have given rise to new qualities of contact, related to the concepts of elevation and the creation of physical centres that connect bodies to each other. The practice of these movement concepts is a source of inspiration when composing. He calls this research process, aimed at the creation of a dance technique, method, or language, Contact to Creation. The focus concerns the concept of gravity, investigating this in depth and discovering unexplored aspects. On the other hand, we must add the energetic expression that moulds the bodies, since this is never unnoticed in the creative processes. The movement supposes the transmission of an element with which it has been previously connected, movement is a direct expression of what happens inside, by an internal and irreversible necessity.

Social commitment led Fridman to generate projects like *Rizoma* (2012). From the company's perspective, dance is not understood as something alien to the world's conflicts, many of which are born from a disconnection: with oneself, with nature, with other people. *Rizoma* aims to develop a lasting network among its participants. Since its premiere during the Festival Paris Quartier d'Été, this ecological macro-performance has travelled to several locations (Spain, France, Holland, Italy, Colombia, Hong Kong). Its format has evolved, and today there are two versions: *Nido* (2016) and *A Piedi Nudi* (2018). In each, a group of about 100 people are involved, united by their passion for movement.

This project is a homage to birth, usually performed at dawn. It focuses on the essential processes of dissolution and solidification in nature, listening to our immediate place in it, without control or domination, and is based on the use of natural tools: bodies, voice, wind, sunlight. A symbolic existential birth must take place in every *Rizoma*, inspired by our reality and relationship with the universe. After around two weeks of working intensively with the company, performers develop fluid and emotional choreography based in *contact language*, generating *human landscapes* which express a powerful evolving nature. The dancers resemble lost particles that find each other, and in this meeting something new starts to grow. The beginning of this work is shocking, performers vocalise the final words that they might have to express in life, until they fall to the floor. From that point, nature must work in each participant. Sometimes, the dancers seem like a field of flowers, a group of zebras searching their space, an erupting volcano, a sensual and aromatic garden, or a great mushroom.

Rizoma was conceived to bring nature to the places where it has been forgotten: chaotic and frenetic cities, asphalt floors, alienated and neurotic faces, dehumanised lives. This piece can be born and plugged into any space, filling the empty spaces, growing like the grass does, in the middle of things. Fridman has developed a language which is a metaphor for the possibility that we human beings have of finding new channels of communication, which enable us to face conflicts with new solutions. Dance is confirmed as a way of knowing a complex reality and finding our place in it. Human landscapes are distilled, in which the responsibility of the individual, the need to connect with nature itself, and the questioning of relationships are combined.

Antonio Ramirez

Biographical details

Born in Pardess Hana, Israel, 1980. **Studied** with a local Israeli folklore company he joined aged seven; later joined Ido Tadmor Company; the Kibbutz Contemporary Dance Company; and Vertigo Dance Company of Jerusalem, where he also studied contact. **Career:** Aged 26, settled in Madrid, started his own projects and founded Sharon Fridman Company. Has created work for other companies including Vertigo and Kukai Dantza; work is also in the repertory of National Ballet (Paraguay), Compagnie Jus de la Vie (Stockholm), Collettivo Cinetico (Italy), Bora Art Project Company (Seoul), Theater Bielefeld, LaMov Dance Company, and the Spanish National Dance Company. In October 2018, became artist in residence at the Francisco Rabal

Theatre, Town Hall of Pinto. Currently working on development of his own technique within the field of contact improvisation: 'Contact to Creation'. **Awards** include Spanish Max Awards, 2015 and 2019.

Works

Covered Red (2000); *Anna* (2001); *Waiting* (2003); *The Creation* (2004); *Play Boy* (2005); *Carlos & Me* (2007); *Q Project* (2008); *Shakuff* (2010); *Al menos dos caras* (2011); *Hasta donde …?* (2011); *Rizoma* (2012); *Inner* (2013); *Free Fall* (2014); *Stable* (2015); *All Ways* (2016); *Nido* (2016); *Barro* (2017); *Dialogo Primo* (2018); *A Piedi Nudi* (2018); *Erritu* (2018); *Dose of Paradise* (2020).

Further reading

Interviews: with Anna Trevisan, 'Sharon Fridman. This is the Place', *ABC Dance*, 25 July 2015; Victoria Gallardo, 'El vuelo en picado de Sharon Fridman', *El Mundo*, 2 October 2015; Romain Bigé, 'Catching the Fall: An Interview with Sharon Fridman on Contact Improvisation and Choreography', *Contact Quarterly*, Summer/Fall, 2016; Agencia EFE, 'Sharon Fridman refleja en "All Ways" su filosofía de trabajo y vida', *El Confidencial*, 20 October 2016; Ori J. Lenkinski, 'All ways to Connect', *The Jerusalem Post,* 1 August 2018.

Articles: Ora Braman, 'Dance Review: Sharon Fridman', *The Jerusalem Post*, 5 December 2011; Roger Salas, 'En la habitación sin vistas. Al menos dos caras', *El País*, 20 June 2012; Roger Salas, 'La caída de la casa de Sharon', *El País*, 17 November 2012; Michael Lake, 'Review: Compañía Sharon Fridman, Spanish Troupe Showcases Dynamic Contact-Dance in Halifax', *The Coast*, Halifax, 7 October 2017; Francesca Marotto, 'Review: Compañía Sharon Fridman', *The Wonderful World of Dance*, 18 July 2018; Janine Parker, '"Community" Takes on New Meaning in Work of Compañía Sharon Fridman at Jacob's Pillow', *The Berkshire Eagle*, 27 July 2018.

EMANUEL GAT

The work of Emanuel Gat and his multidisciplinary collaborators can be considered an ongoing investigation into the possibilities and openings of the choreographic process as a shared practice of inquiry about modes of relationality and communal living. Gat's work is affirmative and generative in the way it folds and unfolds many possible 'choreographic environments', where the performers interact among themselves and with other choreographic elements.

According to my experience of his process, 'environment' defines a space inhabited by a set of structures, in which the choreographer and the performers intervene by formulating and responding to tasks through active decision making, thus defining and modifying the environment itself. In this way, it is a space for promoting change and experimentation. In Gat's work, choreography exposes continuities as well as transformations of possible modes of interaction. Movement, generated by the dancers and co-organised by Gat, activates and layers sensations, emotions, ideas, energies, and ethical values. He states, 'To understand choreography, is to understand "what is". The actual thing taking place, happening, during the creative process, as well as when performed' ('#what is', *Choreographer's Notes*, emanuelgatdance. com, 25 December 2018). Whether with his collaborators in Emanuel Gat Dance or with other companies, or his interventions across visual arts, music composition and writing, Gat's work articulates an ongoing process of enquiry about the stakes of choreography itself and as research on possible ways of reassessing existing modes of knowing and relating – among dancers, with audiences, and in larger social terms.

Gat's choreographic system is ever-evolving. Here 'system' does not indicate systematisation but suggests attention towards the emergence of organisational practices and relationalities. Never a product, each choreography is a journey-in-progress, made of shifts, variations, returns, departures. Indeed, Gat often returns to previous works as opportunities to re-interrogate the choreography and the choreographic method. Since *Brilliant Corners* (2011), energetic relations among dancers became an engine for investigation of modes of group mobilisations and non-hierarchical collaborations. *Winter Voyage* (2004) is a male duo where, without touching, the bodies ultimately attract one another in their sinuous paths. *The Rite of Spring* (2004) engages with Stravinsky's *ostinato* through the perseverance of the relationality among five dancers. By employing the fluid, continuous movements of Cuban salsa, Gat plays with direction changes and exchanges of partners with a growing sensuality, intensified by the proximity of the dancing bodies moving within the limited perimeter of a carpet. In *SACRE* (2015), a revisited version of *Rite*, the spatial limitation often explodes when the exit of one dancer from the carpet also pulls the other dancers out, unsettling the space of the ritual and invalidating any teleology of the sacrificial victim.

Within *3for2007 // My Favorite Things* (2007), a three-part work including a duo and ensemble for nine dancers, particularly memorable is Gat's solo (to John Coltrane's *My Favorite Things*), where his body, in quasi-meditative kinetic continuity, acts as a dynamic sound box for the simultaneous and multidirectional counterpoints of the jazz masterpiece. Gat's process of devising a choreographic system open to ongoing variations resonates with Coltrane's composition, a piece the musician continuously reworked.

In 2007, Gat left Tel Aviv and installed his company at the Maison de la Danse d'Istres, France. *Silent Ballet* (2008) marks a shift in his choreographic process. The exposure of gestural cues and movement correspondences among the eight performers, in silence, allowed the emergence of a specific temporality. The dancers' decisions of offering and taking cues, of engaging in and disengaging from group interactions, produce a sense of corporeal counterpoint. Pauses, hesitations, anticipations, accelerations among the dancers expose a non-prescriptive choreographic logic.

The sense of dynamic interrelation among performers was already visible in the 2006 work *K626* (titles typically refer to his music, here Mozart's *Requiem in D minor, K. 626*), where a single dancer's cue activates a spatial shift in the whole group. By the time of *Brilliant Corners*, while the sense of ensemble remains, individuals more clearly emerge as part of an interconnected collective. Gat does not impose movement phrases or technical references in the studio. He organises the work by giving tasks for performers to elaborate individual and shared solutions. The tasks, which can be as simple as maintaining a certain distance between the bodies, do not aim to design final products nor assume an ideological status of the body. Indeed, tasks generate and progressively modify the environment in which the performers move. New questions emerge from the dancers' personal investment, creativity, and relationality.

> Just the simple question of what might be the next best move. / At every single moment of the process, and regardless of my own opinion about the whole. / The choreographic process moves forward through the endless number of times we answer that one question.
> (*Choreographer's Notes,* emanuelgatdance.com,
> 10 August 2017).

Brilliant Corners shows the continuity between individual and collective decisions, which rely on full-body sensorial attentiveness. This allows the 11 dancers to move together and differently across the stage, through reciprocally informed activity which activates individual and group shifts in an ongoing flow of cues and signals. Each performer seems to caress the space (with a hand, a foot, the surface of the back, etc.), creating a dense environment of correspondences. During rehearsal and performance, the process articulates as an experiment, an open field in which dancers practise decision-making. This system has a dynamic quality in the way it folds and unfolds in the environment. The dance happens in its kinetic becoming.

After his exploration of collective movement, GOLD (2015) zooms into the forces that inhabit each member of a community. Dramaturgically empowered by a montage of the multi-layered sound documentary *The Quiet in the Land* by Glenn Gould and his 1981 version of the *Goldberg Variations*, the choreography challenges the fluid unfolding of the spatial and physical relations of *Brilliant Corners* by tackling moments of friction and intimacy, showing how individual dancers can at one moment disengage from the group and the next lean on another body. *Plage Romantique* (2014) continues Gat's research towards structuring a dance in the most non-hierarchical way possible, adding a playful sense of complicity among the nine dancers. The use of microphones, with which the performers call each other's names, intensifies their presence through the sonic expansion of their breath.

In *Sunny* (2016), Gat and his collaborators further broaden the possibilities of choreography with a dance performance that is simultaneously a live concert-DJ set by Awir Leon (a.k.a. Gat's long-time dancer François Przybylski) and a fashion show, where the processes of structuring and improvising interact with each other. *Sunny* mesmerises in how it slips away from definitions and categorisations, avoiding any systematisation of genre.

The stakes of such openness are tested in *Story Water* (2018), performed by Emanuel Gat Dance along with the musician-led Ensemble Modern of Frankfurt. This is Gat's most upfront manifestation of a political stance in relation to Palestine and Israel. He has often been asked why he does not choreographically engage with the Israeli-Palestinian conflict. While on his social media he is very vocal about his personal political stance, in his choreography he warns against 'dance making which presents itself as "political"; [it] is in most cases bluntly abusive, manipulative, and disempowering towards both the performers, and its audience' (*Choreographer's Notes*, emanuelgatdance. com, 11 June 2017).

Gat's choreographic process does not unfold thematically. In the fourth part of *Story Water*, a projection shows a series of statistics without commentary; these illustrate the regime of segregation in the Gaza Strip. Dancers and musicians are in spatial continuity with the audience. A dancer holds a stopwatch and activates it when the director, who entered within the group of 12 dancers, initiates the action, mobilising a generous accumulation of individual and interconnected experiences. Whenever our gaze stops on the clock, we are reminded of the shared experience of time that we are producing together.

Dancers and musicians actively communicate throughout the event, eluding the exclusive control of the set elements that are still part of the performance (such as the music scores of Pierre Boulez, Rebecca Saunders, and Gat himself, the lighting design, etc.). Similarly, the projected text, announcing the titles of the parts that structure *Story Water* (Choreography; Music; People; Gaza; Dance!), does not merely work as a caption; instead it points out sites of intervention or experiences that require an active assumption of responsibility and reciprocal accountability.

The dancers that join Emanuel Gat Dance combine technical wit and creative curiosity. Each brings specific sets of skills to foster the collective action. At the same time, their skills are transmitted and shared during the rehearsal process, so that the reciprocal exchange simultaneously expands the individual dancer as well as the group's possibilities. Gat's works combine compositional clarity, energetic and emotional intensity with a sense of indeterminacy given by the progressive de-hierarchisation of the choreographic process. By unravelling authoritarian relations among the elements in a choreographic work, and exposing how relationships form and unfold on stage, Gat and his collaborators share with the audience an expansive eye on how we organise our communities in our joint experiences of time.

Melissa Melpignano

Bibliographical details

Born in Ḥadera, Israel, 7 March 1969. **Studied** conducting briefly, at the Rubin Academy of Music (now Jerusalem Academy of Music and Dance) after three-year mandatory military service 1987–1990. **Career:** following the suggestion of his partner, visual artist Yifat, Gat, took first dance workshop with Israeli choreographers Nir Ben Gal and Liat Dror; six months later, aged 23, abandoned his music studies to join their company. Started choreographing in 1994; in 2004, established his own company, Emanuel Gat Dance, resident at the Suzanne Dellal Center in Tel Aviv; in 2007, settled in south of France, moving his company to the Maison Intercommunale de la Danse in Istres. Associate Artist of the Festival Montpellier Danse, 2013; Associated Choreographer, National Scene of Albi, 2016; and Associated Choreographer, National Theatre of Chaillot, Paris, 2018–2021. Regular guest choreographer for ballet and contemporary companies including Paris Opera Ballet, Sydney Dance Company, ICK Amsterdam, Tanztheater Bremen, Le Ballet du Grand Théâtre de Genève, Ballet de Marseille, The Royal Swedish Ballet, Polish National Ballet, Ballet de Lorraine, Cedar Lake, Ballet British Columbia, and Ballet de l'Opera de Lyon. **Awards** include a New York Dance and Performance Award ('Bessie'), 2006.

Works

Four Dances (1994); Polipopipop (1996); Ana wa Enta (2003); Two Stupid Dogs (2003); The Rite of Spring (2004); Winter Voyage (2004); K626 (2006); Trotz dem alten Drachen (2007); 3for2007 // My Favorite Things (2007); Through the Center (2007); Windungen (2008); Silent Ballet (2008); Hark! (2009); Winter Variations (2009, further exploration of Winter Voyage); The Revised and Updated Bremen Structures (2010); Observation Action (2010); Satisfying Musical Moments (2010); In Translation (2010); Preludes et Fugues (2011); Brilliant Corners (2011); Organizing Demons (2012); Time Themes (2013); Morgan's Last Chug (2013); Danses de Cour (2013); Corner Études (2013, further exploration of Brilliant Corners); It's People, How Abstract Can It Get? (2013); The Goldlandbergs (2013); Transposition #1 et #2 (2013); Sunshine (2014); Ida? (2014); Plage Romantique (2014); SACRE (2015, revisited version of The Rite of Spring); Gold (2015, revisited version of The Goldlandbergs); Trinity (2016); Sunny (2016); Duos (2017); TENWORKS (for Jean-Paul) (2017); LOCK (2017); Works (2019, new work developed from TENWORKS); Separate Knots (2018); Next (2018); Story Water (2018); The Circle (2019); YOOO!!! (2019); LOVETRAIN2020 (2020).

Further reading

Interviews: with Veerle Corstens, 'Interview with Emanuel Gat: "It's Only in the Studio that We Realize What the Flavor and Texture Will Be"', body-in-revolt.tumblr.com, undated; 'Interview with Emanuel Gat – NEXT', ICK Amsterdam, vimeo.com, 11 October 2018; Agnès Izrine, 'Danse et musique: éspace de dialogue. Entretien avec Emanuel Gat', La Terrasse, journal-laterrasse.fr, [French], 23 February 2018; 'Interview with Emanuel Gat and Ensemble Modern', Festival d'Avignon, 72e édition du 6 au 24 juillet 2019, vol. 10, 2019 [French and English]; 'Interview d'Emanuel Gat / WORKS, Théâtre de Chaillot', vimeo.com, [French], 8 May 2019; Podium Dans, 'Podium Dans 3.7 Emanuel Gat', 2019, vimeopro.com/beatthedutchfilms [Dutch and English]; 'Emanuel Gat Dance Heads Home for Suzanne Dellal's 30th Season', Times of Israel, 2019.

Articles: Lise Smith, 'Review: Emanuel Gat in Winter Variations at Sadler's Wells', londondance.com, 4 November 2010; Theodore Bale, 'Dancing Out of the Whole Earth: Modalities of Globalization in "The Rite of Spring"', Dance Chronicle, 31 (3), 2008; Lyndsey Winship, 'Emanuel Gat: Works Review – Moving Mysterious Dance is a Delight', The Guardian, 12 November 2019; Katja Vaghi, 'It is Only a Pale Winter Sun: Emanuel Gat's SUNNY at the Staatsballett Berlin', bachtrack.com, 19 December 2019.

Books: Philippe Verrièle et al., Emanuel Gat: Cet espace où danse la musique, Paris, 2019; Rosita Boisseau and Laurent Philippe, Danse contemporaine, Lyon, 2016.

JACOPO GODANI

Jacopo Godani, the Italian choreographer and Director of the Dresden Frankfurt Dance Company (which replaced The Forsythe Company in 2015), has not lost an ounce of vitality since he was a young boy chosen to be a student of the Mudra Maurice Béjart School in 1986. Since then, he has toured Europe, and been invited to create work in Israel, US, Canada, and Australia.

Although dance started as a hobby, in two years his teacher Loredana Rovagna of La Spezia Dance Studio Centre coached him to enter Béjart's prestigious Brussels school. His choreographic career began in Mudra with *Oomingmak* (1986), which was accepted into the school's choreographic repertoire and performed during the end of season tournée in the most important theatres of Belgium. Following the creation of *Drastiquement Brutal* (1989) for the company Archipel Sud (Belgium), he was invited by Serge Rangoni, then Director of Atelier Saint Anne, as Resident Choreographer. This was a fundamental step: starting his personal avant-gardist research to find a purpose and a new expressive language.

At the age of 20, Godani joined the Ballett Frankfurt directed by William Forsythe and was immediately involved with the small group of dancers who created choreography for his ballets. 'Billy gave us the ground for self-development, it was a marvellous experience and I will be eternally grateful' (in Angela Testa, 'Forsythe for Godani', *Dance & Culture*, web-magazine n°7, 2015). Simultaneously his freelance activity developed (to the point of leaving his dancing career in 2000), allowing him to practice all the activities that surround the choreographic role: lights, scenography, costume design, creative cooperation with musicians, administrative activity, and last but not least, dancer's preparation.

In 2002 he was nominated for best choreographer at the Nijinsky Award Monaco Dance Forum. That same year, *After Dark* (2002) with the Bayerisches Staatsballett of Monaco won the Tanz-Woche-Preis. The following year, he was nominated for the Benois de la Dance Award.

Godani bases much of his knowledge on self-taught learning and doesn't intend to be a teacher to his dancers. He considers that creative ferment matures with life experiences and grows, consequently, in the social sphere: for him, this means not waiting for knowledge that comes from above. He believes a dance company is not a dance school, and achieving success is something one must create for oneself.

Godani's research is contained in a ballet concept in which he continues to express physical power, virtuosity, sense of beauty, dynamics, and a level of spectacle; he intends to continue to create in this field, without following any dance style or previous influence, remaining still and always avant-garde.

> What Forsythe has brought to the dance world has been incredible. In my opinion, it does not concern dance style as much as his philosophy. How to open up and change, even at a social level, to work with a ballet company ... possibilities are unlimited.
>
> (in Angela Testa, 'Forsythe for Godani',
> *Dance & Culture*, web-magazine n°7, 2015)

And in these unlimited possibilities he transforms the inherited Italian cultural experiences and those absorbed abroad with time and study, without throwing anything away. During the years he has changed the way he summarises his background, from using classical culture, Greek-Roman tragedies, beauty inspired by nature or by theatre aesthetics, to creating allegorical and evocative pieces with an aesthetic taste that leads to pictorial inspirations, as in *Satelliting* (2019), which offers Caravaggesque impressions. About his dance he claims, 'it has strongly changed the ways of expression, we are working on more complex and sophisticated materials, neoclassicism has developed in a way nearly uncodifiable; we do not remain grounded to a language, we always move forward' (in Angela Testa, 'Aspettando Godani ..., Equilibrio Festival 2017', *Dance & Culture,* website, 2017). This approach can be found in *Extinction of a Minor Species* (2017).

So dancers' bodies become chains in perpetual and flexible transformation, as in *The Primate Trilogy* (2015); chains that break in pieces and then reconstruct connections, depending on how the dancers merge and divide, never being satisfied by the achieved shape, like the ensemble choreographies of *Moto Perpetuo* (2016). The search for movement which goes beyond the usual possibilities of the body is taken to the extreme by the use of objects, such as leg prostheses (in a new version of *Extinction of a Minor Species*, 2018) or very high-heeled boots (*Ultimatum*, 2018). These also limit performance and make difficult the movement of dancers who need specific training and extreme attention in their use. In *Alter Ego* (2019), he expresses it in costumes that amplify the expansion of form and movement. One of the latest works, *Satelliting* (2019), demonstrates exceptionally slow movement of the body, not showing it clearly or in its entirety. What matters here is only to grasp some salient aspects picked out by the LED lights, held or worn by the dancers themselves.

Godani is an abstract composer, more interested in what initiates movement than in what is moved; his research is always towards something more transcendent than narration or sentiment because it tends to catch the cause and not the effect, using the body as a precise rhythmic instrument as, for instance, in *Moto Perpetuo* (2016). His is a sophisticated, composite, scientific, often innovative dance, with a tension that springs from the intensity and the pressing search for interpretative precision, pushing bodies increasingly towards untried movement ability in which every unexplored body angle seems to take on a life of its own, such as he developed in *Ultimatum* (2019) too.

The unique gesture of the hands is an unequivocal signature found in all his works; for example *Anomali One* (2005), *Light Years* (2010), *Spazio-Tempo* (2010, 2012), or more recently *The Primate Trilogy* (2015) and *From Now On* (2018). The use of the hands becomes communicative, evocative, or even scenographic. For instance, in the divertissiment entitled *Stormo* (2019), the dancers, standing among the orchestra, seem to play music and, at the same time, direct the musicians with arm and hand movements; in *Alter Ego* (2019), the dancer in the middle of the stage seems to communicate to the others through his frantic moving hands; and in *Satelliting* (2019), a dancer's hands make black butterfly wings with Chinese shadows that obscure the lights and conclude the show.

The spatial organisation of the group is usually very neat and is another of his obsessions. Disjointed, sharp, sudden movements find a harmonious roundness in the waves that fluctuate through vibrant bodies, as in *The Primate Trilogy* (2015) or in *Ultimatum* (2018), and are an exhibition of research at a molecular level, 'a show all choreographed, not even a bit of improvisation, in which the way movement is transferred is all cerebral. It is an abstract work on pure body mechanics and dynamics and musical artistic interpretation' (in Angela Testa, 'The Primate Trilogy for the prime company', *Dance & Culture*, website, 2015).

The audience is not the focal point of Godani's research; his investigation feels strictly necessary as a personal path, even if it doesn't meet public blessing. In spite of this, his desire would be to tear down the fourth wall and offer rehearsal open doors: 'just like people going to museums to admire accomplished works, likewise we should allow people to see first-hand a creation in the exact moment of its development. Bring back the people to the world of dance' (in Angela Testa, 'The Primate Trilogy for the prime company', *Dance & Culture*, website, 2015). Godani's dance, which is often created together with music produced by contemporary composers (very often in close collaboration with the 48Nord duo), reaches the audience like a rock song: if it works, it touches you directly, without interpretation. Music, used in contrast or in harmony with movement, offers vibrant energy from which dancers draw vitality and dynamism; very often it is created and used as if it were provoked by the dancers' own movement to emphasise the difficulty of translating the sharp and abrupt gestures of the body into a spasmodic tension, both in space and toward the other, as in *The Primate Trilogy* (2015), or the dancer's body itself becomes an instrument, as in *Stormo* (2019).

Mise-en-scène, also important to Godani, always has remarkable impact. He uses darkness as substance and light in endless possibilities; as a chisel to sculpt and to polish body contours, to show them more clearly, or to wrap them up in a soft haze. These lights, designed by Godani, together with his costumes, 'something in between a superhero and science fiction as long as it shows a body', (in Angela Testa, 'The Primate Trilogy for the prime company', *Dance & Culture*, website, 2015), totally involve the audience.

The Godani language synthesis could be summarised in this image: Dresden Frankfurt Dance Company is like liquid mercury taking on different shapes, merging, splitting, creating countless balls of different sizes; dancers are fluid, extremely pliable and respond to the choreographer's need to experiment (in Monica Ratti, 'La Dresden Frankfurt Dance Company è mercurio liquido', *Dance & Culture*, website, 6 February 2017). All his dancers are exceptional performers, and today they have a performance smoothness that neither undermines nor subdues the inflexible lines of his language. For example, in *Echoes from a restless soul* (2016) with Maurice Ravel's pieces from *Gaspard de la Nuit,* we experience a baffling descriptive malleability that translates itself into a liquid, fluctuating poetry of movement. Like a Picasso, struggling to find a line through which the underlying concept, the fundamental idea, finally finds expression: this is, in essence, Jacopo Godani's work.

Angela Testa

Biographical details

Born in La Spezia, Italy, 9 October 1967. **Studied** ballet and modern dance at the Centro studi Danza, 1984; and visual arts for three years, Fine Arts School of Carrara. In 1986, accepted at Maurice Béjart's international dance centre Mudra in Brussels. **Career:** professional debut in 1988, performing with several Paris-based contemporary dance companies. Formed his own Brussels-based company and began his choreographic career, 1990. From 1991 to 2000, Godani was a leading soloist with William Forsythe's Ballett Frankfurt and collaborated with Forsythe on the creation of many of Ballett Frankfurt's pieces. Has choreographed works for The Royal Ballet, Bayerisches Staatsballett, Compañía Nacional de Danza, Nederlands Dans Theater, Royal Danish Ballet, Ballet British Columbia, Le Ballet du Capitole de Toulouse, Corpo di ballo del Teatro alla Scala, Royal Ballet of Flanders, Ballet de l'Opera national du Rhin, Finnish National Ballet, Semperoper Ballett, Sydney Dance Company, 'The Project' Israeli Opera & Suzanne Dellal Centre, Het Nationale Ballet, Aterballetto, Les Ballets de Monte Carlo, ŽfinMalta, and Cedar Lake Contemporary Ballet. Appointed Artistic Director and Choreographer of the Dresden Frankfurt Dance Company, 2015. **Awards** Tanz-Woche-Preis, 2002.

Works

Oomingmak (1986); Drastiquement brutal (1989); C'était Ainsi (1990); V.T.S/ O.T.S (1991); Cosmic Punk Adventure (1995); Sleepers Guts Part 3 (1996); Skinks (1997); Radical/Mistaken (1998); The Voice Ghost (1998); Mars in Aries (1999); Monocroma Oculto (1999, 2001); Zero-Point Energy (1999); Digital Secrets (1999, 2003); Kid Dynamo (2000); Aeon's Run (2000); Animal Trigger (2000); Twilight Arias (2001); Magnitude 9 (2001); Noces (2001); Cult Race (2001); After Dark (2002); Getting Started (2002); Pas des deux (2002); Kid Dynamo II (2002); Zero Point Energy (2003); Syndrome (2003); Life Forms (2003); Beyonders (2003); Baby Gang (2004); Blackout (2004); Jacopo Godani Evening (2004); StaticoConfuso (2004); Contropotere (2005); Subliminal Instant (2005); Anomaly One (2005); Prototype Hero (2005); Elemental (2006); Symptoms of Development (2006, 2007, 2013); Scenes de Force (2007); Soirée Godani (2007); Simulations (2007); Polimerae (2008); Unit in Reaction (2008); Conflit Acceleration (2008); Uncontaminated (2009); La Stirpe di Leonardo (2009); Da Ora in Poi (2009); AURA (Anarchist Unit Related to Art, 2009, 2012, 2013); Spazio-Tempo (2010, 2012); 47 (2010); Atto di Forza (2010); Light Years (2010); Raw Models (2011); Ex Nihilo (2011); Sacre (2012); The Primate Trilogy (2015); C.O.R.E. (2016); Moto Perpetuo (2016); Echoes from a Restless Soul (2016); Metamorphers (2016); Postgenoma (2017); Extinction of a Minor Species (2017); Fading Features (2017); High Breed (2017); AL DI LÁ (2018); Prototype Hero (2018); Unit in Reaction (2018); From Now On (2018); Girl's Dance (2018); Ultimatum (2018); Framing Reality (2018); Alter Ego (2019); Satelliting (2019); Stormo (2019).

Further reading*

*note that at the time of publication, Dance & Culture, cited below, is building a new website

Interviews: with Erin Brannigan, 'The Human as Animal', realtime.org.au, 22 Mar 2011.

Articles: Gerald Siegmund, 'Jacopo Godani or the Energy of the Air', *Ballet International*, October 1999; Gerald Siegmud, 'On Stage: The Clone, a Creature', *Ballet International*, August/September 2000; Erin Brannigan, 'Enter the Real World', realtime.org.au, 22 April 2014; Angela Testa, 'Jacopo Godani, un selfmade man italiano alla guida della Forsythe Company', *DanzaSì*, December 2014; Pia Savoie, 'Ballet BC is World Class in a Spectacular Godani/Inger/Walerski Bill', bachtrack.com, 25 January 2015; Angela Testa, 'The Primate Trilogy for the Prime Company', danceandculture.it, 3 October 2015; Stephan Eckel, '5, 6, 7, [Tanz] – Jacopo Godani's dreiteiliger Ballettabend', bachtrack.com, 17 November 2016; Angela Testa, 'Godani's Triumph in Rome', *Dance & Culture*, danceandculture.it, 3 February 2017; Sarah Batschelet, 'Animal Instinct, Humanity and Some Serious Hustle', bachtrack.com, 13 February 2017; Angela Testa, 'Quando il Teatro fa il tutto esaurito per la Danza, quella di Jacopo Godani', danceandculture.it, 15 April 2018; Cintia Borges Carreras 'La audacia coreográfica de Jacopo Godani hace vibrar al Tetro Real: Dresden Frankfurt Dance Company', bachtrack.com, 23 April 2018.

MARCO GOECKE

Marco Goecke does not make a secret of his anxieties. Since childhood, when he felt lost while having a very high fever, fear is the strongest feeling he knows: 'I have many fears, that is a big subject in my life. As if I'm full of something that needs to be exorcized' (De Jong 2017). In the documentary *Thin Skin* (2016), he talks about his overwhelming panic attacks, but they are a huge source of creativity for shaping his universe on stage. Working with people dampens and softens his feelings of fear and loneliness. Goecke does not have to invest a lot to produce that fear onstage. 'It's because the dancers have it too and also spectators feel that fear' (De Jong 2017). He has created many solos, even within pieces for more dancers, like *Nichts* (2008), where a group of dancers appear and disappear, often leaving behind a solitary dancer. He explains that using solos has to do with himself; each solo symbolises what he is. In his world on stage we see creatures, sometimes referencing insects or birds, maniacally struggling, arms and hands razor sharp shaking, shivering, and fluttering, nervously searching, moving with little steps in high speed. In an abstract way his work is about parting, loneliness, desperation, but with tenderness and a lot of humour. As Paul Lightfoot, Artistic Director of the Nederlands Dans Theater, sees it, 'There is darkness, but it also has extreme hope in it' (poddedeux.com, 15 December 2018). For Goecke, his work is about redemption from fear, the fear is transformed into beauty (*Thin Skin* 2016). *Walk the Demon* (2018), created for the Nederlands Dans Theater, is a typical Goecke-ballet, in which the dancers emerge from clouds of smoke, tormented souls, driven by something from inside. The accompanying music is a mixture, this time string quartets and ballads. Movements are nervous with a lot of obsessive repetition, but also lyrical phrases. Sometimes the dancers use their voices, whispering or screaming, which makes them more human, in particular in combination with the seductive, but also desperate, ballads. The male duets especially are very moving. They touch and embrace each other, but soon they part again. The last duet ends in an embrace, but for how long?

In the Netherlands, Goecke's work is well known. Even when spectators are used to his movement language, the dark atmosphere and the magic, his choreographies are never boring; the audience tend to sit on the edge of their chairs, surprised again by a masterpiece. He has an enormous productivity, mostly working in Germany (Stuttgart Ballett, Ballett der Staatsoper Hannover, Gauthier Dance) and the Netherlands (Scapino Ballet Rotterdam, Nederlands Dans Theater), where he has held positions as Choreographer in Residence, Associate Choreographer, and Ballet Director. He also choreographed for many other companies worldwide. He created his first work, *Loch*, in 2000 for Stuttgart Ballett. As early as 2003 he was awarded the Prix Dom Pérignon for *Blushing*. In 2004, Pina Bausch invited him to show *Blushing* and *Mopey* (2004) at the Tanztheater Festival in Wuppertal. After seeing *Blushing* on video, Ed Wubbe, Artistic Director of Scapino Ballet Rotterdam, recognised his talent and invited Goecke to Rotterdam where he created the enthusiastically received *Der Rest ist Schweigen* (2005), followed by many other works. *Blushing* also led to a choreography request from John Neumeier, resulting in *Beautiful Freak* (2005), a sad piece about lonely people, a masterpiece according to German critics. In 2006 he won the Nijinsky Award for the most promising choreographer in the international dance field. After this running start he continued creating works at an amazing tempo, piling up award after award, like the Swan award's most impressive dance production of the year for *Midnight Raga* (Nederlands Dans Theater, 2017) and the Danza & Danza prize for best choreography for *Nijinsky* (Gauthier Dance, 2017). *Wir Sagen uns Dunkles* (Nederlands Dans Theater, 2017) was nominated for the Benois de la Danse. Jiří Kylián stated in the documentary *Thin Skin*: "Marco shouldn't be put in some category. Marco is unique. It's not easy to label him".

This uniqueness has developed from his "little knowing", as Goecke explains in the documentary *Podium Dans*. His career as a dancer was short and choreographers with whom he worked did not inspire him. He received his dance education in Germany and later in the Netherlands at the Royal Conservatory in The Hague, which is classical ballet-oriented. His dream was to become a classical dancer. His first engagement was at the Deutschen Staatsoper Berlin, but he could not deal with the regime and soon moved to the smaller Theater Hagen. Because their repertoire was old-fashioned and he was frustrated in his efforts to become a dancer, he started to make his own work. He was convinced he had to stick with himself, not copying other dance vocabularies, but create something that stands out (Embrechts 2008).

Goecke's almost unbearably intense dance language is based on fragmentation. References from classical ballet are perceptible, but in his world the legs are secondary. The incredible fast movements of arms and hands are disconnected from the lower half of the body. The nervous shaking, shivering, fluttering, spasms and trembling of all body parts, razor-sharp rotations of hands and arms, sharply angular and twitching torsos, are typical of all his work, as well as lightning speed repetition, sudden changes in tempo, and ultra-fast pattering feet to appear or disappear. His complex dance language is executed with great precision, sharpness, and close attention to detail.

The choreography and costumes are gender-neutral. In nearly all his works, the dancers wear black trousers, the men bare-chested, the women in skin-coloured tops. This gives a focus on the upper body, enhanced by the dark lighting and never fully illuminated corners. In collaboration with Udo Haberland, his lighting designer since 2003, Goecke creates a twilight atmosphere in which dancers materialise out of the darkness and then are submerged by it, in which movements sharpen and fade away.

When asked why he likes the darkness on stage so much, Goecke answered that it has to do with infinity, the space that moves back. That it is suspenseful. Going to the theatre has something to do with nightfall and darkness and also with something festive (Podium Dans 2017). This night-time on stage often seems threatening, but there is also magic when sparks of light suddenly glow in the hands of the dancers (*Beautiful Freak*), or when black painted walnuts fall out of black cabinets and cover the floor (*Der Nussknacker* 2006). Goecke surprises by using unusual materials like rustling autumn leaves (*Nichts*), black balloons (*Sweet Sweet Sweet* 2005), rose petals (*Le Spectre de la Rose* 2009), or popcorn (*Hello Earth* 2014) spread over the floor, dancers with bunches of white balloons (*Pierrot Lunaire* 2010), or throwing flour (*Supernova* 2009). These mysterious things stir the imagination.

The black trousers in the subtlest variations, mostly designed by Michaela Springer and/or Marco Goecke, have their surprises too:

covered with walnuts (*Der Nussknacker*), flowers (*Bravo Charlie* 2007), or with fringes of glittering soft tinkling beads (*Wir sagen uns Dunkles*). Sounds made by these materials, or created by loud pitter-patter, rhythmic breathing, beating on bare torsos, and shrieking or quacking voices of the dancers contribute to the atmosphere in a humorous or painful way. The music, often selected late in the making process, adds to the mood. Goecke's movement style, alternating between breathtaking pace, slow motion, and freezing, suits any kind of music, like Bach, Jeff Buckley, or Jimi Hendrix. He explains: 'It is not my aim to interpret the music. I use the mood of the music. It has to do with emotions' (De Jong 2017).

Combining different music styles in the same piece brings an intriguing layer to the dance and opens up many associations. Although some critics have problems explaining movement that seemingly makes no sense except to be different and ugly (Hochman 2019), mostly his work is interpreted as a space of secrets. Underneath you feel the drama of human emotions: the pain, loss, loneliness, craziness, tenderness, and hope staged and interchanged with absurdist moments.

The majority of Goecke's works are less than thirty minutes, but he also creates full-evening pieces, like the dark fairy-tale *Der Nussknacker*, the award-winning *Nijinsky* (2016) and *Songs for Drella* (2011), co-created with Ed Wubbe, all performed by a large ensemble. Solos like *Mopey* (2004) and *Äffi* (2005) are performed globally and challenge the dancers to excel technically as well as expressively. His duets, either embedded in a choreography or autonomous, are deeply moving. In *Firebird Pas de deux* (2010), to Stravinsky, the Firebird with her fluttering hands and twitching head, is longing for her 'prince'. When he appears, they shyly start moving synchronously but isolated. When they come closer, with jerky and shaking movements, anxious, vulnerable, but also curious, a brief inconvenient embrace follows. Immediately they separate, motionless, looking at each other with a long farewell gaze in silence. In *Midnight Raga* (2017), Goecke created freaky solos for Guido Dutilh and Alexander Anderson (NDT 2) to Ravi Shankar's sitar music, followed by an intriguing duet on the blues of Etta James, using the same intense, shaking language. The nervous longing to touch each other, the tenderness in a quick kiss takes one's breath away and evokes deep emotions.

For his incisive performance in *Wir sagen uns Dunkles*, Guido Dutilh won the Swan for the most impressive achievement in dance (2018). He completely internalised the obsessive movement style, transforming into an inhabitant of Goecke's universe. It is fascinating to watch Guido performing, and when he was asked how he reaches that state of being, he explained (personal communication with author, 28 January 2020) that it all has to do with honesty:

> Marco either demonstrates, gives us tasks, or refers to stories he tells us. The stories often involve celebrities he admires or situations in his own life and tend to give a humorous perspective to his fears. We try and translate these elements until we find something that resonates with him. He makes sounds of excitement or fear which guides us to the essence of each movement, of each little shift. He is poking and stirring things up on [an] emotional as well as technical level. It is very, very intense. During the rehearsals, but also on stage, with Marco in the wings, we are breathing together. He becomes part of the dancer.

Jorge Nozal, another NDT dancer, talking about his experience while creating *Thin Skin*: 'He challenged me to be the truest version of myself, through which he could be the truest version of himself as a choreographer. It was extremely personal' (NDT Programme 2015).

Over time we can notice development in costumes and lighting. The darkness as well as his interest in high speed movements in his early pieces had to do with uncertainty, explained Goecke. For the audience, this made it hard to see exactly what was happening (Podium Dans 2017). But in Udo Haberland's more recent lighting designs we can see every detail of the dancers. The prevailing colour for the costumes is still black, but sometimes the dancers materialise out of the dark background in grey or even red costumes. An interesting change is how Goecke evokes feelings of fear and loneliness. In his early work these feelings are expressed in solos and in ensembles without contact between the dancers. But more and more, dancers try to communicate in pairs and threesomes, searching for tenderness. As Paul Lightfoot expressed: 'There is darkness, but it also has extreme hope in it'.

Liesbeth Wildschut

Bibliographical details

Born in Wuppertal, Germany, 12 April 1972. **Studied** at the Ballet Academy Cologne and the Heinz-Bosl-Stiftung, Munich; then at the Royal Conservatoire, The Hague. **Career:** began as a dancer at the Deutschen Staatsoper Berlin and at the Theater Hagen, where he created his first choreography *Loch* in 2000; followed by works for the Noverre Society and in 2002 the New York Choreographic Institute. Choreographer in Residence at the Stuttgart Ballet (2005–2018) and Scapino Ballet Rotterdam (2006–2011); Associate Choreographer, Nederlands Dans Theater (since 2013); Artist in Residence, Gauthier Dance Stuttgart (since 2018); Ballettdirektor at Ballett der Staatsoper Hanover (since 2019). Has choreographed for Peter Boal and Company, Leipzig Ballet, Les Ballets de Monte Carlo, Norwegian National Ballet, Pacific Northwest Ballet Seattle, Les Grands Ballets Canadiens de Montréal, São Paulo Companhia de Dança, Staatsballett Berlin, Zurich Ballet, Gärtnerplatztheater Munich, National Ballet of Canada, Maggio Danza Fiorentino, Deutsche Oper am Rhein, Gauthier Dance, Finnish National Ballet, Stanislavsky Theater, Wiener Staatsoper, Paris Opera. Invitations for festivals: 20 Years Tanztheater Wuppertal, Jacob's Pillow Festival, Venice Biennale, International Dance Festival NRW, Movimentos festival Wolfsburg. **Awards and honours** include Prix Dom Pérignon, Hamburg, 2003; Cultural Award of Baden Württemberg, 2005; Nijinsky Award, Monte Carlo, 2006; Choreographer of the Year, *Ballett/Tanz*, 2015; The Swan award, 2017; Danza & Danza prize, 2017.

Works

Loch (2000); *Chicks* (2001); *Chick* (2002); *Demigods* (2002); *Blushing* (2003); *Ring Them Bells* (2003); *Mopey* (2004); *Ickyucky* (2004); *Sweet Sweet Sweet* (2005); *Äffi* (2005); *Beautiful Freak* (2005); *Der Rest ist Schweigen* (2005); *Alles* (2006); *Viciouswishes* (2006); *Der Nussknacker* (2006); *Sonnett* (2007); *Bravo Charlie* (2007); *Alben* (2008); *Suite Suite Suite* (2008); *Whiteout* (2008); *Nichts* (2008); *Supernova* (2009); *Fancy Goods* (2009); *Fur* (2009); *Le Chant du Rossignol* (2009; new version 2015); *Spectre de la Rose* (2009); *Tué* (2009); *Pierrot Lunaire* (2010); *Orlando* (2010); *Vuurvogel Pas de deux* (2010); *For Sascha* (2010); *Songs for Drella* (2011, with Ed Wubbe); *Place a Chill* (2011); *Dearest Earthly Friend* (2011); *In sensu* (2011); *Garbo Laughs* (2012); *Black Breath* (2012); *And the Sky on that Cloudy Old Day* (2012); *Dancer in the Dark* (2012, with Louis Stiens); *Nap* (2012); *I Found a Fox* (2013); *Late Bird* (2013); *Peekaboo* (2013); *On Velvet* (2013); *I found a Fox II* (2013); *Hello Earth* (2014); *Deer Vision* (2014); *Minute Made* (2014); *Sigh* (2014); *Smokey Sarah* (2014); *Sah ein Knab'ein Röslein stehn* (2014); *Thin Skin* (2015); *Cry Boy* (2015); *Lonesome George* (2015); *Black Swan Pas de deux* (2015); *Valse* (2015); *All Long Dem Day* (2015); *Greyhounds* (2015); *Lucid Dream* (2016); *Woke Up Blind* (2016); *Nijinsky* (2016); *Petruschka* (2016); *Midnight Raga* (2017); *Wir sagen uns Dunkles* (2017); *Dance/Jazz Fusion Vol. 2* (2017); *Walk the Demon* (2018); *Almost Blue* (2018); *La Strada* (2018); *Infant Spirit* (2018); *Ungarischer Tanz Nr. 1* (2018); *Dogs Sleep* (2019); *The Heart* (2019); *Kunstkamer* (2019, with Sol León, Crystal Pite, Paul Lightfoot).

Further reading

Interviews: Sander Hiskemuller, 'Redder van de dans', *Trouw*, 18 March 2008; Francine van der Wiel, 'Aan de benen niet toegekomen', *NRC*, 5 December 2008; Interview podium dans, NPO2 Extra, vimeopro.com, 2017.

Articles: Annette Embrechts, 'Gooien met een contrabas', *Volkskrant*, 13 November 2008; Ali Mahbouba, 'Moving Being, Gods and Dogs and Nichts', *Dance Europe*, February 2009; Lambrecht Wessels, 'Netherlands Dance Theatre Programme III is Utterly Unmissable', *Bachtrack*, 13 February 2014; Andrew Blackmore-Dobbyn, 'Nederlands Dans Theater: An Affirmation of Our Humanity', *Bachtrack*, 17 November 2016; David Mead, 'Goecke and Clug's Contemporary Takes on Stravinsky Classics Petrushka and Sacre', *SeeingDance*, 2 December 2016; Manon Lichtveld and Bas Westerhof, *Thin Skin*, WDR/ARTE, vimeopro.com, 2016; David Mead, 'Dancing Emotion: Nederlands Dans Theater in Taiwan', *SeeingDance*, 28 February 2017; Ali Mahbouba, 'Nederlands Dans Theater 2', *Dance Europe*, 1 July 2017; Fritz de Jong, 'Schubert is mooi, maar niet genoeg. Choreograaf kiest voor klassiek én rock', *Het Parool*, 9 November 2017; Katja Vaghi, 'First Time in Berlin: Gauthier Dance in Marco Goecke's Nijinsky at the Haus der Berliner Festspiele', *Bachtrack*, 27 January 2018; Maggie Foyer, 'Defining Contemporary Dance Today: Nederlands Dans Theater in London', *SeeingDance*, 2 July 2018; Michael Hasted, 'Nederlands Dans Theater triple bill – saisonnier', *Arts Talk Magazine*, 28 September 2018; Jerry Hochma, 'NDT 2: Contemporary Dance Art, from Zany to Angst', *Critical Dance*, 16 January 2019; Joy Wang, 'Goecke, Lidberg and Cherkaoui at the Paris Opera Ballet', *SeeingDance*, 27 February 2019; Sarah Batschelet, 'Zurich: Marco Goecke's New Age Nijinsky', *Bachtrack*, 11 March 2019; Maggie Foyer, 'A Ballet Legend Finely Drawn: Ballett Zürich in Marco Goecke's Nijinsky', *SeeingDance*, 1 April 2019.

Books: Nadja Kadel (ed), *Dark Matter*, Königshausen & Neumann, Würzburg, 2016.

EMIO GRECO AND PIETER C. SCHOLTEN

Emio Greco and Pieter C. Scholten met in 1995 and arrived at the realisation that something was lacking in the dance landscape. Next to the virtuoso body and the conceptual body, they missed a place for the intuitive body. They wanted to develop a new dance vocabulary and dance dramaturgy in which there is room for vulnerability and the physical impulses of the body. Starting from a *tabula rasa* they developed a new 'dramaturgy of the flesh' to investigate the principles which underlie the intimate intentions of gesture and the impact on the body and the spectator. Their thoughts were condensed into the manifesto *The Seven Necessities* (1996), which communicates the aesthetic premises and foundations of their work with an emphasis on a belief that creativity is incarnated in the body, while movement is self-sufficient and creates time, space, and multi-layered meanings. The eloquence of the body that communicates at various levels is characteristic of their work. Greco and Scholten work intuitively, but rhythm, tempo, and dynamics are orchestrated with precision.

Their first work *Bianco* (1996), performed by Greco, developed from their desire to explore the inner mechanisms of the body. This was followed by a second solo, *Rosso* (1997), and a duet, *Extra Dry* (1999). Together these formed the trilogy *Fra Cervello e Movimento* (Between Brain and Movement). In the solos, Greco shows a curious, searching body and creates the impression of being amazed at how his muscles tense and relax. He explores the possibilities of a joint, the displacement of weight, and surrenders to the inimitable effects of the movement of limbs, torso, and head, at times stressing their autonomy, for instance by disconnecting the direction the limbs move into and the direction of view. As philosopher Antoon van den Braembussche described (2001): 'At the one extreme there is the perfectly controlling mind, subjecting the body to the will of the dancer ... [at] the other, there is the body's resistance to obeying the mind and the will, a body that follows its own desire and madness, erupting in spasmodic disorder, spontaneous tics and jerks'.

Greco explored the notion of the 'escaping body' here, where the moment between a movement and the realisation of the mind that observes that movement is postponed, opening an intuitive interspace between the instinctive impulses of the body and their conscious registration and control. Greco and Scholten have, since then, been playing with the interspace and friction between instinct and discipline, freedom and restriction, sacred and profane, the mastery of academic dance and the uninhibited urge of the flesh.

In *Extra Dry* (1999), Greco was joined by another dancer. In this *solo for two* – a relationship with 'the other' was added, leading to exploration of themes like disunity, dualism, and dichotomy. The dancers explored their individuality while surrendering to the dynamism of the duet, their bodies propelled by one and the same impulse, moving side by side but never really touching. Connected through their breathing, they followed the same spatial and temporal paths, punctuated by a variety of physical expressions: minimal gesture and technical virtuosity, crescendo intensity and silence, speed and stasis. Just as in their duet *Double Points: Two* (1998), synchronicity and interdependency were explored. Greco and Scholten defined synchronicity as a 'dual utopia': a continued attempt to become 'one body' that coincides with space and time – as distinguished from merely moving in unison.

This was elaborated in group works like *Conjunto di NERO* (2001) and *Rimasto Orfano* (2002) and became an important factor in their dramaturgical approach to the dynamics of light and sound in relation to body language: the confrontation with other dancers, with the music, or with elements such as sound, light, and darkness became the focus. In *Conjunto de NERO*, lighting concealed an unknown presence while revealing another presumed absence, creating an interplay between the individual shadows of the dancers. Loud sounds seemed to stop the fast-accelerating dancers in their tracks.

The specific approach, towards the intuitive body underlies the 'Double Skin/Double Mind' (DS/DM) dance method initiated in 1998 when Impulstanz Vienna invited Greco and Scholten to coach professional dancers. DS/DM aims to discover the sensitivity of the body and is based on four essential principles: *Breathing*, *Jumping*, *Expanding* and *Reducing*. These prepare one for new physical and mental awareness in which intention and form coincide. Physical challenge, heightened concentration, and breathing exercises allow participants to focus on the processes in the body, achieving form or letting it go. This allows a deeper awareness of the specificity of one's body and the potential effects of personal, social, cultural, and political impacts on this. This method forms the starting point for each individual performance and became the source for various research projects. In 2017, teacher training for DS/DM was set up, which has taken the method beyond ICK, to other companies and academies.

In addition to the establishment of a 'dramaturgy of the flesh', Greco and Scholten focused on the relationship between dance and other art forms. Through their *Double Points* series (developed since 1998), consisting of études, research materials, and sketches, they explored the artistic boundaries of dance by confronting the company's vision with that of other experts, dance makers, and artists. As Scholten puts it (ickamsterdam.com): 'We invite "the other" onto our playing field: the other with whom you may clash and merge at the same time, who can disturb, disrupt and take you out of your comfort zone'.

In 2004, a project with Swiss composer Hanspeter Kyburz entitled *Double Points: +*, focused on dance, music, and interactivity. Greco's body, carrying sensors, allowed him (through movements ranging from subtle and precise hand gestures, to a crashing to earth of the entire body) to influence the pitch and dynamics of electronic sounds. At other moments, he reacted freely to the schemes proposed by the musicians. The project invited the transformative influence of each other's artistic domain, while simultaneously investigating the distinctions. This research was continued with American composer Michael Gordon, for in *[purgatorio] POPOPERA* (2008), and with French composer Franck Krawczyk, who made free adaptations of Bach's *St Matthew Passion* for *[purgatorio] IN VISIONE* (2008), *Passione in Due* (2012), and Mahler's *Kindertotenlieder* for *Appearance* (2017).

Interaction and disruptive frictions between disciplines also formed the basis for the collaboration with Schaubühne am Lehniner Platz (2001). Greco and Scholten worked with actors and dancers, an experience that was deepened in their direction of Pasolini's *Teorema* for Toneelgroep Amsterdam (2003). They took the interdisciplinary experiment beyond the performing arts, when they worked with fashion designer Jean Paul Gaultier, Italian perfume creator Alessandro Gualtieri (you PARA | DISO perfume), and Dutch chocolatier CHOCOdelic (EXTREMALISM Raw Chocolate). Examining the relationship between brain and movement, Greco and Scholten addressed the phenomenon of *synaesthesia*, in which senses become mixed: sounds are seen, colours tasted. They wondered whether dance can be experienced as tangible, and whether it can be smelled or tasted. The creative approaches for perfume and chocolate were prompted by a process similar to the breathing exercises in the DS/DM method. The ingredients of perfume and chocolate were determined simultaneously with the components of the choreography.

These interdisciplinary projects gave rise to a trilogy inspired by Dante's *Divine Comedy*: HELL (2006), *[purgatorio]* (2008), and *you PARA | DISO* (2010). HELL is an extreme journey investigating bodily exhaustion and the strength to rise again, in an opulent and charged setting. *[purgatorio]* POPOPERA creates a hybrid atmosphere between a concert and dance where dancing bodies play the electric guitar, dancers mutate into instruments, and raging guitars become fragile flesh-and-blood sound-boards. PARA | DISO unfolds unfamiliar aseptic worlds in which dancers connect and organise themselves by tracing the sounds, echoes, and vibrations of each other's movements.

In 2012, the site-specific performance *Addio alla Fine*, after Fellini's film *E la Nave Va*, initiated a chain of performances with the motif 'The Body in Revolt', in which dance was to lay bare new connections with the self (our own body) and society (other's bodies). Here, the body is conceived as a 'social body', sensitive to social changes such as globalisation, digitisation, crisis, and fragmentation. Exemplified in *Extremalism* (2015), 30 dancers organise themselves anarchically in harmonious, wild, and orderly compositions, shifting positions, subdividing into men versus women, tall versus short, Asian versus European. At times a cluster of bodies looks tiny in the background, like the anonymous soldiers of a strategy game, and then a group is in the foreground, radiating individuality. These constantly varying configurations and spatial layouts, evoke social and political-religious associations and show the tension between mass and individual, order and chaos, vulnerability and strength, good and evil.

Parallel to 'The Body in Revolt', a second motif developed: 'Le Corps du Ballet' (The Body of Ballet) emerged from the confrontation of their intuitive movement vocabulary with the precision and virtuosity of classical ballet. The task was to find a way to intersect the presumed clashing energies and forms. This resulted in an unexpected form that retained their individuality and ultimately released a vibrant wave of energy. This project was re-created for Les Ballets de Monte Carlo (2011), Het Nationale Ballet (2013), and Ballet National de Marseille (2015). More confrontations followed in works created for Ballet National de Marseille: *Momentum* (2016) and *Les Cygnes et les autres* (2018). The latter, based on the oeuvre of Marius Petipa, was an ode to ballet and a commentary on its constraints. They related Petipa's aesthetics to the current dance culture and explored its relationship by answering Petipa's well-known dance phrases with the long, wavy extensions and fast pace from their own movement language – for example, by having the proud, dynamic, and feminine Kitri solo from *Don Quixote* danced by a man on pointe amidst an entourage of women. Apart from the obvious contrasts in movement language, parallels also stood out: elongated lines of the limbs, symmetry, and the academic basis.

Initiatives developed alongside the company's regular productions included the launch in 2004 of interdisciplinary documentation and archival research within the company and projects involving other movement practices, beginning with *Beyond Seoul* in 2009, inspiring the establishment of the International Choreographic Arts Centre (ICK Amsterdam) as a format in which education and research assume a prominent place alongside creation. ICK functions as an inspiring creative environment for numerous visiting and resident choreographers and was recognised as the Amsterdam City Dance Company in 2013.

From the experiences at ICK, Greco and Scholten implemented their idea of organisational synchronicity. Between 2014 and 2018, ICK and Ballet National de Marseille joined forces to develop collaborative initiatives: these promoted the advancement of contemporary dance and cross-border development of talent; organised joint festivals in Marseille and Amsterdam; and developed a European-funded project on dance education and digital technologies: *Map to the Stars* (2017–2019).

From the outset, Greco and Scholten contributed to 'the memory of the dance'. Since writing their *Seven Necessities* manifesto, they have maintained an attitude of questioning the relevance of dance and the body, for the arts and for society. In 2003, they initiated a series of *Dance and Discourse* Salons, informal gatherings with international interdisciplinary professionals. One of the salons explored the implications of archiving dance. This raised questions regarding the value of dance and how to access it as a unique form of embodied knowledge. These research projects started with the *Notation Research Project* in 2005, in which themes related to documentation, notation, and transmission were explored.

Eventually an international team of researchers brought together expertise in documentary filmmaking, notation systems, interactive media design, gesture analysis, and cognition studies. They researched ways to document movement, and also the intentions and meanings of dance. In October 2007, the results were presented in the book, *(Capturing) Intention,* and in the *Interactive Installation Double Skin/Double Mind,* a simulation environment in which Greco and Scholten's DS/DM dance method can be experienced. A further collaborative interdisciplinary research project, *Inside Movement Knowledge* (2008–2010), used the outcomes of *(Capturing) Intention* as a case-study to continue exploring methods of dance documentation, transmission, and preservation with a new consortium of researchers.

Another research project *Pre-choreographic Elements* (2009–2014) focused on the pre-phase of choreography where movement is created, shaped, and tested, but is not yet part of the selection and ordering process. This deepened reflection on dance methods by analysing the terminology used during the process of transmission established within the dance company. *Abracadabra, bridging, leaving aura, mapping, rhythm on, undulation,* and *vacuum* are some terms defined and explored, providing insights into ways of dealing with the body, time, space, and interactions with other dancers. As one result, the *Pre-choreographic elements* are used as improvisation tools for other choreographers to create with.

Greco and Scholten's focus on language gives rise to an evolving archive of systematically categorised words called the *ABCdaire,* which serves as the contact point for the collaboration with Motion Bank, in a project that develops digital technologies to support artist-led documentation, analysis, and transmission of dance practice. These connections provide a shared engagement regarding the political relevance of embodied knowledge and inclusion of alternative epistemologies such as intuitive, non-verbal, and embodied forms of knowing.

Greco and Scholten continue to query the relationship between dance/choreography and society by choosing 'back to the future/the future is back' as their motto for the new decennium. In 2019, they presented their diptych *Appearance-Disappearance,* which led them

113

to complement *The Body in Revolt (2.0)* with *Rücksichtslos Idealisme (Uncompromising Idealism)*. They find themselves in a place between past and future, between melancholy and utopia. As they wrote in an essay, *The Body in Revolt 2.0* in 2020: 'While utopia is the longing for something to come, melancholy feeds the longing for something that has been. But we carry the experiences of what has passed in our bodies. We will propel our dancing body into the future with melancholy as a source of knowledge and intuitive power'.

Bertha Bermúdez, Scott deLahunta,
and *Francesca Magnini*

Biographical details

Born: Greco in Brindisi, Italy; Scholten in Vlaardingen, Netherlands. **Studied:** Greco undertook dance training at École Supérieure de Danse de Cannes Rosella Hightower; Scholten studied drama. **Career:** Greco performed with Ballet Antibes Côte d'Azur; then 1993–1996 with Jan Fabre. From 1996–1998, worked on productions with Japanese choreographer Saburo Teshigawara. Scholten specialised in production of theatrical works focusing on historical characters including Oscar Wilde, Yukio Mishima, and Pier Paolo Pasolini; then collaborated with international choreographers as a dance-dramaturge. In 1995, Greco and Scholten created first work together, the solo *Bianco* and wrote the manifesto *The Seven Necessities* featuring 7 principles of dance. In 1996, founded their dance company in Amsterdam; from 2009 transferred this to the International Choreographic Arts Centre (ICK), which offers space for talent development, education, and research. From 2014–2018, they were also directors of the Ballet National de Marseille. **Awards** include Philip Morris Arts Prize, 1999; Sonia Gaskell Prize, 2001; Herald Angel Award, 2001; Teatro del Mundo Award, 2001; Premio Danza&Danza Award, 2003; Time Out Live Award, 2004; Meilleur Spectacle de Danse, 2006; VSCD Dance Awards, 2007, 2012; Dioraphte Dance Award, 2011.

Works

Fra Cervello e Movimento: Bianco (1996); *Fra Cervello e Movimento: Rosso* (1997); *Double Points: Two* (1998); *Fra Cervello e Movimento: Extra Dry* (1999); *Double Points: One* (1999); *FRA* (film, 1999); *Conjunto de Falda y Chaqueta* (2000); *Double Points: NERO* (2000); *Conjunto di NERO* (2001); *Double Points: SchauBühne* (2001); *Piano di Rotta* (film, 2002); *Rimasto Orfano* (2002); *Double Points: Bertha – The Bermúdez Triangle* (2002); *Teorema* (theatre, 2003); *Double Points: +* (2003, 2005); *Orfeo ed Euridice* (opera, 2004); *Double Points: Hell* (2005); *HELL* (2006); *The Assassin Tree* (opera, 2006); *Double Points: Rudi* (2007); *[purgatorio] POPOPERA* (2008); *[purgatorio] IN VISIONE* (2008); *Double Points: 7* (2008); *Double Points: Tsjaikovski* (2008); *Imagined Hell* (2008); *Double Points: ROCCO* (2008); *BEYOND Seoul* (2009); *Double Points: Janine*

| *Martin* (2009); *Double Points: OUTIS* (2010); *you PARA* | *DISO* (2010); *Le Corps Du Ballet* (2011, 2013, 2015); *Double Points: Orgel* (2011); *La Commedia* (2011); *Nardini Cascate* (2011); *ROCCO* (2011); *Imagined Purgatorio* (film, 2011); *Passione in Due* (2012); *Addio alla Fine* (2012, 2013); *Double Points: Extremalism* (2012); *Great Expectations* (2013); *Double Points: VERDI* (2013); *L'Étranger* (2013); *One Man Without a Cause* (film, 2013); *De Soprano's* (2014); *One Man Without a Cause* (2014); *Boléro* (2015); *Extremalism* (2015); *Macbeth* (theatre, 2015); *Passione* (2015); *Momentum* (2016); *Paradiso Revisited* (2017); *7EVEN* (2017); *Corpi Ingrati* (2017); *Appearance* (2017); *ROCCA* (2018); *ZIEL* | *ROUH* (2018); *Non Solo Medea* (2018); *Les Cygnes et les Autres* (2018); *Disappearance* (2019); *All Over Acts of Love* (theatre, 2019); *Sweet Like a Chocolate* (2019).

Further reading

(See also ickamsterdam.com and insidemovementknowledge.net)

Interviews: 'Pre-choreographic Elements: Scott deLahunta in Conversation with Bertha Bermudez, Choreographic Documentation', *International Journal of Performance Arts & Digital Media*, 9 (1), 2013.

Articles: Scott deLahunta and Frédéric Bevilacqua, 'Sharing Descriptions of Movement', *International Journal of Performance and Digital Media*, 3 (1), 2007; Scott deLahunta and Norah Zuniga Shaw, 'Constructing Memories. Creation of the Choreographic Resource', *Digital Resources: Performance Research*, 11 (4), 2007; Scott deLahunta and Norah Zuniga Shaw, 'Choreographic Resources Agents, Archives, Scores and Installations', *Performance Research*, 13 (2), 2008; Maaike Bleeker, 'What if This Were an Archive?', *RTRSRCH*, 2 (2), 2010; Gaby Wijers et al., 'Extra Dry (1999) Emio Greco | Pieter C. Scholten: Inside Movement Knowledge Documentation Model', *RTRSRCH*, 2 (1), 2011.

Books: Alexander Baervoets et al., *Danssolo/Solodans,* Cultureel Centrum Maasmechelen, 1999; Antoon van den Braembussche, *It's Life Jim but not as We Know It. A Philosophical Approach on Emio Greco | PC's Trilogy*, Amsterdam, 2001; Ada D'Adamo, *Emio Greco/PC*, Palermo, 2004; Carlotta Plebs, *Quando il corpo è curioso: la danza di Emio Greco/PC*, Catania, 2006; Maaike Bleeker et al. (eds), *De Theatermaker als Onderzoeker*, Amsterdam, 2006; Marion Bastien et al., *(Capturing Intention). Documentation, Analysis and Notation Research Based on the Work of Emio Greco | PC*, Amsterdam, 2007; Ingrid van Schijndel et al., *Company in the School. Between Experiment and Heritage*, Amsterdam, 2007; Fransien van der Putt and Pieter C. Scholten, *ICK and the Other*, Amsterdam, 2008; Bertha Bermúdez et al., *ICK and the Academy*, Amsterdam, 2009; Annet Huizing et al., *From Cross to Nobody, The Infinite Journey of a Music-Dance Project*, Amsterdam, 2010; Virgilio Sieni, *Dialogo Dialogue*, Firenze, 2009; Francesca Magnini, *INSPIRATION Emio Greco | Pieter C. Scholten. The Multiplicity of Dance*, Rome, 2015; Vito di Bernardi and Letizia Gioia Monda (eds), *Proceedings of the International Conference 'Imagining Dance. Bodies* and *Visions in the Digital Era'*, *Sapienza University of Rome*, 3–4 December 2015, Bologna, 2018; Maaike Bleeker, *Transmission in Motion: The Technologizing of Dance*, London, 2017.

JOHAN INGER

When asked how he engages with an audience in an interview with *GRAZIA* Magazine, Johan Inger states, 'I have to think about the audience because I want to communicate something. I want to reach and move them. That doesn't mean that I don't want to challenge them; there's nothing worse than when a story becomes literal and flat' (unattributed, 2019).

Influenced by mentor and Swedish choreographer Mats Ek, who worked extensively in adapting classical narratives, Inger's work represents an architecture of tensions that invites storytelling and imaginative thinking. His repertoire amalgamates vocabularies from various movement languages and reinvents them to express a style current in the field of embodied research – a language both found and created with the dancers he works with, using ballet vocabulary and modern techniques. Inger was principal dancer for many years at Nederlands Dans Theater (NDT), under the leadership of Jírí Kylián; the movement vocabulary and etymology of his work derives from this training in ballet and modern, though executed with a casual ease.

The composition of narrative and choreographic structure requires an inherent tension that motivates conflict. The Freytag Pyramid suggests that stories begin with an inciting incident, rising action, conflict, then resolution. In this way, Inger has been telling stories since 1995 when he created *Mellantid* for Nederlands Dans Theater 2 (NDT2) while still dancing for NDT. The ballet, which begins with six dancers standing together for a family portrait, is not straight forward, so much as it is interested in excavating the understatements of its supposed memory and inviting the audience to engage with their own interpretations. There is a whimsical aesthetic to the choreography that forecasts the trajectory of Inger's interest in showing how movement engages in the act of remembering. In one scene, a line of roses falls from overhead, landing perfectly erect having been made with darts to land directly into the Marley floor. A young female dancer collects them, offering them to a male dancer who grabs her and carries her across stage. She drops the roses and they land again, erect, this time bunched like a bouquet. *Mellantid* won the Philip Morris Finest Selection Award in 1996 for Contemporary Dance and was nominated for the Laurence Olivier Award in 2001 for Best New Dance Production. It ends with a single dancer standing upstage, his arms out imitating the wings of an airplane, before running to the lip of the stage, then blackout. Thematically, it is not so much the present and past that Inger introduces but a gaze toward the future that his later choreographies continue to suggest.

In 2001, Inger choreographed *Walking Mad* to Ravel's 'Bolero' for NDT. It is an accumulation of scenes and characters set against a moveable and malleable wall covering the span of the stage. Characters pass through and behind it. The wall collapses and in one scene becomes a deck on which two characters, one male the other female, question their likeness and reflection. The wall, upright again, closes to create a 'V' enclosure. The music's volume lowers, becoming almost inaudible, although the metronomic beat of the score continues to be heard as though from afar, focusing attention on a single dancer inside the enclosure who demonstrates a reaction to the otherness of the setting. In various scenes, Inger's movement is humorous and casual, referring to classical form but suggesting something opposite to its technical rigour. For example, shrugged shoulders with a developé of the leg, rocking of the hips in deep second position, and the whimsical playfulness and fluidity of the floor work. Inger's language refers to human gesture as much as it is interested in the pendulum of the body's core. In *Walking Mad*, Inger disrobes archetypes and invites the audience to a more intimate narrative. He asks viewers to take a closer look at the person and dancer. The ballet received the Lucas Hoving Production Award in 2001 and the Danza & Danza Award in 2005 after it was performed by the Cullberg Ballet.

Inger uses scenography as a function in design and also as an element that confronts the cast with an obstacle to react to. For example: the inclusion of a moveable wall, as in *Walking Mad*; in *Out of Breath* (2002), choreographed for NDT2, in which a slanted wall seems to be buried halfway through the floor, introducing a destructed setting whose axis has tilted; and in *B.R.I.S.A.* (2014), where a carpeted floor covers most of the stage and a wind-blower is cast as both prop and character. In these examples, moveable walls and carpeted stages are not only the setting but also an inciting incident. They set the beginning of the story and help create a construct that paves the possibility for various points of view. There is hardly a single, straight forward story going on at once. Every dancer provides a playfulness and dramatic tension in gesture and physicality, and the effect is that the choreography reverberates with thematic atmosphere created by multiple voices.

In 2011, Inger choreographed *Rain Dogs* for Ballet Basel. Set to music by Tom Waits, it is an abstract commentary on our relationship to the world and to others. In one scene, what seems like black ash falling from above alludes to the remnant echo of a destroyed society under a tragedy of its own creation. In another, a toy dog emanates smoke as it sits centre-stage under a spotlight and a voice-over of Charles Bukowski recites a poem about middle-class America. It is in these methods of understatement and allusion that Inger gives essence to the choreographic worlds he creates, offering space for the audience to question and ponder the circumstances he introduces.

What is most constant in Inger's work is a movement language that unveils human form, in the technical demand of classical training fused with an original choreographic voice that celebrates contemporary authorship. In *I New Then*, choreographed for NDT2 in 2012, Inger begins to incorporate spoken words for the performers. A soloist grunts and groans while reacting to a pair of dancers in a romantic embrace, trying to find words to express his desire for engagement. In many of Inger's works the choreography paints a soundtrack with moving bodies, but in *I New Then* the dancer is engaged with his own ability to create music, expressing an effort to find the right language for his reaction.

In *Bliss*, created for Aterballetto in 2016, the seventeen dancers are members of an orchestra, transcribing the rhythmic nuances of Keith Jarrett's *The Koln Concert, Part One* from 1975. Inger organises various stories at once, limning strokes of movement design like that of a Jackson Pollock painting across the stage a chorus of colour, tempo, and qualitative utterances. In the program, Inger writes: 'We are, all of us, no matter how experienced, related both to each other and to the music that give us voice'. Music, when it reaches its crescendo, does not fill the theatre so much as it transcribes the orchestration of the choreography's compositional parts. Here you detect Jírí Kylián's influence, a choreographer known for his ability to illustrate a moving landscape that helps audiences *see* music. Something else to recognise is that Inger is interested in expressing joy without dismissing the inherent truth of tragedy and human grief, emancipating a freedom in movement under the constraints of more pressing concerns and questions.

In 2015, Inger worked with Compañia Nacional de Danza in Madrid and created his first full-length evening work, *Carmen*. In 2017, he choreographed *Peer Gynt* for Theater Basel, juxtaposing Henrik Ibsen's play with his own biographical point of view. The scope of these works is larger than his earlier creations, filled with various scenes and changes in scenography. Due to this larger canvas, the plot structure expands and twists. There is nothing more evident than this in clarifying that Inger works, and thinks, like a novelist.

When writers begin their devotion to the craft, they often occupy the space of a short story as a vehicle to discover their voice and style. If shorter choreographies are the equivalent to short stories, then full-evening ballets are equivalent to novels. In thinking of these two disciplines in a similar light, choreographers face the challenges that novelists do in their intention to offer something new to the field. Like a novelist, Inger questions which point of view he wants to use, as well as which architectural shape is best for the story he wants to offer. The work becomes a vessel of communication for the audience to interpret, an organisation of parts that helps suspend disbelief, and ultimately helps them consider his work as relevant in contemporary and choreographic thinking.

Mario Alberto Zambrano

Biographical details

Born in Stockholm, Sweden, 1967. **Studied** at the Royal Swedish Ballet School; and National Ballet School of Canada. **Career:** Danced with Royal Swedish Ballet, c. 1985–90; and Nederlands Dans Theater, c. 1990–2002. Began choreographing in 1995 for Nederlands Dans Theater 2, Cullberg Ballet, Ballet Basel, Royal Swedish Ballet, Gothenburg Ballet, Ballet de Monte-Carlo, Compañia Nacional de Danza, Aterballetto, Theater Basel, Lyon Opera Ballet. **Awards** include Philip Morris Finest Selection Award, 1996; Lucas Hoving Award, 2001; Danza & Danza Awards, 2005 & 2016; Carina Ari Award, 2013; Benois de la Danse Prize, 2016.

Works

Mellantid (1995); *Sammanfall* (1996); *Round Corners* (1997); *Livnära* (1997); *Couple of Moments* (1998); *Hurry Slowly* (1999); *Among Others* (2000); *Dream Play* (2000); *Arcimboldo* (2000); *Walking Mad* (2001); *So Now Then* (2002); *Out of Breath* (2002); *Home and Home* (2002); *Pneuma* (2003); *Phases* (2003); *Within Now* (2004); *As If* (2005); *Negro con Flores* (2005); *Empty House* (2005); *Blanco* (2006); *Point of Eclipse* (2007); *Position of Elsewhere* (2009); *Dissolve in This* (2009); *Falter* (2010); *Tone Bone Tone* (2010); *Stabat Mater* (2011); *Rain Dogs* (2011); *In-Exact* (2011); *I New Then* (2012); *Sunset Logic* (2012); *Tempus Fugit* (2013); *B.R.I.S.A.* (2014); *Rite of Spring* (2015); *Carmen* (2015); *Now & Now* (2015); *One on One* (2015); *Bliss* (2016); *Sweet Sweet* (2017); *Peer Gynt* (2017); *Birdland* (2017); *Under a Day* (2018); *4 Karin* (2018); *Petrouchka* (2018); *Impasse* (2020); *Don Juan* (2020).

Further reading

Interviews: with unattributed, 'Walking Mad', *GRAZIA Magazine*, April 2019; Karen van Ulzen, 'Limelight Johan Inger', *Dance Australia*, danceaustralia.com April 2019.

Articles: Margaret Foyer, 'Johan Inger', *Dance Europe*, 53, June 2002; Janet Smith, 'Ballet BC Program One dances from sombre abstraction to playful delights', straight.com, 3 November 2017; Jesús Valinas, 'CND's Carmen is a Mind-Expanding Work of Art', *Independent*, 2018; Carolien Verduijn, 'De Impasse Van Oneindige Vooruitgang', *Theaterkrant*, 2020; Francine van der Wiel, 'NDT2 toont met werk Naharin creatief proces in werking', *Nrc.nl*, 2020; Nanska van de Laar, 'Een eigenzinnige en sterke dynamiek', *Uit*, 2020.

SHOBANA JEYASINGH

Shobana Jeyasingh has been creating dance for over 30 years, mostly via the medium of the company that bears her name (Shobana Jeyasingh Dance). Her work is resolutely thematic, and although ungoverned by linear narrative, it is invariably inquisitive, taking a deep dive into an eclectic range of issues concerning interculturalism, science and art; it is always demanding. Jeyasingh not only interrogates her subject but challenges her dancers, her audiences, and herself.

Born in Chennai, India, Jeyasingh grew up in Sri Lanka and Malaysia before settling in the UK, in 1981. Her life has followed an intercultural trajectory of otherness: a Christian in India; a Tamil in Sri Lanka; an Indian in East Malaysia (where she went to a Chinese School and was taught by Scots); and an Indian in Britain. This multiplicity of origins has layered a legacy of identification with everywhere but nowhere in particular.

Jeyasingh's highly individual work is most often seen in theatres but it has also been set on the Champs Elysées (*Defilé*, 1989); in a Palladian monastery (*Outlander*, 2016); an Age of Enlightenment courtyard (*Counterpoint*, 2010); and several historic churches (*TooMortal*, 2012). Her choreography has been expressed in overlapping thematic cycles, beginning with the mathematical influences of her bharatanatyam training (especially *Configurations*, 1988, through to *Making of Maps*, 1992); and shifting to the arts, finding material in such diverse inspirations as a Renaissance masterpiece (*Outlander*, 2016), Rodin's sculptures (*études*, 2016), and Schiele's paintings (*Staging Schiele*, 2019). A fascination with science fiction (*Phantasmaton*, 2002) has led to collaborations with academics from many disciplines including cell biology (*Strange Blooms*, 2013; *In Flagrante*, 2014), neuroscience and robotics (*Trespass*, 2015), digital technology (*[h]interland*, 2002), and virology (*Contagion*, 2018), each of which has tended to envisage a futuristic evolution of human potential.

Inevitably, her work has also been informed by her personal experience as a British Asian woman, exploring conflicts between diverse personal and cultural origins. Whatever the subject, Jeyasingh's art is rooted in her evolving vision of culture and society, and her themes have often referenced issues of interculturalism, including its culinary impact in *Just Add Water?* (2009), where movement sequences were inspired from memories of home cooking amongst the multi-national group of six dancers.

Jeyasingh is not comfortable with her work being regarded as a fusion of East and West, preferring the alternative concept of hybridity, reinforced by Homi K. Bhabha's concept of the 'third space', in *The Location of Culture* (1994). Where *fusion* implies the application of a forced formula, *hybridity* offers a more fluid intermingling that retains the qualities of its formative influences and finds something new.

After initially working from a bharatanatyam base, Jeyasingh's choreographic process became progressively dislocated from the ornate aspects of her classical formation, which she came to view as a potent trap, both for socio-political and personal reasons. 'Being 'pinned down' within such a rubric was discomfiting for Jeyasingh, causing her to 'wriggle' creatively, an exercise she identified as a 'supremely diasporic ritual'...' (Shiromi Pinto in Avanthi Meduri, 2008). It is also important to reference the other influences that have underpinned her intellectual interrogation of dance: her mother was a maths teacher (*Correspondences*, 1990, was inspired by the short life of Indian mathematician, S. Ramanujan); and Jeyasingh's university education encompassed Shakespeare and Renaissance Studies, the latter at Master level.

Jeyasingh's choreographic process began by setting work on her own body, which led to it being transferred onto others in the studio, but she came to accept that movement generation was most satisfying when developed in collaboration with her dancers, some of whom have been with her for many years (notably Avatâra Ayuso – now Jeyasingh's Associate Artist; Sunbee Han; Noora Kela; and Sooraj Subramanian). Jeyasingh separates her choreographic practice into creating *sequences*, where her role is to give guided tasks, stimulating dancers to work with her in creating small sections of movement, which she then develops into *phrases*; the conceptual resin that bonds the accepted sequences together.

Complex numerical systems, developed in relation to bharatanatyam traditions, formed the basis for Jeyasingh's early works. *Miniatures* (1988), a solo choreographed on herself for a TV documentary and expanded later that year into *Configurations*, marked Jeyasingh's transition from dancer to choreographer and the founding of her company. It also introduced the unwanted label of being an Indian choreographer doing cross-cultural collaboration with western music (she had commissioned Michael Nyman to write what became his *Second String Quartet*, composed around an elaborate rhythmic structure, which she had pre-determined); a burden that Jeyasingh continually sought to offload. Although thoroughly immersed in bharatanatyam, she does not view it as an Indian form so much as a rhythmic system. From the beginning, her choreography has been infused by a sense of her dancers' fighting with the space around them, accentuating the weight of their movement rather than any sense of ethereality.

Jeyasingh has cited certain science fiction films (*Bladerunner, The Matrix, Terminator 3: Rise of the Machines*) as formative influences on her choreography. She took the notion of memory being bits of chemistry that could be implanted within a human brain from Philip K. Dick's *Do Androids Dream of Electric Sheep?* (1968), the book that inspired the *Bladerunner* film. Another influence was Donna Haraway's *Simians, Cyborgs and Women* (1991), a collection of ten essays, including the *Cyborg Manifesto*, which predicts the development of a post-human hybrid of organism and machine (conjuring classical imagery such as mermaids, centaurs, and the half-man/half-lion *Narasimha* avatar of the Hindu god, Vishnu). These were Jeyasingh's starting points for *Phantasmaton* (2002), in which the varied glances of a bharatanatyam dancer were linked into the creation of a haunting digital goddess by Jeyasingh's regular film-maker, Pete Gomes.

Faultline (2007) considered the cultural dislocation faced by British Asian youth in a choreographic mix of contemporary dance, hip hop, martial arts, and bharatanatyam. Uppermost amongst many triggers for *Faultline* were the deep-seated anxieties in the multicultural climate after the London bombings of 2005. Another influence was Gautam Malkani's novel, *Londonstani* (2006), exploring the thin veneer between vanity and violence in the street culture of British Asian 'rude-boy' gangs who manifest through the peacock posturing of the young men at the beginning of the work. Jeyasingh found the stylised and vernacular base of *Londonstani* to be reminiscent of another futuristic film, Stanley Kubrick's *A Clockwork Orange* (1971).

Music was the trigger for *Bruise Blood* (2009). It arose from Jeyasingh's contact with vocal performer Shlomo and their shared connection with the music of Steve Reich and, in particular, *Come Out* (1966), which repeats the words 'come out to show them', spoken by a young black man (Daniel Hamm) who, having been wrongfully arrested during the Harlem riots of 1964, punctures and lets out his 'bruise blood' as evidence of being assaulted by the police. This incident led Jeyasingh to a more general creative concept of dancers offering up their own bodies as evidence.

2Step (2008) took Jeyasingh's choreography outdoors, performed on the steps of St. Paul's Cathedral to celebrate the Olympic Games' Handover from Beijing to London; and it stayed in the open for *Counterpoint* (2010), performed in the courtyard of London's Somerset House, where the movement of 20 female dancers interacted with the water-flow dynamics of 55 fountains. She continued in unusual venues with historic church interiors for *TooMortal* (2012), where another all-female cast (six performers, dressed in flame red) danced within the pews, conjuring imagery of mermaids ploughing through the waves, vampires awakening from their coffins, or their backs arched over the sides of the pews like dying swans draped over fallen tree trunks. In a surreal shift of emphasis, they become a synchronised swimming team without the obligatory nose clips but with the same emotionless expressions, plunging in and out of the dark recesses of the pews. Originally made as a fundraising solo for an Elizabethan Church in Stoke Newington, *TooMortal* was then taken up – as part of the 2012 Olympic Festival – by Dance Umbrella, which has a long history of commissioning site-specific work, and by the Venice Biennale, which had not.

Nonetheless, Jeyasingh was invited back to Venice and another religious setting for *Outlander* (2016), performed in the Palladian Refectory at the San Giorgio monastery, once the home of Paulo Veronese's monumental painting, *The Wedding Feast at Cana*, which was plundered by Napoleon. Jeyasingh drew influence from the multicultural banquet portrayed in Veronese's exuberant masterpiece for three consecutive solos, performed along a specially designed catwalk with a digital projection of the painting stretched across one wall.

Jeyasingh focussed on the cellular processes of plants in *Strange Blooms* (2013), her eight dancers embodying a botanical theme in arms that drift and curl like tendrils, bodies that wrap around each other like stems, and changing group patterns as if spores are being blown away in the breeze. This cycle of scientific enquiry was continued as part of the Knowledge Producers programme at King's College, London, following a presentation of *Bruise Blood* to six science academics; their individual commentaries became the scripts for film portraits in *Translocations* (2014), directed and edited by Gomes.

In Flagrante (2014) was another filmed work (directed by Ravi Deepres), commissioned by Professor Marina Wallace of the University of the Arts in London, to run alongside a European exhibition, entitled

Lens of Life. Working with leading geneticist Professor Kim Nasmyth, Jeyasingh's brief was to bring science and choreography into an open dialogue by capturing the tension, instability, and fast-moving energy of cell division in the performance of a solo dancer (Ayuso).

Her fascination with the hybridisation of artificial beings and humans, led Jeyasingh to investigate how she could mediate academic enquiry into Artificial Intelligence and robotics to clarify her art. Working with the Department of Natural & Mathematical Sciences at King's College and The Bartlett School of Architecture, Jeyasingh intended a robot to be programmed with certain behaviours and movements that would enable a duet to be choreographed, for it to perform with a human (another articulation of the hybrid). It was an idea ahead of its time and funding limitations led to the construction of just a robotic arm. The resultant *Trespass R&D* project (2015) became a choreographic exercise in dealing with elements of chaos and unpredictability.

Jeyasingh returned to cultural interactions with *Bayadère – The Ninth Life* (2015), a radical imagining of the classical ballet, *La Bayadère* (1877). Drawing on stories of the first temple dancers (bharatanatyam was originally a temple dance) to visit Europe, as recorded in 19th century texts by the French writer and critic Théophile Gautier, Jeyasingh examined how the story of *La Bayadère* has exerted a lasting exotic allure for Europeans and how this still affects the Indian diaspora today.

Material Men (2015) is a virtuoso piece made on two diverse performers of that diaspora who chose to dance very differently (Subramanian, a classical bharatanatyam dancer and Shailesh Bahoran, a hip-hop performer). Through their shared ancestry of indentured labour, they helped Jeyasingh create a divergent experience, represented in the contrasting contained style of bharatanatyam and the explosive quality of hip hop.

In 2016, Jeyasingh created *études*, a solo (performed by Kela) responding to the exhibition *Rodin and Dance: The Essence of Movement*, curated by Dr Alexandra Gerstein at the Courtauld Gallery in collaboration with the Musée Rodin, which explored Rodin's fascination with dance and bodies through experimental sculptures made towards the end of his life.

Although *Contagion* (2018) was co-commissioned by 14-18 NOW, the UK's arts programme to honour the First World War centenary, Jeyasingh ignored the war between humans to commemorate the contemporaneous Spanish influenza pandemic, which killed almost four times the number of people than the war itself. Her choreography reflected the genetic structure of a virus: rapid, random, and constantly shape-shifting. In a strangely prescient forewarning of the coronavirus pandemic, which postponed the intended March 2020 premiere of Jeyasingh's debut as an opera director (*Until the Lions: Echoes from the Mahabharata*, Opera National du Rhin, Strasbourg), Jeyasingh concentrated her focus on the battle between virus and cell and, furthering her fascination with science fiction, the metaphor of alien entities invading human bodies.

Staging Schiele (2019) was a germ that spun organically out of *Contagion*, given that Egon Schiele died, aged 28, from the Spanish flu, just three days after his wife, who was pregnant with their first child. Schiele's paintings included a large quantity of unflinching female nudes and, although tastefully clothed, time after time the rawness of his art is clearly articulated in the dancers' contorted poses: the male artist's sexually intrusive gaze on these women is a traditional aspect of art, but in Schiele's paintings his naked women stare back defiantly – a motif that Jeyasingh adopted too.

Music has always been the spur to Jeyasingh's choreography. She has developed important collaborations with composers, notably Glyn Perrin (*Romance … with Footnotes*, 1993, *Transtep*, *Bruise Blood*, and – with Niraj Chag – *Where is Dev?*, 2012); Orlando Gough (*Late*, 1991, *Just Add Water?* and *Staging Schiele*, described by the composer as an 'opera of anxiety'[in Roy, *Surface Tensions* Podcasts, 2019]); Gabriel Prokofiev (*Strange Blooms*, *Bayadère – The Ninth Life*, and *Terra Incognita*, 2014, choreographed for Rambert); and two enigmatic electronic musicians, Scanner, aka Robin Rimbaud (*Faultline* with Errollyn Wallen, and *Outlander*) and Cassiel, aka Nick Rothwell (*Counterpoint* and *TooMortal*, the latter remixing James MacMillan's *Tenebrae Responsories*). Jeyasingh remains loyal to many creative collaborators, most notably the costume designer, Ursula Bombshell, who has worked on numerous projects over the company's life, and lighting designers, Guy Hoare, Lucy Carter, and more recently Fabiana Piccioli.

Throughout her choreographic career, Jeyasingh has never presented prettiness, harmony, or resolution, and her productions rarely offer comfortable viewing. She generally works with tension and counter-tension, experimenting with the contortion and twists of the body that create those dynamic movements; it is unsurprising that the series of podcasts that define her career to date are entitled *Surface Tension* (referencing her eponymous dance work of 2000).

Graham Watts

Biographical details

Born in Chennai, India. 26 March 1957. **Studied** Bharatanatyam with guru Valluvoor Samuraj Pillai; came to UK in 1981, attained a BA in Shakespeare Studies and MA in Renaissance Studies, University of Sussex. **Career**: Toured internationally as a solo performer and founded Shobana Jeyasingh Dance, 1988. Honorary Master of Arts, University of Surrey, 1995; Honorary Doctorates: De Montfort University, Leicester, 1995; University of Chichester, 2015. Research Associate at ResCen, Centre for Research into Creation in the Performing Arts, Middlesex University, from 2006. Associate Company, Southbank Centre, London, from 2018. Creates work for other companies, including: Rambert; Sonia Sabri Dance Company; Random Dance Company; City Contemporary Dance Company, Hong Kong. **Awards and honours:** Digital Dance Award 1988; London Dance and Performance Award, 1988; Arts Council's Women in the Arts Award, the Prudential Award for Dance, and £100,000 Prudential Premier Award for the Arts, all 1993; Time Out Awards, 1993 and 1996; Member of the Order of the British Empire (MBE), 1995; NESTA Dream Time Fellowship, 2004; Asian Woman of Achievement Award, for contribution to arts in the UK, 2008; Award for Excellence, International Institute of Dance and Theatre, 2014; Woman of the World Award, 2017; National Dance Award, 2019; Commander of the Order of the British Empire (CBE), 2020.

Works

Miniatures (1988); *Configurations* (1988, revised 2012); *Janpath* (1988); *Defilé* [also known as *Défilé*] (1989); *Correspondences* (1990); *Byzantium* (1991); *Late* (1991); *Making of Maps* (1992); *Romance … with Footnotes* (1993); *Duets with Automobiles* (1993); *Raid* (1995); *The Bird and the Wind* (1996); *Palimpsest* (1996); *Intimacies of the Third Order* [also known as *Intimacies of a Third Order*] (1998); *Memory and Other Props* (1999); *Fine Frenzy* (1999); *Surface Tension* (2000, DVD 2005); *Web* (2001); *Phantasmaton* (2002); *[h]interland* (2002); *Curve Twist Gaze* (2002); *Curve Chameleon* (2003); *Café Event* (2003); *Polar Sequences* (2003); *Neon Dream* (2003); *Triptych Self* (2003); *Foliage Chorus* (2004); *4Squares* (2004); *Transtep* (with Lisa Torun, Filip Van Huffel, Rasphal Singh Bansal, 2004); *Debris* (2004); *Flicker* (2005); *Transtep 2* (2005); *Pop Idle* (2005); *Skin Deep* (2005); *City:zen* (with Mui Cheuk-yin, 2006); *Counterfeit* (2006); *Exit No Exit* (2007); *The Dancer's Cut* (2007); *Faultline* (2007, DVD 2008); *Taxon* (2007); *Sibuya* (2007); *2Step* (2008); *Breach* (2008); *Body Talk* (2008); *Just Add Water* (2009); *Bruise Blood* (2010); *Detritus* (2009); *Re:Mix* (2009); *Counterpoint* (2010); *Dev Kahan Hai?/Where is Dev?* (2012); *TooMortal* (2012); *Strange Blooms* (2013); *Translocations* (2013 on SJD website, but the resultant film shown only once, 21 March 2014); *In Flagrante* (2014); *Terra Incognita* (2014); *Bayadère – The Ninth Life* (2015, revised 2017); *Trespass R&D* (2015); *Material Men* (2015); *Outlander* (2016); *études* (2016); *Dance Beneath* (2016); *Here* (2017); *Material Men redux* (2017); *Contagion* (2018); *Staging Schiele* (2019); *Until the Lions: Echoes from the Mahabharata* (opera, 2020).

Further reading*

*For sources prior to 2000, see Stacey Prickett, 2nd edition of *Fifty Contemporary Choreographers*.

Interviews: Anne Sachs, 'Sowing Seeds', *Dance Theatre Journal*, 17 (2), 2001; Gerald Dowler, 'Out of the Suitcase …', *Dancing Times*, September 2008; Terence Handley MacMath, *Church Times*, 29 June 2012; uncredited, 'There's a Lot of Drama Inside Cells', Brighton Dome website, 28 September 2015; Carmel Smith, londondance.com, 9 January 2017; Ka Bradley, 'Instead of a Camera Frame I Have the Stage', *The Observer*, 5 October 2019; Maya Pindar, *The Wonderful World of Dance*, 26 October 2019; Sanjoy Roy, *Surface Tension* Podcasts: Series 1: 'Configurations', 14 March; 'Faultline', 16 May; 'Counterpoint, Too Mortal and Outlander', 15 July; 'Science and Science Fiction', 19 September; 'Staging Schiele', 25 November; 'Staging Schiele: Bonus Episode', 28 November (all 2019); and 'The Dancer's Cut', 9 January 2020.

Articles: Diana Evans, 'Subtle Movements and Small Details', *Dance Theatre Journal*, 16 (1), 2000; Andrée Grau, 'Dance and Cultural Identity', *Animated*, Autumn 2001; Lorna Sanders, 'Shobana Jeyasingh', *Dancing Times*, September 2001; Maggie Foyer, 'Shobana Jeyasingh', *Dance Europe*, June 2002; Shiromi Pinto, 'No Man's Land – Exploring South Asianness', Symposium Report, June 2004; Shiromi Pinto, 'Lightning Strikes in the Same Place', *Pulse*, Spring 2005; Shobana Jeyasingh, 'Much More Talk, Talk, Talking than Dance', *Pulse*, Autumn 2005; Avanthi Meduri, 'Labels, Histories, Politics: Indian/South Asian Dance on the Global Stage', *Dance Research*, 26 (2), Winter 2008; Alexandra Kolb, 'Akram Khan, Lloyd Newson, and the Challenges of British Multiculturalism', *Dance Research*, 36 (2), Winter 2018; Shobana Jeyasingh, *South Asian Diaspora Arts Archive*, sadaa.co.uk, undated.

Books: Paul Allen, *Art, Not Chance: Nine Artists' Diaries*, London, 2001; Valerie Briginshaw, 'Hybridity and Nomadic Subjectivity in Shobana Jeyasingh's Duets with Automobiles', *Dance, Space and Subjectivity*, New York, 2001; Christopher Bannerman et al. (eds), *Navigating the Unknown: The Creative Process in Contemporary Performing Arts*, Middlesex, 2006; Janet O'Shea, *At Home in the World: Bharata Natyam on the Global Stage*, Middletown, CT, 2007; Janet Lansdale (ed.), *Decentring Dancing Texts*, London, 2008; Jens Richard Giersdorf and Yutian Wong (eds), *Routledge Dance Studies Reader (Third Edition)*, Oxford/New York, 2019.

AKRAM KHAN

The work of British Bangladeshi dancer and choreographer Akram Khan defies neat categorisation, existing in the 'intersection between political and philosophical negotiations of multiple identity locations'

(Mitra 2015). Khan's trajectory, from a young dancer rooted in the north Indian classical dance form kathak to iconic British contemporary choreographer, is marked by a continuous dialogue between disparate techniques, cultural histories, and artistic collaborations. He refutes dichotomies of "East" and "West" to engage with what Bhabha termed the third space of diaspora (*The Location of Culture*, Routledge, 2004), through works that interrogate the boundaries of cultural, political, and physical identity.

Born in London in 1974 to parents recently immigrated from Bangladesh, Khan grew up on Bangladeshi folk dances and Michael Jackson music videos. His identity was shaped by a daily confluence of often contradictory cultural narratives and practices. His mother enrolled the seven-year-old Khan in kathak dance classes under Sri Pratap Pawar, a doyen of the Lucknow *gharana* (style), which emphasises subtlety, grace, and nuanced emotional expression. Kathak combines *nritta* (abstract movement including footwork and compositions that focus on line and rhythm) with elements of *nritya* (stylised storytelling through mime and codified gestures), informed by a variety of cultural traces tied to both Hindu and Muslim aesthetics and spiritualities. Kathak is steeped in a logic of circularity reflected in a cyclical understanding of time, in the reciprocal exchange of emotion between performer and viewer, and in the quintessential *chakkars* (heel spins) derived from Sufi whirling practice. Mitra (2015) suggests that 'in kathak's syncretic, chequered and trans-ethnic history ... Khan's own multi-ethnic identity and intercultural perspectives were rather appropriately reflected and nurtured'. He performed his traditional debut concert aged 18. His involvement in Peter Brook's adaptations of the Hindu epic, *The Mahabharata* (theatre, 1987; film 1989) was a critical early exposure to intercultural theatre centred around white experiences of non-white cultures, a framework that Khan's later work upturns.

Khan's studies at De Montfort University and the Northern School of Contemporary Dance was his crash course in Western dance techniques, including ballet, Graham technique, Alexander and other release techniques, contact improvisation, and physical theatre. These techniques clashed with his kathak training by challenging kathak's innate verticality, rootedness, and unidirectional relationship with the floor. He began to engage with movement that explored the horizontal plane, introduced new flexibility to the spine, repositioned the centre of gravity and expanded interaction with the floor. This period of exploration created what Mitra calls a 'muscular, skeletal and sociological tension' within Khan, that contributed to the distinct 'confusion' of movement and method that Khan self-describes as his primary aesthetic. This style is not simply 'contemporary' kathak, nor a superficial blending of Western contemporary dance with 'Asian' seasoning. It is a syncretic style of movement emerging from Khan's unique corporeal position that makes visible the ambiguous state of diasporic subjecthood itself.

The beginnings of this 'confused' aesthetic are visible in Khan's solo *Loose in Flight* (1995) and its film version (1999), an auto-ethnographic work transposed against the backdrop of London's Docklands, a culturally specific site of migrant life. Vigorous floor movements and acrobatic leaps explode out of neat, upright kathak resting positions, which Khan continuously returns to with a sense of both relief and repression. Kathak continued to ground Khan's early solos, *Fix* (2002) and *Polaroid Feet* (2001) for example. Later, collaborative works including *Torobaka* (2014) with flamenco artist Israel Galván and *Gnosis* (2010) with Taiwanese dancer Fang-Yi Sheu centred the rhythmic technique and fluid grace of kathak.

One key principle that emerges in Khan's contemporary work is the purposeful disruption of kathak's physical techniques. For example, in his first evening-length group work, *Kaash* (2002), dancers begin recognisable kathak phrases only to create dysfunction between fluid upper bodies and hyper-rigid lower bodies. Khan disrupts the foundational agreement between the quality of rhythmic syllables (*bols*) embedded in Nitin Sawhney's score and the quality of bodily comportment (*ang*) traditionally performed to those syllables that marks virtuosic kathak dance (Sushil Saxena, *Swinging Syllables: Aesthetics of Kathak Dance*, Sangeet Natak Akademi, 1993). The dancers undercut the torrent of bols that rush over them, creating a disharmony that becomes a recurrent theme in Khan's choreography: He states: 'For me contemporary dance was about breaking the perception of where the parameters were about right and wrong. It was about breaking all the rules that were set in my body' (Samantha Ellis, *The Guardian*, 22 April 2004).

Many of Khan's works take myth, history, and autobiography as starting points for explorations of identity, politics, and subjectivity. Some, like *Gnosis* (2010) and *Until the Lions* (2016), grew from traditional narratives like the Hindu *Mahabharata*, while *Xenos* (2018) and *Dust* (2014) are inspired by historical events like World War I. Others take events from Khan's own life to explore various aspects of the diasporic life condition, such as *zero degrees* (2005) and *DESH* (2011). Instead of illustrating linear narratives, Khan is concerned with the generation of *rasa*, the psycho-somatic communion of audience

129

and dancer through the shared experience of emotion that is central to Indian classical dance practice. According to Mitra, Khan's rasa emerges through an understanding of the body as itself a site of knowledge, and not simply as a tool for communication based on fixed codes.

Khan's 90-minute solo *DESH,* for example, is a masterful expression of embodied knowledge, history and socio-political strife, through a mixture of dance vocabularies, animation, and stage design. *DESH* ('homeland' in Bengali),

> lays bare Khan's turbulent relationship with his father as analogous to his relationship with Bangladesh. The piece moves seamlessly between London and Bangladesh, and in both these evoked locations we witness Khan's isolation and restlessness as he relentlessly searches for a sense of belonging.
>
> (Mitra 2015)

DESH engages with multiple characters including Khan's father, a teenage Khan, an imaginary second-generation niece, a young boy from a Bangla folktale, and an adult Khan. Together with visual artist Tim Yip, lighting designer Michael Hulls, writer and poet Karthika Nair, and composer Jocelyn Pook, Khan creates what Mitra calls an 'alternative aesthetic ... that operates at the boundaries of each art form, blurring their individual characteristics and heightening their ability to reach out to audiences at multidimensional, emotional, cultural and sensorial levels'.

Khan deploys the methods of physical theatre and multi-modal *tanztheater* to allow new work to emerge from the conversation between transnational bodies, subjects, and identities. Duets, including *In-I* with actress Juliet Binoche and *Sacred Monsters* with ballet artist Sylvie Guillem, open new doors for Khan: 'Even though the common denominator is my body in duet with another body, my body is changing because of them' (Guy Cools, *body:language #2 Akram Khan,* London: Sadler's Wells, 2012). He opens a conversation with another Muslim diasporic subject, Belgian-Moroccan Sidi Larbi Cherkaoui, in *zero degrees,* where the two men combine spoken and gestural monologues, duets across multiple dance vocabularies, and interactions with uncanny moulds of their own bodies to trace a history of border crossings, confrontations, and conciliation that exists uniquely between their subject positions.

Khan also follows a dialogic approach in *bahok* (2008), a group work generated between '8 dancers from diverse cultures, traditions and dance backgrounds: Chinese, Korean, Indian, South African and

Spanish ... speaking different languages both with their bodies and tongues' (akramkhancompany.net). Unlike Khan's earlier works, *bahok*'s choreography was not transferred onto these dancers; movement, sequences, and storylines emerged from anecdotes shared among them. A similar approach occurred in *Outwitting the Devil* (2018), an ensemble production bringing together six dancers from different cultural histories and vocabularies to co-create an illustration of man's circular ability to destroy and create, inspired by the Epic of Gilgamesh. According to Khan, who at this point is transitioning from performing to choreographing for others: "I have awakened to a new way of dancing. And that is to dance my ideas through the bodies of others ... who carry their histories and complex emotional experiences within them" (personal communication with the author). Khan's work does not exist in a vacuum of his own artistic vision – producer Farooq Chaudhry, composer Nitin Sawhney, dramaturges Guy Cools and Ruth Little, and other international artists have remained in his circle of collaborators for many years.

Khan's position as a key figure in the British contemporary dance scene is evidenced by high-profile commissions, including his contribution to the 2012 Olympic Games Opening Ceremony in London, and for English National Ballet his 2014 *Dust* and his 2016 reimagining of *Giselle*. This work was set among migrant workers toiling in sweatshops, merging ballet technique with the expressive hands of kathak dance. Khan replaced the storyline with provocative imagery to cultivate emotionally resonant moments: 'the fluid weave of bodies that rise protectively around the dying Giselle, the human threshing machine created by the Wilis as they wield their warrior staves, their feet drumming lethally on pointe' (Judith Mackrell, 'Giselle review', *The Guardian*, 28 September 2016).

Khan also bridges the mainstream British dance and South Asian classical dance spheres through his role as curator, organising mixed bills of classical and contemporary Indian dance through programs like the Darbar Festival at Sadler's Wells and *Carnival of Shadows* (2020).

Khan's iconoclastic approach to both Indian classical and British contemporary dance has reshaped the field of dance in the UK through a distinctly border-crossing aesthetic. He destabilises the genres of classical and contemporary by centring the multiplicity and ambiguity of his own embodied subject positions. Through his unique combination of multiple movement vocabularies, exuberant theatricality, and intentional collaborations across dance languages, Khan has brought the question of difference to the centre of British contemporary dance.

Shweta Saraswat

Biographical details

Born in London, 29 July 1974. **Studied** Bengali/Bangladeshi folk dance with his mother as a child. Trained in kathak under Sri Pratap Pawar, London, beginning aged seven, performed his solo debut concert (*rang manch pravesh*) at age eighteen. Studied contemporary dance and ballet at De Montfort University (1994–96) and finished his dance degree at the Northern School of Contemporary Dance (1996–1997). **Career:** Toured internationally as a teenager with Peter Brook's production of *Mahabharata* 1987 to 1989 and appeared in the televised version in 1989; performed as a kathak soloist in the 1990s and early 2000s; established Akram Khan Dance Company with Farooq Chaudhry in 2000; choreographer-in-residence and associate artist, Southbank Centre, London (2001–2005); associate artist, Sadler's Wells Theatre, London (2009–present); associate artist, Mountview Academy for Theatre Arts, London and Curve Theatre, Leicester. Choreographed for the 2012 London Olympic Games opening ceremony. **Awards and honours** include Jerwood Foundation Choreography Award 2000; Time Out Live Award 2000; Critics' Circle National Dance Awards 2000, 2002, 2005, 2012, 2013, 2015, 2018, and 2019; Doctorate of Arts, De Montfort University 2004; MBE for services to dance 2005; South Bank Show Award 2005; Excellence in International Dance Award 2007; Helpmann Award 2007; Honorary Doctorate of Letters, Roehampton University, 2010; Honorary Fellowship, Trinity Laban Conservatoire of Music and Dance, 2010; Age Critics Award 2010; Danza & Danza Award 2010; South Bank Sky Arts Award 2011; Distinguished Artist Award 2011; Lawrence Olivier Awards 2012 and 2019; Herald Archangel Award 2014; New York Dance and Performance Award ('Bessie') 2014; Fred and Adele Astaire Award 2015; Honorary Doctorate of Music, University of London 2015; Culture & Theatre Award 2016; Eastern Eye Arts Award 2017; Dora Mavor Moore Award 2018.

Works

Loose in Flight (1995; film version 1999); *No Male Egos* (1999); *Desert Steps* (1999); *Fix* (2000); *Rush* (2000); *Related Rocks* (2001); *Polaroid Feet* (2001); *Kaash* (2002); *Ronin* (2003); *Red or White* (2003); *A God of Small Tales* (2004); *ma* (2004); *Zero Degrees* (2005); *Third Catalogue* (2005); *Sacred Monsters* (2006); *Variations for Vibes, Strings and Pianos* (2006); *Lost Shadows* (2007); *Bahok* (2008); *In-I* (2008); *Confluence* (2009); *Gnosis* (2010); *Vertical Road* (2010); *DESH* (2011); *Abide with Me* (2012); Olympic Games Opening Ceremony, London (2012); *iTMOi* (2013); *Dust* (2014); *Torobaka* (2014, reworked as solo *Toro*); *Desert Dancer* (2014); *Techne* (2015); *Until the Lions* (2016); *XENOS* (2018); *Kadamati* (2018); *Giselle* (2018); *Outwitting the Devil* (2019); *Curry House Kid* (2019); *Chotto Xenos* (2020); *Father: Vision of the Floating World* (2020).

Further reading*

*See also sources in Stacey Prickett, 2nd edition of *Fifty Contemporary Choreographers*.

Interviews: with Hanna Weibye, 'theartsdesk Q&A: Choreographer Akram Khan', *theartsdesk.com*, October 2014; Katie Razzal, 'Akram Khan: 'My Body Has Been My Voice' – BBC Newsnight', *YouTube*, February 2018; Parbati Chaudhury, 'Akram Khan – On Curating Darbar Festival', pulseconnects. com, 30 November 2018; Rebecca Liu, 'To Move is to Hope': How Choreographer Akram Khan is Democratizing Dance', *Prospect Magazine*, April 2019; '21 Questions with Akram Khan', *YouTube*, April 2019.

Articles: Josephine Machon, 'Akram Khan: The Mathematics of Sensation – The Body as Site/Sight/Cite and Source', *(Syn)aesthetics*, January 2009; Royona Mitra, 'Akram Khan Rewrites *Radha*: The "Hypervisible" Cultural Identity in Kylie Minogue's *Showgirl*', *Women & Performance*, March 2009; Royona Mitra, 'Decolonizing Immersion', *Performance Research*, October 2016; Shanti Pillai, 'Global Rasikas: Audience Reception for Akram Khan's *Desh*', *The Drama Review*, August 2017; Alexandra Kolb, 'Akram Khan, Lloyd Newson, and the Challenges of British Multiculturalism', *Dance Research*, November 2018; Roslyn Sulcas, 'Coming to Chicago: A "Giselle" that Speaks to the Present', *The New York Times*, 15 February 2019.

Books: Lorna Sanders, 'Akram Khan's *ma*: An Essay in Hybridisation and Productive Ambiguity', in *Decentering Dancing Texts* (ed. Janet Lansdale), Basingstoke, 2008; Guy Cools, *In-between Dance Cultures: On the Migratory Artistic Identity of Sidi Larbi Cherkaoui and Akram Khan*, Valiz, 2015; Royona Mitra, *Akram Khan: Dancing New Interculturalism*, Basingstoke, 2015; Royona Mitra, 'Akram Khan on the Politics of Choreographing Touch', in *Contemporary Choreography: A Critical Reader* (eds. Butterworth and Wildschut), London, 2018.

AMIT LAHAV

Amit Lahav, choreographer, designer, writer, and theatre director, is founding Artistic Director of Gecko. His works invite us to feel moved by the pain and ugliness of power, relationships, and loss through story telling that touches on the archetypal and the individual. But Lahav is not afraid to be optimistic, and he is also driven to seek and share the hope and light that inevitably emerges through the cruelty of human behaviour.

Gecko creates total physical theatre. These inter-disciplinary works are about the human condition; family conflict, internal struggle, survival, and social conditions; inequality, migration, and climate change. Sound, set, story, and choreography combine to produce 'a global sensibility that reaches deep into our universal emotional patterning' (Lahav 2019). Works such as *Missing* (2012) and *The Wedding* (2017) move from the personal to the universal, reaching beyond age, gender, class, or national identity: 'This company have the extraordinary capability to pierce the heart of a subject and essentially remind us what it is to be human' (The Reviews Hub, 2018).

Lahav is concerned with relational intimacies and global themes in tandem. The resulting choreography is both simple and complex, difficult to summarise but aiming straight for the heart. Describing working on *Institute* (2014), Lahav explains that his choreography provides an orderly frame within which characters express emotionally free behaviours full of trauma and *dis*order. Moments of intense emotional expression are balanced dramaturgically through a character's story without alienating the audience. This enables the choreography to be explosively unshackled at crucial moments, moving beyond narrative:

> I'm always trying to get to the most poetic potential. Where audiences can be as individually predisposed to interpretation as possible. The movement is not highly descriptive in terms of the scene but it might be a gateway into the expressive possibilities of the moment.
>
> (Lahav, 2019)

In Gecko's work, intimate minutiae of the ritualised behaviours of daily life are often featured to express the common quest for togetherness, order, and security on an individual level. These glimpses of a search for hope, trust, and security echo the larger challenge posed by the dangers of global politics and environmental calamity. The patterns of everyday life implicitly connect the self to the wider world.

Movement is the universal dialect that connects Gecko's international and multilingual cast (mainly trained dancers rather than actors). Choreographies interweave recognisably folky, historic, or cultural references that connect to our own memories and experiences. These overlap with complex gestural sequences, manifesting their own sensory logic. We recognise ourselves in authentic, everyday gestures and in the fragility or strength of the performers' coordinated breaths. These cut through the fragmented narrative, rattling or reassuring us, and leaving us at times just a little perplexed.

Gecko's choreography emerges through exploring key narratives, relationships, and other elements through improvisation around an initial idea. It builds on non-hierarchical collaboration across dance, theatre, sound and set design, focused on how together they might serve the narrative or emotional state being developed. His work is always driven by emotion, engendered through physically expansive storytelling designed to establish strong empathy with his audiences. Light humour and playfulness remind us that the performers are human too. This builds trust, enabling the storytelling to venture into deeper emotional territory.

Lahav's devising process uncovers authentic emotional expressions. He spends hours creating an atmosphere in which the performers feel physically, emotionally, and imaginatively prepared. These emotion explorations are not scene- or character-based, but an all-out personal exploration (from their internal world to an external expression); anger, for example, should pour out of every cell in the body and every moving part should reverberate with it. Lahav explains:

> I use emotion-based exploration, and given that all emotions are physical, it will inevitably produce a physical template for a particular performer to build on. Once we are connected with the rhythms and shapes of a certain emotion, we can start to construct a choreographed journey. Breath and vocalisations become the glue which bind the performers together and give structure.

Movements are precise even when appearing throwaway or naturalistic. Body shape, gesture, and rhythm are balanced with stylised motifs and synchronised breath. Choreography, rhythm, and direction in space, together or alone, is always specific to a scene. It has its own rhythm, often led by and punctuated by the breath. It embodies a world being created, providing context for movement. 'There is no extraneous movement or decoration. Each moment or choreography has been meticulously crafted by interrogation of the idea or emotional state we are exploring' (Lahav, 2019).

Watching a Gecko show is exhilarating and confusing, like waking from a powerful dream: fragments of story, disintegrating or half-formed moments, snatches of conversation in multiple languages, and a timeline that feels like someone is intermittently leaning on the remote control. This disruption keeps the audience in a purposefully unresolved state of intrigue but with enough relatable, emotional provocations to hold their attention and allow the performance to reach them on a universal emotional level: 'it is intoxicating and once you have been seduced by the sinuous rhythms of Amit Lahav's production, it is hard not to be swept up in its strange, propulsive energy' (Lawrence, *The Telegraph*, 2018, on *Missing*).

This is a risky business. Lahav would see it as a failure if the audience felt lost or intimidated, or were in agreement on a singular narrative: he speaks of a difficult balance being struck between comfort and discomfort, being guided and left alone, sign-posted and lost (2019).

The works swirl between languages, often with exchanges in multiple dialects, denying the audience access to any consistent linguistic logic. The resulting ambiguity opens a space for interpretation more entwined with our own realities and priorities. Lahav forgoes the prescribed fixed logic embodied in narrative spoon-feeding, drenches movement with intention, and layers action with 'mutterings' (Lahav's expression): sometimes audible, sometimes almost imperceptible. This muttering enhances the movement and facilitates the intention.

Lahav has a three-year cycle of creation for each work. Research and development to build and balance the fragmented narratives and emotional arcs continue throughout its life. The reflective process is a core component of his reiterative working practice. It starts with Lahav, then draws upon the whole team as well as audience and other partners. Collective reflection enables deeper excavation and supports the ongoing labour of discovery: as Lahav describes it, the 'process of discovery, of searching, however difficult, however glorious that is, the process of creating our own world, our own story, our own script. That is Gecko'.

Lahav's long-term collaborative partnerships with performers, designers, composers, and producers are robust enough to flex through extended processes of play, trial, and error. Collaborators share ownership of the material they create together. There is no separate choreography or movement direction credit for his shows. He explains that movement, acting, puppeteering, and the stage management of the show's journey are all facets of the same endeavour: to find the truth of the moment and find its most potent outlet.

Experiences with two seminal theatre makers, David Glass and Lindsay Kemp, have influenced Lahav's work. *The Lost Child* (1999) was a socially engaged project with David Glass Ensemble in South America and SE Asia. It had lasting impact on his approach to connecting with others on a meaningful emotional level. With no shared language or cultural knowledge and working in the midst of painful childhood trauma, co-creating theatre allowed new connections to be made. Authentic expressions of joy and grief emerged as part of the shared non-verbal communication: the children's drawings, play, and stories came straight from the heart.

Lahav found this emotional honesty and courage profoundly moving and seeks to find this intensity in his stage works. The emotional authenticity of these children's relationships reminded him how, as privileged and distracted adults, we block, struggle with, and manage our emotional selves. Such formative experiences helped him to understand how emotional communication can happen quickly and directly. Universal human emotions such as fear, joy, love, and anger connect us regardless of cultural and linguistic markers. This experience gave Lahav the confidence to explore poetic expression of our universal emotional landscape.

Lahav worked intensively with Lindsay Kemp over a number of years. Kemp's complex, bold, and irreverent performance-making relied on 'felt' connections, and he refused to compromise on playing out his truth. Lahav was impressed by how Kemp manipulated and guided his audiences through emotional sequences enabling complex reactions. He enjoyed Kemp's luxurious world of highly stylised performance: tantalising, romantic, and provocative. This influence can be seen in Lahav's more recent works, *Missing* and *The Wedding*, as he plays expertly with intertwining contradictory emotions. The contract signing in *The Wedding* sees the joyful act of multiple marriages overlaid with the seriousness of individuals signing away their lives and smiling brides being dragged around the stage, their eyes full of dread. In *Missing*, the couple are exhausted by switching between their previously intoxicating romance and their increasingly toxic present.

Glass and Kemp both influenced his fascination with rhythm, emotional repertoire, and comedic play in stylised (Kemp) and internal (Glass) processes. For his part, Lahav considers movement work, often led by audible, coordinated breathing, to be the fundamental source of the poetic body. For example, at the end of *Institute,* three performers flock through space, sweeping changes of direction punctuated by reaching arms and long, low strides. Their exaggerated breath is amplified, their arms reaching up towards the orange, sun-like sky: Lahav can't resist a hopeful ending. The power of rhythmic, communal breathing is in this simplicity. At its simplest, we all breathe.

Gecko's works leave us roused and inspired to reimagine how we live, but Lahav wants his work to be experienced beyond those who share his worldview, to draw others into the conversation. Global politics, human connections, migration, and mental health are key themes in his work. Lahav's aim is not only to present his own thoughts on this but to provoke conversation and ultimately affect social change.

Sue Smith

Biographical details

Born in Rehovot, Israel, 1972. Family emigrated to UK, 1973, after the Arab-Israeli war. **Studied** at the Cockpit Youth Theatre, London, aged 18; trained in acting, Rose Bruford College (1992–95), traditional drama study (Stanislavsky, Brecht, Chekov, Shakespeare) and elements of physical theatre, clowning, and comedia dell'arte. **Career:** created comedy street performance group, Quick-Change, while at College; founded own company, Gecko, 2001. Performed with range of companies: including Box Clever Theatre Company (Theatre in Education), 1995–2000; Lindsay Kemp, 1996–1998; *Barnham* (musical, 1998); Steven Berkoff, 1999; Green Candle, 1999; David Glass Ensemble, 1999–2001. Also worked with disenfranchised children and adults, David Glass's Lost Child Project: Thailand, Cambodia, Vietnam, Laos, Argentina, Brazil, Naples; and The Chemical Brothers for live and filmed projects. **Awards** include Time Out Critics' Choice of the Year, 2002; The Guardian Pick of the Fringe Award, 2002; Special award in Sarajevo for outstanding theatre, 2002; Time Out Live Award, 2003; Total Theatre Award, 2005; Fox Fellow, 2010; Peter Brook / Equity Ensemble Award, 2016.

Works

Ramayana (touring production, 2000–2002); *Taylor's Dummies* (2002); *Inside* (2003); *The Race* (2004); *The Arab and The Jew* (2007); *Depth Charge* (2008); *The Overcoat* (2009); *Missing* (2012); *Institute* (2014, filmed adaptation, 2019); *The Time of Your Life* (for BBC4 TV, 2015); *The Wedding* (2017); *Egon Schiele: Dangerous Desires* (film, dir: Teresa Griffiths, 2018).

Further reading

Interviews: with Hannah Dolan, warwickartscentre.co.uk, 8 May 2014; Alex Wood, theatrebubble.com, 15 November 2016.

Articles: Lyn Gardner, 'Gecko: The Theatre Company Divorcing Post-Brexit Britain', *The Guardian*, 4 April 2017; Daniel Pitt, 'Beyond Borders: Amit Lahav and Gecko', springbackmagazine.com, 4 September 2018; Ben Lawrence, 'Gecko; A Triumphant Return to Battersea Arts Centre', *The Telegraph*, 12 September 2018; Maryam Philpott, 'The Wedding – YouTube', thereviewshub.com, 28 May 2020.

Books: Gecko Theatre Resource Packs, geckotheatre.com; Alex Mermikides and Jackie Smart, *Devising in Progress*, macmillanihe.com, 2010; Nick O'Brien and Annie Sutton, *Theatre in Practice* (2nd ed), London, 2018; Rachel Hann, *Beyond Scenography*, London, 2018; 'Gecko: An Organic Journey', in *The Twenty-First Century Performance Reader*. 1st edition (eds. Brayshaw, Fenemore and Witts), London, 2019.

ROSEMARY LEE

Rosemary Lee's choreography deals with the qualities of 'intimacy' and 'humanity', reflected through the diversity of her work, which includes large-scale productions with huge casts, as well as profound encounters in the form of solos and duets. Lee often works with both trained and untrained dancers, creating performances that defy binary categorisations of 'professional' or 'community'. Her interest in simple forms of movement with a strong choreographic concept creates possibilities for deep engagement by performer and audience alike and have led to a sense of her work as being a reflection on what it means to be human. Lee occupies a special place in the landscape of 21st century British dance, not least because of her ability to create performances for non-professionals with high production values but also to share and articulate her dance making process through performance, research, and documentation that furthers understanding of the field of dance and choreography.

Lee describes her practice as 'moving portraiture'; she works closely with her dancers to bring out their individuality and presence. Attention to detail is acute and her process rigorous, not in a way that is reliant on physical techniques but understanding how form and presence work together in performance. Lee's own experience of performance throughout her career informs this. Somatic practices are key to her choreographic process, using approaches such as ideokinesis – the use of guided imagery to inform movement qualities and create a sensitivity of touch between bodies. She creates new relationships between the viewer, the site and the performer.

Lee's interest in working with people of different ages and untrained dancers was influenced by her training at the Laban Centre (now Trinity Laban) in London, 1978–1981 and her exposure to the radical practices of Judson Dance Theater in the 1980s. Rudolf Laban's work informed dance education in the UK, for example valuing 'the individual's own choice of movement, and self-initiated vocabularies' (trinitylaban.ac.uk/history/rudolflaban). Lee describes her experience of viewing highly technical dancers as "remote from my own experience ... I couldn't be them. I felt that could ostracise a lot of people, so I was already looking for an aesthetic that included all ages and experiences, before I saw work influenced by Judson Church" (personal interview with author, 24 September 2010). This was underpinned by her childhood experiences in Lowestoft as part of 'amateur dramatics' which demonstrated the value of people from all walks of life creating something together. The combination of these influences cemented her desire to make work with a social conscience.

Informed by the ideology that art had a vital role in society, the 1980s saw an explosion of Community Arts practice and policies which influenced the opportunities available to artists such as Lee. Site specific-theatre of the era was often made with large casts in order to be 'spectacular' and demonstrate participation on a grand scale, something that inspired her to create choreography that was epic but also intimate – creating more subtle levels of engagement for the audience.

In 1987, Lee was Artist in Residence at 'Jointwork' in Oxford, where *New Springs from Old Winters* (1987) involved a large-scale performance in the town hall, preceded by a procession of over 200 people, including members of Oxford Youth Dance and a large local network of untrained dance enthusiasts. This was her first work as a director and began her trajectory as a choreographer who could integrate the conceptual, practical, and ethical concerns of participatory dance. Themes from this piece have been revisited and re-configured, for example *Egg Dances* (1988), conceived for the stage, became a seminal piece of dance on screen in 1990.

Egg Dances featured a cross-generational cast, from 9 years old to 70. This work, which premiered at *The Place*, London, used minimal movements; simple shifts in weight, lifts and counterbalances learnt from somatic approaches such as contact improvisation. Images of different-aged bodies supporting each other's weight created a powerful sense of the possibilities for human beings relating to one another. Several large-scale pieces with groups of all ages followed, including: *Haughmond Dances* (1990), involving a cast of 237 local people in a ruined abbey; *Ascending Fields* (1992), set in an empty tyre depot off the M6 motorway; and *Banquet Dances* (1999), part of an event called *Take Me to the River*, which led the audience to three site-specific performances by boat.

The stage work *Passage* (2001) had a mixed age cast but also incorporated Lee's increasing interest in working with film. It had a large backdrop of screens featuring close-up portraits of the performers and expansive landscapes. It was her final work with film-maker Peter Anderson; a collaboration born in 1995 when she co-produced, with Anderson, an acclaimed dance for camera titled *boy*.

In *boy*, Lee's method of 'choreographic portraiture' created a piece that allowed the dancer – nine-year-old Tom Evans – to be entirely himself in movement terms: 'Between close ups and long shot we can piece together gesture, intention, space and terrain in this beautiful depiction of the intensity of child's play – the choreography remains true to the un-thought, incipient actions of childhood ...' (Erin Branningan, *RealTime*, 23, realtime.org.au/archives, Feb–March 1998). Working with body and landscape is characteristic. The film focuses on Evan's perceptions of his surroundings – a Norfolk beach, discovering this viscerally through jumps, rolls and falls. Close-up camera shots allow viewers to engage with the textures of the site as

Evans himself does; wide angles show a small boy in a huge landscape. Commissioned by Arts Council England and BBC 2, dance for camera was still emerging as a form in its own right. The film has been cited in international publications on screen dance – cementing *boy* as a definitive part of Lee's oeuvre and the emerging genre.

The concern with both intimate portrait and epic landscape, and the relationship of these, continued to inform Lee's site-based practice. She created several critically acclaimed choreographies *Common Dance* (2009), *Square Dances* (2011), *Without* (2013), *Calling Tree* (2014), *Passage for Par* (2018), and *Circadian* (2019).

Common Dance took place in Greenwich's historic Borough Hall, London; Lee's concept took root in the idea of 'common ground' – finding shared spaces and values amongst diversity, something that was being eroded in contemporary societies and urban spaces. Movement vocabulary was drawn from stripped back folk dance and somatic practices that encourage 'listening to the body', a quality that pervaded the work, as Welton writes in 2010: 'Through air, floor, space and silence, the company entreated the audience to listen, and in coming to attend to this silence the audience stretched back towards them'. Sanjoy Roy articulated the particularity of the choreography and casting: 'We sensed their [the performers'] uniqueness and multiplicity, as well as their common humanity … it was revelatory, like being shown both the wood and the trees … it could only have worked with this mixed motley cast' (*The Guardian*, 3 November 2009). The cast was made up of 50 professional and non-professional dancers aged between 8 and 83, with a choir from Finchley Children's music group singing a score composed by Terry Mann. The flow and energy of the group of dancers operated as a chorus, rather than privileging individual virtuosity, demonstrating the hopeful potential for togetherness and collaboration in other areas of life.

Common Dance was the basis for a ground-breaking DVD and symposium (created with Martin Welton, Queen Mary University, 1 December 2012) entitled 'On Taking Care', which illuminated Lee's processes of creating choreography. In *Common Dance*, personal and political conceptions of touch were embodied through the way that Lee choreographed the interactions between this inter-generational temporary community; opening up the possibility for human contact restricted in other areas of social life.

In 2014 Lee began a collaboration with Simon Whitehead that led to *Calling Tree*, a durational performance with several iterations in and around different trees in significant locations, identified by the potential of these ancient trees as gathering points. Visually striking, performers were placed within the boughs of an ancient leafy tree, ascending and descending its great height through the use of harnesses; they danced, sang, and repeatedly called out snippets of text, such as *'branches twist out of me, leaves whisper in my ribs'*, whispered in amongst the hum of cars and the city in the distance. The slow unfolding of this web of sound and movement created subtle reflections on the nature of the relationship between people and place. Public gathering or 'commons' such as the parks and gardens where *Calling Tree* has been performed are a feature of Lee's outdoor work: *Square Dances* (2011) performed in four public squares in central London; *Under the Vaulted Sky* (2014) for Milton Keynes International Festival in the city's 'Cathedral of Trees'; and *Liquid Gold is the Air*, a video installation that followed.

Lee's desire to create relationships between people, space, and screen chimes with the interdisciplinary nature of much contemporary art and her evolving relationship with visual art practice is demonstrated by innovative collaborations with film and installation artist Nic Sandiland. In 2001 they created *Remote Dancing*, inviting individual audience members into enclosed corridors where their movements instigate an intimate pas-de-deux between body and technology with an onscreen dancing partner. Lee suggests that through the neutrality of this space, participants became aware of their own presence and potential action in a state of receptive waiting for their digital partner. In *Apart from the Road* (2001), an interactive installation built into the fabric of Barking library (before moving to Hammersmith and Whitechapel libraries), Lee worked with poet Chrissie Gittens as well as Sandiland to place tiny video screens, TV monitors, and video projectors revealing a collection of whispered poems and miniature dances by 180 children, creating 'dancing, aural portraits' of each one. This work responded to the library and its social context to bring attention to hidden personal stories in a highly urban site.

Lee's work is often driven by multi-layered approaches to people and place. In 2018, she was commissioned to create a new work as part of a visual arts initiative 'Groundwork', that bought internationally acclaimed art to Cornwall. *Passage for Par* was performed on Par Sands beach. This site was chosen because of its social demographic, one of the poorest areas in Cornwall, echoed by the paradoxical image of a kaolin factory humming at one end of the beach and a picturesque cliff face at the other. Lee's choice of location is never arbitrary; work is tailored to the place, and movement vocabulary arises from this specific relationship. In the case of *Par* this was taken from minimal bouncing folk steps, similar to *Common Dance*, but particular to Breton and Cornish styles of dance. Thirty women cast from across the UK and Europe took part in this work. The women remained physically connected, with linked arms throughout, as they snaked their way across the vast expanse of sand. Lasting over two hours, *Par* allowed the audience to connect to the piece as they would a changing land-scape, a sunset, or a slow-moving creature inviting a different mode of attention. As usual Lee's process was rigorous in how the landscape shaped the choreography, informed by the changing tide and weather conditions, down to the timing of the event itself and the detail of how the dancers placed their feet. The dramatic vision of this line of women along the shore inspired unspoken stories of waiting and longing.

Each iteration of performance is a refinement of Lee's concerns to engage and reflect on humanity's relationship to its environment through a democratic aesthetic and relationships that encourage listen-ing and connection:

> The state I try to find myself in when creating – a receptive state, open to the forest of possibilities and hyper attentive and sensi-tive to the present – is the very state I want to help the audience experience. The artist, the performer and the audience could be sharing the same state. This receptive place for me is one of infi-nite openness.
>
> (Lee, 'Do you think dance can change the world?',
> *Juice*, 55, 2003)

Lee's choreography is a vehicle for connection in such a way that if you are involved in her work, it happens almost imperceptibly, but inevi-tably, that you will leave the event with a greater sense of relatedness to others and the world around you, receptive to the infinite openness.

Ruth Pethybridge

Biographical details

Born 14 January 1959, Lowestoft, Suffolk. **Studied** a BA at The Laban Centre (now Trinity Laban) London, (1978–81); ideokinesis, improvisation, contact improvisation at 'Movement Research' and with various teachers, New York. **Career:** in New York (1982–86) danced with Spoke the Hub Dancing and Marta Renzi Dance Company; in the UK, created participatory works with Sally Sykes (1986–88); founder member of Sue MacLennan's Occasional Dance Company (1985–1991). From 1985, is an independent artist; DanceEast Associate Artist 2014–16. Part of ResCen, Middlesex University 1998–2019, and senior Research Fellow at CDaRE (Centre for Dance Research) Coventry University (2015–present). **Awards and honours:** Bonnie Bird Choreography Award 1988; Digital Dance Awards, 1989, 1991; Time Out/Dance Umbrella Award 1991; Choreography for the Camera Award, Moving Pictures Toronto 1995; Arts Council Fellowship 2000–2002; SouthEast Dance Fellowship 2012–2014; Bonnie Bird New Choreography Research Award 2013; Jerwood Choreographic Research Project Award, 2013; WorkPlace Artist 2013–2020; Honorary Doctorate, Roehampton University, 2014; Festival Prize, Light Moves Festival of Screendance 2015: Honorary Lifelong Member of People Dancing (formally Foundation for Community Dance), 2016; Fellow of Trinity Laban 2016.

Works

They Are Wreathed (1981); *She Treads with Clanging Mysteries* (1985); *Mirror Mirror on the Wall* (with Sally Sykes, 1986); *Cold Comfort* (1986); *New Springs from Old Winters* (1987); *Feathered Snippet* (1987); *Moments Shoreline* (1987); *What the Eye Doesn't See* (1987); *Easily Led?* (1988); *Memoirs of a Cast of Thousands* (with Sally Sykes, 1988); *Egg Dances* (1988; video with Peter Anderson 1990); *Tenderhooks* (1989); *Escape Routes* (1989); *Seize the Thread* (1990); *Haughmond Dances* (1990); *Duel in a Teacup* (1990); *I Need a Calm Sky* (1991); *Pensthorpe Performance Trail* (1991); *Stranded* (1991); *Ascending Fields* (1992); *We Are Singing Our Farewell and Our Puzzlement* (1993); *Heart Home* (1993); *Cedar* (film 1993–94); *The Galliard, Every Morning Before Breakfast* (1994); *Exhale* (1994); *boy* (film, with Peter Anderson 1995); *Greenman* (film, with Peter Anderson, 1996); *Treading the Night Plain* (1996); *Silver* (1997); *Three Studies in Courtship* (1997); *Litany* (1997); *Chapel Dance* (1998); *Infanta* (film, with Peter Anderson, 1998); *One to One* (solos for Rosemary, collaborations with invited choreographers, 1999–2004); *The Banquet Dances* (1999); *Brink* (2001); *Dancing Nation* (film, with Peter Anderson 2001); *Passage* (film, with Peter Anderson 2001); *Apart from the Road* (installation, with Nic Sandiland, 2001, 2004); *Studies 123 and 4* (2001); *Beached* (2002); *Snow* (film, with David Hinton, 2003); *Remote Dancing* (installation, with Nic Sandiland, 2004–2008); *Stereo Dances* (with Nic Sandiland, 2004–2008); *Night-Plane* (2005); *The Suchness of Heni and Eddie* (2002, and DVD 2008); *Lightwalking* (2007); *Library Dances* (2009); *Common Dance* (2009); *Square Dances* (2011); *Melt Down* (2011); *Without* (installation, 2013); *Under the Vaulted Sky* (2014); *Calling Tree* (with Simon Whitehead, 2014); *Liquid Gold is in the Air* (installation, with Roswitha Chesher, 2015); *Rising* (2016); *Passage for Par* (2018); *Circadian* (2019); *Threaded Fine* (2020).

Further reading

(see rescen.net and independentdance.co.uk for further articles)

Interviews: with Sue MacLennan in Butterworth and Clarke (eds), *Dance Makers Portfolio, Conversations with Choreographers*, The Greenhouse Effect, 1998; Martin Welton, 'Rosemary Lee', in *Performance and Community* (ed.

McAvinchey), Bloomsbury, 2014; 'Starting with Sight: A Conversation between Rosemary Lee and Anna Heighway', *The International Journal of Screendance*, 8, 2017; Jacky Lansley, 'Other Voices', *Choreographies*, Intellect, 2017; 'A Balancing Act. Victor Merriman Interviews Rosemary Lee', *Animated*, Spring/Summer, 2019.

Articles: Rosemary Lee, 'The Possibilities Are Endless', *Animated*, Spring 2004; Ruth Pethybridge, 'Rosemary Lee Common Dance', *Dance and Age Inclusive Practice*, Foundation for Community Dance, 2010; Martin Welton, 'Listening as Touch. Paying Attention to Rosemary Lee's Common Dance', *Performance Research*, 15(3), 2010; Rosemary Lee and Niki Pollard, 'Writing with a Choreographer's Notebook', *Choreographic Practices*, 1(1), 2011; Gemma Collard-Stokes, 'Finding Common Ground through Language and Movement: Examining the Role of the Writer in Rosemary Lee's The Suchness of Heni and Eddie', *Research in Dance Education*, 13(2), 2012; Rosemary Lee, 'On Taking Care', (interactive DVD) ResCen, artsadmin. co.uk, 2012; Rosemary Lee, 'Vaulting Ambition; How to Create a Large Scale, Site-Specific Dance Piece', Dance Blog, *The Guardian*, 11 July 2014; Martin Welton, 'Making Sense of Air. Choreography and Climate in Calling Tree', *Performance Research*, 23(3), 2018.

Books: Rosemary Lee and Niki Pollard, *Beached: A Commonplace Book*, Middlesex, 2006; Christopher Bannerman, Joshua Sofaer, and Jane Watts (eds.), *Navigating the Unknown*, Middlesex, 2006; Diane Amans (ed.), *An Introduction to Community Dance Practice*, London, 2017; Vassiliki Karkou and Sophia Lycouris (eds.), *The Oxford Handbook of Dance and Wellbeing*, Oxford, 2017; Simon Ellis, Charlotte Waelde, and Hetty Blades (eds.), *A World of Muscle, Bone and Organs: Research and Scholarship in Dance*, CDaRE, e-book, 2018; Rosemary Lee and Ruth Pethybridge, *The Routledge Companion to Dance Studies* (eds. Prickett and Thomas), London, 2019.

LIV LORENT

Since graduating from Trinity Laban Conservatoire for Music and Dance, London, in 1993 (formerly the Laban Centre for Movement and Dance), Liv Lorent has created close to one hundred works. Many of these have incorporated her trademark of using multi-generational casts and performers of varying technical training. This is one of the aspects of her work that has endeared her to the communities she engages with and maybe one of the reasons why the Poet Laureate, Dame Carol Ann Duffy, described her on a BBC Radio 4 programme (*Women's Hour*, 6 October 2018), as 'a national treasure'. She demands the highest standards from those she works with and never patronises the non-professional dancers. Instead she pushes them beyond what they imagine possible, as one 80-year-old community dancer observed, 'If Liv tells you you can do it, you can!' (Paul RW Jackson, 2006).

Shards (1993), Lorent's prize winning graduation work at Trinity Laban, was selected to represent the UK in the Deuxiéme Rencontres Choréographiques Internationale in Fougeres, France, and as a result of this she founded balletLORENT. The somewhat unusual name was chosen because she felt it implied a certain degree of theatricality and spectacle that she felt was lacking in British dance at the time. Her work is eclectic. The dancers have a firm grounding in ballet and a range of contemporary techniques to which are added, when needed, aspects of burlesque, ballroom, aerial work, gymnastics, and physical theatre. A key aspect is the age range of dancers she employs; some began their careers with her in the late 1990s and are still performing with the company, while the apprentices are recent graduates. This gives the company a familial feel that is often missing from project-based companies. There is a physical and aesthetic heritage which the older dancers can pass on to the younger, something more often seen in a ballet company. This results in a homogeneity of style, instantly recognisable, though never moribund. Added to the core company works, there have been many which have included community casts aged from infancy to nonagenarians. This is the physical mix that enables Lorent to create her art.

After the boost of going to France, Lorent set about learning her craft and her audience by touring small venues in London, where she built a loyal following. Then in 1995, she became an Associate Artist at The Place Theatre, London. It was here that she began honing her craft and where she was head hunted by Janet Archer, the director of Dance City, the National Dance Agency based in Newcastle upon Tyne, in north-east England, to which the company relocated in 1996. Though no longer based at Dance City, they remain in the city as an integral part of the dance ecology of the region.

Lorent's approach to choreography is unorthodox. She has never been drawn to performing and in the studio demonstrates as little as possible, not wanting to allow her body 'to fall into the luxury of comfortable or familiar movement' (Paul RW Jackson, 2006).

Hers is not a task-based approach. In the studio, she talks to the dancers as they are moving, cajoling them into a rich vocabulary, which she uses as a sculptor would her hands, trying to convince them that they can shape their bodies into the images she sees in her mind. It is therefore for the dancers to find the line through the technicalities, which are often extreme. She wants them to find answers that suit their own bodies. This approach produces rich rewards and her work, neither shape based, nor gesture based, is at once sensual, sometimes erotic, often violent yet tender. Like her compatriot Anne Teresa de Keersmaeker, Lorent's work has a theatricality, drawing on many traditions, but ultimately on the pain and glory of the human condition. Lorent describes being energised by the 'unselfconscious magic' that multi-generational casts bring to her work. Their input informs, their ability determines content, and their individuality enhances the aesthetic. For her, the movement of young children can have a 'purity, and sometimes feral truth' that she will ask her trained professionals to emulate. With elders, she often finds a 'great purpose and economy in how they move' and 'a tendency to not be decorative for its own sake, or pretentious or over stylised or sexualised' (Lorent's descriptions are from an email to the author, 20 January 2020).

Her sense of theatre has been helped by collaborating with a range of costume, set, and lighting designers such as Nasir Mazhar, Malcolm Rippeth, Neil Murray, and Phil Eddolls. The profile of the company was raised, for example, by collaboration with Michele Clapton who designed the costumes for *Game of Thrones* and Murray Gold who composed the music for the reboot of *Dr Who*. All have contributed to the unique look of the company and in the creation of its fantastical worlds. The sensuality of the dancer's body is important to Lorent; in a number of works she asked her performers to appear naked, and is particularly keen that the costumes enhance, not obscure, their bodies.

Lorent is a musical choreographer, and like Mark Morris, Richard Alston, or Paul Taylor, she uses the widest possible range of musical scores. A balletLORENT performance can be an illuminating musical event. For example, she has used music that includes Tartini, Janacek, Ravel, Schnitke, Max Richter, Astor Piazzolla, and Jimi Hendrix. Unlike Mark Morris she does not read music, but like Graham or Ashton before her she has an innate understanding of the music's personality and how to make that visible. She listens to the music repeatedly, so that when she arrives in the studio she does not need to bind the movement in complex counts, rather the phrases of movement meld effortlessly with the phrases of the music in a way that seems wholly appropriate and organic. Since 2012 she has developed a fruitful relationship with composer Murray Gold, who has become a key collaborator.

Her company is well known for its site-specific work. One of the most ambitious was *Ballet in Shriek* (2000), presented inside one of the towers of Newcastle upon Tyne's iconic bridge. Lorent is also interested in drawing in new audiences to dance and to new spaces; *The Ball* (2002) was also performed in non-traditional dance spaces including Trafalgar Square, London. Beginning as a performance and ending in a party, *The Ball* was a unique attempt to break down the boundaries between high and low art. *La Nuit Intime* (2006) was designed to be performed in intimate club settings.

Lorent has made work for other companies, including collaboration with Scottish Dance Theatre for whom she made two works including the widely acclaimed *Luxuria* (2004). For Singapore Dance Theatre, she created *Into the Mouth of the Orchid* (2001) and for the Ballet Boyz she created *Propeller* (2006). Outside of dance she has created movement for drama and musical theatre. In 2018 she was movement director for *Great North Star*, the closing performance of the Great Exhibition of the North, broadcast internationally.

Beginning in 2012, Lorent began work on a trilogy of family friendly works based on Grimms' fairy tales, *Rapunzel*, *Snow White* (2015) and *Rumpelstiltskin* (2017), reimagined for the 21st century by Dame Carol Ann Duffy and with specially commissioned music by Murray Gold. These classic tales allowed her to create dance stories that were relatable to multi-generational audiences, with an exciting cast of already recognisable characters and protagonists to engage a younger audience. *Rumpelstiltskin* was filmed for streaming by the Arts Council England funded web source, The Space.

In a very early piece of handwritten publicity for her company, Lorent wrote: 'We want to deliver great dance for all', (balletlorent. com/archive), and as Lorent celebrates more than 25 years of creativity, she can be proud to have fulfilled this desire.

Paul RW Jackson

Biographical details

Born in Namur, Belgium in September 1972. The family moved to the UK in 1979. **Studied** at the Arts Educational Schools in Tring; then a BA in Theatre Dance at the Laban Centre for Movement and Dance (now Trinity Laban Conservatoire of Dance and Music), graduating 1993. **Career:** Founded own company, balletLORENT in 1993. She has choreographed for other companies: including Scottish Dance Theatre, Singapore Dance Theatre, Fevered Sleep, Ballet Boyz, and Newtons Ladder. Associate Artist, Northern Stage, 2018–20; National Strategic Partner, Sadler's Wells Theatre, London, from 2018 ongoing. **Awards and honours** include Jerwood Choreography Award, 2001; The Arts Foundation Choreography Award, 2005; MBE for Services to Dance, 2014.

Works

Shards (1993); *ROT* (1994); *Sextet* (1994); *9½ Minutes* (1994); *Critical Mass* (1994); *Sketch for New Work* (1995); *X (The X Factor)* (1995); *Albatross* (1995);

Axis (1995); *'Wounds Too Bleeding Flesh Where Angels Land'* (1996); *Precipice* (1996); *PassAge to Passion* (1996); *Flesh, Liquid, Bones* (1997); *Some Still Small Voice* (1997); *Octopus Hotel* (play, dir. Neil Murray, 1997); *Thief of Lives* (play, dir. Ed Robson, 1997); *Life Stories Dancing from the Heart* (1997); *Moments in Filigree* (1997); *Biopsy* (1997); *I Say Me, but I Could Say Man, Any Man?* (Tim Rubidge, 1998); *Uni-verse* (1998); *Threepenny Opera* (musical play by Bertolt Brecht, dir. Neil Murray, 1998); *Solo* (1999); *La Famille (2 versions)* (1999); *Ballet in Shriek* (2000); *Strange Glitter* (2000); *A L'instance de devenir* (2001); *Life Stories* (2001); *Into the Mouth of the Orchid* (2001); *Fractions* (2001); *The Ball* (2002); *I'm Forgetting You* (2002); *Street of Strangers* (play, 2002); *My North, My South, My East, My West* (2002); *Such Sweet Thunder* (2003); *The Ice Ball* (version of *The Ball*, Newcastle City's New Year's Eve Celebrations, 2003); *Non* (2003); *Tall Stories* (with Dodgy Cutch, 2003); *La Vie des Fantasmes Erotique & Esthetique* (2004, also an extract *Mercedes* 2004); *The Goodbye Rituals* (2004); *Luxuria* (2004); *Ferryman* (2005); *La Nuit intime* (2006, as *la nuit intime* 2009); *Propeller* (2006); *La Penumbra* (2006); *Tigers Bride* (play, dir. Neil Murray, 2006); *Angelmoth* (2006); *Tenderhook* (2007); *Stone, Paper, Scissors* (play, dir. Neil Murray, 2007); *Designer Body* (2008); *MaEternal* (2008); *The Bloody Chamber* (play, dir. Neil Murray, 2008); *Crush* (2009); *Peter Pan* (play, dir. Erica Whyman, 2009); *The Borrowers* (play, dir. Erica Whyman, 2010); *Blood, Sweat & Tears* (2010); *Underneath the Floorboards* (2011); *Rapunzel* (2012); *The Night Ball* (2013); *Snow White* (2015); *Love Struck* (2015); *Cyrano de Bergerac* (play, dir. Lorne Campbell, 2015); *Peter and the Wild Flowers* (2016); *Rumpelstiltskin* (2017); *Hope is a Thing with Feathers* (2017); *Great North Star* (2018); *After Dark* (2018); *Hold on Let Go* (play, 2019); *Sirin* (2019); *The Lost Happy Endings* (2019).

Further reading

Interviews: with Rosie McKenzie, 'I Was Inspired by the Rule-Breaking Women in Dance', blog.sadlerswells.com, 8 March 2018; James McGillivray, 'Giving Communities a Voice through Collaboration', *Animated*, Spring/ Summer 2019; Anna Winter, 'Liv Lorent', *The Stage*, 9 November 2019.

Articles: Paul R.W. Jackson, 'Of Ballet [boyz] and Spectacle', *Dance Now*, 15(3), Autumn 2006; Sanjoy Roy, 'balletLorent: Angelmoth Review', *The Guardian*, 26 February 2008; Ian Palmer, 'Blood Sweat and Tears', *Dancing Times*, 25 October 2010; Kristy Stott, 'Rapunzel', whatsonstage.com/salford-theatre/reviews, 27 April 2014; Sanjoy Roy, 'balletLorent: Rumpelstiltskin Review, Sensual Retelling of Grimm Fairytale', *The Guardian*, 1 April 2018.

RUSSELL MALIPHANT

Poised, elegant, poetic, thoughtful; these are some of the words critics use to describe the work of Russell Maliphant. They could apply equally to his own way of dancing. With a choreographic career that spans almost thirty years, preceded and paralleled by a career as a dancer, Maliphant is a staple of British dance. He works continually and understatedly, generally on small scale and minimalist productions, with notable exceptions such as *The Rodin Project* (2012). The power of his productions comes from elaborate integration of movement, music, and light.

Maliphant was born in Canada in 1961 and trained at The Royal Ballet School in London. He danced with Sadler's Wells Royal Ballet (1981–1988), leaving to perform with DV8, Michael Clark, Rosemary Butcher, and Laurie Booth. His studies of anatomy, physiology, and biomechanics, as well as training in the Rolf Method of Structural Integration (Rolfing), inform his choreographic work, which is also influenced by other practices such as ballet, contact improvisation, yoga, capoeira, and tai chi. An unlikely – but self-confessed – influence is the flow of the partnering work of British choreographer Sir Kenneth MacMillan, with whom Maliphant had the opportunity to work in Dance Advance, an independent venture he was part of just after his years at SWRB. From his work in DV8, with choreographer Lloyd Newson, he took interest in showing dancers 'as real people in all our complexities' (Maliphant, 2019). Through his work with Laurie Booth he learned 'about the use of space, working with a motif, repetition, energy, and focus' and also practised improvisation extensively (also 2019). His own company, Russell Maliphant Dance Company, has existed since 1996, but he also creates work for and with other artists and companies such as Sylvie Guillem, Robert Lepage, Isaac Julian, BalletBoyz, and Lyon Opera Ballet.

While there are clear influences from the people he has worked with, Maliphant has developed a particular style that is easily recognisable. It includes classical ballet elements such as line, *épaulement*, and head positions, but is also influenced by Body-Mind Centering in the use of breath, by Rolfing in the use of fascia and floorwork, and by contact (English National Ballet, 2018). He expands on this: 'Classical dance is traditionally lighter and more upwardly oriented, whilst contemporary is generally more oriented down, relating to the earth. I am trying to draw on and expand through that range' (Maliphant, 2019). Sanjoy Roy (2009) describes Maliphant's style as 'quite an amalgam', stating that he is 'an abstractionist' working 'with the physics of action and interaction', but insists 'it never feels forced; you can't see the seams'. There is a clear interdependence of movement with light and/or music, benefitted by his long-term collaborators, lighting designer Michael Hulls, costume designer Stevie Stewart, or composer Andy Cowton. Dana Fouras, performer, researcher, and collaborative assistant in the company, also occasionally creates or arranges music for his work. His choreographic approach is facilitated by an analytical approach to movement, which also allows him to work with other vocabularies, such as kathak with Aakash Odedra (*Cut* 2011) or hip-hop with Dickson Mbi (*The Rodin Project*; *Traces* in 2013).

Maliphant's choreographic career started in 1991 with his solo *Evolving Paradigm*. This initiated his trademark solo and duet works and his collaboration with Michael Hulls, whom he met when working with Booth. Soon he began choreographing slightly larger works on commission. With the foundation of his company, Maliphant began to develop a choreographic signature, starting with *Unspoken* (1996), the first full-length collaboration with Hulls. Some of his seminal works emerged from this moment: *Shift* (1996), *Two* (1997), or *Critical Mass* (1998) are examples of works which are still performed today. These early works showcase his attention to detail and his ability to choreograph a seamless flow of interaction, between light, music and movement, between the dancers, or both. At this point his work was noticed by William Trevitt and Michael Nunn, then George Piper Dances, now the world-famous BalletBoyz. Trevitt and Nunn were eager to dance *Critical Mass*, and managed, apparently after having to convince Maliphant (Parry, 2001). In 2001 they finally performed this piece, which was in turn noticed by ballet superstar Sylvie Guillem.

Her interest led to *Broken Fall* (2003), a choreography for the BalletBoyz and Guillem, and the beginning of a new series of works for Maliphant. *Push* was created in 2005. This evening of dance included new works as well, *Two* and *Shift*, the former a solo origi-nally created for Fouras in 1997, and the latter Maliphant's solo from 1996. The evening included a new solo for Guillem, and *Push*, a duet for Maliphant and Guillem. *Solo* is a nine-minute piece to Spanish music by Carlos Montoya. It exquisitely portrays Guillem's body and technique, and Maliphant's eye for choreographic grace, control, and powerful simplicity, with a flavour of Flamenco inspiration spicing them both. In *Push*, what emerges most clearly, and exemplified to transfixing lengths, is Maliphant's ability to choreograph seamless flowing partnerwork. For thirty-two minutes, to Cowton's music and Hulls' lighting, the spectator is lulled into bliss by the way both dancers work together in impossible, and impossibly light and nuanced, lifts. The production won a Time Out Award, Southbank Award, Olivier Award, and a Critics' Circle National Dance Award. Maliphant and Guillem continued their collaboration in *Eonnagata* (2009), a more the-atrical endeavour than Maliphant's usual work, with director Robert Lepage and costume designs by the late British designer Alexander

McQueen. While this collaboration was challenging for all involved, Maliphant encountered more narrative, more complex costumes and a faster creative period than he was accustomed to (Mackrell, 2009). Some of Maliphant's working signatures, such as his soft but powerful movement quality are identifiable, but the result was a mix between sword fighting, cross-dressing, kabuki theatre, dance, theatre, and martial arts which received equally mixed reviews.

One (1998) and Two are perhaps the clearest examples of Maliphant's studious approach: he has transformed the solos by staging them with two or three dancers, Two x Two (2001) and Two x Three (2003), or by building second parts as in One Part 2 (2002). Revisiting works keeps his approach grounded on analytical attention and exploration of choreographic possibilities, as well as allowing him to go deeper into the work through collaboration with different dancers. This is facilitated by use of video-editing software, which allows him to explore the material in depth, and to re-organise improvised material into choreographic sequences (Maliphant, 2019).

Talking about his long-term collaboration with Maliphant, Hulls explains that the detailed work of the choreographer is 'about the quality of the darkness', because you want to focus the spectator's attention (Moran, 2017). A stunning example of this was the work Afterlight (Part One) (2009), created on dancer Daniel Proietto and commissioned for a gala commemorating the centenary of the Ballets Russes at Sadler's Wells. Hulls, in conversation with Ismene Brown, states that the work is 'inspired by Nijinsky and the Ballets Russes', but is not about them (2009). This indicates a key feature of Maliphant's work: narrative is there, underlying the work, embedded in the interaction between the elements, but not obvious. Emotional aspects are embodied in the work itself. As British critic Luke Jennings observes: 'you don't have to know the story of Nijinsky's descent into schizophrenia to be profoundly moved' (2009).

Afterlight (Part One) is an exemplar of Maliphant's aesthetic and his process. From Nijinsky's poses and drawings, Maliphant developed the basic movement motif of the spiral, which was then embodied by Proietto through tasks concentrating on movement following the fascia. This results in a minimalist continuous hypnotic sequence of movements, structured in a circular fashion: starting very small, to cover the whole space, then finally returning to a small space. Hulls and Jan Urbanowski created an atmosphere of clouds turning around and on Proietto, through the light animation projected from above the stage. This follows the same spatial structure as the movement, and serves to hide and almost disjoint the dancer's body through the use of shadows. The return at the end is not quite to the same place, however. After seeing him freed and expansive around the open space, the audience sees Proietto despairing at being caged again, until he, like the lights, slows to fade away.

Maliphant turned *Afterlight* into a full-evening work, creating *Afterlight (Parts 2 & 3)* in 2010. *The Rodin Project* (2012), later adapted for film and re-titled *Erebus*, is a work partially about the sculptor's life, partially about Rodin's sculptures and how they portrayed the body. This follows Maliphant's now usual tension between narrative and abstraction. The 20th anniversary of the collaboration between Maliphant and Hulls was celebrated through *Conceal | Reveal* (2015), an evening including *Spiral Pass* (2014), *Broken Fall* (2003), *<<both and>>* (2015), and *Piece No. 43* (2015). All of these works exemplify the generative collaboration between these two artists and the inextricable nature of their contributions.

Since 2017, Maliphant Dance Company has produced seasons of work at the Print Room at The Coronet, West London. *Maliphantworks* – as these performances are titled – has already had three successful performances, the last one in February 2020. In *maliphantworks2*, a new duet, *Duet* (2018), between Maliphant and Fouras was presented, which demonstrates the established understanding between these artists. In other developments, Maliphant was appointed Guest Artistic Director 2019/2020 for the UK's National Youth Dance Company. He also collaborated with composer Vangelis to create *The Thread* (2019), a commission by Sadler's Wells, where Maliphant's masterful ability to sculpt space and bodies is both challenged and spiked by Greek folk dance, and by use of a much larger ensemble than is usual in his own productions. According to Sarah Crompton,

> [a]s the music thuds, [the dancers] sway, arms linked, before moving off like an endless snake ... winding around the stage. They travel so smoothly they look as if they are on wheels, but if you look closely you can see their feet are carving delicate, intricate steps.
>
> (2019)

This reimagining of folk dance, again in Crompton's words, is a link 'between past and present, moving and intense' (2019); it is also a testament to Maliphant's commitment to continuous exploration of the art form through cross-stylistic collaboration, and to his visual, almost magical, aesthetic. Also in 2019, his own company created *Silent Lines*, for which he returned to video animation, this time by Panagiotis Tomaras, to project 'ideas and images from inside the body ... to create spaces and textures within the stage environment ... [which are] manipulated by the dancers' movement' (Maliphant, 2019). Maliphant lets the audience see on stage the elements of his inspiration for movement ideas. For *maliphantworks3*, Maliphant, Fouras, and Tomaras also worked on another collaboration, *The Space Between* (2020).

Through an erudite approach to dance, Maliphant is able to conjure up magic on stage, collaborating to create beauty and atmosphere through light, music, and astounding possibilities of movement.

Lucia Piquero Alvarez

Biographical details

Born 18 November 1961, Ottawa, Canada; **Studied** ballet, tap, and modern dance at The Patricia Newman School of Dance; went to Royal Ballet School, 1977. Studied anatomy, physiology, biomechanics 1991–1994; Rolfing Method of Structural Integration 1994; contact improvisation, yoga, capoeira, and tai chi. **Career:** Danced for Sadler's Wells Royal Ballet, DV8 Physical Theatre, Michael Clark Company, Laurie Booth Company, Rosemary Butcher. Created work for other companies. Associate Artist Sadler's Wells 2005; Associate Artist Wycombe Swan; DanceEast Resident Company. **Awards and honours** include Time Out Awards 1991, 2006; Arts Council Fellowship, 2000; Time Out Live Award, and People's Choice Award, Festival de la Nouvelle Danse, Montreal, 2002; South Bank Show Dance Awards, 2003, 2006; Critics' Circle National Dance Awards, 2003, 2006, 2009, 2013; Olivier Award, 2006; Honorary Doctorate of Arts Plymouth University, 2011; South Bank Sky Award, 2015.

Works

Evolving Paradigm (1991); *Relative Shift* (1992); *Corpus Antagonus* (1994); *Paradigm* (1994); *Recoil* (1995); *Unspoken* (1996); *Shift* (1996); *Decoy Landscape* (1997); *Two* (1997); *Critical Mass* (1998); *One* (1998); *Liquid Reflex* (1998); *Knot* (2001); *Two x Two* (2001); *Sheer* (2001); *Trio* (2002); *Torsion* (2002); *Stream* (2002); *One Part 2* (2002); *Broken Fall* (2003); *Choice* (2003); *Two x Three* (2003); *Transmission* (2005); *PUSH* (2005); *Solo* (2005); *Flux* (2006); *Cast No Shadow* (*Small Boats* and *True North*, 2007); *Afterlight (Part One)* (2009); *Eonnagata* (2009); *Afterlight (Parts 2 & 3)* (2010); *The Rodin Project* (2012); *Fallen* (2013); *Spiral Pass* (2014); *Second Breath* (2014); *Here and After* (2015); *<<both and>>* (2015); *Piece No. 43* (2015); *Duet* (2018); *Other* (2018); *The Thread* (2019); *Silent Lines* (2019); *The Space Between* (2020).

Further reading

Interviews: with Laura Barnett, 'Portrait of the Artist: Russell Maliphant, Choreographer', *The Guardian*, 25 March 2008; Sarah Crompton, 'Dana

Fouras and Russell Maliphant: Back in Step', *The Guardian*, 6 September 2015; 'Lest We Forget: Russell Maliphant on Second Breath', *English National Ballet*, 18 July 2018; Lindsey Winship, 'Go with the Flow: The Mesmerising Moves of Russell Maliphant', *The Guardian*, 21 February 2019; Jennifer Jackson 'Russell Maliphant Shares His Inspiration for Silent Lines', *The Wonderful World of Dance*, 9 March 2019; Anna Winter, 'Choreographer Russell Maliphant: 'The Work is about Sensing the Body, that It's Pulsing with Blood''', *The Stage*, 9 April 2019; Karine Hetherington, 'Interview with Choreographer and Dancer Russell Maliphant', *artsmuselondon*, 20 January 2020.

Articles: Jann Parry, 'Ballet Boyz Just Want to Have Fun', *The Guardian*, 9 December 2001; Judith Mackrell, 'The Name's d'Eon. Chevalier d'Eon', *The Guardian*, 19 February 2009; Sanjoy Roy, 'Step-by-Step Guide to Dance: Russell Maliphant', *The Guardian*, 4 June 2009; Luke Jennings, 'In the Spirit of Diaghilev', *The Guardian*, 18 October 2009; Ismene Brown, 'Lighting Designer Michael Hulls. Olivier Award-Winning Genius with Light and Dance Explains His Art', *The Arts Desk*, 14 April 2014; Lyndsey Winship, 'Push/Sylvie Guillem & Russell Maliphant, Coliseum – Dance Review', *The Evening Standard*, 31 July 2014; Sarah Crompton, 'Russell Maliphant and Vangelis: The Thread Review – Reimagining Greece', *The Guardian*, 24 March 2019; Mark Monahan, 'Silent Lines, Russell Maliphant Dance Company, Sadler's Wells, Review: Like Watching Flesh-and-Blood CGI', *The Telegraph*, 19 October 2019; Mark Monahan, 'maliphantworks3, Coronet, London W11, Review: Light Entertainment in the Best Possible Way', *The Telegraph*, 7 February 2020.

Books: N. Stewart, *Choreography and Corporeality. Relay in Motion* (eds. Thomas DeFrantz and Philipa Rothfield), London, 2016; N. Moran, *The Right Light. Interviews with Contemporary Lighting Designers,* London, 2017; Russell Maliphant Dance Company, *Company Resource Pack*, 2019.

DADA MASILO

In *The Bitter End of Rosemary* (2011), Dada Masilo continued her interest in exploring Shakespeare's heroines, interrogating Ophelia's backstory. She wanted to give expression to Ophelia's madness, to reveal her extreme vulnerability and to highlight not the crazed babbling of a woman gone mad, but the lucid, articulate understanding of her situation. The work is infused with layers of music, song and fragments of speech that weave around each other. She begins with breath as her melody, and as a cry wracks her body, she turns to face the audience with a huge wire crucifix around her neck. It seems to drag her down and as she removes it, she starts to recite extracts from Ophelia's famous soliloquy. These are interspersed with a score created for her by Philip Miller. This startling solo indicates Masilo's fearless approach to performance and willingness to challenge expectations.

Masilo comes from Soweto (South Western Townships), established in the 1930s as part of the apartheid policy of separating black and white citizens under the Urban Areas Act (1923). Born there in 1985, Soweto had grown into a sprawling city near Johannesburg. In terms of framing her childhood and cultural influences, urban and imported traditional and rural dances coexisted and were performed and practised widely by a myriad of youth and cultural groups in Soweto. She began dancing traditional and township modern dance with an all-girl group called The Peacemakers in Meadowlands. They performed at The Dance Factory in Newtown, in 1996, as part of the Arts Alive Festival. Masilo encountered director Suzette le Sueur and was invited to join their Saturday youth training programme.

The apartheid government had created Provincial Arts Councils in the main cities in each province, where theatres housed companies solely dedicated to European art forms (ballets, operas, theatre productions and musicals) appealing to the tastes of white audiences. Eventually several artistic and cultural organisations arose in protest and developed alternative dance and theatre forms, often under dangerous circumstances. The Dance Factory was established at the Johannesburg City Hall in the late 1980s and then relocated to the Newtown Cultural Precinct in the early 1990s. Housed in a disused warehouse, it became an organisation dedicated to fostering and showcasing *all* forms of dance, in particular the nurturing of dance with a South African identity.

It was here that Masilo began formal training in ballet and contemporary dance in 1997, and throughout her school days at the state-funded National School of the Arts in Braamfontein, Johannesburg. She experienced a variety of forms, performing in works created by Soweto Dance Theatre's co-founder Jackie Mbuyiselwa Semela, Sello Pesa, Swedish choreographer Mari-Brolin Tani, contemporary dance pioneers PJ Sabbagha (The Forgotten Angle Theatre Collaborative FATC), and Gregory Vuyani Maqoma (Vuyani Dance Theatre).

During 2003, Masilo was a trainee at Jazzart Dance Theatre in Cape Town (under the leadership of Alfred Hinkel), after which she spent two and half years at the prestigious P.A.R.T.S. School in Brussels on a scholarship, before returning to South Africa. She stated: 'I wanted to dance. I learnt so much but found the intellectual and conceptual stuff limiting. There is more passion here, we can be more open'. She wanted to learn a new way of moving: 'I didn't go with the intention of being a choreographer ... But we had to do it there and I wanted to find something that would challenge me. I discovered the notion of fusion and this has become my obsession' (all quotations unless otherwise indicated, are from a personal interview with the author, 10 September 2019).

Fusion has become the hallmark of Masilo's work – she uses the classical aesthetic and its narratives, melding them into new forms with an African character and a feminist attitude. At the heart of her work lies her need to tackle pressing social issues which South Africans confront daily. Her first work, *Dying, Dying, Dead* (2006), a contemporary dance solo, was created as a tribute to her aunt who died from HIV/AIDS. Using Saint-Saëns' music from *The Dying Swan*, Masilo performs in a short white tutu, her upper body naked. The work sought to expose the degradation and despair that thousands of AIDS sufferers endured daily in South Africa. Thabo Mbeki, then President, had instituted a devastating policy of denying the existence of AIDS and refusing access to life-saving antiretroviral drugs. Ultimately, she used *Dying, Dying, Dead* to comment on the lonely deaths of ordinary people. This work evolved:

> Two years later, at the height of the Thabo Mbeki Aids denialism, *Dying, Dying, Dead* developed into a darkly elegiac trio danced in black. That work morphed again into *Swanicide*, the profoundly moving finale of *Swan Lake*, which premiered in 2010 after its initial incarnation [as] *Umfula Wa Ma Dada* (2009).
>
> (Adrienne Sichel, 'Mzansi Moves', *Independent Online*, 4 September 2012)

On being awarded the Standard Bank Young Artist for Dance in 2008, she created *Romeo and Juliet* with assistance from two of her artistic mentors, Sabbagha and Maqoma. The young ad hoc company of twelve, many of whom were trained at The Dance Factory with Masilo, became the hit of the National Arts Festival, Grahamstown (now Makhanda). Using Prokofiev's score, she drew on ballet and contemporary vocabularies, setting the work in Elizabethan times, with men in tights and doublets and women costumed in ballgowns and masks. This was fleshed out by the infusion of contractions, weighted energy, dynamic ensemble work, and intense spasmodic shuddering contrasting, with more lyrical and restrained moments. Reflecting modern ideas of love, deceit and betrayal, Masilo entered the realms of popular culture by making ballet accessible through her own African identity.

Masilo's trademark performance quality embodies movements performed at high speed and with breath-taking rhythmic complexity. Her performances have been described as electric, even extravagant. She is tiny. Her small frame belies her age and she is honed and muscular. She sports a 'chiskop', (shaved head), a look she has deliberately embraced as an act of defiance against the politics of ballet. This feature sits at odds with her enviable classical technique and often surprises people. She doesn't look like a conventional ballerina.

In a country where the dancing African body is always under scrutiny, Masilo has shaken up the classical canon, infusing a technique involving hyper-flexibility, challenging the pursuit of perfection and the stereotypical sylph-like body with a grounded African-ness. She chooses her dancers carefully, looking for quirky eccentricities, variety of body shape and an ability to create the material with her. She builds on their personalities, and rehearsal periods are intense. For *Carmen* (2009), Masilo stripped down the ballet vocabulary by intertwining flamenco and contemporary dance, shedding the romanticism and exposing a society wracked by sexual violence and the brutality of rape. The bold flamboyancy and thrusting of hips and pelvises brought street-wise Joburg moves into sharp focus. Here lies the power of her process and engagement with the classics; she has the knowledge, the technique, the clarity of vision to re-invent, cut, stitch together, and make something new that still retains its origins.

In addition to her dancers, Masilo also acknowledges the importance of her mentors and teachers whom she has drawn on during the making of her works such as Le Sueur, Dianne Richards (her first ballet teacher and former Principal Dancer with Festival Ballet, London), David Thatanelo April (a graduate of Moving Into Dance, Afrofusion expert, teacher and choreographer) and Sabbagha, whom she describes as her dad.

In 2010, aged 25, Masilo created her now-famous African version of *Swan Lake*, which premiered at the National Arts Festival and deals with issues of homophobia and the ravages of HIV/AIDS. She asked her young cast to interrogate issues around homosexuality and to listen to each other's stories: 'It's very important to hear what everyone is going through, e.g. homosexuality. It's so dangerous for gay men and women in South Africa; it's not even safe for them to catch taxis at night. We discuss a lot of things; my role is a facilitation of the process and personalities'. Masilo performed Odette, while Siegfried was portrayed as a homosexual who is only interested in a male Odile. She plays with the notions of concealing and revealing, referring to the erotic nature of ballet, and tips outdated gender roles on their heads.

In *Swan Lake*, the entire cast is costumed in white tutus, the men bare-chested. Masilo's choreography blends pointe work with rhythmically challenging indigenous dance forms such as mapantsula (township jive) and the workers' gumboot dancing. The cast is vocal, using voices and bodies, summoning traditional Zulu dance stamps, flipping their pelvises, rupturing the idealised nature of ballet: 'Masilo illuminates a common conception of white identity as being noted for its restraint, its silence, and its stiff upper-lip, compared with blackness as free, loud, social and vocal' (Steven Van Wyk, 'Ballet Blanc to Ballet Black: Performing Whiteness in Post-Apartheid South African Dance', in Sharon Friedman (ed.) *Post-Apartheid Dance: Many Bodies Many Voices Many Stories*, 2012). In the final scene, to music by Arvo Part, Masilo's company commits mass suicide, hence the reference to *Swanicide*, with the entire cast wearing floor-length black skirts and the women revealing their breasts.

Nudity is a key factor in much of Masilo's work, whereby she breaks a strict African taboo. For example, her mother refused to see her acclaimed solo *The Bitter End of Rosemary* because her daughter danced naked. 'Nudity is seen as such a negative thing in our communities especially amongst the older generation; it's not OK to even talk about nakedness' (Masilo interviewed by Tammy Ballantyne, *Business Day*, May 2011). For Masilo, it was the only way she could illustrate how society and religion place restrictions on women's bodies and perpetuate the culture of subservience and obedience. Her decision to dance naked highlights her desire to explore how differently she could move in space sans embellishments and expose Ophelia's defencelessness as she slides further into madness, and ultimately an escape from all inhibitions.

Masilo then began a rewarding collaboration with William Kentridge, which resulted in *Dancing with Dada* (2011) and *Refuse the Hour* (2012), which she performed in several European cities. Masilo revealed that after *Swan Lake,* she wanted to do something different, inhabit another space. Kentridge introduced her to highly conceptual, deeply aesthetic, and site-specific engagements in a visual arts way, as opposed to the pure theatricality of dance theatre. In *Refuse the Hour,* she was part of a cross-genre, collaborative team, and the large-scale work involved live music, projections, film, and dance. The multilayered, improvisational approach offered an important learning experience which she has applied to her own creative processes.

In 2017, she returned to the classics with a retelling of *Giselle* (2017). Her main concerns were the bringing out of different voices and characters on stage, not just Giselle's narrative. Here Myrtha is black, young, androgynous and gay and is portrayed as a sangoma (traditional healer); when Bathilde is in a rage she is deft with a sjambok (a long, stiff whip made of animal hide), the brutality and violence are visceral. The wilis are brought into a sharp, South African context as avenging African spirits of the underworld.

Masilo describes how she approached the use of African rituals and symbols:

> I had to sit with the elders and ask if Llewellyn (Myrtha) could use the fly-whisk (symbol of power and virility) if he's not a sangoma. It's about learning the rules and breaking them but not in an insensitive way. I asked Ann Masina (opera singer and performer) who is really a practising sangoma to watch my rehearsals – it's her voice you hear singing in the 2nd Act.

The score, by Philip Miller, references Adolphe Adams' original music but with African influences.

The traditional tale of betrayal of young love with its themes of lust, anger and revenge becomes a reflection of the brutal landscape of protests and strikes, of a people unwilling to keep forgiving, of the ever-increasing gap between rich and poor. By introducing colloquial vocabulary, Masilo frees up the strict classical form, giving the themes an African aesthetic.

In 2020 she will premiere *The Sacrifice*, based on Nijinsky's *The Rite of Spring* (1913), at The Joyce Theater, New York. Between continuing overseas tours of her major works, she has been workshopping the early stages of *The Sacrifice*, dealing with African rituals, particularly those around cleansing, tribalism and community.

She has asked Miller to compose the music, this time with three live musicians. The dancers have been trained by Tswana dance specialists, teaching the rhythms of the traditional dances of the Tswana-speaking peoples, and incorporating elements from the San, such as foot rattles, staccato stamping and clapping with outspread fingers.

Her commitment to shifting the boundaries in her movement vocabulary cements her influence alongside potent female dancer-choreographers such as Mamela Nyamza, Nelisiwe Xaba, Lliane Loots, Thandazile Radebe and Athena Mazarakis. Masilo has plunged into territories many have feared to interrogate; she embodies a bridge between her own history and context in a very troubled South Africa and stories that have been told and re-told for centuries. She summarises her choreographic vision succinctly: 'I want people to feel, I want people to come to the theatre and not watch a spectacle, I want them to leave feeling something … to see work that is visceral. It's easy to show off, but more difficult to bring people into your space'.

Tammy Ballantyne

Biographical details

Born in Soweto, Johannesburg, 21 February1985. **Studied** at The Dance Factory and The National School of the Arts, both in Johannesburg; Jazzart Dance Theatre, Cape Town, 2003; P.A.R.T.S., Brussels, 2004–2006. **Career:** danced and taught at The Dance Factory as a teenager; created first solo, 2006; from 2007–2011 she worked with The Forgotten Angle Theatre Collaborative performing in new works by Sabbagha such as *Macbeth, Back, Deep Night*; and experimenting with her own choreography, while touring and teaching; in 2008 began choreographing large-scale works which have toured internationally across Europe, USA, UK, and Canada since 2012; collaborated with William Kentridge on *Dancing with Dada* (2011) and *Refuse the Hour* (2012); has toured internationally to Europe, USA, and Australia; she performs in her own works and is Artist-in-Residence at The Dance Factory. **Awards** include a Gauteng MEC Award, at the FNB Dance Umbrella, 2005; Standard Bank Young Artist Award, 2008; South Africa Women in the Arts Mbokodo Award, 2015; Danza&Danza Award, 2017; the Prince Claus Next Generation Award, 2018.

Works

Dying, Dying, Dead (solo, 2006); *The World, My Butt and Other Big, Round Things* (2007); *I Just Want to Be a Princess for One Day* (2007); *Love and Other Four-Letter Words* (2007); *Romeo and Juliet* (2008); *Carmen* (2009); *Unravelling Carmen* (2009); *Umfula wa ma Dada* (2009); *Swan Lake* (2010); *Dancing with Dada* (coll. with William Kentridge, 2011); *The Bitter End of Rosemary* (solo, 2011); *Refuse the Hour* (coll. with William Kentridge, 2012); *Death and the Maidens* (2012); *Giselle* (2017); *The Sacrifice* (2020).

Further reading

Interviews: with Bongekile Macupe, 'Getting to Know: Dada Masilo', *The Sunday Independent*, Johannesburg, 9 September 2012; Kgomotso Moncho, 'Moved by Her Body's Emotions', *Mail and Guardian*, Johannesburg, 26 September 2014; Prince Claus Fund, 'Louder than Words with Dada Masilo', *YouTube*, 18 December 2018; Shirley Ahura, 'Interview with Dada', *lucywritersplatform*.com, 22 September 2019.

Articles: Adrienne Sichel, 'A Slow Dance with Death', *The Star Tonight*, Johannesburg, 25 July 2006; Matthew Partridge, 'Dancing with Dada', *Wanted* magazine, August 2011; Julie Crenn, 'Dada Masilo – Yinka Shonibare: Upending the Classics', *Seismopolite, Journal of Art and Politics*, 5, (seismopolite.com) 15 May 2013; Adrienne Sichel, 'Dada Masilo's Firecracker *Carmen* Turns Up the Heat', Johan Myburg's blog *Taadaa*, September 2014; Adrienne Sichel, 'Enigmatic Bodyscapes – Sampling South African Dance', *Critical Stages, The IATC Journal*, 13, June 2016; Roslyn Sulcas, 'Dada Masilo Turns Tchaikovsky on His Head in "Swan Lake"', *The New York Times*, 1 February 2016; Robyn Sassen, 'Quintessential Giselle in Masilo's Hands', *robynsassesnmyview.com*, 25 June 2017.

Books: Georgina Thompson (compiler) and Adrienne Sichel (ed.), *FNB Dance Umbrella 20 Years On*, Johannesburg, 2009; Fariba Derakhshani and Barbara Murray (eds.), *Prince Claus Fund Next Generation Laureate*, Amsterdam, 2018; Adrienne Sichel, *Body Politics: Fingerprinting South African Contemporary Dance*, Johannesburg, 2018; Jay Pather and Catherine Boulle (eds.), *Acts of Transgression Contemporary Live Art in South Africa*, Johannesburg, 2019; Kathrina Farrugia-Kriel, *The Oxford Handbook of Shakespeare and Dance* (eds. Lynsey McCulloch and Brandon Shaw), Oxford, OUP, 2019.

WAYNE MCGREGOR

McGregor's body of work prior to 2010 was well documented by Helena Hammond in the second edition of *50 Contemporary Choreographers*. This third edition concentrates on the huge diversity of work produced within the decade 2010–2020 with his cutting edge company Random Dance, considered his own physical laboratory, renamed Company Wayne McGregor in 2017; with The Royal Ballet at Covent Garden, London, where he has been Resident Choreographer since December 2006; and with other independent commissions, theatre and opera productions, film, television and music videos, site-specific work, and digital/online projects which are referenced as part of his prolific oeuvre.

In juxtaposing the sinuosity of contemporary dance to a fractured postmodernism, the early McGregor style was distinguished by its rattlesnake speed, flickering detail, and extreme and often distorted physical articulation. In it, you could see vestigial flashes of disco, techno, hip hop, and martial arts, as well as an echo of the work of poststructuralist choreographers like William Forsythe (Jennings, 'Wayne McGregor CBE: The rock star of ballet steps up', *The Observer*, 2 January 2011). From 1992, McGregor borrowed from every area of exploration and practice. Computer technology, film theory, architecture, medicine; nothing was too esoteric or obscure.

Take, for example, *FAR* (2010), which was inspired by Roy Porter's book *Flesh in the Age of Reason*, a history of 18th century explorations into body and soul. As David Jays details (*The Sunday Times*, 2010), the age of enlightenment, medical advances, and anatomical rigour brought radical philosophical inquiries into the mechanisms of thought and emotion. McGregor's approach was sympathetic to the idea that the mind cannot exist without the body, whilst flesh is animated by thought and feeling. But what did it look and feel like? Lisabel Ting describes classically clean lines that were pushed to the extreme, with splits extending way past 180 degrees, knees turned out, and shoulders almost popping out of sockets. Each dancer's limbs racing to get across the stage as fast as possible, without crashing into each other. The sheer unusual, alien quality of the movement made it fascinating to watch (*Straits Times*, Singapore, 15 October 2014).

McGregor is articulate. Increasingly fascinated by the field of cognitive theory and its application to choreography, he undertook research projects with scientists at Cambridge University, the Massachusetts Institute of Technology, and the University of San Diego. Audience and critical reactions were mixed. Sometimes the works were seen as perplexing or alienating, but many more celebrated McGregor's innovative style, and the awards and the commissions mounted. In the New Year's honours list, 2011, McGregor was awarded the CBE (Commander of the Order of the British Empire) for outstanding services to dance.

He is also prolific. In 2011 and 2012 he worked for the Paris Opera Ballet, and in London created *UNDANCE* (2011) with the artist Mark Wallinger at Sadler's Wells; he choreographed *Carbon Life* (2012) with the songwriter Mark Ronson for the Royal Ballet and directed Max Richter's new chamber opera *Sum* at the Linbury. He also devised and directed Big Dance for London's Olympic Games 2012. In interview with Debra Craine, (*The Sunday Times*, 15 June 2012) he expressed the rationale for his participation in Big Dance:

My background is working with young people and community groups, and I have a zealot's passion for encouraging creativity.... I only agreed to do it if it could be a creative project, I didn't want to do something where everyone learnt a single routine ... This has involved a whole range of teachers teaching dance over eight weeks with Hofesh Shechter and Kate Prince giving choreographic sessions. It is a skill-sharing exercise in which we are empowering groups to work creatively, to generate their own pieces. So it's 1,000 choreographers rather than 1,000 dancers. We have all age groups and all styles, from line dancing to Bollywood and hip-hop, and I want everyone to make something. Then I will work with their material, I will shape and recompose it to make a 45-minute piece that I would be happy to share with the world in Trafalgar Square.

An inveterate collaborator, McGregor has created startling onstage worlds with numerous composers, lighting and fashion designers, authors, dramaturgs, architects and film makers. His engagement with science is not tokenistic but serious long-term research, he and his dancers becoming lab subjects for neuroscientists, cardiologists and experimental psychologists.

By 2013, it was evident that collaboration had become the influence for a huge range of McGregor works. He created *Atomos* for Random Dance, where a cognitive scientist filmed and analysed the choreographic process in the studio, studying how the group communicated, interacted, memorised and made decisions. The work was structured through building up 'atoms' of dance material; in the studio, his Random dancers constantly engage with challenges to think of new ways of moving; his dance language is informed by a collaborative ingenuity and exploration, led by his own physical vision. He is leading a lab, not teaching steps; he sets creative tasks, observes the outcome, then modifies and reconstructs the material; he puts together solo material to create brief duets or trios that merge, exist in the moment and then dissolve.

Atomos opens with a sense of community under threat. The music, from ambient duo A Winged Victory for the Sullen, morphs through slow-moving harmonies. Judith Mackrell is clear that the scientific research never weighs down the sheer inventiveness of his extraordinary abstract choreography which links the dancers in circles, lines, and clusters, variations of a theme of communality. But it then starts breaking them up into single, heroic lines of movement – almost as preparation for the apocalyptic middle section, in which a fiery red light and footage of an exploding industrial plant dominate the stage. The final third feels like aftermath: a robotic section, in which the neon-lit dancers have the clipped, angular appearance of alien lifeforms, followed by a poignantly lyrical coda. So abstract is all this, Mackrell opines, that it's open to any interpretation – or none at all (*The Guardian*, 10 October 2013).

McGregor is excited by working in other media; opera, film, video, or installation. He made two music videos with Radiohead's Thom Yorke: *Lotus Flower* (2011), where the singer flails artfully in completely choreographed but inimitably Yorke style, and *Ingenue* (2013) for his Atoms for Peace supergroup. A 5-minute music video of *Ingenue* was released via YouTube on 28 February 2013, directed by Garth Jennings, choreographed by McGregor, performed by Thom Yorke with Random Dance's Fukiko Takase.

In August 2013, at the Roundhouse in London, Conrad Shawcross's installation *Timepiece*, with big steel structures, moving at different speeds, lights attached, cast huge shadows on the surrounding pillars.

McGregor created *Azimuth* with ten dancers performing singly or in groups, to complement and interact with the sculpture and light, taking their cues from its swinging, relentless pulse. As ever, it is a thought-provoking and intense piece of work.

He made *Borderlands* for the San Francisco Ballet in January 2013. Janice Berman (*San Francisco Classical Voice*, 30 January) wrote an affirmative review suggesting that McGregor's partnering all but defies description. The women are lifted and tossed with dangerous vigour. A woman is whirled and snapped around the shoulders of her partner, then pushed out to his side before, somehow, arriving between his feet. This move has a geometric, toothlike quality: all points and sharp edges. Often, though, after such a manoeuvre the dancers do something more balletically conventional with speed before returning to jutting hips, involuted legs, twists of the spine, arabesques beyond 180 degrees. Toward the end, a foursome faces the audience and the two dancers in the middle raise their eyes to the light in a rare suggestion that, just maybe, human vulnerability outstrips kinetic inevitability. Wendy Perron (*Dance Magazine*, 23 October 2013) interviewed McGregor about creating a collective imagination for the cast: 'We're inventing it together. I'm curious to see what they're feeling or thinking when they're watching or performing the work. Building that language gives you those anchor points that hopefully make the work more cohesive'.

Much has been written about McGregor's Resident Choreographer relationship with the Royal Ballet, particularly his first three works: *Chroma* (2006), *Infra* (2008), and *Limen* (2009). He is clear about his intentions:

> Both consciously and unconsciously my residency at the Royal Opera House (ROH) with The Royal Ballet has attempted to question assumptions about ballet; how it is made, what it communicates and how far one can explore the form in order to unleash a fresh perspective for the dancers, collaborators, and the audiences. I believe that although some … critics insist that there are specific formal rules that must be adhered to for new work to be valid, I have, in the spirit of restless curiosity, wanted to explore and test what these artificial boundaries are.
>
> (Butterworth and McGregor, 'Wayne McGregor: Thwarting Expectation at the Royal Ballet', *The Oxford Handbook of Contemporary Ballet*, 2021)

In *Live Fire Exercise* (2011), the key elements are Michael Tippett's richly textured *Fantasia Concertante on a Theme of Corelli* and a setting consisting of an artwork by John Gerrard. This takes a US military training exercise in the desert and transmutes it into a strange, slow-moving tableau of lorries crashing, a plume of flame rising from the explosion, stones rolling across the foreground. Although the image is of an African desert, it makes one think of Afghanistan and Iraq. It creates an alien landscape in which McGregor's six dancers, in Lucy Carter's half-light, grapple with the choreography of conflict, to suggest images of combat and its aftermath.

Carbon Life (2012), and *Machina* (2012) follow, and *Raven Girl* (2013), his first exploratory narrative work. *Woolf Works* (2015) was McGregor's first full-length production for The Royal Ballet, and he defied expectation by producing a triptych of three novels rather than one holistic narrative. Inspired by the life and chosen writings of Virginia Woolf, each of its acts is based on a novel – *Mrs Dalloway* (1925), *Orlando* (1928), *The Waves* (1931) –interspersed with autobiographical elements of Woolf's own life, her diaries/notes and recordings. McGregor's innovative, unconventional approach truly captures the essence of Woolf's modernist prose; each section offers a particular, distinctive style and aesthetic. His creative team included composer Max Richter, dramaturge Uzma Hameed, film artist Ravi Deepres, with set design by Ciguë and We Not I, lighting design by Lucy Carter, and costume design by Moritz Junge.

In the same year, *Tree of Codes* (2015) for the Manchester International Festival introduced more complex collaborations, where his company dancers joined forces with those from the Paris Opera Ballet. As Paul Vallely pronounced,

> it is fecund with human creativity.... it has a stunning succession of simple visualisations by the artist Olafur Eliasson, and a stark but highly evocative minimalist musical score from the remix artist-turned-composer Jamie xx.... With fluidity and deceptive ease the dancers shift through muscle-defying depictions of the geometry perceived by the human brain – the contours of the alphabet, the cubes and crystals of science – and on to create an allusive history of humankind in snapshot sequences.
>
> (*The Independent*, 5 July 2015)

The piece toured widely internationally where the different locations offered transformation for performers and audiences.

McGregor repeated the notion of combining dancers from two distinct companies in +/– *Human* (2017, with dancers from The Royal Ballet). +/– *Human*, an experiment with digital artists

Random International, performed at the Roundhouse. 'I've had it in my head for ages to do something with drones, although apparently we're not allowed to call them drones, they're autonomous flying objects'. They are diaphanous, spherical globes, a metre-and-a-half across: 'They fly very softly and elegantly, and they have algorithms based on swarming and flocking' (Lyndsey Winship, *Evening Standard,* 2 August 2017). He choreographed a short dance piece performed inside the installation with 15 dancers from his own company and the Royal Ballet. Visitors could watch the spheres from a distance – or walk in among them, interacting with the flying objects in a really beautiful, poetic way.

A major new work, *Autobiography,* premiered in October 2017 to celebrate the 25th anniversary of his own company. The work is far from a traditional autobiography; instead, the starting point is the sequencing of McGregor's own genome. The choreographer was interested in examining the body at a cellular level by sequencing his DNA. The experience has, however, made McGregor muse on life's bigger questions. 'It really made me think about mortality and immortality. The central question of what it is to be alive and why we want to extend life. What that made us do in the studio is to work much more sensorially than I would normally do' (Lyndsey Winship, 2 August 2017).

In *Living Archive: An AI Performance Experiment* (2019), McGregor collaborated with Google Arts & Culture engineers to develop an artificial intelligence-powered tool that creates original dance movement. The algorithm was trained using thousands of hours of video from the choreographer's previous works over 25 years. The technology also learned the distinctive way each of McGregor's company dancers moved. Cameras captured dancers' solos, detecting the forms of their individual poses, and then it provided suggestions for the next choreographic sequences, displaying them on screen like stick-figure avatars. The choreographer can then make choices. Every time *Autobiography* is shown, it is different, which is a huge challenge for the dancers. Nothing is fixed; it is organised in 23 chapters, following the pattern of chromosomes.

It is clear that building bridges to other disciplines and reaching out to creative individuals who are unused to working in dance has been a lifelong interest and vision for McGregor. No doubt in the next decade he will persist in pushing boundaries, challenging perceptions, questioning assumptions, experimenting and continuing his delight in making bodies misbehave.

Jo Butterworth

Biographical details

Born in Stockport, Cheshire, in 1970. **Studied** at Bretton Hall (University of Leeds) and the José Limon School, New York. **Career:** founded his company Random Dance while Choreographer in Residence at The Place, 1992; Random Dance became Resident Company at Sadler's Wells Theatre, London, 2002; AHRB/ACE Research Fellow in Cognition and Choreography, School of Experimental Psychology, University of Cambridge, 2003–4; Resident Choreographer at the Royal Ballet from 2006; the UK government's first Youth Dance Champion, 2008; Innovator in Residence at University of California, San Diego, 2009; choreographed for San Francisco Ballet, Stuttgart Ballet, NDT1, English National Ballet, La Scala Theatre Ballet, Paris Opera Ballet, Gothenburg Ballet, Ballet Zurich, Bolshoi Ballet, Boston Ballet, National Ballet of Canada, Alvin Ailey American Dance Theater, Rambert, Australian Ballet, Bayerisches Staatsballett, American Ballet Theater and New York City Ballet. **Awards and honours** include Arts Foundation Fellowship 1998; Time Out Awards 2001, 2003; IMZ Dance Screen Award 2002; Laurence Olivier Awards 2004, 2007, 2016; International Theatre Institute Award 2009; Prix Benois de Danse 2009; *Ballett Tanz* Choreographer of the Year 2009; Movimentos Award 2009; Excellence in International Dance, International Theatre Institute, 2009; Critics Circle Awards 2004, 2006, 2007, 2009, 2010, 2015; CBE (Commander of the Order of the British Empire) for outstanding services to dance, 2011; The Progress 1000 (Dance, London), 2011, 2012, 2013, 2014, 2015, 2018; Golden Mask Award, 2012; Dance Magazine Award, 2014; *The Sunday Times* Makers of the 21st Century, 2014; Helpmann Awards, 2014; Manchester Theatre Awards, 2015; Sense Award, 2015; Danza&Danza Magazine Award, 2018; D&AD Award, 2018; Gross Family Prize with Jlin for *Autobiography*, 2018; In 2017 Studio Wayne McGregor moved into newly created studio space at Here East, Queen Elizabeth Olympic Park. McGregor is Professor of Choreography at Trinity Laban Conservatoire of Music and Dance; awarded an Honorary Fellowship of the British Science Association, 2017; an Honorary Doctor of Science from Plymouth University, an Honorary Doctor of Letters from University of Leeds and in 2019, was made an Honorary Doctor from University of the Arts London and University of Chester; is part of the Circle of Cultural Fellows at King's College London.

Works

Xeno (1992); *Xeno 123* (1993); *9.7 Recurring 2% Black* (1994); *Artificial Intelligence* (1994); *Labrax* (1994); *Sever* (solo, 1994, as duet 1995); *AnArkos* (1995); *CeBit Dances* (1995); *For Bruising Archangel* (1995); *Jacob's Membrane* (1995); *Dragonfly* (1995, 2004); *Cyborg* (1995); *A Little Night Music* (theatre, 1995); *Slam* (1996); *Cybergeneration* (1996); *Vulture (Reverse Effect)* (1996); *Urban Savage* (1996); *8 Legs of the Devil* (1996); *Bent* (film, 1997); *Encoder* (1997); *Bach Suite* (1996); *Neurotransmission* (1997); *Skinned Prey* (1997); *x2* (1997); *Chameleon* (1997); *Black on White* (1997); *S.I.N.* (1995); *The Millennarium* (1997); *53 Bytes in a Movement* (1997); (1997); *A Trial by Video* (1998); *Angel*

(1998); *Medusa* (1996); *Intertense* (1998); *INTER:ACTION* (1998); *Sulphur 16* (1998); *Zero Hertz* (1999); *Equation* (1999); *Net/Work Narrative(s)* (2000); *The Field* (2000); *Telenoia* (2000); *A Fleur de Peau* (2000); *Aeon* (2000); *The Trilogy Installation* (live web cast of *The Millennarium, Sulphur 16, Aeon,* 2000); *Symbiont(s)* (2000, 2001); *Velociraptor* (2001); *Brainstate* (2001); *Detritus* (2001); *Codex* (2001); *Duo:Logue in Three Parts* (2001); *CastleScape* (2001); *HIVE* (2001); *Digit01* (2001); *11 Digital Mantras* (2001); *HoriZone* (film, 2001); *Nemesis* (2002); *Phase Space* (2002); *BodyScript* (2002); *Game of Halves* (2002); *L.O.V.E.* (2002); *PreSentient* (2002, 2019); *Chrysalis* (film, 2002); *Alpha* (2003); *2Human* (2003, 2009); *Nautilus* (2003); *Bio-Logical* (2003); *Binocular* (2003); *Xenathra* (2003); *Polar Sequences 3* (2003); *Qualia* (2003); *Series* (2004); *AtaXia* (2004); *Dance USA* (film, 2004); *Dice Life* (film, 2004); *Cloaca* (theatre, 2004); *Aladdin* (theatre, 2004); *The Woman in White* (theatre, 2004); *EDEN | EDEN* (2005); *Engram* (2005); *The Midsummer Marriage* (opera, 2005); *You Can Never Tell* (theatre, 2005); *Tremor* (film, 2005); *Amu* (2005, also as *Amu@Durham,* 2006), *Ossein* (2006); *Skindex* (2006); *Dido and Aeneas* (opera, 2006); *Much Ado about Nothing* (theatre, 2006); *Chroma* (2006, 2008, 2010, 2013, 2016); *Harry Potter and the Goblet of Fire* (feature film, 2005); *Erazor* (2006); *Genus* (2007, 2009); *[memeri]* (2007); *Kirikou et Karaba* (theatre, 2007); *Nimbus* (2007); *Proprius* (2008); *Infra* (2008, 2010, 2012, 2018); *Entity* (2008); *Renature* (2008); *Dyad 1909* (2009); *Dyad 1929* (2009, 2012, 2013); *Limen* (2009, 2011), *FAR* (2010); *Outlier* (2010); *Yantra* (2010); *UNDANCE* (2011); *L'Anatomie de la Sensation* (2011, 2015); *Twice Through the Heart* (Opera, 2011); *Carbon Life* (2012, 2016); *SUM* (Opera, 2012); *Machina* (2012); *Amber* (2012); *Big Dance* (2012); *Atomos* (2013); *Borderlands* (2013, 2014); *Azimuth* (2013); *Raven Girl* (2013, 2015); Gareth Pugh London Fashion Week (2014, 2017); *Tetractys – The Art of Fugue* (2014); *Kairos* (2014, 2015); *Alea Sands* (2015); *Closer* (Theatre, 2015); The Brit Awards (2015, 2016); *Tree of Codes* (2015); *Woolf Works* (2015, 2017); *Obsidian Tear* (2016, 2018); *Multiverse* (2016); *The Legend of Tarzan* (film 2016); *+/– Human* (2017); *Autobiography* (2017); *Autobiography Edits* (2017); *Atomos* film (2017); *Yugen* (2018); *AfteRite* (ABT 2018); *Bach Forms* (2018); *Fantastic Beasts: The Crimes of Grindelwald* (film 2018); *Mary Queen of Scots* (film 2018); *Sweet Charity* (Theatre, 2019); *Living Archive* (2019); *Orpheus and Eurydice* (Opera, 2019); *Inferno* (first act of *The Dante Project*) (2019).

Further Reading

Interviews: with Claudia Rocco, 'Action Star Learns Merits of Tenderness', *The New York Times,* 7 February 2010; Debra Craine, 'How Wayne McGregor Made the UK Dance', *The Times,* 15 June 2012; Wendy Perron, 'Wayne McGregor', *Dance Magazine,* 1 April 2013; Lyndsey Winship, 'Inside Choreographer Wayne McGregor's Brain', *London Evening Standard,* 17 September 2013; Alexandra Desvignes, 'In Conversation with Wayne McGregor', *Bachtrack,* 27 October 2014; Tom Brown, 'Transcript – Full Interview with Wayne McGregor', *Dance Journal HK,* 15 October 2015; Sven Schumann, 'Wayne McGregor on Being a Choreographer', *purple*

MAGAZINE, Issue 24, Winter 2015; Debra Craine, 'These Dancers Are Not Stupid. They Won't Do Whatever I Say', *The Times*, 21 October 2016; Ari Stein, 'Wayne McGregor: The Politics of Movement', *52-Insights.com*, 27 April 2017; Lyndsey Winship, 'Wayne McGregor on Mixing Dance with Drones and Creating a Show Inspired by His Own DNA', *London Evening Standard*, 2 August 2017; Claudia Pritchard, 'Wayne McGregor Interview: We All Have a Physical Story', *The i*, 7 August 2017; Ruaridh Nicoll, 'Wayne McGregor: 'Dancers Are no More Unfaithful than Other People', *The Observer*, 26 August 2017; David Jays, 'The Body is a Living Archive: Wayne McGregor on Turning His DNA into Dance', *The Guardian*, 3 October 2017; PORT Magazine, 'Mind and Body: Wayne McGregor', *PORT Magazine*, 6 September 2018; Nick Byrne, 'Wayne McGregor', *King Kong Magazine*, Issue 9, 2020; Andrey Bashtovy, 'Genetics and Minimalism: Choreographer Wayne McGregor Goes to Ukraine for the First Time', *The Village*, 6 March 2020.

Articles: Alan Blackwell, Scott deLahunta, Wayne McGregor, and John Warwicker, 'Transactables', *Performance Research: On the Page Issue*, Allsopp and Mount (eds), 9(2), 2004; Roslyn Sulcas, 'Wayne McGregor & Alexei Ratmansky Premieres, New York City Ballet', *The Arts Desk*, 16 May 2010; Scott deLahunta, Wayne McGregor, Philip Barnard, et al., 'Points in Mental Space: An Interdisciplinary Study of Imagery in Movement Creation', *Dance Research*, 29(2), 2011; Sarah Crompton, 'Undance: The Supergroup of Modern Dance', *The Telegraph*, 29 November 2011; Laura Thompson, 'London 2012: The Big Dance', *The Telegraph*, 13 July 2012; Wayne McGregor, 'Tips for Thinking Like a Dancer', *TEDBlog*, 14 September 2012; Sarah Crompton, 'Timepiece, Conrad Shawcross/Azimuth, Wayne McGregor, Review', *The Telegraph*, 10 August 2013; Judith Mackrell, 'Random Dance: Atomos Review', *The Guardian*, 10 October 2013; Wendy Perron, 'Wayne McGregor', *Dance Magazine*, 23 October 2013; Paul Vallely, 'Tree of Codes, Manchester Opera House, Review', *The Independent*, 5 July 2015; Judith Mackrell, 'Who's Afraid of Virginia Woolf? Not the Royal Ballet', *The Guardian*, 2 May 2015; Cedar Pasori, 'The Story Behind the Jamie xx-Scored Tree of Codes Ballet', *Fader*, 14 September 2015; Roslyn Sulcas, 'Review: "Obsidian Tear" Is a Choreographic Breakthrough for Wayne McGregor', *The New York Times*, 30 May 2016; Sarah Crompton, 'Steve Reich: Pas de deux', *The Sunday Times* 6 November 2016; Roslyn Sulcas, '"Can You Rotate That?" A Hyperkinetic Spin on "Rite of Spring"', *The New York Times*, 18 May 2018; Daphne Leprine-Ringuet, 'Google's Latest Experiment Teaches AI to Dance Like a Human', *WIRED*, 17 December 2018; Tanya Jayani Fernando, 'The Ekphrastic Body: Wayne McGregor's Woolf Works', *Dance Chronicle*, 42(2), 2019; Makeda Easter, 'Can Artificial Intelligence Become a Choreographer? Wayne McGregor Brings AI to L.A.', *Los Angeles Times*, 10 July 2019; Ada Bronowski, 'English National Opera in Collaboration with Studio Wayne McGregor: Orpheus and Eurydice', *The Wonderful World of Dance*, 14 October 2019.

Books: Steve Dixon and Barry Smith, *Digital Performance: A History of New Media in Theatre, Dance, Performance Art and Installation*, Cambridge, MA, 2007; Jo Butterworth and Liesbeth Wildschut, *Contemporary Choreography a Critical Reader*, London and NY, 2009; Ulrich Dietz, *The New New*, Distanz, 2010; Sarah Crompton, *Sadler's Wells – Dance House*, Oberon Books, 2013; Wayne McGregor, *Wayne McGregor Random Dance*, Silvana, 2014; Scott deLahunta and Philip Barnard, 'Seeing the 'Choreographic Mind': Three Analytic Lens to Probe and Notate Creative Thinking in Dance', in *The Neurocognition of Dance: Mind, Movement and Motor Skills* (eds. Bläsing, Puttke, and Schack), Abingdon, Oxfordshire, 2018; Jo Butterworth and Wayne McGregor, 'Wayne McGregor: Thwarting Expectation at the Royal Ballet', in *The Oxford Handbook of Contemporary Ballet* (eds. K. Farrugia-Kriel and J. Nunes Jensen), Oxford, Oxford University Press, 2021.

MOURAD MERZOUKI

Mourad Merzouki has been Director of the Centre Chorégraphique National de Créteil et du Val-de-Marne, France since 2009, and is today recognised as the choreographer who took hip-hop off the street and onto the stage. Merzouki describes himself as an acrobat using circus skills and a hip-hop breaker, even though he has rapidly blurred boundaries between those different schools to create his own choreographic style.

Born on 6 October 1973 in Lyon, France to Algerian-born parents, Mourad Merzouki grew up in Lyon's *banlieue*, a French suburb historically inhabited by immigrant families. Merzouki started to learn martial arts (karate and American box) and circus at the age of seven. When 15 years old he started to learn hip-hop and joined the breakers dancing on the forecourt of the Lyon Opera. Merzouki was part of this first generation of breakers in France, deeply influenced by the United States where the form started in the 1970s. According to Felicia McCarren, 'hip hop dance forms arrived in France in the early 1980s and were taken up first in suburban and immigrant communities, becoming a forum for debate on assimilation and multiculturalism' (*French Moves*, 2013: xii). During its first decade in France, hip-hop was mostly associated with its dancers' socio-demographic characteristics, the difficulties of their social situation, and the extreme body language they created as a response to their living conditions. Later, the French press (*Le Monde, Libération*) played an important role in changing the status of hip hop, evolving from a dance of social inclusion to a dance considered and appreciated for its artistic qualities and technical prowess.

In 1989, Mourad Merzouki created the hip-hop company Accrorap with his friends Kader Attou, Eric Mezino, and Saïd Chaouki. Their 1994 show *Athina*, that premiered during the Lyon Dance Biennial, helped transpose hip-hop dance from street to stage and gain institutional validation. It is no surprise that almost twenty years later, Merzouki was invited to be the Associate Choreographer of the 2012 prestigious *Montpellier Danse* festival. In a promotional interview, Merzouki mentioned the importance of such an invitation for someone who was not trained in a traditional conservatory of dance. For him, this invitation was an effort from the institution to promote the aesthetic diversity of 21st century dances and the importance of blurring the limits of his own school. Yet, he challenged the theme of that year's festival, Mediterranean, in order to go beyond the amalgam between hip-hop and North African culture. 'Hip-hop is not only about the Mediterranean. Yes, most of the hip-hop dancers are of immigrant descent, like me. And some come from the Mediterranean. But not only. We can't forget the ones from Asia, South Africa and other parts of the globe' (author's translation from interview, 2012). Merzouki insists on how hip hop is an art that facilitates conversations at a global level. For him, the Mediterranean has to be rethought through the diversity that is at the core of contemporary hip hop.

Agwa (2008) is a good example of this quest to challenge movement traditions and the cultural and racial discourses attached to them. Performed by 11 male dancers from Rio de Janeiro, *Agwa* addresses the issue of clean water accessibility, mass productions, and use of plastic in Third World countries. Plastic cups, raincoats, and gumboots are among the props used as creative constraints. In one scene, dozens of plastic cups are aligned on the ground, challenging the dancers as they try to navigate amongst them. These plastic cups give a dramaturgic purpose that adds sound and rhythm to the dance. Another scene shows the dancers wearing gumboots, which became a political accessory as originated in South African gold mines where codified taps were used by black miners deprived of conversation. Yet, this piece based on water also reveals how fluidity and liquidity are part of Merzouki's conception of dance. *Agwa* mixes hip hop with capoeira, samba, bossa, and electro music and values the variety of influences within Brazilian culture. Similarly, in *Yo Gee Ti* (2012) ('organic' in Mandarin), Taiwanese and French dancers confront their traditions, mingling hip-hop with contemporary dance, traditional Taiwanese dance and classical ballet. When asked about the challenge of working with Taiwanese dancers without being able to communicate in

Mandarin with them, Merzouki answers: 'No need to have an alphabet to communicate. Dance is our form of communication' (author's translation from interview, 2014).

This desire to challenge his own genre has been visible since the beginning of his dancer's career when Merzouki worked with contemporary choreographers based in France, first with Maryse Delente in *Choré-couleurs* (1991), then with Jean-François Duroure in two pieces: *Le savoir vivre* and *La nuit partagée* (1992–1993). His collaboration with Josef Nadj in 1993 was cut short because of the repercussions of the war in the former Yugoslavia. These choreographers are among a long list (Gallotta, Montalvo, etc.) to be inspired by and collaborate with hip-hop dancers. Influenced by his work with these choreographers, he imagined and designed in 2009 a new place of creation in Bron, France: the Centre Chorégraphique Pôle Pik. This space is dedicated to the encounter of hip-hop with other performance arts (theatre, dance, music, circus, magic and puppetry), and to choreographic development. A few years later (2013), he created the hip-hop festival Kalypso based in Ile-de-France, which became an artistic stepping-stone, highlighting hip-hop dance as a constantly evolving art form.

Merzouki's recent works move beyond a dance of integration performed by *banlieue* artists to explore new connections between dance and other mediums. *Pixel* is a 2015 piece that uses a high-tech production, rich in different technologies, in which Merzouki worked closely with two digital French artists, Claire Bardainne and Adrien Mondot. Together, they complexified dancers' relationship to time and space, using illusion and *trompe l'oeil* techniques to challenge both physical and symbolic perceptions. Limits between virtual and reality are blurred, creating a dream-like atmosphere where virtual pixels (made visible on stage by interactive technologies) create new forms of architectures. Dancers interact directly with the digital installations: dancers' movements are amplified by the virtual space when the dots move apart in response to the dancer's motions; the dots expand the movements or challenge them. Such a technological level put at the service of dances traditionally associated with economic and social poverty reflects the broader political project of this artist. In addition, *Pixel* premiered shortly after the *Charlie Hebdo* attacks. This timing had a significant impact on the reception of this piece.

> Far from the negative media images of North Africans, far from the media coverage of young French men and women engaged in jihad, and yet – unfortunately – somewhat close to them in the

public imagination, this hip-hop uses new technology to create and diffuse a space of integration and community.

(McCarren, 2018)

By using abstraction, Merzouki makes minorities visible and challenges anti-Muslim media discourses. Another recent piece that explores new connections with other mediums is *Folia* (2018). Inspired by 17th and 18th century Neapolitan tarantella and virtuoso folias, Merzouki confronts acrobats and hip-hop performers with contemporary and ballet dancers (two of them using pointes) with the addition of a whirling dervish who concludes the show. In *Folia*, Merzouki also decompartmentalises music by mixing baroque and electronic music through live musicians and one opera singer. Conducted by the artistic director of Le Concert de l'Hostel Dieu, Franck-Emmanuel Comte, *Folia* emphasises more than ever the plurality of choreographic and musical languages, creating a new standard embedded in *métissage*.

Merzouki is recognized today as a choreographer who did not hesitate to take some distance from *banlieue* stereotypes and biographical elements expected from second-generation immigrants. Looking back over Merzouki's almost thirty-year career, we can appreciate how he keeps pushing the limits of hip hop further by confronting it with other genres, mediums, and traditions. The very fact that Mourad Merzouki is present in this edition of *Fifty Contemporary Choreographers* shows not only how his work is recognised beyond hip hop, but it also shows how much contemporary dance was transformed and reshaped by hip-hop artists such as Mourad Merzouki.

Lucille Toth

Biographical details

Born on 6 October 1973 in Lyon, France to Algerian-born parents. **Studied** martial arts and circus at the age of seven and starts hip hop at 15. **Career**: Danced with Maryse Delente, Jean-François Duroure, and Josef Nadj; began creating work in 1989 with Accrorap company he co-created with Kader Attou, Eric Mezino, and Chaouki Saïd; founded Compagnie Käfig in 1996. Director of Centre Chorégraphique National de Créteil et du Val-de-Marne since 2009; created the Centre chorégraphique Pôle Pik in 2009; created hip-hop festival Kalypso in 2013. **Awards and honours** include Author of the message of the 32nd International Dance Day under the aegis of UNESCO, 2014; Medal of Honor from the City of Lyon, 2013; Officer in the Order of Arts and Letters, Promotion by the Minister of Culture and Communication Frédéric Mitterrand, 2011; Creators Without Borders Trophy 2008, awarded by the Minister of Foreign and European Affairs, Bernard Kouchner, 2008; Culture

Enlightenment Trophy in the Dance category, awarded by Le Progrès and Télé Lyon Métropole, 2006; Prix Nouveau Talent Chorégraphique, awarded by the SACD, 2006; Knight of Arts and Letters, appointment by the Minister of Culture and Communication Renaud Donnedieu de Vabres, 2004; Prize for Best Young Choreographer at the Wolfsburg International Dance Festival, 2004.

Works

Athina (1994); *Käfig* (1996); *Génération Hip-Hop* (1997); *Rendez-vous* (1997); *Récital* (1998); *Pas à Pas* (2000); *Le Cabaret urbain* (2000); *Dix Versions* (2001); *Le Chêne et le Roseau* (2002); *Mekech Mouchkin – Y'a pas de problème* (2003); *Corps est graphique* (2003); *La Cuisine* (2004); *L'adapté* (2005); *Terrain Vague* (2006); *Tricôté* (2008); *Agwa* (2008); *iD* (2009); *Des chaussées* (2009); *Correria* (2010); *Boxe boxe* (2010); *Yo Gee Ti* (2012); *Käfig Brasil* (2012); *Pixel* (2014); *7Steps* (2014); *Cartes Blanches* (2016); *Boxe boxe Brasil* (2017); *Récital Colombie* (2017); *Danser Casa* (2018); *Folia* (2018); *Vertikal* (2018).

Further reading

Interviews: with Rosita Boisseau in *Panorama de la danse contemporaine. 90 chorégraphes*, Paris, 2006; 'La culture pour tous passe aussi par l'exigence pour tous', *www.lestroiscoups.com*, 18 September 2009.

Articles: Anna Kisselgoff, 'Dance Review: Hip-Hop Head-Spinning, but with a French Twist', *The New York Times*, 16 May 2002; Marie-Christine Vernay, 'Mourad Merzouki: Fédérer les énergies', *Libération*, 30 November 2009; Laure Cappelle, 'Mourad Merzouki, the Ambassador of French Hip-Hop', *Financial Times*, 21 March 2014; Laure Cappelle, 'Lyon Dance Biennial, France – Review', *Financial Times*, 15 September 2014; Laure Cappelle, 'Raw Talent on Show at France's Kalypso Hip-Hop Dance Festival', *Financial Times*, 1 November 2016.

Books: Claudine Moïse, *Danseurs du défi. Rencontre avec le hiphop*, Arles, Indigène Editions, 1999; Roberta Shapiro, 'La danse à l'envers', in V. Nahoum-Grappe, O. Vincent (dir.), *Le goût des belles choses. Ethnologie de la relation esthétique*, Paris, 2004; Rosita Boisseau, *Panorama de la danse contemporaine. 90 chorégraphes*, Paris, 2006; Felicia McCarren, *French Moves. The Cultural Politics of Le Hip Hop*, London and NY, 2013; Felicia McCarren, 'Minority Visibility and Hip-Hop Choreography', in *Contemporary Choreography, A Critical Reader*. 2nd ed. (eds. Butterworth and Wildschut), London and NY, 2018; *Petit Larousse Illustré 2019*, French and European Publications Inc., 2018.

ROCÍO MOLINA

Flamenco dancing has a rich cultural and technical history; recent associations with dance tourism belie the serious body of scholarship generated in the field of *flamencology*. Debates rage about purity of form, authenticity and ethnic origins. Within this contested arena an influential new type of *bailaora* has emerged: Rocío Molina. An avant-garde provocateur and experimental choreographer, Molina provokes both uproar and admiration. By building upon the style of *Flamenco Nuevo* popularised by Joaquín Cortés and Sara Baras, Molina is a commanding performer and choreographer open to a wide range of artistic influences. Her charisma chimes with the traditional Flamenco pantheon of 'great artists' who exert a hypnotic power. At 26, she received Spain's National Dance Prize. Molina presents herself within the framework of traditional flamenco references while simultaneously challenging presumptions, broadening flamenco's openness to other art forms, aesthetic references, movement vocabularies, gender norms, and their political implications. Molina states: 'I am not trying to innovate. I just want to be myself' (Cappelle, 2017). As an openly gay woman this 'self' is a challenge to the Flamenco establishment. Throughout her career she has returned to themes of transformation, identity and the performativity of self-hood.

Born in Malaga in 1984, Molina's mother was a ballet dancer, and she began dance training at age three. While studying at the Royal Dance Conservatory in Madrid, she was exposed to a range of dance styles including folk dance, ballet and *escuela bolero*. Molina was precocious. By 12, she had appeared on national television demonstrating an accomplished technique, confidence and charisma beyond her years (Canal Sur, 1996). Once graduated, Molina performed internationally in ensemble flamenco companies and began to choreograph. She is seldom alone on stage, often joined by musicians and singers or other dancers. Nonetheless, her choreographic practice is clearly focused on her role as soloist, tailored to her body's capabilities and preferences. Alastair Macaulay (2010) describes her distinctive qualities:

> Every part of her body dances, often within the same phrase, as if in ricochets and crosscurrents, and she amalgamates melting softness with academic rigor, so that her most startlingly experimental moves look classical. Frequently she moves limbs and torso so as to oppose sharp angles with curved lines.

Whether performing in a bull-ring, with her ruffled *traje de flamenco* trailing in the dust of her aggressive footwork, or in black leggings and bare feet, she is virtuosic performer. Traditional technique is displayed with astonishing speed: her tightly held upper body, sharp staccato foot and heel work (*zapateado* and *taconeo*) are combined with hand clapping, thigh slapping and finger snapping, enabling her whole body to become percussive and reverberate with rhythm. *Entre paredes* (2006) was her first choreographic work and in 2008 *Oro viejo* received critical acclaim, with many traditional elements of *ópera Flamenco:* red and black gypsy dress, onstage musicians, singers, guitarists, and two supporting male dancers. This trio masterfully performs classical flamenco vocabulary with drilled synchronicity. Yet Molina plays with the boundaries of *ópera Flamenco*; for a moment her male dancers passionately dance together, a forewarning of the provocative choreographic voice taking aim at traditional Flamenco stereotypes. Reinforcing this, an additional movement quality emerges in transitional moments: a pose inspired by Michael Jackson, a contemporary contraction, a flowing balletic arm. In her small mincing steps, swinging her fan like a pendulum, humour also surfaces. This playful, ironic tone will become a characteristic quality of her choreography.

Molina is conscious of her body as it strains at the bounds of tradition. She states: 'I felt early on that my body was forcing me to leave traditional flamenco codes behind' (in Cappelle, 2017). Aiding this departure, in 2009 Molina's partnership with theatre director Carlos Marquerie signalled a creative turning point, 'an entirely new approach' (in Zellinger, 2017). This led to a theatrical and conceptual turn in Molina's artistic practice and an increase in dramatic ambition. *Cuando las piedras vuelen* (2009) emphasised a new athleticism, aesthetics of the everyday, and symbolic theatricality: footwork is literally spotlighted and framed as she dances in red shoes inside a small box. An opening film shows Molina lying on white stones in black bra and briefs; later her singers crouch, beating these white stones with white tap shoes. Molina, dressed in sweater and leggings, swivels on a bar stool, her bare feet dancing as she rotates behind them.

In 2010, *Danzaora* brought new emphasis on theatricality, culminating in a wine glass being crushed under foot; while a companion piece *Vinática* (2010) develops a theme of personal metamorphosis. Here, dressed in black, Molina dances with her back to the audience, long braided hair swinging, she faces a chalked body outline that she begins to attack like a punching bag. Angular backbends performed in profile, followed by isolated, circular arm movements seem mechanical and modernist rather than a traditional *braceo* (circular movement of the arms). Desultory wandering and standing still with her arms crossed puncture sequences of classical flamenco shapes and patterns, sculptured poses fall away into everyday movements as she allows her arms to swing loosely in parallel. What began stylistically as a mix of theatrical, flamenco, and everyday fashion in *Cuando las piedras vuelen* becomes movement vocabulary in *Danzaora* and *Vinática*.

Bosque Ardora (2014) marks a further increase in dramatic ambition. Set in scenery of live trees, Molina explores an ambitious range of thematic, movement, and visual references. Beginning with slow crouching movements in a fox's mask, she experiments with dramatic use of silence and slow-motion actions which punctuate speedy footwork variations. As she snakes across the stage accompanied by a melancholic trombone, a hypnotic focus and slow-motion gestures make her hands look like gnarled tree roots and echo vocabularies found in Japanese butoh. Later, slinking hips and stilettos evoke images of midnight cabaret and jazz clubs. *Bosque Ardora* breaks away from the tradition of the virtuoso flamenco soloist supported by backing dancers, and Molina crafts some carefully choreographed interactions. Partnered by two male dancers, Molina transforms from Artemis, into a fox, a witch, burlesque dancer and dominatrix as she straddles her male partners in a Darwinian game of survival, alternating between hunter and prey. Explicitly inspired by Pina Bausch, a key innovator of German *Tanztheater*, *Bosque Ardora* clearly absorbs a Bausch-inspired blend of drama, symbolic scenery, humour, the quotidian, interrogation of gender roles, and an overarching sense that movement is motivated by strongly felt emotion and memory.

While *Tanztheater* may seem an unusual Flamenco bedfellow, both traditions emphasise feeling, emotion and improvisation as key to dance's experimental energy and power. Flamenco improvisation builds on the concept of *Duende,* a Spanish term for a heightened state of emotion, expression, and authenticity, and is integral to Molina's choreographic process. Emilio Belmonte's 2017 documentary follows Molina as she performs a series of public improvisations (*Impulso*) which double as public interactions. A range of settings enrich Molina's choreographic imagination: public streets, prisons, manicured gardens, nightclubs and ancient ruins. Lengthy and gruelling, her intense, trance-like concentration is interrupted as members of the public hand her items to shape her unfolding performance – a cigarette, wine-bottle, walking stick or text-message. Molina draws from a Flamenco tradition of ecstatic improvisation, but is keen to remove its mystical connotations. Molina self-consciously displays her labour, struggle, and sheer physical effort: when her *Impulso* is filmed she encourages the camera lens to zoom in on the sweat as it rolls down her face.

Belmonte's documentary followed Molina as she created *Caida del Cello* (2016) while artistic associate of Chaillot National Theatre, Paris. In an *Impulso* recorded in 2015, she uses her long voluminous taffeta skirt to become an abstract sculpture: as the skirt completely envelops her she stomps, extending one arm from material folds. She wraps the skirt around her legs to become pantaloons, she holds the hem in her mouth, she flexes her arm muscles in the pose of bodybuilder and stutters across the floor in tiny steps, swinging her arms like a mis-behaving, mechanised puppet. *Caída del Cielo* developed from these sessions, and with a willingness to use everyday gesture and weighty, earth-bound movements, it reflects contemporary dance, conceptual, and performance art worlds. Molina also dances barefoot and performs a striptease, shedding her traditional white dress to face the audience in quiet stillness. This is her most overtly sexual piece to date: she wears bondage gear, leather thongs, and plastic skirts. The reference to falling (*Caída*) in her piece's title is more than nominal; *falling away* from classical flamenco structures is embodied in her curving, crum-bling upper-back and bare feet. She *falls apart* as she drags her limp body across the stage leaving a trail of red blood. Even then, rhythm is irresistible, and she starts tapping the floor; this instinctual desire to turn the world into something percussive is the motivation that brings Molina upright into another virtuosic variation. In doing so Molina creates a 'kind of carnal, poetic dramaturgy' (Newman, 2017).

The human voice is integral to Flamenco from the singing of tradi-tional songs to the raucous *jaleo* (shouts of encouragement) of onstage musicians and audience. Molina's increasing use of the spoken word builds on this tradition while using it to comment on issues such as identity, gender, sexuality and flamenco itself. In a 2014 *Intermezzo* performed at the Flamenco Biennale, Molina whispers 'chiribi, chir-ibi' to the singer Rosario La Tremendita, and this exchange becomes a dramatised form of extended conversation addressing the audience. This is further developed in Molina's 2017 TedX talk *Soy impura, soy danzaora, (I'm impure, I'm a dancer)* (September, Madrid, 2017). She pulls a cue card from her simple black shirt dress only to throw it to one side and perform a rapid footwork sequence, ending as she draws a leg slowly upwards into a balletic balance. Falling out of this pose, she saunters across the stage addressing the audience in conversational tones and everyday gestures. She works through a series of mini-mon-ologues, interspersed with dance sequences, including speed-skating arm circuits and comedic falls: when she falls on her back, legs splayed above, she pauses, stretching and flexing her ankles in circles before flipping onto her stomach and addressing the audience again.

In *Grito Pelao* (2018), Molina develops this theatrical dialogue and transforms the personal experience of pregnancy into performance. The piece documents her decision to have a child through artificial insemination: only performed during the first seven months of her pregnancy, its performative duration aligns with Molina's physical journey. Bathed in delicate sinuous lighting resembling a web of bodily tissue, *Grito Pelao* is a series of passionate and tender duets between Molina, the singer Sílvia Pérez Cruz and her mother, Lola Cruz. Molina and Pérez Cruz's duet builds a passionate physical intimacy, the latter wraps herself around Molina, guiding her arms as she sings, and they writhe together as one body on the floor. In contrast, when Molina dances with her mother Lola Cruz, they mirror each other, and she holds her as though she is made of glass, emphasising intergenerational, maternal protectiveness. As such, Molina continues the move away from traditional Flamenco synchronisation. Throughout *Grito Pelao*, Molina's swollen belly is exposed over the lowered waistband of her flamenco skirt embodying her stated aim to 'deconstruct this flamenco image of a supernatural body' (Cappelle, 2017). Molina's voice becomes increasingly strident in *Grito Pelao,* turning into 'a feminist scream, an elemental cri de coeur' (Luke Jennings, 2017).

Molina continues her vision of taking the essence of Flamenco, making it new. She takes pride in the fact that Flamenco has always included powerful women: 'There's no code to say a woman can't lift a man or grab him, like I do in my new work. That gives you courage to do what you want, to be authentic to yourself' (in Mackrell, 2014). By mining this history and reconfiguring it into relevant contemporary shapes that explicitly address the politics of identity through spoken word, aesthetic reference, and movement vocabulary, Rocío Molina continues to forge an avant-garde path.

Erin Whitcroft

Biographical details

Born in Malaga in 1984. **Studied** at the Royal Dance Conservatory, Madrid. **Career:** performed with flamenco's leading figures, including: María Pagés, Miguel Poveda, Antonio Canales, and Israel Galván. Aged 17, made her London debut at the annual Sadler's Wells Theatre's Flamenco Festival; performed internationally: including Europe, New York, Singapore, Seoul, Moscow, Taiwan. Associate of the Chaillot National Theater, Paris, 2014–2015; worked with choreographer and hip-hop dancer Honji Wang and Sébastien Ramirez to create *Felahikum*. Collaborations with the contemporary art world, include Carlos Marquerie, Mateo Feijóo, and Jean Paul Goude, with whom she designed a project for the brand Hermes, Shanghai, 2017. **Awards and honours** include Giraldillo Awards (2008, 2016); Best Dancer Award, Seville Biennial (2008); Critics Choice Prize (2009); Spanish National Award for Dance (2010); Gold Medal awarded by the Province of Malaga

(2011); Province of Malaga, Max Awards (2015, 2017, 2019); British National Dance Awards (2016, 2019).

Works

Entre Paredes [Among the Walls] (2006); *El Eterno Retorno* [The Eternal Return] (2006); *Turquesa como el limón* [Turquoise as a Lemon] (2006); *Almario* (2007); *Por el decir de la gente* [As People Say] (2007); *Oro viejo* [Old Gold] (2008); *Cuando las piedras vuelen* [When Stones Fly] (2009); *Vinática* (2010); *Danzaora y vinática* (2011); *Afectos* (2012); *Bosque Ardora* (2014); *Impulso* (2015, 2016, 2017, 2019); *Felahikum* (co-choreographed 2015); *Caída del Cielo* [Fallen from Heaven] (2016); *Impulso: Rocío Molina vs. Storyboard P.* (2016); project for Hermes (with Jean Paul Goude, 2017); *Grito Pelao* (2018).

Further reading

(see also the company website rociomolina.net)

Interviews: with Sonia Martínez Pariente, 'Interview with Rocío Molina. Flamenco Dancer', *deflamenco.com*, 4 January 2008; Judith Mackrell, 'Rocío Molina: Flamenco and Beyond', *The Guardian*, 15 October 2014; Lyndsey Winship, 'Rocío Molina Reinvents Flamenco', *The Economist*, 31 August 2017; Ezekiel Oliveira, 'Rocío Molina: "My Work is Intuitive"', *Five Lines: A Contemporary Dance Initiative*, 3 October 2017; Laura Cappelle, 'Flamenco with an Individual Stamp', *The Financial Times*, 11 October 2017; Susanne Zellinger, 'Indomitable', *Tanz im August*, 5 January 2017; *Impulso* (film, 2017); Justine Bayod Espoz, 'Why Rocío Molina Will Only Perform Her Latest Work While She's Pregnant', *Dance Magazine*, 15 October 2018.

Articles: Alastair Macaulay, 'Leading the Audience into Flamenco's Heart', *New York Times*, 25 June 2009; Julio Bravo, 'Baryshnikov at the Feet of Rocío Molina', *ABC Culture*, 14 February 2010; Alastair Macaulay, 'A Passionate Tradition is Made Livelier through Irreverence', *The New York Times*, 15 February, 2010; Judith Mackrell, 'Rocío Molina: Bosque Ardora review – a flamenco chameleon defies stereotypes', *The Guardian*, 17 October, 2014; Luke Jennings, 'Rocío Molina: Fallen from Heaven Review – a feminist flamenco scream', *The Observer*, 15 October, 2017; Barbara Newman, 'Stamping on Flamenco', *Dancing Times*, October 2017; Laura Cappelle, 'Rocío Molina: Grito Pelao, Avignon Festival – Poignant, Sensual', *Financial Times*, 12 July 2018; Frank Scheck, 'Impulso', *The Hollywood Reporter*, 17 October 2018.

MARK MORRIS

Mark Morris's historical importance was that initially his work united what were two divergent trends. One was traditional modern dance, with its weightiness, musicality, and liberal humanism. The other was the postmodern sensibility – with its insistent irony, self-conscious historicism, and political emphasis – which dominated American art, including dance, in the 1980s. When Morris began showing his work to New York audiences, these two trends followed separate paths. Morris's work bridged the divide. It was up-to-date, full of 'styles' and mordancy, and taboo-breaching (particularly gender-violation: unisex dances, women lifting men, etc.). Yet it was dance, modern dance: plastic, musical, fundamentally earnest. And the combination seemed completely natural.

In view of Morris's education, it was natural. Born in Seattle, Washington, in 1956, he was the third and last child of an ordinary middle-class family, his father a teacher, mother a housewife. Aged eight, he received the *coup de foudre* at a performance of José Greco's flamenco troupe and began lessons in Spanish dance. Thereafter most of his training was in folk dance. He began ballet training at the age of 10, but his primary dance education was in flamenco (which he also studied in Madrid in 1974) and Balkan dance, which he learned when, aged 13, he joined Seattle's Koleda Folk Ensemble, a troupe devoted to Balkan forms. For three years, Koleda was socially and artistically the centre of his life. From them he learned how he wanted a dance ensemble to look – like regular people, full of human variety – and how he wanted the dancing body to look – sturdy, solid, with weight held low and the feet flat on the ground. From the post-1960s spirit with which the members of Koleda imbued their dances, he learned the utopianism that characterised his later work. Finally, Balkan dance and also flamenco, both highly sophisticated musically, taught him to see dance as grounded in music.

Morris had almost no training in modern dance, with the result that he was never affected by its generational disputes, never saw himself as needing to throw off the past. He had grown into a bad-boy type (loud-mouthed, provocative) and forthrightly homosexual. Yet from ethnic dance he learned all the values that enabled him to become an unselfconscious practitioner of modern dance, and to place his new style sensibility in the service of that old form.

Morris began choreographing at the age of 14 and made dances for school plays and recitals. In 1976, aged 19, he moved to New York, and danced with various modern dance troupes for seven years. In 1980, he founded the Mark Morris Dance Group and by 1986, the year he turned 30, he was being reviewed by national magazines, two major ballet companies had premiered dances by him, and he had been the subject of an hour-long Public Broadcasting Service television special. He was a foremost young choreographer in the United States.

In 1988 Morris moved his troupe to Brussels, replacing Maurice Béjart's Ballet of the 20th Century as the resident dance company of Belgium's national opera house, the Théâtre Royal de la Monnaie. They spent three turbulent years there, receiving, for the most part, harsh reviews from a press unaccustomed to American modern dance. Meanwhile, the company experienced painful internal changes. Their first generation yielded to its second. Veteran dancers quit, new dancers arrived, the company became larger, younger, more technically skilled. Despite these disruptions, during the Belgian years Morris created eleven dances, including two masterpieces, *L'Allegro, il Penseroso ed il Moderato* (1988), to Handel's oratorio, and *Dido and Aeneas* (1989), a danced version of Purcell's opera. In recognition of this show of strength and courage, he was awarded a MacArthur Fellowship in 1991. Shortly afterwards, they returned to New York, becoming the fourth-largest modern dance troupe in the US and probably the most discussed.

One of the first impressions is the seeming naturalness of his dances. His dancers look like the varied people one might meet on the street. They move with weight and effort; they squat and strain; they hurl themselves into the air. This gives them a note of vulnerability, of candour, and also an extreme physical immediacy, compounded by the fact that the dances are often performed to live vocal music, so that the music too reverberates with the force of the body. This is profoundly visceral choreography. However, naturalism for Morris is an artistic strategy: largely abstract, a structure of open symbols. Though the dancers may drag themselves across the floor by their arms – which they do in Morris's popular *Gloria* (1981, rev. 1984) – they do so in a line of seven, in canon, in imitation of the music's structure.

The basis of Morris's choreography is music. From adolescence he has been a passionate and erudite music-lover. He has set works to the music of more than 60 composers, together with many popular songs. He favours baroque music, by reason of its structural clarity, emotional directness, and danceability – he set five dances to J.S. Bach, including *The* (2015). And since his youth he has shown a fondness for choreographing to the West Coast experimental composers: Harry Partch, Henry Cowell, Lou Harrison. His taste remains eclectic, for example *Pepperland* (2017) to Ethan Iverson's setting of Beatles' songs and *Sport* (2019) to music by Satie. It is because a piece of music has given him choreographic ideas that he decides to use it, and the dance reflects the musical structure – he usually choreographs with the score in hand. Musical ensembles become dance ensembles; musical solos, dance solos. Rhythm, harmony, counterpoint, dynamics, and key structures all become part of the dance. While 'music-visualising' is characteristic of his work, the relationship between the music and dance structures tends to be elastic. If music is his muse, the source of his choreography is the imaginative process – a compound of thought and emotion, experienced as movement images. This process is something that an external pattern can only influence, never dictate. The pattern is necessary to him, however. Morris has almost never commissioned music. The music is usually pre-existent; he has to hear it in order to want to make a dance.

A number of Morris's finest works are narrative. *One Charming Night* (1985) tells of a vampire seduction; *Bedtime* (1992) of the theft of a child by a goblin. *Dido and Aeneas* and *The Hard Nut* (1991) which is the name of Morris's *Nutcracker*, tell the usual tales. Other dances, if they do not have stories, have clear subjects, in keeping with their vocal text: love (*New Love Song Waltzes*, 1982; *I Don't Want to Love*, 1996), death (*The Vacant Chair*, 1984), fear *(Behemoth,* 1990; *The Office*, 1994), dreaming (*Bedtime*, 1992), religious feeling *(Gloria; O Rangasayee*, 1984; *Stabat Mater*, 1986; *Strict Songs*, 1987; *Beautiful Day*, 1992; *Jesu, Meine Freude*, 1993); and 1960s nostalgia and celebration (*Pepperland*, 2017). Another persistent theme is community, group love. Morris is not especially interested in romantic love. He has created few love duets – notably for instance in *A Garden* (2001), and *Jenn and Spencer* (2013), a duet for company dancers Jenn Weddel and Spencer Ramirez. While he uses 'subject matter', he tends to develop it not in a literary or linear way, but in a musical way, through the repetition and development of movement themes.

Morris's works tend to have double emotions. They present opposing sides of an experience simultaneously: sorrow and dryness (*Love Song Waltzes*, 1989), reverie and absurdity (*Ten Suggestions*, 1981), exultation and anguish *(Stabat Mater*, 1986), brassiness and horror (*Lucky Charms*, 1994). As an overarching opposition, he tends to use beautiful old music –putting the audience into a worshipful mood – in combination with blunt, vernacular movement, which disrupts that mood. This doubleness is not offering a simple irony. It is quite earnest, but he is also witty and unsentimental, and there is a streak of darkness in his vision of life. Many of his dances have great pathos, as in *Layla and Majnun* (2016), based on a love story where the relationship is never consummated, but won from difficulty, from a criticism of pathos.

Morris is remarkably prolific. Since 1980, when he founded his company, he has created more than 160 works – about five per year.

This includes 15 classical ballets for the Joffrey Ballet, Boston Ballet, American Ballet Theatre, Paris Opéra Ballet, Les Grands Ballets Canadiens, Houston Ballet, and, most frequently, the San Francisco Ballet. He has directed several opera productions. (In *Orfeo ed Euridice*, Iowa City, 1996, and *Platée*, Edinburgh, 1997, there was copious dancing, but the singers too were onstage. *Dido and Aeneas*, Brussels, 1989, and *Four Saints in Three Acts*, London, 2000, were through-danced, with the singers offstage.) He has also created dances for operas directed by others, notably Peter Sellars's *Nixon in China* (1987) and *The Death of Klinghoffer* (1991). His rifle-toting ballerinas in *Nixon* were much admired.

Morris's style has changed over time. In 1985–86, when he began his immersion in baroque music, he became more interested in tight, complex dance structures, both as a reflection of that music and as a container for themes of grief. Morris was the star dancer of his company, until in 1986, he broke his foot. Now he began to design dances in accordance with how it would be to look at them, and for specific dancers rather than for a notional general dancer based on himself. He took himself out of certain pieces, though went on creating superb roles for himself. In *Dido and Aeneas*, he played both Dido and the Sorceress – the greatest role of his career. At 52, he danced occasionally, in specialised parts, but in his 60s he no longer performs.

Another turning point was the period in Brussels. With the resources of the national opera house at his disposal, Morris doubled the size of the company, and commanded set and costume shops, orchestras, and choruses. His work expanded in every way, not just in size but in clarity and boldness. For example, in *L'Allegro*, *Dido*, and *Behemoth* there is no fat; it is impossible to imagine the dances offering any greater imaginative force. At the same time, his style changed; he had many new dancers and studios of his own, so that he could train them. He began teaching company ballet class every morning, for another influence of this period was ballet. He was also caught up in a burst of creativity, with ideas newly clear to him. His dances took on a new look, something more formal, more designed and legible, with the body more 'worked', the steps more complicated, the rhythms more difficult and exact. This change had been building for years, but in Brussels it was noticeable, partly because one saw it on new dancers, untrained in the older, shaggier style.

Since Brussels, his work has not altered as much. Stories and emotions are there in his work but must be inferred. With important exceptions, his work is increasingly abstract, for example, in *Sport* (2019), Jack Anderson states that 'choreographed sports emphasised crawling, falling, whirling and wiggling' (2019: 69). One notable development of the 1990s was Morris's exploration of new media: dance on video (*Falling Down Stairs* and *Dido and Aeneas*, both 1995 for Rhombus Media); opera (*Orfeo*, *Four Saints*, *Platée*); and musical theatre (*The Capeman*, 1998).

One thing has never changed in Morris's work, and that is its amalgamative nature. David White, founding director of Dance Theater Workshop, where much of his early work was produced, opined 'Mark is a sort of car crash of personalities. There's this working-class guy and there's this music scholar guy, and there's this folk-dance guy and this gay guy, and they've all washed up into the same body' (in Joan Acocella, 1993). His work, likewise, is a great gathering-in. While Spanish and Balkan dance, together with ballet, have been major influences, he has been affected by Asian dance, European court dance, and figures of American modern dance. Though music is the law of his mind, he is also passionately involved with stories, which work by an opposite logic. While his is a very modern mind – sophisticated, ironical, self-critical – he is also attached to old values, old music: Bach, Handel, and the things they felt were important. This is not to say that Morris can't be pigeonholed. He can be. He has a specific style, specific concerns. But his habit has always been to join opposing things. This makes his work more difficult and more durable. It also produces a generosity of vision that has endeared him to the public.

Joan Acocella (updated by Lorna Sanders)

Biographical details

Born in Seattle, Washington, United States, 29 August 1956. **Studied** flamenco dance from age nine, with Verla Flowers, and ballet with Perry Brunson in Seattle. **Career:** Danced with semi-professional Balkan dance troupe, the Koleda Folk Ensemble, from age 13 to 16; later danced with numerous companies, including Eliot Feld, Lar Lubovitch, Hannah Kahn, and Laura Dean; founded Mark Morris Dance Group in 1980, became resident company of the Théâtre Royal de la Monnaie, Brussels, 1988–91; co-founded, with Mikhail Baryshnikov, White Oak Dance Project, in 1990. The Mark Morris Dance Centre, Brooklyn, New York, opened in 2001. Has choreographed for numerous companies, including Joffrey Ballet, Boston Ballet, American Ballet Theatre, Les Grands Ballets Canadiens, Pacific Northwest Ballet, San Francisco Ballet, and Paris Opéra Ballet; has also directed opera. **Awards and honours** include New York Dance and Performance Awards ('Bessie'), 1984, 1990 and 2007; Guggenheim Fellowship, 1986; MacArthur Foundation Fellowship, 1991; *Dance Magazine* Award, 1991; Olivier Award, 1998 and 2002; *Evening Standard* Award, 1997; New York State Governor's

Award, 2001; *Time Out Live* Award, 2002; Critic's Circle National Dance Awards (UK) 2002; Doris Duke Award, 2002 and 2016; Fellow, American Academy of Arts and Sciences, 2005; New York Mayor's Award for Arts and Culture, 2006; WQXR Gramophone Special Recognition Award, 2006; Samuel H. Scripps Award, 2007; Independent Award, Brown University Club of New York, 2007; Member, American Philosophical Society, 2008; International Society for the Performing Arts' Distinguished Artist Award, 2012; Benjamin Franklin Laureate Prize for Creativity, 2012; inducted into Vanderbilt Whitney Hall of Fame, National Museum of Dance, New York, 2015; *The Times* Arts Award, 2017.

Works

Barstow (1973); *Zenska* (1975); *Brummagem* (1978); *Rattlesnake Song* (1980); *Castor and Pollux* (1980); *Dad's Charts* (1980); *Ten Suggestions* (1981); *Etudes Modernes* (1981); *I Love You Dearly* (1981); *Gloria* (1981); *Rattlesnake Song* (1981); *Canonic 3/4 Studies* (1982); *Jr. High* (1982); *New Love Song Waltzes* (1982); *Not Goodbye* (1982); *Songs that Tell a Story* (1982); *Bijoux* (1983); *Ponchielliana* (1983); *Caryatids* (1983); *Celestial Greetings* (1983); *The Death of Socrates* (1983); *Deck of Cards* (1983); *Dogtown* (1983); *Minuet and Allegro in G* (1983); *The 'Tamil Film Songs in Stereo' Pas de Deux* (1983); *Come on Home* (1984); *Forty Arms, Twenty Necks, One Wreathing* (1984); *Love, You Have Won* (1984); *My Party* (1984); *Championship Wrestling after Roland Barthes* (1984); *O Rangasayee* (1984); *Prelude and Prelude* (1984); *She Came from There* (1984); *The Vacant Chair* (1984); *Vestige* (1984); *Frisson* (1985); *Handel Choruses* (1985); *Jealousy* (1985); *Lovey* (1985); *Marble Halls* (1985); *One Charming Night* (1985); *Retreat from Madrid* (1985); *Aida* (1986); *Ballabili* (1986); *Esteemed Guests* (1986); *Mort Subite* (1986); *Mythologies* (1986); *Pièces en Concert* (1986); *Salomé* (opera by Richard Strauss, 1986); *Shepherd on the Rock* (1986); *Stabat Mater* (1986); *Nixon in China* (opera 1987); *Scarlatti Solos* (1987); *Sonata for Clarinet and Piano* (1987); *Strict Songs* (1987); *La Folia* (1987); *Drink to Me Only with Thine Eyes* (1988); *Die Fledermaus* (opera 1988); *Fugue and Fantasy* (1988); *L'Allegro, il Penseroso ed il Moderato* (1988); *Le Nozze de Figaro* (opera 1988); *Offertorium* (1988); *Orphée et Euridice* (opera by Gluck, 1988); *Dido and Aeneas* (1989; television version, 1995); *Love Song Waltzes* (1989); *Wonderland* (1989); *Behemoth* (1990); *Ein Herz* (1990); *Going Away Party* (1990); *Motorcade* (1990); *Pas de Poisson* (1990); *The Death of Klinghoffer* (opera 1991); *The Hard Nut* (1991); *A Lake* (1991); *The Marriage of Figaro* (also dir., 1991); *Paukenschlag* (1992); *Beautiful Day* (1992); *Polka* (1992); *Three Preludes* (1992); *Bedtime* (1992); *Excursion to Grenada: A Calypso Ballet* (1992); *Grand Duo* (includes *Polka,* 1993); *Home* (1993); *Mosaic and United* (1993); *Jesu, Meine Freude* (1993); *A Spell* (1993); *Falling Down Stairs* (film, 1994; stage, 1997); *The Office* (1994); *Lucky Charms* (1994); *Rondo* (1994); *Maelstrom* (1995); *Quincunx* (1995); *Somebody's Coming to See Me Tonight* (1995); *Pacific* (1995); *World Power* (1995); *Three Russian Preludes* (1995); *Orfeo ed Euridice* (1996); *I Don't Want to Love* (1996); *Rhymes with Silver* (1997); *Anger Dance* (1997); *Waltz in C* (1997); *Platée* (opera 1997);

The Capeman (musical 1998); Medium (1998); Greek to Me (1998); Dancing Honeymoon (1998); The Argument (1999); Dixit Dominus (1999); Sandpaper Ballet (1999); Flight (1999); Zwei Harveytanze (1999); Peccadillos (2000); Four Saints in Three Acts (opera 2000); Sang-Froid (2000); From Old Seville (2001); A Garden (2001); Gong (2001); V (2001); Later (2002); Foursome (2002); Kolam (2002); Resurrection (2002); Something Lies Beyond the Scene (2002); Non Troppo (2003); Serenade (2003); Idomeneo (Act III ballet, 2003); All Fours (2003); Sylvia (2004); Violet Cavern (2004); Rock of Ages (2004); Cargo (2005); Candleflowerdance (2005); Up and Down (2006); King Arthur (2006); Mozart Dances (2006); Italian Concerto (2007); Orfeo ed Euridice (opera 2007); Looky (2007); Joyride (2008); Excursions (2008); Romeo and Juliet, On Motifs of Shakespeare (2008); L'isola Disabitata (2009); Empire Garden (2009); Visitation (2009); Cease Your Funning (2009); Socrates (2010); The Muir (2010); Petrichor (2010); Festival Dance (2011); Renard (2011); Beaux (2012); A Choral Fantasy (2012); A Wooden Tree (2012); Kammermusik No.3 (2012); Jenn and Spencer (2013); Crosswalk (2013); Spring, Spring, Spring (2013); Curlew River (2013); Acis and Galatea (2014); Words (2014); Whelm (2015); The Letter V (2015); The (2015); After You (2015); A Forest (2016); Layla and Majnun (2016); Pure Dance Items (2016); Pepperland (2017); Numerator (2017); Twelve of 'em (2017); Little Britten (2018); The Trout (2018); Sport (2019); Arrows. Eros (2019).

Further reading

(*For sources prior to 2000, see Joan Acocella, 2nd edition of Fifty Contemporary Choreographers)

Interviews: with Beth Genné, 'A New Home for Mark Morris', Dancing Times, October 2001; Janet Lynn Roseman, Dance Masters: Interviews with Legends of Dance, London and New York, 2001; Meryl Cates, 'Mark Morris Dance Group Returns to the UK', Dancing Times, April 2010; Susan Bedall, 'Review: Layla and Majnun', Dance Australia, 16 October 2018; Jonathan Gray, 'Landing in the Right Spot', Dancing Times, March 2019.

Articles: Debra Craine, 'The Ruling Class: Twenty Years of Mark Morris', Dance Now, Winter 2001/2; Mark Morris, 'Creating Sylvia: Eros Triumphs over Diana in Mark Morris' New Work for San Francisco Ballet', Dance Magazine, May 2004; Zoe Anderson, 'Mark Morris Anniversary', Dancing Times, May 2006; Deborah Jowitt, 'Mark Morris Matches Wits with Beethoven and Ives', The Village Voice, 25 August 2009; Deborah Jowitt, 'Message from Mark Morris: Look, But Don't Forget to Listen', The Village Voice, 2 March 2010; Alastair Macaulay, 'A Romp Through the Barn', The New York Times, 19 August 2011; Joan Acocella, 'Doubleheader', The New Yorker, 15 April 2013; Gia Kourlas, 'Mark Morris's Legacy Plan', The New York Times, 24 April 2018; Jonathan Gray, 'Pepperland', Dancing Times, May 2019; Jack Anderson, 'Notes from New York', Dancing Times, September 2019.

Books: Jeffrey Escoffier and Matthew Lore (eds.), *Mark Morris' 'L'Allegro, il Penseroso ed il Moderato': A Celebration*, New York, 2001; Janet Roseman, *Interviews with Legends of Dance*, New York, 2001; Rose Eichenbaum and Clive Barnes, *Masters of Movement: Portraits of America's Great Choreographers*, Washington, DC, 2004; Joyce Morgenroth, *Speaking of Dance: Twelve Contemporary Choreographers on Their Craft*, New York, 2004; Vida Midgelow, *Reworking the Ballet: Counter-Narratives and Alternative Bodies*, London and New York, 2007; Stephanie Jordan, *Mark Morris: Musician – Choreographer*, Alton, 2015; Mark Morris and Wesley Stace, *Outloud; A Memoir*, London, 2019.

OHAD NAHARIN

'The Illusion of beauty/ And a thin line that separates between madness and sanity/ The panic behind the laughter/ And co-existence of fatigue and elegance'. This sentence opens *Echad Mi Yodea*, one of Naharin's most recognised compositions [this version appears in *Decadance* (2000). *Echad Mi Yodea* was originally composed for *Kyr* (1990)]. The dancers stand still in a wide position, in dim light, as if to expose themselves to the audience, and before their figures alter into sitting on the chairs behind them (leaning forward, as if they are defeated), the words suggest that we look into the complexity beyond appearances. The introduction refers to beauty as semblance, and the narrator (Ohad Naharin) directs our awareness towards the possibility that impressions and human qualities may overturn. This is an invitation to shift attention to the involvedness of processes which initiate behaviours – as well as to observe and to imagine what expressions hide, convey, expose or compromise. This request is exemplary of how the choreographer Ohad Naharin invites his audience and dancers to use their sensitivity and imagination for exploring bodily movements and human performances. Although his movement vocabulary is constantly evolving and his choreographic works are very different from each another, Naharin's artistic signature can be defined as multilayered textures and qualities of movements composed into a nuanced and complex physical presence.

Ohad Naharin is the house choreographer of Batsheva Dance Company and was its artistic director between 1990–2018 (with a short break during 2003–2004). In addition to his choreographies, Naharin is also the creator of Gaga, an evolving movement research, developed in order to better communicate choreographic ideas with the dancers he works with. The Gaga research enables Naharin to explore systematically movement possibilities beyond a set vocabulary, and it supports the dancers in enriching their interpretation of the dance. Nowadays Gaga is the main practice of the dancers of Batsheva Dance Company and the Batsheva Young Ensemble. It has also spread to the larger field of dance practices worldwide and is practised by both dancers and non-dancers. In line with the opening introduction of *Echad Mi Yodea*, the practice shifts the dancers' attention from the appearance of gestures into the processes that initiate them.

Gaga incorporates Naharin's pedagogical approach towards dancing. Accordingly, excellence transgresses the commitment to following established forms. Instead, the creative effort of dancing is directed towards increasing the dancer's physical comportment through somatic awareness. He states: 'what is unique about Gaga is the demand to listen to the body before we tell it what to do, and the understanding we must go beyond familiar limits on a daily basis' (Heymann 2015, 0:43:30). In place of practising routines of movements in front of mirrors, Gaga's vocabulary compromises metaphorical instructions like 'float!' with the request for bodily listening (for example, the instruction 'move from your spine!'). The dancers systematically explore their feelings in order to fulfil, realise and embody those instructions. The emphasis on researching movement as a process of coordinating images and feelings, intentionally and perceptively, accelerates the articulation of gestures and extracts their expressivity (Katan 2016).

Naharin's formal training as a dancer started late, when he was already 22 and apprentice to the Batsheva Dance Company in Tel Aviv. Batsheva was at that point a daughter company of Martha Graham, who served as its first artistic advisor (1963–1975). In 1974 Graham staged *Jacob's Dream* (1974) for the company in Tel Aviv; the role of Esau was created for Naharin. Following that experience, Graham invited Naharin to join the Martha Graham Dance Company in New York. After ten months, Naharin stayed in New York and studied at The Juilliard School of the Arts and The School for American Ballet. In 1978 he was accepted as a dancer in the Béjart Ballet of the 20th Century in Brussels and remained for one year.

Naharin was born in 1952 in Kibbutz Mizra – a socialist and agricultural environment. His father, Eliav Naharin, was an actor who nurtured a career in psychodrama. His mother, Sofia Naharin, was a dance, music, and Feldenkrais instructor, a student of Moshe Feldenkrais, the founder of the Feldenkrais method, and of Noa Eshkol, a choreographer that developed, together with the mathematician Avraham Wachman, the Eshkol-Wachman Movement Notation. In interviews with Deborah Friedes Galilli (2015), both Naharin and his mother recall exploring playing, music, rhythms, and dance when he was a child. Analysing Gaga and Naharin's choreographies, it seems that his parents' professional backgrounds have inspired his ongoing approach to dance. As in psychodrama – his work advances the articulation of feelings as artistic action; like the Feldenkrais method, Gaga emphasises physical awareness; and in correspondence with Eshkol's mathematical examination of movement beyond stylistic conventions, Naharin's movement and choreographic research foster the breaking of habits, the revealing of new possibilities, and the acquiring of new patterns of movement.

Over the years, Naharin's choreographic pieces have been recognised for their surprising sense of drama, great timing, and rich physical nuances. His choreographic debuts, the solos, *Pas de Pepsi* and *In Common,* and the duet *Haru No Umi* were performed in 1980 at the Kazuko Hirabayshi Studio. Corresponding with timely influences from Pina Bausch's dance theatre, the movement in his early works had a dramatic exchange with the logic of the human situations they affected and proposed. The choreographer Reggie Willson, who danced in the Ohad Naharin Dance Company in the 1980s, describes the movements Naharin created as full and luscious: 'especially at that time it was deep and heavy and weighted, it had emotion in it, it had a feeling in it' (Heymann 2015, 00:36:05). During the time that Naharin worked as an independent choreographer in New York (1980–1990), he was invited to create pieces for Batsheva Dance Company, The Kibbutz Contemporary Dance Company, Nederlands Dans Theater, Sydney Dance Company, Pittsburgh Ballet Theatre, and Grand Théâtre de Genève. His choreographies during that period had a strong sense of physical freedom and flow – for instance, the rolling jumps in *Black Milk* (1985) – alongside dramatic compositions that collected rhythmic timings into a poetry of human happenings. For example, in one episode of *Tabula Rasa* (1986), there is a movement sequence from a line of dancers, who are shifting their weight in slow motion from one leg to another and moving their hands in front of their faces. The collective timing of sensitive and intimate gestures within this composition made the dancers appear as fragile individuals and an attentive collective at the same time.

In 1990 Naharin was appointed artistic director of Batsheva Dance Company. His first work *Kyr* ('Wall', in Hebrew, 1990), involved a live act of the rock band 'Nikmat HaTraktor' (The Tractor's Revenge) on stage. *Kyr* seemed like a powerful expression of life in Israel. Its most recognised sequence, *Echad Mi Yodea*, is a rock interpretation of a song from the Passover Haggadah, which is composed from a repetitive and cumulative counting of identifying beliefs. In Naharin's dance, the Jewish imperative of retelling the tradition transforms into an expressive movement between composure and explosion. Over and over again, the dancers erupt from their well-organised seating order, and throw their clothes on stage as if they are trying to peel the shells of a forced identity. The live music on stage, the dramatic lighting of Avi Yona Bueno, and the fresh and powerful dance created a remarkable work that brought new, young, audience to the dance theatres in Israel. The Israeli critic, Gaby Aldor, writes that *Kyr* was a door opening to a new dance in Israel. It generated a fresh feeling that instead of conveying the tradition or presenting a political problem, the dance enfolds the world with its pain and comfort (Aldor 2017). *Kyr* paved the way for Naharin's early artistic works for Batsheva Dance Company [among them *Mabul* (1992), *Anaphase* (1993) and *Zina* (1995)] as 'Gesamtkunstwerk' – a total work of art, in which music, lighting, costumes and movements correspond and tailor a complete and compelling event.

The establishment of Gaga over the years as a systematic movement research has refined the coexistence of diverse qualities in Naharin's choreographic works, into a nuanced style of movement. The precision of flow between distinctions – like explosive power and yielding – requires from the dancers who perform his works a sense of alertness, availability, and complex coordination. As a result, his choreographies consistently manifest a composite expression with a flow of meanings. In addition, although Naharin deals with complex political issues and life matters, he carefully avoids delivering a simple and didactic position concerning actual events. As he often states: 'nothing is more dangerous than an idea, if it is only one idea' (Aldor 2017). The artistic commitment and the creative emphasis in Naharin's choreographies are on multifaceted approaches to movement; the value of his dances is entailed within the ever-changing process of dancing and the sensitivity it inspires. In line with Gaga's pedagogy, his dances are composed for the audience to look and feel beyond the habits of their usual perspectives.

It is apparent that Naharin's request to develop a sensitive and engaged spectatorship among the viewers of his works has become a choreographic concern. In *Naharin's Virus* (2011), for instance, he uses Peter Handke's anti-theatric play *Offending the Audience* to direct the audience's attention to the qualities of movements and behaviours well beyond their theatrical and symbolic representations. In addition, the compositions of gestures in his works keep the audience alert to actual developments. One example among many is from the final duet of *The Hole* (2013); a female dancer leans on her knees and sends her arm to a male dancer as if she is pleading. The male dancer treads on her outstretched palm, and then she leads his moves like a mother who takes care of her child. The composition changes from a moment of begging into humiliation and then briefly transforms it into a moment of support and personal strength. The transformation of gestures in this sequence intimates a bigger story beyond what the moment encompasses.

With compositions that use the feeling of storytelling without leading to a conclusion, the dance generates complex feelings of mystery and intimacy. These expressions break the expectation and anticipation of watching the dance, and provoke self-awareness, encouraging the audience to follow the gestures of others. Inspirational values like attentiveness, open-mindedness and reflectivity in Naharin's dances are tailored by all choreographic elements. In *The Hole*, meaning flourishes also by the specific spatial arrangement and the seating positions of the spectators. The work takes place in an octagonal room, and the dancers break onto and underneath the stage and pop up from the ceiling and the walls. Thus, in each singular moment the viewer cannot encompass the whole space and becomes aware that what they see is fragmentary. The limitation of a point of view reveals it as a singular perspective. Likewise, Naharin's compositions tend to lead the attention of spectators in unexpected manners, which differ from one work to another.

Considering Naharin's body of works as a whole, he is a choreographer who not only fosters contemplation of human qualities, habits and possibilities but also how people – dancers, non-dancers, spectators and practitioners – may improve them.

Einav Katan-Schmid

Biographical details

Born in Kibbutz Mizra, Israel, 22 June 1952. **Studied** at the School of American Ballet, The Juilliard School, and with Maggie Black and David Howard, 1975–1976. **Career:** joined Batsheva Dance Company as a dancer in 1974; performed with Martha Graham Dance Company, 1975; and with Maurice Béjart's Ballet of the 20th Century, Brussels, 1978. Choreographed for his own small troupe in New York, Ohad Naharin Dance Company, 1980–1990; also created work for Batsheva Dance Company, the Kibbutz Contemporary Dance Company, and Nederlands Dans Theater, Sydney Dance Company, Pittsburgh Ballet Theatre, and Grand Théâtre de Genève. Artistic Director of Batsheva Dance Company 1990–2018, established the Young Batsheva Ensemble and developed Gaga movement language. Currently Naharin lives in Israel and continues to create for Batsheva Dance Company, as their house choreographer. **Awards and honours** include

Chevalier de l'Ordre des Arts et des Lettres, France, 1998; New York Dance and Performance ('Bessie') Awards, 2002, 2003; Israel Prize for dance, 2005; Jewish Culture Achievement Award, The Foundation for Jewish Culture, 2008; EMET Prize, 2009; Samuel H. Scripps Award, 2009; Dance Magazine Award, 2009. Honorary doctorates from the Weizmann Institute of Science, 2004; the Hebrew University, 2008; Juilliard, 2013; and Ben Gurion University of the Negev, 2019.

Works*

Haru No Uni (1980); *Pas de Pepsi* (1981); *Interim* (1981); *In Common* (1981); *Inostress* (1983); *Black Milk* (1985); *Sixty a Minute* (1985); *Tabula Rasa* (1986); *Chameleon Dances* (1987); *Sinking of the Titanic* (1989); *Passomezzo* (1989); *Queens of Golub* (1989); *King of Wara* (1989); *Arbos* (1989); *60 a Minute* (1990); *Kyr* (1990); *Axioma 7* (1991); *Mabul* (1992); *Perpetuum* (1992); *Off White* (1992); *Opening Ceremony* (adapted as *Anaphase*, 1993); *Dancing Party* (1994); *Paselet HaChalomot* (1995); *Kaamos* (1994, 2009); *Z/Na* (1995); *Yag* (1996); *Two Short Stories* (1997); *Diapason* (1997); *Sabotage Baby* (1997); *Zachacha* (1998); *Quotations 1–9* (1999); *Moshe* (1999); *Minus 16* (1999); *Decadance* (2000); *Naharin's Virus* (2001); *Plasticine* (2001); *Mamootot* (2003); *Camooyot* (2003); *Playback* (2004); *Three: Bellus, Humus, Secus* (2005); *Telophaza* (2006); *Furo –* (created with Tabaimo 2006); *George & Zalman* (2006); *Max* (2007); *Order* (2007); *Project Five* (2008); *B/olero* (2008); *Hora* (2009); *Sadeh21* (2011); *Session* (2011); *Decale* (2012); *The Hole* (2013); *Project Secus* (2014); *Last Work* (2015); *Venezuela* (2017); *2019* (2019).

*Works and dates cited here were provided by the Batsheva Dance Company

Further reading

(*For sources prior to 2005, see Batsheva Dance Company website at batsheva.co.il/en/home; company archive at archive.batsheva.co.il/eng; and Gaga movement language at gagapeople.com/en)

Interviews: with Wendy Perron, 'Truth in Movement', *Dance Magazine*, October 2006; Tomer Heymann, *Out of Focus*, Heymann Brothers Films, 2007; Tomer Heymann, *Mr. Gaga*, Heymann Brothers Films, 2015.

Articles: Deborah Jowitt, 'Ohad Naharin Brings the Gaga to BAM in Max', *The Village Voice*, 11 March 2009; Einav Katan, 'The Total of the Expanse Exceeds the Sum of Its Parts', *Dance Today*, 21 December 2011 (Hebrew); Jenny Stevenson, 'Contemporary: Sarah Foster Sproull: Exploring Gaga Technique', *DANZ Quarterly: New Zealand Dance*, 28, 2012; Rachel Howard, 'Ohad Naharin in San Francisco', *The Hudson Review*, 68(1), 2015; Deborah Friedes Galili, 'Gaga: Moving Beyond Technique with Ohad Naharin in the Twenty-First Century', *Dance Chronicle*, 38(3), 2015; Einav Katan, 'Connect Effort into

Pleasure: Overcoming the Perceptual Gap Between Body and Mind', *Dance Today*, 28, 2015 (Hebrew); Eric Mullis, 'Dance, Philosophy, and Somaesthetics', *Performance Philosophy Journal*, 2(1), Winter 2016; Meghan Quinlan, 'Gaga as Metatechnique: Negotiating Choreography, Improvisation, and Technique in a Neoliberal Dance Market', *Dance Research Journal*, 49(2), 2017; Hiie Saumaa, 'Ohad Naharin's Sensual, Somatic Gaga', *Dance Chronicle*, 40(3), 2017; Louis Laberge-Côté, 'The Porous Body: Cultivating Malleability in Traditional Dance Training', *Journal of Dance and Somatic Practices*, 10(1), 2018; Andrew Sanger, 'Gaga as Embodied Research', *Research in Dance Education*, 20(1), 2019; Helen Singh-Miller, 'Gaga, Give Me More: The Spectrum of Human Movement in Two Dances by Ohad Naharin', *Feldenkrais Research Journal*, 6, 2019.

Books: Henia Rottenberg in Martha Bremser and Lorna Sanders (eds.), *Fifty Contemporary Choreographers*. 2nd ed., London and New York, 2011; Einav Katan, 'Move and Rest in Peace: "Pathosformel" in Mamootot, a Dance Work by Ohad Naharin, Batsheva Dance Company, in Ulrike Feist', in *Et in Imagine Ego* (ed. Markus Rath), Berlin, 2012; Mary Ellen Snodgrass, entry on Naharin, *The Encyclopedia of World Ballet*, London, 2015; Einav Katan, *Embodied Philosophy in Dance: Gaga and Ohad Naharin's Movement Research*, London, 2016; Gaby Aldor, *Naharin* (Hebrew), Tel Aviv, 2017.

GIDEON OBARZANEK

For many of us, our first enjoyable dancing experience is at a house party. Emblematic of his later work, Gideon Obarzanek's dance career began unconventionally as a teenager when he discovered an interest in dance as a party guest.

Few Australian choreographers have created as eclectic a body of work as Obarzanek. From 'kaleidoscopic patterns' and 'frenetic, body-flinging chaos' (Chloe Smethurst, 'This tangled web we weave', *Dance Magazine*, November 2011) to 'refreshingly in-your-face … [and] blackly humoured', (Kate Sands, 'Bonehead', *Arena Magazine*, (29), 1997), Obarzanek's choreography resists definition whilst enjoying wide audience support and prestige. His diverse body of work – spanning dance, theatre, film, and installation – has come to represent a particular Australian aesthetic: independent, nontraditional, and maverick.

Obarzanek was born in Melbourne in 1966 to Jewish parents. Soon afterwards his family moved to Kibbutz Gal-On in central Israel. As part of the socialist-kibbutz lifestyle, Obarzanek shared his living quarters and possessions with the other children. Living separately from his parents in the children's dormitory, Obarzanek credits this experience in part for his resilience and collaborative way of creating dance work (Susanna Ling, 2018). It was also his first exposure to folk dance.

Obarzanek's return to Melbourne, aged eight, saw him struggling to assimilate with his peers (Michelle Potter, *A Passion for Dance*, 1997). With encouragement from his mother, Obarzanek began taking dance classes before auditioning for the Australian Ballet School (ABS) whilst finishing high school. Deferring a university course in marine science, Obarzanek accepted a place at ABS and trained in classical ballet and Graham technique, graduating in 1987. Hinting at his suspicion of institutions (in CreativeMornings HQ, *Gideon Obarzanek: Minimal*, youtube.com, 21 July 2014, he later described ABS as a 'very conservative, rigorous school'), Obarzanek found release in his first choreographic opportunities and developed *Heat* (1987), a quartet for four men.

Obarzanek continued to indulge his passion for creating whilst dancing with the Queensland Ballet, then Sydney Dance Company, throughout the late 1980s and 1990s. Feeling stifled by a lack of opportunity to choreograph under their respective directorships, Obarzanek eventually left to forge an independent career – his works from this period include *Slow Me Up, Speed Me Down* (1993) for Kibbutz Contemporary Dance Company, and *Petrol Head Lover* (1993) and *Cool White Fridge Knocked Over* (1995) for Nederlands Dans Theater 2.

Following his European work, Obarzanek returned to an Australian scene fraught with inflexibility for independent dance artists and makers. Inspired by a more European model, Obarzanek went about developing a 'platform for [himself], but also for other people to make work' (in Poptech, *Gideon Obarzanek digital moves*, youtube. com, 21 March 2010), which, with help from Garry Stewart, became Chunky Move.

His first work with this fledgling company was 1995's *Fast Idol*, performed in Sydney. In a similar vein, *Bonehead* (1997) integrated early hallmarks of Obarzanek's choreographic style with references to pop-culture, mass-culture, and a violent cinematic quality evocative of the pulpiest fictions (Potter, 1997). For *Bonehead*, Obarzanek styled the dancers in a violent and discordant frenzy, with the performers flipping between extreme displays of technique and jarring theatrical characterisations.

Chunky, as the company became known colloquially, emerged in a schizophrenic fury reflective of Obarzanek's own ironic/idealistic worldview. Relocating to Melbourne in 1997 when an opportunity arose for the Victorian State Government to fund a high-level dance company, Obarzanek began a lengthy tenure as Chunky's inaugural artistic director, creating several acclaimed pieces, including the Bessie Award-winning *Tense Dave* (2003).

Obarzanek's choreographic process is task-oriented, where the dancers in the work are presented with research and movement provocations in order to produce material. Inherent to this approach is a process of abstraction. Noting that his works vary in their capacity for narrative structure, or even elements of narrative, Obarzanek treats the dancer as an entity beyond identity; an abstract defined by their contribution to a movement language.

Mortal Engine (2008) served as a compelling synthesis of technology and dance in this state of high abstraction. For this work Obarzanek returned to his partnership with German engineer Frieder Weiss, utilising infrared cameras and complex projection technologies. Muted, mutable, and darkened forms scatter across the stage like scarabs; bodies vibrate in electric light and Robin Fox's brilliant green lasers close the work with startling linearity. Building on the earlier success of *Glow* (2006), *Mortal Engine* augments the former in scale and length. Described at the time as 'unlike anything its audience has seen before' (in Penelope Broadbent, 'Mortal Engine | Chunky Move', australianstage.com.au, 2009), this work stands as an essential example of Obarzanek's intersection of loneliness and corrupted idealism with technology. The choreography itself is a testament to the frenetic quality that characterised much of Obarzanek's early canon.

Obarzanek left his role as CEO and Artistic Director of Chunky Move in 2012, citing a series of 'emotional situations' that stemmed from conflicts between the business side of running the company and his creative ambitions (Westle, 2016). He felt ready to move forward in developing his choreographic style.

Given his belief that choreography is group-authored, Obarzanek's process might be described as communal. This interest in the group is particularly evident in *Assembly* (2011), his final work as Artistic Director of Chunky Move, representing his grand farewell. Working in collaboration with the Victorian Opera, the small dancing ensemble gathered on a large staircase whilst 50 singers chanted *a capella*; the dancing bodies thumping out their own percussive contribution in a mixture of trained and amateur dancing. *Assembly* had a baroque sensibility of voice and awe, an *agape* quality that diffused the rapidity of his earlier pieces in favour of a particular dignity; an attempted return to the sublime. Notably pared back compared to his more highly technological works, some commented on the disconnect between the vocals and the choreography leading to a feeling of isolation (for example, Kuzminksy, 2011).

After leaving Chunky Move, Obarzanek became resident artist of the Sydney Theatre Company. His major work, *Dance Better at Parties*

(2013), which Obarzanek wrote and directed with choreography by Jessica Prince, again touched on his central themes of aloneness and connection. In 2014, this work, which follows a middle-aged man's attempts to learn Latin dance, was turned into a documentary-drama film. Collaborating with fellow writer/director Matthew Bate and producer Rebecca Summerton, *I Want to Dance Better at Parties* won the Dendy Award for Best Film at the 2014 Sydney Film Festival, a testament to Obarzanek's skill outside the dance studio.

Obarzanek foregrounds himself as a central figure in the Australian arts scene, particularly through festival curation. From 2015 to 2017 he served as an artistic associate to the Melbourne Festival and as co-curator of XO State at the Asia-Pacific Triennial of Performing Arts. Obarzanek has most recently worked as the outgoing chair of the Melbourne Fringe Festival; and in 2020 he takes a new role as co-artistic director and co-CEO of the New Melbourne Festival alongside Hannah Fox. Since his time with Sydney Theatre Company, Obarzanek has continued to direct and choreograph, including a collaborative effort on *Attractor* (2017) with Lucy Guerin, which was awarded two Helpmann awards. In *Attractor*, the movement rhymes with the guttural, haunting cries of the musicians centre stage. Rave meets rite, the performers flick and collapse as sweat flies from focused brows and bodies bounce along the floor like stones on a lake.

His latest stage work *Us 50* (2019) was performed as part of Sydney Dance Company's 50th anniversary celebration season and featured ex-company dancers moving amongst the current ensemble. The movement is en masse and often angular or ecstatic. Arms reach out and drift across the chest dreamily, only for elbows and feet to quickly shift in regimented patterns. The dancers follow one another, and their gazes are obvious to the audience – a kind of lineage manifesting in their maroon-coloured dance.

As his career shifts into a new leadership role with the forthcoming Melbourne Festival, we can pause to wonder whether Obarzanek's signature free-spiritedness will persist. With his passion for collaboration and mutability, and a lingering desire to dance better at parties, it seems we can safely hope so.

Hamish McIntosh

Biographical details

Born in Melbourne, Australia, 1966. **Studied** at the Australian Ballet School, graduating in 1987. **Career:** joined Queensland Ballet 1988–1991; worked under Graeme Murphy at Sydney Dance Company. Worked as an independent artist and choreographer with companies including Nederlands Dans Theater. Founded Chunky Move in collaboration with Garry Stewart in Sydney, 1995; company relocated to Melbourne, 1997; Artistic Director and CEO of Chunky Move until 2012; resident artist, Sydney Theatre Company 2013. Artistic associate, Melbourne Festival 2015–2017; co-curator XO State, Asia TOPA 2015–2017; chair, Melbourne Fringe Festival 2015–2019; co-artistic director and co-CEO, New Melbourne Festival from 2020. **Awards** include Prime Minister's Young Creative Fellowship, 1996; New York Dance and Performance Award ('Bessie') 2005; Helpmann Awards, 2008, 2017; Australian Council Fellowship, 2013; Sydney Film Festival Dendy Award, 2014.

Works

The Heat (1987); *Drift Office* (1988); *Mr Crowther and the Wallflower* (film, 1989); *Sleep No More* (1991); *Siesta to Dusk* (1991); *You've Got Me Floating* (1992); *Sand Siren* (1992); *Sweetheart* (1993); *Slow Me Up, Speed Me Down* (1993); *Petrol Head Lover* (1993); *Saccharin Suite* (1994); *While You're Down There* (1994); *Play Dead* (1994); *Cool White Fridge Knocked Over* (1995); *Fast Idol* (1995); *Lurch* (1996); *Bonehead* (1997); *Corrupted2* (1998); *Wet* (1998); *All the Better to Eat You with* (1999); *Corrupted* (1999); *Disco.very* (2000); *Soap* (2000); *Antistatic* (2000); *Hydra* (2000); *Crumpled* (2000); *100% Off* (2001); *Wanted: Ballet for a Contemporary Democracy* (2002); *Clear Pale Skin* (2002); *Closer* (2002); *Three's a Crowd* (2003); *Tense Dave* (2003); *I Want to Dance Better at Parties* (2004); *Singularity* (2006); *Glow* (2006); *Dance Like Your Old Man* (film, 2007); *Mortal Engine* (2008); *Two Faced Bastard* (with Lucy Guerin, 2008); *Faker* (2010); *Connected* (2011); *Assembly* (2011); *There's Definitely a Prince Involved* (2012); *Dance Better at Parties* (play, 2013); *I Want to Dance Better at Parties* (film, co-dir., with Matthew Bate, 2013); *L'Chaim!* (2014); *Stuck in the Middle with You* (film, 2016); *Two Jews Walk into a Theatre* (play with Brian Lipson and Lucy Guerin, 2016); *Once Upon a Time in the Western Suburbs* (film, 2017); *Attractor* (2017); *Bangsokol – A Requiem for Cambodia* (2017); *One Infinity* (2018); *Us 28* (2018); *Recital* (2019); *Us 50* (2019).

Further reading

Interviews: 'Interview with Israeli Choreographer Gideon Obarzanek', *Dance Australia*, June/July 1999; with Chunky Move, 'Assembly Interview with Gideon Obarzanek', youtube.com, undated; Fran Kelly, 'Gideon Obarzanek: Outgoing Artistic Director of Chunky Move', abc.net.au/radionational, December 2011; Andrew Westle, delvingintodance.com/podcast, 6 December 2016; Susanna Ling, 'Gideon Obarzanek, choreographer: My life', finearts-music.unimelb.edu.au, 27 April 2018.

Articles: Susan Reiter, 'Dance; Making the Most of the Awkward and Threatening', *The New York Times*, 7 October 2001; Hilary Crampton, 'Postures and Gestures', theage.com.au/entertainment, 20 May 2006; Anonymous,

'MIAF: Two Faced Bastard, Interpreti Veneziani Baroque Ensemble', theatrenotes.wordpress.com, 14 October 2008; Anonymous, 'Review Dance Massive: Inert, Mortal Engine', theatrenotes.wordpress.com, 7 March 2009; Judith Mackrell, 'Venice Festival: Where Dance Comes to Debate', *The Guardian*, 9 June 2010; Irina Kuzminksy, Assembly, 'Chunky Move and Victorian Opera', danceaustralia.com.au/review, 11 October 2011; Erin Johnson, 'Chunky Move's *Mortal Engine* in London', bachtrack.com, 22 October 2012; Gorkem Acaroglu, 'Cyborg Presence in Narrative Theatre', *Australasian Drama Studies*, 65, 2014; Elizabeth Ashley, 'The Connection Between Movement and Sound in Gideon Obarzanek's 'Recital', dancemagazine.com.au, 28 February 2019; Michelle Potter, 'Bonachela/Obarzanek', 'Sydney Dance Company', michellepotter.org, 4 November 2019.

Books: Michelle Potter, *A Passion for Dance*, Australia, Canberra, 1997; Jane Goodall in Jane Collins and Andrew Nisbet (eds.), *Theatre and Performance Design: A Reader in Scenography*, London and New York, 2010.

DIMITRIS PAPAIOANNOU

Greek choreographer Dimitris Papaioannou was the creator of the Opening and Closing ceremonies for the Athens Olympic Games (2004) and has since achieved a worldwide reputation as a chore-ographer. A visual arts graduate and student of the Greek painter Yiannis Tsarouchis, his works are full of visual imagery, irony, and striking references to art history. They exist as creations at the inter-section of visual theatre, dance theatre, experimental movement, and even circus. Judith Mackrell and Lyndsey Winship (2018) com-ment that 'Papaioannou has the skills of an illusionist', while Leonetta Bentivoglio (2018) notes that his universe on stage has 'a hallucinatory tone in the manipulation of the bodies, in the masterly composition of the nudes, in the prodigy of Botticellian or pre-Raphaelite fairies that sprout from heaps of leaves', creating layers of ideas, images, sensa-tions, and meanings for audiences to experience.

Starting as a performer for Analia, a Greek dance-theatre company, from 1982, Papaioannou's early dance knowledge is linked to his New York experience in 1983. He took classes in Erick Hawkins tech-nique and studied Japanese butoh with Maureen Fleming at La MaMa Experimental Theatre Club, inheriting a sense of energy flow and inner awareness of body movement. His apprenticeship with theatre director Robert Wilson in the production *Orlando* (1989), in Berlin, sharpened Papaioannou's visual clarity and sense of form on stage. He is also an awarded comic designer, a practice which acquainted him with how to use condensed and fragmented means in narrating a story through images.

In 1986, he co-founded Edafos Company with the dancer Angeliki Stellatou. The company, which disbanded in 2002, produced 17 works that changed the identity of contemporary dance in Greece. Edafos Company created a reputation for presenting aesthetically distinctive works characterised by striking stage images and a profound emotional impact on audiences. This first period cultivated some of his main choreographic features, like poetic imagery, use of repetition, visual 'tricks', and an intense body consciousness.

Since his first works, such as *To Vouno* [*The Mountain*] (1987), Papaioannou focused on minute detail in movement and in the distribution of energy in and out of the body. *Domatio 1 and 2* [*Room 1 & 2*] (1988) were performed by a diverse group of performers: Papaioannou and Stellatou, the actor Stavros Zalmas, and the dancer Nikos Dragonas. Movements such as undressing, walking, sitting, and lying were executed in a repetitive, slow manner within a simple stage setting consisting of a bed and table. These early works exposed a raw energy and idiosyncratic language based on stage actions instead of dance steps, while the use of nudity gave them a sensual appeal.

Teleftaio Tragoudi tou Richard Strauss [*The Last Song of Richard Strauss*, 1989], a collaboration with visual artist Nikos Alexiou, was a duet for Papaioannou and Stellatou on themes of love and loneliness. This work was incorporated into several subsequent choreographies and presented a female performer with red palms repeatedly washing her hands in seven troughs placed around the stage space, embracing a male figure with fierce urgency for love until he finally leaves her. *Ta Tragoudia* [*The Songs*] (1991), was set to a music selection ranging from Greek rembetica song (an urban style of early 20th century music) to Gluck and Richard Strauss; slow-paced movement, the use of objects such as the branch of a tree, and materials like water, were used to create dream-like images or hallucinatory effects that activated emotion. For example: a girl climbed up on a tall man-tree, a resonance for human relationships; a man crawled on a table facing a mirror that became a watery surface. These images were the result of detailed scenography, lighting design, and choreographic craft with roots in Papaioannou's performance, visual arts, and graphic background.

The next production *Ta Feggaria* [*The Moons*] (1992), based on Sappho's poetry and Fokine's *Le Spectre de la Rose* (1911), made explicit Papaioannou's inclination to use art history references and surreal images to activate the spectators' imaginations. The work exposed the performers' white painted bodies in slow motion to build tableaux vivants. His interest in white bodies and flesh lies in their visual effect; his painterly interest in contrasts and contour of forms on stage are evident in his early works. Especially in *Dracula* (1997), he presents a totally white work (white bodies, costumes, scenery, floor) in which the character of Dracula, as in Coppola's movie, has a black figure following his steps like a shadow.

Papaioannou sometimes makes allusions to ancient Greek sculptures, especially in the way that half- or fully-naked bodies stand; an idea thoughtfully explored in *Primal Matter* (2012), in which a black-suited performer manipulates the naked body of another, setting him in positions similar to sculptures. On other occasions, paintings are his reference point; the female figure in *Human Thirst* (1999), suggestive of the Virgin Mary in Giotto or de la Francesca paintings, or the dancer with the octopus in *Moons* resembling the fisherman fresco from Santorini. Through these visual quotations and use of lighting, which gives texture to the dancers' skins, he plays with the flesh and materiality of the real bodies on stage.

Edafos Company had a multidisciplinary character and collaborative ethics. Papaioannou's inclusion of non-dancers comes from a fascination with their movement qualities, due to his appreciation for non-refined movement, natural ways of moving, and raw energy in deportment. His performers are often dancers, actors, athletes, or hip-hop dancers, seen in early works like *The Songs* (1991) and *Moons* (1992), or in recent pieces like *Nowhere* (2009) and *The Great Tamer* (2017). His creations are often accompanied by visual compositions which give the atmosphere and the elements of the choreography, animated on stage through the live presence of the performers. Papaioannou is often involved in the set, lighting and costume design, make-up and the set-up of productions. As a result, his works bear the signature of an artist who combines different art forms in one craft, while he opens up his areas of responsibility to disperse his choreographic authority.

Midia [*Medea*] (1993), based on the Greek myth and commissioned by the Cultural Centre of the City of Athens, was Edafos Company's big success, marking a turn to storytelling. On four high tables/platforms set on a stage full of water, the story of Medea unfolded through a close relationship to excerpts from Vincenzo Bellini's operas. As the music reaches its peak, 'Medea kills her children by dashing two hand puppets to smithereens. Their red innards fall into the ankle-deep pool below, the "sea" that Jason, portrayed as a priggish 19th century admiral, has crossed' (Kisselgoff, 1998). This combination of music, song, and stage action builds an intense experience for the audience, full of emotion. By 1995, Edafos Company was well funded by the Greek state, and *Medea* proved to be Papaioannou's signature piece for the 1990s.

Storytelling through scene-by-scene plot development and a combination of music and action, supported meaning-making in a series of narrative works: *Iphigenia at the bridge of Arta* (1995), *Xenakis' Oresteia – The Aeschylus Suite* (1995), *Dracula* (1997), *The Storm* (1997), *Human Thirst* (1999), and *For Ever* (2001). However, two works of this period differ: *Enos Leptou Sigy* [*A Moment's Silence*] (1995) and *Monument* (1997). The first used compositions by notable Greek composers (Giorgos Koumendakis and Manos Hadjidakis) and dealt with the subject of the AIDS epidemic. It explored male gay sensitivities, desire and death by using text, music, song, dance, and visual imagery to build a multisensory experience; the latter, a solo for Katerina Papageorgiou (currently known as Kat Válastur), was inspired by Expressionist dance and images of early 20th century dancers taken by the Greek female photographer Elli Sougioultzoglou-Seraidari.

In 2004, having disbanded Edafos Company, Papaioannou created the opening and closing ceremonies of the Athens Olympic Games. A young boy in a boat floating on a lake in the middle of the Olympic Stadium, pieces of statues hanging in the air before forming a Cycladic sculpture, performers as figures from Knossos or archaic Kouroi, the god Eros flying above the lake, are some elements of this ceremony that 'could not be a story – it could only be the unfolding of a dream sequence' (Papaioannou's website).

After this experience, Papaioannou turned to large-scale productions, a context where his artistry could gain new momentum, and at the same time he abandoned his role of performer. *2* (2006), produced in collaboration with Konstantinos Vita, an electronic music composer, explored contemporary urban life from a gay perspective, with a large cast of male performers. It set the context for his next stage of development. *Medea (2)* (2008), a re-approach to the choreographer's trademark work, was commissioned by the Greek Ministry of Culture. Papaioannou restaged his original choreography with a new cast; he removed Bellini's music and colour from the props, leaving a cold white setting, a soundscape, and flat lights. This gave a harsh and visceral approach to the story, signalling a shift in his aesthetics to offer an almost post-human atmosphere on stage. *Nowhere* (2009), a commission by the National Theatre for its renovation, was a large-scale exploration of the stage mechanisms, its space and theatre, as apparatus for 26 performers who operated within and against a 'space-machine' (Greek National Opera press release). In the vast dimensions of the theatre stage, the human body became a reference point, a component whose motion was activated and affected by the environment. Humans, machinery, theatrical space, and actions existed interdependently in a dark heterotopia. *Inside* (2011), in contrast, explored time and duration. It was a six-hour-long performance in the form of a loop, during which the audience could enter and leave at any time. In a setting depicting the interior of a house and a window offering a 24-hour view to the city landscape, this urban meditation of everyday actions, such as walking, lying, looking out of the window, built a visual and temporal rhythm on stage. This experiment in transferring the performance situations of a gallery onto the theatrical stage proved too controversial for spectators.

Returning to minimal materials, in *Primal Matter* (2012), Papaioannou again became a performer. In this male duet he plays with the manipulation of the human body in a detached and ironic manner, creating body images linking to a range of references from broken statues to posthuman robots. In *Still Life* (2014), the myth of Sisyphus gave him the impetus to contemplate the absurdity of life and the contradictions of human existence. Through poetic images which unfold in a juxtaposition of ideas, provocative combinations of materials with human bodies and a vast transparent fabric hanging above the stage, Papaioannou created a work full of existential angst. In *The Great Tamer* (2017), this angst turns into histrionic comment on the history of mankind. He describes the work as 'a children's comic for adults. It is a self-made circus in someone's head. Someone who saw the history of the world being written on the bodies of those who loved and on people's art' (Onassis, 2017). *Since She* (2018) paid homage to Pina Bausch's Tanztheater seen through his personal writing, while distilling some of its essential elements, like absurdity and humanity.

In general, his interest in space-body architecture, human proportion, and use of costumes, props, lights, bodies, and objects has led him to constructing a world on stage which operates paradoxically, for it 'turns over the layers, literally and metaphorically' (Boisseau, 2017). It is a universe inhabited by a range of polymorphic creatures which dissolve into a series of images based on detailed precision, transformation, ambiguity, and trickery. Papaioannou's artistic motivation lies in a constantly alert state: 'I am trying not to know what I am looking for, or even better, I am trying to be available for every interesting thing produced by accident while searching' (Onassis, 2017).

Steriani Tsintziloni

Biographical details

Born in Athens Greece, 21 June 1964. **Studied** with Greek painter Yannis Tsarouchis before enrolling at the Athens School of Fine Arts. **Career:**

gained recognition as a painter and comic artist before entering the field of performing arts as a performer, choreographer, director, and designer of sets, costumes, make up, and lighting; first performed in the Greek dance company Analia; co-founded and choreographed for Edafos Company (1986–2002) in Athens. In 2004, created the opening and closing ceremonies of Athens Olympic Games; in 2015, created the Opening Ceremony for the Baku First European Games; in 2018 invited by Tanztheater Wuppertal to create a full-length work as the first choreographer for the company after Bausch's death. **Awards and honours** include 5th Biennial of Young Artists, 1990; Greek National Dance Awards, 1994, 1999, 2001; Golden Cross of the Order of Honour, 2005; Danza&Danza Award 2015; Special Prize of the XVI edition of the Europe Theatre Prize, 2017.

Works

The Mountain (1987); *The Raincoat* (1987); *Room I & II* (1988); *The Last Song of Richard Strauss* (1990); *The Songs* (1991); *The Moons* (1992); *Medea* (1993); *Theodora* (theatre, 1994); *Iphigenia at the Bridge of Arta* (1995); *Xenakis' Oresteia – The Aeschylus Suite* (1995); *A Moment's Silence* (1995); *Nefeli* (dir, stage show, 1995); *The Brothers Grimm Fairy Tales* (1996); *Dracula* (1997); *Monument* (1997); *The Storm* (1997); *Human Thirst* (1999); *Tree* (dir. stage show, 1998); *Volcano* (dir. stage show, 1998); *The Return of Helen* (opera, 1999); *La Sonnambula* (opera, 2000); *A Tale* (dir. stage show, 2000); *For Ever* (2001); *2* (2006); *Medea 2* (2008); *Nowhere* (2009); *Inside* (2011); *Primal Matter* (2012); *Still Life* (2014); *The Great Tamer* (2017); *Since She* (2018); *Sisyphus Trans Form* (site specific, 2019).

Further reading

(see also Papaioannou's Official Site: dimitrispapaioannou.com)

Interviews: with Klementini Vounelaki, 'Dimitris Papaioannou. Sta misa tis zois mou', *Lifo,* issuu.com/maglifo/docs/38 (in Greek), 12–18 October 2006; *Behind the Wall,* (Documentary film, dir. Nefeli Sarri, prod. Argonaftes AE and ERT AE), 2019.

Articles: Anna Kisselgoff, 'When Warmth Rises Above Hatred', *The New York Times,* 17 September 1998; Theophilos Tramboulis, 'Useful Contradictions', *Athens Contemporary Art Review,* 9, 2007; Greek National Theater, *'Nowhere' Press Release,* nt.gr/el/news/, 2009; Leonetta Bentivoglio, 'Since She', *La Republicca,* 28 May 2018; Judith Mackrell and Lyndsey Winship, 'Top 10 Dance Shows of 2018', *The Guardian,* 17 December 2018; Rosita Boisseau, 'Dimitris Papaioannou's Descent into Hell [La descente aux enfers de Dimitris Papaioannou]', *Le Monde,* 21 July 2017; George Sampatakakis, 'Bodies of Truth: The Terrible Beauty of Queer Performance', *Journal of Greek Media and Culture,* 4(2), 2019.

Books: Association of Greek Choreographers, *Choros*, Athens, 2004; Eleni Fessa-Emmanoueccl (ed.), *Choros kai theatro [Dance and Theatre]*, Athens, 2004; Pavlos Kavouras (ed.), *Folklore kai Paradosi. Zitimata ana-parastasis kai epitelesis tis mousikis kai tou chorou [Folklore and Tradition. Issues of Re-presentation and Performance of Music and Dance]*, Athens, 2010; Vassilis Vamvakas and Panagis Panagiotopoulos (eds.), *H Ellada sti dekaetia tou '80. Koinoniko, Politiko kai Politistiko Lexiko [Greece in the Decade of the 80s. Social, Political and Cultural Dictionary]*, Athens, 2010; Stegi Onassis, *The Great Tamer*, Athens, 2017, issuu.com (in Greek); Steriani Tsintziloni, in Penelope Petsini and Dimitris Christopoulos (eds.), *Lexiko logokrisias stin Ellada [Lexicon of censorship in Greece]*, Athens, 2017; Stegi Onassis, *Since She*, Athens, 2018, available at issuu.com/stegi.onassis.cultural.centre (in Greek and English).

CRYSTAL PITE

Crystal Pite is synonymous with powerful dance, either in the form of large numbers of dancers on stage, or through visually enticing but subtle works for fewer dancers. Articulate, emotional, detailed, her work speaks clearly and is, according to Pite herself, her first language (Royal Opera House, 2017). Underlying all her work is a game of words and movement, of meaning and symbolism and intense physicality. Critic Zöe Anderson has described her work as 'mov[ing] between contemporary and neoclassical dance, with a sharp eye for distinctive, emotionally driven movement' (2017), and Clement Crisp recognises that she holds a strong 'fascination with massed humanity as symbol and theme' (2017). Mass humanity is used within her works for evident choreographic power and craft, and, as Crisp describes, as the narrative line of the work, such as in her approach to migration in *Flight Pattern* (2017), or in symbolic representation of conceptual content such as in *The Season's Canon* (2018).

Pite's use of all the elements of performance is also highlighted by reviewers: Michael Upchurch, 'The musical score, the lighting, the set – all brilliantly dovetail with the action on stage' (2011); or Matthew Jocelyn, 'Pite's work integrates original music, text, rich visual design' (2009). Her company's website cites Judith Mackrell from *The Guardian*: 'Pite structures her work with a thrilling intelligence and choreographs with a detail that makes you feel passion and unease under your own skin' (Kidd Pivot, 2020). The company describes how their 'work is assembled with recklessness and rigour, balancing sharp exactitude with irreverence and risk' and how the 'distinct choreographic language [is] a breadth of movement fusing classical elements and the complexity and freedom of structured improvisation' (Kidd Pivot, 2020).

Born in Canada, Pite developed her career as a dancer in Ballet British Columbia and then with William Forsythe's Ballett Frankfurt. And although she confesses to have played unknowingly with choreography from a young age (Banff Centre for Arts and Creativity, 2015), her first work was presented in 1990 for Ballet BC's choreographic workshop. Early works for companies such as Ballet BC, Alberta Ballet, or Les Ballets Jazz de Montréal already show the essential contrasts which will recur and develop throughout her career: between small detail and large flowing movement, between the gestural and the symbolic, between the highly theatrical and the purely abstract. Pite continued to develop her choreographic and dancing careers in parallel until 2011, when she started to concentrate fully on choreography. Certain aspects of her work can perhaps be traced to her time under Forsythe's direction: an interest in pushing limits, the idea of leaving space and time for the dancer's improvisation, the complexity of her work's conceptual development. However, her style has since developed in many other directions. Her creative process is defined as a double entanglement: of the opposing forces of conflict and connection at the level of the body as well as in the subject matter. Tension, especially, Pite finds necessary and energising. Connection, she says, is what dance is for, it is about being human (Banff Centre, 2015).

Since 2008, Pite has developed a close relationship with Nederlands Dans Theater as Associate Choreographer. She has created ten works (one in collaboration with Paul Lightfoot and Sol León) for both NDT 1 and 2. *Plot Point*, created for the company in 2010, was nominated for the Benois de la Danse award. She has also created work for many companies and artists including Cullberg Ballet, Ballett Frankfurt, Les Ballets Jazz de Montréal, Cedar Lake Contemporary Ballet, and Louise Lecavalier/Fou Glorieux. Most recently she has created large-scale works for ballet companies: *Emergence* (2009) for National Ballet of Canada, subsequently restaged for Pacific Northwest Ballet and Scottish Ballet; *Flight Pattern* (2017) for the Royal Ballet; and *The Season's Canon* (2018) for Paris Opéra Ballet. These works are created in short periods and often make use of 36 or more dancers. Pite explains that a simple idea with a small variation, multiplied times 36 bodies on stage, creates immense complexity. *Emergence*, *Flight Pattern*, *The Seasons' Canon*, and *Body and Soul* (for Paris Opera in 2019), are witness to the intricacy, beauty, and power of her work, and also to her ability to transform the aesthetic of ballet bodies and companies while maintaining the interest of ballet audiences. Perhaps her own career as a ballet dancer helps with this, even though she confesses to Laura Cappelle that she still feels 'like an outsider' (2017).

Flight Pattern is a twenty-five-minute ensemble piece which premiered at the Royal Opera House, London, in March 2017, and restaged in May 2019 to great critical acclaim. It is set to the first movement of Henryk Górecki's *Symphony No. 3* (1976), known as the Symphony of Sorrowful Songs. Critic Lindsey Winship describes this piece as 'get[ting] to the bone of human experience' (2017). Pite uses 36 dancers, using repetition, canon, simple pedestrian movements – such as rocking back and forth – in varying group formations. These are interspersed with individual gestures which capture both the narrative thread and the specific attention of the audience. Sculptural lighting by regular collaborator Tom Visser forms spaces and times through elements such as doors which open and close, snow, and differently coloured atmospheres. However, neither the space nor the costumes locate a specific place or era, allowing for a powerful – if not unproblematic – sense of universality to emerge. The amount of activity on stage is almost overwhelming at points, desperate, with the dancers breaking into small groups and then reuniting with the larger ensemble. Only brief moments allow the audience to breathe through stillness, slow motion, and powerfully emotional rebounds. The sheer simplicity of these moments alters the spectator's emotions. Pite's masterful orchestration of the dancers is evident: the larger ensemble breaks into two, three, four groups, front and back, side to side, all connected but performing slightly different sequences. When they are all together the unison is not perfect, highlighting the sense of humanity further. Kristen McNally and Marcelino Sambé signify the clearest narrative line, both in her solos and in the moments they dance together. McNally's solo to the soprano voice physicalises the weight of loss and grief, no less through the weight of the long coats the other dancers place on her. Sambé's final solo is both despair and fight, through clear reaching, curving, shaking, or flicking movements: an example of resilience which hauntingly closes the work. Crisp explains how Pite builds a world of 'energy and despair' (2017), and an emotional portrayal of the current humanitarian crisis, and the work is described on the DVD brochure as a 'poignant and passionate reflection on migration' (Opus Arte, 2020).

With her own company, Kidd Pivot, founded in Vancouver in 2002, she can really explore the subtleties of her style. She explains the name of her company: *Pivot* for precision, specificity, rigour, skill, a movement that changes your direction and hence your point of view; *Kidd* for the outlaw, the pirate, that which is reckless, chaotic, unpredictable. These productions are smaller in cast and usually have six dancers – the number of people, she says, who can hold a dinner conversation without subdividing into smaller groups (Royal Opera House, 2017). Pushing the bodies of her dancers to the limit, Pite and her 'Pivots' explore articulation, manipulation, qualities of movement. There are images which emerge within her work with Kidd Pivot but also transfer elsewhere: shaking, staccato movement, use of tableaux, bodies being moved 'against their will', unison, precise hand and arm positions and gestures, rocking back and forth … The message is clearly embedded and laid out in both what is present in the movement – thought articulated in her dancers' bodies – and what is absent: the hand that nearly touches, the body that almost falls, the indication of what might be, the tension, once again.

Her biggest play, however, is in the narrative. Not only because she freely plays with language in the works – through inspiration in poems, voice-over, lip-syncing, speeches, voices narrating the movement sequences; but because she continuously reinvents narrative devices. In most of her own company pieces, Pite divides the work in two acts: the first highly theatrical and almost linearly narrative, the second exploring the narrative and themes in 'pure' dance. This second act is where the work enters the 'real world', the human act (Public Salon 2014). Although it might seem further detached after a clear, witty, humorous first act, these second acts are Pite's real revolution of dance. She has already given the narrative, she does not worry about her audience not understanding, and she can give free rein to the intensity, the emotionality, the visceral power of dance. Through these structures, she says, dance reaches out to people, because they know this language of emotion already (Public Salon 2014). Pite intends to offer the 'audience a variety of ways to get into a piece', using 'anything to get people in the same world as each other' (Cappelle, 2017). Interestingly, she seemed to reverse this order in *Body and Soul* for the Paris Opera in 2019, where the first two acts seemed more human – with truly humane, touching moments – and the final act moved into a pop-infused insect world, Pite's sense of theatricality and risk evident in this particular endeavour.

Pite says there is doubt and terror in her creative process, and her own sense of conflict is beautifully fleshed out in *Dark Matters* (2009). But these generative doubts and tensions give Pite's audiences the richness of her productions. And after a full act of heart-wrenching narrative-in-movement, it is the little humane moments which show clearly the genius of this choreographer: the hand changing from shoulder to chest when Cindy Salgado holds Jonathon Young in *Betroffenheit* (2015); Marcelino Sambé stopping to put a hand on

Kristen McNally's shoulder in *Flight Pattern*; or the final, sublime stitch between puppet and puppeteer in *Dark Matters*.

Lucía Piquero Alvarez

Biographical details

Born 15 December 1970, Terrace, British Columbia, Canada. **Studied** in Victoria, British Columbia under Maureen Eastick (Pacific Dance Centre) and Wendy Green; in the Banff Centre Summer Programmes; in the School of Toronto Dance Theatre Summer Programmes. **Career:** Dancer with Ballet British Columbia (1988); dancer with Ballet Frankfurt, under William Forsythe (1996). Featured in Forsythe CD-ROM Improvisation Technologies (1999). Founded Kidd Pivot (Vancouver, 2002). Given a residency at the Künstlerhaus Mousonturm in Frankfurt (2010–12). Created work for companies such as Nederlands Dans Theater, Cullberg Ballet, Ballett Frankfurt, National Ballet of Canada; collaborated with Electric Company Theatre and Robert Lepage. Associate Dance Artist of Canada's National Arts Centre; Associate Choreographer with the Nederlands Dans Theater since 2008; Associate Artist at Sadler's Wells, London since 2013. **Awards and honours** include Banff Centre's Clifford E. Lee Award, 1995; Paul D. Fleck Fellowship in the Arts from The Banff Centre, 2004; Bonnie Bird North American Choreography Award, 2004; Isadora Award for Choreography, 2005; Rio Tinto Alcan Performing Arts Award, 2006; Jessie Richardson Theatre Award, 2006; Governor General of Canada's Mentorship Program, 2008; Dora Mavor Moore Award, 2009 and 2016; Jacob's Pillow Dance Award, 2011; Dora Mavor Moore Award, 2012; Canada Council for the Arts' Jacqueline Lemieux Prize, 2012; Olivier Award for Outstanding Achievement in Dance, 2015; Critics' Circle National Dance Award, 2016 and 2018; Georgia Straight Critic's Choice Innovation Award, 2016; Prix Benois de la Danse, 2017; Olivier Awards for Best New Dance Production, 2017 and 2018; Dance Magazine Award, 2018; Grand Prix de la Danse de Montreal Laureate, 2018; Critics' Circle National Dance Award, 2018; Chrystal Dance Prize, 2019.

Works

Between the Bliss and Me (1989); *Reflection on Billie* (1992); *In a Time of Darkness* (1993); *Shapes of a Passing* (1994); *Two Dances for Jane* (1995); *Pendulum* (1995); *Quest* (1995); *Moving Day* (1996); *Field: Fiction* (1996); *Hopping the Twig* (1998); *Excerpts from a Future Work* (2000); *Tales-New and Abridged* (2001); *Short Works: 22* (2001); *Uncollected Work* (2003); *Double Story* (2004); *The Stolen Show* (2004); *Xspectacle* (2004); *Pilot X* (2005); *Lost Action* (2006); *Arietta* (2006); *Lone Epic* (2006); *The Second Person* (2007); *Frontier* (2008); *10 Duets on a Theme of Rescue* (2008); *Matter of a Maker* (2008); *Dark Matters* (2009); *Emergence* (2009); *The You Show* (2010); *Plot Point* (2010); *Lost Action, Trace* (3D adaptation, 2010); *The Tempest Replica* (2011); *Solo Echo* (2012); *Parade*

(2013); *Betroffenheit* (2015); *In the Event* (2015); *The Statement* (2016); *The Seasons' Canon* (2016); *Flight Pattern* (2017); *Partita for 8 Dancers* (2018); *Body and Soul* (2019); *Kunstkamer* with Paul Lightfoot and Sol León (2019); *Revisor* (2019).

Further reading

Interviews: with Luke Jennings, *The Guardian*, 22 September 2013; for Public Salon Vancouver, 5 March 2014; Sarah Crompton for *The Telegraph*, 21 April 2014; Dominic Girard for Banff Centre for Arts and Creativity, 2015; Emma Southworth for the Royal Opera House, 9 February 2017; Laura Cappelle for *Dance Magazine*, 16 March 2017; Rachel Beaumont, for the Royal Opera House, 27 April 2017; Cathy Levy for National Arts Center Dance, 6 March 2019.

Articles: Zöe Anderson, 'Flight Pattern, The Royal Ballet, Royal Opera House, London, Review: It Has Immense Scale and Ambition', *The Independent*, 19 March 2017; Clement Crisp, 'Crystal Pite's Flight Pattern at the Royal Opera House, London – Profoundly Moving', *Financial Times*, 19 March 2017; Michael Upchurch, 'Review: 'Dark Matters' at On the Boards is Spellbinding Dance', *Seattle Times*, 18 February 2011; Matthew Jocelyn, 'Choreographed by Dance Sensation Crystal Pite. Dark Matters', *Canadian Stage*, 2009; Lyndsey Winship, 'Flight Pattern, Dance Review: Crystal Pite's Extraordinary Talent Shines in Royal Ballet Triple Bill', *Evening Standard*, 20 March 2017.

Books: P. Dickinson, 'Narrative Pivots: Text and Movement in Crystal Pite's Dance-Theatre', in *Narrative in Performance* (eds. B. Sellers-Young and J. R. McCutcheon), London, 2019; L. McJannet, 'Incorporating the Text: John Farmanesh-Bocca's Pericles Redux and Crystal Pite's the Tempest Replica', in *The Oxford Handbook of Shakespeare and Dance* (eds L. McCulloch and B. Shaw), Oxford, 2019; L. Piquero, 'On Physicality and Narrative: 'Emotional Universality' in Crystal Pite's Flight Pattern', in *The Oxford Handbook of Contemporary Ballet* (eds. Kathrina Farrugia-Kriel and Jill Nunes Jensen), Oxford, forthcoming 2021.

ALAIN PLATEL

Alain Platel's choreographic career began as a bet between friends. The provocation? A 1984 trip to the theatre to see Maurice Bejart's new work; in response Platel created a series of amateur performances that brought together friends and family as performers. The founding of a small company ensued, given the ironically grandiose name of *les ballets C de la B*. This origin story is an often-repeated founding myth because it highlights two crucial factors shaping Platel's choreographic approach: a collaborative working practice and confidence in his role as outsider.

Without formal dance training, his background in psychology and experience working at a cerebral palsy centre for children left an indelible mark on his movement vocabulary and thematic interests. Platel's productions include both 'amateur' and untrained dancers, aiming to exploit the aesthetic traction that arises between differently trained bodies: aerialists dance with contortionists, tenors sing alongside dancers who are themselves singing, purposefully out of tune. In *Gardenia* (2010), for example, seven retired drag artists in formal suits drift across the stage, slowly undressing to reveal frail, aging bodies. As they pose in freeze-frame style the pop song *Forever Young* plays. Built upon the concept of a cabaret performance and upending mainstream narratives, a young trained dancer becomes the 'outsider' in this group. As *Gardenia* shows, Platel is indebted to an aesthetic and creative practice established by Pina Bausch's *Tanztheater*, and like Bausch, his work revels in combining a multiplicity of artistic modes: integrating spoken word with mime and comedy, juxtaposing sudden violence with lengthy, languorous duets; meshing religious iconography with neon shopping signs.

Platel is a dance director who facilitates, edits, and moulds raw material developed through research, improvisation, questioning, and conversation. His role in the studio has been described as that of 'catalyst' or 'empathic witness' (Cooper Albright, 1997; Stalpaert, Cools & De Vuyst, 2020). Not based around a single signature, his collective approach challenges the language of dance learnt at leading conservatoires. By bringing together a diverse range of collaborators with rich and varied experiences, and offering them freedom to experiment, his company established an environment that fostered unusual creativity. As a result, *les ballets C de la B* is also a dynamic artistic platform producing choreographers such as Sidi Larbi Cherkaoui, Hans van den Broeck, Christine De Smedt, Koen Augustijnen, and Lisi Estaras.

From 1984 to 1989, Platel and his collective experimented with humorous works such as *Stabat Mater* (1984), in which two men try to seduce the same woman only for her to choose an enormous cream cake. *Bonjour madame …* (1993) was the first time Platel was credited as director and engaged professional dancers. It toured internationally for four years. During this time, Platel began working with writer Arne Sierens creating work for a youth theatre and with dramaturge Hildegard De Vuyst. Developing an unusually close working relationship, De Vuyst acts as narrative architect, translator, editor and critic.

Platel returned to *les ballets C de la B* to create *Wolf* (2003). Combining performers with varied technical backgrounds, *Wolf* marks the beginning of an increasingly sociological approach where Platel constructs miniature societies on stage. Three suited men play water glasses while a woman bangs cymbals and marches across the stage screaming; in another corner a dancer walks on his hands dangling a plastic garden chair from one foot. Amongst this seemingly random chaos, an ecstatic duet bursts forth: a male and female dancer, both in floral dresses, leap in synchrony as onstage musicians stamp their feet and drum metal shutters creating a cacophony. A dancer in tiara and tutu performs développé and chainé turns (gestural references to *Swan Lake*), later re-emerging in lurid red bathing cap with red devil's horns. In stilettos her legs stroke the floor, performing deep lunges and yogic stretches with a small, fluffy dog tucked into her bathing suit. *Wolf* explores themes of poverty, marginality, gender, and social conflict. Set to music by Mozart, tension builds as a dancer ends his solo with a direct address to the audience: "I don't really like classical music". As dancers loiter and drink from beer bottles, they try to round up the twelve loose dogs wandering the stage. The piece also probes the power dynamic between humans and animals in a stage set that resembles an abandoned shopping mall complete with wire fencing, graffiti, metal shutters, and shop-front video display. *Wolf* established an aesthetic that would reach its climax in *tauberbach* (2014) set on a rubbish dump.

Ways of describing Platel's work as collage reflect the multiplicity of meanings and aesthetic references. De Vuyst describes Platel's choreography as counterpoint, explaining the complexities as 'two images that cancel each other out or contradict each other' and 'give rise to conflicting emotions, so that judgement must be suspended. With Platel, an unclear message is not vague but disturbing' (Stalpaert, Cools & De Vuyst 2020). These disturbances require audiences to take on the role of 'witness'. Lengthy running times reinforce the disciplined concentration Platel expects from audiences, mirroring the physical effort of the dancers as they groan, gasp, and sweat.

A distinctive form of manic movement emerges across Platel's works. In *vsprs* (2006) set to a jazz arrangement of Monteverdi's *Vespers* by Fabrizio Cassol, and inspired by mental asylum footage, a series of flamboyantly drawn characters – a pop star, 60's model, and contortionist – convulse in spasmodic, virtuoso variations that resemble seizures. As the music fades, the dancers desperately drag each other up a stage set of icebergs made from white underwear. In *vsprs* extremity extends to facial expressions and the dancers contort their faces in myriad distortions and shapes of silent cries. Platel's frequent use of nudity also intensifies these hysterical bodies' vulnerability.

This movement vocabulary creates a new way of presenting the body, and Platel's emphasis on hyperphysicality draws inspiration from medical discourses. He explored Tourette's syndrome in *La Tristeza Complice* (1995) while for *Out of Context: For Pina* (2010), he highlights specific movements associated with dyskinesia and dystonia: spasms, convulsions, tics, chattering, grimacing. Platel argues in an interview with Paula Citron (2010), that 'there is also a poetic side – a beauty and power in the misshapen and malformed'. By utilising a range of movements associated with differently able bodies or illness, Platel unleashes their expressive qualities and challenges their status as peripheral or abnormal. His work produces a type of extreme technique described by Kélina Gotman in 2012, as participating in an 'alterkinetic turn', extending the range of bodily movements. Gotman argues that Platel's choreography emphasises 'movement and all its discontents: abled, disabled, virtuosic, technically proficient, amateurish, and expansive'.

Platel's collaborative model extends globally. Since 2001 his company regularly visits Palestine bringing their dancers and the Royal Flemish Theatre together with local artists to create collaborative work, including *Badke* (2013). A successful Congolese tour of *pitié!* (2008) preceded *Coup Fatal* (2014), which involved thirteen musicians from Kinshasa. Asked to respond to baroque composers, they created a concert style performance inspired by the exuberant energy and movements of the 'sapeur' or dandies of Kinshasa. The cultural collisions and appropriation Platel encourages are a source of critical anxiety (see Kasner, 2018), but he believes that appropriation, when embedded in collective working practices, is ethical. Platel calls this approach 'bastard dance' by asking dancers to copy movement phrases from each other in an appropriative chain of exchanges subconscious (Stalpaert, Cools & De Vuyst 2020).

This commitment to collaboration and appropriation penetrates works which are not direct cultural collisions. In *pitié!* (2008), Platel worked with composer Fabrizio Cassol to integrate African and baroque influences into his interpretation of Bach's *St Matthew Passion*. This piece exemplifies the importance of music to Platel's creative process and use of live musicians as a dramatic element; as Mackrell (1999) observes, 'Platel often sets his works to noble music – Purcell or Bach – and this has the unexpected effect of giving his characters lyric flight without sentimentalising them'. As dancers emerge from plastic tarpaulins with tin cups and tattered clothes, the tensions between sacrifice, suffering, and pleasure are explored. Athletic solos of acrobatic flips alternate with spitting, stuttering, and the failure to master relatively simple movements. Thus, while one dancer falls, another becomes an aerialist, suspended from the ceiling, spinning gracefully. When the piece rises to its final climax the company becomes one body groaning, shrieking, and stumbling in a succession of rhythmic bursts.

Platel returns to this aesthetic in *nicht schlafen* (2016). Mahler is mixed with African polyphonic chants; the stage could be a refugee camp or resting place for itinerant travellers, but soon a fight erupts and the dancers viciously tear each other's clothes off and claw at faces. Eventually they stomp and shout in exaggerated displays of bravado as though warning off the next attacker. Centre stage, Berlinde De Bruyckere's large sculpture of three dead horses piled on a plinth, is a stark reminder of death and ritualised animal sacrifice. Critics have suggested that Platel should be considered in the context of Artaud's 'Theatre of Cruelty' where theatre is an attack on the senses and liberation of the subconscious (Stalpaert, Cools & De Vuyst 2020). *Requiem Pour L.* (2018) pushes these ethical boundaries by including a commissioned film of the final moments of a woman's life.

Platel's political urgency and ambition has increased over time. In 2007, *Nine Finger* explored the perspective of an African child soldier while *C(H)OEURS* (2012) responded to the Arab Spring and Occupy movement. Created for seventy members of the Teatro Real chorus, *C(H)OEURS* demonstrates Platel's move towards large-scale works, such as the 2018 community performance of *Le Sacre du Printemps* for 300 townspeople. In *C(H)OEURS* a large loudspeaker hangs over the centre of the stage, handwritten placards are raised by the choir as though it's a protest; towards the end of the piece, two small boys are passed corpse-like above and through the choir's raised hands. Two dancers perform a tender duet of synchronicity, with enveloping and interwoven limbs rising amongst the choir lying on the floor. The fallen choir raise their palms to reveal red stained palms, as the dancers leap weightlessly above them. Using lyrical, graceful movements and Grecian aesthetics contrasted with the visible signs of violence and protest, *C(H)OEURS* builds an atmosphere of tragic grandeur. Continuing his evolution as a socially engaged choreographer, Platel is updating *C(H)OEURS* to respond to current affairs in 2020.

Erin Whitcroft

Biographical details

Born in Ghent, Belgium in 1956. **Studied** psychology, pedagogy, mime, and courses in modern dance; he is a self-taught director. **Career**: first worked in child psychiatric hospitals and a centre for children with cerebral palsy. Created the collective, *les ballets C de la B*, 1984; in 1991 Platel left, returning in 1993 to produce *Bonjour madame* ... their breakout success; this brought state funding; Platel left a second time in 1999 and then returned as Artistic Director, overhauling the staff and sharpening the company's focus on the avant-garde. Began collaborating with writer Arne Sierens and the youth theatre Victoria, creating theatrical productions; founded *The Best Belgian Dance Solo* competition for the Stekelbees Festival. In 2018 helped create a community performance of *Le Sacre du Printemps* with Lisi Estaras and Quan Bui Ngoc involving 300 townspeople. **Awards and honours** include Prix Saint Denis, 1990; KONTAKT International Theatre Festival Prizes, 1995, 2007, 2018; Hans Snoek Prize, 1996; Mobil Pegasus Prize, 1996; Flemish Océ Prize, 1997; Time Out Live Award, 1998; Lycea Prize, Rencontres Internationales de Seine Saint-Denis, 1998; Masque d'Or de la Production Etrangère, Canada 1999, 2002; Prix Europe Nouvelles Théatrales, 2001; Chevalier of l'Ordre des Arts et des Lettres de la République Française, 2001, upgraded to Commandeur, 2015; Prix Ubu pour la Meilleure Production Etrangère 2001; Frank Van Acker Prize, 2002; Ballet-Tanz Magazine Award, 2006-2007; Dora Mavor Moore Awards, 2011, 2018; San Francisco Dance Screen Festival Award, 2013; Champagne Prize 2014; Grand Prix de la Danse, 2015; Flemish Culture Prize, 2015; Herald Angel Award 2009; Gold Medal, Royal Flemish Academy of Belgium for Science and Art, 2016; Catalan Performing Arts Critics Award, 2017; Special Jury Prize, Belgian Prix de la Critique, 2017. Honorary Doctorates: University of Artois (France) 2012 and University of Ghent, 2016.

Works

Stabat Mater (with Ethel Thuyn, Johan Grimonprez, Pascale Platel, 1984); *Lichte Kavalerie* (with collaborators, 1985); *Mange p'tit coucou* (with Alexander Claeys, 1986); *Alchemie* (1987); *Architectuur als buur* (1988); *Emma* (with Alexander Claeys, 1988); *O Boom* (with Johan Grimonprez, 1989); *Mussen* (1991); *Bonjour madame* ... (1993); *Moeder en kind* (with Arne Sierens, 1995); *La Tristeza Complice* (1995); *Bernadetje* (with Arne Sierens, 1996); *Iets op Bach* (1998); *Allemaal Indiaan* (with Arne Sierens, 1999); *Because I Sing* (2001); *Wolf* (2003); *vsprs* (with Fabrizio Cassol 2006); *les ballets de ci de là* (film, 2006); *Uit de Bol/Coup de Choeurs* (2006); *Nachtschade* (2006); *Nine Finger* (with Fumiyo Ikeda and Benjamin Verdonck, 2007); *pitié!* (with Fabrizio Cassol 2008); *Out of Context - for Pina* (2010); *Gardenia* (with Frank Van Laecke, 2010); *C(H) OEURS* (2012); *tauberbach* (2014); *Coup Fatal* (with Fabrizio Cassol 2014); *En avant, marche!* (with Frank Van Laecke, 2015); *nicht schlafen* (2016); *Requiem pour L.* (with Fabrizio Cassol 2018); *Le Sacre du Printemps* (with Quan Bui Ngoc & Lisi Estaras 2018); *C(H)OEURS 2020* (2020).

Further reading

(see also lesballetscdela.be)

Interviews: with Judith Mackrell, 'Horror that Started as a Joke', *The Guardian*, 7 December 1999; Monika Navarro, 'Choreographer Alain Platel: "I Seek What Unites People, not What Divides Them"', *l'Humanite*, 3 March 2006; Hildegard De Vuyst, 'An Interview with Alain Platel about pitié!', lesballetscdela.be, August 2008; Rob Kraatz,'Interview No.7: Alain Platel', Ueberbuehne.de, May 2014; Tejas Rawal, 'Alain Platel Discusses the Challenges of Grappling with Mahler', londondance.com, 27 June 2017; Tomasz Kireńczuk, *'Interview with Alain Platel "On the Need to Be Together"'*, dialogfestival.com, 9 October 2017.

Articles: Adrian Kear, 'Seduction and Translation: Alain Platel in Conversation', *Performance Research,* 7, 2002; Renate Klett, 'Nothing Happens, and Yet Everything Does: The Theatre of Alain Platel', *Theater,* 36, 2006; Alain Platel, 'Diary', lesballetscedela.be, 2007; Alain Platel and Lou Cope, 'Looking Inward, Outward, Backward and Forward', *Contemporary Theater Review,* 20, 2010; Lourdes Orozco, 'Never Work with Children and Animals: Risk, Mistake and the Real in Performance', *Performance Research,* 15, 2010; Hildegard De Vuyst, 'Out of Context – for Pina: Introduction', lesballetscedela.be, 2010; Ryan Platt, 'Human Failure and Humane Exhaustion: The Passion of Alain Platel', *Journal of Performance and Art,* 32, 2010; Kélina Gotman, 'Epilepsy, Chorea, and Involuntary Movements Onstage: The Politics and Aesthetics of Alterkinetic Dance', *About Performance,* 11, 2012; Erin Whitcroft, 'Alain Platel Brings *les ballets C de la B* to Sadler's Wells', Bachtrack, 2 July 2017; Charlotte Kasner, 'Murdering Mozart: les ballets C de la B in *Requiem Pour L.*', Seeingdance.com, 20 March 2018.

Books: Joe Kelleher and Nicholas Ridout (eds.), *Contemporary Theatres in Europe: A Critical Companion*, London, 2006; Hildegard De Vuyst (ed.), *Les Ballets C. de la B,* Tielt: Lannoo Uitgeverij, 2006; Guy Cools, *Imaginative Bodies: Dialogues in Performance Practices*, Amsterdam, 2016; Bill Bissell, *The Sentient Archive: Bodies, Performance, and Memory,* Connecticut, 2018; Kélina Gotman, *Choreomania: Dance and Disorder*, Oxford, 2018; Alain Platel, *Requiem Pour L.*, Amsterdam, EPO Uitgeverij, 2019; Christel Stalpaert, Guy Cools, and Hildegard De Vuyst (eds.), *The Choreopolitics of Alain Platel's les ballets C de la B: Emotions, Gestures, Politics*, London, 2020.

ANGELIN PRELJOCAJ

Internationally, Angelin Preljocaj is probably the best-known French contemporary dance choreographer of the generation who came to prominence during the 1980s. His company frequently performs in the world's major theatres and festivals, and he has created works for ballet companies including New York City Ballet, Opéra de Paris, and Berlin Staatsoper. He seems equally appreciated by contemporary dance and ballet audiences. Born in France of Albanian immigrant parents, he learnt classical ballet and studied both European and US modern dance techniques. As he admits, the twin poles of his creative process are German expressionism and US abstraction (in Bettina Wagner-Bergelt, 1996). His works are often set to European classical music, or to scores by contemporary composers. He has a particular affinity for the music of Prokofiev and Stravinsky which inspired him to choreograph some dynamic, intense works. While Preljocaj is an intellectual, his work is never cerebral but is direct and strips away formal conventions to focus on basic human needs and drives. It often combines abstract passages of characteristically angular and asymmetrical choreography with fragmented dramaturgical structures that hint at narrative without telling stories. While not a minimalist, his work sometimes takes on a ritualistic quality, or proceeds with an irresistible, almost machine-like inevitability that gives it a disturbing or menacing edge.

Preljocaj's parents were political refugees who, following threats, had escaped from Albania. He was born shortly after they settled in France and grew up feeling Albanian at home while speaking French at school and with friends. Having studied ballet from an early age, he turned to contemporary dance taught by Karin Waeher, a pupil of the great German choreographer Mary Wigman. After studying in New York at the Cunningham studio, he worked for the Centre National de Danse Contemporaine in Angers, directed at the time by ex-Cunningham dancer, Viola Farber.

Of all the US companies who, during the 1960s and 1970s, had acted as catalysts for the revival of European modern dance, Europeans recognised in Cunningham's work a continuation of the European avant-garde tradition of Dada. They found in his hybrid fusion of ballet and modern dance movement a way of adapting and developing the modernist tradition of post-war European ballet choreography. Cunningham's influence on the 'new wave' of French contemporary dance in the 1980s can be found in the cool, crisp clarity with which choreographers like Preljocaj developed their own somewhat idiosyncratic, fragmented styles.

After dancing with Farber, Preljocaj spent three years as a member of Dominique Bagouet's company. The French Ministry of Culture set up 'national' dance centres and companies based throughout the French regions and Bagouet was based in Montpellier. He was probably the most innovative and influential pioneer of the French 'new wave', Preljocaj working with him at a key early stage in its development. When Preljocaj left Montpellier to start making his own work, some saw this as a betrayal.

Preljocaj first attracted attention in 1984 when his piece *Marché Noir* won first prize at the international choreographic competition at Bagnolet. In 1985, his newly founded company was established in Champigny-sur-Marne with regular funding from the Ministry of Culture, and he created *Larmes blanches*. This title is ambiguous, meaning 'white tears' (*larmes*) while sounding like 'white weapons' (*l'armes*), and this uncertainty was also present in the choreography, which seemed poignantly idiosyncratic but also aggressively impersonal. Made for two men and two women, and including same-sex duets, it was set to baroque music played on the harpsichord, whose quasi-mechanical ticking combined with the choreography's complex, geometrical precision to give the piece a modernist quality. The movement material consisted of tiny obsessive gestures, unexpected sideways hops, and sudden collapses, often performed in nervous but uncanny unison.

In contrast with the fastidious surface of *Larmes blanches,* Preljocaj's version of *Les Noces* (1989) was a fast-moving, menacing ritual to Stravinsky's jarring, discordant choral music. Originally choreographed in 1923 by Nijinska for the Ballets Russes, Preljocaj retained the piece's premise but abandoned the ballet's libretto. He made an abstract ensemble piece for five couples who sit on, jump over, or upend five benches, and play violently with five life-size rag dolls that are dressed like brides. As Anna Kisselgoff observed in 1991: 'There is nothing exploratory or learned about the relationships on view; the couples throw themselves into each other's arms or laps with a regularity that implies pre-ordained roles – male-female confrontations ruled by instinct'. *Les Noces* drew the attention of the film director Roman Polanski whose discussions with Preljocaj formed the basis for a 1992 book of interviews.

The younger generation of more conceptually oriented French choreographers in the 1990s criticised Preljocaj's generation for pretending they were developing new movement vocabularies, like those found in works like *Larmes blanches* and *Les Noces*, when these were derived from established historical traditions. This is, however, to misunderstand the way the French 'new wave' experienced their newly found choreographic freedom as an alarming loss of certainties. The resulting aesthetic of boundarylessness was particularly resonant when many Europeans were suffering the unsettling and disorienting effects of globalisation and the collapse of soviet communism. In 1993 Preljocaj described choreography as a way of accessing the unknown: 'Only the language of the body can bring out the difficult transmission of the unspeakable. What seems so magnificent to me about the craft of choreography is its potential for grasping the unspeakable and unnameable, and expressing meanings in its name' (in Aline Apostolska, 1993).

The 1980s saw several modern re-workings of well-known ballets, including Mats Ek's *Giselle* (1982) and *Swan Lake* (1987) for the Culberg Ballet, and Maguy Marin's surreal *Cendrillon* (Cinderella, 1985) for Lyons Ballet, who commissioned Preljocaj, in 1990, to make a new version of *Roméo et Juliette*. Setting this in a dystopian future, Preljocaj collaborated with cult fantasy and sci-fi illustrator Enki Bilal. Their Capulets became a rich elite, living in a futuristic gated-community patrolled by helmeted, leather-clad security men with guard dogs. Tybalt and his crew let off steam on excursions to attack local vagrants – the Montagues. Thus, while the Capulets wore tight black clothes and moved in a brutal, angular way that recalled Nazi goose-stepping, the Montagues wore soft, loose grey shirts and tattered trousers, and moved with provocative insouciance. The encounters between the two gangs had the same menace as those between Sharks and Jets in Robbins's choreography for the musical *West Side Story* (1957). Preljocaj counted on audience familiarity with Shakespeare's play, Prokofiev's score and with previous versions of the ballet. This, however, also gave him opportunities to trouble their sense of the familiar by introducing disorienting elements and abstracting or ritualising scenes. The role of the Nurse became two sinister female minders whose dancing had an almost robotic, clone-like, mirrored symmetry. The climax of the bedroom scene saw four duplicate couples emerge in the background, moving in perfect synchronisation with Roméo and Juliette's passionate embraces.

Following this success, Preljocaj was commissioned in 1993 to create an evening of work as a tribute to the Ballets Russes, for which he revived *Les Noces* and created characteristically idiosyncratic versions of *Le Spectre de la rose* and *Parade*. In 1994 the Paris Opéra commissioned *Le Parc*, around the idea of 18th century aristocratic libertinage danced to music by Mozart, and Preljocaj explored the same theme in 1998 with *Casanova*. He re-choreographed two more Ballet Russes ballets, both with Stravinsky scores: *L'Oiseau de feu* (1995) for Munich Ballet, and, in 2001, *Le Sacre du printemps* for dancers in the Berlin Staatsoper supplemented with his own dancers. The final sacrifice of the Chosen One in *Le Sacre* was initiated with a rape scene as she struggled to get away but was assaulted by male and female cast. As she tried to resist they held her, tore off her clothes, left her completely naked and ashamed. Such explicit scenes of sexual predation and violence proved controversial.

Preljocaj created several works that celebrate the male dancing body. In 1988, with film maker Cyril Collard, he created the short dance film *Les Raboteurs*, inspired by an impressionist painting by Gustave Caillebotte of workmen planing floorboards with their shirts off on a hot day. Preljocaj's choreography emphasised the contrast between its intense physicality and the mundane nature of the event, Preljocaj himself dancing as one of the three workmen. The film also invented a bourgeois couple who sipped wine while voyeuristically watching them working. Preljocaj returned to the spectacle of intensely physical, half-clad male bodies in his 2001 work *MC 14/22*. The title refers to the story of the Last Supper: St Mark's Gospel, chapter 14, verse 22 reads: 'take, eat, this is my body which is given for you'. It began with the cast of semi-naked male dancers ritualistically washing one another and ended with defiant, heroic choreographed sequences set to the sounds of bombs and helicopters. Preljocaj seems to believe that the male dancing body is attractive both for female and gay male spectators; the bourgeois voyeurs in *Les Raboteurs* being matched by a disembodied female voice in *MC 14/22* whispering mystically about male erections.

In 1994, Ballet Preljocaj was invited to Toulon. Shortly after the move, a prominent member of the far right, anti-immigration Front National was elected Mayor of Toulon. Ballet Preljocaj's plans to undertake outreach projects with poor North African immigrants in the city's suburbs caused the Mayor to cut their funding and mount a vicious campaign against the company. The Ministry of Culture intervened and in 1996 Ballet Preljocaj relocated to Aix-en-Provence.

In 1998, Preljocaj was made a Chevalier of the Légion d'Honneur. The rebellious outsider had become an establishment figure. Asked to name his favourite choreographer (in Dominique Frétard, 2003), he replied Jerome: Robbins and Bel, the latter having danced for Preljocaj in the late 1980s. Preljocaj's work had developed from the edgy, impersonal radicalism of works like *Larmes blanches* into the more explicitly humanist intentions of *Near Life Experience* (2003), a work inspired by the breathlessness Preljocaj had experienced while climbing Mount Kilimanjaro without the aid of oxygen. He remains extremely productive, often making more than one new work a year. He has received prestigious invitations from major ballet companies, including the Paris Opéra, La Scala, and the Bolshoi Theatre in Moscow to create new works or to restage his most successful pieces. As Dominique Frétard indicates in 2003, as soon as Preljocaj reaches the rehearsal studio he forgets everything except the task of choreographing: 'When I have before me my dancers, then I am inspired by what vibrates in their bodies, which is biological and organic. The dance pours out of this forgetting'.

Ramsay Burt

Biographical details

Born in Sucy-en-Brie, France, January 1957. **Studied** classical ballet, then modern dance with Karin Waehner at the Scholia Cantorum, and at the Cunningham Studios, New York, 1980; also studied Noh in Japan, 1987. **Career:** Joined Quentin Rouiller Company in Caen, then worked at Centre National de Dans Chorégraphique at Angers, 1981–82; dancer for Dominique Bagouet, 1982; choreographer, making first work, *Adventures colonialis* (in collaboration with Michel Kélménis) in 1984; established his own company in Champigny-sur-Mer and du Val-de-Marne, 1989; the company, now known as Ballet Prelojcaj-Centre Choreographique National de la Région Provence, based in Aix-en-Provence from 1996, moving into new purpose-built premises, Pavillon Noir, 2006. Has created works for Lyon Opera Ballet, Ballet de l' Opéra de Paris, Munich Ballet and New York City Ballet; and work staged by companies worldwide, including Helsinki Ballet, Gulbenkian Ballet, Finnish National Ballet, Ballet of La Scala, Nederlands Dans Theatre, São Paulo Balé de Cidade, and Staartsoper, Berlin. **Awards and honours** include First Prize, Concours de Bagnolet, 1984; Grand Prix, 1992; Prague Video Festival Prize, 1993; Benois de la Danse, Moscow, 1995; New York Dance and Performance Award ('Bessie'), 1997; Chevalier of the Légion d'Honneur, 1998; Grand Prix International de Vidéodanse, 1999; Grand Prix du Film d'Art, 2003; Order of Merit, 2006; Cristal Globe, 2009; Samuel H. Scripps/American Dance Festival Award for Lifetime Achievement, 2014; elected to Academie des Beaux Arts, 2019.

Works

Marché noir (1984); *Larmes blanches* (1985); *Peurs bleues* (1985); *A nos héros* (1986); *Hallali Romée* (1987); *Le petit napperon bouge* (1987); *Liqueurs de chair* (1988); *Les Raboteurs* (film, 1988); *Un Trait d'union* (1989, film 1992); *Les Noces* (1989); *Amer America* (1990); *Roméo et Juliette* (1990); *La Peau du Monde* (1992, extract presented as *Sand Skin*, 1993); *Hommage aux Ballets Russes: Parade* and *Le Spectre de la rose* (1993); *Le Parc* (1994); *Petit essai sur le temps qui passe* (1995); *L'Anoure* (1995); *Annonciation* (1995); *L'Oiseau de feu* (1995); *Roméo et Juliette* (1996, 2015); *Paysage après la bataille* (1997); *La Stravaganza* (1997, 2015); *Centaures* (1998); *Casanova* (1998); *Personne n'épouse les méduses* (1999); *Portraits in corpore* (2000); *Le Sacre du printemps* (2001); *MC 14/22 (ceci est mons corps)* (2001); *Helikopter* (2001); *Near Life Experience* (2003); *Annonciation* (film, 2003); *Le Songe de Médée* (2004); *'N'* (2004); *Empty Moves (Part I)* (2004); *Les 4 saisons …* (2005); *Grendel* (opera, 2006); *Fire sketch* (2006); *Haka* (2007);

Empty Moves (Parts I & II) (2007, with *Part III* added 2014); *Eldorado (Sonntags Abschied)* (2007), *Snow White* (2008), *Le funambule* (2009), *Siddharta* (2010), *And then, One Thousand Years of Peace* (2010), *Ce que j'appelle oubli (What I Call Oblivion)* (2012); *Royaume Uni* (2012); *The Nights* (2013); *Spectral Evidence* (2013, 2015); *Return to Berratham* (2015); *La Fresque* (2016); *Polina, danser sa vie* (film, 2016); *Still Life* (2017); *Playlist #1* (2017); *Gravité* (2018), *Ghost* (2018); *Winterreise* (2019).

Further reading

Articles: Anna Kisselgoff, 'A French Company's Version of *Noces*', *The New York Times*, 22 June 1991; Aline Apostolska, 'Angelin Preljocaj: Capricorne', *Saisons de la danse*, March 1993; Gus Solomons, 'Review of Choreography Performed by the Lyon Opéra Ballet at the Joyce Theater, New York City', *Dance Magazine*, December 1994; Bettina Wagner-Bergelt, 'The Classical Choreographer Between Abstraction and Expressionism', *Ballett International*, April 1996; Thomas Hahn, 'You See, Willi!: Preljocaj's *Casanova* in Paris', *Ballett International*, May 1998; Thomas Hahn, 'On Stage: Angelin Preljocaj, Flight 14/22 Delayed', *Ballett International*, May 2001; Anne Gilpin, 'Ballet Preljocaj: *Helikopter* and *Rite of Spring*', *Dance Europe*, June 2002; Dominique Frétard, 'Danse: l'escalade vertigineuse d'Angelin Preljocaj', *Le Monde*, 26 June 2003; Jenny Gilbert, 'Blissed Out!', *The Independent on Sunday*, 9 May 2004; Allan Ulrich, 'Preljocaj Meets Grendel', *Dance Magazine*, July 2006; Victoria Looseleaf, 'Ballet Preljocaj', *Dance Magazine*, July 2009; Darrell Wilkins, 'Blood in the Snow', *Ballet Review*, 37(4), 2010; Kathrina Farrugia-Kriel, *Angelin Preljocaj's* 'Empty Moves (2014) and Transmodern Dance History', *Dance Chronicle*, 40(1), 2017; Graham Spicer, 'Danza in Italia', *Dancing Times*, May 2019.

Books: Jean Bollack, Ismail Kadaré, and Brigitte Paulino-Neto (eds.), *Angelin Preljocaj, Roman Polanski*, Paris, 1992; Isabelle Ginot (ed.), *Danse et Utopie: Mobile 1*, Paris, 1999; B. Raffali, *Preljocaj ou la tentation de l'épique*, Paris, 2001; Guy Delahaye and Agnès Freschel, *Angelin Preljocaj*, Arles, 2003; Dany Lévêque, *Angelin Preljocaj: de la création à la mémoire de la danse*, Paris, 2011; Paul-Henry Bizon, *Angelin Preljocaj*, Paris 2015.

FRANCES RINGS

Frances Rings is a proud Aboriginal woman whose maternal ancestors are from the Kokatha language group, part of the Western Desert language chain that covers much of the southern Australian continent. On her father's side, she is of German descent. She is also one of Australia's most respected and renowned choreographers.

The dance works created by Rings emanate from a living culture that is over 60,000 years old, and one that in the 21st century is forging a powerful and creative contemporary 'songline' (the term refers to the unique knowledges of Aboriginal and Torres Strait Islander peoples, which tell of the law, history, and culture they have created, maintained, and practiced for thousands of years). She describes her choreography through a flowing lexicon of phrases that sing from her imagination with references to Country, Knowledge, Story, and Ancestry. Her inspiration for choreography comes from stories that awaken audiences to the impact of colonial invasion and racism, as well as stories that expose the undeniable connectedness that we share as part of a global humanity. There is a palpable sense of dignified, yet unapologetic, determination to get the audience's attention and draw them into a place where knowledge and emotion can coexist, to shift perspectives and produce a united sense of collective respect. The embodiment of these motivations – the dance – is generated in a 21st century context, while being grounded in footprints of ancient knowledge.

Rings was born in 1970 – only three years after the Australian people voted by referendum to change the nation's constitution granting the country's Indigenous population the right to be called citizens. This was a milestone in Australia's history. Its potent symbolism flamed a level of political agency for Indigenous Australians, that in turn ignited the voices of many contemporary Aboriginal and Torres Strait Islander artists. The work of these artists established a unique form of activism through art making, shaping a vibrant continuum of storytelling that challenges the so-called 'official' history of Australia. As the country struggles with issues like native title, full constitutional recognition, and the impact of dispossession, Indigenous artists focus on bringing the truth of the past – and the reality of the present – to their audiences. Frances Rings is one of these artists.

As a teenager in the mid 1980s, Rings saw an image of a dancer on a poster. The dancer was black. Her feet were flexed, her arms and legs angular and as Rings has noted, 'she looked like me'. Having experienced dance in the form of mainstream musicals, ballet and pop-culture, this was the moment of realisation that inspired Rings to seek and inhabit the world of Indigenous dance theatre, seeing it as a creative, powerful platform where cultural meaning and contemporary dialogue could be embodied and transmitted.

In 1989 Rings went to the National Aboriginal and Islander Skills Development Association Dance College in Sydney, Australia. NAISDA was established by Carole Y. Johnson, an American dancer, who in the 1970s was astounded that there was no choreographic voice for Indigenous Australians. Johnson's initiative attracted students from all over Australia, including Stephen Page, who with his brother Russell, trained at NAISDA just prior to Rings. Stephen Page became the artistic director of Bangarra Dance Theatre in 1991 and engaged Rings as a dancer shortly after. Highly accomplished in western dance techniques, she was a compelling performer and storyteller.

In 2002, Stephen Page invited Rings to create one half of a new Bangarra program entitled Walkabout. Her work for this, *Rations*, explored a period in Australia's colonial history where Aboriginal women were removed from their ancestral lands and trained as domestic workers on cattle and sheep stations, their children forced into Christian-based schooling. During this time, Aboriginal people were prevented from practicing their own agricultural methods and were given rations of white flour, refined sugar, and tea. The impact of the provision of food and shelter, in exchange for free labour, had disastrous effects on their social infrastructure and health. In the Walkabout theatre programme, 2002, Rings asked: 'At what price can a transaction displace a people and a system replace a lifestyle? The passage of goods, a long and winding road to assimilation'.

From this early work, Rings' fascination with innovative design elements – costume, props, lighting, shapes, and sets – became integral to her creative 'dreaming'. In *Rations* the 'Blankets' section pitches the representation of a western symbol of comfort, against a more abstract depiction that suggests hiding from oppression. In *Terrain* (2012), the Spinifex section sees the women moving across the stage with delicate, deft isolations, complimented by the weight of the floor-length die-cut dresses and spindly stick-like headdresses. The effect is a delicate, feminine rendering of the spinifex clumps of dry foliage that Rings observed blowing across the barren surface of Kati Thanda (Lake Eyre), the great salt lake in central Australia that inspired *Terrain*. In 'Salt', a male duo, one of the dancers wears a dramatic piece of spiked apparel on his upper body, accentuating the sharp textures of hardened salt. A most riveting design action occurs in the opening of the work, when the stage explodes from blackout to blinding white light accompanied by a thunderous earth beat, portending the forces of nature that are the most powerful energies in our world.

Rings' works begin with rigorous research periods, visits to locations (often remote), long consultations with traditional owners, communities and families, trawling through historical documents, scientific evidence, academic journals, and film documentation, as well as many hours of deep discussion with the creative team. The actual choreography, the time in the studio with collaborating dancers, is a relatively short process when the whole creative life cycle is considered.

Once a production has been premiered and toured around Australia, it is taken back to the community that inspired it. Rings affirms on the Bangarra Dance Theatre website, 2019, 'there is a beautiful gifting of stories and trust that our people give us. It's a reciprocal relationship – we trust that you are going to tell this story respectfully and in the right way; and that you'll bring it back to us. It's a beautiful exchange'. Observing and adhering to the protocols that guide this type of creative process offers little chance of a choreographic formula or repetition developing, and this is reflected in Rings' body of work to date.

Sheoak (2015) centres around stories of the Allocasuarina, a tree commonly referred to in Aboriginal culture as the 'grandmother tree'. The sheoak has a role in family and community that is about protection, wisdom, and the passing on of knowledge. Children were often left under its protective bough while parents gathered food. The tree was especially important in holding the soil structures in environments that were battered by weather. But this work also includes unapologetic statements about the body's relationship to place, and the cultural erosion that occurs with family breakdown, and dispossession – a place where cultural care, like that provided by the sheoak, is missing.

As a colonised land, Australia tells its postcolonial history from different perspectives and towards different objectives – political, economic, social, cultural – and those perspectives are repeatedly contested as more voices join the discourse. In *Unaipon* (2004, restaged in 2019), made for Bangarra Dance Theatre, Rings challenges the history of racism and human rights, embedded bias and belief systems. David Unaipon's life exposes a story that receives scant attention in the official histories of Australia, yet his portrait is on the face of the Australian $50 note. Rings explores the life journey of one man – a traditional man who spoke his language, practiced his culture, who was a scholar in western classical studies, a scientist whose inventions innovated the wool industry, a government advisor, and a Christian preacher who respected all religions. Yet over the course of his life, he was not recognised as a citizen. In Rings' iteration of David Unaipon's story, in three sections 'In the Beginning', 'Science', and 'Religion', the movement language is derived from internalised explorations of information gathered in research. With the minds and bodies of the dancers steeped in cultural information, the quality of the choreography is imbued with an unfettered honesty, exposing truths that have fallen from the historical record, giving voice to a People who have been repeatedly silenced.

This theme is evident in *X300* (2007) which examines, from an Aboriginal perspective, the British testing of atomic weapons conducted in the Maralinga area of South Australia from 1956 to 1963. Through an agreement with the Australian government, and without consultation with the original custodians of the site, the Maralinga Tjarutja people, the testing went ahead. Contamination was significant and sacred sites were annihilated. People became ill from the fall out. Women miscarried their unborn babies, and when tribal lands were fenced off people could not return to their homeland. Rings approached this story with care and respect, while making no concessions to the horror of the assault on the land and the people. In the section 'Tracking', the soles of a group of women's feet face the audience and press gently into an imaginary earth. This dissolves the notion of what is seen on the surface of the land – the British and Australian governments claimed there was nothing there – and speaks to the ancient history of people 'walking the land', the land that gives people life and purpose. As a result of the tests, ancient waterholes, cared for by the Maralinga Tjarutja people for thousands of years, were poisoned. The work *X300* is immediately frightening and confronting, and told through dance, is a powerful and palpable human to human interaction.

Rings' choreography is eloquent, often mesmerising and technically complex. In *Unaipon,* the section titled 'Motion' illustrates the concept of perpetual motion where the dancers weave intricate, fast paced, and seamlessly coordinated pathways around each other. In 'Reflect', a section of *Terrain,* a solo female performs a poetry of movement that is both fragile and evocative of 'the sacred realm where earth and sky meet' (*Terrain* theatre program, 2012). Rings' choreography has a unique capacity to tell stories of Indigenous culture through the abstract medium of contemporary dance, into a realm where Indigenous people can participate in their traditions as well as the modern agenda of issues they experience, and where non-Indigenous people can join in this celebration of recognition, and learn.

Rings has created works for Bangarra Dance Theatre and for other First Nations' dance companies in Canada and New Zealand. She has also received commissions from a number of ballet and contemporary dance companies in Australia and been involved in several independent projects. She is passionate about the development of young Indigenous artists and for two years was the Head of Creative Studies at NAISDA Dance College. Now Associate Director of Bangarra Dance Theatre, alongside her mentor Artistic Director Stephen Page, she creates works with important messages to convey, in order to build a world that listens to the past, values the wisdom of ancient knowledge and works to a meaningful agenda of reconciliation.

Shane Carroll

Biographical details

Born in Adelaide, South Australia, 1970. Descendent of the Kokatha Tribe and also of German descent. **Studied** at the National Aboriginal and Islander Skills Development Association (now called NAISDA Dance College) from 1989–1993; also studied Graham and Horton techniques at the Alvin Ailey American Dance Centre, New York, USA, in 1995. **Career:** Danced with Bangarra Dance Theatre 1994–2006; also with Leigh Warren and Dancers, Meryl Tankard, and Legs on the Wall Company. First choreography, *Minymaku Inma* was for Bangarra's Dance Clan program, 1999; much of her choreography has been for Bangarra Dance Theatre; choreographed works for NAISDA Dance College; West Australian Ballet, Sydney Festival, Tasdance; performed with New Zealand's Atamira Dance Theatre; and forged relationships with Kahawi Dance Theatre, Toronto, Canada. Appointed member of Dance Board of the Australian Council for the Arts, 2005. Film credits include central role in the documentary, *The Widower*, 2004 (dir. Kevin Lucas); television presenter for Indigenous Current Affairs and Media programmes, including ABC's *Dance 4 Film* series with Channel 4 in the UK, 2008. Appointed Head of Creative Studies at NAISDA, 2017–2018; returned to Bangarra Dance Theatre as Resident Choreographer, 2010–2015 and Associate Artistic Director, 2019. **Awards and honours** include Deadly Award for Female Dancer of the Year, 2003; Helpmann Awards, 2003, 2004, 2010, 2013, 2016, 2017; Ausdance Award, 2004; Betty Pounder Green Room Award, 2011.

Works

Minymaku Inma (1999, in collaboration with women from the Central Desert region of Australia); *Rations* (2002, restaged 2006); *Bush* (co-choreographed with Stephen Page, 2003); *Unaipon* (2004, restaged 2019); *X300* (2007); *Debris* (2007); *Belonging* (2008); *Remembered of Us* (2009); *Artefact* (2010); *Forseen* (2011); *Breathe* (2011); *Terrain* (2012, restaged 2016); *Sheoak* (2015); *Your Skin, My Skin* (2014); *Kamu* (2015, restaged 2016); *From Sand to Stage* (2016); *Restoration* (2017); *Storyplace* (2018); *Shapeshift* (2018); *SandSong* (co-choreographed with Stephen Page, 2020).

Further reading

(see also Bangarra digital archive: Knowledge Ground, at bangarra-knowledgeground.com.au)

Interviews: with Rose Niland, *The Cultural Concept Circle*, theculturalconcept. com, 2012; Martine Hart, *Engaging Women: Frances Rings*, engagingwomen. com, 2015; Stephen Page, *Terrain: Interview with the Choreographer, Frances Rings*, Film, Bangarra Dance Theatre, Kanopy Streaming, 2016; Maxim Boon, *Frances Rings: Seeing County Through Her Father's Eyes*, limelightmagazine. com, 3 March 2016.

Articles: Michelle Potter, '9 July 2015, Canberra', michellepotter.org, 15 July 2015; Maxim Boon, 'Review: *Lore* (Bangarra Dance Theatre)', limelightmagazine, 17 June 2015; Steve Dow, 'Family Trees', *The Saturday Paper*, 13 June 2015; J. Albert, 'A Look Back on 30 Years of Collective Dreaming of Bangarra Dance Theatre', *Vogue Australia*, December 2019.

Books: S. Burridge and K. Dyson (eds.), *Shaping the Landscape,* London, 2011.

LIA RODRIGUES

Lia Rodrigues is a dancer/choreographer based in Rio de Janeiro, Brazil. Born in 1956 in São Paulo, she studied Ballet and History at the São Paulo University, the oldest university in Brazil, and in 1977 she set up her first dance group, Grupo Andança. She then travelled to France for her first professional engagement with Compagnie Maguy Marin between 1980 and 1982, where she participated in the creation of *May B.* Returning to Brazil in the late 1980s, Rodrigues worked with João Saldanha in the Atelier de Coreografia.

Lia Rodrigues is now Artistic Director of the Lia Rodrigues Companhia de Danças (LRCD) founded in 1990 in Rio de Janeiro. Company activities since then have included dance laboratories, creations, classes, and rehearsals. From 1992–2005 she directed an annual festival of contemporary dance, Panorama de Dança; the festival continues to this day as one of the most prestigious in Latin America. During 40 years of professional and artistic life, Lia Rodrigues has dedicated herself to training and artistic creation, with touring and commissioning from many major world capitals. Mixing militancy and utopias, she believes in the synergy between art and social processes.

Since 2004, her company has been involved in developing educational and artistic activities in Maré favela, one of the biggest slums in Rio de Janeiro, in partnership with the non-government organisation Redes de Desenvolvimento da Maré. Thanks to this collaboration, she has dedicated herself to the development of dance in this favela; the Arts Centre of Maré was opened in 2009 followed by the Free Dance School of Maré in 2011. For Lia Rodrigues, (liarodrigues.com), to make art in Brazil is an ongoing process of affirmation, investment, and resistance. She was awarded the medal of Chevalier dans l'Ordre des Arts et des Lettres from the French government in 2016, and won the SACD Prize for Choreography. In the Netherlands, she received the Prince Claus Award (2014).

Historically, dance in Brazil was greatly limited by military dictatorships from 1930 to 1946 and from 1964 to 1988. In the early 20th century, Russian ballet instructors laid the foundation for the later establishment of Ballet Brazil and other movements. In the 1940s and 50s Russian and German instructors introduced modern dance to Brazil; there was also a strong influence from German Expressionism in theatre, as many Europeans fled to South America to escape the World Wars.

Brazil's 20th century was either strongly coloured by cultural colonialism or subjected to censorship by a dictatorial government, and these influences prevented Brazilian artists from creating works that reflected their true voices. From the 1940s, the national state ballet companies sometimes performed contemporary works but most performances were traditional repertory works. As Nayse Lopez ('Supporting Contemporary Dance in Brazil' *Performing Arts Network, Japan*, 19 March 2012) describes, during the 1960s and 70s, government censorship was necessary for dance works. When a dance work premiered, censored works were simply described as 'violating the morals of society'. In short, they were ordered to cease performances because there was nudity.

As Brazil was essentially closed off from the rest of the world, so information about the movements of political activism in Europe and North America in the 1960s and 70s was scant and dated. Only when the country was freed of the dictatorship did Brazilians begin to see artistic works showing greater diversity; the first truly contemporary dance works, such as those created by Lia Rodrigues, began to appear as Brazil entered the 1990s.

Rodrigues was evidently influenced by her three years with Compagnie Maguy Marin, a French choreographer less interested in conventional dance movement, more in bodily expression that distils movement into drama. *May B* (1982) was a choreographic homage to the playwright Samuel Beckett, and contained both a sense of fantasy and of the absurd, as Anna Kisselgoff ('The Dance: May B by Marin', *NYT* 19 February 1986) illustrates: 'Like Beckett, she works with archetypal characters ... and using universals, makes the human condition look very specific'. Rodrigues' sojourn in Paris, her creative involvement in this work and the opportunity to tour and perform in Europe was invaluable, and strong links with France are maintained to this day.

Other influences on her choreography came from well-known Brazilian artists and thinkers such as Lygia Clark, Hélio Oiticica and Mário de Andrade. All shared critical questions about the alleged purity of national or individual identity, showing how such an identity is tangled up in what is supposedly other to it, borrowing and amalgamating ideas from other cultures. In fact, for them one must abandon the notion of pure identity altogether in favour of something else, namely, a mestizo identity, one that is not only crossbred but always changing, becoming (João Cerquiera da Silva Junior, 2017).

Early work by Lia Rodrigues for LRCD includes *CATAR* (1989), *Gineceu* (1990), *MA* (1993), *Folia* (1996), *Resta* (1997), and *Folia II* (1998). *CATAR* was described by Fabiana Britto (Revista Dançar, 1990) as a choreographic jewel where

> design and realisation harmonise perfectly. The entrepreneurial elements of the theatre are integrated into the choreography. The music ... the light, with defined foci and the use of the face muscles composing with the choppy and rhythmic movements, make this one of the best moments of the Dance Movements Festival promoted by SESC / Anchieta de São Paulo.

During the 1990s the company performed in major Brazilian contemporary dance events, and participated in festivals in France and Tel Aviv, Israel with *MA* and *Folia,* and in the summer of 2003, at the Brighton Festival in the UK. Dorothy Max Prior's illuminating review of *Aquilo de que somos feitos* (What we are made of, 2002) elucidates:

> All human life is here in this extraordinary performance ... an evolutionary journey that takes the human body from abstract objectified form to vital, world-changing social and political being. We start with a series of tableaux, presenting the human body as sculpture, the performers making shapes that focus our attention on the bony curve of a spine or the angle of an elbow. We move from this abstracted view of line and form to human interaction, where bodies meet – creating shapes but also forming physical relationships with hints of both sensuality and humour. We are by now acclimatised to the selection of naked bodies right in front of our faces – but unprepared for the next stage, where the performers shake and roll themselves into the audience. We have moved into the arena of human emotion; expression of need and response.
>
> The sudden appearance of a clothed, speaking performer is another shock. No longer the naked ape, the human being is consumer and commentator on her world. As she walks amongst us, she recites a litany of sound-bites – 'The children of Iraq ... Britney Spears ... September 11th ...' – each pronouncement

given equal weight. Eventually, all are clothed, and come together in an ensemble finale that presents the human being as all-powerful when united and joyous in the celebration of life and defiance of oppression.

In 2004, Rodrigues began to work in residency at the Complexo de Favelas da Maré in Zona Norte, a region of 16 favela (slum) communities with 140,000 inhabitants, largely underprivileged. Not simply offering outreach programmes, the LRCD company relocated into this marginalised community, found a warehouse to create an arts centre (Centro de Artes da Maré, or CAM), and began to create all their art works there. By 2009, CAM became the place to rehearse, create and present the company's pieces, offer a programme of free dance classes to an estimated 300 students, organise artistic events and performances by choreographers from Europe and elsewhere.

In interview with Marcos Steuernagel in 2011, Lia Rodrigues described the works that had already been performed there: *Encarnado* (2005), *Pororoca* (2009), *Aquilo de que somos feitos*, and *Formas Breves* (2002). She demonstrates well how she was able to relate to local inhabitants, help develop their aesthetic understandings, and share her own:

> people's reactions were amazing. In the break between performances, sometimes people would come talk to me, and normally what I heard the most was: 'I don't understand. What do you mean?' So I would say: "Many people tell me they don't understand what we do, so I would like you to know that this is the place where you don't need to understand, can you imagine? A place where you can be free. It's a place where you can sit, receive something, where it's OK to not like it – Can you imagine? – you can hate it, you can leave, stay, you can cry. That's the interesting experience.

The company continued their European touring; marketing for the Festival d'automne, Paris 2005 stated:

> Art is a form of confrontation, and Lia Rodrigues wages her battle on the frontlines of her genre, a fusion of visual arts, dance and performance art. In Brazil, her dance troupe, the Companhia de Danças, performs in some of the country's remotest regions and Rodrigues, a tireless advocate of society's underdogs, is a common

sight in the urban *favelas*. *Creation* is her latest journey on the road beyond convention.

In the last decade, the dimension of artist training has become an increasingly important aspect of her company, particularly as she often employs young dancers with little previous professional experience. Silvia Soter, professor and company dramaturge, defines the concept of artist training as 'a process which includes informal teaching-learning strategies and an exchange of knowledge between the choreographer, other artists, invited teachers and the members of the company' (Soter and Pavlova, 'ELDM in Rio de Janeiro', in Butterworth and Wildschut *Contemporary Choreography*, 2017).

In the last decade, the trilogy *Pororoca* (2009), *Piracema* (2011), and *Pindorama* (2013) have toured internationally to superb reviews. Cecily Binford (australianstage.com.au) felt pushed to the limits of sensory endurance at a performance of *Pindorama* in Perth:

> Nothing in my years of reviewing have given me any framework for the type of performance that Lia Rodrigues has created.... We reviewers are sometimes at a loss for words when it comes to visceral performance experiences, left only to advise readers: 'you've got to experience it yourself'. When a work leads you into new territory that leaves an impact on your psyche, words become functionally inadequate, and the process of putting descriptors on moments seems unworthy. Nevertheless, we try.

Binford describes a nude woman emerging from a dark corner, pouring a two-litre water bottle over her head.

> She begins to crawl at an achingly slow pace, over the plastic, popping the balloons under her body as she goes, splashing water in small pools across the sheet. The other performers hold the sheet, ... moving it slowly, creating ripples across its length. They move it faster, faster, increasing the pace and force of their movements until the woman in the middle is tossed around like a fish on rocks. We are sprayed with mists from the sheet; the sound of the whipping plastic is deafening. We're all caught in a storm.

The latest work, *Fúria* (2018), was a co-production with Chaillot – Theatre national de la Danse, Paris, devised by the company during the latest Brazilian elections in Autumn 2018, depicting a transformative process moving from celebration to uprising and war, calling for radical change. Nine dancers set off on a journey,

> transforming the stage into a fragile and fluctuating territory. Switching between pack-like group, autonomous organism and sum total of individuals left to confront themselves with the loneliness of their flesh, they attempt to create different worlds – and to turn the stage into a universe which is run through with paradoxes ... (Chaillot.com).

As the driving force behind Centro Arte da Maré, Rodrigues continues to make work that is inventive and virtuoso, but also complex, political and socially committed.

Jo Butterworth

Biographical details

Born in 1956 in São Paulo; **Studied** Ballet and History at São Paulo University; **Career:** set up her first dance group, Grupo Andança in 1977; travelled to France for her first professional engagement with Compagnie Maguy Marin between 1980 and 1982, where she participated in the creation of *May B*. Returned to Brazil in the late 1980s, Rodrigues worked with João Saldanha in the Atelier de Coreografia; founded the Lia Rodrigues Companhia de Danças (LRCD) in 1990 in Rio de Janeiro. In 1992 she also created an annual festival of contemporary dance, Panorama de Dança, which she directed until 2005; in 2004, her company moved to Maré favela, one of the biggest slums in Rio de Janeiro, in partnership with the non-government organisation Redes de Desenvolvimento da Maré; the Arts Centre of Maré was opened in 2009 followed by the Free Dance School of Maré in 2011. She continues to work in France, and to tour internationally. **Awards and honours** include the medal of Chevalier dans l'Ordre des Arts et des Lettres from the French government in 2016, and the SACD Prize for Choreography. In the Netherlands, she received the Prince Claus Award (2014) and the 2017 Bravo Bradesco Award.

Works

Catar (1989, 1991); *Gineceu* (1990); *MA* (1993); *Folia* (1996); *Resta Um* (1997); *Folia II* (1998); *Aquilo de que somos feitos* (2000, 2001); *Dois e um dois* (2001); *Resgate* (2001); *Formas Breves* (2002, 2003); *Contra aqueles difíceis de agradar* (2005); *Encarnado* (Incarnat, 2005); *Hymnem* (2007); *Chantier poétique* (2008);

Pororoca (2009); *Piracema* (2011); *Exercício M* (2012); *Pindorama* (2013); *Para que o céu não caia* (For the Sky not to Fall, 2016); *Fúria* (2018).

Further Reading

Interviews: 'Interview with Marcos Steuernagel', hemisphericinstitute.org, 15 July 2011; Clovis Domingos, "Arte é uma Palavra pra desencardir do Hábito', 27 October 2012 obscenica.blogspot.de/2012; *Gilles Amalvi for the Festival d'Automne à Paris 2013*, English translation by Claire Tarring kfda. be; Tiago Bartolomeu Costa, 'Brasil: A Educação Liberta', publico.pt, 23 October 2014.

Articles: Dorothy Max Prior, 'Lia Rodrigues Companhia de Danças', *Total Theatre Magazine*, Issue 15-2, Summer 2003; Nayse Lopez interviewed by Takao Norikoshi, 'Panorama Festival: Supporting Contemporary Dance in Brazil', *Performing Arts Network, Japan*, 19 March 2012; Cicely Binford, 'Pindorama | Lia Rodrigues Companhia de Danças', *Perth Reviews*, australianstage.com.au 9 March 2016; Oonagh Duckworth, 'Fúria – Lia Rodrigues' pzazz.theater, 25 May 2019.

Books: Rodrigo Garcez, 'Antropofagia Nômade e Etica no Processo Criativo em Lia Rodrigues', *V Reunião Científica da ABRACE – Associação Brasileira de Pesquisa e Pós-graduação em Artes Cénnicas*. São Paulo: Memória Abrace Digital, 2009; Christine Greiner, 'Researching Dance in the Wild: Brazilian Experiences' in *Planes of Composition: Dance, Theory, and the Global* (eds. André Lepecki and Jenn Joy), London and New York: Seagull Books, 2009; João Cerquiera da Silva Junior, *Reflections on Improvisation, Choreography and Risk-Taking in Advanced Capitalism*, Kinesis 8, University of Helsinki, 2017; Silvia Soter and Adriana Pavlova, 'Escola Livra de Dança da Maré in Rio de Janeiro: A Ground to Share' in *Contemporary Choreography: A Critical Reader* (eds. Butterworth and Wildschut), 2nd edition, London and New York, 2018.

TERO SAARINEN

On a hazily lit proscenium stage, the silhouette of a man approaches. As the luminosity increases, dancer Tero Saarinen becomes distinguishable, traversing seemingly unknown ground in uninterrupted bound and weighty slow motion. His upper body is bare, and a layered white skirt covers his pelvis and thighs. Counterposing the support his legs offer, Saarinen's body flows from one vaguely slanted form to another. His arms extend horizontally and hover in the air, with pointed fingers. Eventually, he opens up into wide and low leg stances, backward arches, arms circling and reaching behind the head, as if to take him into flight. The impact is one of deep concentration.

Following the rising intensity of Stravinsky's *Rite of Spring*, Saarinen produces increasingly vigorous circular movements and turns. Retaining focal clarity in the flow of the grounded dance, his torso undulates in diverse directions, arms gesticulating angularly. He travels down stage, with strenuous and impressive progression at floor level – hands on the ground, his torso, pelvis and legs are thrown into the air in different directions. An alley of bright white light highlights and frames the dance. Back on his feet, teetering on in-turned feet in jerky motions, refined footwork pushes him to regain balance. This motional odyssey attests to the physical prowess and sensitivity of his performance. As the music reaches its climax, intermittent flashes of light capture dramatic falls to the ground and poses with wing-like arms reminiscent of Fokine's *The Dying Swan* (1907). Moving imagery is projected briefly onto Saarinen's body. His flowing skirt reflects the light, and seemingly turns Saarinen into a monstrous machine. Finally, he whirls around like a dervish, ending with several high leaps. Seen in bursts of light his image is left hovering in mid-air, as the performance ends in darkness and silence.

This impression of an intimate spectacle, relentless intensity, distinct virtuosity and attractive grotesqueness, remains after seeing Finnish dancer and choreographer Saarinen perform his choreography *HUNT* (2002). Commissioned by the Venice Biennale, the work was a collaboration between Saarinen, media artist Marita Liulia, lighting designer Mikki Kunttu, and costume designer Erika Turunen. Dance critic Anna Kisselgoff (2004) considered *HUNT* the most moving performance of the Lyon's Biennale de la Dance in 2004, and according to Rauhamaa (2014–2015) it was one of the top ten performances in New York in 2006.

During the years he toured with the work, Saarinen received the Movimentos Dance Prize for Best Male Performer in Germany and the award of Chevalier de l'Ordre des Arts et des Lettres by the Ministry of Culture in France. According to Saarinen (in Jyrkkä, 2005), aside from aging and death, *HUNT* addresses our relationship with digital technologies and the information society that we live in. Before he last performed it in 2013, aged 48, he had done so 174 times in 83 cities. The seminal work is representative of many aspects of Saarinen's oeuvre: his quality as a performer, passion for the intuitive power dance entails, intimate interlinking of dance and music, appreciation of the dance heritage, and an ability to foster generative artistic collaboration.

Saarinen was first internationally acknowledged when performing the solo *B12*, choreographed by Jorma Uotinen. It earned him the first prize in the contemporary division of the 1988 *Concours international de dance* competition in Paris. This launched his international career and invitations to perform helped him present his own solo work. Saarinen is a dancer for whom 'physicality, even physical distress' have been important (Rauhamaa, 2014–2015). In a documentary directed by Thomas Freundlich, *Rooted with Wings* (2018), he states 'every time I dance, I try to probe depth, primal forces within me'. Saarinen explores these forces in the solo work he creates as a freelance artist, *Ondekoza* (1989), *Kehtolaulu [Lullab]* (1990) and *Takana [In the Past]* (1992), as well as in a later piece *Vox Balaenae* (2011). Owing to Saarinen's performance quality, he has been offered opportunities to perform solo work by exceptional choreographers. These include *Déjà vu* by Murray Louis, previously performed only by the choreographer and Rudolf Nureyev. Carolyn Carlson (Carlsson in Finnish) choreographed *Travelling* (1998) and *A Man in the Room* (2002) for Saarinen. She also restaged her solo *Blue Lady* from 1983, addressing the feminine life cycle and emotions. Inspired by Kabuki theatre's onnagata roles in which males perform as women, a performance approach in which Saarinen had trained, Carlson reconsidered the issue of gender and paid specific attention to Saarinen's androgyny (Tawast, 2008). He first performed *Blue Lady [Revisited]* at the *Biennale de la Dance Lyon* in 2008.

Saarinen has been the artistic director of *TSD* since 1995. Known as *Tero Saarinen Dance & Company Toothpick* for its first seven years, his vision was to work more collaboratively with artists who shared his values and to support his choreographic endeavours and commissions; the *Finnish National Opera*, Tampere-based *MD Mobita Dansco*, *Kuopio Dance Festival* and *Batsheva Dance Company*. Important collaborators from the early years of the company include lighting designer Mikki Kunttu, dancers Henrik Heikkilä, Sini Länsivuori and Satu Halttunen, and producer Iiris Autio. The company quickly developed into a well-organised and networked establishment that appreciates collaboration, shared values and risk-taking but which underlines the importance of joy in working in a community (terosaarinen.com). *TSD* produces its own works and tours, but it also licenses work for other companies and teaches Saarinen's movement technique (Krabbe, 2010–2011).

Collaborations have produced 16 original group pieces, many of which have received international accolades. He has the skill of structuring individual and groups of dancers into dynamic inter-relationships; and has repeatedly addressed themes related to the tension between the individual, communities and society, and views about masculinity. As his career developed, commissions from Nederlands Dans Theatre (NDT1), French ballet companies in Lyon, Marseille and Lorraine, the Gothenburg Opera Ballet in Sweden, and the National Dance Company Korea have followed.

Saarinen's virtuosic and original performance style forms the basis of his choreography. His is a 'choreographic handwriting ... that demands virtuosity combined with the pursuit of sensitivity in movement motivated by music' (Rauhamaa, 2014–2015). Saarinen's performance and choreography entail sustained motion that plays with the ebb and flow of interweaving bodies and groups, as well as utilising strong shifts in weight and balance. The style epitomises influences from European contemporary dance that became part of his signature; the uniqueness of each dancer's body, and an increased sensitivity to its experiential stances diversified the movement vocabulary of European contemporary dance (Kaiku, 1998). Between 1986–1992, Saarinen spent his first professional years as a dancer at the Finnish National Opera and Ballet. Then he became acquainted with Finnish contemporary choreographers, including Tommi Kitti, Marjo Kuusela and Jorma Uotinen, who influenced his approach. In 1988 Saarinen was also a visiting dancer at the Helsinki Dance Company, whose artistic director was Carolyn Carlson.

In the early 1990s, he became interested in minimalistic expression and Japanese art and studied Kabuki theatre at the Fujima School in Tokyo. He took classes with butoh dance originator Kazuo Ohno in Yokohama, learning to appreciate the impact of the subconscious dimension, our ancestors and the traditions of the past. Ohno's approach and view of life left an indelible mark on Saarinen and strengthened his understanding that a dancer is a medium for shared and unspoken forces (Saarinen in Jyrkkä, 2005).

These influences are noticeable in Saarinen's movement style: disciplined virtuosic skill, detailed movement articulation, deep concentration, flowing motion, subtle footwork, outreaching arms, and a contracting and arching torso. By 2000 it had become so crystallised that his long-time collaborating dancers from *TSD* had begun to teach the style as a technique for other dance professionals. Titled TERO Technique, the approach aims at honing dancers' sensitivity of their own motional bodies and further nourishing their individual movement competence. Relying on the previous skills of the dancers attending classes, the teaching explores bodily weight to expand the dancers' ability to move on the threshold between balance and off-balance. Awakening the responsiveness of the feet as well as fostering an alert and concentrated body are focal to the training. Saarinen aims at attaining such observational attention in which 'even the skin is curious and alive' (terosaarinen.com).

Important group works include the early *Westward Ho!* (1996), *Petruschka* (2001), and *Borrowed Light* (2004). The latter was inspired by the radical American religious group the Shakers. Having viewed a documentary on Doris Humphrey's choreography, *The Shakers* (1931), Saarinen was struck by the ascetism and communal values of this group whose ceremonies involved quivering and shaking and who sang old English folklore songs. In *Borrowed Light*, Boston Camerata sang rhythmic and lyrical Shaker songs live on stage whilst a group of eight male and female dancers, performing mostly in their gendered groups or alone, explore their devotion and belongingness to each other and the community. The movement expresses longing, struggle and hope: groping large arm movements, arms reaching high upwards with spread fingers, heavy and trailing feet pressing on the ground. The somewhat manic repetitions of the motion and monotone chanting occur on a bare, dimly lit stage (Yli-Honko, 2005). The Village Voice considered the work one of the best of the decade and the Boston Globe described is as powerful, elemental, unforgettable (teroasaarinen.com). Parts of the choreography are also documented in the film *A Chair Fit for an Angel* directed by Raymond St-Jean in 2014 (Rauhamaa, 2014–2015).

More recent pieces in which Saarinen returned to explore masculinity include *Morphed* (2014), a work for eight male dancers with music by composer Esa-Pekka Salonen and *Breath* (2018), a duet for himself and accordion player Kimmo Pohjonen. In the latter both male performers well into their middle-ages, dance, emit vocal sounds, and play instruments, while playfully testing their physical and expressive powers. In larger format, *Kullervo* (2015), commissioned by the Finnish National Opera, is a major work for 27 dancers and 65 singers and is based on the Finnish national epic the Kalevala and Jean Sibelius' early composition *Kullervo (Symphony Op. 7)*.

Saarinen has been of the most internationally known Finnish dancer-choreographers for more than two decades. He continues working with his collaborators to fulfil his mission:

> I believe dance and movement are imprinted in people's DNA. Dance brings people together with its intuitive power. People have used dance to speak to the gods, to make crops grow and to achieve communion with nature. Physical talent is present in everyone, if we just surrender ourselves to it. But we are so distanced from our own bodies (in Rauhamaa, 2014–2015)
>
> *Leena Rouhiainen*

Biographical details

Born in Pori, Finland, 7 September 1964. **Studied** dance with Liisa Nojonen at Pori dance school, 1980–1982; and the Ballet School of the National Ballet, 1982–1986. Studied Nepalese dance in Katmandu and Kabuki Theatre and Butôh in Japan in 1992. **Career:** Dancer at the Finnish National Ballet 1986–1992. Since 1989 he began touring the world with solo works and as a visiting soloist for Helsinki City Theatre Dance Company 1989–1991. Founded Tero Saarinen & Company Toothpick in 1996, from 2002 known as Tero Saarinen Dance Company. Has also choreographed for other companies, including Batsheva Dance Company; Helsinki Dance Company; the National Ballet of Finland; Dance Theatre Dansco; P.D.C. Pori Dance Company; Sirkus Bohemia; Lyon Opéra Ballet; Göteborgs Operans Ballet; Ballet National de Marseilles; Nederlands Dans Theater (NTD1); Ballet de Lorraine and Opéra National de Lorraine; Nordwest/Tanzcompagnie Oldenburg; Tanztheater Bremen; Saitama Dance; National Dance Company of Korea; Ghetto Exposed; and Dance Theatre MD. **Awards and honours** include the Concours International de Danse Prize, Paris, 1988; ITI Ballet Competition Silver medal, Helsinki, 1991; Phillip Morris Ballet Flower Award,1993; Jury award, Les Nuits de la Danse d'Istres competition, France, 1996; Ministry of Culture and Education, Finland prize, 2001; Culture Prize, City of Helsinki, 2002; International Movimientos Dance Prize, Germany, 2004; Chevalier de L'Ordre des Arts et des Lettres, France, 2004; Pro Finlandia Medal, Order of the Lion, Finland, 2005; The Finnish Cultural Foundation Award, 2008; Jean Sibelius commemorative coin, 2015.

Works

Ondekoza (solo, 1989); *Kehtolaulu* [Lullaby] (solo, 1990); *More Milk* (1991); *Takana* [*In the Past*] (solo, 1992); *Vajonneet* [*The Sunken*] (1993); *Hurmaa 1* (1993); *Lifewheel* (1994); *Wanha* (1994); *Flock* (1994); *Lelulaatikko* [*Box of Toys*] (1995); *Sirkus Bohemia* (1995); *Big Flock* (1996); *Westward Ho!* (1996); *Daydream People* (1996); *Kohta* [*Passage*] (1997); *Overdosed Mood* (1997); *Un/ Do* (1998); *Gaspard* (1999); *Could You Take Some of My Weight …?* (1999); *Pulcinella* (1999); *Wavelengths* (2000); *Sini* (2001); *Kaze* (2001); *Petrushka* (2001); *HUNT* (solo, 2002); *Even More Milk* (2002); *Transfigured Night* (2002); *Georgia* (2003); *The Captain* (2004); *Borrowed Light* (2004); *Huukit* (2006); *Frail Line* (2006); *Mariage* (2007); *Next of Kin* (2008); *Scheme of Things* (2009); *Double Lives* (2010); *Absent Presence* (2011); *Vox Balaenae* (2011); *MESH* (2014); *VORTEX* (2014); *Morphed* (2014); *Kullervo* (2015); *TRAIL* (2015); *Loopit* (2017); *Zimmerman Trio* (2018); *Breath* (2018); *Third Practice* (2020).

Further reading

(see also Tero Saarinen Dance Company website, terosaarinen.com; Dance Info Finland, tanka.danceinfo.fi/tanka-en-US; areena.yle.fi; and danceinfo.fi/finnish-dance-in-focus)

Interviews: in *Rooted with Wings*, documentary film, dir. Thomas Freundlich, Lumikinos Production, 2018; in *Kuusi kuvaa: Tanssitaiteilija Tero Saarinen edustaa kulttuurivientä parhaimmillaan*, radio broadcast, edited and complied by Laura Satimus, Yle Radio 1, 2018.

Articles: Anna Kisselgoff, 'Critic's Notebook: Dance Festival Reveals the New and the Unknown', *New York Times*, 6 October 2004; Karolina Yli-Honko, 'Borrowed Light (Tero Saarinen) Helsingin Juhlaviikot 2005: Askeettista kauneutta hämärän loisteessa', Liikekieli.com, 2005; Claudia La Rocco, 'Brooklyn Convocation of Shakers (and Movers)', *The New York Times*, 9 November 2007; Minna Tawast, 'Carlson Passed the Blue Lady onto Saarinen', *Finnish Dance in Focus*, 11, 2008–2009; Katarina Krabbe, 'Dance – An Economic Engine', *Finnish Dance in Focus*, 12, 2010–2011; Oksana Khadarina, 'Tero Saarinen Company – Westward Ho!, Wavelengths, HUNT – Washington', dancetabs.com, 17 March 2013; Raisa Rauhamaa, 'The Power of Dance is the Fiery Core of Tero Saarinen's World', *Finnish Dance in Focus*, 15, 2014–2015; Nicholas Minns, 'Tero Saarinen Company, Morphed', writingaboutdance.com, 11 September 2017; Hilary Maxwell, 'Helsinki's Tero Saarinen: A Choreographer with Curious DNA', *Dance International*, Fall 2018.

Books: Jan-Peter Kaiku, *Valokuvan tanssi. Suomalaisen tanssin kuvat 1890 – 1997 (Dance in Finnish Photography)* (eds. Hanna-Leena Helavuori et al.), Oulu: Kustannus Pohjoinen ja Teatterimuseo, 1998; Tero Saarinen, *Tanssintekijät – 35 Näkökulmaa koreografin työhön* (ed. Hannele Jyrkkä), Helsinki, 2005; Hannele Jyrkkä, *Etsijä – Tero Saarisen tie nykytanssin ikoniksi / The Hunter – Tero Saarinen, the Icon of Contemporary Dance*, Helsinki: Siltala Publishing, 2020 (forthcoming).

BENOIT SWAN POUFFER

Artistic director and choreographer of two high-profile repertory companies, Rambert and Cedar Lake Contemporary Ballet, Benoit Swan Pouffer has also worked across a broad range of performance contexts; musicals, cabarets, films, television shows, and commercials. Seeking a less formal approach to viewing contemporary dance, Pouffer has brought the audience into closer contact with the dancers through 'immersive' installations and taken the art form out to other performance arenas, such as festivals and concerts.

Pouffer characterises his work as 'very physical' and as having 'a sense of theatricality within the body'. He asks the dancer to be in 'a certain state of emotion which will translate through the body and create a thread through the work'. Pouffer describes dance as a live painting, where the space is the canvas, the dancers are the paints, and their intention and drive determine the intensity of the colours.

Going into the studio, he knows the theme and tone of the work, and 'steps come easily'. Pouffer describes the lighting as an important extra performer on stage, underscoring the work's mood and the expressive, emotional qualities of the movement. He wants the audience to feel what they are seeing (interview with the author, August 2019).

Pouffer was born in Paris, France, in 1974, of mixed-race parentage. His last name is pronounced 'Pouffère', with a soft 'e' and 'r' as in *compère*. During his years in the United States, he was known as Swan because Americans had difficulty pronouncing his first name, which lost its accent and acquired a hyphen (Benoît-Swan).

As a young dance student in Paris, Pouffer was profoundly affected by seeing a videotape of Alvin Ailey American Dance Theater. It was the first time he had seen 'black dancers dancing together … amazingly … elegant[ly] … it showed me my future' (in Katie Derham, 2019). After gaining his diploma at the Paris dance conservatoire, Pouffer, aged 18, went to New York City to study at the Ailey school. Then, from 1994 to 2004, he danced professionally with US companies composed predominantly of African-American dancers, including eight years with the Ailey company.

Brief mentions of his choreography start appearing in the New York press in 2001: a duet for Earl Mosley's Diversity of Dance; a solo for an Ailey benefit performance. In December 2003, Pouffer made a sextet, *Parts of Us*, for the preview performances of a new company, Cedar Lake Ensemble, founded and financed by Walmart heiress Nancy Laurie. The ensemble's announced launch in June 2004 fell through, and in August, Pouffer was appointed its resident choreographer.

In March 2005, he was involved in *Raw*, a two-hour-long performance about death, produced by Cedar Lake's artistic director, Jen Ballard, and a team of writers. Critics were unimpressed but Marilyn Stasio (*Variety*, 15 March 2005) singled out Pouffer's 'sinuous (and strenuous) choreography' as the 'real attraction'. *Raw* took place in a warehouse in the Chelsea art-gallery district of New York City that Laurie was converting into a theatre, rehearsal studio and offices. She appointed Pouffer as the new artistic director, and he programmed a mixed bill to mark the theatre's opening in October 2005.

The company, known as Cedar Lake Contemporary Ballet from 2006, had no repertoire to fall back on, and so Pouffer choreographed four works in quick succession. *Seed* (2005) was made for the inaugural mixed bill, and *Between Here and Now* (2006) for the following season's dream-themed bill. His hour-long *Hammer* (2006) explored a Nietzsche quote about posing questions with a hammer. *Vastav* (2006), which premiered at Jacob's Pillow, was inspired by an arranged marriage Pouffer had witnessed in Algeria and the women danced on pointe. Critics responded unfavourably to these works, but dance bloggers found more of interest in them.

In 2007, Cedar Lake had a critical and popular success with Ohad Naharin's *Decadance,* and the company's artistic identity came into focus. Pouffer gained a reputation for commissioning emerging, Europe-based choreographers who were unknown or rarely seen in the US, most notably Crystal Pite, Hofesh Shechter, and Sidi Larbi Cherkaoui. His own work absorbed influences from the choreographers he brought in.

With a distinctive curating policy in place, Pouffer ceased to choreograph for Cedar Lake's seasons and instead focused on its annual installations (2006, 2008–2012). These aimed to disrupt the conventions around attending dance performances by making audiences less passive. Spectators could wander around the theatre (stripped of its seating and wings) and choose their vantage points on the various performance areas. The installations allowed Pouffer to experiment and develop as a choreographer. To take the pressure off him, critics were not invited, although dance bloggers were invited to *Glassy Essence* (2008) and attended others.

The installations consisted of a series of unrelated vignettes gathered around a theme. The visceral choreography unspooled in a continually shifting thread; movement sequences were rarely repeated. The movement was often frenetic and fierce, with dancers shooting out their limbs, flinging energy. They thrashed in jerking movements and writhed through rapid isolations. Duets, same sex and mixed, could be fast and combative, or slow and sensual, and exhibited a wide variety of lifts (by the men). A recurring set was a long, over-large table, which dancers sat at, leaned on, danced upon, and emerged from underneath. Another was a climbing wall with foot holes and protruding blocks, which allowed dancers to dangle and pose in unusual shapes. Getting dancers off the floor was a preoccupation, and Pouffer used cables, flying harnesses, swings, and latex 'slings' to suspend dancers while they carved shapes in the air or partnered those below.

A high-profile project for both company and choreographer was the Hollywood film *The Adjustment Bureau* (2011), in which actor Emily Blunt played a Cedar Lake dancer. She trained with Pouffer, whose choreography earned him a nomination for the Astaire Award for Choreography in Film. Pouffer also collaborated on short dance films with photographer Erez Sabag and director Loïc Maes and choreographed commercials using Cedar Lake dancers.

Performances of Pouffer's last two 'stage' works for the company took place at the Festspielhaus in Baden-Baden, Germany. The subject of *on this planet* (2010) was our inability to escape gravity 'despite our attempts to reverse this universal phenomenon' (Pouffer's programme note, translated from German). Dancers were lifted, carried, and held up, or climbed on each other, but inevitably remained earthbound. In *Nu* (2013), the eight men began in tunics threaded with elastic cords, which they used to manipulate and extend each other's movements. They then removed these tunics, as if shedding their skin, to reveal leotards printed with an anatomical drawing of the torso's skeleton and muscles. *Nu*'s two sections contrasted strength and vulnerability, combative and supportive interactions, youthful recklessness and mature consideration.

In May 2013, Pouffer left Cedar Lake to embark on a career as a freelance choreographer. His most frequent collaboration was with Franco Dragone, the director known for his Cirque du Soleil and Las Vegas shows. Pouffer choreographed *Paris Merveilles* (2015), Dragone's new cabaret for the Lido de Paris, and *La Perle* (2017), his circus spectacle in Dubai. In 2015, Pouffer revamped *Taboo*, Dragone's existing cabaret in Macau, China, and in 2016, was his assistant director on a televised concert by Russian popstar Philipp Kirkorov, staged at the Kremlin. Pouffer credits Dragone with teaching him theatre techniques, such as how to control the stage picture, used in his subsequent work.

In 2013, Pouffer choreographed his third musical, *Soul Doctor*, about a folk-singing rabbi, which had an eight-week run on Broadway. Also in 2013, he melded singer Gala and four dancers in sculptural groupings in her music video 'Taste of Me'. He used contemporary dance again in Ellie Goulding's live-streamed concert for American Express Unstaged in 2015, and created a fast, ballet-based, male duet for *So You Think You Can Dance*.

While at Cedar Lake, Pouffer had choreographed for student dance companies and Ailey's junior company, Ailey II, and in his freelance years, he made several pieces for commercial dance schools. He continued his affiliation with JUMP Dance Convention, teaching at conventions and creating pieces for their closing show, and other conventions and studios in New York and Paris.

In 2018, Rambert, Britain's leading contemporary dance company, asked for Pouffer's assistance in setting up Rambert2, a new master's-level student company, run in partnership with the Rambert School. Concurrently, Mark Baldwin, Rambert's artistic director, resigned, and Pouffer stepped in as guest artistic director. Pouffer was appointed artistic director of Rambert in December 2018.

That year, Pouffer made *RAMBERT x GAIKA*, a one-off piece for the Wilderness festival, where the audience sat on the grass around the stage. Rapper GAIKA was incorporated into the work, interacting with the dancers while singing tracks from his debut album. Pouffer's choreography responded to the mood of his edgy lyrics and dense electronic music.

The two collaborated again on *Grey Matter* (2018), Rambert2's first world premiere, which had a commissioned score. Inspired by his mother's Alzheimer's diagnosis, *Grey Matter* was unusual in Pouffer's contemporary dance work for having defined, repeated movement sequences, used to underscore the theme. A female dancer drifted in and out of sharing this material with the group, and at a point where she froze, other dancers manipulated her through the pattern. At other times, individuals guided her in making her way around the space. *Grey Matter* used one of Pouffer's recurring devices of pulling the dancers into a tight group. From there, individuals leaned into or fell out of the group, or the dancers moved as a single, sculptural entity, connected by hands on shoulders or backs. Although sharp and driving in its energy, the work had a sense of community.

In 2019, Pouffer was involved in two BBC television shows. As creative advisor on the competition *The Greatest Dancer*, he created an emotive piece to Freya Ridings' song 'Lost Without You', sung at the piano with the Rambert dancers around her. For the drama *Peaky Blinders*, Pouffer made a brief pastiche of a *Swan Lake* pas de deux. Subsequently, he choreographed *Red Right Hand* (2019) for the first Legitimate Peaky Blinders Festival in Birmingham (UK), drawing on scenes from the popular series and its menacing tone.

Noting that his piece for *The Greatest Dancer* was viewed by a broader audience than those at live dance performances, Pouffer said, 'For me, it's important that I do this type of work. My responsibility is to do [it] to a high level. I want to make sure that the technicality and the artistry are there within this medium'. Reflecting on his crossover into other media and arenas, Pouffer explained, 'I like to go everywhere. To me, dance is dance. Mr Ailey said it: dance comes from the people and we have to deliver it back to the people. And that's been my mantra'.

Chris Jones

Biographical details

Born in Paris, France, in 1974. **Studied** at Conservatoire national supérieur de musique et de danse de Paris, 1991–93, and Alvin Ailey American Dance Center, New York, 1993–94. **Career:** 1994 to 1997, dancer with

Complexions Contemporary Ballet (New York), PHILADANCO! The Philadelphia Dance Company, Donald Byrd/The Group (New York); dancer, Alvin Ailey American Dance Theater, 1997–2004; resident choreographer, Cedar Lake Ensemble, New York, 2004–05; artistic director, Cedar Lake Contemporary Ballet, 2005–2013; freelance choreographer, 2013–2018; guest artistic director and then artistic director, Rambert, London, 2018. Has also choreographed for Dragone Productions, Earl Mosley's Diversity of Dance, New York Theatre Ballet, Mobile Unit of The Public Theater, Ailey II, Rutgers University's Mason Gross Dancers, NYU's Second Avenue Dance Company, STEPS Repertory Ensemble, and other student groups, as well as three musicals: *Dangerous Beauty*, Pasadena Playhouse; *Amazing Grace*, Goodspeed Opera House; *Soul Doctor*, Broadway. Work has appeared on television shows: *So You Think You Can Dance*, *The Greatest Dancer*, and *Peaky Blinders*; and in the feature film *The Adjustment Bureau*, 2011. Creative advisor on first series of *The Greatest Dancer*, 2019. Choreography in different contexts: installations; short dance films; advertising commercials for Bentley, Macy's, My Old Navy, 2(X)IST, among others; 'MJ Evolution' photo shoot for *Lemon Magazine*, 2012; two online instructional videos for teachers for Stage Door Workshops, 2015; Tracy Reese fashion show, Spring 2015; and fashion shoots for *Paper Magazine*'s 'Mrs America', 2016 and *Sunday Times* newspaper, 2018. Visiting artist: New York University, Rutgers University, Marymount Manhattan College, and University of Hartford.

Works

Duet, Earl Mosley's Diversity of Dance (title unknown, 2001); *Beautiful Places* (co-choreographer 2001); title unknown, Alvin Ailey American Dance Theater Benefit (2001); *Untitled* (co-choreographer, Dance on a Shoestring, 2003); *Drawing Mad* (solo, 2003); *Parts of Us* (2003); *Raw* (2005); *And Those …* (2005); *Seed* (2005); *Between Here and Now* (2006); *Hammer* (2006); *Vastav* (2006); *3 Thursdays* installation (co-choreographer, 2006); title unknown (Dance on a Shoestring, 2007); untitled (dance film, *Fly Magazine*, 2007); *Glassy Essence* installation (2008); untitled Salt Lake City installation (2009); 'Iran Inside Out' installation (2009); *Show Me* (2009); *On this Planet* (2010); *Winter 2010 Installation* (2010); *Still Here* (2010); *For All of Us* (2010); *2011 Installation* (2011); untitled Dallas Installation (2011); *Cedar Lake 360°* installation (co-choreographer, 2011); *The Adjustment Bureau* (film, 2011); untitled work (television, *So You Think You Can Dance*, 2011); *Dangerous Beauty* (musical, 2011); *New Work* (2011); untitled work (video, The Collective/JUMP Dance Convention, 2011); *2012 Installation* (2012); *Rusty* (2012); *Knead* (2012); *Amazing Grace* (musical, 2012); *Birds, Butterfly, Crystal, Iconic – Black, Iconic – White* (short dance films, 2012); *P.L.A.S.T.I.C.* (short dance film, 2013); *Nu* (2013); *Soul Doctor* (musical, 2013); Gala's 'Taste of Me' (music video, 2013); *Equilibrium Phase II with Prelude* (installation, 2014); *Four* (2014); *Paris Merveilles* (cabaret, 2015); *Taboo* (cabaret, 2015); untitled duet (television, *So You Think You Can Dance*, 2015); 'Explosions' and 'Love Me Like You Do', *American Express Unstaged: Ellie Goulding* (live-streamed concert, 2015); Tracy Reese Spring Show (fashion show, New York Fashion Week, 2015); *Street* (aka *Ebony*) and *Dance* (aka *Chromat*) (short dance films, 2015); Philipp Kirkorov's birthday concert (2016); *Romeo and Juliet* (play, 2016); *Fresco* (2016); *Grant Us Peace* (2016); *La Perle* (circus show, 2017); *The Garden is Becoming* (2017); *Upside Down* (installation, 2018); Rambert's Summer Installation (curator, 2018); *RAMBERT x GAIKA* (2018); *Grey Matter* (2018); Freya Ridings' 'Lost Without You' (television, *The Greatest Dancer*, 2019); untitled duet (television, *Peaky Blinders*, series 5, episode 4, 2019); *Red Right Hand* (2019).

Further reading

Interviews: with Katie Derham, 'Benoit Swan Pouffer', *Sound of Dance*, BBC Radio 3, 20 April 2019; Laura Dodge, 'Democratising Dance', *Dancing Times*, May 2019.

Articles: Anon., 'Edgy and New', *Pointe Magazine*, 2007; Khara Hanlon, 'From Movie Studio to Dance Studio', *Dance Magazine*, 26 August 2010; Rachel Elson, 'Director's Notes: A Taste of Europe', *Pointe Magazine*, 30 July 2012; Charmaine Patricia Warren, 'Benoît-Swan Pouffer Choreographs New Broadway Show', *New York Amsterdam News*, 18 July 2013; Elizabeth Zimmer, 'Benoit Swan Pouffer Goes from Ballet to Broadway in "Soul Doctor"', *Metro USA*, 27 August 2013; Oscar Héliani, 'Benoît-Swan Pouffer: Nos Boys ne sont plus des faire-valoir', *Têtu*, May 2015; Richelle Harrison Plesse, 'Behind the Scenes of the Lido de Paris', FranceToday.com, 7 November 2015; Emma Byrne, 'I'd Love to Go on Strictly – Dance is for the People', *Evening Standard*, 7 May 2019.

HOFESH SHECHTER

Hofesh Shechter is a choreographer and a composer best known for epic pieces, that transform theatre auditoriums into mosh pits – part dance show, part rock gig.

His movement style, described variously as earthy, animalistic, urban and gritty, is hard to characterise. References to folk dancing, to neo-classical ballet, laid-back moves from club culture – all have equal value across his repertoire. As Bruno Guillore, long-term collaborator and Associate Artistic Director of Hofesh Shechter Company (HSC) describes

> Hofesh is a choreographer in search of totality – this means expressing yourself with your body and with your inner world as fully as you can. Totally forceful, totally vulnerable, totally simple, totally instinctive. All of this in the attempt to create something

that resonates within us and generates emotions. Perhaps due to his Israeli–German heritage, his work is often thought to have political subtexts. Shechter gently responds: 'My work is no more political than anyone else's. We are all in this world together – the circle of life and the endless cycle of war affects us all in some way or another'.

(personal interview with author, April 2010)

Shechter has been a British resident since 2002, when he joined Jasmin Vardimon Company as a dancer. He left to create his own work, which is self-deprecating, often confessional in style and accompanied by a quick wit. It ensured him a speedy trajectory into the mainstream UK dance scene. *Fragments* (2003) attracted some international attention, but in 2004 Shechter was a Place Prize finalist with *Cult*, which won the audience vote for 5 of its 10 performances. *Cult* featured a voice-over straight from the therapist's couch, red dresses, suits paired with socks, a man dressed as a gorilla, and movement that was as sensuous and meaty as it was ethereal and fleeting. The confessional voice-over – a motif that appears in many of his works – was teamed with fluid movement that morphed bodies and groupings seamlessly.

After graduating from the Jerusalem Academy of Music and Dance, where he had switched from the classical music to dance, he moved to Tel Aviv spending three years with Batsheva Dance Company: 'It was this experience that grew me as a young dancer, and as a young man. Ohad [Naharin] was a huge influence for me' (personal interview with author, May 2009). This was followed by National Service in the Israeli army, after which he spent a year in Paris as a drummer in a band before arriving in the UK.

Shechter's use of the floor is integral to his style. 'I've got this natural urge to use the floor fully. In respect of sensations, it connects me to a sense of comfort, security, of endless possibility. Perhaps balancing a feeling of restricted possibilities when standing' (HSC company document, February 2012). He also talks of 'soft rolling feet' when he works; and the notion that the floor and body are interconnected, symbiotic, as illustrated in *Uprising* (2006). Danced by seven men, it begins with an immensely loud, pounding industrial beat and a large bank of fierce bright lights shining directly into the auditorium. Out of the shadows stride the men, travelling downstage to balance in retiré before melting and crumbling back into the shadows. The lolloping, crouched 'monkey' runs, heavy pelvis and hunched back, the seamless relationship between dancers' bodies and their passage into and out of the floor, are motifs that evolve through his later works.

The interplay in his works between what audiences can or cannot see (dancers melting into and out of shadows, lighting guiding the eye to see fragments of movement in detail before the scene plunges into darkness), is a filmic influence that Shechter often references. 'A huge influence for me is Stanley Kubrick – the aesthetics and the timing of his story-telling is something that I just adore. There is something so brave and bold in the way that he's doing it' (Shechter, Matches Fashion Podcast: The Collector's House, Episode 53, July 2019). His collaborations with lighting designers, most notably with Lee Curran, who echo these filmic influences have helped build his reputation for visually atmospheric pieces. His stage is inhabited by murky back alleys, hazy darkness, suffocating stillness – layering images to build the 'worlds' he refers to in his pieces.

In *The Art of Not Looking Back* (2008) Shechter's own percussive soundtrack coupled with John Zorn's screaming and choking composition, are overlaid with snatches of strings that build and soar, in a work with challenging subject matter – his own childhood abandonment. A stripped-back piece for six women in a white space, it was more gutsy and visceral than his earlier works; 'I really wanted to challenge myself, and my audience, who at that time saw me as a very 'male' choreographer ... I wanted to work with strong female energy' (Shechter, Uprising/The Art of Not Looking Back, A resource pack for teachers and students, HSC, May 2012). At the end, the dancers rewind their movement, as if fixing glitches and righting wrongs;

> the clamorous electronic soundtrack gives way to an Urdu song of extraordinary sweetness, and the women begin to backtrack through the choreography. As their movements accelerate to near inhuman speeds, it is like watching the home movie of a life unravelling.
>
> (Judith Mackrell, 'Hofesh Shechter Company, Brighton Dome', *The Guardian*, 18 May 2009)

Ultimately it was a work of hope, despite its painful theme. This is a notion Shechter returns to often, 'I want people to leave the theatre thinking that it's going to be ok. That we are all in this together' (Hofesh Shechter's SUN, a resource pack, HSC, November 2013).

In his 2009 work *In your rooms*, Shechter's development as a composer grew, with the introduction of live music. The work featured an ensemble of five musicians on a floating platform; a combination of drums and strings in a rousing sound-score underpinned with his self-effacing commentary in voice-over; and ten dancers. (Extended for Sadler's Wells Theatre, London, using 8 musicians and 14 dancers). His trademark humour is cut through the piece, never more so than three minutes in, when all dancing and music halts and his voice-over states '*Let's start again .... I can do much better than that ....*' There is a pause, followed by an unapologetic '*... erm.... no. I can't*'. The piece whirs into frenetic action again.

His first full-length piece, *Political Mother* (2010), announced his ambition of scale. Beginning in murky darkness with the startling image of a warrior in armour committing harikuri, it then bounces the audience through scenes reminiscent of a prisoner of war camp, a gaggle of gutsy entertainers, an embattled couple. It involves a screeching dictator in uniform, a rock star, an execution, frenetic military clad drummers, and musicians floating mid-air on a vast unlit scaffolding. The dancers surge through the space, morphing between worlds of agony and ecstasy, driven on by the loud pulsating score (some venues offer earplugs and warn that noise levels may exceed 100 decibels). An artwork, by the artist FOS, slowly revealed in neon lights across the backdrop, states *Where there is pressure there is folk dance*. The final scenes offer a fast motion, poignant rewind of the piece, a choreographic tool reminiscent of his earlier 2008 work. These closing moments are accompanied by a gentle song as the house lights are raised, before plunging the auditorium into darkness as the entire cast make a curtain call to thrash guitars, often to standing ovations. Swift changes in tone keep the audience off balance to the last.

Noting that some of the themes of his work to date – oppression, sublimation, loss – were seen as gloomy, Shechter set out to make a funny piece. Though humour finds its way into all his work, the result, *SUN* (2013), was dark and brooding. Images and the language of colonialism and slavery wrestled alongside a score weaving excerpts of classical music with his own driving and rolling percussive rhythms. Pierrot costumes, white clown wigs, a man driven to madness – it is a work where all is not quite as it seems. *SUN* culminates in a final scene reminiscent of slapstick Commedia dell'Arte humour, the entire cast putting on a tongue-in-cheek 'finale' for the crowd, to the dying chords of the 'Arrival of the guests at Wartburg', from Wagner's *Tannhäuser*. '*Now ... here is your fucking finale ...*' Shechter tells us in voice-over. Where *Political Mother* was his large-scale crowd pleaser, *SUN* divided critics and audiences alike. Shechter tackles difficult images and our chequered history, sometimes with deft nuance and at other times with full-throated aggression.

Imagery is writ large in *barbarians* (2015), a piece in three parts. A group of automatons dressed all in white crash and melt through the space, morph into one homogenous group, then break out again into satellites before being sucked back into the whole. Movement motifs that are recognisably Shechter-like – the softness with the floor, a released lower back – are coupled with classical port de bras and pointed tendus puncturing the earthiness of his more recognisable movement language. The second part was created in an underground studio, at night-time, Shechter wishing to push his and the dancers' limitations. It brings a change of pace as five dancers in gold cat suits improvise, breaking the fourth wall by engaging in conversation with the audience, in a piece that changes at each performance.

The piece ends in a quiet duet. It's a discombobulating evening of work, ending with a whimper whilst encompassing everything from nudity, profanity and rage to gentle calm. Shechter had set out to challenge himself (and his audiences): 'After all, what is "good" art? We have no idea. It's absolutely culturally subjective … I'm ripping my heart out and trying something experimental … and it can go horribly wrong' (Lyndsey Winship, Hofesh Shechter talks #HOFEST', *London Evening Standard*, 2 July 2015).

Grand Finale (2017), a rabble-rousing piece, was a return to critical acclaim. With the band clad in black tie and shabby life jackets, themes and imagery of a sinking ship and drowning threaded their way throughout. Dead bodies piled up against the huge tomb-like walls designed by Tom Scutt, and dancers waltzed to Lehar's *The Merry Widow* under a rainfall of bubbles. Later, fleeting images are glimpsed – suffocated bodies in the back of a truck, a couple kissing, a man about to be shot against a wall. Hofesh's cinematic lens was gaining clarity and confidence in these fast changes of pace and emotion. And once again his work probed deeply into the human condition, in all its glory and horror.

Shechter's trajectory from a teenage would-be rock star to a choreographer commissioned by high-profile dance companies is surprising to him. His 'loser mentality', (Shechter, unpublished interview with author, April 2010), lives deep in his psyche, and emerges in all his works, from images of downtrodden prisoners in *Political Mother,* to poking fun at himself for notions of excruciating self-obsession (*'Hofesh … stop talking … be quiet'* the robotic voice-over chides in *barbarians*). His approach when creating is total, immersive, intense. His desire to make audiences feel something – to question, to unpick, to unravel – is at the forefront of his process. 'I want audiences to be awakened, to experience my work from the gut. Trusting the gut is to me like trusting nature, or God … a source, a spark. Trusting a higher and better force than our limited oppressed cultured minds' (HSC website,

October 2018). His movement language comes from an emotional starting point, making his work accessible to so many – the sense that we are simply watching ourselves on stage.

Of his complex and arresting musical scores, Shechter states it as a case of necessity, 'Music is such a big part of my choreography that I don't think I could create an entire piece to someone else's score' (Robertson, 'Hofesh Shechter, The Crouching Tiger: How Israeli Hofesh Shechter became the Biggest Beast in British Choreography', *The Independent*, 16 May 2010). Looking back to the first time he showed work professionally, he remembers feeling excitement at the thought that people would hear his music. 'Getting into choreography, one of the more attractive things for me was that I would be able to make the music for it … I'm deeply excited about presenting music plus dance. It's not a secondary thing' (Monahan, 'Hofesh Shechter: steps from another direction', *The Telegraph*, May 2010).

Shechter's work is loved by many, found challenging by others. His ability to make us laugh, weep, even dance out of auditoriums is powerful. He shines an unforgiving light on our human frailties, whilst also making us question ourselves. His work reminds us that nothing divides us as much as all the things that unite us. He states (interview with author, May 2010):

> For me it doesn't matter if the foot is like this, the arm held so … those details come later. At its heart my movement comes from emotion. If it then translates into an emotional response for the person watching that movement, then I am doing my job well.
>
> *Lucy Moelwyn-Hughes*

Biographical details

Born in Jerusalem, Israel, 3 May 1975. **Studied** piano from age six, followed by folk dance. Studied dance at the Jerusalem Academy for Music and Dance. Aged 18, joined Batsheva's Young Ensemble, under Ohad Naharin. After relocating to Paris, he studied drums and percussion and played with rock band The Human Beings. **Career:** Danced professionally with Batsheva Dance Company and with Jasmin Vardimon Company. Following his early works, *Fragments* (2003), *Cult* (2004), and *Uprising* (2006), The Place, Southbank Centre and Sadler's Wells Theatre, London, commissioned him to create *In your rooms* (2007). Founded Hofesh Shechter Company in 2008, now company in residence at the Brighton Dome and Shechter is an Associate Artist at Sadler's Wells. Has staged and choreographed works on leading international dance companies – including Alvin Ailey American Dance Theater, Batsheva Ensemble, Candoco Dance Company, Cedar Lake

Contemporary Ballet, Nederlands Dans Theater 1, Paris Opera Ballet, Royal Ballet, and Royal Ballet Flanders – and choreographed for theatre, television and opera. **Awards and honours** include Critics' Circle Award, 2007; Tanz Magazine Award, 2018; OBE for Services to Dance, 2018; Dora Award, 2019.

Works

(See hofesh.co.uk for Hofesh Shechter's full music credits)

Fragments (2003); *Cult* (2004); *Uprising* (2006); *Motortown* (play, 2006); *In Your Rooms* (2007); *The Arsonists* (play, 2007); *Saint Joan* (play, 2007); *The Fools* (2008); *The 10 Plagues* (2008); *Dog* (2008); *The Art of not Looking Back* (2009); *Political Mother* (2010); *Political Mother: The Choreographer's Cut* (extended version, 2011); *Survivor* (with Antony Gormley 2012); *Violet Kid* (2012); *Two Boys* (opera, 2013); *SUN* (2013); *Dust* (2014); *Barbarians – Part I: The Barbarians in Love,* Part II: *tHE bAD,* Part III: *Two Completely Different Angles of the Same Fucking Thing* (2015); *Untouchables* (2015); *Orphée et Eurydice* (opera, 2015); *Disappearing Act* (2015); *Clowns* (2016); *Fiddler on the Roof* (Broadway musical, 2016); *Grand Finale* (2017); *Wolf* (2017); *Corpse de Ballet* (2018); *Clowns* (film, BBC 2, 2018); *SHOW* (Shechter II, 2018); *Vladimir* (2018); *Contemporary Dance* (2019); *POLITICAL MOTHER UNPLUGGED* (reworked revival, Shechter II, 2020); *Double Murder* (2020).

Further reading

Interviews: with Hanna Weibye, 'Q&A: Choreographer Hofesh Shechter', theartsdesk.com, 15 March 2014; Candice Thompson, 'At the End of All Things: Hofesh Shechter on His Latest Work', dancemagazine.com, 7 November 2017; David Jays, 'Interview: Hofesh Schechter', theatrevoice. com, 10 May 2018; Laurine Mortha, 'Hofesh Shechter on His Creative Process', bachtrack.com, 17 May 2018; David Jays, 'In Conversation with Hofesh Shechter', blog.sadlerswells.com, 20 June 2018.

Articles: Judith Mackrell, 'War Was Coming Through the Window', *The Guardian,* 12 January 2009; Allen Robertson, 'The Crouching Tiger: How Israeli Hofesh Shechter became the Biggest Beast in British Choreography', *Independent,* 16 May 2010; Geraldine Higginson, 'Upping the Volume', *Dance Australia,* October/November 2019.

Books: Sarah Crompton, *Sadler's Wells Dance House,* London, 2013; Jenny Bunker, Anna Pakes, and Bonnie Rowell (eds.), *Thinking Through Dance; The Philosophy of Dance Performance and Practices,* London, 2013; Guy Cools, *Imaginative Bodies: Dialogues in Performance Practices,* Amsterdam, 2016.

GARRY STEWART

Garry Stewart's work has been described as ballistic, high octane, and gymnastic, a deliberate forcefulness delivered with exuberant athleticism by his dancers. Such responses do not however communicate the depth of the issues with which he engages. Deeper concerns of humankind's relationship with self and sentience, and with the union of the self with nature, are recurrent and underlying themes that remain in dialogue throughout his decades of work.

Whether his background in remote rural Australia impacted on Stewart's creative work is difficult to discern. Arguably it created a resolve to invest everything in shifting from the outback to the city and from university student to choreographer, resolve which sparks commitment driving each of his projects. It is infectious and permeates the culture of all who commit to working with him. His dance vocabulary has favoured extreme physicality, informed by break dance, martial arts, and gymnastics. Stewart's interest in these heightened forms of physical expression stems from a desire to challenge what dance offers. It is informed by a deep understanding of the body as a highly expressive instrument that can distil and communicate human emotion with palpable alacrity, to the point that during some performances his audience appear to be holding their breath, waiting to give a collective exhale at the end.

Stewart's life in outback New South Wales began as the youngest son living on the cattle station where his father worked as a stockman. Whilst studying social work at the University of New South Wales he nurtured an interested in the arts, attending a contemporary dance performance by Sydney Dance Company which opened his eyes to a whole new world. In response to this compelling visceral experience, in a life changing moment, Stewart decided to pursue a career as a dancer, eventually gaining a place at the Australian Ballet School. He joined Australian Dance Theatre (ADT) in 1986, a company to which he would return as Artistic Director in 1999.

Stewart danced with Expressions Dance Company based in Brisbane during 1987, returned to Sydney in 1988 to work with Kai Tai Chan and then worked as an independent dancer in Spain. Having already created short works in choreographic workshops, it was the creative process that really captured Stewart's interest. He eventually returned to Sydney where he turned his attention to choreography alongside studying new media and cultural theory.

Stewart's early work was created as an independent artist, predominantly in Sydney. Founding his own company in 1998, *THWACK!*, he created two works which had second iterations when he returned to ADT; *Plastic Space* (1999) which combined dance and film in an exploration of attempts to comprehend the cosmos, and an early version of his seminal work, *Birdbrain*.

Stewart's first work as Artistic Director for ADT was a televised commissioned work for the International Millennium Broadcast, performed by dancers and a violinist whilst abseiling down the mainsail of the Sydney Opera House. The performance was viewed by an estimated one billion people. His full-length *Birdbrain* (2001) became a phenomenon, maintaining the position as the most performed Australian contemporary dance piece. In the words of UK dance critic Judith Mackrell, *Birdbrain* 'could only have been imagined by a choreographer genuinely in thrall to the ritual of *Swan Lake*' ('Australian Dance Theatre', *The Guardian*, 9 May 2003). *Birdbrain* is not so much a deconstruction, but rather a distillation of this classic ballet. His wry and ironic postmodern approach reconstitutes the well-known narrative, questioning the culture of classical ballet itself. Poignant moments have been extracted and reshaped. Choreographed with humour and wit, dancers work in tight formation. The cygnets wrestle, the 32 fouettés are divvied amongst several cast members who wait patiently in line for their turn, and the story is conveyed through words printed on T-shirts. A contortionist mimes the story, to ensure the audience keeps pace. *Birdbrain* remains a testament to Stewart's capacity to bring contemporary relevance to a well-known classic.

G (2009) is another reworking of a classic. Stewart takes a nonlinear approach to the narrative of *Giselle* and exposes an emotionally charged subtext that draws reference from images of women incarcerated in the infamous Pitié-Salpêtrière Hospital in Paris during the 1700s. For the duration of G, the dancers, dressed in green costumes, cross the stage in an unrelenting stream beginning with solemn walks which rapidly escalate. Bourrés become runs which quickly turn into airborne tumbles as the dancers deliver traveling scenes of desperation, madness and unrequited love. Moments of perfectly formed classical lines are distorted and reinstated, interspersed with humorous quips at peasant frivolities and haughty aristocracy. G challenges the portrayal of women in the classical canon, showing them as physically powerful and capable of domination. Instead of the ethereal otherworldly qualities in the ballet, here the women are earth-bound creatures that scratch and claw, whilst silently mouthing profanities. The choreography is at times ugly and the women in particular dance movements that appear to shudder with effort and visible trauma. Portrayed as fighters, they rarely conform to archetypical notions of beauty associated with classical ballet. They hurtle themselves in daring tumbles that crash into their male prey, deftly bringing them to the ground.

Stewart's work can be grouped under key headings that defy chronological orderliness, but are nonetheless connected. *The Age of Unbeauty* (2002) and most recently *Objekt* (2016) address objectification, the ability of humans to subjugate each other. *Be Your Self* (2010) and *Proximity* (2012) address self-hood, the body and human interconnection. *Birdbrain* and *G* are deconstructions of classical ballet narratives. *Devolution* (2006), a collaboration with Canadian roboticist Louis-Philippe Demers, grew from a series of tasks that investigated evolution and metamorphosis. As humans and robots compete for ascendency in *Devolution* it can be viewed as a precursor to his Nature Series. *The Beginning of Nature* (2016) led to his latest work *South* (2019). An adjunct of his Nature Series, *Multiverse* (2014), a work with 3D animation in an exploration of quantum physics, could claim infancy in *Plastic Space*.

As a front runner to a series that investigate humankind's relationships with each other, Stewart explores acts of human violence in *The Age of Unbeauty*. Extending the extreme physicality of his dance vocabulary, the work exposes the dichotomies that exist in the terror wrought by humans alongside our imperative need for each other. Next, drawing from *The Tibetan book of Living and Dying* by Sogyal Rinpoche, and Elizabeth Kubler-Ross's work *On Death and Dying*, the exploration of terror in *The Age of Unbeauty* is resolved in *Nothing* (2003), which explores death, loss and mourning. *Nothing* is less violent and explosive than *The Age of Unbeauty* and includes scenes that depict solemn ritual. Movements that are animalistic and contorted then soften as though the dancers wish to shield themselves from the inevitability of death.

Objekt was originally created in collaboration with Tanzmainz. Here Stewart positions the human body as an object of art and then, at times, brutally portrays objectification. The work teeters cleverly between beautiful and uncomfortable, then compelling and abhorrent. In one scene dancers carry each other strapped in harnesses hanging upside down with seemingly no regard for their welfare. The work revisits the scenes of violence and suppression first explored in *The Age of Unbeauty*, however, this time the choreography is imbued with less physical violence but rather depicts psychological menace.

Believing that dance works best in partnership with other disciplines, Stewart has collaborated with practitioners from fields as diverse as architecture, robotics, film, photography, 3D animation, video technology, and linguistics. Notable collaborations include: *Held*

(2004) with New York based dance photographer Lois Greenfield; *Be Your Self* with leading architectural firm Diller Scofidio and Renfro; *Devolution* with roboticist Louis-Philippe Demers and media artist Gina Czarnecki; and *Proximity* (2012) with French visual and interactive programmer Thomas Pachoud. These collaborations place dance in other contexts augmented by technology and design.

In *Held* (2004), Lois Greenfield, the photographer is on stage. Her spectacular images, immediately relayed to two huge screens, reveal moments that usually pass by too fast for spectators to register. Caught or literally held in time for an elongated moment, her photographs capture gravity-defying twists and spins, with the resulting images appearing unattainable as dancers hang in impossible positions in the air. The work typifies Stewart's reciprocal approach to collaboration; dance and photography are central.

Proximity is an exploration of the body and intimacy. Visually stunning and design-centric, spectators are forced to choose whether to watch the live bodies interacting on stage, or the larger than life projected images that are augmented with video effects which entangle bodies in intricate webs and create dust-like trails, rendering a perfectly combined visual experience of interconnectedness.

Devolution was one of the most ambitious stage productions for dancers and robotics ever made. Here Stewart investigates the fragility of sentient beings in a futuristic world. Robots dominate the stage, some in threatening proportions and with a seemingly unstoppable disregard for the safety of the humans dancing amongst them. Swarms of small bots evoke visions of bot plagues as the choreography suggests a malfunctioning evolutionary cycle in a post-dystopian age.

Multiverse (2014) was the result of a collaboration with Motion Lab at Deakin University where Stewart was Thinker-in-Residence in 2013. The choreography communicates the impossibility of string theory as dancers interact with vast 3D images that sometimes envelop the audience. The animations meld the audience and dancers together in a surreal world. In contrast to the sublime beauty of the animation, the choreography is often awkward and illogical, as dancers twist, threading their limbs through strange movement pathways.

Stewarts' collaborations extend to Australian composers including Luke Smiles, Brendan Woithe, and Hugh Benjamin. The music evolves in tandem with the choreography as the music is flexibly crafted to match the palette and timbre of Stewart's work. The creative process for *Be Your Self* (2010), composed by Woithe, included videoed sections of choreography sent from Adelaide to the composer in Sydney, returned with new musical compositions attached. This toing and froing with music in close dialogue with the dance resulted in a score that obsessively and minutely frames the action.

Be Your Self deepens Stewart's reflection on self-hood and intersperses dance with the spoken word and film. Inspired by conversations with a Buddhist teacher, the work begins with quirky explorations of the human body where the physical self is turned inside out. Dancers squirm, breathe noisily, appear to vomit, then fling unruly arms and legs whilst their torsos ricochet off the floor. The unique movement vocabulary is informed by break dance moves. In the second part, Stewart examines the emotional body creating an uncomfortable world, filled with tension and sexual domination. Sexually evocative movements show dancers clinging and grasping at each other in desperation, quickly morphing into violent rejection. The set is a pristine white ramp, designed by New York architecture firm Dilis Scofidio & Renfro, through which dancers emerge, arranged carefully to appear as beautifully synchronised works of art. The set also acts as a projection screen for film that bookends the work.

In Habitus (2016), Stewart shifts focus to challenge how we habitually relate to objects, introducing spectators to a world of things through an assemblage of small scenes that recontextualise the stuff of everyday life. Stewart creates a world defined by sofas, books, tables, chairs, and language, not utilised in conventional ways, to demonstrate our obsession with material possessions. Books pile up and down in deft synchronicity. Dancers fly over and onto furniture, sofas are dragged, shoved, and upended. Having descended into chaos the work ends as a lament for the natural world, the choreography in the closing section a precursor to Stewart's Nature Series.

The Nature Series is a group of dance works and films inspired by the ramifications of climate change in a rapidly changing world. The first, *The Beginning of Nature* (2018), is a poetic handling of the intrinsic relationship between humans and Earth. The choreography draws humans into the fabric of nature by referencing rhythms found in nature, such as night and day, the seasons and tidal action. Recurrent themes such as growth, decay, birth, and metamorphosis are crafted into sublime patterns of movement. In one section, dancers form lines holding long green painted sticks, which they shape to form a cage, a trap, then a forest. Percussive movements synchronised with audible breaths, in unison and then counter point, indicate communication beyond language associated with flocking and swarming. They maintain a strong sense of cohesion, working in tight formation at times with arms outstretched as though in flight, then quickly contracting their limbs as though sensing danger. For the libretto, Stewart collaborated closely with first nations Kuarna language custodian Jack Buckskin.

The allegory *South* (2019) explores the climate crisis by referencing explorer Douglas Mawson's ill-fated journey to the Antarctic in the 1900s. A set of huge white cubes is constantly and meticulously re-configured by dancers to evoke human endeavour, in an ever-changing landscape. Conjuring scenes of dangerous terrain, this work captures the dramatic nature of the expedition and is the closest that Stewart has ventured into narrative form.

Elizabeth Old

Biographical details

Born in Gunnedah, New South Wales, Australia, 19 May 1962. **Studied** at the Bodenwieser Studio; the Tanya Pearson Classical Academy, Sydney, 1982–84; Australian Ballet School, Melbourne, 1984–86; and the Susan Klein School of Dance, New York. Studied video at the University of New South Wales; and Media and Communications at the University of Technology, Sydney. **Career:** performed in drag shows, 1982–84; made his professional debut with Australian Dance Theatre, 1986; also dancer with Expressions Dance Company 1987, Queensland Ballet, and One Extra Company 1988. First choreography as a student, 1985, then creating works for One Extra, Darc Swan, Chunky Move, Sydney Dance Company and several tertiary dance courses, 1991–1998; founded own company *Thwack!* 1998; artistic director, Australian Dance Theatre, from 1999. **Awards and honours** include Robert Helpmann Scholarship, 1998; Australia Council for the Arts Fellowship, 1999; Australian Choreographic Centre Fellowship, 1998, 1999; Australian Dance Awards, 2002, 2004, 2005, 2006, 2008; Adelaide Critics' Circle Award, 2002; Helpmann Awards, 2004, 2006, 2019; IMZ Dance Screen Award, 2005; Reeldance Award, 2006; Ruby Awards 2006, 2012; Australia Council Award for Outstanding Achievement in Dance, 2015; Winston Churchill Fellowship, 2017.

Works

Conversation with an Ironing Board (1985); *Zen Do Some Nothing* (1986); *Childscape* (1987); *N.Y.* (1988); *The Year My Leg Broke* (1991); *The Sex, Flesh / Love, Lust Axis* (1992); *Arlene Harper* (1992); *The Kweer and the Unfamilia* (1993); *This* (1993); *The Velocity of Sex* (1995); *Bonded* (1995); *Spectre in the Covert Memory* (1995); *West Side Story* (1996); *THWACK!* (1996); *Danger is Imminent* (1997); *Two Step Crush* (film, 1997); *Birdbrain* (evolving versions, 1998, 2000, 2001); *Fugly* (1998); *Smiles Miles* (film, 1998); *Amnesia* (1999); *Space* (1999); *Plastic Space* (1999); *Currently Under Investigation* (1999); *Housedance* (1999); *Monstrosity* (2001); *The Age of Unbeauty* (2002); *Nothing* (2003); *Held* (2004); *Nascent* (film, 2005); *Present Tense* (2005); *Devolution* (2006); *Honour Bound*

(2006); *Infinity* (2008); *G* (2008–09); *The Sydney* (2009); *The Centre and Its Opposite* (2009); *Un-Black* (2009); *Be Your Self* (2010); *Worldhood* (2011); *Choreography* (2014); *Proximity* (2012); *Multiverse* (2014); *Collision Course* (film, 2015); *The Choreography of Emotions* (film, 2015); *Habitus* (2016); *The Beginning of Nature* (2016); *Objekt* (2016); *Doppleganger* (2017); *South* (2019); *The Circadian Cycle* (film, 2019).

Further reading

Interviews: with Lee Tran Lam, 'Nothing If not Inspired', *Limelight*, July 2003; Mark Baechtel, 'The Body Heroic', *Anchorage Daily News*, 7 April 2005; Karen van Ulzen, 'Limelight', *Dance Australia*, October/November 2005; Erin Brannigan, 'Dance Evolution in the Land of Robotics', *RealTime*, February/March 2006; unattributed, 'Jack Buckskin & Garry Stewart', ABC Radio National, 2019; 'Garry Stewart Celebrates 20 Years at the Helm of Australian Dance Theatre', *Adelaide Messenger*, realtime.org.au, 2019.

Articles: Karen Van Ulzen, 'Man of Extremes', *Dance Australia*, August/September 1999; Jack Anderson, 'Taking Liberties with Ballet's Archetypes', *The New York Times*, 6 January 2002; Ashley Hay, 'Frieze Frame', *The Bulletin*, 10 August 2004; Zoë Anderson, 'Birdbrain', *The Independent*, 8 March 2005; Jacqueline Pascoe, 'A Cry for Justice', *Dance Australia*, October/November 2006; Jane Howard, 'Multiverse Review – Dancers Play with 3D Projections and Optical Illusions', *The Guardian*, 11 July 2014; Jane Howard, 'Garry Stewart Celebrates 20 Years at the Helm of Australian Dance Theatre', *Adelaide Messenger*, 2019.

Books: Alan Brissenden, *Fifty Contemporary Choreographers*, 2nd ed. (eds. Martha Bremser and Lorna Sanders), London and New York, 2011.

MARESA VON STOCKERT

Choreographer and visual artist, Maresa von Stockert creates work that reflects on the complex social, political, and environmental questions of our time. Her thought-provoking perspective, attention to detail, and focus on intimacy invites others to see, feel and reflect on the intangible exposed in her work. Von Stockert unfolds an environment that can range from the poetic, tender and delicate to the absurd, cold and grotesque.

Her work crosses art-form boundaries and defies general classification. Although rooted in contemporary dance, her choreography combines visual and performance art, object manipulation, physical theatre, sound design and text. Whether for the stage or open air, site-responsive or on film, her pieces are uncompromisingly tailored to the chosen contexts. 'Maresa von Stockert has a choreographic sensibility that's all her own, a mix of intellectual and sensory scrupulousness that makes her work strikingly original' (Mackrell, 2010).

Her artistic trajectory demonstrates an interest in the physical dialogue between the human body and its surroundings; objects, architecture, and landscape. Underpinning this process is recognition of the tension that can evolve from the interaction and interdependency between the animate and the inanimate. In collaboration with her performers she applies a process of dynamic sculpturing that merges bodies, materials and environments in constant flux, driven by the overarching concept of each work.

As much a visual artist and 'metteuse en scene' (orchestrator of elements of production) as choreographer, she defines her work as being 'drawn to the process of amalgamating different artforms. I long for paintings in motion; movement poetry; metaphors of doubt; a circus of the senses – a play between rest and restlessness of bodies, thoughts, sounds and materials' (all quotations are from an unpublished interview with the author, 2019). Von Stockert creates multi layered, cross art-form pieces – 'Gesamtkunstwerk' (bringing together differing art forms into one work: Richard Wagner in *Das Kunstwerk der Zukunft*, Leipzig, Otto Wigand, 1849) – perhaps unconsciously channelling Bauhaus concepts and gestures towards her German heritage. Her work captures the Zeitgeist, interrogates contemporary issues that have current resonance. Yet she also touches upon universal feelings that are not bound by time and place in her own interpretation of what makes us human.

Born and raised in Germany, von Stockert moved to the UK in 1992, torn between going to university to study literature in Germany or dance in the UK. Having chosen the latter, she integrated her passion for the written word in her work. Authoring her own texts, she introduced voice-over, utilising a deadpan tone that understated, rather than overdramatised, the tragicomic she observed in everyday existence.

Her seminal early work, *Grim(m) Desires* (2004) used literature as a starting point. Having chosen five known fairy tales as source material, she merged archetypes and applied dark humour to re-write the tales from her own psychoanalytical viewpoint. In *Marjorie's World Unhinged* (2006); *Glacier* (2008); and *T(r)apped* (2009), she evolved the use of voice-over and included spoken dialogue on stage. Her texts never explain but complement the movement vocabulary. 'I used text for what I felt only words could express; and movement to convey what I could not put into words'.

Commissioned by the late Jules Wright (Wapping Project), *Grim(m) Desires* was von Stockert's first site-specific piece and first full-length work.

> At Wapping Hydraulic Power Station I started to understand the full potential of framing bodies within architecture: playing with what could be hidden and seen, highlighting performers or body parts between Victorian brick walls, doorways and arches. I explored the great height of the space suspending dancers from ceilings. Performers ran sideways along walls experimenting with changes of perspective, such as the birds' eye view of a dining scene on the vertical. I had a fascination for playing with the viewer's sense of orientation and with architecture from unusual viewpoints.

Von Stockert's play with perspective and corporeal ambiguity is also evident in her theatre pieces. In *Marjorie's World Unhinged*, a performer allows us, via a tiny hand-held camera, an intimate close-up view of her body and movements, projected large onto a screen. Later in the piece, von Stockert uses camera feedback to turn a single dancer into an endless line of performers. The reoccurring image of the conveyor belt features in many of von Stockert's works, a fictional portrayal of individuals trying to escape Kafkaesque systems of conformity. Performers moving at a production line serve as a metaphor for mass production, consumerism, and the loss of individuality. Immersed in complex rhythms, chain reactions, and detailed gestures, performers appear ruled by the miniscule, cut off from the bigger picture. In addition, she utilises objects and materials as destructive forces, obstacles keeping bodies apart or distorting their movements. Objects turn into manipulators and performers are manipulated. Material overload triggers chaos or a breakdown that gives a broadening of perspective, a revival of the humane, tender and sensual. Thus, through her use of materials she subversively reveals the immaterial and often comments on materialism itself.

Masquerade (2011) marks a turning point. Moving away from spoken and recorded text she focuses entirely on the subtlety and fragility of the body and psyche. The work is inspired by Freud's interpretation of dreams and the Surrealist movement of the mid-20th century. The performers, from their twenties to sixties, interact with delicately sculpted faces and prosthetics of their own body parts, investigating the human frame – physique and ego. The result is an ambiguous, dreamlike psychoanalytical reflection on aging and the subconscious. A duet between two performers, one young male and a mature woman, is performed twice. When we first see this, the woman wearing the mask of a child appears like a little girl playing with her father who lifts her playfully, her feet never touching the floor. The second time we see the same action, now unmasked, it is a frail woman held above ground by a male partner who could be her son. The scenes' movements are identical and portray physical dependency, yet each carry various meanings, reflecting on the process of aging as well as echoing distorted undertones of the Oedipus complex.

In von Stockert's first outdoor promenade piece, *Seasaw* (2010–2012), audiences walk for several kilometres, viewing eight performance vignettes that playfully dissect existential questions exploring the impact of man on nature and vice versa. One scene shows a group of performers who move like a flock of oil-drenched birds as they try to take flight, their limbs and physicality distorted by the slippery, black liquid engulfing them. The movement gradually dies down, the dancers' gestures and oily skin becoming blurred and faint under a transparent sheet of plastic that finally covers them up.

Seasaw toured nationally and internationally, von Stockert working site-responsively to adapt the piece to each location she encountered, sculpting moving bodies into the vast landscapes of coast lines and framing them in the architecture of the outdoors. Viewers watch some vignettes closely, others they witness from above or below, or from afar. Dancers are seen in the distance throwing sand or soil as they dig holes into the earth they kneel on. By the time the audience walks closer, each performer has retreated into his/her cavity in the ground, head and torso buried upside down. Only their legs remain visible pointing towards the sky, slightly swayed by the breeze. With an unusual eye for depth of field, detail and sensitivity, von Stockert relates the movement or stillness of the human body with that of the object, landscape and architectural form, to turn these into sensual experiences. With her next two works she remains in the public realm. *Fragile* (2013) includes contemporary circus, dance, and a large-scale outdoor set. *Belonging(s)* (2014–17) integrates local communities into a touring promenade piece, tailor-made for each location. Both works show that she is unafraid of taking risks and challenging herself, searching for the unknown and untried in each production.

In 2014 von Stockert entered a new phase, creating a triptych of major pieces that segue one into the next, beginning with the outdoor work *Belonging(s)*, followed by the stage piece *Constructions of Thin Air* (2018), and culminating in the film and installation-based gallery work *Come and Gone* (2019–21). Despite varying greatly in form, concept and content, these works have a common thread: they are reflections on the ephemeral nature of our existence and environment, on the constantly changing notions of home, family and identity which evolve with age and circumstance. All three pieces are created together with a diverse and intergenerational cast of performers.

Belonging(s), led audiences in and outdoors, responding to its surroundings, integrating local communities, architecture, and landscapes. Von Stockert is drawn to locations that are weathered by negligence. Her work provokes questions around our sense of place by reimagining the abandoned and initiating a conversation between the familiar and the unfamiliar. In *Constructions of Thin Air*, the performers are sculptors as well as architects of their surroundings. Using cardboard boxes as construction material, they move and are moved by the rooms and ruins they create, momentarily captured like fleeting memories in window frames that get pulled away or collapse with the fragile walls they sit in.

Whilst the set comes alive in constant transformation, performers handle one another as inanimate material. They drag, pull, push, and carry one another, sometimes tenderly, often in a matter of fact way, through opening walls and into dark corners. The constant shift between detached rawness and intricate sensitivity creates an emotionally charged choreography out of seemingly everyday movements. The objectified human being is a reoccurring concept in von Stockert's work. The tension between the passive and active, the intimacy of gesture and the symbolic sculpting of the space, highlights both the inhumane and humane within the performers' ambiguous relationships.

The final work, *Come and Gone*, consists of 16 short films embedded in soundscapes and installations. Through the eye of the camera, von Stockert further elaborates on the themes of loss, longing and belonging. 'Different layers of interpretation are played with: the microcosm of the family nucleus with its complex relationships being as present as reflections on global issues, such as the displacement and migration of people'.

The medium of film suits von Stockert's work. The camera allows her to zoom in on minutely subtle gestures that would otherwise go unobserved. Physicality appears even further reduced, the lens focusing on the very essence of a simple gesture — such as the faintest touch between performers, the movement of the eyes — distilling its meaning and emotional content. The use of camera stimulates von Stockert's interrogation of depth of field and scale of location. Editing the films herself, she engages with another non-linear choreographic process, featuring the fruits of research she undertakes when working outdoors: experimenting with utilising wind, rain and heat as movement catalysts between performers and objects, she adds decay and disintegration of materials into concept and physicality. Marking her entrance into the visual arts world, von Stockert's films for gallery settings sensitively capture the fleeting nature of our circumstances and existence with a delicate yet intense sense of longing that is her very own.

David Steele

Biographical details

Born in Germany, December 1972. **Studied** contemporary dance at Trinity Laban, London, UK, 1992–93; with Bessie Schoenberg, at Jacob's Pillow Dance Festival, USA, in 1994 and 1995; and with Viola Farber and John Jaspers at Sarah Lawrence College, New York, USA, graduating with an MFA, 1996. **Career**: Worked briefly as a freelance dancer in London and as a teacher and choreographer in Germany, then founded own dance company in London in 1999. Choreographer in Residence, at London's Southbank; and Associate Artist at The Place, London, 2002–04; DanceEast, Ipswich, 2005–08; DanceDigital, Chelmsford, 2008–10; and Crying Out Loud, London, cryingoutloud.org, since 2012. Artistic Director of her company Tilted Productions, becoming a UK National Portfolio Organisation in 2012. Tours nationally and internationally, and since 2012, creates many works in artistic residencies: in the UK, including 101 Outdoor Arts, DanceEast, and Seachange Arts; and in France including Atelier 231, at several Centres Nationals des Arts de la Rue, La Breche, and Pôle National des Arts du Cirque. In 2018/19, undertook an extensive research period, evolving her work to include films and installations for gallery settings. Since 2019 has lived and worked in the UK and France. **Awards** include a UK New Choreography Award, Bonnie Bird Choreography Fund, 2001; a Jerwood Choreography Award, 2002; and a Time Out Live Award, 2005.

Works

Like Nobody's Business (2002); *Hairy Days* (2002); *La Sardina* (2003); *Beyond the Seven Seas* (2003); *Nightmares in Black & Green* (2003); *Polystyrene Dreams* (2004); *Grim(m) Desires* (2004); *Luciano Berio Installation* (2004); *Julie and the Wolf* (2004); *More Grim(m) Desires* (2005); *Marjorie's World Unhinged* (2006); *Anonymous Creatures* (2007); *Glacier* (2008); *TrAPPED* (2009); *SEASAW* (2010–2012); *Masquerade* (2011); *Fragile* (2013); *Belonging(s)* (2015–2017); *Constructions of Thin Air* (2018); *Come and Gone* (2019/20, exhibition opening in 2021).

Further reading

(see also the artist's website: maresavonstockert.com for further reading)

Articles: Judith Mackrell, 'Masquerade – Review', *The Guardian*, 16 February 2010; Derek Purnell, '*SEASAW*', *Animated Magazine*, Winter 2012; Maresa von Stockert, 'A Short Insight by Maresa von Stockert', *Arts Espace Public*,

November 2014; Rachel Elderkin, 'Review, Constructions of Thin Air', *EXEUNT MAGAZINE*, exeuntmagazine.com/reviews, 14 March 2018.

Books: Marc Villemain and John Ellingsworth, *Over the Channel: Artistes et espace publics transmanche*, (in French), Montpellier, 2013; Maresa von Stockert, 'Grim(m) Desires, Maresa von Stockert, 2004', *The Wapping Project on Paper*, London, March 2014.

JO STRØMGREN

Four male dancers, dressed in black-and-white striped football gear with huge numbers on their backs, appear on a dark stage. Abruptly they start moving with a language that is physical, hard, unrefined and raw – adjectives associated with masculinity. They leap, throwing themselves into the game, dribbling, roaring, scoring and celebrating, presenting the culture of football in the guise of contemporary dance. The Norwegian choreographer Jo Strømgren's work, *A Dance Tribute to The Art of Football* (1997), thrusts the audience into the physical, absurd, theatrical, humorous, and sometimes vulnerable interaction between people – characteristics that apply to the majority of his productions.

The huge response to this dance led to more than 130 original works, many of them full-evening productions. The boy from Trondheim, in the middle of Norway, who loved skiing and playing football, became one of Norway's greatest choreographers.

His path to dance began after graduating from High School. Strømgren faced the difficult choice of studying chemical engineering or Russian. However, whilst on student exchange, he took Flamenco classes in Madrid, which opened his eyes to studying the performing arts. After successfully auditioning for the Oslo National Academy of the Arts – Academy of Dance, he commenced a three-year dance studies education, followed by one year of choreography.

His exam performance *Rechts Links* in 1994, foreshadowed what the media proclaimed was, 'Perhaps the most brilliant talent Norwegian ballet has ever seen' (Ljunggren, 1994). Since then, Strømgren has worked with dance, theatre, drama, film and puppet theatre for more than 25 years, mostly overseas, owing to Norway's small decentralised population and limited opportunities for the performing arts. His work has been staged in over 60 countries worldwide, and choreography, theatre direction, and playwriting are the three art forms that define his main occupation.

Strømgren's work is varied. His company, Jo Strømgren Kompani (JSK), established in 1998, has evolved from dance performance to physical theatre. His choreographies for other companies, like the Norwegian National Ballet and the Cedar Lake Contemporary Ballet, have been more conventional. Some are neo-classical in form, like *Suite* (2007) for the Norwegian National Ballet, where the dancers move around, under, over a grand piano placed centre stage. The dancers use classical technique but with twisted movements, broken lines and flexed feet typical of current styles of neoclassical ballet. In other commissioned works like *Gone* (2015) for Oslo Dance Ensemble, Norway, the dance vocabulary is contemporary/jazz; through contractions, releases, rolls, and spirals we see more dynamic movements and a less constrained body.

Another Strømgren feature in several commissioned works is the extensive use of voice-over. The performances are consistently text-based, but the text is not performed by the dancers, nor used as a Brechtian alienation tool. For example, *The Outskirts* (2011), made for GöteborgOperans Danskompani, Sweden, is set in the suburbs, at the end of summer 1964, and the scenography consists of four house walls, with windows. People are curiously watching what is going on outside. *'What felt safest was watching what others were doing. That didn't involve any personal risk. Some even watched those doing the watching'*, the voice-over explains. Small-town secrets are being played out. Something is revealed, something is at stake. The dance is characterised by everyday movements. The dancers walk, stop, put their hands in their pockets; there is an underlying pessimism, touching on human fears of the unknown.

Although the commissioned works differ in genre and expression, the dancing clearly dominates. The language of physical theatre is more predominant in the pieces made for JSK. This clear distinction between his own company and choreographic works for others was deliberate, as he wanted to build a recognisable brand for his own company. Strømgren has, with JSK, developed his trademark by presenting performances at the intersection of dance and theatre, with absurd humour. In most of JSK's performances gibberish is used as a language, often with various dialectical and linguistic associations. In *There* (2001), the language is named 'nonsensical "Sovietic"', set in an interzonal area between East and West. The language hints at geographical location, but also provides associations to the Cold War, to the imminent danger of an East-West confrontation, to prejudiced understanding of the Soviet Union or the East. *There* is one of Strømgren's most frequently performed pieces and represents a turning point where JSK started to use actors rather than dancers.

Strømgren's conscious aim to create his own brand has been criticised. The perception that art becomes inferior if an artist builds a brand, or that he or she is commercial or a sell-out, is very much present in Norway. In 2007 the headline 'This is how they build their art' appeared in one of Norway's biggest newspapers. Exports, branding, and business are terms that are not used in the performing arts, but Strømgren thinks it will come (Eidem, 2007). He argues that branding does not mean deflating artistic value, quite the contrary. If you want to sell art internationally, you'll need a brand and it must be special, original and personal, he claims (personal communication with the author).

'Artistic signature' is another term used as a synonym for branding, but potentially without the negative connotations. One can argue that there is a fine line between signature and stagnation. Strømgren was told by Arts Council Norway, to explore new expressions and not to further develop JSK's signature or branding, including the use of gibberish (personal communication).

Strømgren has stressed the potential conflict between maintaining a personal signature and being in line with ever-changing trends. His mantra from the beginning was to remain untrendy, thus securing a longer life on stages around the world. This deliberate strategy has obviously worked for Strømgren with an ongoing demand for his work, making it possible for him to make new pieces and meet new audiences in different countries. He wants to reach a large audience: 'How can I use and customise my odd and particular expression and make it accessible to as many people as possible?', he asks in another interview (Nipen, 2009). With this statement he also touches on the old, unwritten dogma between high art and popular art – that the less accessible something is, the higher the artistic value it has, a logic which Strømgren strongly opposes.

When Strømgren entered the Norwegian dance scene in the late 90s, he did something different to what had dominated it prior to the 90s and his works were refreshing. The dancer's movements could be rough and coarse with spastic trembling and tremors, reminiscent of something uncontrolled and somewhat frightening. Humour is sometimes simple, in the form of slapstick, or more advanced where we laugh at how hopeless people are in the face of others, and where the laughter hits ourselves, in a kind of self-examination. Strømgren balances the ambiguity – is it serious or just nonsense?

His performances often depart from familiar places or everyday situations, and become an exploration of absurd, small details. On closer inspection, these represent the greater things in life. Big questions are addressed through recognisable everyday situations, wrapped in a physical theatre or dance language, precise timing and unexpected situations. This happens in *The Department* (2004), where four bureaucrats are employed in a small office far inside a government ministry. The language of nonsensical Polish hints at location. With minimal clues to life outside the office walls, they embark enthusiastically on their daily tasks: receiving, decoding and broadcasting information received in their pipeline mail. Suddenly someone spills coffee on a paper message, making it unreadable. Structure and predictability transform into chaos because the bureaucrats are forced to improvise. Stringent and routine movements are replaced by tremors, interruptions, and sudden motions. The performance addresses the lack of transparency and confusion in modern societies – do we really know who is in charge? Strømgren reveals, through movement, the absurdity in the way we behave and interact and how society is organised. Starting points typically involve the familiar places we take for granted – a football pitch, an office, a hospital. In Strømgren's choreographies, however, '*normal*' is upended and seen from unfamiliar and strange perspectives.

Strømgren is one of a generation of choreographers who had their breakthrough in the 90s, and who still dominate the dance scene in Norway. He and his fellow choreographers, Ingun Bjørnsgaard and Ina Christel Johannessen, have helped contemporary dance gain momentum nationally. They have toured abroad extensively with their companies and have contributed to making Norwegian dance visible overseas. Though the independent dance scene encompasses 90% of the total dance activity in Norway, historically there have been limited opportunities for long-term and predictable funding, due to the project organisation approach in the sector.

This prompted Strømgren, active for over ten years and under constant demand abroad, to protest. He wanted greater predictability and financial security for JSK. In 2007, Norway established a 'basic funding for independent performing art companies'. The funding grant was initially referred to as the 'Strømgren grant scheme' because to some extent it was created to suit his company and its needs (Røyseng, 2014). In 2019, the scheme changed. JSK and several other independent dance and theatre companies no longer have long-term support and are facing uncertain futures.

Strømgren has helped contemporary dance become a more popular and accessible art in Norway, no longer just a rare interlude by a visiting company, or an experimental work performed by a small group of aficionados. Staged in our local and national dance and theatre houses, we experience dance which comments on humanity and uses familiar themes like football, the office, the kitchen, the neighbour, and the hospital. The common denominator in all of Strømgren's work can perhaps be said to be its overall pessimistic, yet humanistic, view upon the world. Through all of his performances he pinpoints sides of humanity that leave us with more questions than answers.

Sigrid Øvreås Svendal

Biographical details

Born in Trondheim, Norway, July 1970. **Studied** at Oslo National Academy of the Arts, Academy of Dance 1991–1994. **Career:** choreographic debut in 1994, worked as a dancer and choreographer for Carte Blanche (The Norwegian National Company of Contemporary Dance) 1996–1998. Founded own company, Jo Strømgren Kompani, 1998. Choreographs for other companies: including The Norwegian National Ballet, Oslo Dance Ensemble, Carte Blanche, Royal Danish Ballet, Royal Swedish Ballet, GöteborgOperans Danskompani, Wiener Staatsoperballet, Cedar Lake Contemporary Ballet, Scottish Dance Theatre, Ballet de l'Opera National du Rhin, Staatstheater Nürnberg, Staatstheater Mainz, Cloud Gate Ensemble, Ballet X, and Iceland Dance Company. House Choreographer for Norwegian National Ballet, since 2013. Directed several theatre plays, for The National Theater (Oslo), The National Stage (Bergen), Riksteatret/The Norwegian National Touring Theatre, Hålogaland Theater, Trøndelag Theater, Malmö State Theatre, Philadelphia Live Arts, and Moscow Pushkin Drama Theatre. **Awards and honours** include Norwegian Critics Award, 1998; HEDDA Prizes, Norway, 1999 and 2001; Special Prize, International Fadjr Festival, Iran, 2000; Norwegian International Film Festival Award, 2003; Dublin Fringe Festival Award, 2007; Golden Review Award, Kontrapunkt Festival, Poland, 2009; Belgrade International Theatre Festival, Audience Award, 2009; Rose d'Or, Switzerland, 2010; Lutke International Puppet Theatre Festival Award, 2010; The Cuban Critics Award, 2012; the Telenor Culture award, 2015; Teheran-Mobarak International Puppet Theatre Festival Award, 2016; Golden Stage Cross Award, Lithuania, 2018.

Works

Rechts Links (1994); Schizo Stories (1995); Grinebiteren (1995); Benpibernes Bøn (1996); Con Dolore (1996); Alrekr (1996); Nebendraus (1996); Masculine Mysteries (1997); A Dance Tribute to the Art of Football (1997); Sturm Über Popocatepetl (1997); Peer Pressure (1997); Unreleased Tracks (1997); Alexie (1997); Fiévre (1998); Slakt (1998); Bindingsverk (1998); Ten Years Later (1999); Comfort Living (1999); The Arrival (2000); Eine Winterreise (2000); Placebo (play, 2000); A Dull House (2000); Casse-Noisette (2000); Teruchtraprem (2000); Gorri Gorri (puppet theatre, 2000); The Nutcracker (2000); There (2001); Kraak (2001); Kraak Een, Kraak Twee (2001); The Metamorphosis (play, 2001); Hö-hö (play, 2001); Osmose (play, 2001); Welcome to the Faroe Islands (2002); The Pianist (2002); Una Furtiva

Lagrima (2002); *Lux Aeterna* (2002); *When We Dead Awaken* (play, 2002); *Tok Pisin* (2003); *Destination Moscow* (film, 2003); *Poulimatkassa Reykjavikin* (2003); *Halfway to Ural* (2003); *The Bookshop* (play, 2003); *Beethoven versus Boeing* (2003); *The Department* (2004); *The Masterbuilder* (play, 2004); *Bolero/Pavane* (2004); *Kvart* (2004); *Last Piece by Anybody* (2004); *The Hospital* (2005); *3:8 Limbo* (play, 2005); *En Gorilla søker hjem/The Last Night* (play, 2005); *Luft* (2005); *Some Variations* (2005); *The Convent* (2006); *Polaroid* (2006); *Little Eyolf* (play, 2006); *Around the World in 80 Minutes* (puppet theatre, 2006); *A Doll's House* (play, 2006); *The Orchestra* (2007); *The Consulate* (play, 2007); *Drumming* (2007); *Suite* (2007); *The Statues Are Alive!* (2007); *The European Lesson* (2007); *The Society* (2008); *Coppelia* (2008); *Sunday, Again* (2008); *The Writer* (puppet theatre, 2009); *Herzschmerz* (2009); *Partita* (2009); *The Experiment* (2010); *The Neighbour* (film, co-dir. with Stein Roger Bull, 2010); *The Four Seasons* (2010); *Grosstadtsafari* (2010); *The Wake* (2010); *The Pseudonym* (play, 2010); *The Outskirts* (2011); *The Border* (2011); *A Dance Tribute to Ping Pong* (2011); *Die Insulaner* (2011); *Necessity, Again* (2012); *The Hypnotic Wallpaper* (play, 2012); *The Anniversary* (play, 2012); *The Painter* (puppet theatre, 2013); *Origin of Species* (2013); *Czterdzoesci* (2013); *Winter, Again* (2013); *The Kitchen* (2013); *Orfeus & Evrydike* (opera, 2013); *Minutemade* (2013); *Oslo-losens tidsmaskin* (puppet theatre, 2013); *Sentimental, Again* (2013); *Gaîté Suédoise* (2014); *The Ring* (2014); *Arsen – ein rokokothriller* (2014); *Estrogen* (play, 2014); *The Fairy Queen* (opera, 2014); *The Community Centre* (play, 2014); *Hattrick* (2015); *A Doll's House* (play, 2015); *Lamentate* (2015); *Gone* (2015); *The Confirmation* (play, 2015); *The Virus* (2016); *The Fairy Queen* (2016); *Carmen* (2016); *A Midsummer Night's Dream* (play, 2016); *The Hunters* (play, 2016); *Coco Chanel* (puppet theatre, 2017); *Salve Regina* (co-production, 2017); *Closed* (film, 2017); *Society of Lost Souls* (2017); *The Letter* (2017); *Hinter Türen* (2017); *En dag i Finland* (2017); *The Road is Just a Surface* (2018); *The Door* (play, 2018); *The Disadvantages of Love*, (play, 2018); *Nordens Paris* (play, 2018); *Hunger* (2018); *Sidespringerne* (play, 2018); *The Ministry of Unresolved Feelings* (2019); *The Moon* (2019); *Circus Absence* (co-production, 2019); *The Tired Man* (2019); *Der Unerwartete Gast* (2019); *Spytt* (2019); *The Breakdown* (2020); *The Sound of Contemporary Living* (co-production, 2020); *Zum Sterben zu Schön* (2020); *The Fort* (2020); *Mahler Memories* (due 2021); *The Library* (due 2021).

Further reading

Interviews: with Margaret Ljunggren, 'Fire landet velberget i debut', *Aftenposten*, 18 May 1994; Eidem Åshild, 'Slik bygger de kunsten sin', *Aftenposten*, aftenposten.no/kultur, 13 March 2007; Kjersti Nipen, 'Mediehorene dominerer norsk kulturliv', *Adresseavisen*, adressa.no/kultur, 20 February 2009; 'Coffee or Tea: Interview with Norway's Jo Strømgren about the Society', *Fringe Arts*, fringearts.com, 13 August 2013; Jo Strømgren Kompani, *'About Us'*, jskompani.no/about-us/introduction, undated.

Articles: Daniel Evans, 'A Dance Tribute to the Art of Football', *Canadian Theatre Review*, 159, 2014; Sigrid Røyseng, 'Kulturpolitikk og lobbyisme

– En case-studie av det dansepolitiske oppsvinget under Kulturløftet', *Sosiologi i dag*, 44 (1), 2014; Jo Strømgren, 'Redegjørelse fra Jo Strømgren', *Scenekunst*, scenekunst.no/sak, 16 November 2018.

MEG STUART

Meg Stuart's corpus is invested in deconstructing the body with all its implications, whilst navigating the tensions between theatre and dance. Starting from physical tasks that test the body's limits, Stuart induces altered states of consciousness and then disrupts them as a way to undo and reconfigure patterns of bodying (meaning both the habitual bodily movement and the preconception of the body itself). In breaking down the body into different parts and by putting the body in crisis, she manages to reimagine its multifarious possibilities. She is interested in marrying the conceptual and abstract with the spontaneous energy that arouses movement, as the body emerges in an enticing physical experience.

Born in New Orleans as the daughter of theatre directors, Meg Stuart performed in her parents' productions and later studied Dance at New York University and Movement Research. Invited to perform at the Klapstuk festival in Leuven, Belgium, in 1991, she created her first evening-length piece, *Disfigure Study*. In this choreography, Stuart approaches the body as a vulnerable physical entity that can be deconstructed, distorted, or displaced but still resonates with meaning. Directly inspired by Francis Bacon's art, *Disfigure Study* did not explicitly refer to any of his paintings. Rather, it tapped into Bacon's main aesthetic principle, what Gilles Deleuze called Bacon's 'logic of sensation', in order to refigure what it means to desire movement in a postmodern era and in the wake of the AIDS pandemic deaths. Here Stuart displays influences from postmodern dance in the US: in particular, a rejection of hierarchy regarding people, materials and body parts; and the importance of everyday movement. However, in her subsequent piece, *No Longer Readymade* (1993), Stuart challenges the neutrality of 'readymade' movement and looks at involuntary bodily manifestations as a dance language. By pushing the dancers to their physical limits, she transforms the neutrality of typical cliché movements that convey humanity, such as touching or mourning, into futile pretentions that provoke bodily and emotional states such as nausea, sweat, fever, disorientation, and emotional vulnerability. As dance scholar André Lepecki, dramaturge and scenographer of this work, explained: 'Stuart's works are events aimed at attacking (sometimes rather unceremoniously), and at redressing (sometimes quite touchingly), her audience's affective field' (Allyson Green and André Lepecki, 2018).

Stuart often plays with time in endless actions and irresolvable quests as a way to induce emotional and physical states, both in performers and audience. In *Blessed* (2007), rain destroys the whole scenography over the course of one hour. The influence of disaster is palpable, notably in the way the set design – made of cardboard – is gradually washed away. The relentless water and the performer's perseverance create a brutal sensation. Similarly, in *Running* (1994), the performers run at different speeds in repetitive and endless circles, sometimes grouping together, sometimes running alone. Running becomes the perpetuum mobile for actions to start appearing: a woman runs against the current putting on lipstick; a man carrying a chair runs directly behind her; another tries to light a cigarette; a couple eats a meal together; one person reads while running. Parallel worlds unfold, round upon round the stories interweave, becoming multi-layered and complex. The circularity creates a field for images and déjà vu; a special sense of time is invoked offering interpretations ranging from futility, individual resignation, towards playful refusal of time's authority.

Most of Stuart's physical tasks demand disorientation, defamiliarisation, and failure as choreographic strategies. Stuart demands from the dancer to think the previously unimaginable, to perceive of the imperceptible and to dance the undanceable: for example: in 'looking at your own body as if you were dead' the dancers are asked to imagine that they are all alone in the studio but everything about them is erased (identity, memory, history, training, habits, etc.) and to approach their body as a heap of flesh and bones (Jeroen Peeters, 2010). Similarly, in 'the last person on earth' the dancers imagine they have just regained consciousness after an accident and are the last survivors. Stuart gradually guides them to look with curiosity at their bodies and their surroundings and to re-enter the world by approaching every movement as a new movement that they need to repeat until it becomes their way of functioning in this world. In 'impossible tasks' Stuart asks the dancers to choose an impossible task and try to succeed at it without being literal. She encourages them to continue finding new interpretations of the task until exhaustion. This enables her to move away from constructing dances out of a phrase of material. 'Change' is perhaps her signature choreographic strategy where she asks dancers to enter in a specific emotional or physical state and once they achieve that state, a witness shouts out 'change'.

These exercises help dancers explore their range and avoid gravitation towards a familiar physicality. Improvisation is an important part of Stuart's practice. In her early career, improvisation was used primarily for generating material, whilst lately she has explored improvisation as a catalyst for collaborative synergies and creativity. For example, she initiated several improvisation projects such as *Crash Landing* (1996–1999) and *Auf den Tisch!* (2004–2011) where she invited more than a hundred artists (for both projects) to work together to rethink and reconfigure what improvisation can be as a performance. Stuart's aim was to share responsibility, to make spontaneous decisions that emerge from the dialogue, to be out of control, and to dare to fail – skills that she has built and developed in improvisation and now looked at anew from the perspective of facilitation. In 2016, Stuart hosted *City Lights – a continuous gathering* in Berlin's HAU Hebbel am Ufer, where she invited more than twenty local women artists and scientists to collaborate by sharing their stories and experiences of the city and the theatre itself. Fostering a sense of simultaneity through multiple viewpoints and ideas, and initiating productive debate, Stuart's aim was to facilitate a synergy that could challenge preconceived notions of the woman's gender identity, age and improvisation.

For Stuart, 'individualities are incomplete' (Astrid Kaminski, 2013), and for that reason she has dedicated her process to collaboration as a mode of production. Her company, Damaged Goods, offers a mobile, open structure to facilitate cooperation with different artists and institutions. Since 2016, with Jozef Wouters Decoratelier, Stuart has run a space that accommodates various forms of collaboration and labour, striving to develop a new language for every piece in collaboration with artists from different creative disciplines. For example, in *Celestial Sorrow* (2019), with Indonesian visual artist Jompit Kuswidanant, audience and dancers enter and interact with an immersive, vibrant installation of light. The massive chandelier hanging all over the stage has two functions: firstly, shedding light on one of Kuswidanant's memories of colonial Indonesia, when chandeliers functioned as a symbol of colonial wealth and power, segregated audiences and races; and secondly, becoming the space for Stuart and her dancers to shed light on their own memories, ghosts and traumas (a recurring theme).

In 2019, Meg Stuart was the first choreographer invited to direct the *TanzKongress*, one of the most most important events on the German dance scene that serves as the space for sharing and incubating theoretical and curatorial innovation and creating networking opportunities. Based on her experience as a practitioner and facilitator of collaborative projects, Stuart's contribution to *TanzKongress* was to look into facilitation, to the dance and choreography's social potential inherent in the act of a gathering.

Pavlos Kountouriotis

Biographical details

Born in New Orleans, Louisiana, 15 March 1965. **Studied** dance at New York University and at Movement Research Institute (New York). **Career:** as daughter of theatre directors, regularly performed in her parents' productions; in the 1980s danced with Nina Martin, Lisa Kraus, Frederico Restrepo, Marcus Stern and Randy Warshaw Dance Company; created first evening-length piece, *Disfigure Study* in 1991. Founded own dance company, Damaged Goods, Belgium, 1994; initiated improvisation projects *Crash Landing Auf den Tisch!*, 1996–2011 and *City Lights*, 2016. Collaborated with artists including Jozef Wouters, Garry Hill, Ann Hamilton, Hahn Rowe, Brendan Dougherty, Stefan Pucher, Christoph Marthaler, and Frank Castorf; Artistic Director of the German TanzKongress, 2019; ongoing collaborations with Kaaitheater (Brussels) and HAU Hebbel am Ufer (Berlin). **Awards and honours** include New York Dance and Performance Award ('Bessie'), 2008; Flemish Culture Award, 2008; Konrad-Wolf-Preis, 2012; Tanz Magazine Award, 2014; Grand Prix de la Danse de Montréal, 2014; Golden Lion for Lifetime Achievement, Biennale di Venezia, 2018.

Works

Disfigure Study (1991); *Running* (1992); *This is the Show and the Show is Many Things* (1992); *No Longer Readymade* (1993); *Swallow My Yellow Smile* (1994); *Noone is Watching* (1995); *XXX for Arlene and Colleagues* (1995); *Crash Landing* (1996–1999); *Insert Skin #1 – They Live in Our Breath* (1996); *Remote* (1997); *Splayed Mind Out* (1997); *Appetite* (1998); *Highway 101* (2000); *I'm All Yours* (2000); *Private Room* (2000); *Sand Table* (2000); *Soft Wear* (2000); *Alibi* (2001); *Meg Stuart's Alibi* (2001); *Visitors Only* (2003); *The Invited* (2003); *Forgeries, Love and Other Matters* (2004); *Somewhere in Between* (2004); *Auf den Tisch!* (2004–2011); *It's not Funny* (2006); *Replacement* (2006); *BLESSED* (2007); *Maybe Forever* (2007); *Revisited* (2007); *All Together Now* (2008); *Intimate Strangers, Brussels* (2008); *Walk+Talk #2* (2008); *I Thought I'd Never Say This* (2008); *The Only Possible; City* (2008); *Do Animals Cry* (2009); *Politics of Ecstasy* (2009); *Off Course* (2010); *Signs of Affection* (2010); *The Fault Lines* (2010); *VIOLET* (2011); *Atelier* (2011); *Intimate Strangers, Ghent* (2011); *Walk+Talk #16* (2011); *Blanket Lady* (2012); *Built to Last* (2012); *Atelier II* (2012); *An Evening of Solo Works* (2013); *Sketches/Notebook* (2013); *Hunter* (2014); *UNTIL OUR HEARTS STOP* (2015); *Inflamável* (2016); *Shown and Told* (2016); *City Lights – A Continuous Gathering* (2016); *Study of a Portrait*

(2016); *Atelier III* (2017); *Projecting [Space], Dinslaken* (2017); *Celestial Sorrow* (2018); *Projecting [Space], Berlin* (2018); *Solos and Duets* (2018); *Tanzkongress 2019 – A Long Lasting Affair* (2019).

Further reading

(see interviews and articles at Meg Stuart/Damaged Goods.be)

Interviews: with Gia Kourlas, 'Perseverance in a Collapsing World', *The New York Times*, 6 January 2012; Adam Linder, 'Uncomfortable Zones', *Spike*, September 2014; Frank Bock, 'Crossing Borders Talk: Meg Stuart', *Indepdendent Dance*, 12 December 2014; Pieter T'Jonck, 'Into Uncharted Waters', *De Morgen*, 30 November 2016; Astrid Kaminski, 'Energetic Turn', *Spike*, March 2018; Hans Ulrich Obrist, 'Exhaustion into Transcendence', *Kulturstiftung des Bundes Magazine*, April 2018; 'Meg Stuart: A Refracted Portrait', (video interview), *Walker Art Center* (2019).

Articles: André Lepecki, 'Arts on the Edge of Moving', *Sarma*, August 1995; Robert Ayers, 'Meg Stuart: Not Really Dance', *Dance Theatre Journal*, 15(1), 1999; Gerald Siegmund, 'The Bodies' Desire', *Goethe Institut*, April 2010; Esther Boldt, 'In the Picking Field', *Corpus*, April 2010; Jeroen Versteele, 'Music is Potentially Always a Threat', *Etcetera*, September 2012; Astrid Kaminski, 'Dance Moves', *Frieze*, 2013; Anna Volkland, 'The Worlds of Meg Stuart', *Deutsche Bühne*, March 2014; Smaranda Olcèse, 'Hunter: Meg Stuart', *Inferno*, 2015; Gonçalo Frota, 'Meg Stuart Dances with Her Ghosts', *Público*, January 2016; Allyson Green and André Lepecki, 'Disfiguring Dance, Refiguring the Human', *Skirball*, 2018; Guy Gypens, 'An Essay for "Underneath Which Rivers Flow"', *Secret Gardens*, March 2019; Thomas DeFrantz, 'Supernatural Movements, Assymetrical Encounters: Meg Stuart & Jompet Kuswidananto's Celestial Sorrow', *Walker Art*, November 2019.

Books: Rudi Laermans and Pieter T'Jonck, *Esbracejar, Physical Paradoxes: Vera Mantero & Meg Stuart*, Leuven, 1993; Rudi Laermans, Meg Stuart, Jeroen Peeters and Jan Ritsema, *A-Prior N. 6: Meg Stuart*, Brussels, 2001; Helmust Ploebst, *No Wind No Word*, München, 2001; Pirkko Husemann, *Ceci est de la danse: Choreographien von Meg Stuart*, Xavier Le Roy und Jérôme Bel, 2002; Maaike Bleeker, Adrian Kear, Joe Kelleher and Heike Roms, *Bodycheck: Relocating the Body in Contemporary Performing Art*, Amsterdam and New York, 2002; Jeroen Peeters (ed.), *Bodies as Filters*, Maasmechelen, 2004; Gerald Siegmund, *Abwesenheit: eine performative Ästhetik des Jérôme Bel, Xavier Le Roy, Meg Stuart*, Bielefeld, 2006; Irmela Kästner and Tina Ruisinger, *Meg Stuart – Anne Teresa de Keersmaeker*, München, 2007; Annamira Jochim, *Meg Stuart: Bild in Bewegung und Choreographie*, München, 2008; Jeroen Peeters (ed.), *Are We Here Yet?*, Dijon, 2010; Göksu Kunat and Meg Stuart, *mono.kultur #41: Meg Stuart, Make the First Move*, Berlin, 2016.

SABURO TESHIGAWARA

One sunny day in August 1985, with assistance from colleagues, Japanese choreographer Saburo Teshigawara buried himself in an upright position in a quiet riverbank in Fukushima. With only his head above ground, he surrendered all mobility for eight hours. He actually had to be rescued after it rained, the moisture causing the soil to expand and compress his body significantly, but the exercise allowed him to reflect on the quintessence of movement, how his body communicated and responded to the elements around it both during and after its burial, and that the concept of an autonomous body is an illusion.

That experiment was part of his journey of discovery towards finding his own choreographic philosophy, subsequently developed as 'The Study of Dance Physics' (*buyo butsurigaku*). For Teshigawara, choreography and stage design are not separate arts. Arriving at a form of expression is not a matter of focusing on one element or proceeding in one direction, he believes. Rather, time, light, air, numbers, body, electricity, materials, sounds, text are equivalent materials to be embodied through the dancer. Renouncing the traditional standpoint, he came to see himself and dancers as affective beings subject to the mediation of their surroundings.

After studying sculpture and visual arts, Teshigawara desired to use his own body as the primary material of creation. Aged 20, he began learning ballet and pantomime. While admiring these techniques, he found both overly formalised, narrative and humancentric; while the dividing of dance into categories such as classical ballet, modern dance, butoh, postmodern dance and so on allowed the uniqueness of each form to be expressed, those terms created expectations and erected barriers resulting in a lack of creative freedom.

Despite being faced with the social conservatism of Japanese society, Teshigawara determined to follow his own methods. He worked on interdisciplinary projects with videographers, noise and performance artists but a 1985 meeting with Kei Miyata, who had no formal dance training but with intense physical presence and a keen interest in physical expression, proved pivotal. The couple founded KARAS in search of a 'new form of beauty' in contemporary dance, as it is often described in programme notes. They remain key artistic partners, with Teshigawara the best-known choreographer to have emerged from Japan.

KARAS and Teshigawara came to international attention when he picked up the Innovation Award at the 1986 Bagnolet International

Choreography Competition with *Kaze no sentan* (La Pointe du vent), a work that explored ideas of the body being empty and then feeling that emptiness from within. Evoking the idea of *shitsukan*, a Japanese expression that includes both sense of the material and material qualities, it featured Miyata repeatedly crumbling to the ground as if suddenly deflated, not from the legs but from the head. Teshigawara told interviewer Maimi Sato, 'It was incredibly beautiful to watch. Her body collapsed so smoothly and beautifully. It was like watching a slow-motion film of a giant building collapsing' (August 2008).

The idea of an empty body brought to life by energies from within was the starting point from which Teshigawara developed his unique approach to movement creation. For him, descriptive terms are not about movement as such but refer to an initial change in consciousness or sensibility that enables the performer's body to take on a different material quality or sense, which is then outwardly manifested in movement.

KARAS initially made France its European base but Teshigawara developed a dislike of French contemporary dance and an over-reliance on formalised technique and so switched to Germany. There, he found a creative soulmate in William Forsythe at Ballett Frankfurt, for whom he created *White Clouds Under the Heels, Part I* (1992), with *Part II* following three years later, making Teshigawara the first Japanese choreographer to work at this international level. More commissions followed including *Le Sacre du Printemps* for the Bayerisches Staatsballett in Munich (1999); *Modulation* (2000) for Nederlands Dans Theater I; *Para-Dice* (2002) for the Ballet du Grand Théâtre de Genève; and *AIR* (2003), the first of three works for the Paris Opera Ballet, a piece that used the colours of Paul Klee and explored the relationship between respiration and the music of John Cage.

Teshigawara never simply teaches movement, believing that it is difficult for anyone to mimic movement since everyone's personal technique is inside them and on their own physical axis. He also considers it important that dancers should distance themselves from their technique, relax the body and let go. He prefers to start with exercises designed to rid them of any movement habits, 'removing one's metaphorical protective armour' (interview with Naomi Inata, 2016). He continued by explaining that this might involve asking them to jump or shake their wrists for a long time, and that by taking away form that is ingrained, what is left is the self, even if that leaves people at a loss. Kyoko Iwaki, in a Waseda University conference paper, cites Teshigawara as telling the dancers of the Paris Opera Ballet, working on *Darkness is Hiding Black Horses* (2013), 'Be vulnerable, be honest, you do not need strength and you do not need to pretend'.

In workshops, Teshigawara encourages participants to think of breathing, and how gravity acts on the body in a holistic sense. Only from feeling the body is it possible to move towards conscious understanding, he considers. Breathing exercises are done with the eyes open in order to stop people focusing on the sound. The breadth of the breath and the moments when inhaling and exhaling begin are emphasised, the process becomes a rhythm, which can then be coordinated with movement.

Teshigawara presents major new works each year, made easier by the move in 2013 to KARAS APPARATUS, a new centre housing a 60-seat black-box theatre, a rehearsal studio and a gallery in Ogikubo, Tokyo. At APPARATUS, he produces the Update Dance series that features around ten new short works in 70 performances annually. The venue allows audiences to see more work and its intimacy allows them to get close up and share in the physicality of the dancers. After shows at APPARATUS, Teshigawara talks to the audience, all part of the important process of exposing oneself to the eyes of the public and revealing what lies within oneself.

Teshigawara's creativity extends beyond making movement for the theatre stage. His keen interest in space and the effect it has on performer and audience have led him to create installations and site-specific works. He carefully attends to every element of performance: setting, lights, props, costumes, and music. Among his noted designs are a floor covered with splinters of glass that crack under every step in *Blue Meteorite* (1987), *Flowers of Sand* (1989), *Glass Tooth* (2006), and *Fragments of Time* (2008), the latter a remarkable five-hour solo for Rihoko Sato, presented at the Ikon Eastside gallery as part of the International Dance Festival Birmingham, UK. In 2008, Tesigawara and Sato performed together at the Yokohama Triennale in a cubicle containing millions of glass fragments.

Even livestock has been part of the action. *Oxygen* (2002), a site-specific project for the Klangspuren Festival, Schwaz (Austria) and the Transart Festival in Bolzano (Italy) took place in cattle markets, while *Green* (2003), which won several Japanese dance awards, was danced on a huge pastoral stage with geese and chickens among other animals.

Teshigawara is best known for his highly conceptual dance that tends towards the abstract, but he has also taken on well-known literary works, opera and poetry; Robert Musil's unfinished novel, *The Man Without Qualities*, which he adapted into *The Man Without ...* (2008); the short stories of Bruno Schultz, a Polish Jew who was a writer and painter who died by the Gestapo; the poetry of Juan Ramón Jiménez in *Platero and I* (2014); Samuel Beckett's play *Waiting for Godot* (2015); Kenji Miyazawa's prose poem *Spring and the Demon* (2016); and Dostoevsky's *The Idiot* (2016).

When working with novels or poetry, Teshigawara does not attempt to reproduce or help people to appreciate the original text. Rather he looks through the eyes of the writer to unravel how they lived their lives and why they wrote, or contemplates the message of the subject matter, choosing what is important, identifying which sentences are crucial. He hopes that audiences feel something in the movements of the bodies before them, quite possibly gaining something different in essence from the dance. *The Man Without ...* for example, is an exploratory work that probes and redefines the relationship between word and physicality, rather than a straightforward representation of the original novel. While the text of the work is always there, unfolding in the background, the dance coincides and diverges from it, sometimes paralleling it, sometimes in opposition.

Operas directed and choreographed include *Turandot* (Tokyo, 1999); *Dido and Aeneas* (Venice, 2010); *Acis and Galateia* (Aix-en-Provence, 2011); *Solaris* (Paris, 2015); and *The Magic Flute* (Nagoya, 2016), with dancers from the Tokyo Ballet, in which he replaced the acting scenes with Japanese narrations. Typically, he aims to keep the movement of the singer to a minimum believing that their expression through their singing is enough.

Although he claimed not to be an educator, in 2008 Teshigawara confessed to Maimi Sato to having an interest in other people's bodies and physical expression. Over the years, he has been involved with some notable projects besides the continuous workshops at the KARAS studios. A project with young blind people led to performances titled *Luminous*, and work with middle and high school students resulted in the Dance of Air performance series produced by the New National Theatre Tokyo. A similar S.T.E.P. (Saburo Teshigawara Education Project), initiated in 1995 involved partners in the UK. In Lille in 2004, he created *Prelude for Dawn*, a performance that evolved from a year of workshops with local blind students at the Opera de Lille.

Brilliantly inventive, Teshigawara remains one of the most creative artists to have emerged from Japan. That has not stopped some finding his work unfathomable. Reviewing *Bones in Pages* for *The Independent* on 1st November 1993, Judith Mackrell found him 'brilliant, inventive, precise – but chillingly impenetrable'. That same description was used by Louise Levene, reviewing *The Idiot* for the *Financial Times* on

25th March 2019. She was not alone; the production prompted the observation from Charlotte Kasner in her review for SeeingDance. com that the original novel was 'all but unrecognisable in what is depicted on stage'.

Perhaps that is not surprising given his tendency to emphasise symbol over story and to eschew overt narrative in favour of distilling a work to its emotional essence. He is on record as saying that the purpose of dance is not to communicate information; while admitting to being attracted by how far abstraction can be taken, he equally believes that it should be accompanied by a figurative element. 'What is important with dance is whether it is alive or not', he told Inata. Whatever one's view, there is an underlying freedom to his creativity that never fails to impress. In his 2008 interview with Maimi Saito, he said that "Art must never be inhibited by conservatism", a statement he certainly continues to live up to.

David Mead

Biographical details

Born in Tokyo, Japan, 15 September 1953. **Studied** sculpture and visual arts at graduate level, then ballet. **Career:** Danced independently before forming KARAS with Kei Miyata, 1985. Has also choreographed for Acosta Danza, Ballet du Grand Théâtre de Genève, Bayerisches Staatsballett, CCN-Ballet de Lorraine, Göteborg Opera Dance Company, Nederlands Dans Theater, Paris Opera Ballet. 2004, Dance Mentor in the Rolex Mentor and Protégé Arts Initiative. From 2006 to 2013, taught at the College of Contemporary Psychology, St. Paul's (Rikkyo) University in Tokyo. Since 2014, professor in the Department of Scenography Design, Drama and Dance at Tama Art University. **Awards and honours** include the Concours de Bagnolet Innovation Award, 1986; Japan Dance Critic Awards, 1987, 2000, 2008, 2014; Prix du Public, Festival International de Nouvelle Danse, Montreal, 1989, 1991, 1995; Munich Dance Critic Awards, 1991, 1993; Tokyo Journal Innovative Performance Award, 1993; Japan Culture Art Award, 1994; Japan Inter-Design Forum Award, 1994; Mobil-Pegasus Award, Summertheater Festival, Hamburg, 1995; Japan Festival Fund Award, 1997; Danza&Danza Award, Italy, 2001; Nimura Dance Award, 2001; Asahi Performing Arts Awards, 2001, 2002; First Prize, Il Coreografo Elettoronico, 2004, Napoli International Film Festival, 2004; First prize in Dance category, Festival di Palazzo Venezia, 2006; Minister of Culture Art Encouragement Prize, 2007; New York Dance & Performance Award ('Bessie'), 2007; Purple Ribbon Medal awarded by the Emperor of Japan for outstanding achievement, 2009; Japan Dance Forum Award Grand prize 2010; Tokyo Journal Innovative Performance Award 2013; Japan Dance Forum Award 2015; The Takaya Eguchi Award 2015; Officer of the Order of Arts and Letters of France 2017.

Works*

Constellation (1986); The Pale Boy (1986); Kaze no sentan (1986); The Enemy of Electricity (1987); Blue Meteorite (1987); The Moon is Quicksilver (1987); The Arm of the Blue Sky (1987); Moon Station (site specific, 1987); Saburo Fragment (1988); Nocturnal Thought (1988); Saracens (1988); Ishi-no-Hana (1988); Melancholia (1989); The Wisdom of the Buttons (1989); Even the Once Murdered Waters Swell ... (site specific, 1989); Karada-no-Yume (site specific, 1989); Montage (1990); KITAI (1990); Dance of Air (installation, 1990); AO (blue) (installation, 1990); Bones in Pages (1991, new version 2003); Dah-Dah-Sko-Dah-Dah (1991); NOIJECT (site specific, 1992); White Clouds Under the Heels; Part I (1992); Seasons of Burns (1993); KESHIOKO (film, 1993); T-City (film, 1993); N-EVER-PARA-DICE (film, 1994); Here to Here (1995, 2007); White Clouds Under the Heels; Part II (1995); I Was Real – Documents Vacuum (1996); In: Edit (site specific, 1996); Morning Glory (1997); Q (1997); Vacuum (1997); Petrouchka (site specific, 1997); Absolute Zero (1998); Turandot (opera, 1999); Night Songs (1999); Absolute Zero '99 (1999); Triad (site specific, 1999); Le Sacre du printemps (1999); Light Behind Light (2000); Modulation (2000); Raj Packet – Everything but Ravi (2000); Luminous (2001); Para-Dice (2002); OXYGEN (site specific, 2002); AIR (2003); Raj Packet II (2003); GREEN (2003); Light Behind Light (installation, 2004); KAZAHANA (2004); Perspective Study vol. 1 (film, 2004); Scream and Whisper (2005); A Tale of (film, 2005); VACANT (2006); Black Water (2006); Glass Tooth (2006); Substance (2007); MIROKU (2007); Friction of Time – Perspective Study vol.2 (film, 2007); Fragments of Time (installation, 2008); 36 Dance Books Saburo Teshigawara (2008); DOUBLE DISTRICT (3-D video artwork, 2008); The Man Without ... (2008); Double Silence (2009); Bach and Europe (2009); Obsession (2009); Mirror and Music (2009); SHE (2009); Dido and Aeneas (opera, 2010); Partita No.6 in E minor (2010); A Boy Inside the Boy (film, 2010); Symphonie No.6 (2010); SKINNERS – Dedicated to Evaporating Things (2010); Saburo Fragments (2011); Coup de coeur de René Martin (2011); Pierrot Lunaire (2011); Acis and Galatea (opera, 2011); Mercury Moon (2011); Eclipse (2011); REUNION – Goldberg Variations (2012); Organ (Breathing Physics) (2012); Sacre Russe (2012); Breathing – Power of Transparency (2012); DAH-DAH-SKO-DAH-DAH (2012); Dancer R's Cell (2013); Spring, in One Night (2013); Infinity ∞ The Universe of Pipe Organ (2013); L'heure exquise – PARIS x DANCE (2013); Dodo (2013); Second Fall (2013); Darkness is Hiding Black Horses (2013); Metamorphosis (2014); Empty Hour Glass Sanatorium (2014); Eyes Off (2014); LINES (2014); July Night (2014); Sleep (2014); Broken Lights (video installation, 2014; site specific version, 2018); Landscape (2014); The Age of Genius (2014); Perfume (2014); SOLARIS (opera, 5.3.2015); The Man with Blue Eyes (2015); HARI (2015); Merzbow (2015); Water Angel (2015); On a Sunny Day (2015); Waiting for Godot (2015); Tranquil (2016); Cinnamon (2016); Echo of Silence (2016); Tristan and Isolde (2016); The Idiot (2016); Recontres musicales d'Évian (2016); Illumination (2016); The Magic Flute (opera, 2016); up (2016); In an Autumn Garden (2016); Sleeping Water (2017); Pointed Peak (site specific, 2017); Flexible Silence (2017); ABSOLUTE ZERO 2017 (2017); Howling at the Moon (2017); Brandenburg Concerto No.3 (2017); Grand Miroir (2017); J.S. Bach – Partita

#2 (2017); *Absolute Absence* (site specific, 2018); *Transparent Monster* (2018); *Shirobe* (3.5.2018); *One Thousand Years After* (2018); *Pygmalion* (opera, 2018); *Festival Berlioz* (2018); *La Symphonie Fantastique* (2018); *Pierrot Lunaire* (2018); *Lost in Dance* (2018); *Remains of a Cloud* (2019); *The Hand of Paul Klee* (2019). Numerous short works have also been made in the *Update* series at KARAS APPARATUS since 2013.

★ Published sources vary. The order of works and dates cited here have been compiled primarily from the KARAS website and Saburo Teshigawara's official CV, the most up-to-date sources at the time.

Further reading

Interviews: with Gerald Siegmund, 'The Invisible Moment', *Theatershrift*, 8, 1993; Ian Bramley, 'Standing Still to Move', *Dance Theatre Journal*, 16(2), 2000; Maimi Saito for *Performing Arts Network Japan*, performingarts.jp, 29 August 2008; Amélie Bertrand, 'Saburo Teshigawara: 'Notre corps est flexible et fragile. Sa force est là', dansesaveclaplume.com/pas-de-deux, 22 October 2013; Naomi Inata for *Performing Arts Network Japan*, performingarts.jp, 2 November 2016.

Articles: Saburo Teshigawara, 'White Time' *Theaterschrift*, 12, 1996; Christiane Berger, 'Profile of Japanese Dancer and Choreographer Saburo Teshigawara', *Ballettanz*, February 2002; Katie Phillips, 'Teshigawara/Karas', *Dance Now*, 13(4), Winter 2004/2005; Clark Lunberry, 'Dance of Light and Loss', *A Journal of Performance and Art*, 38(2), May 2016; Sae Okami, 'Toward New Forms of Dance: Transcending Both the Everyday and Work with a Choreographer', *Wochi Kochi Magazine*, November 2018; Kyoko Iwaki, *Buddha, Heidegger and Atmospheric Choreography: Teshigawara Saburō and the Recosmisation of Being*, Conference paper, researchgate.net, 2020.

Books: Christiane Berger, *Körper denken in Bewegung. Der Wahrnehmung tanzerischen Sins bei William Forsythe und Saburo Teshigawara*, Bielefeld: Transcript, 2006, (German); Saburo Teshigawara, *Light and Specific Gravity*, KARAS, 2006 (German).

JASMIN VARDIMON

At the start of *Yesterday* (2008), Jasmin Vardimon's tenth year retrospective, it takes a few moments to comprehend what is emerging from the semi-dark stage. A woman's voice pours a mournful Portuguese melody into the darkened space; slowly the light increases and there she stands with a long fishing rod thrust out into the audience. She hovers high above the stage because she balances on the soles of a man's feet as he lies with legs extended upwards supporting her. Behind, a screen fragmented into strips shows clips from earlier company performances, spilling out disintegrating and incomplete images from the past. As the light increases and the song is drowned out by increasingly loud electronic pounding music, threatening figures emerge from the depths, rolling, sliding, twisting in unison, only to be swept away as a screen with projections slides across and they vanish.

Although more fragmentary than most of Jasmin Vardimon Company's performances, this brief recollection is characteristic of how Vardimon combines layers of design, sound, and technology with movement to create an image-laden and multi-perspectival spatial dynamic. The potential for brutal human (or digital) interaction sits next to scenes of reflection, intense vulnerability and gloriously joyful solo and choral dancing. She tells stories, but these rarely appear as linear. The fractured narration is structured through rapid changes in perspective, scene shifts, and contrasting movement qualities drawn widely from highly stylised dance, but equally from gymnastics, martial arts, everyday actions or sport. Her choreography is not easily pinned down. It derives from many sources that are constantly enlarged and refreshed by her international performers, who contribute material from personal movement training and experience, stimulated by the ideas for each new production. Like the opening scene from *Yesterday*, Vardimon's pieces leave audiences with questions rather than resolutions. Why does the woman stand on that man's feet? How does the fishing line relate to the audience? Who comes crawling so threateningly from the back of the stage?

Vardimon's choreography is often labelled expressionist. It is evident from the full-scale work *Lullaby* (2003) through to *Medusa* (2018), that passionate experiences of extreme emotion are generated through repetition of powerful movements, through intimate performer contact or in group formations that traverse the space. Critics link this element of Vardimon's work to the choreography of Pina Bausch. However, although Vardimon admired Tanztheater Wuppertal, the primary roots for the expressionist aspects of her work arise from her upbringing. Born in 1971 and brought up on an Israeli kibbutz in the Hefer Valley, Vardimon remains appreciative of the creative education she received, tailored to encourage independence of thought and to respond holistically to each child's needs. The classes in rhythmic and improvised dance, popular in the kibbutzim across Israel, were strongly influenced by European emigres fleeing from an increasingly Nazi controlled Europe. German expressionist dance, Ausdruckstanz, was introduced by dancers and choreographers, especially Gertrude Kraus who had worked with Bodenweiser and Laban prior to settling in Israel. At fourteen, after success in athletics and gymnastics, Vardimon focused on dance, including ballet, Graham technique, and dance improvisation. She was selected by choreographer Yehudit Arnon to join Kibbutz Contemporary Dance Company (KCDC) and performed with them for five years, enriched by performing with visiting internationally renowned choreographers, such as Mats Ek, Daniel Ezralow, Suzanne Linke and Gideon Obarzanek.

JVC productions are labelled dance-theatre and Vardimon favours the term 'performer' over 'dancer' to emphasise the necessity for company members to work with narrative, voice and text. Vardimon's formative years brought her into intimate contact with theatre through her father, director/producer for the left wing political Tzavta theatre in Tel Aviv, encouraging her to see visiting theatre artists such as Peter Brook, Sankai Juku, and Laterna Magika. Narratives also had a presence through Vardimon's experiences on the kibbutz, where residents had important and emotionally disturbing stories to relate of their emigration to Israel escape the persecutions and devastation of Nazi controlled Europe. For her full-length work *7734* (2010), which focuses on extremes of human cruelty, Vardimon researched genocides across the world and drew significantly on her recollections of those accounts of the holocaust. In particular, her mentor Arnon's memories of surviving the death camp Auschwitz-Birkenau, including the time she was cruelly punished for refusing to dance for the Nazi guards.

Winning the British Council choreography prize was the catalyst for a move to the UK, where Vardimon established her own company Zbang and developed a making process that proved enduring. Rather than starting with music, using its rhythmic structures and melodies as determining factors, each piece was seeded from a concept and an idea of a place. For instance, in *LureLureLure* (2000), a campsite with the pleasures and potential dangers of family life, for *Lullaby* (2003) a hospital as a space of high emotion, fear, vulnerability and exposure to predators, set against relief at recovery or joy at a birth. Performances emerged from collaborations with actors, dancers and designers, signalling her move into a new form of dance theatre, closely allied to physical theatres pioneered by Lloyd Newson with DV8, Charlotte Vincent or Wendy Houston.

PARK (2005) shot JVC into wider public awareness. It combined detailed character observation with a visceral response to an urban park and its architectural components – fountain, fences, lamp and bench. It typifies Vardimon's unflinching observations of the distressing, touching, violent, and humorous swirl of social interaction. The tensions bound within a contemporary city site were played out in microcosm as individuals' conflicting demands and sense of spatial ownership collided, erupting into brutal encounter. Props and set design are multi-referential: the fence becoming a prison as well as a protector; the basketball a weapon one minute and an instigator of a delightful bouncing choral dance the next; the fountain, a welcome washbasin for the homeless man and a place of despair and death in the final scene. The movement is fast paced and intensely athletic. It switches at speed between moments of vicious attacks of sexual domination, sudden tenderness in a skating duet, vulnerability as the homeless man requests 'spare love', or slapstick humour when the woman who is encrusted in a lifetime of clothes strips off layer after layer. As with all Vardimon's pieces, the multiple narratives are accessible but, as they interweave, the linearity of storytelling is disrupted by splinters of absurdity or magic. For instance, the mermaid crowning the grandiose statue in the fountain suddenly comes alive, slips off, and is next found energetically undulating her tail – the repurposed sleeping bag. So, although the performers play characters, uses of costume or prop that help determine characterisation are deliberately exposed in self-referential acts that stimulate multiple connections.

Stage sets are similarly embedded in the choreography with their material properties exploited, movement potential explored, and metaphoric resonances exposed. Vardimon brings set elements into the early devising process to test out their feasibility as structural partners for the performers, in a form reminiscent of contact improvisation. This draws attention to the impact of the built environment as representative of socially and politically determined rules, and as a material performer that functions practically and imaginatively. In *Jusitia* (2007), a collaboration with playwright Rebecca Lenkiewicz, the narrative is ostensibly about a trial concerning a domestic murder, the audience cast as jurors, but the 'facts' are brought into question as scenarios move through the stage set, designed by Merle Hensel. Each scene is within a walled segment of a whole circular construction that sits on a revolving stage platform, allowing scenes to be turned back and forward in time and space as material is added or revisited. Even the therapy room chairs, when the legs are inserted into holes in the wall, can be climbed, a route of escape from one scenario to another. The whole stage space is activated, and its rotations perform the instability of memory and personal narration, revealing or hiding its segments' contents in cycles that eventually bury the truth.

Music and multimedia technology play vital roles, contributing layers that have emotional or atmospheric impact in tune with the performer's actions, or that run counterpoint to the narrative. Guy

Bar-Amotz, visual media artist and Vardimon's partner is central to the media and design input, as well as acting as associate director and occasional dramaturge. Visual media contribute to the performance concept as in *Justitia*, where projected text of an unreliable stenographer or a questionable confession challenge the veracity of the written word over action or dialogue. In *Yesterday,* one character draws a felt tip line connecting her body scars which is live fed onto a huge screen. The rapid escalation of technological development is continually harnessed by Bar-Amotz as he and Vardimon collaborate with artists such as Jesse Collett who contributed video animation of a shadow puppet play for *Freedom* (2012).

Early works, *Therapist* (1997), *Madame Made* (1998), and *Tète* (1999) had original scores by Fabienne Audeoud; and Jules Maxwell for *LureLureLure* (2000). Later, Vardimon adopted a more open relationship with music that allowed her to play with an eclectic range of choices, during and after choreographic development. Finalising selections with sound designers towards the end of production prevented the dominance of music and afforded easier integration of sounds or recorded text. An exception was made for the opening of *7734,* closely choreographed to Richard Wagner's *Tannhäuser* overture, itself a deliberately provocative choice given his anti-Semitic views. Music selection, however, actively contributes to the intense discourses residing in performance and, as with the dramatic physicality of the dance, can disturb.

A preferred working process proved no barrier to alternative creative collaborations. Vardimon fulfilled opera commissions in London for the Royal Opera House (ROH), *Tannhäuser* (2010 and 2016) with director Tim Albery, and the same opera for Lyric Opera of Chicago (2015). The collaborative work with minimalist composer Graham Fitkin for ROH2's OperaShots in the Linbury Studio produced *Home* (2012), an opera with a libretto co-written by Fitkin and Vardimon, performed by three dancers with a live band and two singers on stage. Monochrome animations by Collett projected onto three walls depicted an increasingly invaded domestic space that a young couple desperately attempt to hold together. The disintegration of home was also central in a new venture as she choreographed for pop singer Paloma Faith's music video, *Loyal* (2018).

Vardimon maintains close connections with Sadler's Wells Theatre, London as Associate Artist from 2006, and develops strong engagement with communities in Ashford, Kent, where she is based, awaiting the completion of purpose-built performance studios. The stability of such a space, continuance of funding and the loyalty of her performers and collaborators is hard won and is linked, maybe, to her upbringing that engrained the values of education and sharing creative skills and opportunities. Vardimon consistently nurtures new generations of performers and creatives through establishing training opportunities, including the JV2 Professional Development Course and as the first artistic director of the National Youth Dance Company.

Since 2015, Vardimon has embarked on artistic journeys that continue to expand her creative possibilities. *MAZE* (2015), a collaboration with Turner Contemporary Gallery, Margate, won an Exceptional Award from Arts Council England. Bar-Amotz and designer/architect Ron Arad filled the space of the Winter Garden theatre with massive foam blocks that created an erratic maze-like structure with disintegrating sides and eerily leaning contours. This extended Vardimon's interest in the audience's role in the creative construction of performance by bringing participants into direct interaction with performers from JVC and JV2 as they appeared from holes, travelled in unison, made offers, told secrets, or moved at speed from grounded floor rolls to balance on wobbly chairs, surfing and scrambling to high vantage points. In this venture Vardimon brought a fresh movement-based aesthetic to the trend for immersive theatre, popularised by companies such as Punchdrunk, WildWorks and dreamthinkspeak. Both *Pinocchio* (2016), Vardimon's first work for a young audience, and *Medusa* (2018) take classic stories and adapt them with new perspectives – contemporary concerns with child self-agency and power, the climate emergency, and women's assertion of strength in the #MeToo generation. Preparations for the next decade include ideas for a work inspired by Lewis Carroll's *Alice in Wonderland*, focusing on adolescence; a film that includes performers from diverse communities; and plans for the new studios.

Libby Worth

Biographical details

Born in Kibbutz Ein Hahoresh, Israel, 1 February 1971. **Studied** at Ulpan Menashe Dance School and in the Sadna, Kibbutz Contemporary Dance Company directed by Yehudit Arnon. **Career:** Danced with the Kibbutz Contemporary Dance Company, 1990–95, also working as choreographer on independent creations; founding dancer, choreographer and director, Jasmin Vardimon Company, UK, 1997. Choreographed *Tannhäuser* (2010 and 2016) for the Royal Opera House and for Lyric Opera of Chicago (2105); and *Home* (2012) for ROH2 Linbury Studio's OperaShots season, with composer Graham Fitkin. First Artistic Director and Choreographer for the UK National Youth Dance Company, 2013. Commissions include with Bitef Theatre Belgrad; Hellenic Dance Athens; Candoco; WID; Bare Bones; Transitions; and curated the Dance Ballads Festival at the Ovalhouse. Choreographed the video for Paloma Faith's song *Loyal* (2018). **Awards and honours** include a British Council Award, 1995; Colette Littman Scholarship Award, 1997; The London Arts Board 'New Choreographers' Award, 1998; Jerwood Choreography Award, 2000; Jerwood Foundation's 'Changing Stages' Award, 2004; Dimitrije Parlić Award and Serbia's Choreography Award, 2013; The International Theatre Institute Award, 2013; Arts Council England's Exceptional Award in partnership with Turner Contemporary, 2014; Kent Culture Award & Canterbury Award, 2014; Honorary doctorate from Royal Holloway, University of London, 2014; Honorary fellowship from the Institute Arts Barcelona, 2018.

Works

Lo Tinaaf (1991); *Master Morality* (1992); *Mr. Hole in the Head* (1993); *Echo Isn't There* (1995); *Therapist* (1997); *Madame Made* (1998); *Tête* (1999); *LureLureLure* (2000); *Shabbat* (2001); *Ticklish* (2001); *Oh Mr. Grin* (2002); *DisEase Room* (2002); *Lullaby* (2003); *Park* (2005, 2014); *Justitia* (2007); *Because* (2007); *Yesterday* (2008); *Tannhäuser* (opera, 2010); *7734* (2010); *Home* (opera, 2012); *Freedom* (2012); *Tomorrow* (2013); *Atlantis* (TV drama 2013); *Yesterday* (2013); *In Between* (2013); *Tomorrow* (2014); *Tannhäuser* (opera, 2010, 2015, 2016); *MAZE* (2015); *Pinocchio* (2017); *Medusa* (2018); *Body Map* (2019).

Further reading

Interviews: with Christos Polymenakos, 'Jasmin Vardimon's Justitia', *Highlights Magazine*, 37, November – December 2008; Elad Samorzik, 'The Responsibility that Comes with Freedom', *Haaretz*, 4 May 2012; Nione Meakin, 'With Freedom Comes Great Responsibility', *The Argus*, 19 November 2012; Laura Enfield, 'Dancer and Choreographer Jasmin Vardimon: Park', *East Essex and West Essex Guardian*, 11 November 2014; Graham Watts, 'Jasmin Vardimon's Pinocchio', *Dance Tabs*, 19 November 2016; Graham Watts in '# MeToo Medusa', *Dancing Times*, 22 October 2018.

Articles: Michelle Kennedy, 'An Examination of Critical Approaches to Interdisciplinary Dance Performance', *Research in Dance Education*, 10(1), February 2009; Ori J. Lenkinski, 'Mixing Art, Dance and Life', *The Jerusalem Post*, 21(46), 21 May 2012; Claire Hampton, 'Dance Theatre: An Anti-Discursive Illustration of an Embodied Existence', *Skepsi*, 5(1), 2012; Alexandra Desvignes, 'Jasmin Vardimon: Inspirations, Aspirations and the New PARK', *Bachtrack*, 9 October 2014; Royona Mitra, 'Decolonizing Immersion: Translation, Spectatorship, Rasa Theory and Contemporary British Dance', *Performance Research*, 21(5), 2016; Tim Casson, 'JV2: Dance-Theatre Training and the Importance of Versatility', *Theatre, Dance and Performance Training*, 7(1), March 2016; Graham Watts, 'Inner Worlds of Emotional Generosity', *Dancing Times*, 14 June 2017; Emily May and Armando Rotondi, 'Adapting

'Medusa' myth in the Liquid Modernity Age', *The Theatre Times*, 14 October 2018; Abigail Hammond, 'Evolving Methodology – Designing Costumes for Jasmin Vardimon's Immersive Work *Maze*', *Studies in Costume & Performance*, 4(2), December 2019.

Books: Paul Johnson and Sylwia Dobkowska, *Justitia: Multidisciplinary Readings of the Work of Jasmin Vardimon Company*, Bristol, 2016; Libby Worth with Jasmin Vardimon, *Jasmin Vardimon's Dance Theatre: Movement, Memory and Metaphor*, Abingdon, 2017.

CHARLOTTE VINCENT

Choreographer Charlotte Vincent is refreshingly emphatic about her commitment to feminism which informs every element of her artistic practice, from the day-to-day running of her company, to whom she employs and how she works with them. She has given a voice to women in dance across generations, casting a much-needed spotlight on women's issues, and fighting to raise the profile of female-led arts practice in the UK.

A very personal message about how women artists carry on in the face of failure both in domestic and professional life, struggling with poor wages, pressures around fertility, child-rearing and ageing was conveyed in *If We Go On* (2009), by musicians and performers who stuttered over unfinished sentences and fragments of song, or stumbled over splintered movements. Dance phrases included a balletic duet where the dancers lost control, flailing around the space unable to balance, and a solo in which the performer's grounded, supple technique dissolved into the frenzied spasms of a panic attack.

The naturally sporty Vincent was exposed to amateur dramatics, tap and ballet before moving on to study English Literature and Drama at Sheffield University. Vincent founded her company Vincent Dance Theatre (VDT) in 1994 and makes powerful, provocatively political dance theatre for stage, film and online. Vincent's dance language includes athletic, risk-taking partner work and eclectic mix of theatre, text, physical theatre, movement, film installation and film. Recently she has distributed her work widely in participation contexts and online (via Digital Theatre + and YouTube) to extend its use, accessibility and reception.

Collaboratively devised and cross-disciplinary, her works blend movement, spoken word, music and film, building material around individual performers, using their strengths and vulnerabilities, experiences and stories. Each project includes extensive periods of research, social engagement and professional development which empower everyone involved, affect change and give voice to those whose value is often overlooked. A choreographer who sets her goals on making a difference through her practice and creating dance theatre to inspire change, she is driven by passion and energy: Vincent affirms, 'What is written on the body and felt in the heart drives what I make, with emotion forming a kind of common currency' (Teresa Brayshaw et al, 2020).

Her dance theatre, with its provocative questioning of society and uncompromising content, offers an essential alternative to the contemporary dance scene. While commitment to social engagement and empowering the vulnerable drives her work as a choreographer, her extensive landscape of practice takes on multiple roles, including facilitating and teaching classes and workshops, producing and directing shows, campaigning for parents' rights, designing her own sets, writing performative texts and documentation for each work, mentoring young artists and being a mother to her son.

Post-university, Vincent lived and worked in the north of England. In the mid 1990s, Yorkshire Arts and theatres in Sheffield were supportive of experimental performance, showcasing artists such as Forced Entertainment, DV8, Nigel Charnock and Wendy Houston. Within this fertile environment Vincent cut her teeth, both as an artist and choreographer/director. She developed socially engaged work with prisoners, people with special needs and unemployed (including out-of-work miners in Northumberland) in northern cities, where she was "witnessing social injustices first-hand" (personal interview with author, December 2019).

Her work draws on autobiography and the wider community, strands which tend to be intertwined in every production. Themes are loosely based on significant experiences in her own life, interpreted and devised with her ensemble of collaborators: falling in and out of love, *Falling From the High Rise of Love* (1999); painful divorce, *Broken Chords* (2005): exploitative relationships/sexual inequality, *Intercourse* (1994); failing, *If We Go On* (2009); and mother/child relationships, *Look At Me Now, Mummy* (2015/2008). More recently a focus on socially engaged practice concentrates on care-experienced children, *In Loco Parentis* (2020); the impact of substance misuse, *Art of Attachment* (2018); and the destructive effects of social media on young people, *Virgin Territory* (2016/17).

In her early career, working out issues around trust, responsibility, vulnerability and virtuosity, Vincent explored the format of intense duets. Here, in collaboration with another performer she investigated the human condition and personal relationships using highly athletic contact work, gesture and pedestrian movement, always encouraging her partners to engage emotionally in the work. Examples of this characteristic form and content are seen in *Intercourse* (1994), an exploration of desire, greed and sexual exploitation, performed through fiercely physical partnering and moments of reflective stillness; *Glasshouse* (1998/2015), a dance film in which a couple battled out their differences from dawn to dusk in the confines of a glass house, literally climbing the walls and falling on top of each other; *Broken Chords* (2007) where eight couples engaged in stunningly sensuous and lyrical dancing, viscerally communicating the pain and fall out following divorce; *Falling From the High Rise of Love* (1999) performed by five dancers and actors, who interrogated the extremes of emotion and physical risk-taking around falling in love in endless collisions; *Drop Dead Gorgeous* (2001) which investigated how pain functions as an instrument to shift our awareness of others, performed by six dancers on a punishing surface of slate stones.

Vincent's preoccupations with the 'shelf-life' of a performer, ageing and degeneration were visible in *Punch Drunk* (2004), which explored the faded glamour of vaudeville and burlesque shows; and *Caravan of Lies* (2000), a lamentation for bodies no longer able to perform athletic, virtuosic technique. What developed was a distinctive physical language, a hard aesthetic through which she attempted to speak the truth and reveal the realities of many lives. Sometimes shaking audiences to their core, Vincent's productions intend to provoke dialogue and self-reflection.

Vincent is interested in juxtaposing choreographed movement on one body with another who is speaking or simply standing still on stage. This layering of dance with everyday actions extends the form into one that can be understood by a wide range of people. The process for finding material begins with extended periods of improvisation, based on tasks in which the performers explore partnering, text, costumes, and real-world objects in various environments, in the studio or outside location, experimenting with partnering, group interactions or individual solos. After about seven weeks, Vincent then starts editing, structuring, collating and composing material for the final production.

In 2012, questioning how women deal with motherhood, infertility, visibility, childlessness and loss, Vincent created *Motherland*, a cross-generational piece in which women and men struggle through life, death, birth, and gender politics, all witnessed by a 12-year-old girl. The work, which included live music, singing, dance and performance, covered emotional territory: humour, despair, love, violence and relied on graphic imagery, which included one woman enacting repeated miscarriages, or the physical despair of a cross-dressing man trying to fit in. The continuous sprinkling of soil across the stage was a metaphor for fertility and rootedness, along with leaves that appear in several of Vincent's productions, such as *Virgin Territory* (2016/17) and *Let the Mountains Lead you to Love* (2003). Vincent's approach to set design is deliberately low-tech, ethical and un-ornate, favouring objects from the real world, such as desks, chairs, blackboards, and recycled sets and props. She prefers muted and earthy colours which suit the tone of her work, although this trend was bucked in *Virgin Territory* (2016/17), where primary colours and sugary pink costumes, dazzling lighting and plastic objects conveyed the synthetic fake worlds of social media.

Becoming a mother in 2014 demanded a shift in making work and touring, and Vincent moved the company from Sheffield to Brighton. Over the following 5 years, VDT shifted its focus from a touring company to one that distributed its work on stage, on film and online, to reach out to more inaccessible and diverse audiences. Devising strategies changed as Vincent started to gather stories from people within the community, embedding their individual experiences into the work and soundtrack, their voices informing the devising process.

Work made since 2015 has been some of the most challenging to create, as well as watch. With the inclusion of non-performing members of the community, such as children or young people, ethics of care and rigorous attention to safeguarding policies and chaperoning were put in place. In 2016, after a long research period, Vincent made *Virgin Territory*, first as a live show and then as a film installation. This was a hard-hitting feminist protest informed by Vincent's engagement with teenage girls in relation to their treatment by society. Their testimonies on a range of issues, heard via recordings of their words, included sexting, pornography, body image and female identity. Performed and created by a cast of four young teenagers and four adults, the work included disturbing scenes of sexual abuse, bullying, grooming on social media. It was a chilling yet timely response to how social media impacts on children, hypersexualising them and stealing their childhood, co-opting the very technology that it warns us about. Scenes depicted the teenagers on their phones, taking selfies, posing in titillating costumes, juxtaposing literal and abstract actions – bursts of empowering action, for example, the teenagers run full pelt towards the adults, meeting in exhilarating choreographed collisions. The film, made in 2017, displayed cinematography, dance and performance embedded with personal testimonials which seamlessly spill out across four screens. Split over five screens, close-ups and juxtaposition of imagery made the installation more intense and grittily real than the live performance. While its treatment of edits, blurring and framing was challenging to watch, visual material allowed audiences choices about what they wanted to see. Given the work's sensitive content, Vincent ensured that the younger members were not included in, nor ever witnessed, the making or performing of certain scenes and that their parents were consulted throughout the process.

Working with a similar structure, Vincent turned her attention to the crisis of masculinity when she created *Shut Down*, as a stage performance in 2017 and a film installation in 2018. In a research and development period she conducted conversations with a range of men, then she assembled a courageous cast of adult and young male performers who were unafraid to act out some of the serious dilemmas of being a man, some based on their own experiences. Central to the interrogation of toxic contemporary masculinity was the father/son relationship, based on research with young men struggling with mental health, suggesting that certain problems experienced by young men were related to their absent, violent or depressed fathers. The work transmitted powerful messages through rap, spoken word, text, tight gestural movement and explosive outbreaks of dance action, exposing the exhausting emotional impact of male stereotyping. At one point the dancers stand up-close to the audience, a line of men with different histories but shared realities, carrying the burden of contemporary manhood. Their look is vulnerable, searching, defensive and there is little joy about them as they share snippets of their experiences.

In recent years, Vincent has worked with non-professional and often, vulnerable people working alongside members of VDT. *The Art of Attachment* (2018) was made with women in recovery from substance misuse in partnership with Brighton's Oasis Project, a substance misuse treatment service. The production, developed over nine months, verged on the therapeutic as it enabled performers to explore and represent their uncomfortable realities. During the performance the women, joined by two company members, spoke bravely to spectators about their lives, societal rejection, over-medicalisation by doctors, sexual abuse, and the agony of having their children removed into care. While Vincent acknowledges that making and performing *The Art of Attachment* was demanding and risk-taking in many ways (such projects require her role as facilitator, director, and someone who holds the space when things get tough), she was immensely proud of the women whose courage shone through the trauma. The work gathered a receptive audience of social-care professionals, academics, university students and child development practitioners, whose varying perspectives generated productive responses. Similarly demanding in terms of safeguarding and practices of care in the studio, her latest work, *In Loco Parentis* (2020), is made and performed by children in care, about whom Vincent talks passionately, deeply moved by their resilience, vivid imaginations, and hope.

Vincent celebrates an unusually long career as Artistic Director of her company with which she has created 27 works to date, although in many respects her body of work is one continuous project. The long-term commitment of several company members and core collaborators is reflective of how much Vincent invests in her company: performers such as Aurora Lubos, Janusz Orlik, Robert Clark and Antonia Grove, whose artistry, integrity and sensitivity make them key protagonists in difficult, demanding work, and the consistently mesmerising contributions of film-maker Bosie Vincent, dramaturg Ruth Ben Tovim, lighting designer Nigel Edwards, and composer Jules Maxwell.

Josephine Leask

Biographical details

Born February 1968, in Walton-upon-Thames, UK, moving to West Sussex aged five; mother was a Social Worker. **Studied** English Literature and Drama at Sheffield University, spending the second year at the University of Maryland, USA; graduated with 1st class BA Honours. **Career:** choreographic career began in the North of England: with regional fledgling dance companies Side By Side Dance Co and Dance Republic (Sheffield) making with others, including Gregory Nash and Sue MacLennan; worked briefly with Volcano Theatre, Swansea, Wales. Founded own company, Vincent Dance Theatre in Sheffield 1994, relocating it to Brighton, 2013 as Associate Company at the Brighton Dome and Festival. Delivers professional development and social engagement projects, and directs new work for other companies/individual artists; including Tai Pei's Crossover Dance Company (mature dancers from Cloud Gate); Keira Martin; Gerry's Attic; Bristol (over 65 Dance Company); Senza tempo (Barcelona); Anjali Dance Co with TC Howard (learning disability company); Welsh Independent Dance; Cloud Gate 2; x-IDA graduate Dance Co (Austria); Thrive (for vulnerable young people in Farnham, UK). Mentors and directs small-scale work of mid-career female performer/choreographers: Keira Martin (Leeds), Ella Mesma (London/Leeds), Bridie Gaine (Edinburgh), Nicola Hunter (live artist Newcastle), Anna Klasper (Brighton) and Emma Jayne Park (Glasgow).

Works

Intercourse (1994); *Noli Me Tangere* (1994); *Chthonian Pleasures* (1996); *In Optimo City, The Almost Perfect Town* (1997); *Body:Ink* (1998); *Glasshouse* (1998, revised 2015); *Falling from the High Rise of Love* (1999); *Caravan of*

Lies (2000); *On the House* (2000, revised 2003); *Drop Dead Gorgeous* (2001); *Let the Mountains Lead You to Love* (2003); *Like a Red Rag to a Bull* (2004); *Shifting Intimacies* (2005); *Broken Chords* (2005); *Fairytale* (2006); *Test Run* (2006); *Double Vision* (co-choreographed with Liz Aggiss, 2008); *If We Go On* (2009); *Traces of Her* (2012); *Blurred Vision* (co-choreographed with Liz Aggiss, 2012); *Motherland* (2012); *Underworld* (2012, revised in 2015); *Look at Me Now, Mummy* (2015); *21 Years/21 Works* (2015); *Virgin Territory* (2016); *Virgin Territory Film Installation* (2017); *Shut Down* (2017); *Art of Attachment* (2018); *Shut Down Film Installation* (2018); *In Loco Parentis* (2020).

Further reading

(All interviews/articles below are available on VDT's company website: vincentdt.com/press/)

Interviews: with Susan Cunningham, 'Video Interview with Charlotte Vincent', *Article 19,* 28 November 2005; Wendy Perron, 'Nine Who Dared', *Dance Magazine,* 1 November 2012; Judith Mackrell, 'Vincent Dance Theatre: 21 Years/21 Works Review – Superb Performances', *The Guardian,* 6 March 2015; Lucy Finch-Maddock, 'Interview with Charlotte Vincent', *Art/Law Network,* 4 January 2019.

Articles: Charlotte Vincent, 'Dance and Motherhood: A Pregnant Pause', *Creative & Cultural Skills website,* 21 December 2007; 'Defying Gravity', londondance.com, 1 April 2008; John Highfield, 'Straight Talking', *Danceworks UK website,* 25 March 2009; Humphrey Bower, 'Postcard from London', *Daily Review,* 23 March 2015; Hayley Pearce, 'Women in Drug Abuse Recovery Find Therapy in Dance and Poetry', *The Argus Brighton,* 12 October 2018; Jo Parker, 'Interactive Arts and Art of Attachment', *Art/Law Network,* 22 January 2019; Kendra Houseman, 'Out of the Shadows' blog, 17 March 2019; Emily Gosling, 'Charlotte Vincent Interrogates the "Pornification" of Culture', *Elephant Magazine,* 11 March 2019.

Books: Teresa Brayshaw, Anna Fenemore, and Noel Witts (eds.), *The Twenty-First Century Performance Reader,* London, 2020.

SASHA WALTZ

Often compared to the other key figure in German dance history, Pina Bausch, in Sasha Waltz's works the space and the body as social constructs, rather than the psychological, come to the forefront. If the comparison with Bausch holds for her first trilogy, *Travelogue* (1993–95), with *Körper* (2000), the first part of her second trilogy on the body, the similarities cease. The dances become more abstract, shifting from social to broader questions about the living body, movement, space and humanity as the movement quality becomes less gestural and more internal, defined by clear shifts in muscle tension. One cannot discuss Waltz's works without looking at the spaces in which they were created, as central to the development of her movement material is the relationship with space and the restriction of the moving body in space. Working with limits created by sets, objects or costumes, the design is always essential to the questioning of the body. Waltz's investigations on the body's possibilities for movement, on the source of conscious and unconscious movement, and the centrality of life energy, highlight a notion of the body similar to Maurice Merleau-Ponty's *Chair* (French: living flesh) in space (*Le Visible et L'Invisible*, Gallimard, Paris 1964, 2007). Her work is also intertwined with the independent cultural infrastructures she has helped to develop in Berlin. Each space she accesses informs her artistic signature, as she moves from the small productions at the Sophiensæle, depicting mainly interiors, to larger choreographed operas in main theatres with large objects or structures on stage. Her activity is centred on building bridges between art forms – from composers and conductors to visual artists – and academic research. Each theme is explored in different directions, from sound to mythology and science, so catering to discrete types of audiences.

Daughter of an architect and a gallerist who ran a gallery from the family's home, she experienced different artistic languages that contributed to her signature style and artistic life. Waltz's first interest was in the visual arts. The change of heart did not come with the dance classes of Waltraud Kornhass, a student of Mary Wigman, but by participating as a teenager in a series of postmodern dance workshops. The emphasis on different ways of perceiving and conceiving the body, typical of postmodern dance, fuelled her interest in pursuing a dance career. Between 1983–86, she attended the School of New Dance Development in Amsterdam, renowned for its education in postmodern dance techniques.

Here she started choreographing, an activity that she continued in the newly re-united Berlin after brief stays in New York and Amsterdam, dancing for several companies. In 1993, Waltz and Jochen Sandig founded Sasha Waltz & Guests. The consciously open structure of the company, rotating around her, allowed for interdisciplinary collaborations with different artists to take place, generally in the form of *Dialoges*, but also a company of 14 dancers (as in 2014), with Jochen Sandig as cultural entrepreneur and artistic director, and Yoreme Waltz as dramaturge.

A first phase of research and performances led to her first trilogy, *Travelogues* (1993), which explored the social customs of the freshly re-united Germany. Later, Waltz and the company renovated the Sophiensæle, creating their first independent cultural institution. A former craftsman's building and political meeting place during the 1910s and 1920s, the Sophiensæle is a place for independent theatre and dance experimentation. The opening in 1996 coincided with the premiere of Waltz's *Allee der Kosmonauten* (1996), a dystopic fairy tale of everyday situations, based on interviews with the residents of the Berlin-Marzahn high-rise apartments. In the dance, West and East world perspectives collide in a series of quick, almost violent sketches. Mundane objects are manipulated to create brief, absurd and very witty situations depicting everyday situations. The movement material is mostly gestural, relying on facial expressions and acrobatic stunts.

In 1999, Waltz began to explore the relation between dance and architecture, with the human body seen as a living unit in space. Two large research projects took place, one in the former ballroom in the Sophiensæle (*Dialoge '99/I – Sophiensæle*) and the other in the still empty spaces of the Jewish museum designed by Daniel Libeskind (*Dialoge '99/II – Jüdisches Museum*). Here, together with the sensorial experience of Libeskind's asymmetrical and fragmented design representing the sufferance of the Jewish population, she created a tour of the building filled with ironic but also violent and claustrophobic images; bodies in chains and the piles of bodies in concentration camps strongly affected the numerous audiences attending the event.

In the autumn of 1999, Waltz became co-director of the Schaubühne am Lehniner Platz, with Thomas Ostermeier, Jens Hilje and Sandig. For the first time in Germany, acting and dance had a similar status alternating on stage. Major international contemporary choreographers such as Emilio Greco/Pieter Scholten, Sidi Larbi Cherkaoui and Benoît Lachambre were invited as guests and young choreographers presented their works. The immense rounded stage of the Schaubühne allowed for further explorations on the body in space with the creation of voluminous props that affect the dancers' movement. In *Körper* (2000), still considered Waltz's most iconic work and epitomising her choreographic signature, she puts the bodies under the microscope, squeezing them on an oversized Petri dish in which the dancers move constricted, even climbing the structure by pressing their bodies onto the front glass. Clear echoes of the stirring images of the piles of bodies connected to the Jewish museum are integrated as a discussion on the body, together with references to organ trafficking. The spoken and more gestural sections on the body as a scientific object are juxtaposed with poetic images, created by fluid repetitive trance-like movements of mythical creatures and of tribal living. The naked or almost naked body lost in space becomes the surface upon which to ponder on the body and science, as in *Körper*, or on sexuality and sensuality, as in *S* (2000) or mortality and transcendence, as in *noBody* (2002). With the installation *insideout* (2003), the audience was invited to observe more intimately different human specimens: some of the dancers recalled their life and that of their grandparents, while others danced in a fighting ring in silence and another acted absurdly, eating cables. Her last work at the Schaubühne, *Impromptus* (2004), dedicated to the vulnerability of being off balance, used music by Franz Schubert.

Waltz's need to work closely with music fuelled her urge to leave the Schaubühne and move with her company back to the independent dance scene. Her next work was Purcell's opera *Dido & Aeneas* (2005) in collaboration with the Academy for Early Music and co-produced by three opera houses from Luxembourg, Montpellier and Berlin. For Waltz, the choreographed opera became a new genre. In *Dido & Aeneas*, dance and the moving body play an equal role with music, singing and acting. As in previous works, scenographic objects are central, such as the water tank in *Dido & Aeneas*, symbolising the sea, or the moving floors in Berlioz's *Roméo et Juliette* (2007). Again, the movement material is developed through the physical limitations these objects introduce. Waltz's vision of opera as Gesamtkunstwerk brought her to include dancers in *Dido & Aeneas*, with movements that are gestural and finalised to form tableaux upon the musical tapestry, and then, increasingly, to involve the rest of the ensemble so that with *Roméo et Juliette* and *Tannhäuser* (2014) the singers are given choreographic sequences or tasks, and the abstract dance sequences correlate with the music. Dance and movement are thus more than an extension of singing: dancers become their own living characters.

Alongside large productions of choreographic operas, Waltz continues to choreograph for her company in their new home, the Radialsystem, located in a cultural heritage site, an old water pumps building. It opened in September 2006, with the ad hoc performance *Dialoge 06 – Radiale*. The renovated building hosted the company together with the Academy for Early Music, allowing for cultural and interdisciplinary exchanges to take place. The company thus alternated between larger opera productions such as *Medea* (2007), *Passion* (2010), *Matsukaze* (2011), *Tannhäuser* (2014) and *Orfeo* (2014), and pieces without orchestra developed mostly in the Radialsystem. The company also tours new productions internationally: for example, *gefaltet* (2012) premiered in Salzburg and *Sacre* (2013) in Brussels. In *Kreatur* (2017) and *Rauschen* (2019), Waltz revisits topics from earlier pieces. In *Kreatur*, the exploration of the body is extended to cloud-like unicellular beings that colonise the space (metallic thread costumes by Iris van Herpen). Jerky microscopic movements are then replaced by group dynamics, drawing parallels between unicellular and human interactions, as the dancers dangerously squeeze on top of a staircase leading nowhere. In *Rauschen,* Waltz discusses our relationship with technology through the robotic moves of white-clad personifications of Siri and Alexa. Technology's potential for isolation is contrasted by topless figures in the dark, reminding us of the *Körper* tribal figures, writing with water barrels on the semi-round immense background screen.

In 2016, with Johannes Öhman, she was appointed co-director of the Berlin State Ballet for five years starting from the 2019/20 season. The controversial vision of establishing a contemporary repertoire by bringing the ballet and contemporary tradition under one roof, partially realised by Öhman in previous years, was cut short after the sudden announcement of his departure from 2021, forcing Waltz to resign as well.

From *Körper* onward, objects on stage are streamlined into iconic images, often ambiguous, leading to more interpretations: *Dido*'s water tank connects and separates the characters, and so do the moving floors in *Roméo et Juliette*, whereas in *Medea,* the living bas-relief reminds us of the myth but also overcomes it. An integral part of Waltz's research process is the series of site-specific events, *Dialoge,* in which artists are brought into dialogue with each other and the space. The most well known are those which took place before the openings of museums, such as the Pergamon, the Neues and the MAXXI museum in Rome. These works animated the still empty rooms, playing intensively with the spatial characteristics. The dancers embodied some of the artefacts later to be exhibited in the spaces, for example, the group of dancers dressed as Nefertiti in the Neues Museum.

Waltz's artistic endeavour to bring her work to an audience as diverse as possible, locally and internationally, includes social engagement with children and refugees. Started in 2005 as a module in schools, the Children's Dance Company now features performances with costumes, scenography and musicians, such as *MusicTANZ – CARMEN* (2012) in collaboration with Sir Simon Rattle's Berliner Philharmonic. Initiated as a response to the refugee crisis in 2015, the format *ZUHÖREN* (listening) was started by involving international artists, journalists and political activists to establish intercultural bridges both on and off stage.

Katja Vaghi

Biographical details

Born in Karlsruhe, Germany, 8 March 1963. **Studied** at the School of New Dance Development, Amsterdam, 1983–86. **Career:** Danced in New York City with the companies Pooh Kaye, Yoshiko Chumo & School of Hard Knocks and Lisa Kraus & Dancers, 1986–7, before moving to Amsterdam, then Berlin in 1992. Inspired by the period of German unification; founder with Jochen Sandig of Sasha Waltz & Guests, Berlin, 1993, of which she is artistic director; founding of the Sophiesæle, centre for free theatre and dance, Berlin, 1996–1999; co-director with Thomas Ostermeier, Jens Hilje and Sandig of the Schaubühne am Lehniner Platz, Berlin, 2000–4; founding of the Radialsystem V, space for arts and ideas, Berlin, 2006; joint artistic director with Johannes Öhman of the Berlin State Ballet, 2019–20. Elected to the Berlin Academy of the Arts 2013; has also choreographed for the Opéra National de Paris, Mariinsky Theatre and Berlin State Ballet. **Awards** include the German Critics Association Prize, 2000; Grimme Award, 2000; European Theater Prize, 2008; French Order of Arts and Letters, 2009; Order of Merit of the Federal Republic Germany, 2011; Vision Summit Award 'Arts for Social Impacts', 2011; European Union, European Cultural Ambassador, 2013; George Tabori Prize, 2014.

Works

Travelogue I – Twenty to Eight (1993); *Dialoge – Künstlerhaus Bethanien* (1993); *Travelogue II – Tears Breakfast* (1994); *Travelogue III – All Ways Six Steps* (1995); *Allee der Kosmonauten* (1996); *Zweiland* (1997); *Rötung* (1998); *Na Zemlje* [To the Earth] (1998); *Dialoge '99/I – Sophiensæle* (1999); *Dialoge '99/II – Jüdisches Museum* (1999); *Allee der Kosmonauten* (film, 1999); *Dialoge – La chapelle des Pénitents blancs* (2000); *Dialoge – Schaubühne am Lehniner Platz* (2000); *Körper* [Bodies] (2000); *S* (2000); *Dialoge – Bombay* (2001); *Dialoge 17-25/4* (2001); *noBody* (2002); *Insideout* (2003); *Dialoge – Les Grandes Traversées* (2003); *Dialoge – Paris* (2004); *Dialoge – Passages* (2004); *Dialoge 04 – St. Elisabeth I-IV* (2004); *Dialoge 04 Palast der Republik* (2004); *Impromptus* (2004); *noBody* (film, 2005); *Dido & Aeneas* (2005); *Gezeiten* [Tides] (2005); *Dialoge – Happy Day* (2005); *Dialoge – Bologna* (2006); *Dialoge – Freiburg* (2006); *Dialoge 06 – Radiale* (2006); *Fantasie* (2006); *Solo für Vladimir Malakhov* (2006); *Medea* (2007); *Roméo et Juliette* (2007); *Dialoge – Bangalore* (2007); *Dialoge – Pergamonmuseum* (2007); *Jagden und Formen* (2008); *Dialoge Venedig 08 – Carlo Scarpa* (2008); *Dialoge 09 – Neues Museum* (2009); *Dialoge 09 – Neues Museum* (film, 2009); *Dialoge 09 – MAXXI* (2009); *Continu* (2010); *Passion* (2010); *Métamorphoses* (2010); *Matsukaze* (2011); *Körper* (film, 2011); *gefaltet* [Folded] (2012); *Sacre* (2013); *L'Après-midi d'un faune* (2013); *Dialoge 13 – Kolkata* (2013); *Dialoge 20-13 Festival d'Avignon* (2013); *Sasha Waltz Installationen. Objekte* (2013–14); *Tannhäuser – Und der Sängerkrieg auf Wartburg* (2014); *Orfeo* (2014); *ZUHÖREN: Continu und Gespräche* (2016); *ZUHÖREN: Improvisationen und Gespräche* (2016); *Figure humaine* [Human Figure] (2017); *Kreatur* [Creature] (2017); *Women* (2017); *ZUHÖREN* (2017); *Figure Humaine* (film, 2017);

Kreatur (film, 2018); *EΞOΔOΣ Exodos* (2018); *Dialogue 2018 – Wirbel* [Vortex] (2018); *Rauschen* [Murmur] (2019); *Sym-phonie* (2020).

Further reading

Interviews: with Patricia Stöckemann, 'Für mich kann alles schön sein: ein Gespräch mit Sasha Waltz', *Tanzdrama Magazin*, 26, 1994; Irene Sieben, 'Productive crises', *Ballett international/Tanz aktuell*, July 1996; Malve Gradinger, 'Auf der Suche nach neuen Formen', *Ballet-Journal/Das Tanzarchiv*, June 1997; Jacky Pailley, 'Invité Sasha Waltz: "Je ne suis pas la nouvelle Pina Bausch"', *Danser*, October 2000.

Articles: Katrin Bettina Müller, 'Upstairs, Downstairs, in My Lady's Chamber', *Ballet international/Tanz aktuell*, October 1995; Norbert Servos, 'Aus der Enge ins weite Land: ein Porträt der Choreographin Sasha Waltz', *Tanzdrama Magazin*, 47 (Heft 3), 1999; Irene Sieben, 'Theater jenseits der Sprache: Körper von Sasha Waltz an der Berliner Schaubühne', *Tanzdrama Magazin*, Heft 2, 2000; Arnd Wesemann, 'On Stage: What is Narrated Doesn't Get Under Your Skin, It is Under Your Skin, the "Body"', *Ballett international/Tanz aktuell*, March 2000; Gerald Siegmund, 'Brief and not so Brief Reviews: Sasha Waltz', *Dance Europe*, January 2001; Bernadette Bonis, 'La naissance des corps', *Danser*, May 2002; Philippe Noisette, 'Waltz berlinoise', *Danser*, July/August 2002; Vanessa Manko, 'Sasha Waltz. Focusing on the Body', *World & I*, XVIII (9), 2003; *Garten der Lüste: Die Choreografin Sasha Waltz*. [Garden of Delights: The Choreographer Sasha Waltz] (dir. Brigitte Kramer, goodmovies, 2008); Pedro Kadivar, 'Sasha Waltz, trilogie due corps: une interrogation politique', *Etudes théatrales*, 49, 2010; *Sasha Waltz: A Portrait* (dir. Brigitte Kramer, Arthaus, 2014); Helen A. Fielding, 'Filming Dance: Embodied Syntax in Sasha Waltz's S', *Paragraph*, XXXVIII(1), 2015; Brandon Shaw, 'Phantom Limbs and the Weight of Grief in Sasha Waltz's *noBody*', *Theatre Journal*, 67 (1), March 2015.

Books: Karl Stocker, *Insideout*, Wien, 2003; Verena Keysers, *Sasha Waltz, and Guests* (eds.), *Gezeiten – Sasha Waltz*, Leipzig, 2006; Sasha and Yoreme Waltz, *Cluster – Sasha Waltz*, Leipzig, 2007; Yvonne Hardt, *Sasha Waltz*, Palermo, 2007; Manuela Infante-Guell, 'Performance Documentation 8: *Körper*', *Performance and the Operating Theatre*, 2008; Christiane Riedel and Sasha Waltz, *Sasha Waltz: Objekte, Installationen, Performances*, Ostfildern, 2014; Laura Aimo, *Corpo danza creazione. Sasha Waltz & Guests*, Milano, 2018.

IZADORA WEISS

In Joanna Smymajda's bilingual book on *European Dance since 1989*, dance critic Julia Hoczyk discusses the process of negotiating the identity of Polish dance since the turn of the millennium (2014). She notes that in the early 2000s, different movements in Polish dance shared a departure from ballet and its manner of representing the body, including the reproduction of longstanding plots and narratives. While the roots of choreographer Izadora Weiss can be traced to ballet along those same lines, she undoubtedly created her own style, which critic Graham Watts describes as contemporary narrative ballet (2016, 2017). Hoczyk points out that Weiss created the first autonomous non-ballet performance at the Opera House and transformed the Baltic Opera Ballet into the Baltic Dance Theatre (BTT). The work of Weiss was characterised by a rare 'middle aesthetic', as Hoczyk puts it, 'aimed at a wider public than ballet, on the one hand, and new dance on the other'. (2014). Throughout her oeuvre, 'her movement is always busy and intensely musical but generally it is a means to an end, which is to serve the narrative purpose' (Watts, 2016).

Weiss graduated from the Warsaw School of Ballet and the Frederic Chopin Music Academy. In her early career in the late nineties, she mainly produced choreographies for opera. In total, she has created thirty operas in Poland, which greatly informed her choreographic practice in terms of musicality. Interestingly, Weiss usually writes her own librettos, thus demonstrating her dramaturgical writing skills and testifying to the importance of narrative in her oeuvre.

In 1997, Weiss created her first solo choreography, *Three Dreams*, for the Poznán Ballet in the Grand Theatre in Poznán. Her second choreography *Violin Concerto No. 1* (1998) marked a turning point: watching the performance in 1998, the renowned Czech choreographer Jiří Kylián invited her to join the Nederlands Dans Theater (NDT) to hone her choreographic skills further. Weiss was able to work alongside Kylián, Hans van Manen, Ohad Naharin, Sol Léon and Paul Lightfoot.

Weiss shares Kylián's belief that the narrative potential of the dancing body should be fully explored. A distinctive movement style is developed for each character. Differences in muscle tensions, movement intensities and facial expressions are fully explored and are the major means to convey subtle nuances in the characters' emotions. She avoids any technological *tour de forces* or multi-media tricks. Her stage set generally consists of a black box, with a modestly lit, black dance floor, allowing for the dancers' vivid expressions to be at the centre of attention. Weiss repeatedly makes use of simple, black movable panels to indicate shifts in places of action and to allow characters to appear and disappear smoothly. Another trademark is simultaneity on stage, having different groups of dancers perform at the same time in a different area on stage, revealing different aspects of the story.

Unlike Kylián, Weiss repeatedly relates to repertoire works such as *A Midsummer Night's Dream*, *The Rite of Spring*, *The Tempest*, and *Romeo and Juliet*. Other pieces are based on mythologies and legends, such as *Phaedra*, *Tristan and Isolde*, and *Eros Thanatos*. In her narrative contemporary ballet, Weiss is particularly fascinated by the difficulty of translating into dance the 'big' emotions and anxieties that go with these dramas. Weiss' choreographic work has been greatly inspired by Shakespeare's plays, which Watts described as a '*leit motif* throughout her career' (2017). *A Midsummer Night's Dream* is especially noteworthy, because her debut choreography *Three Dreams*, for the Grand Theatre in Poznán, was derived from an interpretation of this play, and in 2013, another rendition for the Baltic Dance Theatre constituted a highpoint in her career. In this version, an eclectic selection of compositions by Goran Bregović accompanies the vivid contrasts between aerial and floating movements, full of sensuality, confident flirting and explicit eroticism. Weiss received two prestigious awards for the staging of *A Midsummer Night's Dream*, including the Honorary Theatre Award in 2013 and the Music Theatre Award Jan Kiepura for the best choreographer in 2014.

While humour prevails in *A Midsummer Night's Dream*, the rest of Weiss' choreographic work is rather dark and tragic. Her version of the *Rite of Spring* (2011) transposes Stravinsky's libretto to domestic violence, sadistic victimisation, and rape. A cameraman films the dancers' faces, bringing their tormented facial expressions in close-up: a minor conciliation to technological devices, with high emotional impact. In *The Tempest* (2015), the choreography is tailored to Mahler's first symphony, interspersed with the sound of wind. The coming-of-age of the character of Miranda comes with the necessary sorrow. When Miranda-as-a-child ceases to enjoy the playful dancing with her father, she dances some solos expressing the devastating, lonely despair of subsequent adolescent life. And when she falls in love with Ferdinand, Prospero's rage is immense. When, in the end, he accepts their love, Prospero is led to his final destiny: death. Weiss' choreographic narration of *The Tempest* reminds us of the entanglement of life (love) and death. Likewise, in *Eros Thanatos* (2017), Eros – the Greek god of love and sex, and the propagator of life – is intrinsically intertwined with Thanatos – the drive towards death and self-destruction. Here, Weiss was inspired by *Thanatos*, by the Polish painter Jacek Malczewski. The fierce red of Thanatos' dress in the painting is repeated in the dancers' red velvet costumes, which Weiss designed herself. The gesture of gently placing a hand over the deceased character's eyes is repeated every time someone dies. It gives the organic group movements a ritual quality.

Weiss' oeuvre is marked by a fragmentation of assorted musical sources (ranging from Jimmy Hendrix to baroque concertos, and from minimalist music to Goran Bregović). Though she selects and edits the music herself, the choreography does not seem fragmented. For the famous Maltafestival in Poznán, Weiss created a choreography on Vivaldi's *The Four Seasons* in 2000, which was her first collaboration with English violinist Nigel Kennedy. In 2008, Weiss was invited to become director of the ballet company of the Baltic Opera House in Gdańsk, where her production *4&4* premiered, returning to Nigel Kennedy's rendition of *The Four Seasons* for the first half of the performance. This testified that Weiss was changing the face of Gdańsk ballet, 'turning it away from opera ballet to modern dance theatre', (Watts, 2017), in the sense that ballet 'poses' are rendered very emotionally expressive. Ever since *4&4*, her work has not only become more emotionally expressive in its narrative and musicality, but also in her particular movement language, which borrows from other contemporary dance styles. The second half of *4&4* – *Four Attempts at Taming Death* – is inspired by Schubert's *Death and the Maiden*, a work she would revisit in 2013. The dramatic duet between Death (a woman) and the maiden combines a conventional ballet idiom with modern street-dance elements. Their duet is suddenly interrupted by a quintet of male dancers who perform a synchronised dance phrase including hand stands and backflips reminiscent of street-dance battles.

Izadora Weiss has produced a number of choreographies since her debut in 1997. In March 2010, she established the Baltic Dance Theatre (BTT) in Gdańsk. The company has toured extensively, mostly inside Poland. Between 2010 and 2017, Weiss has been especially productive with her company, often revisiting earlier narratives and musical scores. In addition to the cited works by Shakespeare, Schubert and Racine, her work has been inspired by Samuel Beckett's *Waiting for Godot* (*Waiting for …* 2011), Igor Stravinsky's *The Rite of Spring* (2011), Wislawa Szymborka's poem inspired by the painting of *The Milkmaid* by Johannes Vermeer (*Light*, 2014), the legend of *Tristan and Isolde* (2016), and Joseph Conrad's *Heart of Darkness* (*Darkness*, 2017). In particular, issues that inform her work relate to the meaning of life, alienation, existentialism, and later, social dynamics, violence against women, gender equality and sexism. For example, her rendition of *Romeo and Juliet* (2009) is set in modern-day Iraq, where Romeo is an American soldier and Juliet an Iraqi Shia Muslim. The musical score fuses several fragments from Sergei Prokofiev to Liza Gerrard. Visually, myriad projections of Arabic script and other images of everyday life in Iraq accompany the dancers onstage.

Netherlands (2014) forms another remarkable endeavour in Weiss' trajectory. The first part of the project is a triptych of the productions *Clash* by Patrick Delcroix and *Fun* and *Light* by Izadora Weiss. The latter two are inspired by Vermeer paintings. *Light*, to music by Philip Glass, features a female dancer reminiscent of Vermeer's iconic *Milkmaid*, wearing the same crisp, linen cap. Faintly smiling, and with her eyes downcast, she expresses a similar female mysteriousness and vulnerability. She moves gently and with suppressed movements, in contrast to the occasional rude movements of her dance partners. The maid's servitude in housework and in sexual terms is critically explored in this choreography. The second part of *Netherlands* consists of two choreographies by Jiří Kylián, *Sarabande* and *Falling Angels* performed by the Baltic Dance Theatre, and Weiss' choreography *Body Master*, which further explores power relations between master and servant. One blonde female dancer, wearing a similar pink corset-like dress as the milkmaid in *Light*, is shown in her struggles to maintain balance in dynamic group dances, with these dancers dressed in contrasting dark earth tones. Weiss' libretto was inspired by the life of Gordon Craig and his writings on puppetry. In 2015, BDT made their successful debut in London with an interpretation of *Phaedra* at The Place, London.

Over the next six years, the company became more international in its composition, with an 'exciting mix of experience and continuity from the company's core homegrown dancers' (Watts, 2017). In 2016, when the new management of the Baltic Opera decided that ballet should return to its 'secondary' function in opera productions, Weiss sought a new stage for her company. Supported by the Ludvig van Beethoven Association and the Adam Mickiewicz Institute, the company continues to exist, renamed Bialy Teatr Tańca (commonly translated as 'White Dance Theatre', as *Weiss* in German means *white*). The Bialy Teatr Tańca was launched in Saint Petersburg in November 2017. During this transitional phase, Weiss also produced *Darkness* for the Polish National Ballet in June 2017. With her own company of eleven dancers from seven different countries, Weiss created *Eros Thanatos* in 2017 and *Euridice in Hell* in 2018. In the Krzysztof Penderecki European Centre for Music, the company continues to work under the name Weiss Tanztheater in Warsaw. However, the company is still looking for a more permanent solution, because without infrastructure it cannot continue to uphold its reputation.

Annelies Van Assche and Christel Stalpaert

Biographical details

Born in Poland. **Studied** at the Warsaw School of Ballet and the Frederic Chopin Music Academy, with a scholarship in 1999 and 2001 from the Ministry of Culture and the Arts in Poland (MKiS). Internships with Jiří Kylián, Ewa Wycichowska and Jacek Łumiński. **Career**: she choreographed thirty operas which have been presented in Poland, the United States, France, Germany, Luxembourg, the Netherlands and Finland. She made 26 choreographies presented in Poland, UK and Russia. In 2010, she established her own company Baltic Dance Theatre, which was renamed Bialy Teatr Tańca (White Dance Theatre, Weiss Tanztheater) in 2017. **Awards and honours** include Gdansk City Theatre Awards, 2009 and 2014, and for lifetime artistic achievement 2013; Music Theatre Awards Jan Kiepura, 2014 and 2015; Pomeranian Arts Award, to Izadora and Marek Weiss, 2009; Gloria Artis Medal for Merit to Culture, awarded by the Ministry of Culture and National Heritage, Poland.

Works

Turandot (opera, 1996); *The Haunted Manor* (opera, 1997); *Aida* (opera, 1997); *Three Dreams* (choreography, 1997); *Salome* (opera, 1998); *Aida* (opera, 1998); *The Magic Flute* (opera, 1998); *Don Giovanni* (opera, 1998); *Violin Concerto No. 1* (choreography, 1998); *Galina* (opera, 1999); *Nabucco* (opera, 1999); *The Haunted Manor* (opera, 1999); *The Threepenny Opera* (opera, 1999); *Carmen* (opera, 2000); *The Four Seasons* (choreography, 2000); *Eugene Onegin* (opera, 2001); *Aida* (opera, 2001); *Der Freischütz* (opera, 2001); *Aida* (opera, 2002); *Faust* (opera, 2004); *Halka* (opera, 2005); *... from Heaven* (choreography, 2005); *Aida* (opera, 2006); *A Little Princess* (opera, 2006); *Rigoletto* (opera, 2007); *Eurasia* (choreography, 2007); *Don Giovanni* (opera, 2008); *Julius Ceasar* (opera, 2008); *4&4* (choreography, 2008); *Eurasia II* (choreography, 2008); *Eugene Onegin* (opera, 2009); *Romeo and Juliet* (choreography, 2009); *Tre donne Tre destini* (choreography, 2009); *The Magic Flute* (opera, 2010); *Out* (choreography, 2010); *Salome* (opera, 2011); *Madame Curie* (opera, 2011); *The Rite of Spring* (choreography, 2011); *Waiting for ...* (choreography, 2011); *Windows* (choreography, 2012); *Rothschild's violin* (opera, 2013); *Cool Fire* (choreography, 2013); *A Midsummer Night's Dream* (choreography, 2013); *Death and the Maiden* (choreography, 2013); *Fun* (choreography, 2014); *Light* (choreography, 2014); *Body Master* (choreography, 2014); *The Tempest* (choreography, 2015); *Phaedra* (choreography, 2015); *Die Schwarze Maske* (opera, 2016); *Tristan and Izolde* (choreography, 2016); *Darkness* (choreography, 2017); *Eros Thanatos* (choreography, 2017); *La Clemenza di Tito* (opera, 2018); *Turandot* (opera, 2018); *Manru* (opera, 2018); *King of Marionettes* (choreography, 2018); *Euridice in Hell* (choreography, 2018).

Further reading

Interviews: with Anna Legierska, 'Ciemności nie zapadają nagle', *Culture. pl*, 6 June 2017.

Articles: Graham Watts, 'Baltic Dance Theatre – Tristan and Izolde, Death and the Maiden – Gdansk', *Dance Tabs*, 7 July 2016; Graham Watts, 'Izadora Weiss. A Tempest on the Baltic Shore', *Eros Thanatos* and *Darkness* programme, Polish Theater in Warsaw (June–September 2017). English translation at http://www.izadoraweiss.pl; Laura Cappelle, 'Eros Thanatos', *Dancing Times*, 9 September 2017.

Books: Joanna Szymajda (ed.), *European Dance since 1989. Communitas and the Other*, Oxford and New York, 2014 (see chapters by Anna Królica and Julia Hoczyk).

Made in the USA
Las Vegas, NV
29 November 2020

Abbreviations

AOCs	Areas of Concern
BAIT	Bay Area Implementation Team
BARC	Bay Area Restoration Council
BUI	beneficial use impairment
CAFOs	concentrated animal feeding operations
CCC	Cuyahoga River RAP Coordinating Committee
CIAC	Cat Island Advisory Committee
CSO	combined sewer overflow
DDT	dichloro-diphenyl-trichloroethane
DWEJ	Detroiters Working for Environmental Justice
ECCC	Environment and Climate Change Canada
ECF	engineered containment facility
EDF	Environmental Defense Fund
ENVIROPARK	innovative environmental playground

locations and to hone my environmental writing skills in support of accelerating the sustainability transition.

I would also like to thank Catherine Cocks, editor-in-chief of Michigan State University Press, and all her staff for their encouragement and help, and their unique contributions to the production and marketing process. Finally, I would like to especially thank my family for their continued support of my work and my calling to foster stewardship of the Great Lakes.

Acknowledgments

reat Lakes Champions is the story of fourteen people who loved the Great Lakes so much that they devoted their careers to leading grassroots partnerships to clean up the most polluted areas of these freshwater seas. I want to acknowledge and thank them for their service and for sharing their personal stories for this book. I also want to acknowledge the tens of thousands of people, organizations, and businesses that are working to restore polluted areas of the Great Lakes and revitalize communities along the shores of these inland seas. Without all of these grassroots efforts, we could not keep these lakes great nor ensure that they will be a gift to future generations.

This book was written, in part, during writing residencies at Glen Arbor Arts Center in Glen Arbor, Michigan, and the Banff Centre for Arts and Creativity in Banff, Alberta, Canada. I gratefully acknowledge these unique opportunities to write without interruption in such inspirational

Praise for Cold Wonderland:

"T.R. Kelly can write about basketball with the best of them. The world could use more adults like Coach Ernie, whose commitment to young men trying to outrun past traumas, and avoid bleak futures makes for moving entertainment. Part mystery, part coming-of-age, and part middle-aged love affair, Cold Wonderland is Kelly at his best."

~ **Jonathan Evison**, *author of* <u>*All About Lulu*</u>, *West of Here,* <u>*The Revised Fundamentals of Caregiving*</u>, <u>*This Is Your Life, Harriet Chance!*</u>, *Lawn Boy*

The Ernie Creekmore Series

COLD WONDERLAND is the third book in the Ernie Creekmore series featuring a longtime high school basketball coach who calls upon his years of experience, resources and small-town logic to help his fishing buddy and the county's chief criminal investigator solve murder mysteries. The books contain basketball and murder and much more. They are about boys and men, sons and parents, and the confusions of love when we are no longer young.

In the first book, COLD CROSSOVER, recently rewritten, Linnbert "Cheese" Oliver, a hard-luck hero in the Northwest town of North Fork, is reported missing from a late-night ferry. And for Ernie, his father figure, friend and former coach, the news hits hard. Ernie's suffered too much loss and pain in his life—his wife, a state basketball championship, a serious medical malady—and he just can't accept the idea that Cheese might have taken his own life. "The Cheese" was the best basketball player Ernie Creekmore coached in his nineteen years at Washington High School and the best shooter Ernie had ever seen. The unassuming great-grandson of the town's founder, Linn Oliver could do no wrong. He was the talk of the town—until he missed the final shot in the 2000 state championship game. Working with the county's Harvey Johnston, Ernie uses his new contacts in real estate and old hoops resources to trace Cheese's movements. Meanwhile, hints at possible foul play turn up in pieces of North Fork's rough-and-tumble history in fishing, logging and railroading and the past and present violently collide in a series of heart-stopping moments that peel back layers of secrets, gold and twisted family ties that refuse to stay buried.

The second book, COLD BROKER, rewritten and formerly Hovering Above a Homicide, finds Ernie trying to solve the murder of a "helicopter" parent whose body is discovered in a vacant home for sale.

COLD
WONDERLAND

Cold Wonderland

AN ERNIE CREEKMORE MYSTERY
BOOK 3

T.R. KELLY

Crabman Publishing ● Rolling Bay, WA

Published by Crabman Publishing Rolling Bay, WA

Cold Wonderland, Ernie Creekmore Series, Book 3

Dedication

For Robert X

Elementary school foe, high school sidekick and lifelong prankster and hoops analyst. I miss your twisted humor and stunning wisdom. You left us too soon.

ONE

I'VE LEARNED A CRITICAL LESSON IN the nineteen years of directing early Saturday games for aging hoop hackers: it's a hell of a lot easier without a hangover. Today, I managed to nail a solid D-minus.

"Ernie, you look like shit pie." The pudgy Shell station owner waddled toward midcourt, leather ball tucked under his arm. "Man, some of your former players would love to see you now."

I massaged a spot above one of my sideburns and fingered the frayed neck of my jersey. "A bunch of us went for pizza and beer last night after the high school game."

"Bullshit, dude. Your eyes are just trashed."

Why does the worst player with the biggest mouth and the best ball typically show up first? And why am I explaining myself to him as though he were owed an explanation? "Ended up closing Tony's Place. Then some bright soul went to the Red Apple Market for a few cases of PBR and the gang ended up in my den. I'm told I made a couple of six-packs disappear all by myself."

"Nice," he said. "That's what I'm talking about. Now just make damn sure I get in the first game."

As if I had a choice to sit the slob. Everyone honored the early-bird rule: First ten in the door, first ten on the floor. And everyone knew the guy only dribbled with his right hand, hadn't

added a new move in a decade, and couldn't guard your suitcase at the airport.

"And, hey," he added. "I heard the Cheese asked a new guy. I guess the newbie's kid is going be the next hotshot at the high school. From what I hear, maybe you should've waited one more year before hanging it up."

The comment struck me as being as cold as the early March gym. After more than two decades as the head coach of the Washington High School Fighting Crabs in North Fork, Washington, I needed an extended timeout and handed my whistle to a capable assistant at the end of last season. Truth be told, I already missed those kids, and I missed the Tuesday and Friday night rituals and rivalries. What I didn't miss were their parents who absolutely knew what was best for their constantly coddled Camerons yet had no clue how to communicate with them nor the guts to limit their texting and gaming and selfie-goofing time.

More players staggered in, and I did my best to even out the first two teams, delaying my on-court debut until my head stopped pounding. With the first game finally underway, I sprawled across the first three bleacher rows. I loved the stinky, cramped old gym with its creaky floor and ball-marked walls dangerously close to the court. For me, it was as comfy as my den at home. As I rolled backward, two coins spun from my baggy cotton warm-ups. Quarters from Virginia and Alabama. Tired, everyday issues that would not help my collection. I'd seen plenty, just like this morning's usual grunts and groans. I closed my eyes rather than exert the effort needed to collect the loose change.

"You ever gonna pass the fricking ball?" I looked up but could not identify the speaker. Given the number of scrunched faces and shaking heads, several players shared the notion.

Oh, Lord. Already?

First-in Pudgy ambled toward the near basket, raising his palms like a preacher beckoning his congregation to rise. "I

mean, really. Should we just plan on rebounding every time you get it?"

The shooter, a newcomer with golden yellow wristbands a la Rick Barry and a face too pink for the hour, skipped backward on defense, every wavy hair on his head somehow remaining in place. "What are you talking about, man? That was a sweet shot."

Inviting an unknown body to play in a same-gang pickup game was like allowing a friend of a friend to crash in the back bedroom. You never know what you are going to get, and the result can be as brutal as a bad blind date. God knows I've had plenty of both since my wife passed away.

Pudgy, clearly overmatched, rolled his eyes. "Sure as hell been a lot of 'em. I just hope some of your son's will actually go in the basket."

Wristband Rick turned and snarled for all to see and hear. "My kid's gonna light it up. Just you wait and see."

I've had more hits than misses when it comes to new players. Local sons, daughters, and relatives usually know the rhythm and routine: move the basketball, hit the open man, elbows and assholes prohibited. There's no macho embarrassment when guarding a female because the few women who've gotten on the court were more skilled than me, although none had appeared this morning. Former college players and high school stars who knew the drill - pair up and guard each other and let the overweight, knee-braced, balding white guys too slow to consistently get up and down the floor find one another.

Play stopped.

"Gonna play or talk, guys?" an impatient regular grumbled from the practice court. "We got next." Other waiters in the bleachers voiced other variations of *hurry up*.

The slick rookie flicked a *bring it on* gesture which brought an *Are you kidding me?* sneer from more than one man on the floor.

"Hey, figure it out," I barked. "Or take it outside." Then, under my breath, "You'll both fricking freeze before you can fight."

The rows behind me creaked as a trio of men stampeded down toward the court to intervene. The thumping did little for my aching head. Pudgy and Slick Rick jawed toe-to-toe, and I thanked God I was out of range of their breath. After a handful of creative f-bombs and some mandatory superficial shoving, play resumed. Just as the newbie's twenty-five-foot set shot fell a yard short of its target, a dapper figure appeared at the far door, shook his head slowly at the shot selection, and strolled my way. Towering above all he passed, the former coach waved and smiled at two members of the waiting set, including Linnbert "Cheese" Oliver, the best player I ever coached.

Augustine Coatsworth always dressed as if headed to Sunday Mass, even on Saturday. His light pink button-down shirt rested under a crisp navy blazer. Aircraft-carrier-sized penny loafers matched a shiny black belt that encircled olive-drab wool trousers.

"Coach Creekmore, it appears to me that even you might have better shooting range than some of these individuals," Coatsworth said.

I began to push off the pine benches to greet him. His huge hand and sparkling cuff-linked wrist halted my move.

"No, no. Don't get up. It's fairly evident you are better off prone this morning." Leaning forward, he swung his arm and offered a roundhouse handshake. At six-foot-eight, his wiry frame and close-cropped flattop always made him appear more than four inches taller than my six-four. "Perhaps a few adult beverages last evening after the Washington High game?"

Before I could react, he laughed and planted his butt a few seats away. "It appears you have not made any improvement in that department." He pointed toward the players on the court. "Say, didn't you wear wristbands like that at Eastern Michigan?"

"No way in hell," I grunted. "Hell, our control-freak coach wouldn't let that happen."

Coatsworth chuckled and held up his hands in a surrendering signal.

"What?" I said.

He settled in. "Old School Ernie. As if you weren't a control-freak coach yourself. You never came out of that man-to-man defense. I remember the night at the state regionals when a reporter asked why you didn't go to a box-and-one to defend that Silverdale star. You looked at the guy as if he'd just landed from Mars."

Like every coach I'd known, Coatsworth seemed comfortable on prehistoric bleachers that tortured most backsides, including my own. Coaches can sit for hours dissecting minute details and analyzing matchups. Our breed takes comfort in the familiar motions and soundscapes in even the most rundown structure with an iron rim at each end. If delight had a smell, this would be it. Now the delegate for the Washington State Coaches Association, he'd unfolded into the same position countless times in a myriad of gyms, where high school glory and college scholarships hung in the air like the scent of sweat socks and popcorn butter. There was none of that charged atmosphere, however, on our Saturday mornings, where any dreams of the big time had come and gone long ago.

Coatsworth stretched out his legs on the row below and eased his back against the bench behind. "How's your movement?" Coatsworth asked me, his eyes serious now. "The last time we spoke, the MS numbed up your hands and plane travel jacked it worse. Imbibing too many libations doesn't help, either."

"Nah." I waved him off, feeling the lie burn in my gut along with my anger. Getting old was bad enough, and multiple sclerosis added a sucker punch. Stubborn and frustrated, I still lived by the same virile code on the court and in life: never show weakness. "I just don't like getting felt up by those TSA people.

Get me all turned on then leave a guy frustrated. Why? Are you popping for a month in Maui?"

Coatsworth laughed, yet I could tell from his eyes he hadn't bought my story. We had a history, and he was here for a reason, so I cut to the chase. Eyeing him sideways, I said, "I haven't seen you in a year. You're telling me you came all the way to my gym to inquire about my health? I don't buy it. Why the special visit?"

He said nothing, merely smoothed the lapels of his custom coat. His watch probably cost more than my car. What did he need? From me? I didn't like this at all, but who was I to say anything? I was a just-retired coach and part-time real estate agent babysitting a bunch of middle-aged men pounding on each other below a hoop. I had no better plans at the moment, aside from rummaging for a Gatorade in the locker room to ease my pounding head.

"It's early, Coats. What do you want?" I asked, dragging out the words and wondering if I had more aspirin in my bag.

He chuckled. "Subtle as a hemorrhoid, Ernie. You get to the point, that's for sure." He flashed a million-watt smile, but his eyes skidded away.

"If you hadn't noticed, I am aging here. Why the surprise drop-in? I need you to get to the point before one of these overzealous hackers bleeds on the floor, and I have to mop it up." Just as I said that, a muffled voice squawked, "Don't be a dick!" as if to confirm my new mantra in life. I ignored it, mainly because it was aimed at someone else. I also didn't like wasting my time unless I was the one wasting it.

Coatsworth tugged at his tie and withdrew a pamphlet. "Our association has been given two invitations to a select tournament in southern California. The Pacific Waves. It's been around forever."

He handed me the flier, and I eyed the cover. "Sure, I've heard of it. I even know some guys who played in it when they were kids. That was a long time ago."

"Too long," he said. "Our state hasn't been considered for more than a decade. We've always been viewed as a basketball wasteland. Until recently. All the national coaches and recruiters now know there is an abundance of premier players coming out of Seattle and Western Washington. It started with Jamal Crawford, Jason Terry. Lord, then came the flood. Nate Robinson, Marvin Williams, Avery Bradley. On and on."

I laughed and looked away. "And the state's colleges and universities wished the players would all go to school in-state."

"Roger that. I get a call from colleges every week asking to explore opportunities to keep them here. Creative activities, seminars. We need to get more events like the Seattle City Spring Hoopfest that your youngsters played in."

"Well, sending a bunch of kids to the Pacific Waves probably won't help," I said.

He gave me a long look before he continued. "It's a double-edged sword, Coach. We don't want to keep our best kids from playing against the best national competition. Of course, with that comes the attention of some of the best colleges in the country. Candidly, I'd like to see more big-time teams come here, so more of our supposed lower-rung players could get some exposure, too. So few of our kids have the Grade A talent or the financial means to land a spot on an elite traveling team. Granted, we do have some great Grade B kids.

"And, speaking of elite traveling teams, I came here to ask you to consider taking a team to the Pacific Waves. You and your guys made a huge impression on our association at the Seattle tournament last year. Especially that guard Deacon John who came out of nowhere."

I tried to be smug and hide my joy, yet I doubt I'd succeeded. What else did I have to do? Scout kids for my buddies who were college assistants and send them a bunch of filled-in index cards describing their pros and cons? Hell, this could put me back in the coaching game on the big stage.

"Joe," I corrected. "It's Deacon Joe Gonzales. My amazing

Mexican orphan from the Indian reservation. I haven't heard from him in a while, but he might listen to this. And thanks for thinking of me. Maybe this year I can stay in one piece and out of the hospital." I interlaced my fingers and raised my arms above my head. "And away from the cops."

"Your past twelve months have been extraordinary. That parent arrest? Wasn't your fault."

"Maybe I have a face that draws trouble."

He slid closer. "Look, do this for your kids. Christ, do it for me. You'll have total control over player selection, and the association will help you raise some funds. You guys will also have to generate some money. We get a big reduction on the hotel rooms, but some of your parents might have to write a sizable check."

I smirked and looked away. "Few could. I've got paycheck-to-paycheck families who work their asses off and drive twenty-year-old cars. Is that usually how these things go nowadays? I thought the hosting sponsors did more to step up."

"Those days are over because of the conflicts of interest," Coatsworth said. "The sneaker companies had to tone it down. I'm sure some bullshit goes on under the table, but most coaches now break down the costs, then assign a dollar amount to each family."

I cupped a hand over my mouth to hide a grin while weighing the financial challenge of bankrolling a lifetime memory for a handful of gritty warriors. Car washes and bake sales no longer cut it. I had no deep-pocket sugar daddy in the wings eager to spring for airline tickets or splash a corporate name on jerseys and gym bags. I'd have to sell a small community of riverfront cabins to stockpile enough commission cash to make this trip fly. Hell, bring it on.

I then flashed back to the potential card in the hole, but it was a long way from being an ace.

"A joker I played with in college builds homes down there," I said. "Not like the shacks I sell up here on the Skagit River.

Those ocean-view castles you see on rich-and-famous television shows? He knows people and has been after me for years to get down there and check out 'them that have.' Maybe I'll get hold of him and see if he can grab us a place to stay, or at least get a break on a rental or two."

I thumbed through the pages. The pamphlet showed last year's Pacific Waves Tournament that included squads from Miami, Baltimore, New York, Chicago, Las Vegas, and St. Louis, plus several from California.

"Sixteen teams," Coatsworth noted, "all with impressive records. The Seattle Explorers that beat you in the final of the Seattle Center tournament are expected to accept the other Washington state bid."

I'd heard rumors about the funding of the Explorer operation. Why would a coach give so much playing time to a mediocre white guard who happens to be the son of a downtown Ford dealer? Seattle Explorers? Check.

The rafters creaked as the huge boiler fan began to whirl. A warm aroma of musty towels, abandoned lunches, and old cedar paneling blew through the dusty registers behind us. Coatsworth glanced up, then flipped me a *Should we run for cover?* look.

"Our state-of-the-art heating system finally kicking into gear," I said. "It only took an hour. When I opened the doors, you could see your breath in the locker room. You know, when I was coaching, we'd leave that sucker on all day, set the place up like a sauna for visiting teams. Our guys got used to it."

"Ah yes, the steamy Crab Pot," Coatsworth mused. "I remember dreading coming here with my teams. The overheated home of The Fighting Crabs."

I returned to the pamphlet, focusing on the back-cover ad for Diamond Jim Brady's Prime Rib Restaurant in Hermosa Beach that asked, CAN YOUR COACH EAT OUR BIG ONE? The inside pages contained individual team capsules followed by countless two-for-one coupons on pizza, burgers, shakes, and

subs, plus the PACIFIC WAVES ONLY SALE on shorts, sandals, and surfboard rentals. Ads for car dealers, insurance agents and divorce attorneys purchased quarter-pages of space, showing the year the proprietor played with many scrawny-then-portly-now mug shots proclaiming GOOD LUCK TOURNAMENT TEAMS!

On the page behind the double-truck tournament draw stood a tall, smiling man in a sun visor flanked by top-heavy female lifeguards with sparkling teeth holding basketballs. His belly provided a generous slope for a Hawaiian shirt splashed with hibiscus. A headline screamed across the top of the page:

LET US HELP YOU WITH PRIMO SOUTH BAY PROPERTY!

Below the picture, readout lines urged:

PLAY ON THE TEAM THAT ALWAYS WINS!

CALL GORDON ALDERETE, YOUR GO-TO GUY!

SHOREBIRD REALTY, RUBICON BEACH

"God, I can't believe this," I murmured, gripping the side of the bench. "Talk about jeopardizing my health...."

"What do you mean?" Coatsworth asked. "Did you find a friend in there?"

"Far from it." I poked at the picture on the page and tossed him the pamphlet. He snagged it, took a look, and appeared puzzled.

"I'm told the guy is a pillar in the community. Built a shelter for battered women. Organizers tell me they're damn lucky to have him as our tournament director."

"The what?" I said.

He leafed through the pages, then ran his finger down the ORGANIZING COMMITTEE column inside the front cover. Pointing to Alderete's name, he rotated the program page toward me. "You two have a history?"

Linnbert Oliver, light perspiration glistening the matted hair on his forehead, strolled over to take a breather. My shoulders eased with the intrusion. "You want in this game, Coach? Or leave it to me to go the distance?" He sidled over to the state rep and shook his hand. "Great to see you, Mr. Coatsworth."

"Same here, Linn. You're moving well out there."

I shot the youngster a look. "Why? Is there some reason you don't think I have much in the tank this morning?"

"No, simply asking. When I left Tony's last night, you had just about solved the national debt. But it *is* your spot. I subbed, seein' as you've been busy."

"What's it gonna be, Cheese?" came a shout from the court.

"Why don't you continue," I said. "Maybe I'll jump in the next game."

Linn shrugged and ran back on the floor.

Coatsworth glanced my way. "He was one of the best shooters I've ever seen."

"Don't get me started. The Cheese stands alone. Even did some scouting for me after he graduated. Hard to say what I would have done without him."

"Will you invite him to be on your staff for the Pacific Waves? That is, if you accept the position I've offered you."

I closed my eyes and was struck by how much they stung. Figures, they hadn't been open for more than an hour. "That's become a big *if*, Coats. Much bigger now than when you first proposed the trip."

"I don't follow."

I waited a moment and stared right through him. The juices now flowed like a lava stream, rekindling the heat of the delirious moment more than twenty-five years ago. "I nearly killed Gordon Alderete one night with my bare hands. Probably should have."

"Excuse me? Were you hammered?"

"Completely sober. Both of us ended up in the hospital. It could have been a helluva lot worse."

Coatsworth cranked an eyebrow and slumped back. "For chrissake, the main man donates a wheelbarrow of money to this tournament, several times the amount of any other individual or company and you— you're telling me you beat the living shit out of him?"

"And if I see him, I'd gladly do it again. If he doesn't kill me first."

The ball came to Linn Oliver on the wing. His defender played the right side, allowing more room left of the key. Linn dribbled twice, elevated, and launched a frozen-rope jump shot that rammed the back rim and plunged through the net. Game over.

TWO

WHEN THE STATE'S HIGHEST-RANKING basketball administrator shows up in a rural gym, word spreads through a small town faster than the naming of a homecoming queen.

After the Saturday morning session at Washington High, my voice mailbox was jammed with parental pleas and coaches' recommendations. And alleged top-secret player information from men with sinister-sounding voices who didn't leave their names yet were more than willing to help me fill any remaining spots on the roster.

I was already envisioning our run-and-gun attack, flowing down the floor in early evening heat of a summer gym, and we had yet to accept the bid. The event was months away and, despite my misgivings, I'd already begun making a list of Southern California college assistants who'd scouted our area and prep coaches I'd met at clinics. I'd already compiled a research network of high school sports website contributors in case I needed information on teams that might be named to the tournament. Plus, local boosters I wanted on the trip. How sick was that?

"I'm flattered that I am so high on your chaperone list," said George Berrettoni, the proprietor of Tony's Place, North Fork's only riverfront restaurant and bar. "If I didn't have to take Pop back to a family reunion in Jersey, I'd be happy to check out all the bikinis on the beach."

Garrulous George, a former math teacher at Washington High, had doubled as my unofficial basketball scout for more than two decades. His downtown checkered-tablecloth eatery and watering hole remained a community gathering place and dominated the corner site of a century-old block once occupied by the MacTavish & Oliver Mercantile, the first retail outlet built on the banks of the Skagit River in 1877. The place was a goldmine. It featured a private room Kids Korner with shorty tables and crayons, a homemade pasta of the week and a pizza pick-up window for families on the go – or coaches who did not want to be seen.

"It's probably better you didn't make the trip," I said. "You'd probably be a bad influence on the kids."

"Whaddaya mean?"

"They'd wonder how a married man could spend so much time scoping out single women. It might reflect poorly on the coaching staff."

"Look at it this way, Ernie. I'd show 'em how to properly read the entire menu of women without ordering a thing. Now that's useful street ammo that's tough to get anywhere else."

"Especially coming from a source like you. Being a famous restaurateur and all."

George arched his eyebrows and polished an invisible star above his heart. "You got that right. Man, I'm telling you, Coach, if my Evelyn weren't around…."

"You'd still have to take your dad to Newark."

George folded his bar rag into a neat square and placed it down in front of him. "Wait until I get a hold of the dumb cousin who arranged this reunion in friggin' July. I can already smell my sweaty relatives on Seventh Avenue. I'd take a week of nasty gym towels and Coppertone on the beach in a heartbeat." He straightened up and folded his arms. "So, who is going to try to fill my shoes on your basketball road show? As if that is at all possible."

"A difficult task, indeed," I said. "Of course, I've got Linn

and Dr. Timoteo Mesa."

"Your assistants? Hell, they were going anyway. By the way, I'm a better assessor of young men than Dr. Mesa. He knows it, but he won't admit it."

"That surprises me because he's always been so complimentary of your evaluations. He thinks you are an astute judge of talent."

George scoffed and strutted to the other end of the bar to fill a drink order submitted by Stella, a loopy waitress with a new a ratted-hair look. I pulled a pen from my shirt pocket and drew three columns on a napkin: players who had committed to the trip, players still considering, and chaperones. While I welcomed the possibility that some parents would attend, I dreaded spending the better part of a week with others, given the continuous hovering over their kids. And their coach.

"What?" George said upon his return. "You already breakin' down the teams?"

"We don't know all the teams yet, you know that. I'm trying to see who from our gang is going to be in or out."

"The end of July is big-time family time. I mean, just look at the Berrettonis. I think you'll find there will be a lot of people who've already made getaway plans."

He leaned in, turned my napkin so we both could see it, and ran a crooked index finger down the columns.

"Well, looka here." He grinned. "One Diane Chevalier in the chaperone column. I'm betting there might be a little late-night room roulette going on down there. *If* you know what I mean, and I think you do."

I pushed back from the bar. "C'mon George. Don't you think we're smart enough to put it on hold for a week? I mean, the woman's son is going to be down the hall. What sort of message would that send to him? The whole team, for that matter."

"Well, you could put the kids on different floors." He laughed. "Actually, I was wondering about what would happen

if she *wasn't* going on the trip."

"That could use some explanation."

"To tell you the truth, I wouldn't be surprised if 'ol Jessie McQuade didn't slip on a plane to LAX and show up in the bleachers. Maybe even at the hotel."

I massaged my forehead, remembering how infatuated he'd become with Harvey Johnston's secretary, the first woman I had dated since my wife passed away seven years ago. Harvey, the county's chief criminal investigator, rarely missed my high-school games and provided valuable insights both on and off the court.

"George, our relationship has been over for months. We are friends and speak kindly to one another. We've both moved on."

"That's not what Harvey says," George countered. "He says the poor gal is all weepy at the office and can't get you out of her skull. Harvey told me she gets about half the work done she used to."

"We were never together, OK? We dated. I slowed the train down because I didn't want to give her the idea something was down the road for us."

He sniffed, looked away briefly, then leaned across the bar. "Sure, you bet. Now, did you end up with the spiky redhead who cornered you in here the other night?" George's eyes glowed, his enthusiasm unable to curtail any voice reduction.

Squirming on my stool, I discovered only two patrons within earshot, but the white-haired couple appeared too engaged goo-goo-eyed to notice. "She was a very nice landscape architect from Snohomish," I said. "She is new to the area and looking for new clients."

"Wouldn't want to arm-wrestle her, though. Those curved biceps? Sexy. I bet she even had a tattoo. Did she, Coach? Maybe in what we might say, a provocative place?"

Elbows pinned to the bar, my arms formed a tent, fingers flat against both sides of my face. The guy opposite me in the

mirror behind the bourbon bottles appeared familiar. What threw me were the black, uneven whiskers that matched the bags under the eyes.

"It was a mistake, George. OK? Not a personal-best decision. It's something that just happened. What can I say?"

George gripped the edge of the bar with his huge hands. "What I can say is that it's happening enough for me to be amazed. I mean, concerned."

"What are you talking about?"

"Think about it, Coach. You come in here by yourself, get over-served, and then troll or be trolled. How do you think that sits with Jessie? Or is it Diane now? Or who in the hell is now supposed to be . . . number one?"

"They don't know about what I do."

"You dumb, or what? They sure as hell do! You can't keep crap like that quiet, particularly a guy like you in a town like this. It hasn't exactly been your M.O., you know. When you were coaching, nothing like this happened."

I felt my eyes narrowed as my head twitched backward. "Really? I used to come in here by myself, have a beer. . ."

"Have a beer, talk hoop, go over the next opponent's tendencies. You didn't come in and get hammered and then look to hammer anything in a skirt. Or tight jeans." George strutted away to check on the aged lovebirds who covered their gin and tonics, indicating they'd had enough. He punched up their tab, delivered it, and sauntered back my way.

"What's really going on here, Ernie? Got another case of babe deja vu? There's also nothing down the road for you and Diane? Forgive me, Mr. Never Exclusive, but are you seeing anybody else on the romantic front?"

"Diane and I are dating."

"Opposed to say, just boinking others?'

"Go to hell."

"I'm serious! Is it different? Different than with Jessie?"

I glared at him. "God, I don't know. Would you please stop?

It's really none of your business."

"You didn't answer my question. Did you ever consider that I might just care what happens to those ladies?" He dunked a pair of schooners in the soapy tub beside him, bounced them over a cylindrical brush, and ran them through a rinse. "By the way, did you ask Harvey about going on the trip? Next to me, he might be the biggest high-school hoops junkie around."

I thought about my closest friend, a fellow fisherman and a detective for the sheriff's department. "I doubt he can get away. Too busy."

George perused the napkin, reading names and notes upside down. I looked up when Linn Oliver bounded in the door, a brown leather satchel over his shoulder. He saluted from a distance, then zigzagged through a maze of tables to the bar.

"Mr. Berrettoni, how are you tonight?"

"Puzzled, Cheese. Puzzled."

Linn scrunched his face and looked at me. "That happens a lot, Linn," I said. "Trust me."

He shivered his head as if wanting to start over. "OK, well, did you want to look at some of these players now, or grab a bite to eat?"

The charismatic young man in front of me was not only the best athlete I ever coached, but he carried us to a state championship game on a bum knee. I rested him little that night, his last-second jumper bouncing out at the buzzer, and Washington High lost its best shot at a title in any sport for the first time in sixty-seven years.

"Let's do a little bit of both," I said to my now-assistant coach and chief scout who worked as a timber estimator in his family's logging business. "We'll order some food and review the kids until the chow comes."

George aimed his double chin toward a corner table. "Set up shop by the jukebox. I'll get you served." He reached under the bar and slammed half a roll of quarters in front of Linn. "For the music. None of that rap crap, you hear me?"

"No rap songs left here anymore since your father re-did the playlist." Linn peeled off a coin and wheeled toward me. "Call it for the food."

"Wait. Let me see that quarter." I checked both sides under the light. "It's an Oklahoma. Relatively rare."

"Just like a local woman who doesn't know you," George muttered. "In the biblical sense."

"Give it a rest, will ya, for chrissake!" I glared at George. I shifted toward Linn. "Obviously, Nick is in, and Timoteo is in as my trainer and assistant coach. I think I told you he applied to become Trent's guardian."

In between two conversations with diners who stopped by to visit with the famous Cheese Oliver, I explained Trent's living situation since the Seattle tournament and how Timoteo offered to become Trent's legal guardian. With his parents out of the picture, social services located the boy's only known relative, an uncle living in Massachusetts. The man wanted no part of the responsibility. Timoteo stepped up.

"I thought Trent had some uncle on the east coast," Linn said. "Wasn't that who was planning to take him? I'm surprised he's still in the area."

I shook my head. "Didn't happen. The uncle turned out to be a flake they couldn't count on. Anyway, Timoteo expects approval next week. Since Trent is almost eighteen and will get his college years paid for via a basketball scholarship, his financial and domestic needs were not as acute as those of a toddler."

I swapped the coin for a Vermont quarter. Linn won the coin flip and chose the entrée—a combo pizza with a pesto base. We agreed to split a Caesar salad. He dropped the quarter into the machine and dialed up a twangy western tune.

"OK, maybe we start with the big boys in the frontcourt?" Linn said, spreading out his notes. "We've got Trent Whalen and Nick Chevalier, who can rebound with anybody, so I'm feeling good about our strength around the basket. I'd like to

add another big body, but the guy's gonna have to be able to run. We can't be slow. Right?"

I didn't respond, and it took a moment to realize that I hadn't. I'd stopped focusing at "Chevalier." The unanswered question about my status with Diane continued to linger.

Linn flipped his notes on the table. "Coach? What's up? You look out of it."

Stupefied by the catch, I slumped lower. "Sorry, Linn. You're right."

"Right that we can't be slow or right that we need another bruiser under the boards?"

I tried to regroup with an upbeat tone, yet he knew me too well. Linn scoffed at the attempt, spreading his hands with a *what gives?* signal aimed at the momentary trance. "I think if anything happens to either one of those guys, we'd be up a creek. They are tough and healthy, but if they go down, we're going to have to sink a lot more shots because we could get beat on the boards."

"OK," Linn mumbled. "Then a rebounder goes on my to-do list. Now, do you want to work the parent-chaperone column or just deal with the players?"

"I guess we might as well look at the folks," I said. "Diane's in. And –"

"You can bet Diane's in," George blurted, heading our way with a basket of garlic bread. "I like that famous Irishman, Flynn. But I guess Chevalier is probably a little bit French. That's as in French kiss, Linn."

"You're a real asshole. You know that?" I said.

Linn just looked away. George appeared delighted and perused the page, reading names and notes upside down.

"You've got a Rochester in the chaperone-slash-parent's column with a question mark." He poked a crooked finger near the lined margin. "The only Rochester I remember was black, hoarse, and knew Jack Benny."

I shook my head at the reference to the long-dead comedian

and continued to study the page. "You're dating yourself, as usual." I lined the pencil up with the name. "The dad's a real estate developer over in Stanwood. He's been playing on Saturday mornings. Kind of a slick hack with wristbands. Never saw a shot he didn't like. Some of the old boys say he is only planting seeds for his kid."

"Wa-a-a-it a minute," George said. "Out-of-stater? Senior just transferred into the high school?"

I reared up, palms on the table. "Very little gets past you, sir."

He beamed and slapped me on the shoulder. "Just one of the many benefits of owning a bar. Think his name is Kyle, was a tweener size-wise. Can rebound and he's a flat-out, fill-it-up shooter from the corner."

Tugging my chin, I considered the possibilities. Given what I knew about my core picks, we could use the new guy's skills. If he was the real deal and low maintenance.

"One of the priests from Loyola was in for dinner the other night," George said. "He was telling me the mom wanted him to go there, but they couldn't handle the tuition. Apparently, the folks like their Dewar's-rocks. The old man got shitfaced one night and told the padres they'd better pony up a scholarship, but the good 'ol Jesuits wouldn't budge. I mean, those guys got more money than God. I guess Mom staged quite the hissy fit in the hallway."

"Great," I mumbled. "Just what we need. Another candidate who can't pay his way plus a parent with a five-star jerk factor."

Linn dropped his pencil. "Should we move on to this new guy, Rochester? Any chance his parents will head south with us? When he's showed up on Saturday mornings, the father smells like an old brewery."

I gazed at George, who looked ready to unload.

"Not a pair to draw to." George shook his head. "The mom doesn't look like the traveling type. At least for hoops in old high-school gyms. Maybe to Vegas, know what I mean? High

maintenance, lots of mascara, probably got a gold-plated backrest for the bleachers. The dad, Monty, is more than a handful. Gonna be a real pain in the ass to your replacement at the high school."

Linn exhaled and scribbled a note. "Sounds like how Trent's dad used to operate."

"Plus a lot of booze," I said. "I really hope he stays home."

Then we picked the guards, Marcus McGann and Andre Holberton. "OK, I assume the McGanns will make the trip. I doubt if Mrs. Holberton can swing it. Next?"

"The reserves, Jamaal--Booty--Jacobsen and Rochester, who we already talked about. Lord knows how much playing time they'll get. Maybe if we get into an early blowout. It's always tough to expect the folks to go that far and spend that kind of money when their kid sits on the bench most of the time."

"It'll be a big, fat number by the time it's over," George said. A kitchen employee stood nearby with a perturbed bakery delivery driver and signaled for a signature. As George rose, he shook his head. "Christ, you've seen these kids eat."

I pointed to Linn's list, then sat back in my chair. "Like to help Mrs. Holberton if we can. Does she have other kids living at home?"

"Dunno," Linn replied.

"If she can get the time off, I'll find her the money."

Linn cranked an eyebrow and dropped his pencil.

"You seem to come up flush at curious times. Like when helping a young man make the trip of a lifetime he otherwise could not consider."

"Who said I was flush?" I sat back and watched George retreat. "Now, who's left?"

"Point guard," Linn said. "We're set with Deacon Joe, and Marcus can bring it up when Deacon Joe takes a blow."

I cleared my throat and continued to look away.

"What?" Linn said.

"We're not set with Deacon Joe."

"Sure we are."

"He might not be making the trip."

He dropped his arms and forehead on the table. "You've got to be kidding me." Raising up slightly, he continued. "I know he doesn't want people helping him. But there are several of the old boosters out there. All we got to do is ask."

I eased my hands onto my forehead and dragged them down my face. "Not about the dough," I said. "He left a message at my office. It seems his mother doesn't want him to go."

"His mother? It's been years since—"

"Somehow she read about the Seattle tournament. Googled stories about him. A couple of the features got picked up by the state wire services."

Linn rested his chin on his palm. "We've got a got a good team, Coach, but Deacon Joe makes us great. Toss in polite, low maintenance. I mean, c'mon."

"I know," I mumbled. "I also know anybody else we find won't even come close."

"Who else is around?" He stood and began to pace. "I'm not just talking north of Seattle. How 'bout in the entire state?" He shook his head and closed his eyes for a moment, then faced me. "Coach, there's nobody else out there. His caliber? No way. And if we don't know about sleeper prospects, who does?"

The truth hurt, especially coming from a superb judge of talent whose Northwest network rivaled AT&T's. If the Cheese didn't know about a kid, there was no reason to spend time shaking the bushes.

"I don't like how this smells," Linn mused. "Doesn't he want a full ride to a good college? What mother wouldn't want that for her son? I think we better go find him, talk to him. Maybe her, too. Look them both in the eye. After that show he put on in the city, you never know who's going to come after him. Hell, if I were a coach needing a dynamo, I'da been there last month."

THREE

THE MERE MENTION OF LEAVING work for a hoop tournament in July, our prime second-home season, sharpened the tongue of my real estate boss, the Napoleonic Elinor "Cookie" Cutter, a five-foot-two pit-bull negotiator and the most successful real-estate broker in Skagit County. Professional or personal, she typically opened with a tender touch. Then she turned tough. Then stubborn.

"I know you love those kids, Ernie, but you must be joking."

I felt cornered, even though the long hallway in the office was wide open. "Why don't you just wait for one of those popular freaking Christmas tournaments? You know, icy rain and everybody thinking about Santa, gifts under the tree, everything but real estate? Jezuz H. You're supposed to be my go-to second-home guy. You, you're my big dog!"

"I'm absolutely your man during all months of the year." Time to back into the ask. I picked at a stain on my work shirt. Red sauce, lasagna from Tony's Place, last Wednesday. "Except maybe for one week, the middle of next year?" I lied about the duration, but it was a place to start.

"Gawd all Friday. Put yourself in my stylish shoes and think about what you're asking. As soon as the school kids get out in June, all their newly retired teachers turn into full-time fishermen and come asking about your sorry ass. You're the one

with those word-of-mouth river huts that have been in the family for generations. Besides, who else can deal with those crotchety bastards? Plus, the flow of Californicators next year is expected to get near flood stage."

"I don't do flawless teeth and fake boobs."

"Yeah, well somebody has to. You know I need bodies during the summer. This is like a baseball writer requiring time off during the freaking World Series."

"Mariners have never been to the World Series," I replied.

"Cut the crap. You know what I mean."

I prayed her cell would ring or the office secretary would appear with an urgent message. I gave the dream an extra moment, then continued in my top salesperson's tone. "These elite national tournaments are by invitation only," I said, hoping to wow her with the exclusivity. "It's not as if I just cram a bunch of guys in the bus and show up at these things. It's kind of a big deal that any team in this neck of woods gets asked for something like this."

"You're busting my bullshit meter here, Ernie. How many of the coaches at this thing make their living selling recreational property? You're the one who came in here pleading to be my lakes and rivers specialist. Remember?"

I remembered. Peddling riverfront cabins and lakefront homes to a core group of former coaches, teachers and school administrators was my slam-dunk income for years, even while I was still coaching and teaching. Thanks to my dad, a lifelong fly fisherman, I'd also dialed into the rod 'n reel community and nailed nearly every riverfront listing when one of the old boys became too weak to cast. The ample supply of affordable waterfront in northwest Washington lulled local buyers for years. Like flannel shirts and polite drivers, cheap getaway spots came with the region, even for those making a measly wage in the classroom. When one of my guys, or his uncle, aunt, cousin, a friend of a friend or member of the Evergreen Steelhead Association decided to make a move, they came my

way. The network brought Cookie a ton of sales.

Then one day, it all changed. Southern Californians found our rivers, lakes and islands and traded the cost of airfares and rental cars for real estate, blasting my clientele out of the water. Our $65,000 cozy water-ski cabins and island retreats skyrocketed to $200,000 quicker than the short version of "Light My Fire." Savvy Golden State buyers did the math and discovered four hundred grand would buy a lot of plane rides, plus save on freeway headaches. Eager property-seekers flew to Sea-Tac and telephoned agents the minute they hit the tarmac. Throw in the colossal kettle of local tech bucks, and the bargain secrets of old were gone. The consequences, however, were not. Traffic and drive times soared. A kid can go through puberty driving north on I-5 from Tacoma to Bellingham on a Friday afternoon.

I had to start working for my commissions. Some of the qualified, red-hot buyers on those planes were liars. Old coaches and teachers needed to find partners to afford a cabin that now took hours, not minutes, to get to. A headline from the latest North Fork Weekly sparked a variety of coffee-shop conversations:

MORE LA PEOPLE ON LOCAL LAKES THAN SEATTLEITES

Cookie's smoker's cough intruded on my drift. "It's not just the week you'll be gone," Cookie said. "But it's all the B.S. prep you'll do getting ready for the damn tournament. You'll be all-in to this thing, and early. We'll catch you diagramming plays in our weekly staff meetings months before. And the practices. God, you'll practice until their little jockstraps fry."

I turned and coughed into the crook of my elbow, attempting to hide a smirk. Man, did this woman know me? I'd wait to tell her that kids no longer wore jocks.

"What's that shit-eating grin all about? I'll tell you what. If your Cathy were still alive—God rest her soul—she'd never let you abandon me in my time of need. But tell me on the way to my office, because I've actually got some real work to do."

"There was something else that I was going to mention," I said, "but this does not seem like the best time."

She stepped closer, angling her Marlboro breath up in my face. "Bullshit. Let's get everything out on the table right now. There's no time like the present."

She scooted behind her desk and rocketed the top drawer open. A few paper clips flew into her lap. I moseyed toward the window, hands on hips. "Do you remember I told you once that flying in a plane might bother me?"

Unable to locate what she was looking for, she slammed the drawer and slumped into the chair. "As I recall, you thought in-flight air-filtering magnified your MS symptoms."

"Actually, that's right," I said, doing my best to emit genuine concern. "Frankly, it was one of the first things I considered when this tournament surfaced."

She raised both hands above her head. "Bam. There it is. Your built-in excuse. Get Cheese Oliver to do it. Hell, the kids would probably love it. They are more his age, anyway. Dr. Mesa will go with, be your trainer and hard-guy chaperone. Whew, I'd say you're covered, my man."

Looking down, I gripped my chin. "Actually ..."

She straightened up, then tilted her head. "Actually, what?"

I stuffed my hands into my hip pockets.

Her eyes narrowed. "What the hell is it?"

"Given my uncertainties about the plane, I was thinking about driving. Maybe pack up the kids who can afford—"

"Well, think again! And stop trolling like a child looking for an advance on his allowance. I'm not having you take a week off on both ends of this damn tournament."

"Do I receive an allowance? Anyway, it won't be a week. We can drive it in—"

"The hell it won't. I get your operation, Ernie. You'll leave early so the team can get extra practice time in gyms they've never seen. On the rebound, and pardon my so-appropriate pun, you'll find some beach that everybody loves and camp for a few

days. Probably rent goofy surfboards or some god-awful thing."

Dropping to my knees, I feigned paddling on a wave, then assumed the gawky posture of rookie surfer, arms out, flailing for balance. "Why are you so sure about these alleged vacation side trips?"

"Try not to be an asshole, just this once."

I snapped to attention like a Marine with a faded baseball cap and tired blue jeans.

She sighed and gave me a dirty look. "Because I'm a mom, that's why. With persuasive sons. I know what they will try to do. You already know it, but you won't admit it."

"Admit what?"

"You will treat these kids like your own. Children you never had."

"Please, gimme a break."

"You've coached plenty of teams, sure. But how many times have you taken a road trip like this? After those Seattle games? You love these guys."

"Really, Cookie? Now?"

"Hey, you're the guy who started this. Have you even thought about what you are going to do with the women these young studs will attract? Southern California is a helluva long way from North Fork. And I don't mean geographically."

"I think we're getting ahead of ourselves here."

"To the contrary. I'm being realistic. As an employer needing productive people, I've just been informed that your summer is shot. Now, I've got to find a plug for the hole you just dug for me." I knew she'd relent but that didn't mean that she wasn't dead-on right.

"In the meantime, I suggest you craft some fancy answers for the two-job moms who'll want their babies monitored twenty-four-seven *if* they win the lottery and send their Johnny Runnynoses with you. And please, Ernie, don't expect Big River Realty to sponsor this distinguished delegation. Ain't happenin'."

FOUR

THE PLAYERS WHO MADE UP my select team for the Seattle tournament last year grew into a cohesive, efficient unit that far exceeded my expectations. Even though some people say players don't care about all-star games, these guys did. Because they cared about each other and their mission of pulling off an upset over a big-time team. We punished every defense with speed and shooting. Coaches in the stands debated how best to defend us.

The question sat in my gut like a chili burger at midnight: Could we do all of this again, or was that an extraordinary four days destined never to be repeated?

To say the team overcame adversity would be like saying Noah carted a couple of cubs around on a bay cruise. The North Counties Selects rambled through the first three rounds, burying three well-coached teams before dropping the final in overtime against one of the finest collections of talent I'd ever seen. All accomplished despite the arrest of one parent plus a team friend involved in a sexual relationship with a star player. Anybody with a remote notion of what makes team chemistry wanted what we had. Coaches from around the state quizzed me, Linn, and Timoteo for weeks following the event.

Cookie was right. My number of useless days in the office would far outnumber the early guesstimates. It all started with the search for Deacon Joe Gonzales, the five-eight Mexican

American living on the Manzana Reservation northwest of Everett. He was staying with a roofer who took him home when he discovered the young man had been working—and sleeping—at a construction site.

I'd learned that Deacon Joe's world did not revolve around a cell phone. It was among the many things we had in common. His lack of use, however, had more to do with poor reception on the Manzana Reservation while mine was from my inability to locate the device when I needed it.

After days of calls, Linn found that Deacon Joe frequented a Saturday-afternoon open gym in Mukilteo. After getting a signature on a new lakeside cabin listing, I cruised south on I-5 to the waterfront town halfway between Shoreline and Everett. The tiny bandbox of a gym covered the northeast corner of a city park. Its gravel parking lot was lined with beater pickups, a handful of two-door imports with privacy windows, and a half dozen motorcycles. I noticed Deacon Joe's clean green-and-white Dodge right away, the only pickup parked deep in the lot, away from any flying doors from drivers hurrying to join the next game.

Two full-court games were in full swing when I entered. Deacon Joe, stripped to the waist, orchestrated a skins team that appeared to be overmatched against a group of shirts featuring three guys six-foot-five or taller. He pointed his teammates to move farther apart, then passed to his right and set a screen to his left. Solid fundamentals, even in a rag-tag runaway.

"Coach!" he shouted, after fist-bumping his defeated teammates. When he got closer, he extended his hand for a conventional handshake. His grip was firm and his eyes clear. "Remind me to help you with your social schedule, man. Guy like you should be getting slicked up for Saturday night."

I laughed and looked away, pleased and impressed how comfortable this kid seemed in any situation. "I just needed to come down and see if you are still as quick as I remembered."

He grinned, dipped into his gym bag, and wiped his

glistening brown face with a folded white towel. "So, Nick Chevalier's mom's out of town?"

I shook my head, thinking that I was one of two people who knew Diane had grabbed a Friday night flight to Phoenix, her son being the other. "How in the world did you know that?" The lady had leaped into first place on my dating chart, but I had no idea it was common knowledge. Hell, I hadn't even spent time determining when and how she got there.

He grinned and tossed on a T-shirt emblazoned with the catchy name of a local feed store. "Still talk to my man Big Trent." He pointed to the corner. "Let's go sit." We wandered over to the stands while Deacon Joe indicated to the other players that he would sit out the next game.

"People you just played had guys who could fly."

We joked and talked. I caught him up on some of the comings and goings of the North Counties Select kids since last year's Seattle tournament while he laughed me through several of the games he'd played since I'd last seen him. His favorite team was a gang of loggers from Lake Stevens ("either reeked of gas or beer") or a small law firm from Lynnwood ("entitled, prep-ass guys"). Making honorable mention was a not-so-timid church group from Warm Beach, a crusty fishing guide and his office mates from Darrington, and a bunch of young retirees who boated in from Hat Island. I found the detail remarkable.

As the action on the court continued, I launched into the Southern California trip and how we would try to help all players with the funds to get there.

"I got a problem with that," he said.

"Believe me. You're not the only one who will need—"

"Told you. Not with the money, Coach. With the trip. And not the guys. Love the guys. Told Big Trent I'd think hard about it."

"You mentioned your mother contacted you?"

"No idea how she found me. Called where I'm living and left a voicemail that she wants me back. Dunno what that

means." He applauded a pinpoint assist on the floor and shouted, "Good look!" to the passer.

After a long pause, I said, "Do you think she looked you up because she needs you or because you're doing well?"

He turned and faced me, ignoring an errant pass that landed a few feet to his left. "Sure crossed my mind." He was silent for a while and then said, "She *is* my mother." Then, a moment later, "She left a number."

"Are you thinking of trying to see her?" I said.

He leaned back in the bleachers. "I don't know. Maybe. Call her at least. Message said she saw Deacon Joe in newspaper stories. Just knew it had to be me. Probably looked me up on a computer someplace, found out about the Seattle tournament. And this SoCal trip."

I touched him on the shoulder. "Let me know if I can help you in any way."

"Thanks, Coach. I would like to go with you down there, but I just … don't … know."

I bumped him on the shoulder. "For you, I can wait. I won't go looking for another point guard tomorrow."

A couple of players waved to Deacon Joe, indicating the game on the floor was nearly over.

"'Preciate that, Coach. I do." He stood and stretched, elbows high, turning his torso side to side. "Y'know, she said something that hit me."

"Really, what's that?"

"She said if I went to California, some crazy preacher might find me. I would take that to mean my dad."

* * *

MY FIRST DRIFT OF PANIC MOUNTED when three of the players I'd targeted said no because of summer-job

commitments. I needed to lock down another gazelle who could defend, rebound like crazy, and run like a deer. I continued to comb the weekend email list plus other possible candidates collected during extra assignments the past few seasons. You can't take slow guys to an all-star tournament. If you do, they'd better be stud rebounders who can sling the ball out quickly from the defensive boards and then rumble down to join the offense.

I'd heard all about Kyle Rochester, but I didn't know what made him tick. And how quick he was on the court. I did know his previous coach, a former Saturday-morning regular, and I owed the guy a call. My eyes caught a note on Linn's last page of his player evaluation form, three cursory lines scribbled on a coffee-stained sheet. *Junior with an athletic body. Average shooter, exceptional rebounding position, goes after every ball. Really 6-5?*

Frank Shiro, an old Okie who spent twenty years at Marysville High before retiring and taking the Loyola coaching job two years ago, leaned back in his chair in the athletic department as spring-sports kids scampered behind us, preparing for practice. Like many other teacher-coaches, he'd double-dipped from the publics to the privates, drawing a full public-school pension plus a full-time paycheck at Loyola. He remained in the same home with a similar commute time.

"Parents give you static about joining the rival school?" I asked.

"Nobody gives a damn anymore," Shiro said, his huge, calloused palms turning up in resignation "The old sense of rivalry went out with bell bottoms. Hell, you should know that better than anybody."

We talked about other coaching changes and player transfers. Then I asked, "Did the Rochester kid play hard for you or just mail it in?"

"Worked his ass off. All the time. Makeup game, title game, practice. Hated to lose him. He chased every . . . single . . . ball.

Blocks out like a pro."

"But pros don't block out." I laughed. "When's the last time you saw LeBron, anybody in the NBA, block out? Push, shove, lean. But block out?"

He smiled and picked at a callous on a huge brown hand. "If Kyle Rochester doesn't go up for a rebound, you can bet his guy either tripped him or knocked him down. For his size? Kid's quicker than greased shit through a short dog. Got a heart bigger than Texas, too. Much as I hate Texas. But don't get me wrong. The kid can act out, really lose it. On the court and off."

"Never saw him play. I am trying to fill a few more spots on that select team and don't have a helluva lot of time."

Frank angled his head toward the locker room. "He's in there. Getting ready to shoot. Probably stay until the janitor kicks him out."

"Really? The season's over. It's a school night."

Frank fidgeted, glanced down at the floor, then up to the rafters. My gut tightened, feeling negative highlights were on the way.

"Kyle tries to wait for his old man to go to bed. He figures if Monty knocks back enough booze, he'll pass out and leave him alone. The dad makes a list of what he wants Kyle to improve on. There are no positives allowed."

I'd seen it before, but some parents hover lower than others. Frank swung his ring of gym keys and took a deep breath. "Says he doesn't want the kid to get a big head, inflated image of himself. In his mind, we only live by our mistakes, and not a whole lot else counts. It drives Kyle crazy sometimes. I've seen the dad begin his critique the second Kyle walks out of the locker room."

"You gotta be kidding me," I seethed even though I believed it and had witnessed the same conduct before.

"You should have been around Monty when the paid shooting sessions didn't work. He thought everyone simply did not understand the proper way to coach his kid. Because of

Kyle's body, he thought it was obvious he'd become a stellar shooter with his choice of D-One schools. Hey, I wasn't a good enough coach for his kid. That's why he moved him to Washington High. Your successor gets a great kid, but the tradeoff is the dad."

"Ouch," I muttered. "That's a tough way to handle anybody, especially an athlete his age."

Frank turned to face me. "Y'know, I put the kids through a nasty practice one night. Maybe the toughest of the season. Just ran their asses off. I asked Kyle later if that was the hardest part of his week. He said, 'Hell, no. Hardest part of my week is going home in the car with my dad after the game.'"

We talked awhile about my select team roster, the need to find players and define roles. I felt confident Kyle could bang against bigger bodies and rebound, but could he score?

"I think the reason Kyle's got no jump shot now is the old man's expectations. He's too concerned about doing it right, and the mechanics just won't mesh. But I tell you what's going to be dangerous. It'll be the day Kyle's had it up to here." Frank raised a flat hand above his forehead. "Monty gets in his face once too often, the kid could really go off."

FIVE

RICKY "WRONG RIM" WILKINSON came off as one of those rich kids who had more money than brains. Really, who has a wallet full of his own credit cards at seventeen? During our college years, as I watched him squander and then creatively refurbish his cash pile countless times, the scale clearly tilted toward brains.

As a freshman, the six-foot-three smiling cowboy from Roswell, New Mexico, ran a college-football betting scheme in our dormitory that netted him six hundred dollars on the first Saturday of the season. Every week, he'd steal Jimmy the Greek's odds from the newspaper, line up the top twenty games, print two hundred one-page sheets of "The Fabulous Football Forecast," and slide them under dorm-room doors at midnight on Thursday. Entrants picked a maximum of four games; five or ten bucks a game. At the bottom of the sheet in tiny type read, *In the event of a tie, TFFF wins*. After the second week, every printer on campus ran out of paper by noon on Friday.

By the time formal hoop practice started in November, Ricky was the biggest man on campus. Women swooned at his easy smile and came to his room with their checks and late-night picks. On more than one occasion, a young lady darted out his door before breakfast. The floor prefect played three betting sheets a week and never reported any off-hour female visitors. When the daughter of the Dean of the Humanities

College cried to her mom about losing her lipstick money to "a tall, cute con artist who said he loved me," Ricky was forced to close up shop and nearly lost his scholarship. He went from dorm betting cards to backroom card games in downtown Ypsilanti to the roulette wheels in the Native casino while maintaining a 3.9 GPA in Economics. He graduated on time.

As I dialed the number for Pierpoint Builders and waited on the line, I wondered if he'd decided to grow up all over again, maybe return home and take a swing at running the family cattle ranch, enjoy his later years via a slower route. Too many guys grow up fast and burn out young. By the time I got to speak with him, I'd been filtered through two assistants and forced to listen to nauseating office music including a sappy crooner piece about not having met me yet. Perhaps it was part of Ricky's intro.

"Ricky Wilkinson. How can I help you today?"

"By getting out of Dodge," I said.

"Hey, man. I paid you. Maybe you should talk to your guys."

So much for a slower route. I removed the receiver from my ear and winced at it as if the mere motion would clarify the statement. Then put it back. "This is Ernie Creekmore. North Fork, Washington."

"What? You gotta be shittin' me! Old School Ernie?"

"One and the same."

"How the hell are you, man? And sorry about the hello. Some punk is trying to stick my dick in the dirt over a deal that's been done for weeks. Dude should check his direct deposit. That's how we send cash in the new world. Your broker still cut paper checks, Ernie? Sorry, screw that. Anyhoo, to what do I owe this absolutely mofo surprise?"

"Happy to see money in any form," I said. "And you don't owe me a thing. I'm also heading your way."

"Ha! Love you man. Why this way? Not that I wouldn't love seein' you, and all. Too much rain? Shit, last time I was at Sea-

Tac, it was comin' down like a cow peein' on a rock. Chick I was with broke her umbrella. Nearly broke something else 'fore that weekend was over. Know what I'm sayin'?"

"Well, we've had more than our fair share of rain again this year, but I'm coming for hoops."

"Ah, dude. You just made my day. Let me get something to write with." The receiver clunked on a hard surface. A moment later, Ricky shouted, "Tell the dickhead the juice is six percent. Not three, not five. Six! If he doesn't like it, ask him if he tries to chisel his plastic surgeon." Next came the sound of papers being shuffled and jostled close to the phone. "OK, I'm locked 'n loaded. Give me your vitals, babe."

"I'm coaching a team from this region at the Pacific Waves Tournament." I opened a binder to check the dates and assigned hotel.

"The Pacific Waves?" Ricky said. "Man, that's big-time. You must be bringing some real horses. Some hotshots from Vegas won it last year. I caught a couple of the opening rounds at Mira Costa High. They use a ton of venues now because they try to spread out the talent, let people see 'em early, then put later rounds in the bigger gyms. Freaking crowds are incredible; talking new level, man. You need to be a mathematician to understand the damn bracket."

"Let's see here," I said, paging through the book. "We get in the night of the twelfth, and we leave the afternoon of the nineteenth. I guess they're putting us up in at a place called The Shadow Hotel. Supposed to be nice."

"Wowzah, man. You got that right. Top-drawer, baby."

"Good location?"

"Shheeesh! You talkin' fifty-yard line, Rubicon Beach, man. Know what I mean? It's owned by a big-time buckets guy who starred here at Bishop Montgomery High. And the talent in the bar there at night? Dang. There's a bell-cow blonde who shows up there when she's in town. Stewardess, smoking hot. Shit, I've been meaning to pay the bartender to call me when

she shows up."

"Forgive me if I don't pass along all of that valuable information to my players."

"Just wait 'til your farm boys see the babes walking around that lobby. Damn bar turns into a live bait tank at night, man. Your guys won't be able to think straight because all their blood will be in their dicks. Why do you think this cowboy ended up in these parts?"

"You mean you never went home to run the ranch?"

"Too slow, babe. Entirely too slow. This boy needs to live life in the fast lane."

Wilkinson played basketball at an extremely high level. That is, when he didn't close the bar the night before. When our Eastern Michigan team was on the road to play a holiday tournament in Dayton, we checked into the hotel, tossed our bags in the room, and followed the 1960s cover songs banging through our window to a jam-packed tavern across the street. With Ricky leading the charge for "talent," we weaved through the place, taking notice of the sweatshirts and caps from other schools in the event. We landed in an enclosed outdoor patio where the Dayton cheerleaders sat hovering around an open firepit. Ricky surveyed the scene.

"Cocktails for anybody who can stand up!"

The girls leaped from their chairs and pranced, pirouetted, flung their arms around like cops at a busy intersection and pulled their fists tight against their chests. "Go Flyers!" they yelled in unison.

"What are you doing?" I whispered at the time.

"Had to see the legs on the one on the left."

He tossed his credit card on the server's tray that night and told her to "keep 'em coming."

Our college team played its first game at noon the next day. Riddled with illness and injuries, the team needed Ricky, who'd spent the night in the cheerleader van slammed with the brown-bottle flu. When the opening tip caromed his way, he dribbled

the ball down the floor and scored. At the opponents' basket. Two points for the other team. Ricky got his nickname that night, his wayward move providing the only highlight of a miserable game that we lost by twenty-nine.

The phone hit the deck again, and I flinched at the crack. "Dolores," Ricky called. "Tell those assholes we're not holding back any cash for repairs until we get our price. No, no! The deal must be signed all around." A moment later, he came back on the line. "Sorry about that, Ernie. But some buyers are fucking liars. You're in this business, so you know. They say they'll buy the house, but they don't have the balls to pull the trigger, and another agent gets the commission."

"Doesn't really happen that much in this—"

"And the stingy sellers. They'll eat your food, drink your booze, screw your associates, and then take their damn listing down the street to some asshole who suggested a higher asking price than I did. It'll never sell for that, but it's gold to the seller's ears. Know what I mean?"

"That can be frustrating."

He took a deep breath and blew it into the mouthpiece. I imagined him leaning back in his leather chair and watching the waves crash on the sand. "So, how are ya, Ernie? You playing at all anymore?"

"Just with a bunch of guys on Saturday mornings. No more high-powered park leagues for me. But we go full-court, two hours. It's enough."

"Well, it sounds like you're staying in shape. To tell you the truth, I can't remember the last time I've run farther than across the street for a cold one. I try to get out on the golf course every now and then. Love those carts. Nice on the knees."

Ricky said we had to grab dinner during our stay. I asked about possible day trips the players might enjoy. He also mentioned a reunion of our team on the Eastern Michigan campus.

"You been back, Ernie? I haven't seen fucking Ypsilanti

since the day we graduated. I sometimes wonder how in the hell we ended up there in the first place."

"I don't know about you, but it was the only four-year school that offered me a scholarship. And yeah, I've been back. You remember Cathy was a Michigander, a Yooper from Houghton. We used to go back in the summer, stop by the campus. Looks nice. They've done a decent job."

After a long pause, Ricky cleared his throat. I had an idea of what was coming.

"Y'know, I think I've only talked with you once or twice since she passed. You guys had a great thing, a helluva lot better than my three-year fiasco trying to stay married."

I swallowed and waited to make sure I could get out the next line. "Yeah, that was a tough one. I didn't exactly rebound in a hurry. But I'm giving it a shot. It's past time to keep it moving."

"Good to hear, buddy. Good to hear. Say, anybody got a clear shot at first place up there? If not, I got a couple of ladies down here who'll screw your socks off until the cows come home. Thing is, there ain't no cows here, and you don't need no socks. Know what I'm saying? Got them flip-flops, boss. Heh, heh."

I ran a palm over my head. I hadn't defined my situation with Diane to anyone. Even myself. To go there, I'd have to admit that someone had come even remotely close to the comfort I experienced with Cathy. If I was ready, where were the guts to do so?

"There…there just might be," I said. "A woman. And if you play your cards right, you might meet her at that restaurant in the marina."

"OK, boss, you're on." He broke away again, growling out, "Just bring it here!" away from the mouthpiece before returning with a lighthearted "You know, I just can't wait to see your sorry ass."

"Everybody up here is getting fired up for this one. Some of these kids have barely been out of the county. Of course," I said,

"I'd like to get your take on how we play. Maybe you could take some time, help me correct some of the things we're doing wrong."

"You got it."

"Say, before I let you go, have you been on the other side of many real-estate deals with Gordon Alderete?"

When Ricky failed to respond, I envisioned him in another heated sidebar with his office assistant. After a moment, I continued. "Look, it sounds as if you've got a ton of stuff in front of you right now. I won't keep you from making a living, but I just wanted to see if you were going to be around when we—"

"I heard you loud and clear, Ernie." I could feel the tension through the phone. "I just hope I see that son of a bitch in a back room some night. Alone. Just him and me. I'd stick his face in toilet and wait 'till the bubbles stopped." After a short pause he said, "Know what? That's something you should have done more than twenty-five years ago."

SIX

I F OPPOSITES ATTRACT, IT EXPLAINS why Harvey Johnston and I became friends and fishing partners. He built his national reputation as a criminal investigator on thorough research, uncanny recall, and remarkable logic. I operate by the seat of my frayed cords, remember only local athletes who dribble, early American authors, and rock artists of the sixties. He could have calmed both sides in the Cold War, while I'd have thrown Joe Frazier haymakers.

His key ingredients in my world? He loves high school basketball, gives me a heads-up when any of my former players break the law, and even lets me help investigate the reasons why they did when it seems clear that somebody involved would rather talk to a civilian than a cop.

Regrettably, like too many nosy residents of North Fork, he *says* he could care less about my love life yet eavesdrops at any mention of a female and me in the same sentence. The man overprotects all in his purview but takes on a bouncer-like posture regarding Jessie McQuade, his longtime secretary who happens to have a better body than the part-time yoga instructor I'd also been known to see for a variety of physical needs. But there'd always been something especially uplifting about Jessie wearing only a smile that I couldn't forget. I knew our steamy, late-night visits had to stop, but the brakes were so damn hard to apply. I'd checked out months ago but didn't have the guts

to tell her. She'd be the last one in town to get the word.

I nearly choked when I opened the door to Harvey's outer office. Her tight brown skirt stopped a foot above her knee. Thank goodness she sat facing the wall. She swiveled in her chair, beamed, and stood, choosing to stay clear of the open door leading to the inner office. She winked and curled a *come-here* finger.

"Hey, stranger," she cooed. "Take a girl to dinner tonight?" She laid a hand on my shoulder and glided her fingers down my chest. Two ended up wiggling in my lapel pocket. "Then dessert?"

I slowly stepped back and thumbed toward Harvey. She frowned and creased her brows. "Not so loud," I whispered. "Bad night. I'll call you, because we gotta talk." She flattened her lips, pouting. Then, in a voice the entire building could hear, I said, "Nice to see you, too, Jessie. We'll talk soon."

I turned, exhaled audibly, entered Harvey's office, and closed the door. He didn't look up, scouring the legal page in front of him with a pencil. "You've been stringing her along," he said, "and you know it."

The guilt hit home. I flung him the middle finger, high and hard, coupled with a snarl usually reserved for an f-word-slinging heckler slumping in the stands. Both signals came down by the time he glanced up. Harvey didn't deserve either, yet such was my day.

"What are you talking about? We had a fruitful come-to-Jesus a while back. We went all through the exclusivity issue and how I couldn't deal with it, at least for now."

"How kind of you."

"Both of us surfaced better from it—and as good friends."

"Save the standard bullshit." He slammed the pencil down, then swore under his breath when retrieving it from the floor. "It's more than that."

"More than what?"

"Since you didn't have the cojones to tell her you no longer

wanted to see her, romantically, she grills me with the third degree. About what you're doing, if you're assisting with any cases. I feel like I'm being deposed. She's also quite interested in the dates of that California tournament. And other dates. With women. She thinks she's still in the hunt because you never told her she wasn't."

"Christ. Is there anybody who doesn't know about my personal business?" I shuffled over and plunked into one of two uncomfortable oak chairs facing his desk. "I can't believe that. Maybe she wants to make vacation plans to be gone at the same time you're out of the office."

"I've already told her I couldn't take time off to go with you to California. There are two huge cases the district attorney expects me to have tied up with pretty bows by then."

He leaned closer, clutching the pencil in his fist, eraser end up. Its future appeared in jeopardy as Harvey picked up steam.

"I'd be cautious on the women front if I were you," he said. "When you haven't been trolling for years, all of the poles can snap at once as soon as you put the lines in the water."

I shook my head at another curious Harvey correlation and slumped lower. "Give me a break."

"Are you clueless? Get out of your diminutive mind for a second, Mr. Suddenly Available Bachelor. You're a draw. That tends to happen in a small town when you are single and a semi-famous coach whose late wife was everybody's angel."

"You act as if I've become some sort of prime target."

"No one wants advice, only collaboration."

"Herman Melville?" I said.

"Nope. Your buddy John Steinbeck... Look, from all segments of the female population, if the reports I'm hearing from the folks at Tony's Place are true. I can't blame Jessie because she's probably heard the stories and is obviously desperate to be a player in this game you appear to be playing."

I rose from my seat and circled it, stopping opposite his desk. I glared down at him. "Why don't you just say George has

been blabbing around. Again. That's basically what's happened. He's your only source of information on this, and he loves to exaggerate."

Harvey flipped his pencil onto the yellow note pad in front of him. "That's simply not true. I mean, he does exaggerate, and there's little doubt how George takes advantage of any audience, but Patsy also mentioned you had been over-served recently and departed the premises with a woman she would never ask to coffee."

"For godsake. Patsy's a waitress in the restaurant. She. . . "

"She has eyes that can see into that bar," Harvey said. "You don't need to be a professional investigator to make that leap. And you need to be aware of your stature in this community, which appears to be eroding as we speak."

"Unreal." I curled into the chair and dragged my hands down my face, hoping to change the scene. "Is this *All My Children* or North Fork? Maybe I'd better go outside and come back in."

"Can you stop being a jerkball just for a second? Look, I don't know what you are looking for, but if it's a substitute for Cathy, it's not going to happen."

"Lord," I said. "Don't you think I know that? I'm beginning to think you've been spending a lot more time with a certain bartender."

The middle light blinked on Harvey's phone. He scowled, stabbed a button, and made the light go away.

"Sometimes I'm not sure that you do. Maybe on some artificial level, but deep down, I think you're still holding out hope. Either you haven't let Cathy go, or your comparisons are unfair and way out of whack."

"Did you major in psychology or forensic science?"

"How about basic logic? You don't touch a woman for more than five years, begin dating, and within six months you're linked to every babe south of Bellingham. By the way, my sources tell me Diane Chevalier believes she's now in first place

in the Ernie Creekmore Dating Derby. Apparently, she intends to hold that position at least through the summer months."

I felt my face tighten. "I don't follow."

"Because she will be accompanying her son to the tournament."

My mother always encouraged me to visualize a peaceful, calming place before ripping a friend a new one. Closing my eyes momentarily, the north fork of the Stillaguamish lay before me, the sun setting on the valley. A deep breath later, I continued. "I'm sorry, Harvey. I've forgotten why you wanted to see me. And please tell me it has zero to do my love life."

Harvey leaned back in his chair. Its sturdy iron spring groaned with effort. "There are actually a couple of things. First, I really wanted to make that trip. I worked the blasted schedule every which way to try to make things fit. Not only is there the time with the DA, but the domestic calendar's problematic. Martha's dad is headed this way, and it's probably the last time he's going to be physically able to do it. Martha can't handle him alone, nor is it fair I ask her to."

"I totally understand, Harvey. Really. I've known you long enough to know that you'd be the first guy on the team bus if it was at all possible. Don't get me wrong: You'll be missed, but I totally get it. You'll lose out on some laughs, though."

He returned upright in his chair and rummaged through his bottom desk drawer. "There's a lieutenant down there you should meet."

"Why? Do I look like a troublemaker?"

He stopped his search and glared at me. "You're taking ten eighteen-year-old hayseeds to a hard-body beach town where young girls might wear enough clothing to walk on the street. One of your young men could invite a young lady out for an adult beverage. Or something else." He dipped his head lower. "I got his vitals here someplace. Rob Suarez. We started in the bureau together on the East Coast. He might even be smarter than me."

I flinched at the uncharacteristic admission. "Let me write down the day and the time."

"Wiseass." He flipped a manila folder onto the desk, opened it, and waded through scraps of paper that looked like tiny restaurant receipts. He found the one he wanted and began transcribing the information on to a blank sheet of paper. "This guy, he knows his basketball, and his daddy was a grower."

"Citrus?"

"Nope. Avocados. They partnered with an old major-league baseball player on a big piece of land. The old boy even trotted out on Sundays to sign autographs at their farm stand."

I rose from my seat. "Tell me, Harvey. Why did Suarez leave the FBI when you guys were so young? I know your Martha was homesick, but…."

"He lost an eye. One night on the Carolina coast, a Guatemalan drug dealer crushed his face. Rob damn near died."

He handed me the page. "Sounds like a tough guy. Actually, he just might come in handy."

Harvey winced and tilted his head. "I thought you said you didn't expect any problems."

I looked toward the window and then back to Harvey. 'Remember the guy I told you about years ago? The one who hassled Cathy right before we were married?"

"Yeah. Mainly because you beat more than the snot out of him and nearly went to jail. Why the hell do you bring him up now?"

"Because he's going be down there. In fact, he's the freaking tournament director."

He glared at me. "God almighty, Ernie. Why put yourself in this position, knowing the guy is going to be in the spotlight down there? Sometimes I think you've hit rock bottom and started to dig!"

"The kids could use a memory, a week on the beach."

"Don't make it a memory of you pummeling on some old man they've never seen. Move on. What's done is done."

"That would be William Shakespeare."

"Get serious. Just for a minute. You were chosen for your example and reputation. It's not just about you."

Weary of the sermon, I stood to leave. "How about we go down there, the kids put on a show for all the nation to see, and kick ass in the tournament?"

"Sounds like an admirable goal to me."

"Then, I kick the guy's ass."

He rubbed his eyes, then slowly shook his head. After a moment, he continued in a lower tone. "Jesus, man, grow up. What do you think Cathy would want you to do?"

SEVEN

"You're healthy as a horse," said Dr. Timoteo Mesa, as he released his stethoscope, completing my annual physical. "A lot of guys who are fifty-two take meds for something. Or want meds for something."

"Don't forget I take those weekly injections for MS."

"That's a different deal and up to you and your neurologist. The guy you're seeing is a good man. I'm just your friendly family physician."

"Yeah, but I've known you longer."

While I trusted the doctor who managed my multiple-sclerosis care, I valued the opinion of the man the local kids called Tim Table. He served as my basketball trainer, a part-time scout for nearly two decades. On the court, he came between refs and me and saved me countless technical fouls. Off the court, he provided trusted advice. From Ace bandages to sex education, he put kids at ease. That extended as far as taking them in. Case in point: Trent Whalen, whose parents left him high and dry a few years ago.

While slipping on my socks, I said, "Did the neurologist send over my latest scans?"

Timoteo turned to face me and crossed his arms over his spotless white lab coat. "Look, I told you before. I am not the guy to read those x-rays. He is the specialist; I'm not."

"But he says the same thing every time. No real change in

progression. Says I'll probably live a long time with little difference in movement."

"Then why in the hell don't you believe him?" Timoteo moved closer and pointed down at me. "You continue to feel sorry for yourself because Cathy's gone. For some reason, you think your days should be numbered with the MS."

"Bullshit. I put that behind me a long time ago."

"You say you did, but it didn't happen, Ernie, It DID NOT happen. For some reason, you're now drinking your brains out, screwing everything that moves." He sat down on a stool opposite the observation table. "I think there's a piece in you that still feels responsible for her death. And it's crazy. She had complications that nobody could have predicted."

I tied my shoes and sat back in the chair. "You haven't said if you will come on the tournament trip."

He hesitated and pushed away on the rolling seat. "Trent wants to go, but I'm still trying to clear the time. Candidly, I'm a little pissed that you changed the subject."

"I need to tell you something. Something that has to do with the trip." I took a deep breath. "Cathy was assaulted about two years before we were married. I always wondered if it had anything to do with how she died."

"Christ, I am so sorry. How—"

"We were both working at a basketball camp on a lake, not far from her home in Northern Michigan. Former college players from around the country were invited as counselors. Anyway, one night this guy had a lot to drink, took her down to the beach, and jumped on her. He didn't get inside her, but he cracked two of her ribs. I got there just in time and nearly beat the guy to death."

Timoteo dropped his arms and leaned his head against the wall. "Oh my God, man."

"So, guess who's the tournament director of the Pacific Waves?"

"That guy?"

"Bingo. One Mr. Gordon Alderete. If you come with us, you just might be lucky enough to meet him."

He sighed. "Sort of begins to explain your recent behavior." He ran a hand across his forehead. "Look, I get the anger. I really do. But going down there and taking it out on him is not the way to handle this. Especially after thirty years. Why would you set yourself up for that? And in front of your players? What kind of message does that send?" He lowered his voice to a murmur. "Yes, he hurt her. And she's gone. If you're looking for the next Cathy, you will never be satisfied."

"You sound like a freaking shrink. Maybe we should move this session to the couch in your office?"

"Look, man, nobody forced you to come here." Timoteo paced, tugging at his chin. Then he pivoted toward me. "It might be a good idea for you to get back into coaching. Full-time. This all-star trip could be a good first step for you in more ways than one. Learn how to compartmentalize. Manage your emotions. Just like you've always coached our kids to do."

I leaned forward, elbows on thighs. "You know, I've always thought that night was related to how she died. What he did to her on the beach—"

"Nobody could have predicted Cathy's last hours. She had the best possible people at this clinic. Pulmonary embolism is a rare but known complication of pregnancy. She got that clot deep in her leg from the prolonged immobility of the difficult pregnancy."

I shook my head. "You knew her. She was in great shape."

"It can happen to a completely healthy person and be severe, even fatal," Timoteo said. "The docs told you all this. The deep vein thrombus broke off and traveled to the blood supply to the lungs. The clot was large enough and blocked the two main arteries supplying the lungs. Add that to her compromised immune system. It just happened so damn fast. Given all those factors, I doubt an assault many years before had anything to do with her death."

I sat back. "But you don't know for sure. And this is no big-city hospital."

"No, I don't! And, we didn't have time to get her to Harborview in Seattle. Remember?"

"God, do I remember," I muttered.

"I can guarantee you all docs worth their salt would say the same thing about the assault. But you continue to tear yourself up about it, and knowing you're going to see this guy Alderete has made everything worse. You must move on, man." He opened a drawer and chose a notepad and pencil. "I'm going to give you the number of a good person to talk to."

"It's more than that."

"More than what?"

I brushed off my pants as if they were littered with lint. "I should have been there."

"Been where?"

"With her that night at camp. I was asked to play in a pick-up game at the local high school. I knew Gordon had the hots for her, but I went out and played anyway as a favor to the organizers."

"Oh, come on. How in the hell could you have known that it'd go that far? I'm sure there were a lot of guys looking to move on her."

"Still, I could have been there. Prevented it."

He handed me a slip of paper. "Call this person. I think you'll enjoy him."

"A real shrink?"

"Yes, and an avid cyclist. Loves bikes, maybe even more than buckets. Don't take long to do it, either. Put it off, and you're in deep shit. You need to deal with this before you go. Otherwise, I'm going to have to wonder if you accepting this coaching gig is nothing more than a way to get at this guy."

I rose to leave and held up the note. "Thanks for this."

He prolonged a blink and took a deep breath. "Give yourself a break. None of this was on you. And, despite what you want

to believe, it's not on this Alderete guy, either. Forgotten is forgiven."

"Wait. That last part. Gandhi?"

"No, one of your guys. Mr. Lit Teacher. F. Scott Fitzgerald... Look, you have to slow down. You can't keep looking for the next Cathy every night. You'll never find her, and you'll kill yourself trying."

"I thought you said I was healthy as a horse."

"Get the hell out of here!"

EIGHT

I SAT AT THE BAR AT TONY'S PLACE nursing a beer, waiting for a late-afternoon Caesar salad and a big slab of hot garlic bread.

"Didn't see you come in," George said, checking his meat order slip from the butcher. "I'd say you look down in the dumps, but the dump is over by the airport."

I shrugged and spun the cold glass in my hands. "I've got a week to cancel the SoCal hoop trip or lose the deposit. As you well know, I'm not rolling in the green stuff and am on the hook for the up-front dough. I wasn't going to put that risk on a parent."

George flinched and scrunched up his face. "Well, hurry up and do the deal. Pull the trigger."

"Without a freakin' legit point guard? Right now, I got six guys. Six! How on earth can I take a team to an elite tournament and expect to be good with six players?"

George tossed his file on the bar. "I thought the deal with Deacon Joe got handled. Didn't you tell me the Cheese was on it?"

"Linn was going to check on it, but I haven't heard from him." I took a big slug. "Christ, I hate this."

George angled his hairy forearms on the bar. His gold watch glistened on his wrist, leading to long, thick fingers. "How in the hell would you return the cash you raised? What you have? Two dinners here and a couple of car washes at the high

school?"

"Three car washes. And I think the same cars got washed every time."

Jessie McQuade swayed through the dining room toward the bar, destined to grab as much notice as possible. She held her back straight and wore a fabulous light gray skirt in a loose weave, topped by a yellow cotton blouse. She clutched a white sweater in her hand and used a reddish shade of lipstick that matched her flat shoes. She smelled like my neighbor's honeysuckle bush.

"Well, look who's eating alone again tonight," she said, circling a hand on the back of my down vest. "I'd invite you over, but I don't think you'd enjoy the hen session."

I glanced at her, then picked at the salad. "Just as well. Wouldn't be a good conversationalist tonight."

She dragged her arm around me, then dipped in, her nose inches from mine. "Sorry to hear that. Why the frowny face?"

I smirked and reached for a piece of bread. "I don't know if this basketball trip is going to come together. Can't get enough players to commit, and the deadline is right around the corner." I chewed on the bread. She looked in my eyes, then past me toward her table before snuggling close to my ear.

"Well, I'm committed. To wearing my new bathing suit in the sun. You'd better find a way to make this trip work."

"Really, if this happens, my time down there will—"

"Gotta go." She smiled and slipped away.

I flipped the fork against the bread plate, drawing Patsy's attention. She arched an eyebrow. "Girl trouble? I'll take those problems any time with a guy." The comment didn't surprise me. For years I found her kind. But I also found her to be one of those clever people who needed to respond to everything, particularly things they knew little about.

I lifted off the stool, wedged my size-thirteen desert boots between the brass kick rail and the floor, and stretched my calves, alternating right then left, head down, both palms on the

edge of the bar. After a few rotations, I paused, then began again. The voice from behind me sounded familiar and tired.

"I think it's going to take more than one person to move that bar," Linn Oliver joked. "And all of my muscle at the mill just punched out for the day."

I sat back down and signaled him to join me. "Beer? You look exhausted." I signaled for Patsy, who said she'd send George over.

"Crazy night," Linn said. "Had a fully loaded tractor-trailer go off the Stanwood Road last night. Driver said some kid tried to pass a car comin' the other way. Made our guy veer into the ditch. Logs all over the road. Blocked two driveways."

George tied a fresh white apron behind his back and pulled two draught beers from the spigot in front of us. "Sounds like a mess," he said, filling the frosty schooners. He spun two napkins on the bar and placed the beers on them.

"It was." Linn took a gulp and closed his eyes as he savored the taste. "Thank God nobody was hurt." He gazed at George for a moment, and then at me.

"What?" I said.

"And that's not all the bad news."

I feigned a collapse, then focused on the ceiling. "The hits just keep on comin'. OK. let's have it."

"I found out why Deacon Joe's mom got in touch after all this time. Turns out the Seattle Explorers offered her a car." I rested my forehead on the bar a bit too hard. "Pick the model. Open-ended deal, no payments, no strings attached. Probably for as long as he plays on the team."

"Christ." George shook his head. "Recruit the mom and the kid will follow."

I sat up and massaged my neck. "Y'know what? A lot of college coaches recruit the mom. Can't say I'm really surprised by the strategy." I turned to Linn. "But Deacon Joe? I mean, really? Deacon Joe?" The young man grinned so wide that he nearly dribbled his beer. He pinched his nose, and his eyes

watered. I felt the brew could spew from any facial orifice. "What? What is it?"

"The good news," Linn giggled, "was he told her to pick out the biggest, fanciest ride she could find."

"Hey," George broke in. "I'd do the same thing. It's his ma."

"But get this," Linn snickered. "He also told her that he had signed with the North County Selects."

"What?" George asked. "Help me here."

"She hurt him and got really pissed. The reason she contacted him after all these years was that car. She only called when she found out what was in it for her."

He reached into his jacket and tossed a signed hold-harmless agreement on the bar. "I'd like to be there when she tries to pick up the rig." I stared at the paper and exhaled.

"Dust off your flip-flops, son," I said, a grin cracking my face for the first time all day. "Looks like we're goin' to play buckets by the beach."

NINE

It took weeks of creative ass-kissing and a few high-paying commissions before Cookie agreed to cut me loose for the tournament time. And, despite her earlier disavowals, she also cut a serious check to help underwrite expenses. Which didn't surprise me in the least. Besides George and his dad, she's the most generous person I know, yet always makes you sweat before handing you the towel.

After several high-level meetings with parents, chaperones and sponsors, the powers-that-be decided that assistant coach Cheese and I would head up the land brigade of the North Counties Select traveling team bound for the Pacific Waves Tournament in the comfy confines of my 1986 VW bus. The air division, led by Dr. Timoteo Mesa and Diane Chevalier, would fly into LAX, rent an additional van and work out any wrinkles with practice times and hotel rooms before the land gang arrived. Splitting up the troops saved us money and guaranteed some in-bus time, allowing my passengers to get better acquainted. The sports shrinks love to call it team bonding.

Linn and I also decided we'd play overnight stops by ear. While I'd driven to the Bay Area several times in a fourteen-hour straight shot, I'd never deadheaded to the LA basin without stopping for at least a nap. If needed, Linn could easily crank up his cell phone and get a last-minute online rate at a roadside motel or contact our former local sheriff who'd moved

to Paso Robles to grow almonds and grapes. His bunkhouse would fit us all in case we needed to rest five hours north of our destination.

Having Linn in the shotgun seat brought back a variety of memories traveling to games, tournaments, and even the Clallam County Corrections Center to visit a deranged booster/gambler who once beat up Linn and left him for dead. Why? Because he missed the final shot in the state championship game. Cheese rebounded to become the freshman coach at Washington High, coordinate its summer league, and work full-time as the office manager in his family's timber business. If he still suffers ill effects from that fateful time, or from the fateful game, I haven't seen them, and I think I see him pretty clearly.

Linn prepared several comical yet useful documents stuffed into individual folders for our three passengers—Deacon Joe Gonzales, Trent Whalen and Kyle Rochester—including a three-page brief on in-vehicle travel etiquette. It contained a long list of topics that ranged from talk time on cell phones and the need to contribute approved snack foods for frequent consumption, no alcohol and drugs at any time, to their requisite signatures on a sternly worded flatulation proclamation. Linn stated that he was the self-appointed music sheriff and revealed that selections would be heavily weighted to oldies and casual country. Passengers were allowed to use earbuds and personal music players, but not during group discussion periods.

There will be mandatory conversations on basketball and life in general, Linn's note read. *During these designated periods, all passengers are expected to interact and contribute.* I wondered aloud if the traveling bus trip would render college credits. The close quarters did spark conversations never brought up at the spring-break tournament in Seattle because the players rarely gathered outside of practice and games. Any insights into personalities, mannerisms, and preferences were derived from experiences on the court.

The kids quizzed him on an assortment of guy topics, from condoms to barbecued chicken, yet sat captivated by the atmosphere surrounding the title game in the cavernous Seattle Center Showplace. They were also mortified by the thought of a career-ending injury. Kids are like that, expecting a life of springy knees, perfect sunsets, and immortality. I'm sure Linn was like that once upon a time, yet he survived introduction to mortality, and he had no problems with answering every pointed question the kids raised about it.

I cringed at the title-game reference. I thought about it every day, because the loss was on me. I should have rested Linn, forced him to take a break. Exhausted, his jump shot tweaked the front rim and caromed off, eclipsing the dreams of an entire community. We were linked for life, the kid who missed the game-winner for the Fighting Crabs in the state championship and the coach who couldn't get it done with a once-in-a-generation player. But if it took that, and everything awful that happened after that, for us to have the relationship we have today, then I could accept that. And have. And by all indications, Linn has gotten to the same place.

"Shit," Kyle said. "I can only dream about playing at state, getting that far. But having the chance to win it all on a final shot? I'd crap my pants just dribbling down the court."

Linn turned in his seat. "No, you wouldn't. You'd be ready, just as Coach had us ready."

I shook my head, then glanced out my window. "Don't. Just don't go there."

"Had I been set, legs under me, that shot would have gone down."

"Your right knee was trashed!" I shouted. "You played that last quarter on one leg! I was out of my mind for asking you to take that shot." The bus fell silent. Embarrassed, I checked the rearview and nobody made eye contact. All sat sullen, chins down.

Linn filled the void by explaining the logging injury he

suffered the summer of his junior year. A choker cable gave way while on a thinning job for his family's timber company, sending a freshly cut Doug Fir down a slope. It crushed his right knee and pinned him to a rock outcropping. Surgeons repaired the hinge, but it was never the same.

"We'd played three games that week," I said, feeling a need to clarify. All eyes darted my way. "He began to have trouble jumping, changing direction. Hoping against hope, I drew up the final play for him, his favorite spot left of the basket." I looked in the rearview again. "The coach was wrong, guys. Dead wrong."

Linn leaned over and pushed me on the shoulder. I smiled. "But he was still the best chance we had to win. Even on one leg."

After a moment, Deacon Joe said, "Hey, tell me somethin'. It's about your name. How did you come by Linnbert? I mean we're not talkin' Willie or Malcom here."

"Yeah," Kyle chimed in. "And then how'd you become The Cheese?"

Linn laughed and turned in his seat. "Linnbert was my mother's maiden name. Her grandfather came from the outskirts of London and got into coal mining and then timber near North Fork. A real pioneer. One of the businesses he co-founded is where I work now. Anyway, the folks named me Linnbert, but called me Linn most of the time. Linnbert when they were angry."

"And?" Trent said.

Linn grinned and shook his head. The boys waited.

"And?" Kyle said.

The razzing continued with the boys suggesting a variety of creative origins for Cheese. Linn bent lower in laughter, his head nearly grazing the glove box. "He got the nickname from a coach at a kids' hoop camp," I said. "But the guy who actually takes credit for it is the crazy radio announcer who calls the state tournament games. He'd seen Linn play in the semifinals and

was blown away by his performance. Anyway, right before the title game he says, *'I hope all you fans from Flintridge are bringin' the wine, because the George Washington Fighting Crabs are bringin' The Cheese!'* In about one day, the entire town of North Fork had it on their cell phones."

"Huh?" Kyle said. "I don't get it."

"Limburger is a type of cheese," I said. "Sounds like Linnbert."

"Yeah," Trent said. "I knew that."

"Sure you did," Kyle scoffed.

As we drove south on I-5, the troops settled in. Trent questioned Deacon Joe about the open-gym scene in Snohomish County, moved to his living situation, then his early childhood in the LA area. Basketball always seemed to be the comfortable intro into tender topics.

"I mean, a black-looking bro named Gonzales chillin' on the res?" Trent said.

Deacon Joe explained that his Mexican migrant mother married a Haitian preacher who "wasn't the same" after returning from Desert Storm, who disappeared for months at a time. His mother, Juanita, worked the grape vineyards in the San Joaquin Valley town of Visalia before moving to Hawthorne in southern California to be closer to her family.

"When I wasn't playin' ball, I'd help the janitor at my school," Deacon Joe said, apparently unoffended by Trent's comment. "People called me his illegitimate grandson. He showed me how to do jobs right—the first time. That was the worst part about leaving LA. That and my best friend, Terrell."

We bounced along in the bus, barely hitting the speed limit. I continually glanced up at the rearview mirror as the boys exchanged stories. Deacon Joe continued to answer questions about his childhood memories. He described the last time he saw his dad, "maybe ten-twelve years ago." Juanita pushed her husband, Pierre, out the door with a broken bottle, slashing his cheek before he left. Juanita moved Deacon Joe back to Visalia

and eventually to the apple orchards of Chelan.

"Apple harvest was everythin' to everybody," Deacon Joe recalled. "Work sunup to sundown. August through darn near most of October. Didn't see the inside of a classroom 'til it was done. I guess Mom couldn't handle it. Went to a weekend rodeo with some drifter. Never came back. That was a little over two years ago. I'd just turned fifteen."

The rest of the passengers sat mesmerized. I remember feeling the same the first time I heard the story.

"Whoa," Linn Oliver muttered. "Talk about tough times."

"Had she left you alone before?" Trent said.

"She would go away for a few days, but this was different. I hitched up to the Omak rodeo and looked around. Went over to Okanogan. Nobody was much help."

He clamped his arms across his chest and bent lower. After taking a deep breath, he continued. He'd not seen his mother since, and he landed on the west side of the Cascade Mountains as a construction worker.

After a moment, Kyle Rochester broke in. "I'll tell you what." Linn turned down a barely audible Toby Keith CD and turned to look at Kyle. "Having no dad would be OK with me. Sometimes, I can't do anything right." The bus fell silent, the whirl of its tires over the smooth blacktop suddenly louder. "And I know all about broken bottles. Four Roses. He'd make sure to drink it all first, though. Didn't want to waste any."

Linn shifted back in his seat, turned the CD off and raised his eyebrows at me. Of the three players in the back, two lived without parents, and parenting wasn't working for the one who did. While I treasured my dad's lessons, I had no experience on the father end and felt inadequate in an area outside my expertise. I'd dealt with plenty of guy stuff on the court and in the classroom, yet never faced the complexities as the head of a family home. The closest parental relationship I knew was the surrogate relationship I had with Linn because his father, an overworked obstetrician, regularly dealt with the pregnancy

phases of North Fork's mothers. All my passengers were young men. Certainly I could offer something. Had they been females, I couldn't even fake a solution. My problem-solving ability with women seemed nonexistent since Cathy died. I'd been paying dearly for doing nothing about it.

After a long silence, I offered, "Let us know how we can help you, Kyle." A feeble attempt. I wondered if the boys felt it, too.

Kyle's tone was even and matter-of-fact. "Yeah, well you can start help by telling him to stay the hell away from this trip." He let out a short laugh. "He'll probably get hammered, take my mom's credit card, and call the airline. He's got no clue how to work a computer."

A few miles later I said, "Can I call your mom? Would that be any help?"

"I'll try her at work tomorrow morning." I glanced up at the rearview mirror and saw him staring out the window. "You never know what you'll get phoning the house in the afternoon. It used to be just between cocktails and dinner. Now, cocktails can last all day."

As soon as Linn turned up the CW, the boys frowned and inserted their earbuds. Twenty minutes later, Trent popped his plugs and said to nobody in particular, "My dad could be a pain the ass, but I miss him." Deacon Joe and Kyle turned toward Trent as if uncertain what he'd just stated. "He'd get in my ear about my game, but most of the time he was right."

"I bet he didn't corner you after games," Kyle said. "Drunk and pissed. Having to explain every move you made on the court."

"Nah, that didn't happen," Trent said. "My mother was the one who was usually drunk and pissed."

Trent's random thoughts of his father came without hesitation. Linn turned to face him. I spent more time peering into the rearview than checking the southern Oregon road in front of the bus.

"The only times I was embarrassed on the court?" Trent said. "When he started that damn 'Be hard to guard, hard to guard' chant sophomore year. First time I heard it, I was like 'What's up with that?' Made me nervous as hell. Just wanted to find a flow, be smooth."

Kyle piped up from the third seat. "I wonder if that would have been better." Confusion creased his features. "Instead of waiting until after the game to let me have it. Y'know why my dad kept it inside of home? Because he didn't want to slur his words in public. Embarrassed the shit out of him." He paused. "Maybe if he would have gotten more of his anger out during the game, he would have saved my mother some hurt back at the house."

Deacon Joe caught me in the rearview. When we made eye contact, he stared out of the window, a fist cupped around his chin. He said to Trent, "But your dad knew the game, right? Stuff that he was telling you legit?"

"Oh, he knew the game," Trent said. "Great judge of talent, too. Just wouldn't shut up. He could break down the guy guarding me better than my own coach. That was something my mom didn't get."

Deacon Joe squirmed. "Just it. I don't know what my dad knew."

Linn squeezed his eyes with his fingertips and looked my way. I knew the candor surprised him, but he was pleased the kids felt they could air their laundry. One of my goals for the close-quarters group had arrived in spades.

"After a while, my mom wouldn't even come to my games," Kyle said. "Don't think she made one last year. Afraid the old man would do somethin' dumb." He backed up against the side of the bus, his legs extended across the bench seat. "There was a pee-wee game one time at the middle school. Probably a seven o'clock tip. The old man couldn't even stand up long enough to find a seat. God knows how my mother even got him out of there and into the car."

As the bus chugged through the Siskiyous, I pointed out the spot where Cathy and I had spun out behind a jack-knifed semi in the December snow while heading to the Huskies' 1992 Rose Bowl victory over Michigan. All her family made the trip from Traverse City, and the close call nearly ruined our reunion in Pasadena. I lost her a few years later. Ever since, I wished we'd crammed more road trips into those years.

Trent again popped his buds. He eased away from the seatback and leaned closer toward me. "What was it like, Coach? To lose her?"

My foot lifted off the accelerator, and I felt woozy. For a moment, I thought the kid had read my mind. Linn dropped his head and glanced at me.

"I mean, my parents fought and screwed around," Trent revealed. "Somehow, I don't think your situation was the same."

I swallowed hard and hoped I wouldn't have to dab my eyes. *Be careful what you wish for?*

"There's a lot of give-and-take in any relationship," I said.

"But I bet it was like, more even for you," Trent said.

All eyes were on me. Trent moved closer, his arm draped over the corner of my driver's chair.

"It was hard. Still is sometimes." I tried to hold it together. I cleared my throat twice, but the dryness remained. "I think what was important was the mutual respect. We didn't constantly remind each other of our shortcomings. "

"What do you mean?" Deacon Joe said.

"We're bonding, Coach," Linn laughed. Then, in a whisper. "I can feel us bonding. Hey, you'd never get to do this on an airplane."

I felt like I was back in the classroom with every kid's attention dialed into an out-of-school topic. Why didn't they have the same interest in Steinbeck or Faulkner?

"We let the little stuff go," I said. "Stuff she did that bugged me. She knew that I knew, so I didn't slam her about it all the

time. She'd leave two sheets of toilet paper on the roll and never change it."

"Barbara does the same thing," Linn mumbled. "Pisses me off."

"Exactly," I replied. "But you don't slam it down her throat every time, do you?"

Linn shook his head.

I checked the audience. "OK, that's the most basic example you will find. Cathy and I let that stuff go. We saved it for the bigger stuff."

"Like what?" Deacon Joe said.

I ran a hand over my head, wondering if the conversation I had hoped for would ever end. "The woman could not balance a checkbook." I laughed. "Drove me crazy. Every month."

"You mean she overspent the budget?" Trent said.

"We didn't really have a budget," I said.

"What?" Trent said. Kyle winced. Deacon Joe dropped his hands in his lap.

"How can I put this?" I said. "We never had a lot of money, so we never had it to spend. It's not as if we overspent on crazy things."

Kyle replied, "Wait, I thought you said she spent too much money."

"You got me confused, too," Linn said.

I took a deep breath and glanced up at the van's headliner. *How did we get so deep into domestics?* "OK. I never disagreed with the purchases she made. But the timing of some of them was a problem. Sometimes the cash wasn't there to cover the checks. I was a schoolteacher and coach, and she was a substitute nurse. We both knew that the sky was not the limit."

Trent slammed back into his seat, startling Deacon Joe next to him.

"My mom spent like crazy," Trent said. "She didn't give a damn if my dad hadn't sold a house in two months. If she saw something she liked, she bought it. Done deal."

"This is still small shit, Coach," Kyle said. "I mean, weren't you talking about bigger stuff?"

I straightened up and glared into the rearview.

"You got 'em goin' now," Linn snorted. "There are no stupid questions for the teacher. Remember, we're bonding."

I reached out and shoved his shoulder. "It becomes bigger stuff when you both know there's a problem but don't talk about it."

"I thought bigger stuff was like politics, sex, and religion?" Kyle said.

I bit my lip and continued. "Those are topics that need to be discussed and understood. We obviously didn't always agree, but we allowed each other the time to vent. We listened."

"No listening in my house," Kyle barked. "I don't think my dad even hears."

Deacon Joe pulled an apple from his backpack, shined it on his chest, and offered Trent the first bite. The big fella declined with a *thanks anyway* gesture.

"Like to have known my dad was in the stands," Deacon Joe said. "Just once. Didn't even have to be a game. Maybe just a midweek three-on-three. Anything."

"Even if he was on you about your game?" Kyle said. "Constantly?"

Deacon Joe chewed and swallowed. "Just like to show him *what* I could do, man. You know, let him see his kid next to other guys. Just like to see his face. S'all."

We bombed down the backside of the mountains, past roadside communities with old general stores and gas pumps out front. When we reached Lake Shasta, the boys remarked how low the lake appeared with previous water lines soaked into the dark brown perimeter. My eyes danced from Trent to Kyle, to Deacon Joe, to Linn. All were staring out the window. I smiled at the break in the action.

A few miles later, Trent said, "My folks were always fighting about something. Some people are in sync, though,

right?"

After a moment, Linn said, "That's right. I'd like to think Barbara and I are in sync. Bumps? Yeah, but in sync for the most part."

Trent leaned toward Linn, elbows propped on thighs. "So, what would you feel like if you lost her tomorrow? If she suddenly was no longer around?"

Linn eased back against the headrest. I glanced toward him, back to the road, then toward him again. He closed his eyes for a moment.

"I couldn't even begin to tell you how much that would hurt," Linn said. "Can't imagine trying to rebound from something like that. I know I'd never stop loving her."

Trent paused a moment and then said, "But you did, Coach. Right? You had to come back from that?"

I couldn't speak. I bowed lower for a moment, stretching my back, hands gripping the wheel at nine and three. Trent's eyes sought mine, yet I attempted to look away.

I gathered myself. I owed him an answer. "Some days are better than others. How can I put this? Trent, you're probably our best rebounder on the court. You know how some days you turn, block out your opponent, and then go for the ball? Well, sometimes I can't seem to block out as well."

Linn looked at me and blinked hard. His lips flattened.

TEN

THE DISCUSSION ABOUT DADS, COUPLED with the combo aroma of stinky socks, body odor, and stale cheeseburgers, enforced the need for an overnight break. After heated debates over the county's best barbecue and cutest women, I felt a need to clear the air. I asked Linn to dial Artemus Obermeyer.

While Paso Robles was only about five hours from our ultimate destination, the digs were free, and OB had a logical answer for most adolescent challenges. The retired former sheriff of Skagit County had been around the block with booze and women before entering law enforcement. He'd yearned to get back to farming in a kinder climate and grew Zinfandel grapes on a fifty-acre plateau northwest of town, thanks to his thirty-year state pension. We turned west off I-5 onto Highway 41 and reached his ranch shortly before suppertime.

"Last time I saw some of these kids they were playing Pee Wees," OB said, as the boys dropped their bags in the bunkhouse. "Now they probably don't even get carded in a tavern."

"Did you know all the bars in Skagit County now card everybody?" Trent said. "Except for old guys like Coach."

"What?" I laughed. "How in the hell do you know?"

"Say, before I forget," OB said, "Harvey Johnston's office called, wondering if you guys had arrived OK."

"That was good of him," I said. "I know he tried to rework

his schedule to make a couple of our games. I also know he loves swimming in the ocean."

OB tossed me a beer from an icy Coleman cooler, then popped one for himself. I thanked him, then swapped the brew for a can of Coke. "Actually, it was Jessie McQuade who left the message," he said. "Harvey probably asked her to call."

Linn sauntered over. OB wrapped his arm around Linn in a hug. "The Cheese looks like he can still play." OB smiled. "How's your mom and dad? Still enjoying Scottsdale?"

"They love it," Linn said. "They go to San Diego in the summer. Half of Phoenix moves there for July and August to escape the heat. People rent the same house every year. Unbelievable."

"You get down there much?"

"Barbara and I try to go a couple of times in winter. Get out of the rain. No mystery why people live there in February."

"Or November, December, January or—"

"By the way," Linn said, turning to Trent. "They card me every time. Barbara, too. We expect it."

"Well, that's understandable," I said. "Barbara looks nineteen."

"I'll tell her."

"Trying to get served is what guys do, Coach," Trent said. "Gotta give it a shot. Didn't you at my age?"

My face got warmer. "You're what? Eighteen?"

"Not quite, but soon."

"I'm pleased to say I had something to do with that new carding policy," OB said. "For precisely the same reason you're discussing right now. We had so many underage kids drinking and driving that we had—"

"My dad drinks and drives all the time," Kyle snapped, kicking at the dirt "Why didn't you do something about him?"

OB ambled toward me, his suede cowboy boots barely making a sound. "That's some question," he whispered. "These guys don't mess around."

"You should have been in the bus today," I said.

OB moved closer to Kyle, the young man fidgeting at his approach. "Son, it's hard to gauge how much is too much for any man. Most of the time, that's up to the bartender. Drinks affect people in different ways."

"But the bartender can—"

"Now hear me out. It sounds as if your dad's bartender should know better by now. He's putting a lot of people at risk."

"Mom's called the bar, but we're new to the area."

OB shook his head. "A lot is going on and probably won't ever be fixed to our satisfaction."

"Oh, great." Kyle sneered. "So he continues to be a problem for all drivers? Comes home plastered and takes it out on Mom and me?"

"It's more complex than it seems, son. Your dad orders another drink and appears fine. The bartender can cut him off, but he'll catch hell from your dad and maybe your dad's buddies. Bartender loses money as soon as he stops pouring."

"So?" Kyle waved his arms and stared off.

"So, it's difficult for a bartender to stop serving a grown man. Especially if he's a good customer. It's not right, but people are people. They make mistakes and typically give the drinker the benefit of the doubt."

I approached Kyle. "It's hard to put all this on any bartender," I said. "Your dad needs help. Until he gets it, he could drink anyplace. The bar, the car, the garage."

He scoffed. "Tell me about it."

An older woman emerged from the kitchen door, a white apron covering a flowered skirt. OB signaled to her and pointed us to a picnic table on the far side of the house. The boys feasted on grilled chicken and ribs, corn on the cob and coleslaw, and then moved to a nearby firepit for s'mores. The long hours on the road began to set in, and I dozed in the warmth of the campfire.

Trent mentioned that his present temporary living situation

with Diane and Nick Chevalier was working out well. The boys had become good friends and were so familiar with each other's moves on the floor that they each anticipated how the other would react to nearly every challenge. He also explained that Dr. Timoteo Mesa and his wife, Claudia, had offered to become his legal guardians.

"I've known the Mesas for more than twenty years," OB said. "If he and Claudia are successful with their formal application, you could not be in better hands. Except, maybe, for your coach, who hopefully one day will get off his ass and lock down one of the fine women who've been chasing him."

Trent ducked in closer to OB. "The players are kind of hoping he's going to do the deal with Diane."

"I heard that," I mumbled, eyes closed.

The vibration from my cell phone startled me. I dug it out of the front pocket of my jacket, checked the screen, and let the call from the Skagit County's Public Administration Building go unanswered.

* * *

THE NEXT MORNING, LINN STOWED the bags behind the back seat in puzzle-solving stacks with all the agility and fluid mobility of a doorman at the Ritz.

"Are you looking for a tip?" I laughed.

"Can't wait to get this show on the road and get these guys in a gym," he said. "Looking forward to putting this drive behind us. The boys are ready, too, except maybe for Kyle."

"What are you saying?"

"I guess the barbecue didn't seem to sit well. Heard him tossing his cookies outside the bunkhouse late last night."

I stopped and swept at the dirt with a shoe. "Now that you mention it, he did look a little green at breakfast. Where's he

now?"

"Still in the can."

OB followed Deacon Joe and Trent to the bus. Kyle appeared in the doorway, wiping his face with both hands.

"You about ready to blast off?" I yelled.

"I was born ready. I just can't seem to get a little soap out of my eyes."

We said our goodbyes. OB wished the boys well, and they piled into the bus. Kyle rolled on to the back bench seat, knees bent, face toward the ceiling. Heading to the driver's door, OB pulled me aside. "I know boys will be boys, but I don't think bad barbecue was the problem. Somebody got his hands on an adult beverage somewhere, and I got a feelin' that beverage was in my house."

"Good to know," I said. "That somebody hasn't had it easy, but we can't treat him differently."

He turned so the group could hear. "Now, you'd better turn these animals loose on somebody pretty soon," OB said. "Deacon Joe's so ready he can probably dunk."

The morning drive south down 101 brought brown rolling hills sprinkled with ranches surrounded by elegant wood fences and stately white homes, all topped with red tile roofs. Kyle rallied and sat upright by the time we passed the Santa Barbara airport, but passed on our street-taco lunch in Carpinteria. Two hours later, the boys got their first taste of a bumper-to-bumper afternoon on I-405 opposite LAX and soon grew restless about finding another route.

"Welcome to the fast lane," I said. "This is the way it is. All the time."

"Man, I get the road-rage thing now," Trent said. "Always wondered. There's not even an accident."

The canary yellow Chevelle with the babymoon hubs was parked outside Loyola Marymount's Gersten Pavilion, where I'd arranged for a quick shootaround. The practice session brought memories of hot Friday nights in Yakima when we'd

roll in from the apricot orchards, grab a quick shower, and then cruise the strip in search of coeds. If you were lucky enough to be the driver of a car like that, you were better than even money to escort a female companion to the Hamburger Handout. And maybe beyond.

Timoteo Mesa was waiting for us. He held out the keys to our rented team van and pointed to the gleaming Chevy. "Maybe I'll ask the dude if he wants to trade."

The driver with the wraparound shades stood, arms crossed, face to the sky, butt against the driver's door as if drawing energy from both the sun and the vehicle. His smooth, dark brown face featured a staccato stubble that now passed for trendy and gelled black, high-piled hair that would be well received over the hill in Hollywood. Well-developed biceps taxed his charcoal T-shirt and accentuated the matching dragon tattoos on the inside of his forearms. You could smell the street on the man.

"So, I'm readin' online the little man can still play a little bit," the driver said as our quartet paraded in front of the Chevy en route to my bus and the short ride back to the hotel.

The other North Counties kids from Timoteo's van joined the group, stopped and stared, equal parts wonderment and admiration. "C'mon, little man. Take you that long to recognize one of your ol' homies?"

Marcus McGann cocked his head to one side and then to the other. Trent Whalen shot a *No idea* shoulder hike at Deacon Joe, who glared, hesitated, then finally spoke.

"Terrell Dupree? You kiddin' me?"

"Got that right, little man. Right here in the flesh."

The two men slapped, then gripped a handshake before Terrell wrapped his left arm around Deacon Joe and pulled their interlocked fists into his chest with his left. "Been too long, bro."

"How did you know I was here?" Deacon Joe said.

"I still follow the game, man," Terrell said. "The local paper

listed the teams and rosters for the Pacific Waves. Hell, I knew there could be only one Deacon Joe Gonzales."

Deacon Joe dropped his gym bag and shook his head. "I mean right here, right now?"

"Called the paper. Guy gave me a number for the tourney. Tournament rep said your team is staying at the Shadow. Cruised over to the Shadow, and the guy at the desk said you were at LMU. Took me a while to get the info out of him, like he didn't trust me or somethin'. Nice digs, man. You guys must know somebody."

I stepped past Trent and offered my hand to Terrell. "Sounds like you really wanted to find us," I said. "I'm Ernie Creekmore."

Deacon Joe introduced me and all of his teammates who'd gathered in a half circle near the car. After casual fist bumps, Deacon Joe explained that Terrell was his old neighborhood buddy, classmate, and teammate in nearby Hawthorne. The two were always the first to show up at the local playground and played one-on-one games until other players arrived for three-on-three and then eventually a full-court contest.

"Still smell that hot blacktop," Deacon Joe said. "Hear those rusty 'ol chain nets as the ball went through the bucket. Man, those summer days'll melt your shoes."

I smiled and recalled similar games under the Yakima sun, and the countless knee scrapes that came from hitting the sandy deck, compliments of the valley's windblown grit and dirt.

"My mama held me back in first grade," Terrell said. "Thought the extra year would make me the biggest and best. I was the biggest and baddest, but this little man? Always the best. Didn't take it too good. Until I figured out what we could do together."

"Unstoppable," Deacon Joe grinned. He turned away from Terrell, his wide eyes dancing to each of his teammates. "Ran away with the Brick Brothers Two-On-Two tournament. Down in Torrance. Tell you we had a give-and-go move from every

spot on the floor."

"Nice." Marcus McGann nodded. "You guys'll have to show us. Especially what you did from the top of the key. Be great if we could create some more space between the circles."

"No problem." Deacon Joe beamed. He turned toward me, hesitated, glanced at Marcus, then approached me. "What about adding another guard, Coach? Terrell can play forward if we need him, too."

I rocked back and nearly choked. The players stared at me with *could we?* grins as if I had just been given passes to the local topless bar.

Terrell fingered a silver braided chain that culminated with an assortment of keys and fell from a belt loop of his close-cut chinos. Square-toed black boots, one crossed over the other, featured matching silver ankle circles fastened with thin leather straps. I pegged him at six-one, maybe a tad generous given the heavy kicks.

"Y'know, we could use another body," Trent mused. "I'm planning on winning a lot of games down here. Why I came."

"Yeah!" the group responded.

Before I could speak, Terrell bailed me out. "Whoa, whoa. Jus' wait a minute." He limped a few steps, imitating a person with a cane. "This body hasn't run a step in three years. I am definitely not your man."

"Ah, c'mon Terrell." Deacon Joe shrugged and wriggled his arms at his sides. "You can still go."

"Not today, not tomorrow. Ain't gonna happen."

I exhaled and massaged my forehead. I took a moment to explain that Terrell's eligibility probably would have been disallowed because he'd missed the roster submission and that his address was outside Washington state. Inwardly, I felt grimy. I'd manufactured excuses without the slightest hesitation, like a kid caught at an after-game kegger.

"No, I can't show any of them old hoop moves," Terrell said. "Can show you a good time, though. Get you into some

places you won't believe."

Nick whistled, and Kyle Rochester wiggled his hands as if he'd just handled a hot plate. Andre Holberton cackled and made a beckoning motion with his fingers. "Bring it on, baby."

I lifted my wrist and made a big show about checking the time. "Well, we better pack it up because we've got to check in back at the hotel." Pointing the boys toward the bus, I pivoted and shook hands with Terrell, hoping he'd remove the sunglasses so I could see the eyes behind the confident words. No such luck. "Good meeting you."

"S'all right," he said, turning away from me. "Looking forward to this tour-na-ment. Looks like you got some tal-ent." Then, in a louder voice, "Starting with this boy right here." He wrestled Deacon Joe into a friendly headlock. "The Dea-CON is back in town!"

The two repeated the handshake-hug routine, this time with more enthusiasm. The other players offered goodbyes, their intro fist bumps turning to cursory handshakes and backslaps. As they filed toward the bus, Deacon Joe fired a *see you later* finger at Terrell.

"Was gonna tell you," Terrell said. "I've seen him."

As Trent opened the sliding door of the bus and Kyle popped the cargo hood, Deacon Joe turned and spoke. "Say what?"

"You know. The minister."

Deacon Joe winced. "The who?"

"Your old man, dude. Found him pushing a broom at Staples about a year ago."

Deacon Joe raised his head and ran a hand down the side of his face. "You sure it was him?"

"Had that nasty S scar on his cheek, man. Anyway, I told him you were gonna be around."

"So, you saw him—"

"I tol' you. Yesterday, man. I try to give him some stuff to do, bring him some extra cash. I know they can't be paying him

shit at that place. Got him running some errands for me."

ELEVEN

NOW TRAFFIC BEGAN MOVING AT a steady pace, and I followed the directions Linn dictated from his cell. As we curled into The Shadow Hotel's spotless driveway, Linn's jaw nearly hit the floor.

"A Tesla and a Corvette?" he gushed. "What, are we stayin' in some rock-star place?"

"Yeah, baby," Deacon Joe said. "I've only seen that thing in a magazine."

"You've probably seen one," Trent said, "but you just didn't know it."

"No, this is it. Your tournament headquarters, gentlemen."

"Where's the pool?" Kyle said. "Place looks too small to have a pool."

Linn turned and glared over his seat. "You're here to play hoop." Then he glanced to the others. "Can we try to remember that?"

The boys unfolded out of the sliding door and stared open-mouthed, as if arriving at a place they shouldn't be.

I could feel the brows rise across my forehead. "This'll work," I muttered to Linn. "Now let's get these guys settled." We hopped down out of our seats and met at the back of the bus. I flipped open the tail hatch, and the boys separated and grabbed their respective bags.

As Deacon Joe pulled on his backpack, the yellow Chevelle

with tinted windows roared around the corner, stopped for a moment, and then inched at a near idle to the stop sign at the intersection. As we gathered the rest of our gear, the Chevelle rocketed away, its tires burning, sending threads of white smoke flying between matching palm trees on both sides of the narrow street.

"Well, it's been a while since we've seen that," said a trim, suntanned man in black trousers and an open-collar, long-sleeved white shirt. "I'm Myles Turpin, the manager here at the Shadow, and I understand you are the coach. I must apologize for the somewhat rowdy welcome you received."

"Ernie Creekmore." I extended my hand. "How did you know who I was?" Diane Chevalier smiled and waved from the inner lobby. She fit nicely with the other well-dressed people milling about. White jeans, white sandals and a flowing turquoise blouse with sleeves rolled halfway up her forearms. She made men stare, much as I was now. A slump-shouldered guy in an aloha shirt raised a hand to her in a goodbye wave. From behind, I guessed six-foot-seven, balding on top, hair that remained oiled, straight back. As he pecked her on the cheek, she closed her eyes and squeezed his shoulder. The man straightened and glided toward the far end of the foyer toward the restaurant.

Does she shut her eyes when I kiss her?

"Oh, I see you've met some of our group," I said.

"I have," Myles said. "Diane knows exactly what she wants."

"Tell me about it."

"Excuse me?"

"Oh, nothing. Long couple of days."

"No worries, sir. We'll get you guys squared away here right quick."

"Thanks. This is quite a place." A glossy banner showing a rolling blue wave cresting above a basketball covered the back wall above the sliding glass entry. WELCOME TO PWT . . . AND

FUN, SAND, AND SUN!

"We get excited about the Pacific Waves," Myles said. He extended the handles on two mammoth pieces of rolling luggage and hurried toward the front desk. Then, over his shoulder, "Even though it comes at our busiest time of year."

I slung a small leather satchel jammed with receipts and valuables over my shoulder and hustled to keep up. "Good to see tradition has a place."

"A lot of men in the local community played in the tourney. Including my father."

We schlepped our stuff into the lobby, where Nick Chevalier slapped hands and hug pounds with Trent and Deacon Joe. "Can you believe this place?" Nick crooned. "I mean, smell the food. And they'll bring it right here!" He pointed to a waitress offloading a tray of fish tacos and frosty mugs to a lobby table.

I signed in with the desk clerk, who handed me a sheet with the names and room numbers for players. He also handed me individual hoop packs jammed with toiletry samples, water bottles decorated with sponsor logos, and cheap embroidered wrist bands. Parents received Tyvek envelopes filled with shopping incentives at the South Bay Galleria, plus coupons offering two-for-one burgers, cocktails, and a free appetizer with two full-priced meals at nearby restaurants and fast-food outlets.

"Looks like you got the local celebrity," Nick said to Trent.

"Say what?"

"Room assignments have you bunkin' with Deacon Joe."

"S'all good," Deacon Joe said. "You snore, dude?"

"Naw."

"Bullshit!" Nick said. "The guy saws logs, big-time. Sometimes I have to stick in the ol' earplugs. And I don't mean for tunes, man."

Diane appeared from a hallway leading to the hotel's tiny convenience store, reading glasses perched low on the end of

her nose. She folded a newspaper into her purse and peeled a breath mint from a new roll. "Gentleman, let's not forget where we are." She abruptly snapped the glasses into a case, looked up and locked me in with dazzling eyes and a cheerful smile. She dropped her shoulders and exhaled. "Hey, there."

"What? You busy or something?" I joked.

"Don't get me started."

I pointed to the front counter, indicating a need to take care of business with the hotel. The clerk began to speak, but I didn't hear a word, still mesmerized by Diane's class and efficient calm. While Jessie McQuade typically brought dreams of one-nighters in the sack, I realized for the first time that Diane had entered the lifetime-possibility category. Dark hair laced with silver. Admirable figure. A beautiful woman even without makeup. Everybody knows absence makes the heart grow fonder. *But who in the hell was the familiar-looking big guy with the bad legs?*

"Hey! I asked you kindly not to leave your car there." All eyes turned to see a frazzled valet attendant follow Terrell and a heavily muscled bouncer type through the sliding doors. The attendant, who sported the hotel's signature white shirt and black trousers, indicated *I tried* to his boss and returned to his post. On his way out, he passed a young woman on the way in who looked somehow familiar. Maybe it was just the number of kids I'd seen like her in my classrooms. Her brows seemed darker than her hair, flatlined across her face. Strong, straight back and the legs of a dancer, she appeared as tall as Terrell. Hacksawed jean shorts showed more skin than fabric. She shimmy-shook to catch up with Terrell. When she lunged and jammed her silver-ringed fingers into his back pocket to snatch a cellphone, a healthy portion of her bronzed butt escaped its cover. Terrell failed to flinch at the filch.

Myles Turpin tilted his head to one side and stared at me.

Terrell tossed a set of keys to Mr. Muscle, whose longish hair looked like it had been combed back with a hand covered

in crankcase oil. "Oscar, find a spot on the street."

Terrell ducked behind the lady, placed his hands on her shoulder, and aimed her toward Deacon Joe. She squirmed.

"Renee, there's my boy," Terrell said. "Right there." Squinting, he pointed and curled a finger toward Deacon Joe, more of an aim than a point. "Renee, say hey to one fine dude. Grew up with this man." The former schoolmates embraced. Renee managed a barely audible hello, then spun to survey the room as if hired to plan a girls' night out. One of her shoulders gleamed outside a ragged chocolate shirt and held a black textured bag that was either an undersized briefcase or an oversized purse.

"Renee's got friends who can show your boys a good time," Terrell said. "Make 'em feel real good while they're in town."

Trent and Kyle backed against the counter near me, hands on hips.

"I'd feel real good if she'd show me the thong she's got on under there," Kyle whispered. "Probably black. Anything more'd show."

Trent rubbed his chin and appeared transfixed by the area below her studded navel. "And a tattoo. I'm thinking left cheek."

Kyle narrowed his eyes. "Tell you what. Ain't a helluva lot of room in there for more. Moves me from basic horny to genuine heartthrob."

Diane scurried to the middle of the lobby. "We need to get all the players to pick up your keys from me, find your roommates and get your stuff to your rooms. Now."

Terrell grinned at Deacon Joe. "Who's the take-charge homeroom babe? Could have used a rack like that at my school." Deacon Joe shook his head in a *not cool* sign.

Diane continued, "We need to get everybody back down here in thirty minutes for an early team dinner. Coach says you'll be free after that. I know some of you have asked about walking down to the pier. But remember, everybody's got to be

back here at the hotel by ten."

"Whoo-eee." Terrell laughed and whirled toward Deacon Joe, arms out like an airplane banking a turn. His antics brought chuckles from a couple of the players. "Think you can stay up that late, my man? I mean, ten o'clock's pushing it deep into the evening, don't ya think?"

Kyle smirked and cupped his mouth toward Trent. "I hope this Renee's bringin' one of her friends down to the pier. I'd like to get her opinion of the pilings. Including mine."

I grabbed the remaining key cards, a handful of receipts and eased away from the counter. "Take it easy, Kyle," I said. "Don't forget why we're here. I haven't heard you say a thing about basketball since we left Seattle."

"Sorry, Coach. Didn't think you heard any of that."

As I began to cross in front of Kyle and Trent, a distinguished-looking man who seemed better suited in a tuxedo than in his custodial uniform glided through the front door and pivoted left, then right, as if unsure he was in the right place. One of his pant legs was smeared in grease, making it darker than the other. Tight curls, more salt than pepper, highlighted a copper face lined by years of what seemed to be an overabundance of sun and apprehension. Below his left cheekbone sat a small S that looked more like a ranch brand than a scar.

Terrell stopped evaluating the waitresses and glared at the visitor. "What the—"

Renee moaned and pushed away from Terrell. "Mr. Pantel! How can I help you?" She looked like a nurse approaching a confused patient at a senior center. She whipped around. "You leave the man alone, Terrell. He wouldn't be here unless he needed something." Turning back to the agitated man, she said, "Is there somebody you're trying to find?"

Deacon Joe dipped around a trio of players in the middle of the room, squinting toward the commotion. He sidestepped Andre Holberton and slowly raised a hand while mouthing *give*

me a sec.

Terrell snarled and took a step toward the entry. "Man, WHAT are you doing here?" He stopped inches in front of the man's face and popped an index finger into his chest. "Did you make all the stops I told you to make?"

"I said leave him be, Terrell," Renee fumed. "This ain't your warehouse. You hear what I'm saying?"

The man snapped a series of nods, eyes wide. "I did, Terrell. Absolutely. All completed on time. I understood my son—"

Terrell faced him and folded his arms. Oscar strutted back in and shot Terrell a *what's up* signal.

"We got a problem here?"

Renee sashayed closer to Terrell, placing her shimmering black fingernails under his shirt buttons. "We ain't got no problem here at all," she said. "Do we, Terrell?"

Terrell shook off Oscar without glancing his way.

"Now," Renee said softly, turning to Mr. Pantel, "what were you going to say about your son? Before you got so rudely interrupted?" She glared at Terrell, who ignored the exchange because his eyes locked in on his employee.

"Did you sweep all the factory rooms and wash the black Suburban?"

"The tasks were completed," the older man said. "I believe you will find everything to your satisfaction."

Terrell edged closer to Mr. Pantel and continued in a condescending tone.

"Man, I wanted you to wait on this." He glanced over his shoulder. Renee stood, hands on hips, eyebrows flying. He said to the man, "How in the hell did you know where to find me?"

"I overheard a conversation at the warehouse. The young woman answering the phones mentioned to a customer that you were headed to the Shadow Hotel to meet a childhood friend. From what I'd been hearing, I assumed it was my son."

Terrell looked down and ran his fingers through his glistening hair. Mr. Pantel swayed from side to side, trying to

survey the area behind Terrell. He continued, "Yeah, well," Terrell said, "I wanted to explain to him that his dad—"

As Deacon Joe stepped closer, his arms collapsed at his sides. He stared open-mouthed toward the entry, his thin eyebrows launched high on his brown forehead.

"Deacon Joe? Is that my Deacon Joe?" The man slipped past Terrell and eyed the group of young people in the center of the lobby. Terrell turned and followed him. Renee scurried to keep up, her three-inch heels clopping on the stone floor.

"Hey, little man," Terrell announced. "Say hey to your pops."

"Oh, my God," Renee gasped. "I'm so happy for you."

Terrell's icy stare did nothing to reduce her smile.

TWELVE

DIANE REQUESTED A BLOCK OF FIRST-floor rooms, and I made sure that mine was buffeted on both sides by a parent or an assistant coach. I'd learned long ago that sharing an interior wall with a player of any age was not conducive to the ears, regarding both volume and information. Timoteo and his wife flanked me on one side, while Linn Oliver was on the other. Linn and I had planned on bunking together, but his girlfriend, Barbara Sylanski, called us en route, saying she'd booked a flight.

As I juggled car keys, bottled water, and briefcase outside my room, searching for my key card, Diane turned the corner from the lobby and headed toward me, animated in a cell-phone conversation. I raised an index finger to interrupt. She frowned and cranked an eyebrow. "Hang on a second."

Before she could lower the phone, I dropped the briefcase, wrapped an arm around her, and planted a powerful, deep kiss on her mouth while opening mine. It lasted more than five seconds, that pervasive timeframe tattooed on my brain by players unable to inbound the basketball. At about the four count, I opened my eyes and kiss-smiled when hers were still closed. Startled, she shook her head.

"I'm going to have to call you back." Diane looked both ways down the hall and slipped the phone into her purse. "You really have learned how to get my attention. The problem is I

might have to pay the price for putting that woman off."

"It didn't look like you put that guy off in the lobby."

She stopped. Her mouth formed an O of surprise. "Whoa, sir. Just wait a minute here. This call was business. It was about an installation we're doing for a big client in San Diego. The delicate equipment has yet to arrive."

"And the guy in the lobby?"

She took a wider stance and folded her arms in front of her. "Do I detect a bit of jealousy coming from the old coach? Besides, I thought we'd agreed to no affection on this trip." She chuckled and looked away. "Not to say that I didn't enjoy you breaking the rules."

"You didn't really answer the question."

Diane smirked then continued as if detailing facts to a cop. "The man in the lobby and I met a few years ago. One of the West Coast schools showed interest in Nick as an eighth grader. My husband was still alive, and we were new to all the attention. Gordon's interest in Nick seemed genuine, and I thought it was nice that he remembered him."

That first name confirmed my fear and suspicion. I dragged a hand down my face and looked away, recalling tears on Cathy's face as she lay pinned below Gordon Alderete on that beach, her plaid blouse torn, one bra strap pulled down. "Do yourself a favor," I mumbled. "Stay away from the man. A long way."

"What? That's a little dramatic, wouldn't you say? I know you distrust recruiters and agents, but do you ever grant any leeway?"

"Absolutely. But it's hard in this case, believe me. I'll explain later."

Her eyes widened as she stared right through me. A moment later, Diane shrugged it off. "Hey, look at the bright side of all this. If I hadn't run into you, I would have had to ask you for your room number." She glanced both ways, then settled her hands on the tops of my shoulders, cupped and caressed them,

then guided her warm palms down to my waist, looping her thumbs in my belt loops. "You see, I wanted to revisit those rules we made."

Kyle Rochester turned the corner and cleared his throat. Diane's face turned pink. "Ah, I'll dig out that information on meal times and get back to you," she said. "The hotel has set aside a small room off the lobby for our breakfasts, but I need to check on what other meals they have planned and where."

As she hurried away, I fell silent, trying to bury the image of so many summers ago. She pivoted, palms up, and flashed a *well?* sign. "Right," I said. "Just let me know what you find out." She looked at me as if I'd just arrived from Mars and continued on her way.

Smiling, surely with the precious dirt he could now spread to his teammates, Kyle strutted toward me. I jammed-pulled the key card and pushed the door open when the light blinked green. Stunned, I crammed my gear into the room, slammed the door behind me, and prayed Kyle had not caught a glimpse and banked any additional ammo.

Jessie McQuade stood before me, a light brown sheet wrapped around her as if she were headed to a fraternity party at Faber College. When her garb slithered to the floor, she wore nothing but a tiny silver basketball charm on a short sparkling chain. Had the necklace been longer, the ball would have disappeared in a wondrous cavern of shapely flesh.

"As you can see, I came to play." She slipped the chain onto her lips, guiding the ball back and forth slowly on the side of her mouth. She lifted her hands and curled her index finger in a *Come closer* sign. Gone was the weariness of the long drive. Heat returned to my cheeks, though I'd spent little time in the sun.

Dazed, I stepped toward her, uncertain if I'd pick up the sheet and cover her up or wrap my arms around her incredible body. I slid my hands down her arms and on to her amazing hips, remembering how her exquisite curves were so amazingly

soft.

"How did you get a key to—?"

Three heavy thumps on the door sent Jessie flying into the bathroom, clutching the sheet. I paused while she closed the door and then peered into the peephole. Deacon Joe. I opened the door about the width of my body. The young man appeared puzzled when I didn't open it more.

"Did you find your room OK?" I stammered.

"Yeah, just great, Coach. Thanks. I'm all square with Trent."

I hunched my shoulders in a *What do you need?* move and felt terrible as soon as I did so.

"Yeah, say, I was wondering if I could hang out with my dad for a little while. I asked Dr. Mesa, and he said I should probably clear it with you."

"Sure but stay close by. Check out the pier if you want to, but let's not drive too far out until I get some guidelines down with Timoteo."

"Got that. We'll probably just grab something to eat. Stay close."

"Yeah, well, I guess that sounds good to me. Have a great time. And use your head out there."

Deacon Joe winced and moseyed toward the lobby, displaying a different gait than the one that generally got him around. When he looked back over his shoulder, I got the feeling he was wondering more about where I was headed than his time with his father. When I turned back into the room, Jessie leaned out of the bathroom, two hands gripping the sheet under her chin. She grinned like a kid on senior skip day.

"I told 'em I was your wife."

"You what?"

"You asked me how I got the key to get in here. Well, I told the guy at the front desk that I was your wife."

I forced a humorless laugh. "Oh, great," I said, plopping onto a corner of the bed. "Just wait until that gets out. What on

earth were you thinking?"

She sat on the bed next to me, bringing an overpowering scent of roses. "I was thinking you could use a soothing massage after your long trip." The sheet slid from her shoulders. "And maybe a little deeper R and R."

I looked away, annoyed that I'd just asked one of my players to use his head when I wasn't using mine. Ernie, the hypocrite. "You could have called."

"I did call." She rose, fidgeting to keep her cover. "But you never answer your damn cell phone. I don't know why you even bother to have the thing."

I stood, one hand behind my head, and stepped toward the door. "I can't do this. I told you in North Fork I couldn't do this. I thought I was clear about bringing this bus to a stop, but it's obvious I did a lousy job. Sometimes I don't say exactly what I mean, and that's on me. But right now, right now I'm supposed to be in charge of a group of kids, and some might say their parents, who expect me to make responsible decisions on this little road trip. Suffice it to say you have not made it any easier to do that."

"You don't always have to be so responsible, Ernie. Things can be a lot easier than you think."

"Not here. Not now."

She tugged at the sheet, pulling it tighter. "From what I hear, the same rules don't apply to Diane."

I looked down and massaged my eyelids. After a long moment, I gathered myself and faced her.

"I have been wrong in not coming clean with you," I said. "That's all on me, and I apologize. But I need to make a clean break with you, and I am truly sorry it is happening this way. You deserve someone who is all-in with you, and I'm not that guy."

She sniffed and wiped a tear with the sheet. The eyeshadow left a smudge where she held the fold.

"I'm going to go now and try to make things right with the

people at the front desk. I'll tell them there was some sort of misunderstanding, I don't know. When I leave, please get dressed and find a discreet way to exit this building, other than the lobby, in the likely event a member of our party recognizes you."

"Ernie, I—"

"I'm sorry. Please, just do this."

I eased the door open, upset that I was forced to check the hallway for familiar faces, and carefully pulled the handle until the latch clicked behind me before walking down the hall.

THIRTEEN

THE BIKE PATH THAT STRETCHES from Pacific Palisades to Sunset becomes a separate corridor in Rubicon Beach. The old strand sits above the bike path, allowing walkers, leashed dogs, and casual beach cruisers their own lanes while the Lycra-clad road cyclists speed down a narrow concrete thread through the sand below. Surfers, with sand-caked ankles and water dripping from their wetsuits, made their way up the hill to feed parking meters or join the mess on the freeways. Parents ushered kids out of the way of online skaters smelling of Coppertone and street cologne while balancing umbrellas and beach chairs. Gorgeous young women I would have labeled co-eds years ago, those with the drop-dead figures and white T-shirts barely covering their bikini bottoms, yanked cell phones from large straw beach totes. Aging baby boomers in Hawaiian shirts and flip-flops shuffled toward a cocktail stop on Rubicon Avenue.

As I sat staring down at the action and the Pacific from a concrete bench above the strand, I felt as foreign to the culture as my dusty desert boots must have looked to the locals. What also felt foreign, yet undeniably titillating, was the separate and independent lure of the two women I'd encountered in the past thirty minutes. While Diane's intellect and class made her extraordinarily desirable and a better overall fit as a genuine partner, Jessie's bold, in-your-face physicality was an absolute turn-on. Particularly when she was naked. Even when I was

supposedly in an exclusive relationship with another amazing woman, Jessie got me aroused and ready in no time. A natural reaction, yes. I'd gone so many years without a woman's consistent touch and caress that I'd underestimated how much I yearned for it. The trees had gotten in the way of the forest. Time to trim and man up.

"Hey, Coach. Checkin' the talent?"

The singsong delivery was vintage Trent Whalen. He and Nick Chevalier crushed my contemplation and added to the perfect tourist picture I'd begun. Stripped to the waist, they displayed the whitest torsos in sight. Long plaid shorts, street shoes, dark socks and miniature white towels borrowed from a room at The Shadow. All we needed was a camera with a long black strap.

I removed my sunglasses. "Just clearing my head for the week ahead. You guys look like you got it all dialed in."

"I'll tell you what, Coach," Trent said. "I wouldn't mind takin' a few names and dialin' a few numbers."

"I thought you guys were supposed to have early dinner at the hotel?"

"We ran through the chow line, but we wanted to get in the water before the sun went down." He pointed to the volleyball court below. "How does she keep her butt in that suit when she hits?" He shook his head. "Can you believe this?"

Two cuties with barely enough clothing to be legal on a public beach toddled toward the switchback stairs leading to the sand. One pushed silky brown hair off her face and beamed at Nick. The other slowed, bent lower and peeked at Trent over the top of white-framed sunglasses.

"You dudes are tall."

The boys looked at each other as if they had ascended into heaven.

"Believe me, we appreciate observant women," Nick said.

The girls giggled. I felt like I was downwind of a Taylor Swift perfume factory.

"You talk funny," White Sunglasses said. "You go to college or somethin'?" She cranked her neck toward the waves. "Why don't you come and observe us on the beach?"

"We can do that." Trent tugged his chin as if in deep contemplation. "Absolutely. Coach, it's been great. But we gotta go."

Silky Hair stood up a little straighter. "Coach? You guys in town for the tournament or somethin'?"

"Observant *and* perceptive," Nick said, eyebrows high. "A lovely combination, indeed."

More giggles. White Sunglasses considered the statement, bouncing an end of her shades on lips loaded with peachy gloss. "Well, we just might have to come and see you play. We were cheerleaders at Mira Costa High."

"The Home of the Mustangs," Nick replied.

"Hey, I'm impressed." Silky Hair grinned, hands on hips. "How did you know that?"

"I like to be prepared," Nick said. "Always do my research."

I rolled my eyes.

"Of course, we *already* graduated," White Sunglasses added.

"Impressive," Nick mused. "Wow, did you hear that, Coach? Cheerleaders. I would not be surprised if they were students of the game as well."

I smiled, reset my glasses, and slumped deeper into the bench.

"Don't know about that." White Sunglasses laughed. "But we can teach you a thing or two about the beach. Now, take off those shoes. You don't really want anybody to see those down here. Put your socks in 'em and roll 'em up in that washcloth."

"You mean my beach towel?" Trent said.

Silky Hair laughed. "What-ev-ver!"

The boys sat on the strand wall and removed their shoes as if in a race against the clock.

"This sun and that water are going to take a lot out of you,"

I said. "We've got a lot of work to do tomorrow. Did you remember to bring sunblock?"

"Too late in the day," Nick said. "Right?"

I shook no. "Hats?"

Both boys smirked. *Clueless.*

"We've got some screen they can use," White Sunglasses said. "Besides, we're only going to lay out for a few minutes. It'll be chilly down there sooner than you think."

"Did you hear that, Coach?" Nick said. She dug into her purse and handed Nick a blue plastic bottle of Coppertone 30. He began to lather up and passed the cream to Trent. "All of this and sunscreen, too. Kinda unbelievable, wouldn't you say?"

"I would have to agree," I said.

"Maybe you should go get my mom and bring her down here," Nick said, "I'm sure she'd like to see the sunset. Maybe go for a swim. I know she brought a suit."

Four sets of eyes focused on me. After an awkward silence, I said, "Ah, yeah. Sure. Maybe I will."

The girls laughed and guided the boys as they balanced their gear and zig-zagged down the sandy steps on tender feet.

"Don't be late back to the hotel," I said. "Remember the curfew's at ten, but you'll freeze before then with what you've got on."

Trent stopped and looked my way, one forearm clutching his towel-wrapped shoes like a football. He flashed a goofy Heisman Trophy stance, the extended straight-arm, one thigh cranked high and in, and a broad grin. "Looks like we might have found a way to keep us warm." His eyebrows danced. "Anyway, I'm betting my roomie will be the last one back. He was sittin' shotgun in that guy Terrell's ride, and they planned on cruisin'."

* * *

WHILE I'D HOPED FOR A CALMER SCENE when I returned to the hotel, the chaos of check-in day continued. Our families greeted local friends, with some grabbing drinks in the lobby bar. Groups grew larger and louder and activity spilled into the main registration area. I dodged a young kid who darted across the sunken pit in the middle of the lobby seeking to nail his brother in an impromptu game of tag. As he bounded up the top step on the far end, he collided into the crotch of the guy who'd been so friendly with Diane.

Startled, the big man stumbled and forearmed the boy, nearly launching the kid into the pit. "Christ," the man barked. "You damn near crippled me!" His expression changed immediately to a broad smile when a couple toting beach chairs appeared ready to question his behavior. "How are you folks today? I hope you are planning to see some of our tournament games."

He then wheeled around and eyed the youngster, slouched and shuddering on a couch in the middle of the pit. "Son, I'm sorry. My mistake. You just caught me by surprise. Sometimes I just go off. I should not have done that. Will you forgive me?"

The boy pulled himself in, like a bird wrapping its wings around itself. The man swaggered away, his slick-backed hair glowing like a mound of wet black licorice. The arms were a lighter tint than the face and seemed too short for his massive height, giving him the look of a jumbo Pillsbury doughboy. His belly, hidden by a tent-like fuchsia shirt, flowed down and around, revealing a fully inflated spare tire. His clam-digger walking shorts stopped below the knee, revealing thin, scrawny calves. He wore tasseled loafers with no socks.

It was those chicken legs on that beefy torso that sent me down Memory Lane. I remembered them pumping, shifting above Cathy's sprawled body as he assaulted her on the beach that night thirty years ago. *Gordon Alderete, tournament*

director. It came as no surprise that Gordon had become el gordo. And, while I thought I'd prepared for this moment, even prayed for calm, my gut immediately knotted, and a cramp seized the bottom of my foot. Seeing him swat the youngster on the other side of the room hit me as if an opposing coach had punched one of my players. But what he had done years ago had taken a greater toll. I'd always wondered if his crunching on top of her had anything to do with losing her and our baby.

Trent Whalen stepped in front of me. "Coach, you in a zone? I yelled at you twice from the front desk. They need an adult to sign for incidentals. Don't know what it means." I fought the notion of looking away from Gordon. "Articles you might use in the room. Glad you mentioned it. No reason for you guys to use the guest bar, so I'll get Diane to collect the keys."

"Right." Trent grinned. "Wouldn't want any underage guys raidin' the minibar."

Booty Jacobsen's father, an international import-export executive, shuffled through the lobby, exhausted from a flight from Seoul. He was one of those guys who could wear a suit for a week yet look like he put it on five minutes ago. I thanked him for his effort to get here, and we chatted about the tournament field.

Marcus McGann interrupted with a large party of family members who had driven up from Huntington Beach to say hello and get Marcus settled. As I was introduced to his aunt and uncle, Diane crisscrossed the lobby and headed for the elevators, manila files in one hand and a small suitcase in the other. Gordon intercepted her, and she dropped her bag to shake his hand. Smiles all around, then an awkward cursory hug.

My breaths came faster, and I dug my fingernails into the palm of my hand. She showed him some pages from a file as he rested one of his meat-hook hands on her lower back. He dipped lower, attempting eye contact opposite her face. She continued to be pleasant and professional, holding up individual sheets

that probably needed to be filled out and returned to the proper businessperson. Smiles and high eyebrows continued as they worked through the folder. *What had gone on since I hit the road in the van?*

"Coach?" said Marcus's uncle. "It was nice to meet you."

Shaking off the scene, I said, "I'm sorry. Move-in day distractions. I hope you can make some of the games."

"I'm afraid we added to your disruption list. Best of luck in the tournament."

Embarrassed, I nodded. "Not at all. Thanks for coming."

Marcus walked his gang to the door and returned. "Coach, wassup? Seen a ghost? Maybe take a rest. Been a long day." He glanced at Trent and tilted his head toward the door. "And the hits just keep on comin'."

Renee returned, parading through the room like a runway model. She head-flipped her satin hair to the side then smoothed it with a professionally polished hand. She looked like she owned the place or occupied its most expensive suite. When she spotted Gordon across the room, she stared open-mouthed, raised her chin, turned and retraced her steps, spiked heels clicking over the tile floor. His eyes bounced from Renee to Diane until the double doors parted, and Renee slid into the front seat of a black Mustang.

"That girl lookin' for somebody," Marcus said, "And I'm glad I ain't that somebody."

"Think so?" said Booty. "I'm thinkin' she found what she was lookin' for and didn't like it at all."

Myles Turpin, the hotel manager, followed Renee through the exit and watched as her car circled out of the driveway. He turned, crossed his arms, and stared my way as more vehicles delivered arriving guests behind him. I pivoted to avoid his gaze while Marcus and Trent took off for the video-game room. I surveyed the reception area and bar for Diane but could not find her among the many groups chatting and sipping. I prayed Jessie was not among the minglers.

A short lap around the room produced no word or sighting of Diane, so I returned to the entry and posted up by the double doors, a prime spot for observing the lobby and driveway. After giving my cell number to a parent, I leaned against a support pillar and closed my eyes. I felt grateful for the momentary break and was surprised by the depth of my fatigue. A slight shove to my shoulder brought me back.

"Ernie Creekmore? Maybe you remember me. I'm Gordon Alderete."

FOURTEEN

"YOU LOOK GOOD, AMIGO. HOW long has it been? Twenty, twenty-five years?" His curious smile started with a raised, curled lip. Wet, weathered skin showed plenty of outdoor time without sunscreen or sunglasses. Deep crow's feet anchored both eyes. At six-foot-seven, the old power forward looked more like a retired defensive tackle who'd never missed a meal. I estimated his weight at two-eighty. Minimum. He smelled like Listerine and Right Guard.

"It's been thirty. On the nose." I checked his nose, now a too-pretty Greek job that screamed "plastic surgery." I recalled more of a hooked honker the night I broke it. Plus, he's Portuguese.

"Really? That's astonishing. I would never have guessed that."

Wincing, I said, "I guess we all have reasons for remembering times and places." I looked around for a person who could help me discreetly end the conversation, but there wasn't a candidate in sight.

"Amen." He presented a business card featuring his mug set inside the tube of a perfect blue wave. I looked from the card to the person, and back again. The nose, the tan and the raised-lip smile made for a very punchable face. A cluster of liver splotches highlighted his dark, ham-hock forearm. I flipped the card over and flinched at the number of bullet-pointed services

and qualities.

"Geez. Impressive. You've got a lot goin' on." I couldn't recall the last time I faked a shot at flattery.

"Yeah, well, I'm trying to spend less and less time in the office," he said. "Transitioning the real-estate business to a couple of agents who've been with me for years. The goal is to spend more time with community efforts. It's about giving back, amigo. Like this tournament."

"I've seen the asking prices of some of your listings," I said. "Either end of the deal would bring big bucks. A couple of those commissions would have me set for the year."

He snickered and lifted his cell phone from a lapel pocket. The two breast compartments could have held my sneakers. "You underestimate the cost of living down here. Shit, the property taxes alone probably cost more than a mortgage in your wet neck of the woods. Yakima, right?" He scrolled the phone, scowled, and slipped it back in. "Doggone GoPro. Should have shorted that stock." He looked my way.

"Born in Yakima. Living in North Fork now. On the west side, north of Seattle. More water than east of the Cascades. Not only from the sky but also to live on and look at."

"You mean, like rivers 'n lakes?" He shot a thumbs-up to a waitress delivering a Bloody Mary to a pinstripe suit at the concierge's desk. The suit gave her a thorough once-over as if he were measuring her for a bikini. She beamed at both men.

"Rivers, lakes, Puget Sound. If you don't live on it or look at it, you can get to it in ten minutes. Darn near anywhere. That's what I sell. Cabins, second homes. Starting to get a lot more of the people from down here coming up there. Trading miles for dollars."

"Nothin' down here lookin' at the water for under a mil. And that's a shack with a peek-a-boo view out of the bathroom window." After a long moment where I checked the lobby for nobody in particular, he asked, "Aren't you still coachin'? I mean, how did you end up with this gig?"

As much I wanted to tell the guy to go to hell and stay there, I decide to cut him some slack. "Since the last time I saw you, I went home and coached at a small school near Yakima for five years. Helped my dad with the apricot orchard. Took a job with a bigger school in a bigger league and was there for more than twenty years. Quit a little over a year ago. Doing some scouting. The powers that be recruited me for this thing."

He flattened his lips and looked over my shoulder. "Oh yeah? Why did you get into the property game?"

I grinned and looked down. The last thing I wanted to do was leave this guy the impression I couldn't get by on a teacher's salary and a coach's stipend. My house needed a new roof and furnace, and I felt at the time that a second job looked a hell of a lot better than a second mortgage. Besides, Cathy was gone. I had to do something with my extra time.

If Gordon wanted to go fishing about my past, I would, too. Maybe I could find the right moment to set a sharp hook. "My dad's fishing-crazy. He taught me early. Guys in his steelhead gang sold cabins on select rivers, mostly word of mouth. It got to be where more guys were lookin' than cabins available. I live in an area with a lot of primo streams and started to know a bunch of people through coaching and school. Did a little legwork, talked to a few boosters, former players. Got a salesperson's license one summer and went to work. One office run by locals. We do OK with riverfront, lakefront stuff, even some big places on the Sound. But nothin' like down here."

"Yeah, down here," Gordon scoffed. "Where the buyers are liars, and the sellers want the moon."

"Seems I've heard something like that buyer thing before."

"Hell, I ain't the first to say it. You show a guy a thousand properties over three weeks, then he ends up buying from some big-titted babe from another office. That's what's been grindin' on me, pushing me out the door."

We both stood for an awkward moment, pivoting both ways.

"Look, we're having a little reception later for tournament coaches and officials," he said. "I hope you'll stop by. You'll probably know at least a few people there. It'll give you a chance to thank some of the guys who are putting up the big dough for this thing."

Impressed, I tilted my head back, seeking more information. "I heard you put in a great deal of your own money."

He moved closer. Whoever tattooed his fake eyebrows probably crafted another creation on his body where the sun doesn't shine.

"Don't believe everything you hear, amigo. I can be very persuasive, especially with a business owner who has her heart set on a house. You heard of multiple offers? They're on most every house down here. I can get any offer in first place. For a price, amigo. For a price."

"And you can do that, how?"

"Please." He winced, taking a step closer. "Disclose my secret sauce? Let's just say I know people in this business. If I'm the listing agent, I just dress up your offer the best it can be for the seller. Eyeball the other offers when they come in, make yours better. Then your business just happens to throw a few bucks to the tournament, or to Helpline House."

"Glad I *don't* have any customers competing against yours."

He laughed and held up both hands. "That would depend on how much money you got! Just kiddin'. Say, look. I want to get you over to Helpline House while you're down here. It's really become my baby. We're getting some good local press. It's now got a buzz around town."

"It's a hub for food distribution?"

"We started that way in another building. Then I got my hands on a sixteen-unit apartment building next door to Providence Hospital. We completely rehabbed the thing, took it down to the studs. Now it's a home for unwed mothers, some battered. We get referrals from Catholic parishes, St. James down in Sunset, Our Lady of Guadalupe in Hermosa, American

Martyrs here in Rubicon Beach."

"What about the homeless?" I asked, thinking about my Quarter Lady in North Fork. "Women who've spent years on the street?"

"Oh, we'll take others," Gordon defended. "But those are the main feeders. We recruited teachers and instructors for pre-delivery and childcare. Also, pros with computer skills to help them get jobs when they leave. Vons Markets brought in a bunch of cash registers so the girls could train as checkers. Docs are just across the parking lot when it's baby time, or if we have any problems."

Duly impressed, I pondered if Gordon had produced his own personal penance. *Would it suffice for me? And Cathy?*

"Good on you, Gordon. You have to be pleased." He dipped his head with a shy smirk, the first time I could recall any hint toward humble. "Sounds like the place will make a difference." We shook hands, and he slapped my shoulder.

"Y'know, I don't think we parted last time on the best of terms," Gordon said. "I want to apologize for that, even though it was a long time and many cocktails ago."

"It has been a long time, and I appreciate you saying that."

"Yeah, I think it was one big misunderstanding. Remember that girl? Cathy something? She pulled me away from that campfire and took me down to the beach. She was crazy about me, wanted me in the worst possible way. Then you heard us and thought something was wrong. Remember?"

I got up in his grill, my face a few inches from his. Even though he was taller and heavier, I knew if we got into it, he'd tire after two swings. I felt my hands clench as my weight shifted from side to side.

"Whoa, amigo! Is there something I'm missing?"

"That Cathy something?" I lifted my wallet from my back pocket. I eased a college picture of Cathy from the back of the plastic inserts. The creases in the paper did not reduce the joy in her eyes. "She became Mrs. Ernie Creekmore. But, as you

say, that was a long time ago."

Myles Turpin scurried our way, glancing to his left and right. "Coach Creekmore! I'm certain Mr. Alderete still has several important people to connect with today."

"It's OK, My-My," Gordon offered. "We were just finishing up."

Forgive and be forgiven.

* * *

LINN AND BARBARA PICKED THROUGH a bowl of pretzel mix at the bar, each vying for the same target. When Barbara looked up and smiled on my approach, Linn dove in, trying to get the upper hand during the diversion.

"Linn knows I'm only after the cheese nibbles." Barbara smiled, then sipped from a frosty pint. "Now he's grabbing them all for himself."

I felt jealous of their simple game and easy companionship. "Don't tell me you guys are calling this dinner."

"Actually, we ate with the team." Linn swung in a half circle on his high-backed stool. "I stopped by your room shortly after they started serving, but there was no answer."

"Ah, yeah. I just needed some time to myself. The long ride and the close quarters in the bus took more out of me than I thought." I leaned closer to the bar and pushed around the coins near the bowl. "Speaking of quarters, I'm closing in on another set. You've got a New Mexico coin here I could use."

"It's all yours," Barbara said. She handed me the quarter, and she winced when I replaced it with two dimes and a nickel. "Are you still giving your sets to the homeless woman I always see near Washington High?"

I nodded. "She could use at least fifty quarters. A helluva lot more. She's been in a tough situation for years."

"She's camped under the grandstand at the football field," Linn said. "I even found her in the gym on a couple of Saturday mornings. Think she hid in the women's restroom until the Friday-night game crowd cleared out."

I look away, imagining her familiar blue tarps beneath the scoreboard. *There but for the grace of God go I.* Refocusing, I said, "So did I miss anything?"

"A couple of the kids had housekeeping questions, and Diane handled them," Linn said. "Dr. Mesa wanted to know if you wanted ankles taped tomorrow for practice and what time."

I nodded, and he added, "Some of the late-arriving parents were starving, so Diane went out and bought a bunch of box lunches from the deli down the street. She saved one for you. Nobody seemed to know where you went or what you wanted to do about dinner. Some of the kids have scattered, but others are hanging in their rooms." He grabbed the side of the bar, halting his motion. "You OK?"

Barbara suspended the snack-diving. "Anything going on, Coach?"

"Ah, no. Not really. I just needed to get a couple of things squared away. It took longer than expected."

After a moment, Linn said, "I spread the word for the players to meet in the lobby at ten. They're supposed to be back by then anyway. I thought we'd go over the schedule. As you know, there's very little practice time before we start playing games."

"Right, right. Say, have either of you seen Kyle? His stomach turned a little sour during the second half of the road trip."

"Not recently," Barbara said. "But I'm fairly certain he's in the building. A couple of the guys went down to check out the machines in the hotel gym not long ago. Kyle was in that group."

Linn whipped out a notebook and looked down the page clipped to the inside cover. "If he's not there, check 216. He's

rooming with Andre Holberton."

FIFTEEN

THE CONVERTED SINGLE ROOM, ICE-cold, with three mirrored walls, a couple of recycled Nautilus machines and an ancient stair-stepper, is a mandatory yet rarely occupied amenity in every boutique hotel. No soiled towels in the bin, no bottled water missing from the midget fridge. A Led Zeppelin CD blasted from an inexpensive boom box. Maybe the boys left because the tunes were no longer way cool.

I climbed the stairs, zigged a turn toward the numbered rooms that included 216, then zagged down the hall, reviewing my everybody-makes-mistakes talk for Kyle, adding that all team members wanted him to succeed. Ahead, a guy the size of a French armoire blocked the light from the full-length window at the end of the hall. I squinted and swayed, attempting to identify him or any possible partners. When I passed room 220, then 218, Oscar, Terrell Dupree's minder, waved a crooked finger back and forth in front of my face.

"You can't go in there." His breath stunk of cigars and red licorice, which I assumed were his stakeout staples. Maybe he went to the candy indoors.

"Excuse me, I'm just trying to find a restroom," I said, palms up, like a roadie attempting to get backstage.

He circled a finger in a turn-around motion. "You passed it back there, pal." He flicked his chin up.

"I'm sorry. I realize you're probably not a geography major,

but the john is closer *that* way"—I pointed over his shoulder, my arm buzzing his ear—"than *that* way." I stabbed a thumb in the other direction.

"Look, buddy," he hissed, leaning closer, shirtsleeves pulled up to show off overdeveloped arms. "I know who you are." He jammed a finger into my chest, nearly turning me around.

I cocked my head and stared straight at him. I was taller by two inches, but he had me by sixty pounds. Minimum. "If that is true," I said, "then you know that this busy and important person does not like to be touched by strangers in the hallway." As I stepped closer, he sneered and wrung his hands. "I need to use the men's. Now. Get out of my way or I might have to pee on your leg."

He grabbed me by the neck, pivoted, and slammed me into the door. A well-dressed woman in white high heels emerged from a room down the hall, hesitated, and scurried toward the other stairwell. When Oscar stepped closer, I gripped his damp polyester shirt below his shoulders with both hands and kneed him in the nuts, a move I thought was deserving of a WWF highlight reel. As his body lunged against mine, the door opened, and we toppled into the room at Renee's feet.

She screamed. "Jesus, Oscar, what have you done?" She stared down at me. "Ah, what exactly are you doing here?" The view of her straggly shorts from my position would not have made a family newspaper. When I push-rolled the big man off me, he groaned into a semi-fetal position, blocking the closet alcove. Behind me, a figure darted into the bathroom, slammed the door, and flushed the toilet.

"This is not what you think," she said, thrusting her hands in front of her. "I'm not here to party. I came here to talk, but I was a minute too late."

I shook my head. "I guess that's why you needed him outside." I got to my feet and thumbed at Oscar. "In case the talking got a little out of hand."

Myles Turpin turned the corner with the parking attendant and White High Heels in tow and approached the room. Oscar managed to rise to all fours, forehead just above the dark brown Berber, his legs sticking out into the hallway.

"Coach Creekmore, what in the world is going on here?" Turpin said. "We can't allow this type of activity."

"The lady was just explaining that she planned to take the conversation elsewhere," I said. "I wholeheartedly agreed."

Renee snatched her purse from the bed and patted Oscar on the shoulder. "We're outta here." The big man rose, used the doorknob to steady himself, and shuffled off behind her proficient wiggle, a hand to his forehead. Turpin's trio allowed ample space before following. I stepped back into the room, closed the door, and collapsed on the bed. A moment later, Kyle peeked around the bathroom corner like a kid caught in the middle of a dine-and-dash, traces of white powder on the sleeve of his maroon shirt.

"It looks like you've blown your second chance," I said, massaging my eyes. "The booze at OB's place. Now this."

Kyle surveyed the scene and covered his face.

"All before the opening tip of our first game. Congratulations, that's difficult to do." I paused, then looked straight at him. "You let the guys down, big time. It's not like we came down here with a ton of players. The few guys we've got will have to play a lotta minutes."

Kyle slapped the bathroom door. "My dad sends me a text last night, asking me if he can sleep on my floor. Then he sends me a text when we checked in, saying he was getting on a flight. Last thing I wanted. I couldn't handle it, so I scored some blow from Terrell in the parking lot."

I pushed up onto one arm on the bed. "I just wished you would have come to us. Maybe we could have called him and explained what you needed out of this trip. I'll find you a ride to the airport. I suggest you start texting your friends for a ride home from Sea-Tac. Now I've got to think about how to handle

your dad."

He slid into the chair in front of the television and stretched out his legs. He sighed and closed his eyes. "She wasn't here to do dope, Coach."

"Really? Had me fooled."

"She was here to get it back. When she found out Deacon Joe was related to that guy Pantel, she got pissed at Terrell for setting it up. She's just his smokescreen, window-dressing for guys. Won't carry."

"Why the muscle?"

"A couple of twenties from a pretty lady? Cash goes a long way to a guy like Oscar, especially when he's thinking he's carrying out Terrell's wishes. Renee showed up too late for me, though. Already used a little. It's too bad because she would've talked me out of the whole bag."

I stood and pointed to his gym bag outside the bathroom. "Too bad is right. Get your stuff together. I might just have to put you in an Uber to LAX."

He sighed and shook his head. Tears came to his eyes. "Gotta stop screwing up, Coach. Used my dad as an excuse for too long."

I stared at the floor for an extended moment. "Yeah, I hear you. I used an excuse for a long time, too."

"Bet you didn't hurt a team like I just did."

I swallowed hard and looked into his eyes. "I've hurt my share, believe me." After a moment, I said, "Now tell me, did anybody partner with you on this?"

Kyle smiled ruefully. "I'm the only one dumb enough. Other guys were offered, heard about it. Trent got into it with the guy at the door when asked. Marcus and Deacon Joe had to break it up. Got in between 'em."

* * *

I CHOSE TO EAT MY LATE-NIGHT Pad Thai take-out in the lobby, mainly to eliminate even the remote possibility of another private meeting with Jessie. There was the risk that some kid or parent had heard about Kyle, for whom I'd found a midnight flight from LAX back to Seattle, and I didn't want to get into that, at least not tonight, and so far my luck held. I hunkered down on a couch in the corner, looked around for possible meal-killers, and flipped the sports section of *The Daily Breeze* on the vacant cushions to preserve my privacy. Steam rose from the noodles, and the three-star spices dazzled my nose. I closed my eyes and raised the first forkful.

"What, no chopsticks?"

The reserved, direct tone sounded like a stadium rent-a-cop who checks backpacks. I pondered asking the guy to speak up or identify himself. "What?" I said, hoping it would net both.

"Harvey figured you at six-four. Even sitting down, you're the only candidate in the room who qualifies."

I sighed, closed the white food carton, and shook the man's hand, big and bronze like the foreman who ran my dad's apricot orchards. I wondered if he could grip two basketballs at once. "Can't do chopsticks anymore. MS. You must be Lieutenant Suarez."

Rob Suarez could have passed for a fit, six-foot-three Latino movie star with graying hair, despite the wandering glass eye that was a long way from the forest green of his good one. His trench coat worked for the heavy beach fog that felt more like a Seattle drizzle, but I wondered if he kept it in play when the sun came out. When he shuffled into the lobby of the Shadow, two fortysomething women in designer jeans and inflated lips halted their conversation and propped their eyebrows like dedicated fashion police. As they stretched their necks to check him out, the glass eye didn't appear to bother them.

His volume control remained locked on low. He seemed like the kind of a guy who probably didn't even raise it on his

kids. When I folded and moved the newspaper, he dropped onto the sofa and groaned like a much older man. "Bad knees. Plus a long night, and not terribly productive. I'd much rather have been sitting in the stands at the tournament."

"Do you go to the games?"

"Yeah. Try to hit a few every year. It's great because it goes all day and night. Drop in even when I'm working goofy hours and cases. A lot of the old players in the area come back, and most sit in the same seats every year."

Harvey mentioned that Rob starred as a sharpshooting forward at San Diego College, a non-scholarship Division III school. He played professionally for two years in Australia before returning home to his family's avocado farm south of here in Fallbrook. The two men met at the FBI's training academy in Quantico, where Rob graduated number-one in his class. Three years later, both had departed the bureau. Rob headed home to the Southland after losing his left eye. That same summer, Martha Johnston was accosted in Central Park, the last straw for her in Harvey's random assignment in the bureau's New York field office. Harvey divulged more than once that the move back to the Northwest probably saved their marriage.

"Do you still get out and run the floor?" I said.

Rob stood and shed the coat. "Naw, gave it up a few years ago. The knees went first and then the shot. They say the shot is the last thing to go. Well, it really went. It was strange. I felt like I didn't even know the hands shooting it. One day there was just no rhythm, no touch. Now, I get out on the bike when I can."

I flashed to my Saturday morning full-court sessions. They just became more precious. I wondered how many more realistically remained. When I looked up, a grandfather-type shuffled through the lobby hunkered over a brown plastic tray, a white paper cup anchored in each corner. He rested the tray on the cocktail table in front of the fireplace and distributed

cherry-topped drinks to three grinning Brady Bunch kids. "Don't tell your mother I gave you these before bed," grandpa said. *How long until I shuffled and hunkered? I'd love a grandkid to spoil.*

Rob ended the silence with a hushed narrative, a muted alarm interrupting my deep doze. I felt lucky we didn't meet in a loud restaurant.

"Harvey never would have forgiven me if I hadn't looked you up. He thought we have a lot in common, including hoops and farming. In fact, some of the Mexican and Guatemalan families that helped us with the avocados moved up to the Yakima Valley to work apples and apricots. Chances are, you might have known some of them."

When I started to respond, he continued in a procedural-cop voice. "But I need to talk about last night."

For some reason, his wandering eye connoted more intrigue. I pushed back into the sofa. "Tell me about last night."

"Let me first say that I work out of Sunset, but the neighboring departments share information. Torrance, Hawthorne, Rubicon Beach, El Segundo. All are aware of tournament week. Last night one of the Torrance officers stopped and questioned a group of individuals in a yellow Chevelle. The car had been speeding on PCH, quickly changing lanes. No turn signals, heading south toward San Pablo. The officer gave them a break, cited him for the turn signals. The driver claimed he was showing an out-of-town player around town. A mulatto-looking kid with a Spanish name."

"Deacon Joe Gonzales."

"That would be correct. Has this young man been known to associate with questionable characters in the past?"

I sighed and exhaled. "No. Actually, quite the contrary. He's a special kid who has done an amazing job given his circumstances. He grew up in this area. One of his old friends showed up at the hotel."

"Well, let me just say the plate and the car popped up on the

radar," Suarez said. "We believe the car has had more than one plate the past few years. It also has been seen at a warehouse in San Pablo that's been used for private parties, but its primary purpose is to move drugs. We have been targeting another passenger in the car, Terrell Dupree. We believe he took over a piece of the South Bay cocaine and marijuana distribution from one Tony Tautolo, a former bodybuilder who owed a lot of money to the wrong people."

"Did you lock up this guy, Tautolo?"

"I wish. An officer found Two Ton Tony in a Dumpster behind a Taco Bell in Lawndale. I wouldn't be surprised if a member of Terrell's posse put him there. The manager of the store told investigators that the wires to his surveillance cameras had been snipped. Guys knew what they were doing. Found a blind spot on a wall, got on the roof, and cut the cables from behind."

Suarez leaned in and put his hands on his knees. "It's only a matter of time with Terrell. He could very well end up like Big Jess. Your guy needs to know that. I'd hate to have this Deacon Joe in the wrong place at the wrong time. But right now, he's headed in a dangerous direction."

SIXTEEN

Most of the players slept late and blew off the optional team breakfast. I decided to let Deacon Joe do the same before we had our talk. Instead, I glanced at the tournament advance stories in the local paper, then set off to find Pierpoint Builders. I couldn't figure out how to look up the address on my cell phone, so I stopped to ask a woman wiping the tables outside Wahoo's Fish Tacos, down the street from the Shadow.

"You lookin' for a ticket?" the woman said, re-tying a damp red bandanna, her brows arched up in what I took as an expression of routine inquiry.

"To what?"

"Anything. Those guys got tickets to every event you ever heard of. Although the only sports thing going now is the Dodgers, and maybe the ponies down at Del Mar. You could probably get a bet down, too, if you had to, but don't tell them I said so."

"My lips are sealed." I simulated a zip job across my mouth. "Say, I thought it was a construction office?"

"Oh, yeah. They do some grunt remodels. Don't think they've built a home in a while. Say, did you want to order something to go?"

"No. I'm good, thanks. And I get there, how?"

She pointed west. "Down one and over one. Careful, you can miss it if you walk fast."

Pierpoint Builders had the type of peeling, weather-beaten storefront that ranked three rungs below funky, even in the laid-back section of a beach town. No color photos of custom beachfront homes dominated the window, no high-end remodels with white-water, blue-water or horizon views. The only indication that this was a homebuilder office was the faded sketch of a cartoon figure hammering nails on a roof with PIERPOINT written in block letters below it. If my broker ran this shop, she'd shut it down tonight and begin a major makeover in the morning.

The only person seated at a desk in the office appeared to have undergone a personal makeover hours before. Busty and blonde, she knew it and worked it, even though the person she apparently was trying to impress was on the other end of the phone. I grabbed a year-old *Outside* magazine and settled into a cracked vinyl chair with cold metal arms and a burgundy patch that looked like the state of Florida. Yellowed pictures of the Rubicon Beach Pier hung on the wall above me, including one of a giant wave bearing down on the curiously cool octagonal structure at the pier's ocean-side end.

The woman pushed back in her chair and raised both palms, signaling surrender.

"You're speaking with Dolores. No, I'm Mr. Wilkinson's personal assistant." She closed her eyes and shook her head, accentuating long, black lashes. "Actually, the check would be made out to Pierpoint Builders Escrow Account. No, Escrow. Right. E-S-C-R-O-W." She dropped her chin and rested it in the L made by her thumb and index finger. She finished the call and looked up. "English *is* a second language. Now, what can I do for you?"

"I'm looking for Mr. Wilkinson."

"Do you have an appointment?"

"No."

"Is he expecting you?"

"I don't think so."

"Well, I don't think he's available, but I will go back and double-check. Who are you with?"

"The Fabulous Football Forecast."

Her flinch told me I might be important. "Hmmm. One moment, please."

The room's peculiar smell brought me to my feet. I sniffed around trying to nail down a time and place for a similar aroma. There'd definitely been a deep-fat fryer. The greasy air probably rose up the walls and into the ceiling, escaping the pathetic paint job that was once robin-egg blue. My nose explorations gave me away.

"The Oar House," Dolores said, bouncing back to her desk. "Used to be The Oar House. Remember? Anyway, the owner lost his lease, and we were able to move in here. Great location, eh?"

"Location's the key to real estate."

"Mr. Wilkinson said he would try to be right out. He's on the phone at the moment."

I returned to the magazine piece featuring two climbers from Kitsap County, Washington, leading separate expeditions up Mount Everest. One was a former high-school basketball star. I wondered how high he could jump at 29,000 feet.

Ricky popped his head and shoulders into the room first, presumably to see if it was safe to enter. "I'm sorry, but have we met?" The ol' cowboy appeared to have been ridden hard and hung up wet. His perspiring, pockmarked face looked like it had been cleated too many times at the bottom of a scrum.

"Met, played, sang, drank..."

"Oh, Lord. It's Old School Ernie. Dolores, check this guy out. One of the toughest, six-four rebounding white guys ever to play the game of basketball."

"I have been checking him out." Dolores winked. "And I don't give a shit about basketball."

He waved me toward his inner sanctum. "Come on back, man, and tell me what you have been doing with yourself for

the past twenty years or so."

We walked past the front counter and down a narrow hallway reeking with the smell of restroom urinal cakes from two unisex facilities, one on each side. We entered a cedar block, garage-like bunker that had two rectangular picnic tables along the walls with six women who looked like Dolores's sisters.

"Welcome to Wonderland, Ernie. Where the bleached blondes are better lookin' than Alice and twice as dumb. Ha! Better add bitchin' beaches and big bucks, too." He slammed me on the back with a hand that felt more like a mallet. "C'mon into my office."

At six-foot-three, he'd clearly passed the burly category, up a conservative fifty pounds from his playing days. His gray snakeskin cowboy boots had to require the loss of several dozen reptiles, and the blue checkered shirt could double as a tablecloth in a Munich beer tent. His white hair was full and combed straight back. It would look fitting on a big-city attorney in a pinstriped suit. The silver belt buckle rimming his jeans looked uncomfortable, given his midsection.

"Pierpoint seems to be doing a blockbuster business, but I didn't see custom renderings on the lobby wall."

Ricky laughed and thrust his boots up on his desk. One heel was the size of my cell phone. "We build and sell some homes. We do. But I don't have the girls out chasing vacant lots. I found out there's a helluva lot more money brokering tickets than brokering homes."

"Are you still giving odds on games like you did when we were in school?"

"Not really. I got in trouble once, so I've had to lay low on that front. But, for guys like you . . ."

"A leopard can't change his spots."

"I guess you could say I'm that kind of an animal, but I'm not running through the forest telling others about it."

Dolores knocked and didn't wait for permission to enter.

"Mr. Wilkinson, the call you were expecting is on hold. The woman asked me to tell you she did *not* like being placed on hold."

Ricky threw up his hands and stood. "Just another happy client, Ernie. Guess I better take this. Hate to lose the opportunity of a lifetime. But, hey. Buyin' you lunch tomorrow."

We shook hands, and I slid a tournament pass across his desk. It included a ticket to the Coaches' Meet and Greet Cocktail Party.

"Well, looka here! Damn, dude. Youdaman! I'll be the asshole high in the stands screaming how you screwed up."

"A leopard can't change his spots."

* * *

THE FIRST BASKETBALL PRACTICE was a needed gift given the extracurriculars. But when Marcus McGann and Booty Jacobsen cornered me in the entry of the gym and asked to talk for a few minutes, I feared all my problems had yet to pass. The two boys exchanged awkward glances before Booty evil eyed Marcus to start the conversation. Marcus then chose to check the floor tile.

"We heard you sent Kyle packin', and we just couldn't believe it," Marcus said, his head still down. "Specially after what Cheese said about your time in the car. Said it was great."

Before I could respond, Booty said, "You're kinda leavin' us without a lot of players, coach. I mean it's not like we brought a bunch of spare bodies down here."

Andre Holberton dribbled a ball into the entry, stopped, raised his eyebrows, then picked up the ball and hustled through the inner door to the gym.

"I realize everybody is going to have to play more minutes

with Kyle gone," I said. "Particularly you two. But that's just the way it has to be."

"But we really need him," Booty whined. "He can play two, three different positions. You know that. Can you bring him back?"

"Oh, I get it. Believe me. But I needed him more to play by our rules, and he didn't get it done."

Marcus kicked at the floor, his sneaker fetching a quick squeal from the surface. "In the bus coming down," Marcus stammered, "Cheese said you were supportive of all the guys. Why didn't you support him now, give him another shot?"

I tilted my head to the side, took a breath and made eye contact with Marcus, then Booty. "Kyle got two chances. Two large ones. All of you would have. But you have to know the chance bowl is not bottomless. As much as I wanted to keep him, rules are rules. I had to send him home."

Booty smirked and looked away. "I hope his old man doesn't fry his ass for this."

"I plan to check on him as soon as we return home," I said. "I hope you guys will, too."

The rest of the players cruised in sluggish and slow, yet most of the rust and cobwebs dissolved twenty minutes into the session. Except for Deacon Joe. Lazy and aloof, the lightning-quick guard lacked any spark and waltzed through drills, keeping his distance physically and emotionally.

"Dude," Trent said. "You playin' or fakin'?"

"I'm playin', man," Deacon Joe snickered. "Believe me, I'm playin'."

Even at half speed, Deacon Joe guided the offense at a tolerable pace, somehow knowing how to operate on the fine line separating criticism and acceptance. We revisited an out-of-bounds play, discussed the tendencies of our first-round opponent, and announced Marcus would guard its top scorer. After the players divided into small groups for end-of-practice free throws, we packed up the balls and headed back to the

hotel.

Myles Turpin, the hotel manager, signaled to me as we entered the lobby. A man and woman in crisp white trousers and black linen tops stood to his side. Their lively conversation included cops and lots of pointing to their gold watches.

Turpin held up a pausing finger to the couple and turned toward me. "Coach, I'd like to have a word when you have a moment."

Timoteo studied the scene. "I'll get the kids settled, Ernie. You take your time here."

I waved my thanks, handed him my practice notes, and moved to meet with Turpin who pulled on his cuffed sleeves when he saw me coming.

"Coach Creekmore, this is just not working for us."

I squinted at him and folded my arms across my chest. "Really? What is 'this'?" I said.

The tailored and manicured couple shuffled over, inching so close to Turpin that he took a step back.

"Your party, staying in this hotel," Turpin said. "It has become too problematic on several fronts. For example, these guests say they were bullied out of a parking space last night by the same individuals involved at the entry when you arrived."

"Oh, come on." I barked at Turpin. Then, turning to the two slickers, "You do know those people are not part of our group."

"Look," the woman moaned. "We were scared to bring our bags in the door last night, thinking some thug would take a key to our Jag."

I winced. Her entitled whine wouldn't last five minutes in North Fork. Nor would the Jag. "I'm sorry, ma'am, but again, those people--"

Turpin broke in. "Those people are here because you are here. We simply can't afford to have our other guests feel uncomfortable. We would like you to vacate the hotel by noon tomorrow. I'm sorry."

My head dropped. After a moment, I said, "We've got our

first game tomorrow night. Please reconsider."

"I'm sorry, Coach. I'll expect your group to be gone in the morning."

The trio departed. As I contemplated my next move under the lobby's shimmering chandelier, an elderly woman with a tiny black poodle shuffled through the entry and stopped opposite me. She sighed when she considered the four-person line at the front counter.

"I'm sorry to bother you," the woman said. "I've been staying with a friend around the corner. Do you know if the hotel has any rooms remaining?"

"It will tomorrow."

SEVENTEEN

DIANE WORKED OUT A DEAL WITH the hotel to allow some of the parents to remain until the tournament concluded. Linn, Timoteo and I would relocate with the players to other digs. Several voiced their disappointment and aimed it at Deacon Joe. I couldn't blame them. It was the poshest place most of them had ever seen, let alone stayed in. Gordon Alderete telephoned Diane and said he "just happened" to have located a large, furnished home we could use immediately. I found it interesting that he hadn't called me.

The House That Gordon Found screamed pretension. Nouveau-riche on a narrow street in an established neighborhood. Four bedrooms, three baths plus an outdoor shower for sandy beach guests. A typical Spanish-tiled mansion popular in the area, set on a postage-stamp lot on a hill above Highland in Rubicon Beach. Like the house, I looked out of place. The heavy mist had me questioning why I chose sandals.

"Not bad, eh?" Diane said. "The weatherman says this should burn off by one. It will give us a better idea if we have a nice view. "The agent in me immediately noticed the impressive curb appeal. Mainly because the cabins I sell have no such amenity." She frowned, indicating that I should shift to a happier face. "Really, seems like a great find, especially given our circumstances. Glad we don't have a lot of cars to park.

You'd need a valet for a family reunion."

Diane snickered and checked her rental sheet. "Says here there is an alley entrance off Thirty-Third Street. Room for two cars adjacent to the trash enclosure. Garbage collected on Tuesday; recycling on Thursday. No yard waste."

"Good. Didn't plan on pulling weeds, anyway."

As we zig-zagged up the red brick steps, a woman in a bright long white blouse too small to hide her huge breasts, tight designer jeans and Nike running shoes waved to us from her house next door. She smiled and waited for us to draw closer. I thought she might be Dolly Parton's sister. "Hi. I'm Marsha, Marsha McKnight." We introduced ourselves. "Y'all be staying a coupla weeks?" Her lips belonged in a Botox commercial.

"Actually, just five nights, maybe six." Diane said." And we should probably apologize in advance. Several young men from a basketball team will be staying here. With chaperones, of course."

"Oh, I see," she mumbled. "I know Gorda asks for at *least* two weeks most of the time, 'specially during the season. But I know Gorda just *loves* his basketball." She shook her shoulders with delight, a cheerleader at thirty-eight. But more likely forty-seven without the facelift.

I dipped quickly behind Diane as if picking up a coin and whispered, "Everybody just loves Gorda."

She groaned and swiped at me. "Well, you were so nice to catch us and say hello." Diane grinned. "Rest assured, these boys will keep the noise level way down."

"'Preciate that, hon. I really do. Sumthin' don't work, just let me know." It appeared her wink targeted me and did not include Diane. "Maybe I know how to fix it. Bye now." She bounced away, circling her pink rose bushes toward the front door. I could have sworn their scent came from her body.

We approached the entry to our new headquarters, highlighted by a magenta-colored door in a bright blue alcove. The space appeared tight, and I doubted if anyone could

squeeze a piano or a pool table inside. Diane rapped five times in an easy rhythm.

"Gordon said he'd meet us here. I take it that's his car on the street." A white Lincoln rested nearby, its shiny hood aimed downhill, its tires cut to the curb.

"Maybe he doubles as a limo driver. Or leases the rig for proms."

When the door opened, I flinched at the sight of Gordon Alderete, even though I somehow looked forward to the face-to-face, especially after our interaction in the lobby. And his with Diane. His first words took an eternity and came long after a forced smile, preceded by the annoying lip twitch.

"Well, hello. Looks like you found me."

Diane, always charming, appeared charmed. "Thanks for taking the time to meet us. I'm certain you had other things to do."

"No inconvenience, I can assure you." Gordon beamed. "The owner is a close personal friend who travels extensively. He is out of the country at the moment and allows some of my clients to stay here from time to time. It just so happens he left at the last minute, and the home is available this week."

He waved Diane in like the proud owner of a jewelry store, then smacked my back as I passed. "Glad I could do this for you," he said.

"You definitely bailed us out," I murmured. Perspiration lined his forehead in the cool house. A huge aloha shirt covered his gut and looked like a yellow curtain covered with blue parasols. His khaki trousers needed pressing and drooped too low on his shoes.

"I hope this place is gonna work for you and your guys. One room upstairs is a big dorm." He made a grand display with his roundhouse handshake as if I had been called up on stage to receive a prize. His grip felt too soft and moist for a mitt so large. "I'm sure Coach Creekmore has told you we've met on the basketball floor."

"Yes, he has."

"And off of it, too," I said.

Diane eagle-eyed me while digging into her purse. "I'm sure you guys had a lot of games to relive over pizza and beer." She pulled out a cell phone and glanced into the living room which connected to a comfy den. "The home looks to be very well-appointed. Do you mind if I spin through and take a few photos? Wait till my friends in North Fork see this."

"Please, take your time." He pulled out a cell phone and punched it twice. "My only other appointment today is at the Helpline House later this afternoon. I'd love to give you guys a tour of the place. See all of the great things we're doing there."

I could feel my eyebrows move up. I ran a hand over the back of my head. "Sounds like a worthy project. I'm sure the community appreciates your efforts."

"I'll say," Diane exclaimed. "I bet you had to do a lot of recruiting and fundraising. Asking people to part with their hard-earned dollars can be very problematic."

Gordon grinned and sniffed. "Let's just say I can be persuasive when I have to be."

Diane gleamed and darted off toward the kitchen, pivoted, then opened a sliding glass door to the back yard, I peered down the hallway and eyed the family photographs above the stairs.

"You look good, Coach," Gordon said. "What are you doing to stay in shape?" He displayed no notion of an earlier conflict or even a meeting.

"We've got an old-boys game on Saturday mornings," I said. "Local guys, plus some of my former players who've come home. Ride the bike some. Seems to work."

"You can still run the floor? Shit, my knees were blown years ago. Most exercise I get comes from hoisting cold ones."

He snickered and looked toward the sliding door. "And discovering beautiful women."

Diane closed the exterior door and stepped toward the hallway. "Well, I think that little extra room adjacent to the

trash shack could be a nice space for a chaperone. It's a full-size bed—"

"It's actually a queen," Gordon said.

"A queen? Really? That's terrific." She beamed as if she scored free dinners for the team. "So maybe even a couple back there. And they can park literally next to their bedroom." She stopped and considered us. "What are you guys up to? Don't tell me you are still arguing over old basketball games."

"Ernie was just telling me he's the star of a weekly gym-rat game back home. Says the younger guys don't have a prayer of stopping him."

I looked away and smirked. "That's not exactly what I said, Gordy."

He stiffened. "It's Gordon."

"Well, he does stay in shape," Diane smiled. *Did I detect a wink?* "I know it's going to be difficult for him when it's time to give it up." She pulled out her rental page and glanced at Gordon. "I'm going to take a quick peek at the upstairs, and then I'll be out of your hair. If the rest of the bedrooms are as nice as the one outside, this will be a perfect place for us to stay—if the price is right."

As she ascended the stairs, Gordon caught her hand on the banister and placed his hand on hers.

"If you're negotiating the deal, I can guarantee you the price will be right." It was the first time I can remember her blushing. She finished her climb to the second floor.

Gordon's phone buzzed, and he took a call. He held up a finger, mouthed, *Gotta take this*, and circled around toward the den. As he slouched on a couch, I climbed the stairs and went straight through an open doorway to a bedroom that overlooked the alley and parking area. French doors opened on to a cantilevered deck composed of gray recycled plastic boards and outlined with a stainless-steel railing. The sun broke through dank, soupy fog. I stopped the doors open with the two polished rocks provided in a woven basket and bowed over the railing at

the far corner, hoping to see the ocean.

"This would be a nice place to have morning coffee," Diane said, surprising me from behind. She moved her hand across my shoulders and lowered her voice. "Too bad we won't be staying in this room together."

I turned, placed my hands on her hips, and stared down into her bright brown eyes. "Got that right," I whispered.

"Maybe it's the house or just the ocean air, but this place seems so much better for us than the hotel."

"You mean you and me, or the kids?"

"The kids, silly."

"Well, the air was the same at the hotel, but we don't have the lobby distractions." She lifted up on her tiptoes and pecked me on the cheek.

Gordon poked his head around the door, then began to sidle his big body up to the railing.

"Talk about a painful distraction," I said.

Diane pushed me away and hissed, "Do you think that was loud enough?"

"Whoops, sorry about that," he said. "Trying to be a help, not a hindrance." He danced his eyebrows like Groucho Marx. I thought he might fire up a cigar. "Why don't I meet you two lovebirds downstairs?"

After he lumbered out, Diane threw her purse on one of the twin Adirondack chairs at the other end. "Why did you have to say that? He clearly heard you, you know?" She edged closer and crossed her arms. "The guy is going to give us a great house, a great last-minute house. With a view in a great location. And... and you can't get over some manly thing that happened a lifetime ago?"

"Not so loud. There's—"

"I've heard some jerk lines from jerk guys, and what you just said definitely qualifies."

"There's a lot more to it than that." I stepped toward her.

She propped her hands on her hips and gave me a look that

said I'd best keep my distance. "I would hope so! Goodness. It's not as if we have our pick of any great big home around here."

"OK, I admit. It's a great house. Listen, I wanted to tell you about—"

"I mean, we were evicted, Ernie! Evicted. Sittin' on the corner of Desperation and Embarrassment. Then, this nice man bails us out with this castle, and you have the gall to call him a distraction?"

I waited, hoping the breeze would cool her jets. "One year at camp—"

She grabbed the railing with both hands. "Did you ever think what were we going to tell those kids' parents? Not just the ones here, but those back home? 'Hello Mrs. Holberton, the contact information we gave you for our hotel has changed. Why? Oh, we were kicked out for poor deportment. No, we don't know where we're staying. Maybe on the street.'"

I took a deep breath and blew it out hard. "Let me say something, please."

She turned, grabbed her purse, and headed for the door. "Not now, Ernie. You're just going to have to save it."

EIGHTEEN

AN EARLY LUNCH WITH WILKINSON began with the mandatory whatever-happened-to-former-teammates session, and we both had done little to keep up with anybody. While we received word of the passing of our former coach, neither of us made the memorial. Teaching and practices jammed my schedule, funds were tight, and the flight to Detroit was a stretch for a man who taught me a lot about basketball yet little about life.

"Treated me like the asshole I was," Ricky said. "Never did thank him for that."

"Speaking of old boys," I said, "How often do you run into Gordy Alderete?"

He swept his hand on the tablecloth to remove crumbs even though our server had just done so. "It's Gordon, as in sounds so professional Gordon. I love to call him Gordy or Gordo in front of somebody. Really gets his dick caught in a zipper. And I'll tell you what. He's got this area fooled. People think he's a saint for pouring money into this home for unwed moms. But he's still a snake. I got a feelin' *Gordon's* dough comes from the sale of a lot of white dust. He's got some freaking cagey characters under his wing."

"And you know this how?"

"Been in some back alleys myself, y'know? Had a gal bet a ton with me on Nevada State basketball. What chick would bet on an out-of-town college team? Because of the dollars, we

checked her out. Followed her to Gordon's office. Some kind of secretary. Right."

"Gordon went to Nevada State."

"Duh. Still one of its biggest boosters, hoss. Coach lets him in on the weekly media calls. Probably lets him in on a lot more. Like who ain't playin' this week? Can mean beaucoup bucks on a big-boy bet."

I took a sip from my Arnold Palmer. "So how did he get sideways with you?"

"Never forgot what he did to Cathy at camp. I heard about it the next day from another counselor and—"

"Don't want to rehash that now. Trying to move on. What else?"

He grinned and sat back in his seat. "How much time you got? Recession hits, and I got four spec homes listed on the market. Bank is hammering on me and doesn't want 'em back. Hell, they got a lot of builders in the same boat. I work out a program with them, saying I'll get renters for 'em. Month-to month. To pay my monthlies."

"That should hold off any banker for a while."

"But get this. Gordon smells blood. Knows a guy at the bank and goes behind my back, offering cash for one and lease options way below my cost on the other three. Bank says take it, or they foreclose. I end up paying a few bills, then I'm broke. Never really got back into it."

"I take it the neighborhood home builder turned into the neighborhood bookie?"

He laughed and looked toward the ocean. "Hey, I still do remodels for people, mostly smokin' hot single women. Keeps my best subs busy. But the games *do* come a-callin', hoss. Love the action."

"You always did." I sat up in my seat and took another drink. "Maybe you should talk to somebody about how much you love it."

He caught himself from spewing his beer. "No way, hoss.

Ain't there yet. Pays the bills and a helluva lot more."

After a few moments of awkward silence, he continued. "The main deal with Gordon? A USC bet. The same gal comes and wants to go hard on the Trojans against UCLA. Hell, I hate the place on general principles, so I decided to take it. Trojans lose big, I'm loving it, but my cash doesn't arrive. I call the gal. Says she needs a day. The guy who fronts my big action doesn't like it. We're talking dollars way above my pay grade."

"Don't tell me this woman suddenly quits work and quietly leaves the area?"

"No, she's still around. I've seen her in a few bars by the pier."

"But she still hasn't paid the friendly fiddler?"

"*She* didn't, but we eventually got our money."

"Not before you had to break her fingers?"

"Hey, c'mon. Maybe the big boss would, but I'm not going there. Anyway, about a week after the cash is due, I'm sweating bullets. Out of the blue, the office gets a call, saying an envelope will be delivered at noon. I think nothing of it, we get deliveries all the time. Minding my own business, right? I walk out for a sandwich. Here's this yellow Chevy pulling to the curb. Smoke-show Latina gets out dressed to the nines. No smile, all business, big purse. Goes inside, takes out what looks like a brown shoebox, lays it on the counter, and then bails. Didn't say a word."

I stiffened, hoping my interest didn't seem too obvious. "Don't tell me you accepted payment in coke."

"Oh, hell no. Can't stand the stuff. But it didn't look good. Stacks of twenty-dollar bills with rubber bands. The girls in the office got kind of scared. I mean, I'm a homebuilder with legit clients."

"Right."

"And a nasty thirst." He raised and circled his index finger.

I mouthed to the server that my drink was good and then waited as a young couple rose and walked past our table to pay

their bill. "Tell me. Are you into the big boss for big dough?"

He drained the glass and shook his head. "Nah. Was once, but we got it figured out. Try to stay away from the betting action in the spring and summer and pound nails, install cabinets. But college football in the fall? Too tempting. Start jonesin' for that juice. Toss in the World Series and pro football and bam! Bookie's trifecta, hoss."

"Or disaster."

"Hah! Know what? *That* is the time of year I could get into trouble." He laughed and rested a palm on the side of his face as the waitress delivered a frosty brew. After she cleared the empty and wiped a wet ring, he said, "Come to think of it, I damn near went under one year during March Madness. Some brilliant beginner bet Butler and took the points. Your boy here took a big-time hit."

"Has Gordon taken any big hits?"

He considered the question for a moment. "I'm only one of several guys taking action around here. I heard he was into a thug over in Hawthorne for twenty-five K, but who knows? He does have a rep of getting fast cash, and I don't mean your corner ATM." He flicked his eyebrows and bobbed and weaved like a boxer. "Tell you what, though. He took a big hit on the cute co-ed in the office. Senior at LMU. Cornered her coming out of the ladies at Ercoles on Rubicon Ave. Ripped the top button off her blouse. Wish I coulda been there. Would've stuck his head down the john and started flushin'."

* * *

AS I PREPARED TO SCHLEP ANOTHER LOAD of players, balls, snacks, and backpacks to our new headquarters, I second-guessed my magnanimous offer to include Ricky in all tournament festivities. The lunch session provided enough

catch-up material to last a few decades and the prospect of sitting with him, heavily cocktailed for another couple of hours, felt like a fight waiting to happen. Not with me, but with some boisterous braggart who thinks a dislocated toe was the only reason the NBA didn't draft him twenty years ago. I'd forgotten that Ricky turns on every light with a sledgehammer, then waits for somebody to complain about the glare.

Maybe I'm just a piss-poor listener and friend to people my age. Like Diane.

Kids are different. I can hang with kids for hours, hear their troubles, marvel at their wonderment and experiences. But adults? I often look forward to an event, then can't wait to get home. I became so accustomed to the comfortable, silent moments with Cathy that I never realized how many years it took to get there. I mean, how do you return to that place? Was I young enough to relearn the dance with somebody else?

My knees buckled when the leading candidate for that possibility waltzed through the side entrance of the Shadow with Gordon Alderete, one of his big mitts periodically brushing her back, his monster mug dipping low to her face to better hear her delightful words. She smiled way too much and displayed a light orange shade of lipstick I'd never seen.

"Well, look what the cat dragged in," Gordon said, with a slight slur. The tacky saying had long sat atop my can't-stand list, and for years the speaker rested right there with it. "You never got a chance to explain to me how provocative this woman was." He'd covered his aloha shirt with a light jacket and paired it with black slacks.

I shrugged and swept the floor with a foot, my legendary ah-shucks move. "It's not as if we've had a ton of free time, Gordon."

"Oh, Ernie," Diane bubbled. "The fish was simply fabulous. A poached petrale sole with a pinch of lemon. And... and the view. Oh my God, the view was out of this world!"

"Almost as good as that bottle of Chardonnay," Gordon

beamed. "Or was it two?" He bent over close to her when he asked the question, laughed, then so matter-of-factly said, "Really poured well, didn't it?" He pointed at me. "Think it was from one of those wineries up by your place. Yakeema."

"It's Yakima. More than one hundred of them are in that area."

"Really?" he said. "Didn't know hayseeds could grow grapes. Whoops, sorry, Coach." He cranked up that raised-lip smile. It made me wonder if the amount of work done on his face was the result of flashing it in the wrong places and at the wrong times. He waved at a familiar face across the lobby and shot him a thumbs-up.

Diane shook her head and giggled. It was more of a re-set than a genuine show of joy. "Anyway, Gordon took me to this cute little place south of the Rubicon Pier. The cutest little couple run the place. Only about eight, maybe ten tables. White linen tablecloths, cutest local artist work on the wall, some of the kids. It was so—"

"Cute," I said. "Sounds like the cutest place ever."

She shrugged and frowned. "Right." She looked up at me with eyes more sad than glazed. "Why do you have to be like that?"

Gordon sniffed, assumed a wider stance, and began swinging his arms back and forth at his sides. "Tryin' to blow a beautiful day, bro? Just because you weren't included?"

A young, athletic woman in running shorts and a Hennessey's Tavern T-shirt pranced through the lobby bar, then stopped when she saw Diane. The woman flinched and inched closer. Diane looked up.

"I'm sorry," the woman said. She touched Diane's arm. "Do you know these guys?" She then whispered, "Are you OK?"

Diane snapped a few OK bobs, followed by a smile that preferred privacy.

I scratched my head and stared at the floor. "Just a little surprised is all." I pivoted toward Diane. "But more jealous that

you got to take this lady to lunch down here before I did." Diane dipped her head, checked me for a long moment, then gazed into the distance, those light-orange lips now muted and flat.

"She obviously wanted to go, man. Or she woulda said no. Right, babe?"

Babe?

Diane didn't respond. She turned her back on us, yanked a tissue from her purse, and stayed glued to the window.

"Right?" Gordon asked again and still no movement or sound. He smirked at me. "See, now you got her all upset. Christ, you're acting like she's got to ask your permission or somethin'."

My neck popped back. I could feel my eyebrows soar and turned my head to conceal the look.

Gordon turned and clapped his hands. "Well, I gotta go get ready for our big meet-and-greet. You probably heard about it, Coach. Gonna be there?"

I gave him a thumbs-up. "Wouldn't miss it."

He walked closer to Diane and spoke to her back. "I'm kinda hostin' with Diamond Jim. Gotta give a little talk." Turning toward me, he said, "Maybe have another glass of wine. Or somethin' a little stronger."

We sunk into an awkward exit moment, not unlike wondering if the homecoming queen would kiss the king, even though she was going with another guy. Gordon walked over to Diane and put his hands on her shoulders. "See you soon, babe." He then smooched her cheek from behind. He smiled and winked at me, then strutted away. "See you there," he bellowed. "I'll be the handsome dude on the stage."

I waited a moment and approached Diane. "Have you really planned to see him soon? Babe?"

She began walking away, through the lobby and toward the guest rooms. I followed, and she picked up the pace. When I drew closer, she waved her arm behind her back, tissue in her hand. When she waved again, I stopped.

"This is how we left it a few hours ago," I said. "But you were still talking."

I turned, and the white-haired lady with the black poodle I saw yesterday in exactly the same place nearly tripped me with her leash.

"I thought you were told to leave," she sneered.

"I guess by more than one person," I muttered.

NINETEEN

THE COACHES' MEET AND GREET Cocktail Party on the lower level of the Diamond Jim Brady Prime Rib Restaurant drew the usual suspects, plus a few retired players from the area who made a mark in college or stayed just long enough to grab a cup of coffee in the pros. A varied group, in age and body size, stood in clusters outside the banquet room, nursing iced tea or lemonade while others slammed down bottle beers or Bloody Marys. Some seemed about as wide as they were tall, especially the power drinkers. I wondered how they ever got up and down the floor. I'd invited Wilkinson, who cleaned up reasonably well for the event in a magenta bowling shirt with falling pins on the back. Timoteo eyed the crowd, seeking the top celebrities.

"Heard Paul Westphal's supposed to show," Timoteo said. He pivoted and arched his head to his left. "That's Ernie Woods over there. Went to Washington State. Won this tournament with Mira Costa."

A trio of local sportswriters buzzed the huddles, seeking a few old-boy lines for their next post or print edition. One guy said he remembered me from two different occasions, but I could not place him. Somehow, he recalled that I grew up on an apricot farm in Yakima. He said he'd just returned from Australia where he earned a decent living playing and coaching for nearly twenty years. He recalled "lighting me up for twenty-

two" in college, stating the month and year.

"Dated an Aussie in school," the man said. "Followed her home. Lucky girl."

A young writer scribbling nearby flinched, then jumped into the conversation. "Sorry, who'd you follow home to Australia?"

Timoteo closed his eyes briefly and tried to stop a laugh. The writer obtained some cursory ammo and moved on.

"I'm sorry," I said to the unidentified subject. "Where did we meet?"

"Many moons ago. I put on a shooting clinic one afternoon at a coaching camp in Maine." He seemed proud of his work, even now. "You were there with Gordon for a couple weeks, I guess. Speaking of the man," he glanced behind him to see Gordon strut past in a gray seersucker suit, "I guess we're ready to start. The guy has done a great job with this thing and in this community." He walked away, through the doorway leading to the luncheon tables. I never did get his name.

Out of the corner of my eye, I recognized a short, dark-skinned individual in an all-black server's uniform with glistening jheri curls collecting empty glasses and bottles from the attendees on a round tray. I excused myself from Timoteo and Wilkinson and moved toward Pierre Pantel as he began to clear a cocktail table. "Pierre, thanks for coming to practice yesterday."

His eyes darted to every corner of the room. He balanced the tray on the table, looked behind him and turned, using me as a shield to a majority of the group. Some sort of makeup concealer softened his facial scar. "Thank you for all you have done for my son," he whispered. "I can see he enjoys what he is doing."

"It's been a pleasure to—"

He juked as if dodging a thrown bottle. "Terrell doesn't like me taking other jobs. He prefers that I always be available."

I squinted back. "But Terrell's not even here. What do you

have to worry about?"

"You'd be surprised." He stretched to look past me. "At how fast word can spread."

I tried to survey the room without altering my stance. "Obviously some of these guys are going to see you here. What's the big deal?"

He angled his head toward Gordon. "It would not be acceptable if some see me speaking with you. I must excuse myself. I will attend the games, if possible." He collected two cocktail glasses and balled up used napkins.

A microphone shrieked in the adjacent room. "Gentlemen, if you would please take your seats, we've just got a few short messages before we let you go. I know some of you have games this evening."

Pierre ducked away with the tray, weaving toward the swinging kitchen door like a lithe scatback bound for the endzone. I glanced at Timoteo, who shot me a *What's up with that?* shrug. We walked toward each other. "So, his dad's embarrassed to be a waiter? People got to pay their bills. Expensive down here."

"Not embarrassed. More like concerned to be seen with me." I waved at Wilkinson to meet us in the larger room.

"Wait," Timoteo said. "Why?"

"Let's go in. I'll try to explain later."

We found seats near the back of the room at the only table with any vacancies. We extended intros and those seated stood to meet us, three coaches in matching red polo shirts from a San Fernando club and two regional reps from San Diego. One of the suits from San Diego said to send his regards to Augustine Coatsworth.

Gordon captivated the crowd with old tournament game stories, animated after-the-game tavern incidents, and then steepled his fingers on the podium as if praying for the continued support of top-flight tournaments across the country.

"Competitive high-school sports are the closest thing we

have to true rites-of-passage in our culture," he preached. "We need to keep events like this healthy and alive to keep our kids healthy and alive." Boisterous applause followed.

"See how he's got these clowns in the palm of his hand?" Ricky murmured. "If there were a woman here, he'd be talkin' only to her. And hopin' for more later."

"Watch it," I cautioned.

"And speaking of being healthy and alive," Gordon continued from the front of the room, "I wanted to announce tonight that half of the gate proceeds from the *entire* tournament, exactly half, will be going to help the unwed mothers at Helpline House, our new sixteen-apartment facility right here in the South Bay, adjacent to Providence Hospital." Then an even greater round of applause.

Ricky cupped his hand over his mouth. "That ain't shit. By the time the players and parents and old boys get in for free, you might have three paying customers. Big frickin' deal."

I shushed him and cranked my head toward the dais.

Gordon couldn't stop beaming, waving to all the major tournament sponsors, including several athletic shoe manufacturers, his own Shorebird Realty people, and Diamond Jim Brady's Prime Rib Restaurant. Wide-eyed, he worked the room, his head swinging side to side like a happy kid watching a tennis match. "Hey, did you taste those crab cakes? Weren't those delicious hors d'oeuvres today? How about a hand for our host, big Jim himself, sitting right down here? Stand up, Jim, let us thank you properly."

"Boy's on a roll, now," Ricky said. "Here comes the big ask."

After the applause, Gordon turned somber, targeting the tables farther from the front. "I know a lot of you representatives from out of state, out of our area, have asked about how you can contribute to this great week. Some of you coaches, too."

"Doubt even one guy did." Ricky laughed.

I held my hand in a stop motion. "The facility will make a difference," I countered. "I'm trying to give him the benefit of the doubt."

"What doubt?" Ricky said, leaning closer. "What possible doubt? The guy's a slimeball, and we both know it."

I point toward the stage.

"Well, this is your chance," Gordon said. "Right here, right now. Under the centerpieces on each of the tables, you will find an envelope. Please look into your hearts, then dig into your wallets and checkbooks and help us out. Anything you can do will make a huge difference. Anything at all!"

As the room rumbled with sliding chairs and conversation, Ricky stood, extended his arm, reached into his hip pocket, and lobbed his checkbook to the middle of the table. Our tablemates sat stunned, mouths wide open.

"Don't be shy, now! Consider the cause!" Gordon shouted from the podium. "Thanks to all of you for coming to our lunch and our wonderful region. And, please, consider the cause."

Ricky glanced around the table. "You heard him, boys. Consider the cause." He picked up his checkbook, swiped it across the checkered tablecloth, winked at Timoteo and me, and sniggered away. "I'll try to make the game."

TWENTY

WE DREW A NIMBLE, SHOW-TIME team from Las Vegas in the first game of the tournament. It was a late-afternoon session attended by a sparse crowd of parents, college scouts, and other team coaches, along with their sun-burned players curious to gauge the abilities of other teams in their bracket.

The Vegas bunch, from a notorious basketball camp posing as an academic institution, blew us away without running one set play, their raw talent and playground showmanship beckoning our players to watch rather than defend their high-voltage slams and cold-crossover dribbles. For the first four minutes, Vegas staged a no-dunk, no-count clinic. Blinded by a cat-quick defense, our guys needed Federal Express to get the ball upcourt.

I could tell Deacon Joe sensed an early blowout, and so he played like a petulant show pony, sending non-verbals to Terrell and company in the stands. His father cowered around the corner of the bleachers. He wore the same brown uniform and could have passed for the gym maintenance man.

"What the hell was that out there?" Trent roared at halftime. "We didn't come all the way down here to watch. We look slow and stupid." He surveyed his teammates and then glared at Deacon Joe. "Think you're better than us? Then get the hell out!"

Deacon Joe lunged toward Trent, but Timoteo caught the

point guard en route, wrapped him in a bear hug, and swung him toward the showers, his LeBron Soldier sneakers flailing beneath white leggings and knee-length shorts.

"Get those new kicks at a midnight-madness sale last night, bro?" Trent chided. "Because you sure as hell weren't in the hotel."

I decided to let the claim slide for the moment and focus on the second half. Accountability and criticism first needed to be addressed privately and not in front of others, particularly teammates. The prospect of a first-round torch job torpedoing our entire week loomed far more urgent. I tried to tweak the pride nerve so that we could finish on the uptick. When we left the locker room, I had no clue what to expect.

Terrell paraded down a few rows to check in with Deacon Joe. Trent stepped between them and glowered. "Not now." He narrowed his space between Deacon Joe and leaned an inch from his nose. "Let's go."

Nick Chevalier took a thundering charge to open the third quarter that brought a different dynamic to our team. I kept Deacon Joe on the bench, allowing Marcus to bring the ball up, blow past screens, and nail three consecutive jumpers. When Vegas responded by inserting its starting five and double-teaming Marcus, he dumped the ball in low to Trent for easy buckets. Deacon Joe bit his towel and fidgeted on the bench, prompting teammates on both sides to give him more room. Nick continued to spark the defense and cleaned the glass at both ends. By the third-quarter buzzer, we'd chopped Vegas's twenty-eight-point lead in half.

Our five starters, animated and energized by the rally, took a quick seat on the bench during the break.

"See how well you can play when you stop being spectators?" I said.

Trent blurted out, "Let's keep pounding down low and make 'em pay." Deacon Joe shuffled closer, attempting to make eye contact with me for the first time, his hands tugging at the

towel around his neck. He needed to pay the price for his SoCal demeanor, and the team needed to know that he'd been held accountable. *Make him wait.*

Our defensive strategy surprised and confused Vegas and produced two turnovers. I looked down the bench, and Deacon Joe caught my gaze, his face no longer in a first-half scowl. Just then, Marcus's hot hand turned cold, Vegas upped the tempo with a rim-rattling dunk, and we struggled for two minutes trying to chop the deficit to single digits. When Nick picked up his fourth foul, both Timoteo and Linn looked my way. I stood, walked down the bench past all the players, and pivoted.

With Vegas at the foul line, I stopped in front of Deacon Joe. "Go for Andre."

The guard sprinted down the sideline and signaled to the scorer's table, and he took his place at midcourt opposite the Vegas point guard. Deacon Joe licked his fingertips a la Steve Nash and wiped the bottom of his sneakers with an open hand. He checked the stands and lost a step on defense when he gazed too long. The rebound was tipped to the player he was assigned to guard.

"I thought you were ready!" I roared. "Get into it!"

By the time it was over, he'd dribbled the ball off his foot, missed a wide-open Nick on a break, air-balled an off-balance jumper from the corner, and showed no energy on the defensive end. Zero points, zero rebounds, one assist and seven stares into the stands. The team sauntered to the bench, heads down. Deacon Joe was the last player off the court, trailing even our laboring big men.

"Hey, roomie," Trent said as Deacon Joe approached. "Tryin' to kill our rally? Too hungover to care?" Marcus started to reply but slowly closed his mouth and shook his head.

Andre slammed a towel to the floor, wheeled around, and strutted toward Deacon Joe. "Figure it out, man. Or just stay away."

Following the post-game high-five line, one of a trio of

Vegas players headed for the locker room snickered, "This Deacon Joe kid? Looked like Deacon Slow to me."

After changing, Deacon Joe circled around our players and parents near midcourt. Most flashed inquisitive stares. His father caught his eye, stuffed his hands in his pockets, and headed down the aisle toward the side door.

I stepped in front of the player as he headed the other way. "Hey, go thank him," I said. "I'm sure it took a lot for him to show up."

"Yeah, well," he uttered. "That's a first."

"It's a start," I barked. When he moped away, I whipped around and faced him. "Maybe next game, you'll show up."

He turned, head down. "Lot goin' on, Coach."

I ducked in lower, attempting to lock in his attention. "And a lot of it has nothing to do with why we made this trip."

He stopped, leaned back, and rolled his head side to side, eyes peering toward the rafters. "Got people askin' me to make decisions. 'Bout my future."

My shoulders tightened as I pointed at him. "And I've got a lot of our guys asking about this team. And if you want any part in it. Look, I benched you because I had no idea where you were last night. Anything close to that again, and you're done. If you don't want to play, get your stuff out of the house."

* * *

HELPLINE HOUSE SAT AT THE END of one of the finger roads that once led to the massive Providence South Bay Hospital complex in the city of Sunset Beach. The two-story brick building, once a convent for the nuns of the Blessed Virgin Mary who no longer had the numbers to staff the hospital, now enjoyed the quiet of its own block. Its tiny gravel parking lot, jammed with aging sedans, served as a link and walkway to the

southwest wing of "the campus." A new elaborate entry and guard shack funneled vehicles to the east end, ushering visitors to three high-rise parking structures and a free hour of parking.

Diane, still icy from our past two encounters, found the only vacant street parking space within miles directly in front of Helpline House, and eased her rented Ford to the curb. I shook my head, amazed at her luck. "Parking karma." She laughed, yet I knew she was dead serious. "You just have to believe you are going to find a place. You? Well, you are a known non-believer."

She turned off the ignition and touched my hand. "Look," she said, her eyes darting from me to the windshield in front of us as if consistent contact were too painful. "I don't like the way we left each other the past two times. I played a big part, thanks to the wine and several other things."

I swallowed hard. "Like me being pissed at everything Gordon does for you."

"There's that. But he's also helped the entire team."

"With the singular goal of impressing you," I roared. I glared out the shotgun window and took a deep breath. "I don't like it, and I am not handling it well at all." I waited a moment, peeked toward her, and said, "Let's just say I've got a good reason—"

She turned and rubbed my shoulder. "That's sweet, and I appreciate your words." She reached for my hands, held them firmly, and shook them briefly. "I'm afraid I haven't been terribly tuned in to all you are dealing with down here. I don't feel good about that. I promise to be a lot more aware in the next few days." She smooched my cheek.

I nodded and smiled. *Aware and on guard, please.*

We locked the rig and walked up the front steps. She read the message chiseled into the burgundy cornerstone. "*Pro Deo et Patria.*"

"It's Latin," I said. "*For God and Country.* And lord knows Gordon's a patriot. Always got flags on him or around him."

"See," she said, "that's another reason I like hanging out with you. Not many guys would know that."

"Chaplain motto from the war. My dad mentioned it a couple of times. The nuns probably wanted to keep it alive when they built this place."

"And we are striving to keep it alive today." The speaker smiled from an open door to our right. Her hair appeared prematurely gray, professionally cut, and curled sharply at the sides of her face. Her Patagonia fleece top matched her hair and topped black slacks and light blue Brooks running shoes. "Getting our women assistance and working skills helps our community and country. The God part? Well, that is for everyone." She held the door and motioned to come her way. "I'm Lanell Lautze. We're happy you're here."

We shook hands. Diane flourished in moments like this, especially at this hour of the morning. I gladly surrendered the lead. Typical compliments and questions followed, concerning Diane's custom bracelet and embroidered belt and Lanell's heirloom brooch. As I followed Diane in, I glanced toward the gravel lot and balked. In one of the spaces blocked from our street view sat a yellow Chevy, but I couldn't make out the model.

"Ernie, are you coming?" Diane said, Then, to our tour guide: "I just hope we're not too early. We both wanted to come, and Ernie has to meet the kids for practice. So our time is shorter than we'd like."

"No, it's our pleasure," Lanell said. "We especially welcome visitors from out of town. We hope you like what you see and consider doing something similar in your town."

We strolled the first-floor corridor, tasteful lighting bouncing off the recently waxed floor. The fresh, light straw paint balanced the harvest-wheat tone of the floor. "Our first level contains our main working spaces, the cafeteria, and kitchen. The women's rooms and lounge are upstairs. Business offices are in the basement."

Diane asked about the typical patient, percentage of pregnancies, and adoptions. Lanell pointed out that not all women entered the home pregnant and approximately forty percent of them gave up the baby up for adoption. Others were single and needed transitional shelter, mental health care, and other critical services.

"The goal is to help break the cycle of abuse and neglect," Lanell said. "When our women leave here, we hope they have acquired the skills necessary to lead productive, independent and healthy lives. That's a big order, and we can accommodate only sixteen at a time."

I couldn't spot a smudge in the kitchen, even on the large stainless-steel ovens and walk-in refrigerators. A few women gathered at a table in the middle of the cafeteria, water and orange juice glasses in front of them. Two in the group massaged large bellies and shifted in their padded side chairs as a counselor explained a pamphlet on nutrition. I continued to search for a plate or a cup out of place, or a tray piled high with used utensils or greasy napkins.

"Looks like Gordon's helping to fill a need," I murmured.

Both women replied at the same time. "Yes, he is." They smiled at each other and continued toward the education area. We peeked through the small rectangular window of a classroom door, and a saw an elderly Asian woman explaining to a pair of students the attachments of a sewing machine. One woman patted the bandage covering her right eye while the other student gazed out the window for long moments, prompting a nudge from the teacher. Another woman received personal computer instruction in a tiny cubbie that looked like an oversized telephone booth. In the last classroom on the corridor, two women scanned grocery items from a packed shopping cart.

"Our cash registers have been extremely helpful in placing our girls in local stores," Lanell said. "Some get flustered when making change." She turned away from the window and faced

us. "Yes, some need the most basic skills you can imagine. Making change? We take so much for granted, but it takes a long time for some of them to pick it up." She turned back and pointed into the room. "A tone sounds when they reach the bottom of the basket. One of our volunteers will then come through and ask them to make change from various denominations. Again, it can require a lot of practice."

We climbed the steps at the end of the hall to the second floor. "Our clients receive notice about all our tours. We respect their privacy, and they know visitors are critical to us. If they are sleeping or recovering, maybe need some private time, their door will be closed. Those students you saw downstairs most likely left their doors open, as did any who might have been escorted next door to the hospital this morning for appointments or procedures. As you can imagine, some of our moms can be wheeled out of here pretty fast."

We strolled down another clean, cool corridor. The first open door featured an overwhelming scent of peppermint and a baby blue bedspread covered with every imaginable Winne the Pooh stuffed animal. Winnie slippers rested on a brown Tigger throw rug near the bed. No clothes, pens, notebooks, or toiletries appeared to be out of place. How different, I thought, from my team's rental dorm. We shot cursory glances from the hallway into three other rooms. I hesitated, then entered the third.

"You see this plaid bedspread right here?" I said. Eyebrows raised, Diane and Lanell followed me into the room. "This is the exact same one I had in Yakima, Washington. Seventh grade through junior year of high school. Same color, same pattern of squares." I bent down closer, hands behind my back. "Except this one is in a lot better shape. And smells better." Diane groaned and led us back into the hallway.

A curious purple light from the corner room streamed outside the doorway. We glanced in to find a small lava lamp perched on the vanity near the entry. A woman reclined in a

brown Barcalounger angled toward the bed, a pink floor lamp splashing light on the paperback in her lap. As we chatted toward the exit stairs opposite the room, I heard her rise. I assumed she would close the door for privacy.

"What exactly are you doing here?" The voice behind me, quiet yet direct, seemed familiar. I turned and hesitated, trying to place the distinctive face from another place. Renee stared at me, resplendent in black dress slacks, matching pointed-toe flat shoes and a dark blue blouse. Her hair still shined.

"Ah, we're just finishing up a tour," I said. "We'd been wanting to see the facility. If we made too much—"

Lanell darted to the doorway, hands raised. "I am so sorry we disturbed you. We were just leaving."

Renee bowed slightly. "No problem. My sister should be up shortly. She's had a hard time sleeping at night. Naps a lot during the day." She rotated, glanced toward the bed, then turned back to us. "I was just heading to a job interview and hoped to speak with her before I left."

I introduced Diane and Lanell and mentioned that Renee was acquainted with one of our players and his father. Diane crossed her arms and leaned a shoulder against the wall.

"Mr. Pantel found her down near the pier," Renee said. "She was in pretty bad shape. He took her to a shelter run by a priest friend of his. The priest pulled some strings with the chaplain next door at Providence and got her in here."

Lanell apologized again for the intrusion. We excused ourselves, opened the door to the stairwell, and hurried down.

"I was surprised her door was open," Lanell said in a low tone even though no one was in sight. "She's been kind of a mystery. She hasn't said a word to anyone on staff. She just showed up about a week ago with that Mr. Pantel getting her settled. A different kind of man, but a gentle soul."

"I was under the impression there's a long waiting list for these rooms," Diane said. "Quite a few interviews, research involved."

"There is a process," Lanell said. She shook her head and placed a hand on her cheek. "But I'm not privy to what happened in this particular case. I do know she was given the only room with two windows, a view of the garden. I've seen her sister here before. But her only other visitor has been Mr. Pantel, who visits often. At least, when I've been on duty."

Diane pulled me close and waited for Lanell to take a few steps ahead. "OK. That woman, Renee? Did not look like that the other day in the hotel lobby."

TWENTY-ONE

LIFE IN THE LOSERS' BRACKET sucks. It's like planning an exotic vacation and then getting pummeled by rain and rocked by cabin fever. With no chance to win the big trophy, it's difficult for a coach to motivate. Players tend to float and shun crisp execution.

In our second tournament game against the Denver Devils, a few of my guys showed restlessness, and they funneled it in the wrong direction. Trent Whalen pushed and shoved too early and too often, finding himself in foul trouble in the first quarter. Marcus McGann attempted shots far outside his range, hoping that three-pointers would put us on top early and keep us there. Booty Jacobsen dribbled the ball off his foot, trying to make up for the lost play-making skills of Deacon Joe, who stayed on the bench with a too-cool-for-this attitude. Game One revisited. Terrell and his crew slumped in their seats, sending lazy, critical signals to their man below.

By halftime, we'd dug a big hole, and the outlook and vibe felt like worse would be arriving soon and sticking around. I relied on a trusted "respect and responsibility" theme for my halftime talk, but the results netted little improvement. Denver's smoothest player, a six-three Latino with flowing black hair and a deadly baseline jumper, picked us apart even though Cheese Oliver had submitted a detailed scouting report on the kid. We tried three different players, yet none could stay

with him. Not only had he drawn the spectators' attention with his scoring, but he also communicated with his coach and teammates via sign language. When Terrell realized the player's correspondence required more than the usual on-court movements, his gang stood and mimicked the star for several minutes before the irate Denver coach called time-out and stormed my way.

"What kind of BS is that?" he yelled in my face, a dot of spittle landing on my chin. "Your guys up there are classless."

I tried to step back, but he filled the distance. "They aren't my guys," I mumbled.

"Well, they sure as hell are with your guy on the bench." He pointed to Deacon Joe. "There's no place for any of that crap here, and you know it."

The two game officials approached, one with the game ball lodged between his elbow and hip. He glanced at the Denver coach, then stared at me. "That shit stops right now," he whispered. "Or you forfeit. Are we clear?"

I turned and glowered at Terrell and then turned back to the refs. "Crystal," I said.

Terrell circled his finger in the air, indicating to Deacon Joe that the posse planned to split. Deacon Joe acknowledged and mouthed he would meet them after the game. For me, the contest could not end fast enough. Terrell's antics added an extra edge for the Devils while sending us into an embarrassed stupor.

The post-game locker room scene turned ugly with Timoteo needing to separate Trent and Deacon Joe once again. When that situation cooled, Booty crossed in front of me and pushed Deacon Joe into the showers.

"Let's get out of here and leave the stink behind," Trent hollered. "Let him find his own ride."

The players grabbed their gear and headed for the door, followed by Timoteo and Cheese Oliver. Only Deacon Joe remained, head down, hands propped on the tile wall between

showerheads.

I bolted out of the locker room into the hallway, livid about our performance while trying to balance it against the distracting sideshow the players had experienced since arriving. What should I expect? Sun, fun, girls, drugs, old friends. How long would it take them to find any synergy, if at all? Head down, I dashed around a corner and nearly collided with a smiling Terrell Dupree, silver bracelets and rings glittering from both arms below a black chiffon shirt.

"Say, Coach. Wassup? Just waitin' for my boy to be turned loose."

I glared down at him, head tilted. "He should be out in a minute. A couple of his teammates had a message for him."

"Guess y'all waitin' for him to hit his stride. He can turn it on at any time. Talkin' DEFCON One."

"See, we're used to him running at max speed all the time. Seems he's lacked the focus others have had down here."

Terrell shifted his weight and became more animated as if he recalled the missing answer to a quiz. "Oh, just showed him the ol' hood, Coach. Where we used to hang, play. Even went by his old place above the garage."

"Sounds like a short drive. But he didn't return very early." I removed my Washington High Fighting Crabs cap, checked its brim, then replaced it with a firm tug.

"Yeah, I was confused about the curfew thing. Thought it was jus' for boys with parents here. Hope to get the two other brothers involved in the next ride. Your Marcus McGann and Booty Boy Jacobsen. Sure those boys would enjoy the scenery. 'Specially the ladies."

I stepped closer, with one of my sneakers bumping his black square-toed boot. "I'm sure Deacon Joe enjoyed the tour of his old neighborhood." He turned his head and squinted. "But he's here to play basketball. So are his teammates."

"Know that. Talkin' 'bout their free time."

"Their *free* time will be taken up by tournament activities."

I dipped lower, my nose nearly atop his. "Do I make myself clear?"

He sneered, then jiggled his shoulders. "I jus' don't think ya know who you messin' with here, *Coach.* I could be showin' your boy a better way. You really want to stand in the way of that?"

I popped an index finger into his chest. "Steer clear of my guys. We've got four days to take care of business. We don't need any more distractions."

He shook his head. "Ain't your turf, Coach," he said. "Believe your boys old enough to do what they please. Ain't kids no more."

I looked both ways down the hall, then slammed my clipboard to the floor. I reared up, grabbed him with both hands at the chest, and slammed him into the lockers on the wall behind him. His top button ripped from his shirt and dribbled to the beige vinyl floor. "No, you're wrong," I hissed. "They *are* kids. And they're my kids." I eased my grip, shoved him away, and whispered, "Screw with that at your peril."

He straightened up, surveying his damaged shirt. "*My* peril?" he barked. "What the fuck does that mean? My peril? Well, tell you what, old man. You just pissed off Terrell. And nobody pisses off Terrell without payin' a price." He pointed at me. "Big price."

He shimmied once to collect himself and strutted away, turning to snicker over his shoulder.

* * *

PRACTICE PROVED AS DISCONNECTED AND useless as the rest of my morning. Sleep arrived late and was fleeting. I fumbled around early at the house, spilling coffee and unable to locate my bus keys, practice-schedule clipboard and wallet before

eventually borrowing the spare bus key from Linn Oliver. I paid attention to all the misses yet could not attribute them to any one person or challenge. Diane? Gordon? Deacon Joe? Our next opponent? No clarity came to me before meeting the boys on the court. Five minutes into the session, I tripped over myself while backing up on a basic defensive drill. Linn helped me off the floor.

"Why don't you go get a real cup of coffee, Coach?" he whispered. "I can show these guys the lock-down scheme we talked about."

My shoulders slid lower and the tightness in my calf was gone. I thought I'd be embarrassed if I ever left practice early, but the notion never surfaced. "Don't forget their big stud likes to go to his left."

"I know, I know. Marcus will guard him from the top, and Trent can flash up from the low post to help." He turned and handed me the keys to the team van. "Hey, we got this."

I signaled reluctant approval with a casual wave, picked up my sweatshirt and headed out the back door, determined to fix one piece of my scrambled puzzle. While driving back to the house, I rifled through the bus's glove box and console in the remote possibility I'd stowed my keys and wallet there in the past couple of days. I'd changed cars more times on this trip than my underwear and had no idea where my vital possessions could be. Worse, I could not remember the last time I needed my wallet or had even seen it.

I angled the van onto the steep driveway and pulled the door handle. When it didn't budge, I shouldered the panel. *Was it that hard to open on the incline or was I just gassed?* The front door was unlocked, and I was the last one out. Figured. I headed straight to the coffee pot, rinsed out the cold remainder, and reached above the counter for a fresh filter. Near the compressed filter stack sat my keys, yet I could not recall brewing an earlier pot. Perhaps it was yesterday. *Now where in the hell was my wallet?*

The smell of fresh coffee brought a definite sense of reset which I attributed to my first piece of solo time of the entire trip. I cruised through the wash-dry-stow process of breakfast bowls and milk glasses. The Rice Krispies and Frosted Flakes boxes found easy openings in a crowded cupboard. I filled a mug and collected the trash from the downstairs bathroom along with two Snickers wrappers from the den, depositing them in the container under the kitchen sink. I grabbed a garbage bag, topped off the mug, and mounted the stairs.

Given my experience with previous teenage road trips, I found the boys' main dormitory room bordering on acceptable. While earbuds and underwear hung from every possible post, the usual hiding places produced no pot, vape pipes or girlie magazines; the last was easily downloaded to cell phones. Two beds were almost made but perfecting a bunk against a wall needed inspiration few adolescents possessed. Trident won the trash contest followed by Doublemint, Sour Patch Kids, and Butterfinger. I smiled at a Big Hunk wrapper tossed into the intersection of two bed frames, wondering if the taffy-and-nut slab had been cracked and shared as I did with my dad. *When did they have time to buy all this?*

Wedged between a four-drawer dresser and the base of a bunk in the corner of the room, I found two black tablets of identical size, a Kindle E-Reader and a small ledger, the first disguising the second. I knelt on the carpet and opened the ledger in front of me. Written in blue fountain ink inside the front cover read *DJG, Manzana, Washington.* The pages of Deacon Joe's journal chronicled many of his experiences and feelings, including anger and frustration regarding the whereabouts of his mother. While I felt some misgivings about reading his private thoughts, I also felt knowing more about his backstory would help me better understand his current challenges. An early entry from Manzana read:

I went home, waited around, then figured she
wasn't comin back. I wasn't crazy about

*spending another winter in Wenatchee, so a
farmer friend hooked me up with a builder over
here near Granite Falls. Just grunt work, but I
got to sleep at the construction sites and keep
watch. The builder's roofer is a native who lives
on the res and took me in. Big Andre needed
help. It's worked out good. When we're not on a
job, we're cutting cedar shakes. He's taught me
a lot.*

I thumbed deeper into the book. On a stained page with
smudged words, he praised Cheese Oliver and others from the
North Fork team: *The dude don't bullshit me. He solid. Ain't
just about hoops with him. Guys on the travel team strong. Not
fast, smart enough to play, tho.* Another note toward the back
sent me to my feet. I caught a quick breath, cupped my mouth,
and peered down at the book through blurry eyes: *Coach is a
straight-up guy who'd never leave me hangin.*

I slumped on the side of the bed. I felt my head slowly shift
from side to side, wondering about the remarkable motor
driving this black-brown kid living with a native on a
reservation north of Seattle. *And I didn't have the guts to see
and choose what I already had in spades?* My heart sank and
swelled with pride at the same time. It remained in that poignant
place for a few more moments as I fingered through pages with
insightful entries in various colors of ink. I paused again when
I found in red ballpoint:

*People say they feel sorry for me. Shit, no
way. Got it pretty good. Trent workin' through
some bad shit, now livin' with team doc. Good
dude. But still. Trent says buckets all he got now.*

His latest comment, scribbled in pencil and dated this
morning, stated:

*Terrell got bills fallin' out of his pockets!
Never seen so much money on one man. Don't
feel right. Offering me dollars to do a lot of*

things, like wear special sneakers. Don't like my
dad in his shit.

My hands sagged lower. Who wouldn't trip, stumble or crash in at least one of the congested intersections he faced? I squared up the Kindle and journal and replaced them behind the post. Grabbing the trash bag, I continued to cram it with more fast-food cups, toilet-paper tubes, and Q-Tips than I'd accumulate in a month. Rather than risk seepage on the stairs, I gathered and secured the drawstring, hauled it through my bedroom, and opened the French doors to the deck. Medium range shot to the trash shack below. No problem.

Gauging the distance and the strength required to clear the near wall of the enclosure, I slapped the bag on the deck and prepared for a discus-like twirl over the waist-high rail. Swaying twice to gain momentum, I let the bag fly on the third swing. The white package sailed over the wall and smacked into the enclosed area near the base of a green yard waste barrel. Open-mouthed, I squinted below. The bag straddled a huge cream-colored foot wrapped in a cordovan-tasseled loafer.

TWENTY-TWO

Rob Suarez arrived fewer than twenty minutes after I'd phoned him. Once I'd described the body of Gordon Aldrete, he'd instructed me to stay away from the alley and trash enclosure and monitor the area from the second-floor deck. I grabbed a sweatshirt from my room to fight the fog and settled into one of the Adirondack chairs. He cruised around the back corner in his rumpled trench coat, hands in his pockets, and tilted his head when he saw me.

I stood and approached the rail. Then, acknowledging his M.O., I added: "Harvey does the same thing with his hands. Never touches anything the first time through a scene. Just kind of struts on through."

"My boss calls the look Mexican macho."

"Harvey would never be associated with macho. More like disheveled."

He scoffed as if he'd heard it before. "This place will be crawling with cops in a few minutes. You know, the local tourist bureau is going to love you. Probably offer you a public relations job. Nothing but crap has happened since you arrived. Wait until that manager at the Shadow hears what happened *after* you left his place."

I rolled my eyes and suppressed a grin. "Teenagers in hotels? More like who can be the first to break the fun meter. Matter of time."

He straightened up, and his tone turned gritty. "So, did you touch anything?" He opened his coat and lifted two blue gloves from the hip pocket of his trousers.

I shifted my weight, causing a creak in a plank below. "Tried not to. Opened the gate to the garbage using a paper towel. Thought I'd see who was in there. He rented us the place."

"Right. How did you know he was dead?"

"I didn't. I mean, I didn't check him for a pulse, but he looked dead to me. Then I called you."

"I see. So you didn't consider CPR?"

The casual intro now felt far behind us. "I didn't. Seemed to me he was long past that."

"And you're familiar with the procedure?"

"It's a requirement in our district. Came in handy one night for me at a booster party. One of the old boys went down."

He glanced toward the roofs of the neighboring homes, his glass eye oddly rotated toward the trash. "Did you see or hear anybody since you've been here? Anybody peeking out of these windows?" He waved his hand in a circle above his head.

"Not a soul. And I didn't want the team showing up. I called my assistant coach and told him to take the team out to lunch and then to the beach."

He nodded. "Good call." Rob reached into his coat and pulled out a pen and a small ringed notebook. He flipped open the front cover. "How long you been here before you called me?"

"Thinking twenty minutes. Made coffee, picked up some trash, cleaned up after the boys a bit."

"So, nobody came with you?"

"Nobody."

"Have you been back inside since you called me?"

"Just once for a minute. To pee."

"I'm curious. Why did you leave practice before it ended? Kinda strange, isn't it?"

"Couldn't do anything right since I got out of bed. Couldn't find my keys, my wallet. When I tripped over myself at practice, Cheese suggested I take a blow. Felt better since he said it."

"And Cheese is who?"

"My assistant coach, Linn Oliver. Former player."

"Right, right. The shooter. Harvey mentioned him, seen him play. Said he could've been something." He walked the perimeter of the shack, stopping twice to examine the area between the bottom of the wood wall and the pavement. He then circled the house via the narrow passageways leading to the street. He eyed the back entry, then folded his arms and looked up at me.

"So tell me why one of the best investigators on the West Coast allows a high-school coach to tag along on some of his cases. Harvey didn't tell me much, but it's clear he thinks a lot of you."

I leaned on the rail with elbows and tried to clear my throat. "Don't know about that, but I did spend a lot of time in the classroom. And on the court. He knows that I know kids. And like a lot of small towns, some kids caused trouble. Or were victims. My assistant got into an awful deal with a crazy guy."

"Was this *the* Cheese?"

"Same guy. Long story . . . then you have the obvious parent-player issues. One, in particular, turned devastating for everybody."

He held the pen and pad in one hand and gestured with the other as if shooting a ball. "Plus, he's a hoops fan."

"No," I snorted. "Sometimes thinks he's the coach, and the high school is the only game in town. When he didn't agree with my defense, I sure could hear him in the stands."

He checked his watch, then turned back toward the alley, pacing the distance between the shack and the turn-in. He then walked the lane, retracing the path he used when he arrived. He returned to his spot beneath the deck. "I'm going to go look in there for a few minutes." He pointed to the trash area with his

pen, then made a note. "If an officer comes, tell him I'm in there but have them stay out."

"Will do."

My cell phone buzzed, and the caller ID indicated Diane.

"How are you doin'?"

"How are *you* doing? I saw Linn Oliver with the team on the porch down at the Copper Kettle. They were just ordering lunch and then planned on walking out on the pier. He said you weren't feeling well."

"You know, I couldn't get out of my own way. I think I just needed a few minutes to myself. Came home for a bit."

"Well, I hope you're feeling better. I'm looking forward to seeing you and going over some things about Gordon."

I turned away from the parking area and faced the house. "Really? What things about Gordon?"

"Well, there's the invoice for the house that was larger than we thought, and he's also asked me to make a donation to Helpline House. Before I did, I wanted to know if you had already made one."

I heard the gate to the trash area close. "Listen, Diane. I'm going to have to call you back." A police car eased into the parking area. Two officers remained in the front seats, one speaking into a handheld.

"Oh, well, OK. I thought you were alone."

"I'll just call you back." I clicked off.

Rob sauntered up closer to the deck.

"Did I hear you say something about Gordon?"

"It was just my friend with some questions about the tournament."

"I see. Does your friend know Mr. Alderete's present condition?"

"She doesn't. I'm fairly certain you are the only one that knows. Other than me."

"She didn't happen to be the brunette I saw Mr. Alderete talking with in the lobby the day we met."

"Yes. Same woman."

He raised his chin slightly. "Did they have a history?"

I ran a hand through my hair. "They'd met a few times. I just found out about it yesterday."

He put his notebook back into his pocket and followed it with the pen. "Say, did you happen to find your keys and wallet?"

"You know, I feel like a fool. My keys were right next to the coffee pot. The wallet hasn't turned up yet, but I'm sure it will. Hadn't had a chance to really go through the house before you got here."

"Coach, I'm going to come into the house, but I don't want you to move. I'll come up there, get you, and take you out to your van. I want you to sit there, and I'll have an officer come and take your statement."

"My statement?" I babbled. "Why? I just told you all I know, answered all your questions. You have to be bullshitting me!"

"No, sir. Put yourself in my shoes. You come home, and a man is deceased in your yard. He's had a relationship with your girlfriend and he's not, I dare say, one of your closest friends."

"Relationship?! What relationship?"

"Maybe he was here to collect your rent. And you didn't want to pay him . . ."

"You think this is about money? Christ, I don't even pay the bills. Diane does. How was I to know —"

"She does? That's interesting." He took a step toward the back door and pointed up, both eyes aligned right at me. "Look, I don't really know what this is about. What I *do* know is what Harvey told me. The last time you saw the deceased before coming down here you nearly beat him to death."

I sighed and peered down through the deck boards. "I don't believe this," I muttered.

"Stay there. Do not move. This is now officially a crime scene."

* * *

THE COPS SHOWED UP AT OUR COMFY digs on Thirty-Third Street and forced us to drag our gear to our third place in four days. Given that Gordon acted as a rental intermediary with routine access to the house, police chose to tape off the entire property rather than barricade only the driveway and trash area. Blue-gloved officers delivered the boys' bags to the street below the entry where we piled the equipment in the back of the van.

There would be no final group walk-through, yet Timoteo received clearance to accompany one of the officers as he collected the last of the clothes and groceries. Deacon Joe approached Timoteo, concerned that his Kindle and journal might have been left behind. Timoteo assured him that he personally tucked the articles into his duffel bag. Diane stayed clear of the house, still shaken by the incident. She decided to keep Nick with her at the Shadow and found a nearby room for Timoteo and his wife, while Ricky Wilkinson allowed the rest of us to crash in one of his rehab projects—a dusty, two-bedroom duplex in a gulley across the street from an elementary school. I figured we missed the main minivan drop-off by twenty-five minutes. The new tenants will love the light-traffic weekends and the absence of roaring recesses.

As we continued our silent treatment with each other while waiting for Ricky outside the duplex in her Ford, Diane turned and touched my arm. "I owe you an apology," she uttered. "And an explanation. About how I treated you." I turned to her, eyebrows raised. "Well, your crime didn't fit the punishment."

"It's not as if I wasn't a jerk," I said.

"No, you were a jerk, but I needed to respond differently. What I did was way out of line. I am sorry."

"Lunch with another guy without a word about it? Definitely a different environment all around."

"And I don't think I've ever done anything like that before. I definitely was trying to get back at you. It was a weird feeling, and I didn't like it at all. I didn't like me, and I usually never have to say that."

I checked the mirror outside my door to see if Ricky's rig was in sight. "You were pissed that I dissed Gordon at the house? Right?"

She turned so that I could see her entire face. "I did think you were curt." She stopped and shook her head.

"What is it?" I said. "Am I being clueless again?"

"It's just that. . . I don't know. How should I say this?"

"I guess just flat out," I said.

She wiggled in her seat. "When I thought about it, I was upset about us."

"Us? In what regard?"

"We've never really talked about exclusivity. I think I was upset because you never asked that of me or wondered about it. I mean, are we exclusive? Do you want that?"

Jessie and all others out the door? I felt an intriguing relief in the moment of truth someone else provided. I swallowed hard and turned toward her. "I would like that, yes."

Her eyes became misty. "Well, so would I." She stretched and grabbed my hand and smiled. "But tell me. How in the world was I supposed to know that?"

She had a point. I dug for a reply but couldn't fashion a halfway decent one. I settled for the go-to shrug and headshake.

A moment passed. She pulled back her hand and stretched her palms to the headliner. "This week has been a good example to the boys of the damage drugs can do." The change of subject—especially given the subject—pushed me deeper into the seat. "Certainly they'll never forget it. I'm just sorry that they had to see it so up close and personal. And that poor Gordon. My God." She definitely looked for the positive

attributes in everyone, but really brought out the blinders when it came to Gordon.

"So you are convinced drugs are at the root of all of this?" I said.

"Absolutely!" she replied. "What other explanation do you have for any of this? You saw those individuals milling around the lobby. A few of them even showed up at the gym. And weren't you an eyewitness to a transaction in Kyle's room?"

"No, I did not actually see a transaction. But I am interested in how you see Gordon's involvement. Are you thinking his death was accidental?"

She flashed a too-confident look, a facial veneer concealing fear. "The popular saying is 'just in the wrong place at the wrong time.' He most likely got caught in a drug deal gone bad. You know, it *was* at night and in an alley. He's also rented that place to a number of people, and who knows what kind of business they conducted there? Maybe the bad guys confused Gordon for somebody else. A case of mistaken identity."

I shook my head and looked down. "Good lord, Diane. The guy was six-twelve and half a million pounds! There are only so many white whales in one city." I sat back, feeling my mistake. "I'm sorry. I know we're all frazzled trying to figure this out." I was also wondering how much the murder would affect my team. During tournament week, on the court, and for the rest of their lives.

"What?" Diane said. "You don't think this is all about drugs?"

I looked down the street for Ricky's truck, then back to Diane. "I'm not so sure. Gordon knew a lot of people and sunk his hands deep into a lot of stuff. Maybe drugs were part of it, but he did work a lot of angles and some of them might have been too sharp and cut some people." I checked the rear-view mirror. "Like the guy pulling up behind us in this rig."

"You think Ricky had something to do—"

"*Hola, amigos!*" Ricky called, slamming the driver's door.

"*Mi casa es su casa.*"

"Hey, man," I said. We slapped hands and hugged. "You are really bailing us out. I can't thank you enough."

"You bet." He turned to Diane. "Hey, beautiful, I want to hug you too, but I'm too damn dirty. Got this tile dust all over me."

"Give you a raincheck," she said.

"Right. Say, have you been in there yet? Carlos should be finishing up some grout in the back bath. The boys might have to pee outside for a few hours until it dries. Just kiddin', Diane."

She blushed. "Well, I'm sure they've done that at least once before."

"Ernie, this place ain't great, but it's all I got right now."

"Hey, man. Stop apologizing. It's gonna be great."

"Well, I wouldn't go that far. The paint is fresh in the living room, and you'll smell it for a while. You're gonna wanna keep all the windows open. I got some plastic up in the back shower so that's out of commish."

"No problem at all," I said. "Those who want to can shower at the high school."

"Roger that. And, hey, the bath is all squared away off the master, though. Might even meet Diane's standards."

"I'm certain it would, Ricky, yet I am very comfortable at the Shadow."

He asked us to remain outside while he checked with Carlos as to the best rooms to stow our stuff. The young laborer emerged a short time later, sweat and paint staining his coveralls. He removed his protective glasses and revealed the worker's raccoon look. He swatted a dusty Dodgers cap against his thigh, sending residue into his right eye. He grimaced and tried to clear it.

"Muchos problemas," he murmured. "No trabajo hoy."

While I'd felt skittish about asking Ricky for a favor, seeing Carlos walk off the job early moved me into the guilt zone. Having worked the Yakima orchards as a kid, I could sense

when Latino employees were upset even though they'd never say it. Carlos had earmarked his cash, and he'd be shorted today. I voiced my concerns to Ricky and offered to make up the difference.

"Shit no, amigo," Ricky replied. "Hell, he'll just call one of his cousins. Freaking Mexico network is unbelievable around here. He's probably got another job already."

While Diane began cleaning the kitchen, checking the number of utensils, and storing paper towels, I pulled Ricky aside. "I meant to ask you yesterday. Has anybody called you about your history with Gordon?"

"Funny you mention it. Some Mexican guy left a voicemail early this morning. Said he was a lieutenant right here in the South Bay."

"Rob Suarez?"

"Bingo. If I call him back, what should I tell him?"

"Well, when you talk to him, just tell him the truth."

"Yeah, right."

I stepped back. "If you don't call him, I'm sure he'll find you somehow." He grinned and looked away. "Are you telling me you've got something to hide?"

"You mean on this particular case? The guy's a cop, for chrissake. You never know what these guys want. It could have been something that I allegedly did years ago. *Allegedly* did."

I waited, wondering how many times the police have been interested in speaking with Ricky Wilkinson. "Well, I'm thinking it'd be a pretty safe bet that it involves Gordon's demise."

"And I'm a betting man."

"I heard that somewhere."

"And what would lead Señor Suarez to believe that I was involved in any way with one Gordon Alderete?"

I coughed and tugged my chin. "Well, that would be on me."

"How so?"

"There's an investigator back home who's a buddy of mine.

He's helped me when some of my kids got into trouble. He knows all about what happened at that summer camp. I told him you lived down here now and that I was going to look you up."

"Well, he's up there, and we're—"

"He and Suarez go way back. They were in the same class at the cop shop."

"Oh, Christ. You didn't happen to tell your guy that I've been known to take a little action on games..."

"I did not say a word about the bookie business."

"Not a business. It's a hobby. More like sports analysis."

"Right."

Ricky stretched his neck. "Then I have absolutely nothing to worry about."

"Absolutely."

"Is there anything I need to know about this guy?"

"He's a pretty straight shooter," I said. "And, oh yeah, there's the glass eye. Kind of fades right more than left."

His left eyebrow soared. "Now *that's* cool. I look forward to checking it out."

"He's going to want to check *you* out." He winced. His eyes narrowed. "Ricky, he's going to ask you where you were around the time Gordon was murdered."

"That's none of his damn business."

TWENTY-THREE

W<small>HEN THE CALLER</small> ID <small>READ</small> S<small>KAGIT</small> C<small>OUNTY</small> A<small>D</small> B<small>LDG</small>, I let the phone ring out. I didn't need a lengthy clarifying conversation with Jessie about our relationship. Former relationship. When the voicemail light came on a few minutes after the ring, I flipped a *Sports Illustrated* at the phone and continued breaking down the scouting report in front of me. Our next opponent had mauled its previous foe with a rugged inside game, but I felt confident Nick Chevalier and Trent Whalen would bump and scrap and not be intimidated. If I could only get Deacon Joe back in a consistent groove.

The cell phone buzzed again and stopped after two rings. I tossed my pencil down and punched the voicemail button. "If you don't call me back," Harvey hissed, "I'm gonna come down there and step on your neck."

I slumped back in the desk chair and closed my eyes. A moment later, I looked at the digital clock by the bed, then checked the schedule for the day. I took the cell to the bed, slid against the padded headboard, and found the East Coast Mariners game on the TV. I muted the sound and dialed Harvey.

When he answered, I said, "What are you still doing at the office?"

"It's the only place I can close the door and yell at you loud enough. Martha wouldn't let me at home."

"So, are you watching the Mariners? They got a couple of

hits in the top of the third. Might put up some crooked numbers on the scoreboard."

"Don't try to be funny, you dickhead! You're causing a shitstorm on at least three fronts, and the list is getting longer by the minute."

"You mean baseball didn't even make the top three things you wanted to discuss?"

"Damn it, Ernie. Stop pulling my chain! I've got a friend who also happens to be a colleague who says you could be the prime suspect in a murder investigation, a secretary who called in sick the day after she got back from a trip down there, and an upset father who said you sent his kid home on some sort of technicality!"

I snorted and looked at the ceiling. "Can I plead innocent to all three? Kinda like a group plead?"

"I can't believe you think this is all a joke. Rob Suarez called and asked me if I ever heard you say you should have killed one Gordon Alderete. He actually asked me that! And he wasn't kidding."

"What did you tell him?"

"I said no. Because you never did. At least that I could remember. He then asked if I, in my professional opinion, thought you had sufficient motive to kill the guy."

"And?"

"I told him that I couldn't speculate as to your mindset on the day the murder was committed. I told him you had been extremely upset with him about an incident in the past, but I had hoped you had put that behind you."

"Just hoped? You told him you hoped? I know you taught me that everybody is a suspect, but c'mon, man."

The silence on the other end felt more like a gathering storm than a timeout. I visualized Harvey holding the phone high over his head, seeking divine intervention before delivering his next volley. He returned calmer than I anticipated.

"When you helped me with cases in the past, what was one

of the first steps I asked you to take into consideration regarding a suspect?"

"Always look at the big picture over time. Do not rely solely on a person's recent actions."

"Correct. Now, of the conversations that we've had over the years about Gordon Alderete, how many times did you point out the positive attributes of the man?" Harvey asked.

"Well, if you put it that way, very few. I guess."

"What do you mean 'you guess?'" His short-term calm proved short-lived. "You never had a good word to say about the guy in your entire life."

"So?"

"So, I won't lie to a guy like Rob Suarez when he asks me about your big picture regarding the deceased."

"I'd never ask you to lie, Harvey. I just never really realized I was all negative about anybody. But yeah, the pieces of my past with Alderete don't paint a positive picture."

"Right. So any investigator's gonna like you a lot for this. I'm just hoping somebody else moves up into first place. And soon. Too bad it took place in your backyard. It feels to me like that somebody is trying hard to set you up. But who in the hell else down there knows your history with the guy?"

The phone slipped down atop the duvet. I stared at the television. The Mariners turned a double play, but I blanked on who they were playing and where.

"Hey. You still there? Want to call me back on a landline?"

I fumbled for the cell. "No. Sorry. I just dropped the phone." I wavered a moment, trying to clear my head. "There is a guy—"

"Whaddaya mean there is a guy?"

"One of the old boys I played with in college. A loose cannon, a real cowboy."

"Yeah. What about him?"

"He was also at that camp in Maine. He was there the night I got into it with Gordon."

"And he's down there at the tournament?"

"He lives here. Kind of a builder-bookie."

"A what?"

"It's complicated. But he's had some business dealings with Gordon, and they got sideways on more than one. Let's just say they don't spend a lot of Saturdays together."

"Sideways enough to off the guy?" I mulled it over, but the lag tweaked a tender nerve. "Well, if you've had to think that long, I'll take it as a yes," Harvey continued. "Do you think Suarez has talked to the guy?"

"I doubt it. I don't see any reason why he'd already connected the two men."

He paused. "If I were you, I'd find a discreet way to find out if the other guy has left town."

"You mean like the subtle way Suarez has been following me?"

"Well, at least he knows you'll be there until the tournament's over. Now, if you were feeling guilty, you'd probably steal a car and started driving east."

"Yeah, right. I'm just starting to wonder if they will make me hang around after the tournament's over."

"Depends what they've got by then. Unless the cops formally charge you, it'd be difficult for them to keep you from leaving. But I'd get involved if they thought you were a flight risk."

"Oh, thanks." I chuckled. "Keep me under house arrest up in North Fork."

"Don't worry. It won't get to that. But back to your buddy from college. Is he the kind of friend where a call to find out where he is or how he's doing wouldn't be suspicious?"

"You mean Wrong Rim?"

"What are you talking about?"

"Ricky Wilkinson. The cowboy who took a shot at the wrong basket and made it."

"Christ. I'm not lovin' the feel of that nickname." A muffled

crack halted the conversation. I assumed it was the sound of the receiver smacking the desk. Harvey barked instructions away from the phone and returned to talk a moment later. "Look, I got a situation downstairs. But we're not done. You hear me?"

"Loud and clear."

"I can assume Jessie's absence from the office is due to the notorious medical condition known as a broken heart?"

"Let me—"

"And, *and* Lyle and Monty Rochester were on her flight home. Seems Monty got word at the airport about Kyle being dismissed from the team. Turned right around and came home with him. I guess he was heavily cocktailed. Man, is he after you."

I sighed and checked the Mariners game. Seattle's closer surrendered a one-out dinger in the bottom of the ninth. "Tell him he's gonna have to take a number."

"Jessie said Kyle got picked up at SeaTac by a cousin who lives in Arlington. Said the boys were going to work the green bean season at the Twin Cities cannery. Apparently, they planned to live together down there."

"Sounds like a plan," I said. "Give him some space from the old man."

TWENTY-FOUR

THE PHONE RANG EARLY AND OFTEN before I could raise a sleep-drunk arm to the bedside table. My late dream show ended with Diane and me stepping from the crystal-clear ocean, snorkels and fins bobbing at our sides, me admiring how well she wore her bikini.

"Did I wake you up?" Rob Suarez asked.

"No. I had to get the phone."

"What?"

"Forget it," I muttered. I grabbed another pillow and propped up my head. The digital clock's red numerals showed 7:18 a.m. "You don't make calls after eight?"

"You didn't tell me you knew Ricky Wilkinson."

"Is there a question?"

"Well?"

"You never asked."

"God, I hate that answer."

The line went silent, and I didn't care. I closed my eyes and prayed for a dial tone. Didn't happen.

"Harvey said you knew each other in school," he said.

"Then you know."

"What else can you tell me about him? Was he ever arrested?"

"Not that I know of." The scent of fresh coffee drifted into the room. I pictured Timoteo at the controls in the kitchen.

"Commit any crimes?"

I grinned, thinking back to the creative betting scheme Ricky devised in our college dorm. "That's a helluva question. None that he was arrested for." That brought a break in the questions. I changed phone hands and scooted back against the headboard.

"You're not giving me much here."

"Hey," I groaned. "It's early."

"Look," he said. "I am sorry for calling at this hour. But this guy's death caught the eyes of some high-fliers. We need to move on it, produce some leads."

"Doesn't surprise me. Gordon knew a lot of people who sit in comfy chairs."

"OK. Wilkinson has been known to take a few bets around the South Bay. Nothing that we're really excited about, but we know he's involved."

"And?"

"And if he's into gambling there's a possibility he could be into drugs, too."

"He's not into drugs. Does like his games, though." I assumed the muffled commotion at the other end included a shuffling of notes and phone.

"And you know this how?"

I shifted my weight, trying to get comfortable sitting up in bed. "We had a come-to-Jesus about what he did. And he doesn't."

"Could you elaborate?"

"Well, theoretically, let's just say a person got repaid for something. Anything. And that payment came wrapped in a way that seemed suspicious. Maybe even looked like a commodity you did not approve of."

"Go on."

"And that person got really mad about the remote possibility that it was inappropriate. Let everybody know about it. And that such a commodity would never be in his home or associated

with him in any way."

"OK. Understood."

"Why do you think drugs have anything to do with Gordon's murder?" I asked.

"I don't know yet, but they're often a factor. Seem to be a piece in every case we get. I'm just trying to connect some dots. Mr. Dupree has been associated with at least one of your players. You have a longstanding relationship with Mr. Wilkinson. It would seem—"

"Oh, c'mon! That's a huge jump. I hadn't spoken with Ricky for years until this deal came up."

"We're paid to make jumps, especially given Mr. Wilkinson's activities. It's what we do. Sometimes they pay off."

"I thought you guys were doing a deep dive on Terrell. You said he may have broken into the house." My stomach growled. It would be nice to grab a cup from the first pot of coffee.

"He's certainly a person of interest. We're looking into his alibi."

My backside ached. I spun my legs to the floor and sat on the side of the bed. "You may not believe this, but I've got other things to do. Including making sure my players aren't shelled by all this. They came here for fun."

"I'm afraid they'll only remember they stayed in a house where a murder was committed."

"Yeah," I scoffed. "Something they can tell their kids about. Just great."

"I can't imagine the calls you're getting from their parents. They must be fried."

"I got Diane on that. Queen of soothe and smooth. Been going better than expected." I sensed a hesitation, as if Suarez needed a notebook.

"Now that would be Ms. Chevalier, correct?"

"Correct. She's Nick's mom. He's a straight-A student and a damn good forward."

"Right. I believe I saw her at a game, but we didn't actually meet. Now, how are you two associated?"

I swallowed. My throat felt dry, so I took a swig from the plastic water bottle adjacent to the phone.

"Coach Creekmore?"

"Well, as I said, she's a parent of one of my players." I looked away, took a deep breath, and continued. "And she's my girlfriend." I smiled and for some reason added, "And she's a widow."

"I see. Wasn't aware of that. Actually, either of those." He paused a moment and said, "Did she have any previous contact with Mr. Wilkinson?"

"No. I told her about Ricky when we committed to the tournament. They didn't meet until we got here."

"OK. Do you think she would mind if I asked her for a few minutes of her time?"

"I don't see why she would. I mean, you're gonna do it anyway."

"Right. Well, yes, I will be contacting her." Another long pause. I hoped goodbye came next. "Tell me, Coach. Did Ms. Chevalier meet Mr. Alderete down here for the first time, or had they met before?"

I could feel my lips flatten. I closed my eyes and pointed my chin toward the ceiling. "I just found out that they had met before."

"Oh, really. When was that?"

"Several years ago. Gordon somehow discovered Nick at a junior's event. Word was out he was a decent player."

"And what was Mr. Alderete's role?"

"He's a big Nevada booster. Went to gauge the kid's interest in the school. Nothing formal or sanctioned. These meet-and-greets happen all the time."

"It appears these casual evaluations now occur when these boys are quite young?"

"Tell me about it. Kids are gettin' scouted in elementary

school." I stopped, remembering who was on the other end. "Hell, you played. You should know."

"I didn't think they started that early." Another gap in the pinball exchange. I checked the clock and prayed for a quick sendoff. The coffee smelled more inviting. "Did Ms. Chevalier continue the relationship with Mr. Alderete in those several years?"

"I don't think you can describe it as a relationship," I said. "Her husband was alive at the time. Diane said Gordon was helping them through the early recruiting craziness."

"Did she stay in contact with Mr. Alderete after her husband died?"

"No. At least I don't think so."

"Do you know if they ever became romantically involved?"

I leaped from the bed and began pacing the floor. "What kind of question is that?! Hell, no they weren't romantically involved! It was about pee-wee basketball, for chrissake."

"So, you're certain they never dated, saw each other socially?"

"No! I'm not a hundred-percent certain. But there's a snowball's chance they even talked since Nick was a kid."

He waited a moment and then said, "Can you think of any reason why Ms. Chevalier would want Mr. Alderete dead?"

"Oh my God! They hardly knew each other! Why would you ever ask that question?"

"Because he is dead, Coach."

"And everyone's a suspect."

"Everyone's a suspect."

TWENTY-FIVE

LINN AND BARBARA CRAMMED THE boys into the van and headed for pancakes at Polly's on the Pier in Sunset. I met the parents at the Shadow Hotel and answered their questions and addressed their concerns about the fallout surrounding Gordon's murder and the move to the duplex. I headed back to our digs to compile a game plan and work through individual matchups in our next game, but I underestimated the time needed to park. I found myself touring the neighborhood looking for an open spot, fearing that half the afternoon might be wasted in the search.

Ricky Wilkinson said the big joke in the South Bay had become that parking was no longer an issue because there wasn't any. With no driveway or garage, Ricky's renters relied on street spots. Jockeying to get one bordered on an art form. Timing became just as important as location. The combination of specific street-cleaning days, rush-hour restrictions and school-day hours demanded a spreadsheet to determine the possibilities. Add in the enormous number of cars on narrow streets and getting in the door becomes another daily task. I got the message the first time I brought the van home from practice. This time, I ended up three blocks away, under a tree, with my back bumper precariously close to a red-painted curb.

While walking up the sidewalk, I spied a beat-up brown Datsun older than any of my players coasting down the street. I

couldn't decide if the driver of the dusty ride was lost or looking for an address. As it got closer, I recognized Pierre Pantel behind the wheel, and I skipped to the middle of the street to snag him.

"Deacon Joe gave me the address of your place," he said. "It appears I'm on the right block." He showed me the street number on a scrap of paper.

I pointed north. "It's about four houses farther down. Hard to tell because it's a duplex. I'm just going in. Find a place, and I'll meet you there."

"My time is short." He turned the ignition off, and the cooling car made a tinkling sound like popcorn hitting a tin lid. "I simply wanted to see my boy."

"They're all out for breakfast. But why don't you come in for a few minutes?"

"Oh, I don't know. Maybe I'll just be on my way."

I moved closer to the driver's window. "Come on in. If you can park somewhere. I'll make some coffee."

"All right. I'll be in momentarily." He fired up the car and edged away.

About ten minutes later, he bobbed up the sidewalk, brown coveralls over a blue work shirt. His black work boots seemed too big for his feet yet did not curtail his fluid steps. I opened the door. He shook my hand and looked me in the eye.

"Thanks for the invitation."

I picked some of the sofa pillows from the floor in the tiny living room, put them in their place, and removed a *People* magazine from the recliner. The place smelled like leftover French fries and dirty socks. "The kids stayed up to watch *SportsCenter*," I said. "Seems they can't go to bed until they see the top ten plays of the day. Mostly monster dunks." He chose the sofa, and I started to the kitchen to put on a pot.

"I missed all that," he murmured. "Young people watching television. Gathering in groups."

I stopped, head down. "I did, too. No kids in our house. And

I didn't know how bad I missed it until I got into situations like this. I actually love the chaos, but not as much as we've had on this trip." I loaded the coffee and returned to the recliner.

Pantel tossed a magazine on the cocktail table. "How are they doin'? With this Alderete thing?"

I cupped an elbow and pulled it toward my chin, trying to coax a kink from my left shoulder. "Thanks for asking. A couple seemed more upset than the others, and we're taking more time with them. Our trainer, Timoteo, is a doctor but an even better counselor. He's had lots of one-on-one with the boys."

"And my boy?" He stared straight through me, the smooth brown face flawed by the imposing S scar on his left cheek. His tight, glossy curls were perfectly aligned. He looked like an official of a South American country on his day off.

"I think Deacon Joe came through OK," I said. "It's hard to know because it seems he keeps a lot inside."

Pantel blinked hard and looked out the window. A BMW convertible sped by, too fast for the school zone. "He's seen too much," Pantel said, still looking away. He turned to me. "It probably didn't influence him like the other young men."

I crossed my arms and paused. "He and another kid, Trent, seemed to take it best. Trent's had a tough couple of years. They've become buddies. Probably closer than any two kids we've got."

The coffee pot beeped as the final few ounces gushed through the filter. I stood. "You take anything in it?"

"A little milk if it's convenient."

I returned with two mugs and we sat and talked, one man mournful over misused time with a child, the other lamenting not having the chance.

Pierre Pantel took a slug of coffee and spoke of his childhood in nearby Hawthorne. The son of Haitian immigrants, he found the Lord after Desert Storm and began preaching in the San Joaquin Valley town of Selma, "The

Raisin Capital of the World." There he met Juanita, a brown-eyed beauty from Guadalajara who worked the fields with her six siblings and sent their earnings back to family in Mexico. They moved back to Hawthorne where Pierre caught on with an expanding church, but the PTSD regularly surfaced.

"I loved that woman so much," Pierre said. "But in those days, I loved the bottle more. I'd return to her countless times for money and then depart after I got it. I lost my wife, my position at the parish and Deacon Joe. The last time I saw her, she gave me this." He stroked the scar on his face. "She broke my bottle and then stuck me with it. Believe me, I deserved more. The boy saw all of it. After I left, she needed money and went back to working in the fields. Grapes, apples, apricots. She and Deacon Joe ended up your way, and I ended up in rehab. I pray to God my drinking problems are behind me."

I sat back, absorbing his history. And my drinking. I hadn't had as much as a beer since I left North Fork.

"Deacon Joe's got a good head on his shoulders," I said. "He's a tough kid who's going to make a difference."

"Yes, no thanks to me," Pantel scoffed and sipped his coffee. "He's clearly learned to operate on the street. Look at the problems he's caused down here." He slid the mug on the table, drawing a splash-spill. He grunted. "Sorry, so thoughtless."

I sat forward and wiped away the spill as he held up his mug. "Any kid would've been tempted. Money and fast cars mess with the young mind. When you have nothing, it's hard to turn that stuff down."

"Yes, he didn't want to listen. He'd rather parade around with Terrell. My goodness. Terrell thought he was doing him a favor, offering to take him in. Just like he thought he was doing me a favor. Both have been big mistakes." He relaxed and spread his arms on top of the couch.

"I was concerned about Deacon Joe. Especially when he didn't care to play. I mean, your son *always* wants to play. Little

different in the last game, though."

"We spoke. He didn't care to hear anything from me."

"I've learned from years of parent-teacher conferences that kids often don't want words of wisdom from Dad."

He smiled, and his eyebrows rose. "Yes, better to come from someone else. Like yourself. I can't tell you how grateful I am to you and this Cheese fellow."

I waited for a moment. "Don't sell yourself short. There's a way back from this. You've both got a lot of time. More importantly, it sounds as though you both have the interest."

He paused and narrowed his eyes. "Deacon Joe did come around after he understood some of the things Terrell was having me do. When he offered me a job, I was simply too concerned about paying the bills. The situation has deteriorated to where I'd much rather work three jobs than stay with that man."

"We talked briefly at the restaurant. Nice place. I hope that is working out for you."

"It's one of the pieces. My goal is to return to charity work, helping people. I've known the chaplain at Providence Hospital since I was a boy. The facility has expanded such that he finds himself spread too thin. He has appealed to the board of directors to add an assistant minister. I should know soon."

He turned down a coffee refill. Knowing paperwork and roster evaluations loomed ahead, I helped myself to another cup.

"I heard what you did to get that young woman into Helpline House."

Startled, he sat up, looking confused. "Actually, the chaplain got a call from somebody high up and got word to me. But how did you possibly know? Only a handful of people—"

"Diane and I toured the facility the other day. Before we left, we ran into Renee. She happened to be in a room visiting her sister."

He reclined. I couldn't tell if he was pleased for her sister's

safety or concerned about her condition. Maybe both. "Phaedra," Pierre whispered. "Renee's sister's name is Phaedra."

* * *

I GRABBED THE STATS FROM OUR FIRST two games and flopped down on the bed, hoping to spot some tendencies that might help turn us around. Moments later, I was out. The call from Rob Suarez drummed me out of dreamland. I'd been showing Diane how to cast the new flyrod I'd bought her for Christmas on the sunny banks of the north fork of the Stillaguamish River. I fumbled the cell and groaned as I reached to the floor to snag it.

"Have you ever spoken with a Marsha McKnight?"

"Good morning to you, too." I tried to rewind the mental tapes on the name. "Don't think so. Who the hell is that?"

"She was your neighbor on the north side in that rental off Thirty-Third Street. Where we found Mr. Alderete's body. Says she talked to you when you were moving in."

"Right, right. Dolly Parton. Go on."

"Excuse me?" He waited a moment. I rolled over on my side, posted on an elbow. "Anyway, one of my guys went over to her place last night. We interviewed all the neighbors. She thinks she heard somebody in your parking area around dinner time that night. Said she was in the shower and then on the phone in her dressing room and didn't look out until several minutes later. Said she saw a yellow Chevy backing out into the alley. All polished and shiny."

"So, you're thinking maybe Terrell tried to break into this place while we were at dinner?"

"Dinner, or the end of practice, yeah. Definitely wouldn't put it past him. Got any idea what he might have wanted, or

might have been looking for?"

Holding the phone to my ear, I cranked around and sat on the side of the bed. "I hope to God he wasn't delivering some dope to another one of my guys. We already had a situation at the Shadow."

"I've been made aware of that," Rob said. "I was wondering if it was more of a rendezvous with your Mr. Gonzales."

I massaged my forehead. "Lord, I hope not. I was fairly certain he'd split from Terrell."

"But he's still a kid. A vulnerable kid with no money and no real job, right? A wad of cash at the right moment can look pretty good."

I waited, trying to trim my partiality. "I'm still going to side with Deacon Joe. Until I hear otherwise."

"I know you want to support the kid. But given his past few days? I'd say the chances are pretty good he got talked into something. Something not good."

I stood and walked to the hall door, listening for early morning feet. "What do you want me to do on this end?"

"Just make sure you know where the boys are at all times. Especially Deacon Joe. No requests for meals away or visits to the mall. Be casual, but firm."

"We can do that."

"And I'll need a few minutes with each of them. Either at the house or at the gym. In light of what's happened, they all probably expect some time with a cop. Please try not to let them get overly rattled."

"Shit, overly rattled? The damn tournament director was murdered in their driveway! How in the hell can they not be?" I peeked again down the hall, ducked back into the room, and toned it down. "They've had to put up with rumors of the whole tournament being canceled. There's also the minor issue of their coach possibly being a suspect in the case. Somehow my history with Gordon got out." Rob fell silent. "You still there?"

"We got the preliminary report back from the medical

examiner. They put the time of death between noon and eight p.m. You were with your team that entire time. Lunch, game, dinner. Plus before and after."

I took a deep breath, stood in the middle of the room, and dipped my head. "So you actually believed I wanted to kill the guy? And then pulled it off?"

"No, I don't think you killed Mr. Alderete, but we had to rule it out. That's what we do. It's what Harvey is known for. Look, I don't know what you wanted to do to Mr. Alderete at one time in your life. That really doesn't make a difference. We all experience extreme anger at some point in our lives and are capable, *capable* of just about anything."

I didn't want to go there, back to what I might have done that night when the counselors pulled me off of Gordon. "What else did you learn from the medical examiner?"

I heard pages flipping. He answered a question away from the phone. "Sorry about that. Yes, well, somebody bashed him in the back of the head. Right on top of the bald spot. Did you see indications of that when you found him? He also had three cracked vertebrae in his lower back. Curious."

I sat back on the bed, closed my eyes, and tried to rewind the image when I opened the trash gate. "Mr. Alderete was lying face-up. Bloody towel to the side. There were a bunch of plastic bags behind his head and around his body. Mostly black with plastic ties, sopped with blood. A few white bags. Didn't see the back of his head."

"That's an accurate account of what I encountered when I arrived," Rob said. "Most of what you stated is in my report. The medical examiner also raised the possibility that the body could have been dumped there, then dragged a short distance. Reported traces of blood on the pavement."

"Any blood in the house? On the deck?"

More sounds of pages moving. "No mention of that in the report."

I fell silent. My gut hurt for a piece looming outside of our

202 | Tom Kelly

present puzzle. "Tell me something, Rob. How in the hell did this happen?"

"What do you mean, how did this happen? You've been down this road with Harvey. Somebody was obviously upset with Mr. Alderete and lashed out."

"But the guy was six-foot-seven! And probably pretty damn strong."

He seemed to hesitate, pondering an option. "Do you remember any of the players going out back, maybe after you got home from dinner? Perhaps before lunch that afternoon?"

I plunged the phone down to my side, ready to throw it or stomp it into the rug. I took a deep breath and growled, "This has nothing to do with my kids! The big and strong *or* the short and skinny."

"Look, I'm just trying to—

"And we got nobody who sneaks joints. Or anybody who's got a jones of any kind!"

"That you know about." He let that sit, and it felt like a bad batch of spicy chili. "You didn't know about Kyle Rochester. Until you were forced to send him home."

I gnawed on that reasonable statement. "Yes, that I know about. But I *do know* that young men never take out the trash unless you ask them. So, no. Nobody comes to mind."

"Who was staying in the bedroom off the kitchen? The little casita out back?"

"Timoteo and his wife. But they had a date night. I told them to take some time away from the kids. I doubt if they went anywhere near the trash area."

"No worries," Rob said. "I'll catch him today and speak with him about it."

I shuffled back to the side of the bed. "Well, is that it? I need some coffee. We also have a game to prepare for. Can't really expect a lot of spark out of the kids after what they've been through. Three different beds in four days? Christ."

"Before you go. . ."

I groaned and crashed on the bed. Once prone, I took my time raising the receiver to my ear. "OK, let me have it."

"Do you remember the condition of Mr. Dupree's vehicle?"

"Sure. Pristine. Spotless. Not a scratch anywhere. Why?"

"The neighbor. This Marsha McKnight?"

"Right. The bottle blonde with the hillbilly accent."

"When asked to describe the vehicle, she told one of our officers the same thing. Except there was a large depression in the middle of the front hood. Its glare bounced off the alley lights. She said you couldn't miss it."

* * *

TIRED, CRANKY AND IRRITATED WITH no on-court answers in sight, I drove over to the gym to scout the Denver Devils, our likely next opponent. Linn Oliver mentioned on more than one occasion during the week that the club had the third or fourth best roster "on paper" in the tournament. I've learned that in the flesh trumps on paper every time. No written information could replace an in-person visit. Seeing a kid's body language on the floor and his interactions with teammates on the bench did more to assist in my game preparation than a binder stuffed with stat sheets.

Also in the stands that night was an assistant coach from UC-Irvine who'd recruited one of my Washington High players years ago. He pointed out player tendencies, including how the star guard never used his first dribble to advance the ball, content to stand and yo-yo until he appraised his opponent or discovered an open teammate breaking to the basket.

"If you have a quick little guard," the assistant coach said, "you can pressure this guy hard as soon as he gets it and bring his scoring way down."

I jotted down notes on a folded flier I found in my hip

pocket. When the last minutes of the game ticked away, I began to fold the flier. Stunned, I stared down at one of the pages.

"What's up?" the assistant asked. "You look like you just found a phone number you needed last week."

"Oh, it's nothin'," I stammered. "Just looking at something from last year's info."

In the photo featuring a beaming Gordon Alderete stood a cluster of shapely ladies all taxing the limits of their halter tops, all with perfect teeth and flowing, shiny hair. Snuggling at Gordon's elbow stood Renee, the only person in the photo not smiling.

TWENTY-SIX

WHEN MY CELL BUZZED AGAIN before eight a.m., I knew an invitation to a lavish party or a genuine well-wishing seemed remote.

"Turns out one of our Lawndale guys has been tracking your boy, Mr. Dupree," Rob Suarez said.

"Who said he was my boy?" I groaned, trying to sweep sleep bugs from my eyes.

"Since Big Jess was found in that Dumpster, Mr. Dupree's been getting more of our time. Not twenty-four-seven, but more than casual surveillance."

"And it's important to tell me that right this minute because. . . ?"

"One of our guys witnessed a probable drug exchange. He followed the black Suburban to the San Pablo warehouse I mentioned before. Mr. Dupree and a much larger man got out of the vehicle and entered the building."

"Long hair, kinda greasy?"

"Yes. Big shoulders, arms."

"That sounds like Oscar," I said. "One of Terrell's guard dogs. Wouldn't win Best in Show. Strong, but not a Phi Beta Kappa upstairs."

"Yes, well, both men entered and did not leave until several hours later."

I flipped off the covers and stood in my jammies, pondering

jeans or shorts for the morning. "So the boys had a long powwow. So what? Did your man call for back-up, go in and bust 'em?"

"I certainly wish that had been the case."

"Lieutenant, you're killin' me here. From what you have told me about Terrell and company, this sounds like business as usual."

"My message this morning is that, much to my disappointment, the time the two men spent in that warehouse was precisely the timeframe in which we believe Mr. Alderete was murdered."

I reached behind me for the bed, hoping to get there before falling. "Are you saying Terrell now has a solid alibi?"

"That certainly appears to be the case."

I rocked back on the bed and stared at the ceiling. "You're sure he didn't leave that building at all? There's no other exit?"

"We've been around all sides of the property on several occasions. There is only one way in and out of the unit they use. Our investigator was across the street with a visual of the vehicle and entry the entire time."

"Good God," I muttered. "What are you thinking now?"

He didn't wait long. The hound had caught a scent. "Two things. Mr. Dupree wanted Mr. Alderete dead and put a hit out on him. Not unlike what happened to Big Jess."

"And what's number two?"

"That someone used his car to frame you for Mr. Alderete's murder. In either case, given how these guys operate, it makes sense they'd try to cover their tracks."

I paused, recalling my last one-on-one with Terrell. "Hmmm. He did say I would pay the price."

"What? Are you saying he threatened you? When did this take place?"

"After we lost our first game. We got into it in a hallway."

The line fell silent. I bet Suarez wondered what else I could possibly be holding back from him. "OK," he continued. "Were

there other incidents that might connote motive?"

"Not really. But I'll give it some thought." I rose and pulled the curtain, hoping for sunshine but getting another layer of fog.

"Please do." After an awkward moment, he said, "I wanted to ask you something else."

"Fire away."

"Did you ever find your wallet?"

"No. And it's been a pain in the ass. Not only do I not have my license, but I also have to borrow one of Diane's credit cards anytime I want to buy something. Then scribble her signature and hope they don't look at the name on the card. And by the way, tell me you've eliminated her as a suspect."

"Yes. Her whereabouts at the time of the murder have been verified by at least two other persons."

"Great, great police work." He didn't respond. "What about Ricky Wilkinson?" I dipped into the dresser for underwear and a Fighting Crabs T-Shirt and tossed them on the bed.

"Let's just say he has moved to the top of the list. Mr. Wilkinson's up there with another suspected drug facilitator, and Mr. Dupree, of course. Mr. Wilkinson says he has a person who can confirm he was nowhere near the crime scene, but he has yet to identify that person or provide any contact information."

"He tends to keep parts of his life behind closed doors."

"I've got a feeling he better open a few soon, or a big one could be slamming behind him at the state penitentiary." He paused again. I felt another fork in the road looming. "Did you know your wallet was found in one of Mr. Alderete's pockets by our investigators?"

I collapsed onto the only chair in the bedroom. "Is that some kind of trick question? How in the hell was I supposed to know that? And when am I going to get—?"

"Do you remember giving Mr. Alderete your wallet?"

"Hell no! Why on earth would I do that?"

"Can you think of any reason why Mr. Alderete would have

come into possession of your wallet?"

"Christ, no!"

"Perhaps you lost or misplaced it during the week. Maybe you dropped it in the lobby of the Shadow? At the coaches' luncheon?"

I attempted to revisit the timeframe in my mind. "No. I remember having it with me after all that. I always put my wallet and keys down at the same time. I found my keys in the kitchen. The wallet wasn't there."

"The department decided to keep the wallet until we were certain you were not involved. I'll see that it is returned to you as soon as possible." He waited, and I expected the wait. I was beginning to grasp his cop's cadence, his propensity for spacing his messages. "There's something else."

"Geez, I was hoping you were all out of surprises, that I could dress and get on with my day. We *are* in town for a reason, you know. Go ahead, what is it?"

"There was a picture. A small picture of your wife in Mr. Alderete's other front pocket."

I stood and returned to the window. The fog blanketed the schoolyard across the street. "I had one in the wallet. In the plastic windows with the credit cards. Why in the hell had it been taken out?"

"I was hoping you could tell me."

* * *

THE FIRST HALF OF OUR THIRD GAME, a slow bump-fest against a bunch of big-legged kids from Albuquerque, turned sloppy early as both teams missed easy layups and committed stupid fouls. Trent and Nick seemed more eager to push and elbow two freckled farm boys in the middle rather than prance around them and find an open shot. We started Marcus McGann

on their lightning-quick Asian point guard, who found his groove and penetrated our lane, dishing to his teammates for easy buckets. Deacon Joe rode the bench, wearing a pair of weathered high-tops. Terrell and two of his crew swaggered in midway through the first quarter, slouched over three rows near midcourt, scowling and scrolling cell phones. We finished the second quarter by scoring eight unanswered points to cut the deficit to six.

When stumped for a motivating halftime message, I typically re-wound the mental tapes of a memorable comeback. I staggered into the locker room behind the players and scribbled AFS on the whiteboard, three letters that had stuck in my brain for more than thirty years since a stumpy old coach chalked them on a chipped green board. *Always Finish Strong.*

"Just keep it up," I said. "We'll half-court trap the first and third times they inbound the ball. First and third after a basket. Got it? We're going to mix it up and see if they'll turn it over. Now, Linn's got a change on defense, so listen up."

As Linn came forward and explained the new assignments, Deacon Joe stood closer to me, his elbow grazing my side. We had no better attacker in the half-court trap than Deacon Joe, and I knew he wanted to remind me of that fact and his availability. I didn't respond and focused on my assistant's instructions.

"Lemme lock him down, Coach," Deacon Joe whispered. "Please. Let me try."

I ignored him and followed the players out for second-half warm-ups. But as the players were going through their drills, I told Linn we would go with Deacon Joe.

"We've got nobody else who can stop their guy," Linn said. "I just hope he's ready to play."

I signaled to Deacon Joe to leave the court and take a seat. Our remaining players launched a few more practice jumpers. When he came over, I said, "Where are the new kicks? No longer stylin'?"

"Had to make some adjustments, sooner than I thought. Ever do that, Coach?"

Stunned, I briefly closed my eyes and shook my head. "What? I guess not soon enough sometimes. Why?"

"Made a deal with my dad, s'all."

The buzzer sounded to begin the half. Our four starters headed to center court and stared back to the bench, waiting for the fifth. I said, "What's that got to do with sneakers?"

He yanked off his sweatshirt and fired it to the floor beneath our bench. "It's complicated," he shouted as he fist-bumped his teammates. A moment before the tip, he added a long-grip handshake with Trent. As play started, Terrell's posse pounded down the bleachers and strutted out of the building.

TWENTY-SEVEN

THE ALBUQUERQUE KIDS COULD NOT find an answer to our trapping defense. As soon as the ball crossed half-court, Deacon Joe and Marcus doubled the Asian speedster, forcing him to pick up his dribble above the foul line. His teammates failed to break from their spots on the floor and come to his rescue, creating easy steals and turnovers. We won by twenty-three, and it could have been worse. Deacon Joe celebrated with his teammates, collected his gear, and walked out with his father. Timoteo held up the van keys and pointed to the far exit. Linn closed the scorebook and led the players out.

Trent shouldered his bag and turned to Marcus and Nick. "Too bad we lost that first game and got stuck in the losers' bracket," Trent said. "The way we're playin', we could win this whole damn thing."

I waited a moment and pulled Trent aside. "What's with your renewed point guard?"

He paused for others to clear. Dropping his bag, he yanked out a towel and mopped his face and head. "Well, we talked until real late last night. Terrell wanted to test him with a big delivery. We're not talkin' Big Macs. Like it was some sort of initiation. Deacon Joe said he's been tested all his life, why'd he need another one? Then he heard the part about his dad."

"What about his dad?"

"Seems Terrell planned on the old man as the wheelman. Saw the dad-son thing as nice and cozy."

"How did that go down with Deacon Joe?"

"Real shitty. Sorry, but yeah, real shitty. Try to get an ol' homie to do somethin' sketchy with the dad? I mean, c'mon."

Timoteo came back into the gym and hollered, "Hey, Coach, if you guys are ridin' with us, this bus is leavin'."

I held up one finger. "Just give us a minute." Timoteo waved his approval and returned outside.

"So, how did he leave it with Terrell?"

"I guess it got pretty ugly," Trent said. "I mean, I wasn't there, but how often you see Deacon Joe pissed? I mean, like, never. Says he got into it with Terrell, lots of pushing and shoving. A few blows, a little blood."

"Christ, he didn't look hurt."

"S'alright. He came out OK. You know what brought the blows, Coach."

I tipped my chin upward, a *let's-have-it* indicator.

"Guess Terrell said he was the only future the dad had. If they both didn't make the delivery, Deacon Joe's future with Terrell was iffy."

"So what was finally decided?"

"Deacon Joe said he told Terrell to fuck off. Ah, sorry, Coach. But he told him to fuck off and stay the fuck away from the team."

Timoteo bolted back through the door with Linn Oliver behind him. "Ernie, these kids are about ready to eat the upholstery in that van."

"He's right, Coach," Linn said. "They've got pizza on the brain. We're lookin' at a major mutiny here in a matter of minutes."

Trent picked up his bag. "My bad. We're comin'." Then in a lower tone, he said to me, "Anyway, he went and found his dad. The dad took him to a hospital, told him he might get a job there. Showed him around. Deacon Joe said he'd quit Terrell if

his dad quit him. That woman was there, too."

"What woman?"

Trent pushed open the gym door, and we heard a chorus of "Finally!" and "'Bout time!" and "What took so long?" rising from the van. He stopped short of the rig to a bark of "Hurry up!" and turned to faced me. "Know what else? Deacon Joe apologized to me, asked me to forgive him. Said he knew how much this trip meant to me."

Trent tossed his bag into the flat back, to the jeers of the riders, and slid the passenger door open. Everyone played hard-ass and refused to make room for the big guy. "OK, we just won't eat," I said. Several spaces instantly became available. I slid into the shotgun seat, eased back into the comfy headrest, and closed my eyes for one city block when the first f-bomb arrived.

* * *

WE MIRACULOUSLY FOUND A SPOT for the van two houses away from the duplex. The boys spilled out into the fog, burping pepperoni and root beer. As Linn ushered them down the sidewalk, Rob Suarez approached me from the opposite side of the street in a knee-length overcoat.

"You could be in England with that London Fog," I said.

"Not always beach weather at the beach." He stopped near the curb. "Got a minute?" I pointed to the house and began walking.

"Why don't we do it here?" he said.

I stopped and tilted my head to one side. "OK. What's up?"

He dug into his coat pocket and handed me my wallet. "Finally," I snorted. I glanced at him and started thumbing through the sections. "Thanks for bird-dogging this for me. I felt better that somebody actually cared that I got it back." The

cash looked untouched. All credit cards accounted for.

"I think you'll find everything's there." He reached into the front pocket of his trousers. "Except this." He handed me the wallet-size photo of Cathy, taken by our wedding photographer. I felt my head snap back. She looked the same the day she died.

"Why do you think—?"

"Mr. Alderete lived in a three-bedroom condominium not far from here. Ocean view, close to where his body was found. In his locked study, we found one wall filled with photographs of women. Some were well known, glossy eight-by-tens. Studio done, promotional material. Most of the images were enlarged, then mounted."

I slid a hand behind my neck. "So, you think he was going to blow this up and add it to his gallery?"

He pulled a handkerchief from his back pocket and wiped his nose. "Darn fog." He replaced the cloth and said, "Did your wife ever have any sort of contact with Mr. Alderete?"

I looked down and squeezed my eyes. I stared at Suarez. "Yeah, I'd call assault contact."

"I'm sorry," he whispered. He pulled up the collar of his coat and stuffed his hands in his pockets. "How did Mr. Alderete know about the picture?"

"I showed it to him. In the lobby of the Shadow. Thought I'd jog his memory."

"I'm a bit surprised you didn't do more."

I dropped my hands and drew closer. "Man, did I think about it. For *years* I thought about it. And it damn near ate me up!" I stepped back, took a breath and scrunched my shoulders. "Look, I'm getting cold. Why don't you come—?"

"Just one more thing," he said.

I tipped my chin up. "Shoot."

"You are familiar with Renee Sarno, correct? The woman who has been seen with Terrell Dupree?"

"I didn't know that was her last name. I do know the Renee who's been circling, yes." I signaled I'd had enough and began

walking toward the duplex.

"Her mug shot was found on Mr. Alderete's desktop. We have yet to locate its enlargement."

I stopped and turned. I folded my arms and looked to the sky.

"We won't see any stars tonight," Suarez said. "This stuff is too thick."

"Christ, I know that," I said. "And stars are not exactly what I was thinking about." I stared at him. "Whatcha doin' in the morning? The boys have a shootaround at nine."

"Nothing scheduled until one. Why?"

"Why don't you pick me up shortly after nine? Maybe we can find out if that picture was ever enlarged."

TWENTY-EIGHT

When I got inside the duplex, I asked Deacon Joe for his father's cellphone number.

"Might not answer," Deacon Joe said. "Terrell gave it to him. Says for business only." He handed me his iPhone. "Use this. If Terrell traces, number be cool."

I dialed Pierre Pantel. His one-word, hushed-tone responses implied genuine concern and fear. After some prodding, he agreed to meet me on the Rubicon Beach Pier in thirty minutes. When I returned the phone, Deacon Joe froze.

"Comin' with you, Coach," he cried.

"I need you to stay here. Please."

He bristled like a dog sensing trouble. "He's almost clear. Clear of Terrell."

"I know. I just need to ask him a few questions. To make sure he's clear on a few other things."

"I'll get Trent. We'll come back you up. You don't know some of the guys been messin' with him."

"Just trust me on this one. Please."

"I don't know." He looked down with a slow head shake.

"Look. If I don't return in an hour, head for the pier. I promise to be back before that."

His mouth turned down in resignation. "All right. One hour."

I grabbed a jacket and jogged to the VW bus. I needed fewer

than five minutes to drive to the public parking lot adjacent to the pier. The beach crowd had gone, and the bar-restaurant gang now leaned toward cabs and Ubers, leaving a few open spaces for tourists and fishermen. Pierre Pantel rose from a bench near the southern handrail, the Palos Verdes peninsula silhouetted behind him. When I approached, he pulled up his jacket collar and checked behind me for other walkers. We shook hands.

"As you can see, I need to be cautious," he said. Worry and fear tightened his face. "Terrell expected me to persuade Deacon Joe to stay and work with him."

"I'm not sure I understand. It didn't work. Everybody moves on."

"No, Coach. In his eyes, I failed. I expect consequences, but I'm uncertain what they will be."

I turned and gazed north. The lights of Santa Monica had broken through the fog. "Pierre, about those consequences. Did Terrell ask you to set me up? Come to the rental when Gordon was there?"

He looked behind me again and suggested we walk toward the end of the pier. "Not me. But I overheard him talking with Oscar and some others. They talked about tailing Gordon. To accomplish what they wanted to do."

I stopped. "If Oscar was with Terrell, who staked out the house?"

"Terrell does have individuals he can call on. So when it happened, it was not a surprise to anybody."

"Including Renee?"

He turned and raised his hands. "Renee's not in Terrell's camp. Far from it. Terrell calls her his 'cheesecake.' She resents it."

"Enough to set up Terrell for Gordon's murder?"

"Oh, my goodness," he murmured, lowering his chin. "Oh, no. She would never do such a thing. Plus, given what I know about Terrell's organization, it would be too great a risk."

I pinched my chin and stared off, far beyond the end of the

pier. "But not too great a risk to frame me."

Pierre folded his arms and winced. "He clearly was upset with you, for what I don't know."

"Said I would pay a big price."

"Yes, but framing you for murder? I don't know. . . I do know that he was livid with Renee for returning his car with a massive dent. She's pretty much been avoiding him since. I still don't think that would be enough to warrant killing a man." He pivoted and darted to the south guardrail and grabbed it. "Don't look. Two men, near the entry, crisscrossing side to side."

I joined him and feigned a casual conversation. "Any idea who they are?"

"One big and bulky. The other not so much."

"You thinkin' Oscar?"

"Maybe Oscar. Don't know about the other guy."

We waited a few minutes, then strolled to the ocean end of the pier. When we returned, the men had vanished. "You park close by?" I said.

"Not really. Block above Highland."

"I'll drive you to your car."

* * *

I RUSTLED THE BOYS UP AT EIGHT a.m. and lined the kitchen counter with bowls, Cheerios, and Frosted Flakes.

"Betcha Nick is knocking down some of them silver-dollar pancakes this morning at the Shadow," Andre Holberton said.

"Then he's on to an omelet bigger 'n that box," Trent said, pointing to the Cheerios. "Boy can chow."

Linn turned and poured orange juice for all. "Just the benefits of staying with the folks, guys," Linn said. He pointed at his watch. "We only have the gym for an hour, so let's be on time."

"And don't overdo it," I said. "Break a sweat, but don't kill yourselves. Save your juice for tonight. We want to make a statement in our last game here. Remember AFS."

Deacon Joe, Trent, and Andre all smirked and muttered in unison, "Always Finish Strong."

"I'll get there when I can."

Ten minutes later, Rob Suarez double-parked in the street and beeped the horn of a dark blue Chevy Tahoe. I opened the shotgun door and slid in. He'd ditched the trench coat for a khaki blazer and paired it with brown slacks. His oxford shoes appeared new and bordered on orange.

"Nice threads," I said.

"Sun is out in Rubicon Beach. Lucky my good eye isn't colorblind."

"How's it driving with only one?"

"Not as bad as you'd think. Narrow streets with cars parked on both sides?" He waved his hand in front of him. "My biggest problem."

"Should I feel worried?"

He scoffed. "Where to?"

"The rental on Thirty-Third Street. The place we stayed after getting kicked out of the Shadow."

"What? It's still a crime scene. The tape has probably been removed from the street side, but the alley entrance won't be passable."

"I figured as much. Can you get us in?"

"I could get access, but I doubt you'd be allowed. I'll have to feel it out with the investigators once we get there. What are you thinking?"

"Don't really know yet. Couple of things have been gnawing at me. Feel like I better play them out."

He exhaled and raised his eyebrows.

"What?" I asked.

"Harvey said you had good instincts. That something like this might happen."

I pulled the folded leaflet from my pocket and handed it to him.

He arched back. "You want me to see your scouting report on some team? Are you playing these guys tonight?"

"Open it to the middle." He scanned the picture of Gordon with the girls on the beach. "Not only is Renee standing next to Gordon, but she also isn't happy."

He sighed. "It makes you think more about her mug shot that we found on his desk."

His glass eye took on an eerie luminous green shade as if a dim light had been installed behind it. "And we found out something else."

I jerked my chin up in my *Let's hear it* motion. "We have reason to believe Mr. Alderete was buying the drugs and funding the depot south of here while Mr. Dupree organized the deliveries. One of our undercover guys got close to a woman in Alderete's office."

"Close as in eavesdrop or close as in sex?"

"I haven't been privy to all the details, but I assume someplace in between. Why do you ask?"

"Don't you think people tend to be more forthcoming when they are engaged in the latter?"

"Nonetheless, we are discovering more details of the operation."

I arched an eyebrow. "I bet you are." I took back the flier and returned it to my pocket. "So, are you thinkin' Terrell got sideways with Gordon, had one of his thugs deep-six him, and try to pin it on me?"

"More than possible," Suarez said. "And I'll tell you why. Mr. Dupree knew your history with Mr. Alderete. Plus, not only was he upset with you, but he also knew Deacon Joe respects you. Let's assume he went looking for ways to discredit you and at the same time increase the chances that Deacon Joe would join his organization."

I turned in the seat and looked out the window. "Makes

sense. And Terrell covers his ass by being at the warehouse the entire time the dirty deed's goin' down." I could feel my lips flatten. "Hate to see this turn out to be another Big Jess case. Where nobody serves time."

"Excuse me." He sneered. "Nobody yet."

I swiveled back toward him. "Say, anything new on Ricky Wilkinson?"

"We had to persuade Mr. Wilkinson that it was in his best interest to provide us with an account of his locations at the time of Mr. Alderete's demise."

"And?"

"It was ascertained that he was in the company of one Misty Valley, a well-known South Bay exotic dancer."

"Figures," I mused. "I'm sure he'd say she's tops in her field." A moment later I said, "Let's drive over to the house on Thirty-Third Street. If I can look around, I promise to take only a few minutes."

TWENTY-NINE

As we cruised past the front of the rental house where Gordon Alderete's body was found, two young Lycra-clad mothers with kids in strollers shuffled past, their stares probing the residence. An older couple stood across the street, black toy poodle prancing about on a silver leash, the woman pointing at the home animatedly.

"The security tape is down, but the word is clearly out," Suarez said, steering the car to the curb. "Considering the notoriety of the deceased, we can expect quite a few lookieloos." He pointed down the street to two cars edging our way. The drivers leaned across the front seat and away from the wheel, seeking to pinpoint a specific address.

"It's right here, folks," I snickered under my breath. "Gordon's last stand." After a minute, I said, "Let's check the alley entrance."

A uniformed police officer roamed inside the yellow caution tape that reached across the driveway leading to the rear of the house. Suarez spoke to the cop, who said investigators had completed their work inside, but more had to be done on the backside. The officer suggested we park by the main entry. He'd unlock the front door.

Once inside, I recalled the day Gordon first showed the place to Diane and me. I retraced my steps, glanced into all the rooms, then gazed down to the spot where I discovered Deacon

Joe's journal on the floor in the boys' upstairs dormitory.

"Getting what you need?" Suarez said from the hallway.

"No real expectations. Just looking around."

I crossed the hall to my former bedroom, then opened the French doors to the deck and surveyed the crime scene below. Suarez approached from behind.

"You'd get a nice view from here when the sun is out," he said.

"Didn't happen when we were here."

He turned toward me. "You don't always look this confused."

"You should check with my players." I scanned the deck. "I'm done. You ready to go?" Suarez gave me a look that could have either been annoyance or you-wasted-my-time. We waved to the officer below and told him we'd exit via the front door.

I shuffled down the steps and out the door, then walked the narrow passageway between the house and the neighbors on the south side until meeting the caution tape in the back. I reversed my path and cruised the same walkway on the north side to the tape. As I headed back to the car, I spotted a peculiar stone stuck deep in the mud among the pink roses. Shiny and large and partially hidden by the sidewalk, its familiar shape and color brought a jolt of adrenaline.

"Rob? I think you'll want to see this."

* * *

I COAXED ROB INTO ONE MORE STOP, a short jaunt across town to the Providence Hospital complex. Several pieces to Gordon's murder puzzle swirled in my brain, and I felt the need to grab one and slam it in the middle of the ones already in place. The stone in the rose garden and an old saying compounded the mix.

"Thought you couldn't get blood from a stone," I said. "Harvey lamented that for years."

He looked bemused and impressed at the same time. "We've got a new sampling technique, a sort of wet-vac system to collect amounts of DNA on porous surfaces like rocks. The polish should actually be a help. Not as porous." After driving a few blocks, he said, "Another chat with Deacon Joe's dad? I understand he's found a new role that will better suit his background."

"I hope it's a done deal," I said. "But I don't know if any start date's been set. I might see him here today, but I'm not counting on it. If he's not here, then he may be at the game tonight."

He turned toward me and squinted. "I'm confused. We're not going to ask him if he knows anything about the stone we just found?"

I shifted in my seat. "Well, no. But I'm not the investigator here. Are you saying you think he was involved in Gordon's murder?"

"He's one of the principals in this case who's not provided a verifiable alibi at the time of the murder."

"How do you see his relationship to Gordon? Seems he was simply a gofer in Terrell's camp, a pawn to get Deacon Joe to stay."

Rob shook his head as we entered the hospital compound. "I no longer think so. I believe he figured out Gordon was running the show and cut off the head of the snake. In doing so, the organization would fall apart, including Terrell's delivery chores. I believe Mr. Pantel connected the dots and was attempting to protect his son."

"Really?" I snorted and looked away. "Maybe for now. A leopard doesn't change his spots. Terrell picks up with the next dirtbag who can bring him big bucks."

Rob placed the car in park and turned off the key. "So, what are we doing here?" His smile was slow and humorless.

"Candidly, the heat is on to catch whoever did this. It also might surprise you that I've got other things to do. And don't you have a practice?"

I opened my door and pointed to an adjacent building. "Walk with me a moment. There might be somebody here who can help us with some information."

We strolled along a landscaped walkway that ended at the gravel parking lot adjacent to Helpline House. As a nurse exited the back door, I ran to catch it before it closed.

She eyed me warily.

"Lanell Lautze is expecting us," I said.

She raised her eyebrows. "Use the main entrance next time." We acknowledged her with a wave and our thanks, scurried in the door and up the stairs.

I turned to Rob and whispered, "Just happened to be here the other day." He shrugged and followed me as I opened the door at the top of the stairs and peeked down the hallway. The door to the end room was ajar. I leaned in to see Renee again reading in the recliner. I soft-knocked once. She approached the door with the look of a woman in a stalled car with an eighteen-wheeler bearing down on her.

"What . . . what do you want?" she hissed. She wore no makeup, her dark skin smooth and flawless.

"Pierre Pantel said you haven't been around much. I thought I might catch you here." She snuck a look behind her, then stepped into the hallway, pulling the door until it remained just slightly open. "I don't know if you've met Lieutenant Rob Suarez."

"Not yet," Rob said. They shook hands. Her lips flattened, and she blinked long and hard.

"Rob wanted to know if you had a way of contacting Mr. Pantel." Rob looked at me as if I'd asked his girlfriend for a date. "He wanted to ask him where he was when Gordon Alderete was murdered."

"He wasn't anywhere near that house!" She looked away

and put a hand over her mouth. A moment later she wiped a tear.

"And why are you so certain about that?" Rob asked.

A nurse appeared from the far end of the hall, gripping a tray of dishes and food containers. She balanced the tray on one hand and entered a room.

Renee ducked back into her space a moment and reappeared, clutching a tissue. She dabbed her nose.

"Because she drove Terrell's car there that day," I said.

Renee bowed her head.

Rob pushed me on the shoulder and then faced me. "What?" he said. "How did you get that idea?"

Renee pinched her eyes, then said, "Terrell was determined to screw you over. Didn't know how, so I thought I might try to clean up the mess. Like the kid with the nose candy in the hotel. Turns out Gordon says he'll handle you. He didn't want Terrell trashing the house."

"How did you know Gordon was going to be there?" I said.

"I didn't, but I knew he had a key," she said. "He scared the hell out of me. Must have come in the front door."

Rob turned and faced her, his face scrunched. "I missed something. You got in the house, how?"

"I came in off the alley," she said. Then, nodding toward me, "One of the kids probably left the back door unlocked." I smirked and shook my head, knowing I failed to secure it before leaving. "Anyway, I began checking the bedrooms and heard this rumbling down in the living room. I hid in the room straight off the stairs. He staggers up, I hear him fall on the stairs at least once. I go out on the deck and hide in the corner by the window. See he's drunk, absolutely hammered. He slams drawers, pushes stuff around in the closet."

"What did you think he was looking for?" Rob said.

"No idea," Renee whispered. "At first, I thought he might be comin' to plant a ton of pills, get you busted. But he could have easily planted them in your bus."

I looked down the hall, then up at the ceiling. "My wallet," I muttered. "He was looking for my wallet."

Renee tilted her head to one side. "He goes over to the bed and gets down on all fours. Looked painful, took him forever. He reaches between the bedside table and the bed and finds this wallet. God, he needed the table and the bed to get back up. He rifles through the wallet, pulls out a piece of paper. Looks spacey, in a zone. Sticks the wallet in his pocket, opens the door to the deck, staring all the time at the paper."

"He doesn't see you?" Rob said.

She shook her head. "Not yet. He's mesmerized and drunker 'n hell. I pin myself to the wall at one end. He goes to the Adirondack chairs at the other end. When he sees me, he smiles, says we're gonna go inside and mess around."

"Anything like this happen before?" I said.

"Of course." She jeered. "Why I left his office before I got my license. The only reason I agreed to be his smoke show for Terrell was that Gordon promised to finance a house for my sister and me. I couldn't qualify for the loan. Obviously, that didn't happen. I was stupid. Really stupid."

"Take us back to the day on the deck," Rob said.

Renee waited a moment to wipe a tear. She took a deep, audible breath. "When he tried to get up from the chair, I could see that piece of paper was a picture. He put the picture in his pocket, and I rushed over and pushed him back down. He laughed, thought it was a fucking game. He grabbed my arm and wouldn't let it go. Damn curled-lip smile, thinking he'd got me trapped. I reached behind me in the basket and grabbed a rock. I kept telling him to let me go, but he only squeezed harder. He pulled me to him. I gotta use my foot on the chair to keep him away. He used both hands to yank me closer, and I blasted him on the hand with the rock. He got really pissed, booze seemed to be gone. He started to rise. I wound up and nailed him on the back of the head."

Rob and I stared at her, then at each other.

"He was hunched over. I back away, and he grabbed the steel railing. He fell forward, his gut and shoulders over the rail. When he stopped moving, I lifted his legs up and over. Hit Terrell's car below. His back slammed just above the grille, his shoes hit Terrell's hood. I chucked that rock as far as I could toward the street."

Rob sighed. "Sounds like self-defense to me." His phone buzzed, and he looked at the screen. "My boss. Got to take this. Ms. Sarno, I will be right back. Please don't say anything until I return." He stepped into the stairwell.

Renee paused and moved closer. Her arms down straight and pinned to her sides, her hands made tight fists. "Have you ever wanted to beat the livin' shit out of somebody?"

I slowly wiped my face with both hands. "God, yes," I murmured. I paused a moment, remembering the time and place thirty years ago. "Listen," I said, moving a hand behind my neck. "Rob said to wait until—"

"I mean, just beat them to death?" She inched in and raised her chin. "Get 'em on the ground and kick'm in the face? Step on his fucking nuts?! Have you ever felt that way?! Have you?!"

I stared down the hall, holding the years of agonizing loathing and revenge. She slumped against me, whimpering, her forehand rolling against my chest. I placed my hands on her shoulders, then slid them down lower, the light embrace of a stranger bringing an unknown shared comfort and an awkward commonality of pain and sorrow. She pulled gently away, her face bloated with angry red patches.

The door opened behind Renee, and Phaedra Sarno appeared in a nightgown, her dark hair tousled from sleep. Her puffy, gray eyes lacked any sign of hope. A blue-yellowish bruise emphasized her right cheek.

"She did it for me," she muttered. "Renee's so strong. She put the bastard off before. God knows how many times."

Renee stepped to her and wrapped both arms around her. She placed her hands on her sister's hips, looked deep into her

eyes and softly shook her. "I did it for us *both*, Phae," she whispered. "For us both! Don't ever forget that."

Phaedra broke the embrace and faced me. "She did it for me." She pointed to herself. "For me! Because the asshole beat me and raped me right down there on the beach. Then made sure he got me admitted into his own damn recovery center." She leaned into Renee and sobbed into her sister's shoulder before Renee led her back into the room.

Rob opened the door and tucked the phone back into his jacket. "Where's Renee?" he said.

"Went to check on her sister." I waited a moment and then said, "I think you're right about self-defense. Don't see how a jury would see it any other way."

THIRTY

THE NORTH COUNTIES SELECTS CRUSHED their opponent in the fourth and final game of the Pacific Waves Tournament, sending the Seattle Explorers home with a 92-59 floor burn in one of the more impressive slam-downs I'd ever seen. Nick Chevalier grabbed a tournament-record twenty-two rebounds as we allowed our opponents few second chances at the basket. Andre Holberton finally found his rhythm, knocking down his first five three-point attempts, and Deacon Joe Gonzales reverted to his magician mode, dealing thirteen assists, including an alley-oop number to Trent Whalen for a late third-quarter dunk that put us up by thirty and sealed the deal. I told my guys to back off and run down the clock. The Seattle coach cleared his bench, allowing his subs the chance to show their grandkids one day that they once played in the marquee event.

"I finally saw you play a good game," Rob Suarez said in the parking lot. "It's certainly understandable why it didn't happen earlier in the week."

"Tell me about it," I muttered. I turned and faced him. "What's going to happen next? What will you do about Renee?"

He scratched his head. "Mr. Dupree is going down, and soon. She's clearly an accessory in his dealings, even though she might be able to prove she didn't carry or actually deliver. She knew about the operation and did nothing about it."

"What if she helps you convict him and also provides

information on Gordon's operation?"

"That's going to help her, depending upon what she knows and gives up. It may get her off the hook, but I don't know. The goal is to find out who supplied Gordon and stop that train, but she may not have known anything at that level. It's too early to tell." He fixed me with a stare. "How did you know it was Renee?"

I told him what Pierre Pantel had told me about Terrell's anger at Renee for damaging the hood of his car. Given the neighbor's description of the vehicle, time and place, I ventured an educated guess. "Actually, I thought she might have run him over."

Rob gave me a nod and a wry smile. "Well, I gotta hand it to Harvey. He was right about you."

"About what?"

"About how you get people to talk about sensitive things that they'd never say to a cop."

I shrugged. "The years in the classroom, I guess. Kids bring a lot of stuff to school that they sometimes need help figuring out."

"And then they become adults with the same issues." Rob said.

"Sometimes that's true."

Trent bounded from the locker room. "AFS, Coach." He wiped the sweat on his forehead with his sleeve. "Always Finish Strong, and we did. Feels good."

"Yes, you did," I said. "Thanks for stepping up. Great way to head home."

He stepped toward me and lifted his arm for a high-five. I slapped his palm.

"By the way, I called Kyle after the game and told him we finally got things figured out on the court. He mentioned he'd contacted a counselor, a friend of Timoteo's that I knew about. He wanted to me to send you guys his best. Said the time in the bus with you and Deacon Joe meant more than you know."

He smiled and slung his gym bag over his shoulder. "How 'bout that Deacon Joe? Little man's a stud. . . And, hey, did you know that was us on the pier? The other night in the dark?"

"You, what? Well, Pierre and I certainly knew someone was there. Just didn't realize it was you."

"Had your back, Coach. Had your back."

Greg Smithson, the longtime prep writer for *The Seattle Tribune*, attended the game while on vacation with his family. He interviewed several of the players in the locker room for a freelance blog piece on elite tournaments he planned for Labor Day weekend. He corralled me and asked about our itinerary home. I mentioned that some of the kids would remain with me at the duplex for a few days before heading back up the coast.

I'd have loved to drive the highway near Big Sur with Diane, but she planned to fly back with Nick so he could enroll in an Advanced Calculus summer class at Western Washington University. The land brigade would gauge the interest in a trip to Disneyland or Universal Studios, or just kick back on the beach. Trent's new lady friend invited him to be a waterboy at her beach volleyball tournament, and Deacon Joe wanted to visit his dad at his new office at Providence Hospital.

"Your guys played well," Smithson said. "Maybe better than in that Seattle Center affair last year."

"You should have been here earlier in the week," I said.

"Yeah, I see you only won one other game. What's up with that?"

"Where do you want to start?" I mumbled.

"Huh?"

"Nothing. Forget it."

"Your western Washington farm boys distracted by all the bikinis on the beach?"

"Well, there's that. Plus a few other details. Some minor details that might not fit."

He glanced across the room, eyes unfocused. He waited. "Maybe I can get back to you later on some of those details,"

Smithson said. "Put 'em all together and make a nice notes column. But this magazine thing, it's just about the rise of these types of events. Need to keep it about buckets."

"Great idea," I said. "I'm all about buckets." His face tightened as if my message and tone suggested more.

"Right. Well, remind me of those details down the road. I'll get to them sometime." He strode away, notebook in one hand, pen in the other.

How could I forget?

ACKNOWLEDGMENTS

THIS BOOK COULD not have been possible without the following individuals who provided creative insights and useful information for this effort. I called upon them often and their patience, interest and kindness have been extraordinary: Jim Thomsen, Jonathon Evison, Danny O'Neil, George and Jean Johnston, William P. Kelly Alicia Dean, Craig Smith, Linda Owens, Bruce Brown, Kevin Hawkins, Paul Bossenmaier, Sara Sykora, Victoria Cooper, Adam Fuller, Amelia Ramsey, Bob McCord. James Walker Ragsdale, Dr. Robert X Morrell, Dr. Arthur L. Fisher, Joanne Elizabeth Kelly and to high school coaches everywhere who have their hearts in the right place.

ABOUT THE AUTHOR

COLD WONDERLAND is the third book in T.R. Kelly's Ernie Creekmore series featuring the adventures of legendary high school basketball coach turned real estate agent and amateur sleuth.

The first book, *Cold Crossover*, introduces us to Ernie who gets word that his former start player—Linnbert "Cheese" Oliver—has gone missing from a late-night ferry boat. The second book, *Cold Broker* (rewritten and previously published as Hovering Above a Homicide), finds Ernie trying to solve the murder of a "helicopter" parent whose body is discovered in a vacant home for sale.

Before launching into fiction, Tom served *The Seattle Times* readers for 20 years, first as a sportswriter and later as real estate reporter, columnist and editor. His ground-breaking book How a Second *Home Can Be Your Best Investment* (McGraw-Hill, written with economist John Tuccillo) showed consumers and professionals how one additional piece of real estate could serve as an investment, recreation and retirement property over time.

His other books include *Real Estate Boomers and Beyond: Exploring the Costs, Choices and Changes of Your Next Move* (Dearborn-Kaplan); *The New Reverse Mortgage Formula* (John Wiley & Sons); *Cashing In on a Second Home in Mexico* (Crabman Publishing, with Mitch Creekmore); *Cashing In on a Second Home in Central America* (Crabman Publishing, with Mitch Creekmore and Jeff Hornberger), and Bargains Beyond the Border (Crabman Publishing). Tom's award-winning radio show *Real Estate Today* aired for 25 years on KIRO, the CBS affiliate in Seattle. The program also has been syndicated in 40

domestic markets and to 450 stations in 160 foreign countries via Armed Forces Radio. Tom and his wife, Jodi, have four children and live on Bainbridge Island, WA, where they back the runnin', gunnin' Bainbridge High Spartans when not wrestling with three of their five grandchildren.

EPA	Environmental Protection Agency
FWPCA	Federal Water Pollution Control Administration
GLER	Great Lakes Ecosystem Restoration
GREEN	Global Rivers Environmental Education Network
IJC	International Joint Commission
MECP	Ministry of the Environment, Conservation, and Parks
MNRF	Ministry of Natural Resources and Forestry
MPCA	Minnesota Pollution Control Agency
NCR	no carbon required
NEPA	National Environmental Policy Act
NEW Water	Northeast Wisconsin Water (formerly Green Bay Metropolitan Sewerage District)
NWF	National Wildlife Federation
OME	Ontario Ministry of the Environment
PAC	Public Advisory Committee
PAH	polynuclear aromatic hydrocarbon
PCB	polychlorinated biphenyl
RAP	Remedial Actions Plan
RBG	Royal Botanical Gardens
SSEA	Severn Sound Environmental Association
TMDL	total maximum daily load
TRCA	Toronto and Region Conservation Authority
URC	Urban Research Center
WREN	West Michigan Region Environmental Network

Introduction

When astronauts first see the Laurentian Great Lakes from space they are in awe. These freshwater seas represent one-fifth the standing fresh water on the Earth's surface and are a striking feature from outer space. The Great Lakes cover some 94,250 square miles, a combined surface area bigger than the United Kingdom and bigger than the state of Texas. The Great Lakes hold over 5,400 cubic miles of water, enough water, if it were spread out, to evenly cover the 48 contiguous states to a depth of nearly ten feet. They have a combined 10,210 miles of shoreline, greater than the flight distance from Seattle, Washington, to Cape Town, South Africa. It is easy to understand why the Great Lakes are often referred to as the "Third Coast."

When visitors from other countries first see the Great Lakes they often ask if they are saltwater seas. These lakes are truly amazing natural resources that inspire a sense of wonder, serve as the foundation of the

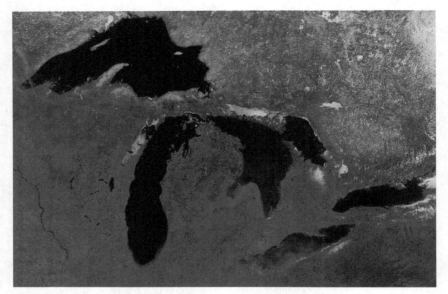

The Great Lakes as seen from space on April 24, 1999

SEAWIFS PROJECT, NASA/GODDARD SPACE FLIGHT CENTER AND ORBIMAGE

Great Lakes region's $5.8 trillion economy, and enhance quality of life for millions of people.

For those of us living near the Great Lakes or periodically vacationing along them, it is easy to understand their attraction. All of us who love these lakes have childhood and adult memories of vacationing along their shores, camping in state and provincial parks on the shores of the Great Lakes, fishing with family and friends, canoeing and kayaking down tributaries, observing birds on their migrations along flyways, and watching the rich hues and vibrant colors of the sun as it dips below the horizon—a classic Great Lakes sunset. These memories forever bond us to the Great Lakes, establishing a connection that makes us long to return, again and again, to their shores. These varied Great Lakes experiences often evoke a sense of authentic personal attachment or belonging to these unique freshwater seas. For many they bring out the emotions of happiness, contentment, and love.

The Great Lakes are exceptional by all standards. Nearly 140 species of fish are native to the lakes and over 350 species of birds have been identified along them. Billions of birds migrate through the Great Lakes each year along the Atlantic and Mississippi flyways. These migrations can be so big that they show up on weather radar screens. The Great Lakes are also home to hundreds of threatened and endangered species, including the Indiana bat, the rusty patched bumble bee, the copperbelly water snake, the piping plover, the Karner blue butterfly, and the northern riffleshell clam. Many of these are found nowhere else in the world. I like to think of this Great Lakes biodiversity as a tapestry. Individual colored threads—each unique and beautiful in their own right—are woven together to produce an exceptional piece of art, more beautiful and much stronger than the individual threads alone. The Great Lakes are like an ecological tapestry, made up of numerous species and habitats. As famed author and environmental activist John Muir states: "When one tugs at a single thing in nature, he finds it attached to the rest of the world." Much like a textile tapestry is a source of pride in the home, the Great Lakes tapestry holds a special place in the hearts and minds of all who live near them or visit them.

Long History of Great Lakes Pollution

It should not be surprising that human use and abuse of the Great Lakes have resulted in considerable impacts and much pollution. Starting in the late 1600s, French fur trappers and traders came to the Great Lakes region in search of beaver to meet European fashion demand for beaver hats. This eventually led to the extirpation of beaver in the Great Lakes Basin. During the logging era in the 1800s, many forests were cut down for farms and to supply lumber for buildings, ships, and mines. These logging practices resulted in substantial loss of terrestrial habitats for birds and other animals and degradation of fish, invertebrate, and aquatic plant habitats in rivers and streams by increasing sediment runoff from the land.

As cities began to develop along the Great Lakes, they began to discharge more and more raw sewage into their adjacent waters. The problem was that these waters where they were discharging their human waste were the very same areas of the Great Lakes where they were drawing their drinking water. This resulted in many waterborne-disease epidemics in the late 1800s and early 1900s that resulted in a substantial human death toll.

During the 1950s and 1960s, increasing inputs of phosphorus to the Great Lakes led to human-accelerated aging of the lakes or what scientists call *cultural eutrophication*. Eutrophication is the gradual increase in nutrient concentrations in lakes eventually leading to high densities of algae, called algal blooms, reduced oxygen levels in the lakes, and major changes in the plants and animals that make up the food web.

There have been numerous benefits of the industrial revolution, including making more goods affordable to more people. However, there were some unintended consequences like the indiscriminate use of toxic substances. Toxic substances can cause death, disease, behavioral abnormalities, cancer, genetic mutations, physiological or reproductive malfunctions, or physical deformities in an organism or its offspring. Also, as these toxic substances are taken up by microscopic plants and move up the food web through invertebrates, small fish, large fish, fish-eating birds, and even humans, they will increase in concentration or what scientists call the process of *biomagnification*. Many people became aware of the effects of toxic substances through Rachel Carson's 1962 book titled *Silent Spring*. This transformational book helped catalyze the environmental movement, helped generate support for the establishment of Earth Day and the banning of certain pesticides like DDT, and forever changed society's approach to toxic substance management. In recent years, there has been considerable concern in the Great Lakes Basin Ecosystem for the introduction of exotic species, like quagga and zebra mussels, and the loss of biodiversity that are weakening of our Great Lakes tapestry.

The terrible impacts of human use and abuse have moved me and many others to devote our careers and lives to remediating the damage and restoring the lakes to health. For over four decades, I have been blessed to work on the Great Lakes in partnership with many outstanding people who have truly made a difference in cleaning up and caring for their home. This book tells the stories of the cleanup of thirteen Great Lakes pollution hotspots and the critical role played by local advocates. These Great Lakes champions are people who have love and passion for the region, who show others the way by example, who have persevered over decades and not given up in the face of adversity, and who have an innate ability and ingenuity to work in partnerships to find a path forward and realize a common vision. These are everyday people making extraordinary contributions to the health and well-being of the Great Lakes. They are not in it for personal acclaim or self-aggrandizement. These are people who simply and profoundly love the Great Lakes and want to pass them on as a gift to future generations. I share these stories because they have so inspired me, and I hope they will inspire you to get involved and care for the place you call home. These stories are based on personal interviews with each of the Great Lakes champions and independent research.

My Great Lakes Journey

Growing up in metropolitan Detroit in the 1960s, I vacationed with my family in northern Michigan, hiking trails and exploring the shorelines of the Great Lakes and many inland lakes. We would go looking for much sought-after Petoskey stones, which are fossilized coral that glisten in water, revealing the six-sided skeletons of once living coral polyps. We also went picnicking in state parks, canoeing, and fishing, and I developed a sense of wonder for the biodiversity and bounty of the Great Lakes. As we prepared to return home, you can just hear my whining—"This is so much fun, do we really have to go home?"

At that very same time, my family loved to explore the outdoors near our home in a Detroit suburb called Allen Park, including canoeing, bicycling, and picnicking on Detroit's island park, Belle Isle. As we fished in the Detroit River, which boasts a world-class fishery in the heart of a major urban and industrial area, we would also scan the horizon for lake freighters, at first tiny and then becoming massive as they passed us. We also explored other city parks and Sterling State Park on western Lake Erie. But our trips to the beach at Sterling State Park were memorable for the wrong reason. I still vividly remember sitting on beach towels with my family on a beautiful summer day as my parents frowned and told us, "Don't go into the water, it is polluted!" To a young boy, these were two polar-opposite experiences. Vacations in northern Michigan took

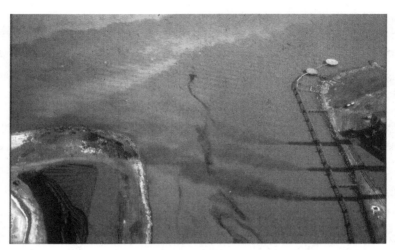

Oil pollution and raw sewage in the Detroit River, 1960s
U.S. ENVIRONMENTAL PROTECTION AGENCY

us to pristine areas. Day trips and weekend excursions took us to places along the Detroit River that were grossly polluted with oil and industrial waste, and to Sterling State Park that had signs warning of polluted water, unsafe for swimming. I questioned: *How can this be? How can one place be so beautiful and unspoiled and the other so polluted? And why don't people care enough and do something about it?*

Then on October 9, 1969, when I was a junior in high school, the Rouge River caught on fire near my home in Allen Park. I remember coming out of my high school with my friends seeing black smoke billowing near the industrial complex in southwest Detroit. My friends and I thought that this smoke was likely from a fire at the Ford Rouge Plant or one of the steel plants. When I got home, I learned the true story. The Rouge River caught on fire because of oil pollution. During the 1960s Ford's Rouge Plant was discharging 900 gallons of oil per day, representing 97.5 percent of the oil ending up in the Rouge River (Vaughan and Harlow, 1965). The impacts of such oil pollution are tremendous. Oil pollution makes the water undrinkable and not safe for swimming. Oil-covered birds and mammals die. It is particularly toxic to fish eggs and larvae, often causing their death. Oil covering shorelines will degrade wetland and riparian habitats. To some, this might not seem all that significant, but one gallon of oil can pollute a million gallons of water. This means that each day oil was polluting 900 million gallons of water in the Rouge and Detroit Rivers, making these waters undrinkable, unsafe for human contact, and killing river life.

We soon learned that sparks from an acetylene torch ignited the oil and oil-soaked debris on the river. Flames shot fifty feet in the air and the Detroit Fire Department required ten fire engines and the fire boat called the John Kendall to contain the fire. You don't extinguish a river fire, you contain it and let it burn out.

Three days later, in an October 12 editorial, the *Detroit Free Press* (1969) had this to say about the Rouge River fire: "When you have a river that burns, for crying out loud, you have troubles. It happened on Cleveland's Cuyahoga, and now it has happened on the Rouge River."

Earlier that year the Cuyahoga River burst into flames, resulting in national media coverage and considerable public outcry. Similarly, the 1969 Santa Barbara oil spill received substantial national media coverage because it was the largest oil spill in U.S. waters up until that time. But other than the *Detroit Free Press* editorial, there was not much media coverage of the 1969 Rouge River fire. Some duck hunters and fishermen spoke out in support of reducing pollution and cleaning up the river, but most people accepted pollution and the river fire as part of the cost of doing business. We were an industrial town, and industry provided decent paying jobs.

But my family felt differently. Sitting around the dinner table sharing meals and discussing current events, my parents taught my sister and me that we all have a responsibility to care for creation and become stewards of the land, water, and all life. Indeed, they taught us that we all have a duty to do our part to care for natural resources and pass them on as a gift to future generations.

In 1970, my senior year at Allen Park High School, public outcry over pollution was increasing throughout the United States. U.S. Senator Gaylord Nelson of Wisconsin, a staunch environmentalist, wanted to unify the grassroots environmental movement and increase ecological awareness. His plan was to organize a national teach-in on environmental issues on university campuses across the nation called Earth Day—April 22, 1970. Nelson's goal was to shine a bright national spotlight on water and air pollution, but he needed help. He recruited Denis Hayes to organize the first Earth Day because of his experience in community organizing and as a student activist against the Vietnam War at Stanford University. Hayes went on to expand Earth Day to more than 190 nations through the Earth Day Network.

Allen Park High School hosted one of countless Earth Day rallies on April 22, 1970. On that day over twenty million Americans demonstrated for clean air and water and a healthy environment. Hundreds of students participated in our Earth Day rally, with some wearing gas masks. Students rhythmically marched in procession into the football stadium with a papier-mâché Earth and time capsule on a stretcher. The message was clear—the Earth was sick and dying. We then buried the mock Earth, symbolizing its death, and a time capsule of goods and information to be shared with generations not yet born. The rally even included a keynote address from a long-time political activist who served as president of the Peace Party—Zolton Ferency. It was quite a moving experience, seared in the consciousness of young high school students.

These formative experiences with pollution of the Detroit and Rouge Rivers and the first Earth Day led me to my career as a Great Lakes scientist and advocate for protecting the environment. Following degrees in biology and aquatic biology from Eastern Michigan University and the University of Windsor, I had an over thirty-year career in assessing the health of the Great Lakes and promoting their stewardship. One of my jobs was with the International Joint Commission (IJC) established under the 1909 Canada–U.S. Boundary Waters Treaty.

The 1909 Boundary Waters Treaty provides the principles and mechanisms for preventing and resolving disputes concerning water quantity and quality along the entire U.S.-Canadian border. Through this Treaty both the United States and Canada must agree to any project that would change the natural levels or flows of any boundary waters. The scope of the Boundary Waters Treaty covers more than 130 rivers and lakes intersecting the Canada–U.S. border that stretches some 5,500 miles, 40 percent of which is water.

Far ahead of its time, the Boundary Waters Treaty also states that waters shall not be polluted on either side of the boundary to the injury of health or property on the other side. As such, this treaty is often described as the world's first environmental agreement. The Boundary Waters Treaty and its IJC were visionary in 1909 and today stand among the world's most successful models for binational cooperation and resolving transboundary environmental issues.

The IJC is an independent advisor to the United States and Canada and works for the common good of both countries in preventing and resolving disputes between the two countries under the Boundary Waters Treaty. The IJC now has over a one-hundred-year history in cooperative problem-solving of boundary water management issues. The IJC uses experts, serving in their personal and professional capacities, to undertake independent fact-finding and to provide advice for problem resolution. Its processes have compiled agreed-upon and trusted scientific and socioeconomic data and have interpreted these data in a public fashion to build broad-based understanding and support for action. More recently, IJC processes have fostered use of a systematic and comprehensive ecosystem approach that accounts for the interrelationships among land, air, water, and all living things, including humans.

The Canada–U.S. Great Lakes Water Quality Agreement was initially signed in 1972 and revised in 1978, 1987, and 2012. It formally recognizes the Great Lakes as an international treasure worth protecting. The agreement has often been described as an evolving instrument for ecosystem-based management. It represents a commitment between the United States and Canada to restore and protect the waters of the Great Lakes and provides a framework for identifying binational priorities and implementing actions that improve water quality and ecosystem health. Canada and the United States are responsible for final decision-making under the agreement and for the involvement and participation of state and provincial governments, tribal governments, municipal governments, watershed management agencies, and other stakeholders.

Since 1973, the IJC's Great Lakes Water Quality Board, the principal advisor to the IJC on matters pertaining to the Great Lakes Water Quality Agreement, has periodically assessed the state of the Great Lakes. As part of these assessments, the board has identified specific harbors, embayments, river mouths, and connecting channels where one of more

Table 1. Beneficial Use Impairments (BUI) as Identified in the Canada–U.S. Great Lakes Water Quality Agreement
Restrictions of fish and wildlife consumption
Tainting of fish and wildlife flavor
Degradation of fish and wildlife populations
Fish tumors or other deformities
Bird or animal deformities or reproductive problems
Degradation of benthos—organisms that live in bottom sediments
Restrictions on dredging activities
Eutrophication or undesirable algae
Restrictions on drinking water consumption, or taste and odor problems
Beach closings
Degradation of aesthetics
Added costs to agriculture or industry
Degradation of phytoplankton or zooplankton populations

jurisdictional standards or general or specific water-quality objectives of the agreement were not being met—pollution hotspots. These objectives and standards were being exceeded despite implementation of pollution control programs. These pollution hotspots were initially termed "problem areas," later Areas of Concern (AOCs).

The list of AOCs changed over time for reasons both good and bad. In some cases, it's because of the implementation of cleanup programs and improvements in water quality. In other cases, it's due to the emergence of new problems or reinterpretation of the significance of earlier reports. The major problems identified have also changed in response to the evolution of scientific understanding of water-quality problems—from recognition of bacterial pollution to eutrophication to toxic substances contamination to loss of habitat and biodiversity. In addition, we've improved our ability to detect and measure problems and made progress in advancing cleanup and prevention efforts.

In 1985, the Great Lakes Water Quality Board, made up of the senior water program managers of the eight Great Lakes states, the Province of Ontario, and the two federal governments, reported that progress had stalled on cleanup of forty-two AOCs (a forty-third was designated in in 1991) and recommended developing Remedial Actions Plans (RAPs) to restore their "impaired uses," which meant making them clean enough to use safely for swimming, fishing, and drinking through an ecosystem approach (International Joint Commission's Great Lakes Water Quality Board, 1985; Hartig and Thomas, 1988). RAPs were then added to the 1987 Revision to the Great Lakes Water Quality Agreement, giving international legitimacy to the program and providing laser-like focus for all stakeholders to work together to eliminate any of fourteen so-called "beneficial use impairments" (BUIs) (table 1). It must be understood that waters are protected for specific uses, and a BUI occurs when people or other creatures can't use waters for their designated purposes. For example, if the fish are unsafe to eat or the waters are unsafe for swimming or drinking, these are identified as BUIs. RAPs were developed in three stages—stage 1 identified BUIs and what was causing them, stage 2 identified what needed to be done to restore uses, and stage 3 provided evidence that uses had been restored.

At the outset, use of an ecosystem approach in RAP development was earthshaking for state, provincial, and federal governments. They were used to implementing water-quality programs in a top-down, command-and-control fashion—telling local communities and industries what they had to do. For example, one of the primary programs of state, provincial, and federal governments was issuing discharge permits to municipal wastewater treatment plants and industries that prescribed the level of wastewater treatment required and the quality of effluent.

Through use of an ecosystem approach in RAPs, all stakeholder groups were charged to work together in a collaborative effort. This truly was an enormous change.

Think of an ecosystem approach as grassroots ecological democracy for cleaning up polluted areas of the Great Lakes. An ecosystem approach brings all stakeholders who impact or are impacted by a natural resource together to sit around a table and reach agreement on what needs to be done to clean up and care for their ecosystem as their home. Can you imagine the difficulty in bringing factory managers, fishing groups, conservation and hunting clubs, port authorities, sewage treatment plant operators, governments, and others together to reach agreement on what needs to be done to clean up their shared waters?

The 1987 agreement literally was a paradigm shift by bringing the ecosystem approach into the mainstream and giving it broad-based acceptance. The first thing is to understand the fundamental distinction between environment and ecosystem. It is like the difference between house and home. We see a house or the environment as something that is external and detached from us. It sits over there. In contrast, we see ourselves in a home or an ecosystem, even when not there. A home is where we raise our children, have family meals, celebrate special occasions, and entertain friends. What we do to our home and ecosystem, we do to ourselves.

Another way of thinking about an ecosystem approach is as a more holistic way of undertaking integrated planning, research, and management of specific places like the Great Lakes. If there was an ecosystem approach to driver's training for four students, the training car would have four steering wheels to show how all need to work together.

While working at the IJC, I became its point person on cleanup and restoration of AOCs. It was an exciting and compelling time when I met many wonderful people. One who was most impactful on me was eminent Canadian research scientist, Jack Vallentyne, equally well known for his globe-trotting persona—Johnny Biosphere. Jack made it his mission to reach and teach 15,000 to 20,000 children annually about the importance of knowing and protecting your personal ecosystem. To get the children's attention, he attached a globe to his back with straps labeled biosphere and ecosystem. Each strap had buttons on it that the school children could push to hear the sounds of animals from different continents. He also wore high top tennis shoes to make sure that children understood that he was a globe-trotter. He so effectively engaged children in understanding that they are indeed part of their ecosystem home and what they do to their ecosystem they do to themselves. Jack understood that efforts to protect our life-support system must start with each child and person taking responsibility for caring for their ecosystem.

An ecosystem approach to driving school
SCOTT RAFT

Dr. Jack Vallentyne as
Johnny Biosphere

Although trained as a scientist, Jack quickly came to understand that scientific terminology was often a barrier to bringing about societal change. He adopted the persona of Johnny Biosphere to communicate scientific knowledge to children and the public in an appealing way. Jack was truly a visionary and an internationally renowned ecosystem educator. He felt strongly that if we are going to change the world and protect it, we must start with the children. I can still hear him asking the question: "Have you been good to your ecosystem today?"

Following fourteen years with the IJC, I spent several years in a variety of positions that enabled me to continue to advocate for the health and well-being of AOCs. For several years, I served as a River Navigator for the Greater Detroit American Heritage River Initiative. This program promoted cleaning up the river, improving public access by building greenways and water trails, revitalizing the waterfront, and celebrating the area's history and culture. As part of this effort, we called for the establishment of an international wildlife refuge. Working with U.S. and Canadian elected representatives and business leaders, we succeeded in establishing the Detroit River International Wildlife Refuge in 2001 as the only international wildlife refuge in North America. Incidentally, the refuge has three AOCs within its boundary—the Detroit and Rouge Rivers and River Raisin—and one at the southern end—Maumee River. Its mission is to protect fish and wildlife and their habitats, bring conservation to cities, and help make nature part of everyday urban life. Each of these jobs offered me an opportunity to further develop and test locally designed ecosystem approaches.

After nearly fourteen years as manager of the refuge, I was given the honor to become a Fulbright scholar and help the United States and Canada look back and evaluate what had been achieved and learned from thirty-five years of cleaning up AOCs. From my Fulbright, I became a visiting scholar at the University of Windsor's Great Lakes Institute for Environmental Research and the chair of the Community Foundation for Southeast Michigan's Great Lakes Way Advisory Committee. In these positions, I am continuing my research on how cleanup of AOCs leads to reconnecting people to these waterways that, in turn, leads to waterfront and community revitalization.

CHAPTER 1

Nelson French

St. Louis River Champion

The St. Louis River is the largest river to flow into Lake Superior with a watershed that covers 3,584 square miles. In total, it flows 192 miles in a circuitous course from its headwaters near Hoyt Lakes to Lake Superior at the twin ports of Duluth, Minnesota, and Superior, Wisconsin—Duluth-Superior Harbor. The lower end of the St. Louis River, where its waters mix with the waters of Lake Superior, is called the St. Louis River Estuary. This 12,000-acre estuary is the largest coastal freshwater wetland ecosystem on Lake Superior and is the most significant source of biological productivity for the western half of the lake. Numerous species of fish, birds, and other wildlife depend on the estuary for their survival. Duluth-Superior Harbor is part of the St. Louis estuary and mid-America's gateway to global trade and the nation's busiest freshwater harbor. More than a quarter million people live and work in the area, and 3.5 million tourists visit every year.

The St. Louis Estuary, the largest coastal wetland ecosystem on Lake Superior
MICHAEL K. ANDERSON

Industrial Development Leaves Legacy Pollution

The Dakota and Ojibwe were the first known inhabitants of the region. French explorers did not reach the region until around the 1650s or 1660s. Two centuries later, American settlers gave Duluth its name in 1856, recognizing Frenchman Daniel Greysolon—*Sieur du Lhut*—who came in 1679 to set up fur-trade routes. In 1871, workers dug a canal so ships could more easily enter the harbor and by the 1900s Duluth's port was handling more tons of cargo each year than New York City. At the turn of the twentieth century, the city experienced tremendous industrial growth: grain processing and shipping, timber harvesting, iron mining, manufacturing, shipping by rail and boat, and shipbuilding. Tycoons such as Andrew Carnegie, Jay Cooke, Andrew Mellon, J. P. Morgan, and John D. Rockefeller helped develop Duluth into an industrial powerhouse

and booming community. Through this period, the St. Louis River and
harbor changed substantially to accommodate shipping and industrial
development along the water. Through human and industrial development, an estimated 7,000 acres of aquatic habitat of this 12,000-acre
freshwater estuary was dredged or filled (Minnesota Pollution Control
Agency and Wisconsin Department of Natural Resources, 1992). The
equivalent of over 5,300 football fields was filled, dredged, paved over,
or built upon. Today, the area is home to the largest dry bulk port in the
United States and is recognized as the largest port on the Great Lakes (U.S.
Army Corps of Engineers, 2015). The navigational channel is regularly
dredged to twenty-seven feet to accommodate the bulk cargo ships that
carry grain, taconite, limestone, timber, coal, and sometimes passengers
to U.S. and international ports. The waterfront was the industrial heart
of both Duluth and the city of Superior. Duluth produced about one-
half billion board feet of white pine lumber in the late 1800s. Heavy

industry—steel foundries and mills and blast furnaces, grain elevators, and shipbuilding operations—operated from the late 1890s through the mid-1900s along the riverbanks, building much of the cities' wealth and giving them their identities. Later, industries that made everything from chemicals and refrigerators to shoes lined the river.

This industrial expansion took a toll on the health of the river. Untreated or partially treated industrial and municipal waste polluted the river and contaminated its sediments. The legacy of industrial development can literally be seen today in Superfund sites, contaminated sediment hotspots, sawmill waste sites, and the loss and degradation of aquatic habitat. Addressing anyone of these environmental problems would be difficult, but addressing them all together in a comprehensive and coordinated fashion would require yeoman's work over many decades. Much of this legacy pollution occurred prior to the landmark environmental legislation of the 1970s:

- National Environmental Policy Act of 1970—considered the "Magna Carta" of federal environmental laws—that requires assessment of the effects of proposed actions prior to making decisions;
- Clean Water Act of 1972—that protects America's waters through regulation of water pollutants from industries, municipalities, and land owners;
- U.S.–Canada Great Lakes Water Quality Agreement of 1972— considered a model of binational cooperation to protect water quality;
- Endangered Species Act of 1973—the essential law to protect all species from extinction;

- Comprehensive Environmental Response, Compensation
  and Liability Act of 1980—the landmark law for cleaning
  up uncontrolled or abandoned sites, called Superfund sites,
  contaminated with hazardous waste or toxic substances.

Then in the 1980s, the era of heavy industry ended, leaving the area's economy devastated along with the environment. The Twin Ports faced the loss not only of their economic base but also their identity. This calamity even inspired a Duluth billboard: *"Will the last one leaving Duluth please turn out the light?"*

River Cleanup

Bearing the terrible burden of a century and a half of industrial pollution, the St. Louis River watershed needed a champion—and it found one. Nelson French was born in Duluth in 1952, but his family moved one year later to Hibbing, Minnesota. Both Duluth and Hibbing are in the St. Louis River watershed. Hibbing is a mining town and home to the largest open pit iron mine in Minnesota called the Hull-Rust-Mahoning Open Pit Iron Mine. Covering five square miles, the pit stretches three miles long, two miles wide, and 535 feet deep. Put another way, it's as long as about eleven Empire State Buildings stacked on top of each other, as wide as a little over seven Empire State Buildings, and nearly as deep as two football fields. Locally people call it a "man-made Grand Canyon." That is one big mine.

Established in 1895, it was one of the world's first mechanized open pit mines. As the name indicates, in contrast to underground mines, open pit mines are on the surface. The advantage of open pit mining is that it is easier and safer to extract ore, compared to underground mines. However, everyone in town witnessed firsthand the environmental impacts of extracting iron ore on that scale. The Hull-Rust-Mahoning destroyed the natural landscape, erasing what took nature millions of years to design. It ravaged ecosystems, destroyed old growth forests, and reduced or eliminated the habitats of many plants and animals, reducing the biodiversity and the beauty of the St. Louis watershed. Pollution from sulfuric acid and other toxic chemicals used or produced in the mining operations poisoned the land, water, and air.

French spent all his childhood summers at nearby Lake Vermilion, where he canoed, fished, watched birds, and did everything outdoors. These experiences gave him a profound appreciation for the natural world. The contrast between Minnesota's largest open pit mining operation and the flourishing wilderness around Lake Vermilion was stark and helped him develop an environmental ethic that would define his career. He notes that his family was also fortunate to be able to travel throughout the country visiting many national parks and natural wonders. Early trips to the Boundary Waters Canoe Area deepened his commitment to the natural world and led him to choose a career in environmental protection and natural resource conservation. French simply notes: "I had a passion for natural resources and an interest in science. . . . I followed my passion."

After graduating with a degree in biology and chemistry from Coe College, he held a series of positions in environmental protection and natural resource conservation. These jobs put him at the center of growing efforts to clean up and restore northeastern Minnesota's despoiled lands, because at the same time much of the industry was leaving the Twin Ports, efforts to clean up the river started in earnest. In 1985, the International Joint Commission's Great Lakes Water Quality Board identified the St. Louis River as one of forty-two Great Lakes AOCs, requiring the development and implementation of a RAP to restore all impaired "beneficial uses." Scientists often compare the health of an ecosystem to that of a patient. Both are healthy when no disease is present, and they are resilient to change and stress. However, for an ecosystem to be healthy, it must also provide beneficial uses or services. The concept of beneficial use impairments comes out of this thinking and has been the driver of RAPs.

The first stage of a RAP requires identifying which uses have been impaired and why. That happened for the St. Louis River in 1992 with the creation of a Stage I RAP; its action plan was completed in 1995. As the scientists were writing the plans, a Citizen Advisory Committee was formed in 1987 to ensure public input and foster an ecosystem approach. In 1996, a river nonprofit organization was created that would eventually be called the St. Louis River Alliance.

Throughout his career, French held several positions in Minnesota government and nongovernmental organizations. He was involved in the early development of the RAP when he served as executive director of the Sierra Club, North Star Chapter's Project Environment Foundation. While at The Nature Conservancy in the 1990s, French participated in several significant land protection projects along the north shore of Lake Superior, including the establishment and expansion of Tettegouche State Park, acquisition of land in the Swamp River watershed, creation of the Swamp River Aquatic Management and Scientific and Natural Areas, and the founding of Sugarloaf Cove Scientific and Natural Area. The last was a particularly good opportunity to permanently protect land for conservation and outdoor recreation, while also encouraging scientific investigations to properly care for these lands.

French then went on to another nongovernmental challenge as executive director of the Kinnickinnic River Land Trust in River Falls, Wisconsin, where he enhanced his skillset in strategic partnership building. Then in early 2011, he learned that the Minnesota Pollution Control Agency (MPCA) had posted a job opening for someone to head up the St. Louis River RAP. He jumped at the opportunity to return to his birthplace in Duluth and take on his dream job of directing the cleanup of his beloved St. Louis River.

While serving as legislative affairs director at MPCA (2002–2007), he worked with the top, cabinet-level administrator of the U.S. Environmental Protection Agency, Mike Leavitt, on the Great Lakes Regional Collaboration, a wide-ranging, cooperative effort to restore and protect the Great Lakes. It became official U.S. policy when President George W. Bush signed an executive order on May 18, 2004. This was the strategy for the federal government to work with the eight Great Lakes states on environmental restoration. More significantly, it laid the foundation for over $2.5 billion that would follow through the Great Lakes Restoration Initiative. Nelson notes, "I really got my sea legs on this collaboration."

The establishment of the Great Lakes Restoration Initiative in 2010 catalyzed the development and implementation of a new combined action and business plan for removing the St. Louis River from the international list of pollution hotspots. Key factors for the success of this business plan included:

- inclusivity: It coordinated efforts between Minnesota and Wisconsin with active participation of the Fond du Lac Band and other stakeholders;

- comprehensiveness and specificity: It identified specific cleanup and restoration actions to restore uses and specified budgets and timelines needed to complete the work;
- aggressiveness: It set an aggressive goal of removing the St. Louis River as an AOC by 2025 that required strong coordination between state and federal agencies and other partners;
- timeliness: It leveraged available funding from existing sources like the federal Great Lakes Restoration Initiative, Minnesota's Clean Water, Land and Legacy Funds, and Minnesota general obligation bond funds in a timely fashion.

Looking back, the RAP process in the 1980s and 1990s built on the success of ongoing regulatory actions that improved water quality, including approximately $320 million to improve wastewater treatment infrastructure, $85 million to remediate contaminated sediment at Wisconsin's Hog Island–Newton Creek and Minnesota's St. Louis River Interlake Duluth Tar sites, and $15 million to acquire and restore more than 16,000 acres of habitat in Wisconsin. But the new RAP took this restoration effort to another level by identifying remaining problems and scoping out collaborative funding for cleanup and restoration efforts. They showed how federal funds from the Great Lakes Restoration Initiative and Harbor Maintenance Trust Funds, which are fees collected from companies that ship goods through the nation's ports and are used to dredge shipping channels, could leverage state and local funds and private sector funding to fully restore all uses through partnerships.

No one could do this alone. Through strategic partnerships, approximately $57 million was raised between 2011 and 2017 for the cleanup of contaminated sediment hotspots and restoration of habitats so that native plants, fish, and birds could thrive. An additional $155–170 million will be needed to implement all necessary cleanup and restoration actions identified in the RAP before the St. Louis River can be removed from the international list of pollution hotspots (French et al., 2018). French noted that raising the $57 million was possible because of the partners' innovative "business plan" approach. It translated a clear collective vision into remedial actions with budgets that were aligned with funding sources (Angelos et al., 2013). French's strategic planning experience at The Nature Conservancy and his many years as a nonprofit executive director with significant accounting, budgeting, fundraising, and government relations experience were instrumental in developing this "business plan" for the St. Louis River AOC. It included accurate budget estimates, funding sources, and firm deadlines for completion of the work.

The establishment of the Great Lakes Restoration Initiative and the 2002 passage of the Great Lakes Legacy Act to expedite cleaning up contaminated sediments in Great Lakes AOCs have been critical to the progress thus far in restoring the St. Louis River AOC to health, and they will be essential to removing all beneficial use impairments by 2025. Today, the river is cleaner for both fish and birds. It provides nursery habitat for forty species of fish in western Lake Superior, including walleye, lake sturgeon, northern pike, and smallmouth bass. It also provides habitat for more than 230 species of migrating and resident birds. And if it is cleaner for fish and birds, it is cleaner for people living in Duluth and Superior.

River Cleanup Leads to Riverfront Revitalization

Duluth is now reconnecting to its river as part of a strategy to expand its economy and create a new identity. According to Don Ness, mayor of Duluth from 2008 to 2015: "There is no question that if not for Lake Superior, Duluth would be defined as a river city. Duluth should be defined by both the world's greatest lake AND the world's largest freshwater estuary. By doing so, we open up many possibilities along the River" (City of Duluth, 2015a). Tourists have long been drawn to the Lake Superior shores along the eastern side of Duluth, where there is a popular walking trail, commercial district, and tourism attractions. Now attention is turning to the city's western side along its riverfront.

Duluth is now building mountain bike and multi-use trails for hiking and biking in spring, summer, and fall and cross-country skiing in winter. These trails are reconnecting residents with nature through restored habitats for native plants and animals, including more than 270 species of birds, improved access roads, trailheads, and parking and restroom facilities, and enhanced neighborhood parks with new playscapes. This effort is being financed by $18 million in bonds from a tourist tax.

By turning toward the river, the city of Duluth is capitalizing on the natural assets and many benefits provided to humans from healthy ecosystems—ecosystem services—like pollination of crops, clean air, flood protection, and more. These natural assets are being made more accessible and attractive through AOC cleanup actions. According to former Mayor Ness, "Most cities put a premium on making life easy; cities like Duluth put a premium on making life interesting" (Ross, 2014).

By promoting world-class mountain biking, skiing, kayaking, and sailing in the city, Duluth is reclaiming its waterfront and inviting people back to the water through investments in public access. There is no better example than the extension of the 3.4-mile Western Waterfront Trail—a walking, hiking, and biking trail that will continue to follow the riparian corridor for an additional ten miles past steel plants, foundries, and refineries. To complete this trail extension, many remediation and restoration projects are needed. The first project to be completed is located at the trail's end in Chambers Grove Park, where a park improvement project was paired with a fish habitat restoration project to greatly enhance the quality of the park and the way park users experience the river. This park makeover for people and wildlife includes an accessible restroom facility, improved parking and access road, an accessible route to the picnic pavilion, an accessible playground, restored wetland and riparian habitats, a wet meadow, and three acres of spawning habitat for native species like lake sturgeon and walleye. Another major initiative is the Grassy Point–Kingsbury Bay project, that has removed 120 years of historic sawmill wood waste and restored 120 acres of coastal wetlands, in-water habitats, and stream channels for native animals and plants right along the trail. Four other remediation/restoration efforts at Erie Pier Ponds, Munger Landing, Spirit Lake, and Mud Lake will soon begin. Collectively, these projects will provide new opportunities for citizens to walk, bike, and paddle amid a wide range of native plants and animals, including forty-five native fish species, mink, beaver, otter, red-tailed fox, white-tailed deer, wild rice, and more, and to reconnect with their St. Louis River ecosystem.

But Duluth cannot rely solely on outdoor recreation to revive its city. Despite the closure of many local industries, the Port of Duluth–Superior contributed $1.4 billion in economic activity in 2017 (Martin Associates, 2018). Ships continue to come and go here, carrying iron ore, taconite, limestone, grains, and other cargo. The port operators have benefited from working closely with the U.S. Army Corps of Engineers to dredge the navigational channel for shipping and remediate sediments contaminated with mercury, dioxins, polychlorinated biphenyls (PCBs), polynuclear aromatic hydrocarbons (PAHs), and other toxic substances.

Where sediments are sufficiently clean, they are being used for habitat restoration. Decades of dredging and filling have displaced wetland and other shallow, sheltered aquatic habitats once common in this area. With well-designed placement of clean sediment dredged from the shipping channels, natural resource managers expect wetland vegetation will return to a site off 21st Avenue West, and with it, the bugs, fish, and birds that live there. For example, since 2013, nearly 1.1 million cubic yards of clean sediment have been used in wetland restoration, including about 700,000 cubic yards deposited at the 21st Avenue West project site and over 300,000 cubic yards at the 40th Avenue West project site. This is a good example of the port's dual roles of enhancing the economy—keeping the shipping channels open—and the environmental quality of the waterfront.

Indeed, the creative partnership between the U.S. Army Corps of Engineers and the MPCA is the one French is most proud of. It must first be understood that historically the corps' mission was to build infrastructure that put them at odds with environmentalists because of environmental impacts resulting from infrastructure projects like building and maintaining shipping channels and constructing harbors, breakwaters, dikes, and jetties to support commerce and industry. This frequently allowed commerce and industry to trump the environment in decision-making. A unique collaboration between the MPCA and the corps turned what had been a proverbial "sow's ear" into a "silk purse." The MPCA had to work through a bias against the disposal of dredged sediments from the shipping channel in Wisconsin waters into Minnesota waters for many years. French and his team worked with several MPCA divisions to develop the scientific and administrative process by which dredged sediments could be approved for habitat restoration in the AOC.

The corps had never allowed this before in the AOC, and there was inertia against changes to this longstanding policy. It must be remembered that the corps functions as a "command-and-control" regulatory agency with a long history of limited flexibility. French notes: "I am most proud of the barrier busting and ground-breaking work that my team did on this issue." For its creativity and uniqueness, the project received a Minnesota State Government Innovation Award.

And the MPCA's partnership with the corps to use dredged sediments wasn't the only case in which restoration initiatives went hand in hand with community and economic revitalization. Most cites have brown-fields—specific lands that were originally developed for industrial purposes—that were contaminated and then left abandoned. Duluth is no exception. The City of Duluth developed a Brownfields Areawide Plan for the Irving and Fairmount neighborhoods, which are adjacent to the St. Louis River and near the port. This plan shows how industry and nature can coexist and contribute to community well-being. Activities include razing old buildings and remediating contaminated soils; providing roads, sewers, and utilities for newer industrial users; improving access to the river; creating new housing; attracting new retail businesses; and enhancing residents' quality of life. In attracting new industries and business to the area, every effort must be made to not make the mistakes of the past and to achieve environmentally sustainable economic development. Throughout the world, there is growing interest in a "cradle-to-cradle" approach to making things. The goal is a circular economy that eliminates waste and ensures the continual use of resources.

Environmental restoration and improved access to the waterfront have led to new developments and national recognition. A $34 million investment converted a cement terminal into a luxury resort (Renalls,

2016), and a \$38 million mixed-use housing development was also built (Council of Great Lakes Industries and Great Lakes Commission, 2018; Johnson, 2017). These new apartments and the hotel on the waterfront led *Outside* magazine to recognize the city for its riverfront recreational opportunities (Helal, 2014; Rayno, 2017). For years, Duluth was losing young people to jobs in other cities. Decent jobs and increased waterfront vitality are now attracting younger people back to the city, where around 27 percent of the population is between twenty and thirty-four years old (U.S. Census Bureau, 2017).

Looking Ahead and Advice

Clearly, the St. Louis River will continue to face threats from human activities, and eternal vigilance will be required to ensure sustainability of the region's ecosystem. The Duluth–Superior community is embracing outdoor recreation as a long-term economic driver, but this will require continued investment in protecting natural resources and building and enhancing outdoor recreational infrastructure. The revitalized nongovernmental organization called St. Louis River Alliance is well positioned to take the lead in implementing the master plan for the new St. Louis River National Water Trail designation awarded by the U.S. Department of the Interior in 2020. The St. Louis River Alliance, the Minnesota Land Trust, and the City of Duluth worked together to create the vision around the St. Louis River National Water Trail and to pull together stakeholders to create the master plan required for the national designation. The Water Trail includes eleven loop trails for paddlers of all skill levels and abilities and is intended for various watercraft use. It encourages recreational boating with the philosophies of environmental stewardship, environmental education, and accessibility for all users. It is readily accepted that this National Water Trail designation is a direct result of a cleaner river.

The work that the area's champions, including French, have already completed provides a model and an incentive for continuing efforts. In terms of what others can learn from the St. Louis River RAP, French says: "Think big, be strategic, engage and gain support of key stakeholders, develop an accurate budget, and set aggressive timelines for actions. After you have accomplished that, market the plan to decision-makers who have the ability to share your vision and make resources available to fund bold and aggressive actions."

French encourages RAP teams and others interested in environmental cleanup and restoration to think out of the box and experiment with new strategic partnerships. He states that:

> In our case we were blessed to have developed an amazing partnership with the U.S. Army Corps of Engineers. The Corps led the engineering and design for most of our projects and provided expertise we would have had a very hard time finding. It also did the construction of many projects. For example, the Corps led both the design and construction of the 21st Avenue West and 40th Avenue West habitat restoration projects. The Harbor Maintenance Trust Fund covered more that 60 percent of the cost for this restoration, thus reducing the need for Great Lakes Restoration Initiative and other funds to complete this work.

Reflecting on top priorities, French believes that threats to the waters of the North Country from possible sulfide ore mining in the Lake Superior watershed and the Rainy River watershed (Boundary

Nelson French, St. Louis River champion
MICHAEL K. ANDERSON

Waters Canoe Area), where mining companies are now seeking permits, are among the most serious issues facing the St. Louis River. The mining company Polymet/Glencore and the Minnesota state government are currently embroiled in a court fight over the future of a proposed copper-nickel mine in the Lake Superior watershed. Twin Metals Minnesota/Antofagasta is also seeking permission to dig a mine on land adjacent to the Boundary Waters Canoe Area. Sulfide ore mining, the process Twin Metals Minnesota would use to mine heavy metals, is well documented for causing catastrophic pollution that poses a serious risk to the wilderness area. The pollutants from acid mine drainage can contaminate the land surface, soils, and groundwater. Needless to say, people must keep on their toes and hold regulatory agencies accountable for their actions.

French's advice to the next generation of St. Louis River champions is "to continue to treasure the natural resources that define your community and region, and continue to invest in clean air, clean land,

and clean water that are crucial for long-term sustainability." In 2018, French received the Department of the Army Commander's Award for Public Service for his support of the U.S. Army Corps of Engineers and the restoration of the St. Louis River. When he first started engaging the corps, some environmentalists were skeptical and doubted whether he could bring about change. However, French and his team persisted and in the end were successful. In an award ceremony, the corps noted that French's unique skills in collaboration and strategic planning brought the vision of using dredged material in the Duluth–Superior Harbor together with providing ecosystem benefits. Further, the corps noted that French's dedication to a shared mission and selfless service to the St. Louis River AOC will provide lasting benefits to the region.

CHAPTER 2

Bud and Vicky Harris

Fox River/Green Bay Champions

reen Bay is an inlet of northwestern Lake Michigan. It is partially sheltered from Lake Michigan by the Door Peninsula in Wisconsin, the Garden Peninsula in Michigan, and a chain of islands between them. These topographical features are the western portion of the Niagara Escarpment—a geological formation that runs from New York state, through Niagara Falls where it gets its name, across Ontario and Michigan's Upper Peninsula, and to eastern Wisconsin. Green Bay is some 120 miles long; its width varies between ten to twenty miles, and it covers some 1,626 square miles. The lower bay is wholly in Wisconsin, and the upper bay is a shared resource between Wisconsin and Michigan.

Ancestors of the Menominee, Ho-Chunk, and other Native Americans inhabited the area for at least 10,000 years, drawn to the area's rich soil and abundant fish, wild rice, and waterfowl. In 1634, French explorer Jean Nicolet met the Ho-Chunk at nearby Red Banks, the earliest reliably documented contact between Europeans and Indians in Wisconsin.

About twenty years later, fur traders arrived. Jesuit priests that visited the bay even earlier wrote descriptions of the bay as clear blue but fringed with green coastal wetlands.

Green Bay has been described as an estuary because, in it, strong temperature, chemical, and biological gradients from the Fox River mix with Lake Michigan waters. It is considered the largest freshwater "estuary" in the world.

The Fox River is the principal tributary of Green Bay and the largest of Lake Michigan. It flows 182 miles from its headwaters in south-central Wisconsin to the northeast and into and through Lake Winnebago before discharging into lower Green Bay. The last forty miles of the river were once wild with rapids. They have been tamed by seventeen locks and dams that trap sediments and pollutants. Intensive agriculture covers much of the watershed that includes one-third of the Lake Michigan basin and delivers one-third of the lake's total phosphorus load.

For management purposes, the Fox River is divided into two basins. The upper Fox River flows from its headwaters to the point it discharges into Lake Winnebago. The lower Fox River flows from the north end of Lake Winnebago to the point it enters Green Bay.

The story of the Fox River/Green Bay ecosystem is one of human use and abuse and some recent recovery. However, much more needs to be done to achieve an ecosystem that supports and maintains ecological processes and a diverse community of animals, plants, and microorganisms. First, it must be recognized that the Green Bay watershed is no small catchment, draining approximately 15,625 square miles. Earliest evidence of human impacts came during the fur trade when European fashion demanded hats made of beaver pelts. During this era, the beaver was extirpated or removed locally because of over-harvesting.

Later in the nineteenth and early twentieth centuries, timber harvesting, papermaking, and agriculture became dominant industries that resulted in major changes in the ecosystem in a relatively short period of time. Excessive nutrient and sediment loadings and organic wastes from sawmills and paper mills were the culprits, overloading the Fox River and causing human-induced nutrient enrichment or what scientists call eutrophication of the waters of lower Green Bay. Indeed, at one time, the Fox River was considered the most heavily industrialized river in North America because over one hundred industries discharged into it and because the lower forty-mile reach received the discharges of thirteen pulp and paper mills—the largest concentration of the paper industry in the world.

Citizen complaints about these severely degraded waters catalyzed decades of scientific investigations. Starting slowly with a few studies and surveys in the first half of the twentieth century, more comprehensive studies began in mid-century with support from the University of Wisconsin's Sea Grant Institute. Such studies have provided the scientific foundation for government-led cleanup programs such as the Lower Green Bay and Fox River RAP initiated in 1985, the polychlorinated biphenyl (PCB) cleanup program, and the more recent total maximum daily load (TMDL) initiative that is identifying the maximum amount of a pollutant that a water body can receive while still meeting water quality standards. Progress has been made, but a fuller rehabilitation of this large-scale ecosystem remains an elusive goal.

Standing at the center of this cleanup and rehabilitation effort have been Bud and Vicky Harris. They are quick to let you know that they stand on the shoulders of colleagues that created and championed ecological restoration concepts for the Great Lakes—people like Henry Regier, John

Magnuson, George Francis, and Paul Sager, to name just a few. Those giants inspired the Harrises and helped shape their thinking for years to come. Such deep thinking on ecological restoration also led to action. Indeed, Fox River and Green Bay represent a true proving ground for adaptive restoration.

Pioneers of Science-Based Cleanup and Rehabilitation of Green Bay

Vicky Harris was raised in a boating family where they spent most summer weekends boating on Lake Michigan or camping—five young children and two adults cramped in a nineteen-foot runabout or a tent. Her parents later upgraded to a twenty-five-foot cabin cruiser that allowed them to take longer trips, exploring popular harbors and islands throughout Lake Michigan. Vicky's father, who loved boating, waterskiing, hunting, and everything about the northlands, and had a degree from the University of Wisconsin in zoology and forestry, built a small sailboat and taught all his kids how to sail, navigate, swim, fish, and overall to love the lake and the outdoors.

Vicky's first trip to Green Bay was on the family boat, down the Fox River from Lake Winnebago to Green Bay. She notes:

> I was about nine years old, and I remember the experience because we had to pass through seventeen locks around the Fox River dams. It was exciting to see the locks being dewatered as we traveled downstream, but the smell of paper mill waste, anoxic water, and dead fish was horrible. My mother bought us all rubber gloves to wear while fending the boat away from the walls of the locks because they were covered with slime molds. What a contrast from the cleaner Lake Michigan water we were used to.

In 1962 her family moved to Green Bay, and her parents sold the boat to help buy a house and start a new business. However, those early water experiences were ingrained in her psyche and would guide the remainder of her life journey.

Bud grew up in Tipton, Iowa. His father was a dentist and wanted Bud to follow in his footsteps. When Bud was seventeen, his father had him assist with tooth extractions on Saturday mornings. Much to the chagrin of his father, those Saturday morning experiences had the opposite effect, and Bud chose not to pursue a dental profession.

Bud's mother was a lover of birds, and he showed an early interest in nature but from a different perspective—hunting and trapping. At the early age of thirteen, Bud started trapping, primarily mink and muskrat, and hunting squirrels and pheasants in the countryside around his home. After dropping out of college to join the U.S. Navy in 1957, Bud returned to finish his bachelor's degree in biology at a small liberal arts college called Coe College. Two professors, one a zoologist (Gene Goellner) and the other a botanist (Robert Drexler) had a profound influence in setting him on his professional course. After graduating from Coe, he got his master's degree and PhD in wildlife ecology and management from Iowa State University under the guidance of Milton W. Weller.

Immediately following getting his doctorate, Bud joined the faculty at the fledgling University of Wisconsin–Green Bay in 1969. As a young ecology professor, Bud remembers vividly his first boat ride on the Fox River in 1971. "It was a rather sour introduction because at that time things were really in what you'd call a desperate condition, it was an eye opener," recalls Bud (Alexander, 2020). At that time, the Fox River was a highly polluted ecosystem with only three species of pollution-tolerant fish—carp and two species of bullhead. Bud began investigating the impact of PCBs being discharged from paper mills on this ecosystem and discovered deformities and reproductive problems in birds. "It was kind of a nail in the coffin to identify that it really was having an environmental impact," said Bud.

At about the same time, Vicky headed off to college. Vicky always loved biology and the sciences in high school. She received a four-year scholarship to University of Wisconsin–Madison and entered their pre-med program, thinking she would go into medicine. During her freshman spring semester in 1970, the campus shut down because of student demonstrations against the Vietnam War. The National Guard was even called in, and student protesters were tear-gassed. Since Vicky's classes were mostly lab courses, it was impossible to complete them, and the students were given "incomplete" grades and told that they could retake the courses the following year. That summer the University of Wisconsin Army Math Building was bombed in protest of military research on campus, and a University of Wisconsin–Madison employee died in the blast. All of this greatly affected Vicky, and she decided to return to Green Bay and enrolled in the new four-year University of Wisconsin–Green Bay campus.

In those early years University of Wisconsin–Green Bay was known as "Eco-U" and had a strong focus on ecology and environmental management, including a young ecological upstart named Hallett J. "Bud" Harris. Initially it was an undergraduate campus, which meant that ongoing faculty research offered some opportunities for student jobs in research that would have been available only to grad students at other universities. Vicky's oceanography professor was conducting research on sedimentation around two new nuclear power plants on Lake Michigan and a coal-fired power plant on Green Bay. She was hired to collect and analyze sediment samples for the next several years. She got hooked.

Vicky abandoned ideas of a medical career and graduated with a degree in ecosystem analysis and a biology major. During that time, she took up scuba diving and loved the underwater and getting an up-close view of aquatic life.

After University of Wisconsin–Green Bay was accredited for master of science degrees, Vicky started her graduate studies in waterfowl ecology and environmental management while also working for the U.S. Fish and Wildlife Service as a student intern. The service was preparing an estuary study of Green Bay and part of her job entailed conducting aerial waterfowl censuses during spring and fall migrations and collecting and analyzing benthic macroinvertebrates to determine what aquatic invertebrate food was available for diving ducks.

Historically, Green Bay had been a major stopover site for migrating waterfowl, particularly diving ducks. But southern Green Bay had become highly enriched with nutrients, or what scientists call eutrophic, by the 1970s. The bay had extended periods of low oxygen levels due to excessive organic wastes from paper mills, sewage treatment plants, and agricultural runoff from the lower Fox River basin. At that time, the water was so turbid with algae and suspended solids that sunlight was unable to penetrate the water column to support underwater plants that were a preferred food of many waterfowl. Low oxygen levels also impaired the invertebrates that lived in the bottom of the bay—clams, snails, and aquatic insects. A general lack of waterfowl food resulted in declining numbers of waterfowl using Green Bay and a shift in migratory routes to other lakes and rivers in search of food to fuel their migration.

These surveys became the subject of Vicky's graduate thesis and she continued to conduct periodic aerial surveys over the next twenty-five years. Flying at three hundred feet over the water in a small four-seater plane was not without risk. They had several close calls when the pilot would dip too low. On one survey they had the misfortune of colliding with a bald eagle which seemed to mistake their small plane for a rival. The pilot tried to avoid the bird, but it persisted and flew directly at the plane taking out their propeller. Thankfully, they were able to make an emergency landing. On another flight which she was fortunate not to be on, the pilot forgot to refuel and the plane had to ditch in the cold bay waters of November. The pilot and U.S. Fish and Wildlife Service staff on board were able to exit the plane before it sank and cling to a floating ice chest from the plane until they were rescued by the crew of a passing commercial fishing vessel.

What brought Bud and Vicky together was their work on and love for Green Bay, and this eventually evolved into a deeper love and they were married in 1981. They had a mutual love of science, a desire to strengthen science–policy linkages to better manage the Fox River and Green Bay, and passion to pass on a healthier Green Bay as a gift to future generations. They have been a dynamic team for over four decades, their unique gifts and talents complementing each other and achieving an impact that has been greater than what they could have achieved separately.

One good example was when the Harrises worked with the Great Lakes Fishery Commission, other Great Lakes scientists, and Green Bay resource managers and stakeholders to examine the feasibility of ecosystem restoration during the late 1970s and early 1980s. They used Green Bay to develop a Great Lakes Ecosystem Restoration (GLER) case study that led to the development of the first rehabilitation plan for Green Bay that helped shape the Lower Green Bay and Fox River RAP in 1988.

An Awakening

When Bud joined the faculty of the University of Wisconsin–Green Bay in 1969, environmental awareness was just starting. That year the Santa Barbara oil spill occurred in California, which was the largest oil spill up until that time in the United States, and the Cuyahoga River in Cleveland, Ohio, and the Rouge River in Detroit, Michigan, caught on fire because of oil pollution. Public outcry nationally over pollution led to the first Earth Day in 1970. Fox River and Green Bay were also highly polluted at that time, and with environmental awareness and public outcry over pollution growing, this gave a young professor an opportunity to undertake relevant science, influence management and restoration of Fox River and Green Bay, and inspire a new generation of environmental scientists working to achieve ecosystem sustainability. Bud's research and teaching interests were broad and interdisciplinary, but his forte was the ecology of freshwater coastal wetlands, with an emphasis on Green Bay. His work has been highly relevant, considering that nearly 50 percent of Wisconsin's original ten million acres of wetlands have been lost to development and land use changes.

In the late 1970s, two of Bud's students observed relatively low reproductive success of Forster's tern while he was the coordinator of the Sea Grant Green Bay Subprogram. Sea Grant partnered with the U.S. Fish and Wildlife Service to mount research on potential impacts of PCBs on tern reproductive success. These definitive studies helped precipitate an unprecedented mass balance study of PCBs in the Green Bay ecosystem that identified where the PCBs were coming from and how much was coming from each source. Bud served as the on-site coordinator for the U.S. Environmental Protection Agency on this study.

This precedent-setting investigation helped solidify the Fox River PCB cleanup of contaminated sediment by the responsible parties at a cost of $1.3 billion.

Bud was never satisfied with just publishing papers in scientific journals. He wanted to make sure that science was guiding decision-making, and he was not afraid to call people out if their position was not supported by science. For example, in 2011 there was a fight over protecting a small wetland tract just down the road from Lambeau Field where the Green Bay Packers play football. Bud argued that "people see what they want to see, depending on their perspective." For Bud and other wetland experts, such wetlands were a rare and valuable resource that provide many ecosystem services or environmental benefits, while supporting a rich array of flora and fauna. To others like developers and some decision-makers, wetlands were an obstacle in the way of job creation, a sadly degraded patch of wasted opportunity. As you can see, Bud saw the other side of an issue that he cared deeply about and was very principled and not afraid to buck the system. Unfortunately, although some small modifications were made to the development, the wetlands were filled. The important lesson is that scientists need to be at the table where such decisions are made to be proponents for wetland protection for all species, including humans.

Lower Green Bay and Fox River RAP

In 1985, the International Joint Commission's Great Lakes Water Quality Board designated the lower Green Bay and Fox River as an AOC. This move elevated the priority for cleanup and gave laser focus to addressing problems such as fish that were unsafe to eat, birds that had deformities, water that was unsafe for swimming, and the disappearance of habitats and many plants and animals that depended upon them. In response, Wisconsin Department of Natural Resources, in cooperation with U.S. Environmental Protection Agency, committed to working with stakeholders to develop and implement a RAP to restore all BUIs. The AOC encompasses the last seven miles of the Fox River from the De Pere Dam to its mouth and from the Inner Bay out to Long Tail Point on the west shore and Point au Sable on the east shore. The area is wholly within the state of Wisconsin.

Vicky joined the Wisconsin Department of Natural Resources in 1982 as the northeast region water resources planner and policy analyst. She prepared watershed management plans for the lower Fox and other rivers in northeast Wisconsin and was the RAP coordinator for thirteen years.

As noted above, the Harrises worked with the Great Lakes Fishery Commission and other scientists and resource managers in the late 1970s and early 1980s to develop a GLER case study that led to the development of the first rehabilitation plan for Green Bay. This foundational work helped shape the Lower Green Bay and Fox River RAP. In keeping with previous efforts to engage multidisciplinary experts and stakeholders in the GLER case study, Vicky established four technical advisory committees and a Citizen Advisory Committee to guide RAP preparation and subsequent implementation. An Outreach and Education Committee was also created to inform and engage the public. This committee focused much of its efforts on addressing nonpoint sources of nutrient and soil runoff that are the root cause of most of the AOC's impairments. The committee even developed a "Baybook" for homeowners with advice on how to reduce runoff that was causing pollution and manage household wastes. They also created first- and fifth-grade school activity books and a teacher guidebook around a cast of cartoon characters known as the "Clean Bay Backers" (a play on their Green Bay Packers football team). The characters were developed by a popular political cartoonist for the *Green Bay Chronicle* newspaper. Each character represented a type of wildlife in the area, e.g., Gretta Goose, Billy Beaver, and Gills Finnegan (a yellow perch), and conveyed messages about how land runoff affected water quality and their habitats.

Between 1986 and 1993, more than one hundred people served on the technical, citizen, and outreach committees to develop the RAP and guide implementation. They represented local governments, agencies, the paper industry, businesses, recreational groups, and conservationists from many walks of life. Vicky notes:

> We were fortunate to have some very capable and influential community leaders take on lead roles. Our Citizen Advisory Committee was initially chaired by a local bank president Jake Rose, and later by Brown County executive Tom Cuene. When the need arose to hold a workshop to merge the more than 120 remedial action recommendations from the technical committees, Jake Rose asked, "How much?," took out his personal check-book and wrote a check to fund the workshop. Tom Cuene advised that to convince local elected officials to approve or take remedial actions, you had to "tell them three times" about the need and rationale for action. By the third time, they begin to believe that the action is their own idea and in the best interest of their constituents.

Bud also played a pivotal role in the RAP. He chaired its Science and Technical Advisory Committee for several years. His successor, John Kennedy from the Green Bay Metropolitan Sewage District, convinced the Sewerage Commission to fund a water quality monitoring program in the AOC beginning in 1986, just as the RAP was getting started. Sewage treatment plants don't usually do that kind of thing, but the program has been invaluable to the RAP and more recently the Fox River TMDL initiative, which identifies the maximum amount of a pollutant that a body of water can receive to restore and protect water quality. In fact, monitoring sites and parameters have been expanded, producing a long-term data set that has been vital in tracking water quality trends in response to remedial actions and introductions of invasive species like zebra and quagga mussels.

The Lower Green Bay and Fox River RAP was first completed in 1988 and was one of the first to be approved by the International Joint Commission. This area had many advantages over other AOCs due to nearly twenty years of Sea Grant research and the GLER ecosystem case study—Bud and Vicky's work. The RAP was updated in 1993 and later updated annually to report progress and identify priority projects for funding and implementation. Indeed, the Green Bay RAP was an early and effective leader in the use of an ecosystem approach and a multi-stakeholder process.

However, Wisconsin Department of Natural Resources' support for advisory committees waned over the years due to lack of state and federal funds. In the lean years, committed stakeholders, particularly the Green Bay Metropolitan Sewage District, Brown County Land and Water Conservation Department, and University of Wisconsin Sea Grant, stepped up to carry on the work of the RAP committees. To this day, over thirty years later, the Outreach Committee, known locally as the "Clean Bay Backers," is still active under the leadership of the University of Wisconsin Sea Grant and has organized six half-day field trips for elected officials and community leaders to showcase RAP projects that are "bringing back the bay." Bud was instrumental in preparing the first two "State of the Bay" reports 1991 and 1993 that summarized the health of the bay and reported on trends in key indicators of ecosystem health. The Harrises later guided development of the most recent expanded State of the Bay report. These reports have been instrumental in synthesizing the science about current ecosystem health, documenting changes over time, translating the science for decision-makers, and building consensus about critical next steps in restoring the bay.

Restoration Accomplishments

The overall lower Green Bay/Fox River restoration effort is an amazing accomplishment in scale and complexity. In total, over $1.6 billion has been spent on cleanup and restoration since 1985:

- $272 million on upgrading wastewater treatment plants and addressing stormwater runoff;
- $1.3 billion on remediating contaminated sediment;
- $21 million on rehabilitating and enhancing habitats;
- $6 million on controlling pollution from agricultural runoff;
- $1.2 million on planning, monitoring, and managing invasive species.

In terms of ecosystem health, there is good news and bad news so far. The good news is that the ecosystem has improved dramatically for fish and other aquatic life. Ammonia levels are down, and dissolved oxygen levels are up in the water. Back in the 1970s when only three species of fish could be found in the river—carp and two species of bullhead—it was essentially a dead system. Today, more than forty species of fish can be found in the Fox River and the lower bay, including trophy fisheries for walleye, northern pike, and spotted muskies, which had to be reintroduced after going locally extinct. Beach closings have lessened, and coastal wetlands have improved somewhat and are considered in fair condition. The bay also supports exceptional waterfowl hunting. The numbers of diving ducks have greatly increased after the invasion of zebra and quagga mussels—one of the few benefits of these invasive species.

The bad news is that phosphorus levels from agricultural runoff are still too high and causing harmful algal blooms. Nitrate and nitrite concentrations are increasing over time. The amount of suspended solids in the water is still considered excessive, chlorophyll *a* levels—a plant pigment indicative of algae—are still too high, and water clarity is still too low. Although much has been done to prevent toxic substances from getting into the water and to remediate legacy pollution since 2013, levels of PCBs, current levels of dioxins, DDT, arsenic, and mercury remain at unacceptable levels. Finally, invasive species, considered a type of biological pollution, continue to impact the food web, and climate change is also impacting the ecosystem.

Regarding the PCB removal results, Bud Harris notes with a smile: "There has been a really marked decline in PCBs in the fish, in the sediment, and in the water column. It will take some time but it's clearly going in the right direction, so I don't think there's any doubt it's going to be successful" (Alexander, 2020). But the Harrises are quick to note that more needs to be done to achieve and sustain a healthy ecosystem. Continued restoration will require continued public and political support.

One project that the Harrises are particularly proud of is the restoration of the Cat Island chain. Rising water levels and a series of severe storms in the mid-1970s eroded a chain of barrier islands in southwestern Green Bay that once protected large areas of coastal wetlands and were home to the greatest diversity of colonial nesting birds in the Great Lakes. Literally, the islands had washed away except for one mere remnant of Cat Island. The Harrises helped champion restoring this chain of islands and the surrounding wetland habitats as one of the RAP recommendations.

In 1994, the RAP Biota and Habitat Advisory Committee held a workshop of fifty wildlife managers from across the Great Lakes to identify the best opportunities for habitat restoration in the AOC. Workshop participants recommended restoring the Cat Islands to their 1960s footprint as the top priority among many other potential restoration activities. The committee chair—Janet Smith, U.S. Fish and Wildlife Service Green Bay office director—and Vicky Harris met with the Green Bay port director and the U.S. Army Corps of Engineers to enlist their cooperation. They worked with the port director who developed a proposal to the Corps of Engineers for island restoration using clean sediments dredged from the outer navigational channel for commercial shipping. The port received an initial grant from the Corps of Engineers to begin planning.

Vicky sampled the sediments in the project area for PCB levels, which thankfully were quite low. The committee wanted to assure the public that any sediments placed during the project would not be higher in PCBs than the existing area and would meet the RAP's goals for sediment remediation. No sediments from the Fox River harbor or remedial dredging were to be used. Local fishermen were also concerned that the restored islands would increase the population of double-crested cormorants, which were already numerous on the remnants of Cat Island

and which they blamed for poor yellow perch recruitment in Green Bay. The Biota and Habitat Advisory Committee gave numerous presentations to interested parties to explain the project and reassure the public that the islands would also be managed for invasive or nuisance species.

Planning, hydrodynamic modeling, and design work took more than a decade and construction of the rock outline of three islands and an access road was not completed until 2013—that's twenty years of meetings, phone calls, proposals, outreach, and planning until construction of the island framework was ready to begin receiving sediments.

The committee was involved during the entire process, providing advice, reviewing plans, holding public meetings, and seeking funds for modeling work. The RAP Biota and Habitat Committee eventually evolved into the Cat Island Advisory Committee (CIAC) under the leadership of the port. The CIAC is a strong partnership between the port, U.S. Army Corps of Engineers, U.S. Fish and Wildlife Service, Wisconsin Department of Natural Resources, University of Wisconsin Sea Grant, University of Wisconsin–Green Bay Center for Biodiversity, and other experts. It provides advice on the timing and placement of dredged sediments, invasive species and predator management, construction of nesting habitat for terns and piping plovers, monitoring, and planning for enhancing habitats.

Over the past seven years, several installments of clean sediments have been hydraulically pumped into the structure after being tested by the U.S. Army Corps of Engineers. The first deposits were very clean sand that provided excellent habitat for shorebirds. The following year observers saw endangered piping plovers using the deposited material, and these birds have since nested each year with encouraging success. In 2020, there were five nests with a total of twenty eggs. However, predation and an outbreak of botulism took a toll, and the seven surviving chicks were collected and taken to a safe site in Illinois. Many other species of shorebirds and water birds have taken up residence or use the island deposits during migration. The island framework is providing wave shelter for recovering submergent and emergent wetland plants, and another project is attempting to restore wild rice and other beneficial aquatic plants in the protected area. Record high water levels in the past couple of years have taken a toll on wetland vegetation recovery and caused some damage to the framework, which was repaired in 2020.

Overall, the initial restoration of the Cat Island chain shows promise in becoming a significant habitat for nesting and migrating birds and should help in the recovery of surrounding wetlands and fish habitat as well. However, it will take as many as twenty to thirty years before enough dredged sediment is available to build the islands back to their planned size and to reach their full potential.

Cat Island chain in Green Bay, Lake Michigan
U.S. ARMY CORPS OF ENGINEERS

Reflections

Good science and long-term monitoring of an ecosystem are crucial to sound decision-making. As the adage says—if you don't measure it, you can't manage it. In Green Bay, they have learned that it can take years to amass the information necessary to tackle major problems.

For example, the use of PCBs was strictly regulated by the U.S. Environmental Protection Agency in the late 1970s because they were found to accumulate in the fat of fish, wildlife, and humans, and they caused reproductive problems and birth defects in fish-eating birds and other wildlife. U.S. Environmental Protection Agency also determined that some forms of PCBs were potentially carcinogenic to humans. Studies of pregnant and nursing women who regularly ate fish from the Great Lakes and Green Bay area had elevated levels of PCBs in their breast milk.

PCBs had been used as a coating for carbonless copy paper manufactured by the NCR paper mill on the Fox River and were also discharged in wastewater from other mills that recycled office wastepaper, or the ends trimmed from rolls of carbonless copy paper. PCBs are not very soluble, and they accumulated in Fox River and Green Bay sediments for decades at levels considered to be harmful to wildlife and humans that consumed fish. It took nearly three decades of study of Fox River and Green Bay sediments, water, fish, and fish-eating birds before a cleanup plan was finally approved. Bud served as U.S. Environmental Protection Agency's onsite coordinator of the Green Bay PCB mass balance study in the late 1980s, which estimated the loading, transport, and fate of PCBs, lead, and cadmium in the bay and predicted the potential results of remediation. Multiple universities and agencies were involved in this extensive study.

It took another seventeen years to dredge or cap more than eight million cubic yards of contaminated river sediments at a cost of $1.3 billion dollars to the paper industry (primarily three mills). Wisconsin Department of Natural Resources estimates that this volume of sediment would fill nearly 700,000 dump trucks that would stretch from Green Bay to London, England, if placed end to end. The project was completed in 2020 and is one of the largest cleanups of PCBs in the United States and probably the world.

Monitoring of areas remediated showed a dramatic 90 percent reduction of PCBs in water, 80 to 90 percent in sediments, and 65 percent in walleyes since 2006. Beginning in 2021, comprehensive monitoring will be conducted every five years to track changes in PCBs in water, sediment, and fish. This life-time monitoring will also be paid for by the paper industry.

Long-term monitoring of Green Bay water quality by the Green Bay Metropolitan Sewerage District (now NEW Water) beginning in 1986 also provided the information necessary to manage the suspended solids and excessive algal problems that impair many beneficial uses of the river and bay. This data set was crucial in developing loading reduction targets for the RAP and subsequently TMDL targets for phosphorus and suspended solids entering the river and bay.

Next Challenges

As noted earlier, the Fox River system, which includes the Wolf River, is the largest watershed flowing into Lake Michigan, draining about one third of Lake Michigan's basin. It is also the third largest watershed in all the Great Lakes. With the cleanup of PCB-contaminated sediments, most of the remaining use impairments are caused by excessive amounts of phosphorus and suspended solids entering the bay from the lower Fox River. Phosphorus fuels algal growth that makes the water unappealing for swimming or other recreation. Harmful algal blooms are common in summer and fall and can release a variety of toxins that may make people and animals sick after they swallow, breathe in, or have contact with the water. Decaying algae and organic solids use up dissolved oxygen in the bottom waters to the point where some areas have extended periods of low oxygen (anoxia) that impair the survival of fish and bottom-dwelling organisms (benthos). The AOC water is so turbid with suspended particles of sediment and algae that sunlight cannot penetrate the water to support submerged aquatic plants that are necessary for fish and wildlife habitat and food. Managing nonpoint runoff of phosphorus and soil erosion from numerous agricultural and municipal sources will be an enormous task if the RAP and TMDL targets are to be reached.

Models used to estimate the reductions needed to meet water quality standards show that the smaller watersheds within this area will need to reduce total phosphorus and total suspended solids loads by up to 80 percent. Dairy-farming operations are the largest source of phosphorus and suspended solids to the river and bay. The Fox River basin has many concentrated animal feeding operations (CAFOs), which generate enormous quantities of manure that is then applied to croplands. While there are regulatory requirements in place for CAFOs and farming practices, enforcement is daunting with limited county staff and resources.

While the U.S. Department of Agriculture and county land conservation departments have encouraged best farm management practices to limit runoff and have shared the cost of implementing them for many decades, efforts have dramatically increased with federal Great Lakes

Restoration Initiative funding, improvements in state regulations, and the TMDL program. The TMDL has spurred new partnerships between farmers, agencies, counties, the Oneida Indian Tribe, NEW Water Sewage Commission, and universities to install and monitor best management practices in the Fox watersheds. Eight farms have been chosen as sites for experimenting with adopting new or improved practices on up to 100 percent of their land. Monitoring the runoff and tile drainage from their fields will show whether these practices are successful in reducing runoff. Emphasis has been on expanding no-till farming, planting cover crops to protect the soil over the winter, rotational grazing, and liquid manure injection over the course of the growing season, rather than spreading all the manure in the fall and winter. Participating farmers have been enthusiastic about the benefits, reporting improvements in soil health, crop production, dairy herd health, and water quality. The demonstration farms also host educational "field days" attended by other farmers, farming professionals, and legislators to showcase their efforts and discuss results.

Although 2019 and 2020 have been the wettest years ever recorded in Wisconsin, it is encouraging that water quality monitoring in the bay by NEW Water shows average concentrations of total phosphorus and total suspended solids over the past five years have been the lowest in decades, approaching the targets set by the RAP and the TMDL. Whether this trend continues remains to be seen. It is very possible that improvements could also be due in part to the eight million cubic yards of nutrient rich sediment that were removed or capped during the PCB remediation over the past seventeen years.

Green Bay ecosystem monitoring and modeling are also underway to assess whether recommended TMDL targets and current best management practices will be sufficient to achieve RAP objectives given the continuing expansion of dairy herds, increasing urbanization, and climate change influences on runoff. Available data and climate change models for Wisconsin show that rain events will continue to increase in frequency and intensity and that more of Wisconsin's winter precipitation is occurring as rain rather than snow. Therefore, it is even more important to maintain crop cover over winter and to prevent spreading manure during wet seasons or on frozen ground.

Substantial additional actions will be needed and will depend on voluntary participation by many more farmers and homeowners. Sewage treatment plants, industries, and municipalities are also being given more stringent limits on total suspended solids and total phosphorus discharges and stormwater runoff to meet their TMDL load reduction targets.

Advice to the Next Generation

The team of Bud Harris as a university scientist and Vicky Harris as a government resource manager and university outreach specialist was critical to making science-informed decisions for cleanup of the AOC. Both had the unique ability to put themselves in the shoes of resource managers and work collaboratively to find solutions, and both made the cleanup of the Fox River and Green Bay their life's work. Their advice is compelling and to the point:

> Be vigilant and never give up the fight for what's right to preserve the legacy of Great Lakes' natural resources. The Great Lakes are the largest and most valuable source of fresh water on the surface of the planet. Speak out and let legislators and community leaders know what you value. The Great Lakes are vast but not immune to pollution or habitat destruction. As human

populations and communities continue to grow, they place increasing stress on the integrity of ecosystems. The next generation will need to continue the work of building more sustainable communities in harmony with nature.

Support and believe in sound science for making wise decisions. But do not be lured into thinking that technology or government agencies can fix any problem. Sometimes the simplicity of what we do in our daily lives or the choices we make as consumers make all the difference—reduce, reuse, recycle.

For the Harrises, good science is essential. But it also must be effectively translated and communicated to the public and decision-makers. This is even more important during these times of social media propaganda and misinformation. They note that science is increasingly under attack by special interests whose primary goals are short-term profits rather than long-term ecosystem and community sustainability. Bud notes: "As we move forward with the restoration of the Green Bay ecosystem, climate change accentuates the need for future research and management to engage an ecosystem perspective, including ecological economics and full cost accounting."

Concluding Thoughts

Just as carpenters have a toolbox filled with many tools to build a house, ecosystem managers need a variety of tools to achieve their goal of ecosystem health and sustainability. Examples of tools used effectively by the many partners in Green Bay include:

- science that understands cause-and-effect relationships;
- the Green Bay mass balance study;

- the TMDL initiative;
- long-term monitoring;
- adaptive management that assesses state of the ecosystem, sets priorities, and takes action in an iterative fashion for continuous improvement;
- inclusive governance that supports ecosystem-based management;
- effective science translation that leads to strong science–policy–management linkages;
- public education and engagement that leads to a stewardship ethic.

Overall, the Harrises are encouraged and hopeful that the Green Bay ecosystem continues to show resilience and is capable of recovery as pollutants and habitat destruction are abated. Recovery of long-standing impairments will not be easy, quick, or without significant investments in improved management practices. They believe that Green Bay's successes to date are in large part due to engaging community leaders and stakeholder groups, continuing public outreach, maintaining an ecosystem approach, and reporting progress.

Today, the Harrises continue to be a force for restoration of the Fox River and Green Bay to benefit both present and future generations of people living in the watershed. Following retirement, Bud served as a consultant for one of the paper companies responsible for the discharge of PCBs to the Fox River. His role for the plaintiff (paper company) was to convince a jury that PCBs did in fact impact wildlife associated with the lower Fox River and lower Green Bay and that the defendant (insurance companies) must in part pay for damages. The jury ruled in favor of the plaintiff.

The paper company's chief executive officer remarked that he wanted to see a visibly cleaner river post-PCB cleanup. When Bud told him

Vicky Harris and Bud Harris, longtime champions of restoring Green Bay
CK PHOTOGRAPHY

that would not happen because the appearance of the river was due to nutrient and sediment loading, not PCBs, the chief executive officer then asked what the next step should be. Bud told him that a watershed monitoring program was needed to locate the most significant sources, and he responded by inviting Bud and colleagues to submit a proposal. Bud recruited a young faculty member with a background in soil science named Kevin Fermanich, to develop a joint proposal. They submitted a proposal which included engaging high school science teachers and students to be a part of the monitoring program along with U.S. Geological Survey personnel. The proposal, calling for just under $1 million, was funded literally over a phone conversation. This project received continued funding amounting to over $2 million, and it set the course for later funding for watershed restoration from the Great Lakes Restoration Initiative.

Bud now serves as president of the Fox–Wolf Watershed Alliance and continues as a long-term member of Wisconsin Sea Grant Advisory Council. In recognition of his long-standing commitment to research and passion for applying science to solving critical ecological and sociological problems, Bud was elected to the prestigious Wisconsin Academy of Science in 2020.

Vicky retired from UW Sea Grant in 2013 but continues to be involved in groups interested in protecting and restoring water quality, including the RAP technical and outreach committees (aka Clean Bay Backers), Wisconsin Sea Grant Outreach Advisory Committee, the Cat Island Advisory Committee, and the Wisconsin Clean Marina Program Technical Team. She served as co-chair of U.S. EPA's Lake Michigan Lakewide Management Plan, a group dedicated to promoting the restoration of Lake Michigan. In 2012, Vicky received the prestigious John R. (Jack) Vallentyne Award from the International Association for Great Lakes Research for important and sustained efforts to inform and educate the public and policymakers on Great Lakes issues. In 2012, Vicky also was recognized by the University of Wisconsin–Green Bay's Environmental Management and Business Institute with an Earth Caretaker Award for her influential career in the sustainability and environmental fields. At the fiftieth anniversary of the Wisconsin Nature Conservancy in 2010, Bud and Vicky were presented with a Gold Star Award for lifetime achievement and lasting contributions to the protection of Green Bay and the Door Peninsula. In 2021, Bud and Vicky were selected as Conservationists of the Year by the Wisconsin Wildlife Federation.

CHAPTER 3

Kathy Evans

Muskegon Lake Champion

M uskegon Lake is a 4,150-acre inland coastal body of water located on the western shore of Lake Michigan in the state of Michigan. Scientists call Muskegon Lake a drowned river mouth because it was formed by erosion of tributary river channels during extreme low water levels. As water levels in the Great Lakes rose, the mouths of such tributary rivers were "drowned." The Muskegon River is Michigan's second longest river, originating at Houghton Lake, the state's largest inland lake in the north-central portion of the Lower Peninsula, and flowing southwest 219 miles into Muskegon Lake before flowing into Lake Michigan.

Muskegon River and Lake helped sustain Native Americans for millennia. *Masquigon* is an Ojibwa word meaning "marshy river or swamp." Today, the city of Muskegon is located along the eastern shoreline of Muskegon Lake in Muskegon County.

During the fur trade era, the Hudson Bay Company found riches in harvesting animals here. During Muskegon's lumber era in 1837–1900, forty-seven sawmills surrounded Muskegon Lake. In fact, when the Great Fire of 1871 devastated Chicago, the city was rebuilt with lumber from this area. At one time during this prosperous era, Muskegon boasted more millionaires per capita than any town in America (Evans et al., 2019). Later during World War II, Muskegon's Continental Motor Company produced tank, aircraft, and automobile engines, giving it a reputation as a foundry town. It is no surprise that Muskegon, throughout its history, has been known as "Lumber Queen of the World," "Port City," and "Riviera of the Midwest." However, its long history of urban development and industrialization led to substantial pollution.

In 1985 the International Joint Commission's Great Lakes Water Quality Board identified Muskegon Lake as a pollution hotspot or AOC. Up until that time, water pollution in this body of water did not receive much attention. But getting on the dreaded list of international pollution hotspots shone a spotlight on algal blooms caused by excessive nutrient runoff from the surrounding lands, closure of bathing beaches because of high bacterial contamination, health advisories on fish because of mercury and PCB contamination, and loss of critical habitats important to the survival of native fish, birds, and plants.

As a result of the lake's being placed on the AOC list, the Michigan Department of Natural Resources committed to working with stakeholders to develop and implement a RAP to restore all impaired beneficial uses. Soon after, Lake Michigan Federation set up a Muskegon office and the state's Department of Natural Resources set up a Public Advisory Council to ensure public input on the RAP and the implementation of

An aerial view of Muskegon Lake
GEI CONSULTANTS OF MICHIGAN

an ecosystem approach, as called for in the U.S.–Canada Great Lakes Water Quality Agreement. One key champion emerged in this grassroots cleanup effort—Kathy Evans.

Budding Conservationist and Environmentalist

As a child, Evans and her sisters were able to explore the natural areas in forested lands along the lakes and streams that led to Bear Lake, Muskegon Lake, and Lake Michigan. The oak pine forest was filled with wintergreen, bracken fern, lowbush blueberry, moccasin flower, and many kinds of mosses and lichens. To an elementary school kid, it was a magical fairy land! Her Mom told her and her sisters not to pick the lady's slippers because they are a beautiful native orchid protected by state law. But the area had been subdivided for development, and as the clearing for roads began, the flowering dogwood trees soon gave way to sassafras, dandelions, and eventually a patchwork of manicured lawns. Her childhood paths and short cut trails soon disappeared and were eventually cut off by backyard fences.

Evans learned about songbirds, fish, wildlife, and waterfowl from her grandfather, who had built a home in the 1920s on the connecting channel between Bear Lake and Muskegon Lake, where he and her grandmother raised a family. This was a very special place for her family on Sunday afternoons. The connecting channel allowed her and her sisters to take a rowboat into Bear Lake. When they pushed off from shore, they would always row rhythmically up the connecting channel, past other homes and cottages, and eventually entered the wide expanse of Bear Lake. To young girls, these nautical excursions were always adventures that inspired a sense of wonder for the great outdoors. They always followed grandpa's advice and never rowed into Muskegon Lake because the winds could kick the water up quickly and it would be too rough for young kids to go it alone. Her grandpa always had fishing poles ready to go at the water's edge just in case the weather permitted and the grandkids were interested. Her grandfather was an avid hunter and fisherman, and a conservationist at heart. He inspired a conservation ethic in his granddaughters by example and by the stories he told.

Her mom's family left Tuscany just before the Great Depression and settled in the city of Muskegon. Nona taught her all about vegetable gardening and let her help, showing her how to water the garden in a way that would keep the soil healthy and not burn the plant leaves. Nona also showed her how to pick dandelion greens in the early spring and how to hunt mushrooms. Whenever she put mushrooms in a pot to boil, she would toss in a quarter and say "a poison mushroom would tarnish silver." Good thing Nona didn't know what a U.S. quarter was made of.

Later, Evans would learn that vast portions of the forests she played in as a child were relatively young forests that rose from the lands that once were logged and that supported oil and gas exploration activities before the 1930s. She learned that the small pockets of open sandy fields within the forest were there because they had been polluted by oil and gas exploration. Plants didn't grow there because of these pollutants.

The formative experiences with her grandparents and the outdoors led her to a career in conservation and environmental protection. Soon after graduating from high school in 1976, Evans took a job with the Michigan Department of Natural Resources at the Gillette Sand Dune Interpretive Center in Muskegon. She worked full-time at the center while attending Muskegon Community College. She married her husband Mark in 1982 and by 1989 had two children under the age of five. They bought a small house on ten acres of rural land with a small creek. Mark Evans worked for the S. D. Warren/Scott Paper Mill, located on Muskegon Lake. Kathy began to learn about the effects of chlorinated organic chemicals, wondering if the Muskegon paper mill was polluting their environment. This was the same time period that Greenpeace was on their Zero Discharge Campaign that called for zero discharge of persistent toxic substances into the Great Lakes. The organization even unfurled a "Zero Discharge" banner on one of smokestacks of a local paper mill. Evans waited and watched in anticipation as the Greenpeace members slowly climbed the smokestack, secured the banner, and captured media attention that raised public awareness of the need to stop pouring persistent toxic substances into our air, water, and land.

This made a lasting impression on her, and she became a champion for the restoration of Muskegon and its watershed.

Following in her grandfather's footsteps, Evans searched out local, likeminded environmentalists and became a volunteer in two different environmental groups. One focused on community and workplace safety and preventing accidental releases of chemicals that could harm employees and the people who lived around chemical plants. Through this group, Evans learned that Muskegon County had more than ten Superfund sites and that one of them was only a mile from the school that her children would be attending. She also learned that the chemical company with the Superfund site near the school was still in operation and that it routinely had "upset conditions" leading to the release of extremely harmful chemicals into the air.

The other environmental group that Evans volunteered with was the West Michigan Region Environmental Network (WREN), which was more broadly focused on environmental concerns in western Michigan. This group provided input and comments on remedial investigations for Superfund sites and a whole host of other environmental concerns that were affecting the health and quality of air, land, and community health. During that time, the Lake Michigan Federation became aware of WREN's activism and urged the group to become involved with the Great Lakes AOCs, two of which were located in Muskegon County—Muskegon Lake and White Lake. At the time Evans did not even know what an AOC was or what it entailed.

But she jumped in with both feet, inspired to make a difference. After serving as a volunteer and then part-time staff for Lake Michigan Federation, participating in the Muskegon Lake Public Advisory Committee,

Evans was hired by the Muskegon Conservation District to manage some grants to help clean up and restore the Muskegon Lake AOC.

Muskegon Lake Remedial Action Plan

With input for the Public Advisory Committee, the initial RAP was completed in 1987. The plan noted that the Muskegon Lake AOC had no apparent impacts on Lake Michigan, but it did produce localized problems, including elevated contaminant levels in certain fishes, contaminated sediments, and degraded habitats. The RAP reported that Muskegon Lake suffered from a long history of pollution, including contamination by petroleum products, mercury, and PCBs. Nutrient runoff from the surrounding landscape caused large algal blooms and harmed the base of the food web. Beaches were unsafe for swimming, fish and wildlife populations were degraded, health advisories were in effect on fish, much habitat had been lost during the lumbering and industrial eras, and there were restrictions on dredging for navigational purposes because of a plethora of toxic substances.

The first water quality improvements were documented following the diversion of municipal wastewater from the lake to the Muskegon County Wastewater Management System in 1973. This 11,000-acre land application system has a capacity of 42 million gallons per day and includes extended aeration, lagoon impoundment, slow-rate irrigation, and rapid-sand filtration. Treated wastewater is discharged to the Muskegon River, approximately ten miles upstream of Muskegon Lake. Between 1972 and 2005, surface lake-wide averages of total phosphorus and soluble reactive phosphorus—key nutrients tied to the accelerated growth of algae—declined from sixty-eight to twenty-seven parts per billion (μg/L) and from twenty to five parts per billion, respectively (Steinman et al., 2008). Average chlorophyll *a* concentration, a pigment found in algae, declined from twenty-five to six parts per billion over the same time period, while water transparency increased from 4.9 to 7.2 feet, as measured by a Secchi disk. These signs of improvement were visible to all who lived near the lake or recreated on it. By the mid-2000s, eutrophication targets for Muskegon Lake were being met or exceeded.

Despite these improvements, major environmental challenges remained, including contaminated sediments and loss of natural habitat. The RAP also laid out plans for remediating these problems. In the early 1990s, the Muskegon Lake Watershed Partnership replaced the Public Advisory Committee. Its purpose was to serve as a community-based, volunteer partnership organization that coordinated all activities to restore the lake and its watershed, and to help promote an ecosystem approach and build capacity. The RAP was updated in 1994 and 2002, and a Stage 2 RAP, identifying necessary remedial and preventive actions to restore uses, was completed in 2011.

Through Evan's involvement in the RAP, she discovered that there was no official organization coordinating the overall cleanup effort. Things were being done, but in a piecemeal fashion. As noted above, despite the improvements in the eutrophication of Muskegon Lake, people still didn't fully understand the severity and geographic extent of contaminated sediments, stormwater, and loss and degradation of fish and wildlife habitat. Many of the Muskegon Lake studies were outdated and isolated in various information repositories in the county and local governmental offices. At the time, this situation seemed totally preposterous to her and she vowed to do something about it. Evans now works at the West

Michigan Shoreline Regional Development Commission, which is the state and federally designated area-wide water quality planning agency under section 208 of the Clean Water Act, where she helped set up a repository that shares information and ensures that the best science is being used to guide cleanup efforts.

Up until the early 2000s, there was no big pot of money or dedicated funding for cleaning up AOCs. But the Muskegon Lake RAP and others played a critical role in laying the foundation for cleanup and restoration, so that people were prepared to act when money did become available through the Great Lakes Legacy Act, enacted in 2002, and the Great Lakes Restoration Initiative, established in 2010. In these years, major cleanup began. Most prominent was the remediation of legacy contamination of sediments in the bottom of the lake at a cost of $48.6 million, including:

- 89,869 cubic yards of contaminated sediment in Ruddiman Creek in 2006 at a cost of $14.2 million;
- 43,463 cubic yards of contaminated sediment at the Division Street Outfall in 2012 at a cost of $10.8 million;
- 44,000 cubic yards of contaminated sediment and soil in the vicinity of the Zephyr Oil Refinery in 2019 at a cost of $17 million;
- 10,600 cubic yards of contaminated sediment and removal of over 2,000 tons of mill debris in Ryerson Creek, followed by covering the entire two-acre area with clean sand, at a cost of $6.6 million (Evans et al., 2019).

Similarly, substantial habitat restoration and conservation work has been completed or is underway in the AOC. More than $22 million has been spent on restoring and enhancing wetland, open water, shoreline, and riparian habitats in four projects (Evans et al., 2019). These habitats are benefiting native fishes like bluegill, largemouth bass, and lake sturgeon. Restored wetlands are bringing back marsh birds. Improved riparian habitats are bringing back frogs, turtles, and mammals like muskrat and mink.

Evans is most proud of the fish and wildlife habitat restoration at Grand Trunk on the southern shoreline of Muskegon Lake and the many community volunteers who made it happen. The area was named for the Grand Trunk Milwaukee Car Ferry Company and served as a loading dock from 1905 to 1978. Before the restoration project, the area was filled with mattresses, automobile doors, and an array of other trash.

Through this restoration project, volunteers from a local paper mill engaged the Lakeside Neighborhood Association, Muskegon Public Schools, conservation organizations, and businesses to transform a literal dump into a nature park and outdoor classroom used by residents, students, and tourists. Over the years, volunteers have removed more than 2,000 pounds of trash and restored seven acres of wetland and riparian habitats for native species of fish, plants, and birds. Volunteers have also placed bird houses and removed invasive plant species that outcompete native plant species. The project was the first fish and wildlife habitat restoration project completed by West Michigan Shoreline Regional Development Commission with National Oceanic and Atmospheric Administration/American Recovery and Reinvestment Act funding through the Great Lakes Commission. There were only three such grants awarded in the Great Lakes Basin at that time and one of only two in the Lake Michigan watershed. The Grand Trunk volunteers held their thirtieth anniversary of the cleanup and restoration of the shoreline property in 2020. The property is now owned and stewarded by the Michigan Department of Natural Resources.

The first beneficial use impairment—"restrictions on dredging activities"—was removed in 2011. "Restrictions on fish and wildlife consumption" and "restrictions on drinking water consumption" were removed as beneficial use impairments in 2013, and "beach closings" was removed as a beneficial use impairment in 2015. In plain language that means that the fish are safer to eat, the water is safer for swimming and drinking, and all contaminated sediment hotspots have been remediated, so there are no longer restrictions on dredging. Only three more habitat restoration projects and one contaminated sediment remediation project remain to be completed. They are projected to be completed by 2022, with a goal of removing Muskegon Lake from the international AOC list shortly thereafter when monitoring data confirm use restoration.

Economic Benefits

Together, pollution prevention, habitat restoration, contaminated sediment remediation, and other cleanup actions have been a springboard for Muskegon to convert areas that were once eyesores detrimental to economic growth into valuable waterfront economic assets. Indeed, cleanup of the Muskegon Lake AOC has been an integral and essential part of waterfront community revitalization. For example, a $10 million restoration project completed in 2009 along the lake's south shore removed 24.7 acres of historical, unnatural fill, restored twenty-seven acres of wetlands, and softened 1.9 miles of shoreline. An economic benefits study found that this $10 million restoration project will generate nearly

$60 million of economic benefits for the Muskegon area over a twenty-year period, or a six-to-one return on investment (Isely et al., 2018).

Another investigation of Great Lakes Restoration Initiative-funded improvements in Muskegon Lake also showed that they have been a critical factor in achieving economic benefits. Muskegon has realized $47 million in completed waterfront developments, and another $300 million are in the works. Interest in water-based recreation has surged, with the customer count at the city's marina increasing by 19 percent just since 2013. And water-based recreation and new waterfront festivals have driven a major increase in tourist activity; revenue from Muskegon County's tax on hotel rooms has increased 45 percent since 2010 (Great Lakes Commission and the Council of Great Lakes Communities, 2018).

Concluding Remarks

There is no doubt that considerable progress has been made in restoring Muskegon Lake over the past three-and-a-half decades. Progress in remediating contaminated sediments and restoring fish and wildlife habitat accelerated with more than $50 million in funding from the Great Lakes Legacy Act and the Great Lakes Restoration Initiative (Evans et al., 2019). More than $20 million more is needed to implement the remaining four projects required to restore all beneficial uses in Muskegon Lake. And Kathy Evans is still involved. She continues to provide staff support to the Muskegon Lake Watershed Partnership and to facilitate coordination of state and federal programs with local governments and community organizations.

According to the plan, all management actions identified in the RAP will be implemented by 2022 with a goal of possible delisting as an AOC shortly thereafter when monitoring confirms all uses have been restored. The Muskegon Lake Watershed Partnership has now developed an Ecosystem Action Plan to guide long-term steward-ship of the lake and the lower Muskegon River watershed from 2018 through 2025. It builds upon the restoration progress made under the Muskegon Lake RAP and through other voluntary and regulatory cleanup programs. In essence, the Ecosystem Action Plan has become the community's blueprint for ecosystem-based management of the watershed and protection of all its natural resources, with a goal of long-term sustainability and never being labeled again as a dreaded pollution hotspot.

Together, the Ecosystem Action Plan and the Muskegon Lake Wa-tershed Partnership will ensure that there is life after Muskegon Lake is delisted as an AOC. The partnership and plan will also ensure a concerted and coordinated effort to achieve the goal of turning Mus-kegon Lake into an economic engine, while improving public access, increasing housing values, and maintaining the integrity of natural resources as articulated in Muskegon Lake Vision 2020. Indeed, all citizens, community leaders, elected officials, and the private sector will have to do their parts and work together to achieve sustainability.

Evans's advice to others pursuing cleanup is that people must be-lieve that cleanup is possible. Contaminated sediment remediation is a challenging but surmountable problem. Early on, one public official asked her: "What do you think you are you going to do, dive to the bottom of the lake and take it out?" The answer was yes. Working with U.S. Environmental Protection Agency's Assessment and Remediation of Contaminated Sediment Program and the Michigan Department of Environment, Great Lakes, and Energy, the Muskegon Lake Watershed

Partnership was able to assess the problem, review options, and achieve cleanup. As Muskegon Lake has shown, taking it out is clearly possible!

Evans notes that there will undoubtedly be new challenges to face. Change is a certainty, and flexibility will be needed to coordinate large-scale, complex cleanup and restoration projects in a large ecosystem like the Great Lakes. Others trying to build the capacity and achieve the coordination necessary for ecosystem-based management will need flexibility, persistence, patience, and most of all a lot of local, state, regional, and federal partners who communicate with one another and bring good science, technical expertise, and practical know-how to the table.

Evans sees that the next challenge for the Muskegon Lake watershed community is to make good land-use and development decisions to prevent harming Muskegon Lake's restored natural resources again. The recent repair of the damage done in the 1800s and 1900s by heavy industry can be easily undone through improper shoreline development, stormwater management, and waste disposal. Community leaders need to go above and beyond what is required and do the right thing. She notes "that sounds cliché, but it's never wrong to do the right thing."

Her advice for the next generation is to sustain the momentum behind the public involvement, education, and growing environmental ethic that has developed over the past three decades or more. It will be less costly and more appealing to the public to keep something good moving forward than to have to start all over again to generate that commitment. The current environmental movement was built from the bottom up. The next generation, which includes Evans's kids and grandkids, watched the cleanup happen, but doesn't have the same experiences of her grandparents or parents, who lived through the degradation of Muskegon Lake and the Great Lakes. Current and future

Kathy Evans, Muskegon Lake champion
MARK EVANS

generations will need to be reminded of our history, how we came to pollute our waters, and what it took to clean them up. Evans feels strongly that we need people to get involved and stay involved in environmental protection and be aware of what is happening to their local ecosystems. Endorsing this insight, Alexander (2006) in his book titled *The Muskegon: The Majesty and Tragedy of Michigan's Rarest River* notes that educating residents about their watershed and connecting them to their river will be essential to creating river stewards.

Evans notes that sustained public involvement and open sharing of information will be essential to avoid backsliding. The Muskegon Lake Watershed Partnership has held a public meeting every month since October 1992. Even when it seemed like there was nothing new to discuss, the meetings were held. By doing this, the community partnership grew stronger and information was exchanged on a regular basis. Stakeholders learned that holding regular public meetings was the best way to stay on top of what was happening to Muskegon Lake, whether it was good or bad. The meetings really helped everyone stay informed.

Evans has been involved in the Muskegon Lake RAP for over thirty-five years and shared her knowledge by participating in basin-wide AOC restoration workshops and conferences of the International Joint Commission, U.S. Environmental Protection Agency, Michigan Department of Natural Resources, and more. The cleanup and restoration of Muskegon Lake could not have happened without her long-term leadership. Her love of Muskegon Lake and the Great Lakes, her deep roots in Muskegon, her ability to foster and build partnerships, and her perseverance were essential to this success. In 2005, Evans received a Great Lakes Commission Outstanding Service Award for her contributions to the cleanup of Muskegon Lake. In 2010, she received a National Oceanic and Atmospheric Administration Restoration Center's Excellence in Restoration Award. In 2013, she received a West Michigan Environmental Council Award for contributions to the protection of western Michigan's natural resources that have left a legacy environmental stewardship. All are well deserved and an inspiration for future watershed stewards.

CHAPTER 4

Keith Sherman

Severn Sound Champion

On the southeastern edge of Lake Huron's Georgian Bay lies Severn Sound. It is a complex of bays and inlets, including Penetang Harbour, Outer Harbour, Midland Bay, Hog Bay, Sturgeon Bay, and Matchedash Bay. The sound covers approximately fifty square miles, with small- to medium-sized cities and towns dotting the shoreline and roughly one-third of its watershed devoted to agriculture. The watershed has a permanent population of about 110,000, rising in summer to about 300,000.

Severn Sound is truly one of the most beautiful parts of Ontario, bounded on the north end by the Georgian Bay Islands National Park, part of the world's largest freshwater archipelago. Here you can gain boat access to 30,000 islands that attract nature lovers from far and wide. It is here where the windswept white pines and granite shores of the Canadian Shield turn to dense deciduous woodland.

There are cruises to and around the waters of the national park from all the larger ports bordering the sound, and it also possesses two of the province's finest historical reconstructions–Discovery Harbour, a British naval base on the edge of Penetanguishene, and Sainte-Marie among the Hurons, a Jesuit mission located near Midland.

Ecologically, the sound supports what scientists call a warm-water fishery in the shallower areas where temperatures are higher. In general, the warmer the water temperature, the less dissolved oxygen is in the water. Warm-water fishes need less oxygen, so they are well adapted to areas like Severn Sound. Living here are largemouth and smallmouth bass, northern pike, muskellunge, walleye, yellow perch, and others. Prior to 1950, the sound also had a cold-water fishery, including lake trout, lake whitefish, and lake herring in the deeper, colder waters with more oxygen. By the 1960s, the cold-water fishery had completely collapsed due to overharvesting of fish, water pollution, and the invasion of sea lamprey. The sound was becoming over-enriched with nutrients in what scientists call accelerated eutrophication. Densities of algae were ten to twenty times higher in Severn Sound than neighboring Nattawasaga Bay, primarily because of the phosphorus coming from sewage treatment plants and agricultural fields. Human development had taken its toll, resulting in considerable concern among residents and vacationers alike.

A Watershed Moment

The Province of Ontario has a long history of involvement with Severn Sound; the Ontario Ministry of the Environment (OME) has monitored water and sediment quality since 1973, the Ontario Ministry of Natural Resources has kept watch on the fish community since 1969, and

Penetang Harbour in Severn Sound, Ontario
SEVERN SOUND ENVIRONMENTAL ASSOCIATION

the Ontario Ministry of Agriculture and Food has been involved with the agricultural community since 1966. In contrast, federal agency involvement in the sound was limited. Up through the mid-1980s, the federal and provincial agencies and the municipalities in the area didn't communicate much, and they did not have a clear focus on restoring Severn Sound.

That all changed in 1985 when the International Joint Commission's Great Lakes Water Quality Board recommended that RAPs be developed using locally designed ecosystem approaches to restore ecosystem health in forty-two Great Lakes AOCs, including Severn Sound. The primary problems or use impairments here were eutrophication and loss of habitat. The federal and provincial governments accepted this recommendation and committed to developing and implementing RAPs to restore all Canadian AOCs. At that time, managers estimated that it would take six months to complete the RAPs. Little did everyone know what an underestimate this was. The Province of Ontario needed a person with passion and expertise who would step outside of the box and work with local stakeholders to clean up Severn Sound. That person was Keith Sherman.

A Champion Emerges

By his own admission, Sherman was a city boy who did not have much opportunity to develop an environmental or conservation ethic. He loved fishing, hiking, and camping whenever he got the chance. But what stirred his interest early on was reading *King Solomon's Ring* by Australian scientist Konrad Lorenz and first published in 1949. The book's title refers to the legendary Seal of Solomon, a ring that supposedly gave King Solomon the power to speak to animals. Lorenz claimed that he too had achieved this feat of communicating with animals. He raised animals in and around his home and observed their behavior. *King Solomon's Ring* describes his methods and his findings about animal behavior and psychology. This book is a beautifully written, delightful treasury of observations and insights into the lives of all sorts of creatures. Lorenz, at that time, did more to establish and popularize the study of animal behavior than any other person, receiving a Nobel Prize for his work in 1973. *King Solomon's Ring* popularized the study of animal behavior and inspired countless young students, including Sherman.

Inspired to learn more, he went on to study aquatic sciences at Queen's University in Kingston, Ontario. While taking classes he learned about the concept of ecosystem health and the monitoring techniques used in assessments. Ecosystem health is a metaphor used to describe the condition of an ecosystem. A healthy ecosystem is one whose physical, chemical, and biological components and their interrelationships are intact, such that it is resilient enough to withstand change and stress.

Early on Sherman worked for a professor who was studying how invertebrates were key biological indicators of ecosystem health in Lake Opinicon, north of Kingston. Following university, he got a contract job with Ontario OME in 1974, assessing the pollution of lakes and streams by discharges from sewage plants, industries, and landfill sites. His first project was to complete the survey and report on the health of a small, vulnerable body of water called Midland Park Lake and make recommendations for cleanup and prevention. This job piqued his interest in cleanup and restoration. Sherman was then hired permanently by OME as a water scientist in 1975, and in this position, he was assigned to survey the quality of the water under the ice in Sturgeon Bay of Severn Sound as part of a long-term study of conditions before the Victoria Harbour sewage treatment plant was designed and built. Little did Sherman know that this project would start a more than forty-year love affair with Severn Sound and its stewardship.

Sherman quickly learned that solving complex water pollution problems requires cooperation. Indeed, he developed a distaste for confrontational approaches that were common early in his career. One example from 1980 was when he was an OME witness in environmental assessment hearings for Colonel Sam Smith Park in Toronto and saw first-hand how adversarial approaches waste time and often delay cleanup. In another experience that year, he presented water quality survey findings at a ratepayers meeting on Musselman's Lake northeast of Toronto. Some people tried to hijack the meeting and confront "the government" about a local landfill issue, but in the end, they were able to refocus on the problem and find some common ground for lake cleanup. This was

Sherman's first exposure to public consultation and stakeholder engagement, and he quickly learned that success in resolving water resource problems requires cooperation and teamwork. As Andrew Carnegie said, "Teamwork is the ability to work together toward a common vision. The ability to direct individual accomplishments toward organizational objectives. It is the fuel that allows common people to attain uncommon results." Sherman has never forgotten these key lessons and has worked to apply them throughout his entire career.

Bringing Stakeholders Together to Develop the RAP

After the federal and provincial governments accepted the responsibility to develop RAPs in 1985, the Severn Sound RAP team formed. At first it was a loose association between Environment Canada, OME, and the Ontario Ministry of Natural Resources. As people realized the size of the undertaking, they set up a more formal RAP team with a wider membership, and Sherman was assigned as the RAP coordinator. He moved to the Great Lakes section of OME's Water Resources Branch in 1986. This was when the St. Clair River "blob"—a large spill of dry-cleaning solvents—was discovered, and the newly elected Ontario Liberal government appointed Jim Bradley as minister of the environment. This spill, which occurred in 1985, came from chemical industries in Petrochemical Valley in Sarnia, Ontario, and it forced the temporary closure of all municipal water intakes from the St. Clair River down to the Detroit River. Minister Bradley made "political hay" out of bad news and secured funding for staffing and projects dealing with industrial effluents as well as a smaller but substantial amount for RAPs. Infrastructure funding for sewage plant upgrades and pumping stations was increased. Other more general programs, such as Ontario's Clean Up Rural Beaches and the federal Great Lakes Cleanup Fund, also provided money for rural projects in Severn Sound. The federal-provincial RAP program also put priority on local public involvement programs, and a RAP Public Advisory Committee (PAC) was formed in Severn Sound in 1989.

As RAP coordinator, Sherman was responsible for coordinating the team's activities, developing and tracking project budgets, and preparing documents in the three stages: 1) problem definition, 2) identification of actions and responsibilities, 3) confirmation of cleanup and restoration. He was also responsible for local administration of the public involvement program through the PAC and the establishment of a Severn Sound RAP implementation office in the area in 1993.

During the early years, one funny story stands out for Sherman. The Georgian Bay Association asked him to give a talk on the Severn Sound RAP at their prestigious annual members' meeting at the Racket Club in downtown Toronto. After making the long trek down from Midland to Toronto, he realized that he had forgotten his suit. Being a good problem-solver (a requirement for being a RAP coordinator), Sherman borrowed one from his brother who lived in the Toronto area. The talk went well. The association newsletter came out shortly after the meeting with a summary of Sherman's remarks and a nice picture of him at the lectern. The caption for the picture read "Sherman wears brother's suit." Who knew the Georgian Bay Association had a sense of humor?

For Sherman, the development of the Stage 1 RAP was particularly enlightening because it led to a cooperative spirit among the federal and provincial agency representatives on the team. The first public meeting in 1988 was a crucial turning point. Everything up to that point between the public and "the government" was confrontational. Advertised with the slogan "we want your input," the RAP public meeting attracted over two hundred people. They listened to the summaries by the various RAP team members, and then the floor was opened to the public. Some people came to the meeting prepared for confrontation. After team members tried to answer one belligerent person, something magical happened. Another member of the public shouted him down and said, "why don't you sit down and listen to the man!" The rest of the meeting turned into a constructive exchange with meaningful contributions to the problem definition they were seeking and an interest in when they could meet again. That is when the RAP team knew it was onto something important and necessary in the Severn Sound area.

The PAC became known locally as a "friendly little monster"—a community-based group of citizens and municipalities that dove into and thoroughly reviewed all stages of the RAP. They were not there to just "rubber stamp" the scientists' plan, but to make sure that it was practical, locally owned, and implementable. This grassroots grounding and the meaningful partnerships were essential for a cleaner Severn Sound.

The cleanup and restoration of Severn Sound had three distinct phases: the federal-provincial RAP partnership to support Severn Sound (1986–1995); a community-based effort with municipal involvement (1993–2002); and a municipal partnership (1997–2009). One key element in the success of the project was an innovative partnership agreement between the federal and provincial governments and the nine municipalities in the Severn Sound area. The partnership became the Severn Sound Environmental Association (SSEA), which is now a joint municipal services board—as defined by Ontario Municipal Act, section 202—representing the local municipalities. SSEA had legitimacy by way of establishment under a municipal act and was trusted throughout the communities. It continues to help guide management decisions related to Severn Sound.

The Stage 1 RAP report was completed and submitted to the International Joint Commission in 1989. The Stage 2 RAP report was submitted in 1993, followed by the Stage 3 report in 2002. The depth and breadth of cleanup and restoration efforts was truly amazing, considering that the area is predominantly rural (table 2). Today, the amount of phosphorus going into the sound has been reduced, and accelerated eutrophication has been halted; habitats for native fish, birds, and plants have improved. The invertebrates that live in the bottom sediments of the sound and the fishery have improved some, and the trumpeter swans once common in the area have been reintroduced. Indeed, Severn Sound is cleaner for fish, birds, and people.

After the International Joint Commission reviewed the reports, it removed Severn Sound from the international list of Great Lakes pollution hotspots in 2003. This success would not have been possible without the concerted effort of the Severn Sound RAP Implementation Office and the commitment to the SSEA. Without the support of the Severn Sound community, especially the municipalities and the farming community, momentum would have slowed, and key stakeholders might have lost interest in commitment to the major remedial actions necessary.

The project that Sherman was most proud of was the phosphorus control strategy applied to Penetang Harbour, along with the habitat restoration projects that became their best example of an integrated approach to restoring beneficial uses. Growth of nuisance algae decreased and, subsequently, water clarity increased—a win–win for Severn Sound. These improvements were highly visible to residents and vacationers and showcased the benefits of cooperation among many stakeholders.

Table 2. A Summary of Cleanup Actions Taken through the RAP to Restore Severn Sound	
SECTOR	**CLEANUP AND RESTORATION ACTIONS**
MUNICIPALITIES	• Phosphorus was controlled by improving processes at sewage treatment plants, upgrading private sewage systems, eliminating sewage bypasses and combined sewer overflows (CSOs), and reducing inputs from agricultural sources. • Through a sewage treatment optimization project, the federal and provincial governments provided technical support and training for municipal operators in all eight treatment plants in the watershed. • Eight municipal sewage treatment plants were upgraded at a cost of Can\$49 million. • To address stormwater, municipalities passed policies to govern new construction and implemented stormwater retrofit and sewer separation projects at a cost of Can\$5.7 million. • To help reduce algal growth in Severn Sound, 3,000 private shoreline sewage systems were inspected and six hundred were upgraded at a cost of Can\$14.1 million.
AGRICULTURE	• Tributary phosphorus loadings from agricultural sources were reduced through farm-level projects to manage manure runoff, treat direct milk house wastes, restrict livestock access to rivers, and improve crop practices at a cost of Can\$4.2 million.
RURAL BEACHES	• Between 1990 and 2002, the federal Great Lakes Sustainability Fund and the provincial Clean Up Rural Beaches program provided Can\$3.4 million for twenty-two restoration projects to clean up sources of bacterial pollution like barnyard runoff, inadequate manure storage facilities, and unrestricted livestock access to waterways; this money leveraged more than Can\$4 million in direct partner funding and nearly Can\$2 million from in-kind contributions.
HABITAT	• Conservation efforts protected 1,015 acres of wetlands and associated uplands. • One hundred thirty-two shoreline habitat restoration projects were completed on streams. • Municipalities adopted natural heritage strategies protecting habitat in planning policies.

Economic Benefits Assessment

Economic benefits assessments played an important role in making the case for implementing cleanup actions and documenting return on investment. People recognized early on that a variety of coordinated actions would be needed to achieve and maintain the desired water quality and that local leaders would need to employ a mixture of funding mechanisms to be able to implement capital improvements and best management practices and to meet operational expenses. Further, community leaders knew that an attractive, safe, useable Severn Sound was a major asset that would allow the surrounding communities to expand tourism and recreation and gain a competitive advantage in the future.

An economic benefits study showed that every dollar spent on restoration projects by the end of 2002 would generate Can$16.34 in benefits, reflecting cost effectiveness of the cleanup effort (Tejani and Muir, 2004). This analysis provided all stakeholders with a compelling rationale to move forward with the recommended actions.

Lessons Learned

Sherman learned many lessons during his nearly thirty years of working on the restoration of Severn Sound. He recommends establishing integrity with stakeholders from the start and always preparing a scientifically defensible rationale for any proposed actions. "By sticking to the science and explaining it well, you can never lose," notes Sherman. A good example was the "evaluative phosphorus budget" developed for the Stage 2 RAP. It identified the controllable sources of phosphorus and demonstrated that everyone had some responsibility for doing their part, without "finger pointing."

He learned from Bob Whittam, their public involvement facilitator, that "nothing is impossible if you don't have to take credit for it." It is always best to let ideas spread. As part of this philosophy, the RAP team and SSEA always recognized the efforts of community volunteers and contributors through annual partner receptions. They even created a Severn Sound RAP honor roll (available on the sound's webpage) that recognizes over 1,000 community and agency people who helped develop and implement the RAP.

Another lesson learned is that facilitating and coordinating projects with stakeholders can be a slow process, so it is important to be patient with the time it takes to make decisions. Groups typically take more time to reach agreement on a solution. Make every effort to get to know the decision-makers in the community and keep in regular touch, and, finally, if possible, never ask one stakeholder to bear the entire cost of a restoration project alone.

Advice to the Next Generation

Sherman's advice to the next generation is "don't forget what you are there to do and why—you are there to restore ecosystem health—making it safe, attractive, and usable by all species, including humans." In using an ecosystem approach, it is important to keep an open mind to all scientific areas of study and value and respect all perspectives.

Recently, Sherman noted that there has been a return to the disciplinary fragmentation or isolation of purpose that was part of the problem that got Severn Sound and other areas on the AOC list in the first place. Think about it as people living in their own unconnected cubbyholes, pursuing their research without talking to each other. Some researchers are becoming more secretive about their designs and findings than ever before, and this protectiveness means other scientists can't build on their work. Therefore, organizations should look for opportunities to collaborate, share information, and network in the spirit of a common vision. They can be scientific fora, State of the Sound conferences, or science and technology transfer sessions, but they must be convened in the spirit of cooperative learning.

The introduction of non-native invasive species into the Severn Sound ecosystem has created new challenges. For example, nuisance algae like *Microcystis* spp. were almost absent in the 1980s and 1990s in the area, but the infestation of zebra and quagga mussels has led to an increase in the abundance of these algae, and their proliferation affects beneficial uses. Clearly, science is the foundation of proper environmental decision-making. A high priority must be placed on continued research, modelling, and monitoring to adequately inform management actions. And there needs to be a mechanism through which scientific research, performed by both academic institutions and governmental research stations, gets translated for resource managers and other stakeholders. Severn Sound badly needs a source of long-term funding, like a foundation, to pay for the necessary research that advances ecosystem-based management. Finally, nonprofit organizations like Severn Sound Environmental Association need sustainable funding to fulfill their critical missions.

The Next Challenge for Severn Sound

It has been eighteen years since the delisting of the Severn Sound AOC. Some decision-makers are forgetting their ongoing commitments to restoring and maintaining ecosystem health and beneficial uses. Protecting

Keith Sherman and his grandson at the celebration of the handoff of the Stage 3 RAP to the International Joint Commission, June 22, 2002
SEVERN SOUND ENVIRONMENTAL ASSOCIATION

the gains made will take ongoing vigilance. Bob Whittam of the Wye Marsh Wildlife Center, who was selected as public involvement facilitator and was well respected in the community, said it best: "Our overall effort and success are excellent, and the RAP team should be commended. However, there is still life after delisting and we should proceed as if we were approved and passed, but forever on probation, lest we become complacent" (Sherman, 2017).

Concluding Thoughts

Severn Sound is one of only nine AOCs to be delisted since 1985. Effective collaboration among all stakeholders was essential to achieve this goal. SSEA has proven to be a particularly effective partnership among federal, provincial, and municipal governments and other organizations to ensure local ownership and acceptance of the cleanup, sustain long-term restoration efforts, and facilitate transition to sustainable development. The one constant during this entire process was Sherman. He provided critical leadership, guided the RAP process from the beginning, kept it on track, and made sure there was a plan for sustainability of the sound. It gives him great personal satisfaction to have been part of a team that restored Severn Sound for future generations. And now he gets to enjoy the fruits of his efforts with his family.

CHAPTER 5

Gail Krantzberg

Collingwood Harbour Champion

Situated on Georgian Bay, Lake Huron, the town of Collingwood was originally a milling center for the sparsely populated farming communities in the area. However, that changed in 1855 with the arrival of the Ontario, Simcoe & Huron (later Northern) Railway. The town quickly grew into a center of commerce because its access to the bay made it ideal for shipments to upper Great Lakes ports like Chicago, Illinois, and Port Arthur–Ft. William (now Thunder Bay). This produced a need for shipbuilding and repairs. Collingwood Shipyards opened 1883 with much fanfare and a special ceremony. It first built wooden skiffs and schooners, and later steel cargo and passenger steamers, including small warships for the Royal Canadian Navy during World War II. It operated as a shipbuilding center for more than one hundred years until overseas competition led to the demise of the industry here. At one point, 1,000 of the town's fewer than 5,000 residents were employed at the shipyards.

Top: View of Collingwood's shipyards in the 1960s

POSTCARD COURTESY OF WILLIAM FORSYTHE/BOATNERD.COM

Bottom: Today as The Shipyards, a European-inspired, waterfront development

TARA PARSONS, FRAM BUILDING GROUP

The Collingwood shipyards closed in 1986 and sat as an abandoned brownfield on the waterfront for nearly twenty years. In 1985, the International Joint Commission's Great Lakes Water Quality Board identified Collingwood Harbour as a Great Lakes AOC because of nuisance algal growth stimulated by excessive phosphorus inputs, habitat and wetland loss, shoreline hardening that provided little to no habitat for fish, invertebrates, and plants, and harbor sediments with contaminants left over from its earlier shipbuilding days that were toxic to aquatic life. At that time, Collingwood Harbour was noticeably different from the waters of Georgian Bay, particularly because it was covered with ugly, smelly floating mats of alive and decomposing algae. Sometimes the harbor even reeked with the smell of rotten eggs because of the hydrogen sulfide gas produced by the bacterial decomposition of the algae. The OME needed someone to lead a grassroots cleanup effort and chose a young Great Lakes scientist with a passion to make a difference—Gail Krantzberg.

The Emergence of a Great Lakes Champion

From as far back as she can remember, Kranztberg has had a deep connection to natural landscapes and their plants and animals. As a child, walking in the woods or paddling a canoe was magical. She spent every summer from the age of eight until her early twenties in nature camps, progressively deepening her love of life and the living world—what scientists call biophilia, the love of nature that leads a person to work on its behalf, locally and globally. She was naturally drawn to science to help find solutions to protect those with no voice, determined to make parts of her world a vibrant place for all life. When on an ecology field trip for one of her undergraduate courses at McGill University in Montreal,

Krantzberg found a quiet time to sit on a large rock in the middle of the woods. As she relaxed, she realized that minerals in the rock were the minerals in her body, that the oxygen in her lungs came from the trees around her, and that those same trees used the carbon dioxide she exhaled to build their food stores. It was an epiphany that she was one with the living and nonliving components of her ecosystem and that they all were linked together through nutrient cycles and energy flows. This striking realization changed her life. It became her religion.

Krantzberg got her bachelor of science degree from McGill University and her master of science and PhD from the University of Toronto in environmental and freshwater science. In 1988, fresh after her PhD, she took a job with the OME as coordinator of Great Lakes Programs and senior policy advisor on the Great Lakes. Immediately, the OME recognized the match between Krantzberg's skillset and the urgent need to coordinate development and implementation of the Collingwood Harbour RAP. Little did she or OME know, at that time, what she was getting into.

Collingwood Harbour Cleanup

Krantzberg's introduction to Collingwood Harbour and her first experiences with residents were memorable. She recalls talking with residents who shared personal stories of pollution: "You want to know where the water line is on your boat? Just put it in the harbor for the day and you'll have a good, green rim. When we worked at the shipyards, we got paid by the number of welding rods we used. So, to make more money, we would throw unfinished rods into the boat slips in the harbor."

Krantzberg's passion for life and all living things, her knowledge and unique talents, and her strong desire to promote stewardship, made her an ideal person to serve as RAP coordinator. She also had to learn how to convey complicated science in plain English, but she had some practice with this. When her younger brother Robert was fascinated that his sister was pursuing her PhD and was determined to understand what scientific puzzles she was trying to solve, she told him that she wanted to understand how toxic metals get into baby insects living in the mud at the bottom of the lakes. To her scientific colleagues, she would have said she was studying the biotic and abiotic factors that mitigate metal bioaccumulation in larval chironomids.

As RAP coordinator, her duties involved representing the governments of Ontario and Canada by working with other local, provincial, and federal experts to provide the community with the technical information it would need to develop the RAP. Krantzberg's role included fostering use of an ecosystem approach, networking among the community and governments to secure funding commitments for the implementation of the plan, ensuring that monitoring tracked the ecosystem response of cleanup actions, and publicly reporting on progress in restoring beneficial uses.

The RAP team, which consisted of engineers and scientists from the governments of Canada and Ontario, under her advice aimed to build the capacity of the Collingwood Harbour Public Advisory Committee (PAC) to define goals for the future of the harbor, select management actions that would eliminate pollution and restore beneficial uses, and align the leadership in the town with stakeholders and governments to finance the implementation of the RAP. The team wasn't supposed to develop proposed remedial actions by itself but to enable the local community to lead the effort. This approach represented something of a change. Governments were used to implementing programs in a top-down, command-and-control fashion. Krantzberg's team turned that approach upside down and called for a bottom-up collaborative process. For the RAP to work, it would have to be locally owned because these PAC members would be the very stakeholders who would have to implement most of the remedial actions. In fact, at one point during RAP development, a senior official in OME expressed deep frustration that such an inclusive process would raise expectations that action would follow. Krantzberg, not too politely, stated that this with exactly the point. That official was quickly silenced.

Stakeholder empowerment and collaboration became the norm. Each member of the PAC came to realize that they would be required to invest in the implementation of the recommended cleanup and restoration actions. The town of Collingwood and its stakeholders—including businesses, civic organizations, environmental organizations, and more—quickly adopted the PAC goal to clean up the harbor and leave a sustainable legacy.

The Collingwood Harbour PAC was incorporated in 1993. A storefront called the Environment Network of Collingwood provided a central location for the activities of the Collingwood Harbour RAP. This space also gave residents an environmental resource library and, most of all, it gave residents and visitors a place to go with environmental questions and concerns. Several years later, the name of the PAC was changed to the Environment Network.

Stakeholders pulled together, with Krantzberg's help and facilitation, and creatively and collaboratively found a way to clean up the harbor. Major RAP cleanup activities included:

- optimizing the local sewage treatment plant with dual alum addition, a chemical used to precipitate or remove phosphorus, to reduce the amount of this nutrient that was causing the growth of excessive algae in the water;
- remediating 257,800 cubic feet of contaminated sediment at a cost of Can$1.2 million to make the harbor safe for invertebrates, fish, and wildlife;
- catalyzing enhanced protection of the existing 237-acre Collingwood Wetland Complex;
- cleaning up the brownfield site left over from shipbuilding so that it could be redeveloped for a mix of community uses;
- controlling invasive purple loosestrife in wetlands so that native plant species could flourish; and
- rehabilitating fish and wildlife habitat in the harbor and watershed by building underwater reefs to provide spawning habitat for native fishes and re-engineering the land–water interface on Black Ash Creek both to prevent erosion and to restore fish and wildlife habitat (Krantzberg and Houghton, 1996).

The Environment Network went on to develop a strategic plan called the Greening of Collingwood that championed pollution prevention for residents, businesses, and industries. To this day, the network operates as a cooperative, providing people with opportunities for work and to learn how they can operate their business or home in an ecologically, socially, and economically sustainable manner.

By 1994, environmental monitoring confirmed that the harbor had been sufficiently cleaned up and all beneficial use impairments eliminated. The unsightly algae were gone, the sediments were no longer toxic to invertebrates, fish, and wildlife, and the wetlands were once again welcoming to birds and other species. Collingwood Harbour became the first site to be removed from the international list of AOCs. It is always hard to be the first at something, but the local community pulled together to reach this significant milestone.

This clearly was a major accomplishment, but Krantzberg didn't rest on her laurels. She also wanted to work with others to transform the community's consciousness and leave a lasting legacy. Her research had shown that the key to success is participatory governance, which involves the people living closest to the resource in the design, implementation, and monitoring of management measures. It also had shown how RAP implementation and progress toward watershed management can continue after an AOC was delisted and leave behind a community with an enhanced capacity to protect the gains made. In her view, governments should view themselves as a vector for community capacity-building.

Krantzberg was able to simultaneously perform her research and to put it into practice. She worked in and through the PAC to get Collingwood not only to accept the shared responsibility for restoration but also to stretch further and begin to change the community's consciousness about the environment. Eventually, that change would catapult it into being one of the most ecologically and socially responsible towns in North America. Not only did the PAC work on technical cleanup issues but also its members and other citizens of Collingwood engaged in a process of education and outreach on environmental issues. Among other projects, they created an innovative environmental playground, ENVIROPARK, on the waterfront. The play structures represent water use in the town in all its manifestations—for industry, for residential needs, for agriculture—and they teach kids how everyday lives affect the environment. PAC members referred to this as "learning by osmosis."

Throughout the RAP process, Krantzberg was able to develop and test the elements that fostered successful collaborative initiatives and sustained a community engaged in place-based action. The PAC and community clearly embraced the ecosystem approach. She became part teacher, part facilitator, and part advocate for people to understand that they are part of an ecosystem and not separate from it. In other words, what we humans do to our ecosystem, we do to ourselves. Krantzberg focused on getting the stakeholders to understand how human activities affect ecosystems and on preparing them to strike a programmatic compromise between detailed understanding of the science and more holistic awareness of ecosystem health. This flexible pragmatism was reflected in the way the Collingwood Harbour RAP was developed and implemented. The opportunity to help build local capacity to achieve consensus and sustain momentum for implementation of the cleanup actions motivated her to advance the action plan that led to Collingwood Harbour to be the first to be removed from the International Joint Commission pollution hotspot list. For Collingwood, people, passion, and partnerships were central to cleaning up the legacy of environmental degradation and emerging as a sustainable community of civic excellence.

Transformation of Collingwood's Shipyards

After Collingwood shipyards closed in 1986, following a 103-year history as one of Canada's busiest shipbuilding centers, it sat abandoned on the waterfront as an industrial brownfield like a millstone around the community's neck. To say the least, it had an uncertain future. Meanwhile, Collingwood and the vicinity adapted to the loss of the shipyards and became better known as a four-season vacation destination, including skiing in the winter at Blue Mountain and golfing, biking, hiking, and many water sports in summer. This attracted vacationers from all over the province and beyond.

Finally, in 2004 the former shipyards site was purchased by a developer that wanted to offer waterfront living in downtown Collingwood, close to restaurants, shops, and services. It took years of environmental assessments and remediation, approvals from all levels of government, and goodwill-building in Collingwood, but finally The Shipyards development was born as a forty-acre mixed residential-commercial waterfront development. This waterfront community will ultimately include more than six hundred homes in a pedestrian village, with condominium townhouses, bungalows, mid-rise condominium buildings, a hotel, retail shops, and restaurants. The development design also took into consideration the RAP with the creation of underwater reefs to enhance fish habitat.

On a lovely Saturday morning in 2004, Krantzberg opened up her *Toronto Star* to find "Launch Your Life" as the headline in the homes section. What caught her eye was an advertisement that residential units were up for sale in the renewed Collingwood shipyards. Within the hour, she and her husband Douglas were driving up to Collingwood. When they arrived at the sales office, she started questioning the representative about the amenities, stating she was hoping to find a marina in the redevelopment to host her boat (which of course was a white lie, she does not have a boat). The sales representative informed her that due to the extensive cleanup of the harbor under the RAP, that a marina was not to be included as it would cause water to stagnate and build up slimy green algae. Krantzberg was clearly impressed that the salesperson knew that. Then Krantzberg asked whether she could just go fishing off the pier (she does not fish; she is a strict vegan). At this point, the salesperson produced a drawing of the underwater reefs that would provide shelter for fish. The drawing was one that one of the RAP staff had actually produced more than a decade earlier. At this point, Krantzberg was getting weak at the knees. Her final question was about green space. And the salesperson quickly noted that The Shipyards also includes a waterfront promenade accessible to all, a seven-acre waterfront park, a community amphitheater, and hiking trials that will eventually link to the Georgian Trail. She was now giddy. Over a decade had passed and a relator knew about the RAP! On the way home, her husband suggested to her that she write up this fascinating evidence that the gains made during RAP implementation were indeed sustained, which she did. Sales started in 2010, and the development is being completed in phases.

It should be noted that the economic downturn of the 2000s led to extension of the construction timeline for The Shipyards. Like many other developments during this time, progress on The Shipyards stalled until investor confidence in the local market returned. However, this redevelopment project is back on track. A municipal fiscal impact analysis of the proposed redevelopment of the former shipyards concluded that in five years there would be a net annual surplus of more than $900,000 to the town of Collingwood alone. "Without the cleanup of Collingwood Harbour in the late 1980s and early 1990s, the revitalization of Collingwood's waterfront would not have been possible," notes Nancy Farrer, director of Planning and Building Services, Town of Collingwood. "Today, our revitalized waterfront is beginning to realize its potential and the social, economic, and environmental benefits are increasing exponentially."

The town of Collingwood clearly also did its part to become a model of excellence for sustainability. Harbourlands Park was created in 2000 and is one of the most beautiful areas in the community. The idea for that park came from one the PAC members, Leona Hall. Residents and visitors alike now enjoy the rugged beauty of a once active shipping/grain storage area. The backdrop of the Collingwood Terminals with its huge white columns rising up from the once wasteland "spit area," now a series of beautifully landscaped walkways and gardens with the local history of the area told on massive granite plinths. Harbourlands Park offers the ever-changing grandeur and scenic beauty of Georgian Bay for the many people who drive or walk to the park. There are benches for reflective moments or to watch the quiet beauty of sailboats filling their sails as they make their way out of the historic Collingwood Harbour.

Krantzberg's Favorite Project

Improved environmental quality, strong interest in waterfront revital-ization, and a commitment to excellence in sustainability enabled the PAC to forge numerous partnerships with the business community to implement a wide range of projects and programs. The PAC organized annual campaigns around habitat rehabilitation and public outreach with the support of service clubs, schools, and the municipality, and with business donations of food, equipment, and advertising. The signature outreach project, ENVIROPARK, was made possible through a consortium of over thirty different local partners, with additional funding from the provincial and federal governments. ENVIROPARK is a five-acre playground, where each structure and the tubes that connect them represent where water is used, treated, and returned to the harbor, with Terri the Trout signs sharing messages of stewardship for the very young and their caregivers. Even the sediment cleanup project brought forward volunteers and local businesses to launch the initial cleanup of the shipyard boat slips, so that dredging could commence. A deeply rewarding moment was on "Harbour Day," a biennial celebration co-organized by the PAC and RAP team. It was during the celebrations of removing Collingwood Harbour from international pollution hotspot list, on board a donated cruise ship touring the harbor, that the then mayor expounded on his delight that for the first time in over eighty years in Collingwood, he could see the bottom of the harbor. Krantzberg noted: "Sure, we invested in sewage treatment plant upgrades to curb eutrophication, but his deep thanks for the work we had all done was a highlight of my entire career."

Lessons Learned

The Collingwood Harbour RAP is a success story in use of a locally designed ecosystem approach to clean up and restore a Great Lakes pollution hotspot. The Environmental Network in Collingwood is an excellent example of capacity building for sustainability and of laying the groundwork for sustaining efforts once Collingwood Harbour was removed from the list of Great Lakes AOCs. Community stakeholders continue to be fiercely protective of the town's excellence in pursuit of sustainability. This is evident in the harbor restoration, brownfield cleanup at the former Collingwood shipyards, and redevelopment into The Shipyards waterfront community.

Commitment from the town of Collingwood to improve environmental performance and establish policies for the purpose of sustainability was very important for obtaining political support, developing policy, integrating policy into operational systems, and manifesting environmental leadership. In this respect, Collingwood is unique in that it had a strong commitment to inclusion that led to community acceptance and ownership of its policies and programs. This characteristic is not common among all AOCs and is fundamental for the success of a RAP.

Community participation calls for people to take part in planning, implementing, and managing their local environment. Community participation should generate a readiness on the part of governments and citizens to accept equal responsibilities in managing their surroundings. The honest inclusion of a community's representatives as partners in decision-making makes for successful community involvement. This was a clear feature of the Collingwood Harbour RAP and the operation of the Town of Collingwood in a broader context.

In establishing the means for community collaboration, senior leaders with local influence, holding responsibility for important functions, were contacted and interviewed. The selection of candidates for the PAC was based predominantly (but not exclusively) on identifying decision-makers who could affect change within the sector or stakeholder group they represented. This is in keeping with the observation that plan effectiveness will be, in part, a function of the inclusiveness of stakeholder and user representation and goal setting. Inclusivity lends legitimacy, stimulates funding, and can galvanize potentially marginalized but important stakeholders through peer pressure. The wider the scope of stakeholder representation, the stronger the performance of the RAP.

Articulating clear and meaningful goals early in the process clearly unites the team. This gives the group the means to overcome conflicts and obstacles during the development and implementation of the plan. Specifying, to the extent possible, quantifiable endpoints or delisting targets that signify success and the achievement of the goals allows the group to recognize progress, prioritize actions, and reach consensus. Next, local ownership is essential. This means that when agreeing to the plan, each member overtly recognizes and takes responsibility for the resource implications for its stakeholder group. Ownership results in pride in delivery, which sustains the process.

Recognition that the local economy and quality of life are inextricably linked to environmental excellence provides an impenetrable shield to the current economy–environment dialectic. The people of Collingwood pride themselves on excellence. Driving north on Huron-tario Street to the harbor, one notices that Collingwood shines, from the architecture, to the landscaping, to the impeccable appearance of its core and its neighborhoods. Its website is perhaps the best evidence: "Welcome to the Town of Collingwood. Collingwood's location is in the heart of a four-season natural playground, on the southern shore of Georgian Bay. . . . The Town of Collingwood offers many economic opportunities; a utopian lifestyle and our natural surroundings make Collingwood an ideal location to live, work, and play."

The PAC also learned that success is contagious. As partners from numerous sectors saw that the RAP was making progress in restoring the harbor, more volunteers stepped up to participate and become part

Dr. Gail Krantzberg working to keep the lakes great
GAIL KRANTZBERG

of the success. They also learned that a strong leader helps the team stay focused on the task at hand. This allows for steady progress in restoring the ecosystem.

The Next Challenge

To protect the environmental gains made and to ensure that the long-term focus is on sustainability, Krantzberg feels that community-based processes must: be cleanup- and prevention-driven, and not document-driven; make existing programs and statutes work; cut through bureaucracy; elevate the priority of water quality protection; ensure strong community-based engagement processes; and be an inclusive, affirming process. RAPs are an unprecedented collaboration of international significance. The passion and dedication of the local community needs ongoing nurturing. Solidarity does emerge, and potential adversaries become allies united by a vision of a shared inspiration to enhance and protect the magnificence that is the regenerated Collingwood Harbour.

Advice for Others

Community groups that enlist a local champion can marshal incentives for others to join the mission. Creative, innovative partnerships and institutional arrangements are needed to stimulate and sustain advances in the cleanup of the AOCs, to control contaminant inputs, restore riparian vegetation, rehabilitate coastal wetlands, remediate contaminated sediment, raise public awareness of individuals' responsibilities, unite governmental with nongovernmental leaders, and make the lakes great.

The Collingwood Harbour RAP employed a combination of human, scientific, technological, organizational, institutional, and resource capabilities to generate and sustain the capacity for the changes required to solve the harbor's environmental problems. The Collingwood Harbour RAP has also been cited as one of the best examples of success in the RAP experiment, in part, because no stakeholder monopoly or opportunism jeopardized the implementation of remedial interventions. Further, the participatory democratic dialogue that enabled consensus and ownership of the RAP has been evidenced again by the commitment of the politicians and civic-minded citizens to ensure the sustainability of the town's economy, environment, and social fabric.

Concluding Thoughts

For her entire career that has now spanned more than three decades, Krantzberg has applied science to help find solutions to protect those with no voice, whether plant, animal, or human. Her passion for science and its application for a better world is indefatigable. She is continuously putting into practice what she had learned and is staunchly advocating for bridging science and public policy to leave an environmental legacy for future generations. Her contributions were recognized in *Canadian Who's Who* in 2017 and by the American Biographical Institute that named her Woman of the Year in 2007. In addition, she has received the 2015 Ontario Volunteer Service Award, the 2007 MacGreen Environmental Award, and the 1998 Amethyst Award for Excellence in Public Service from the Province of Ontario.

CHAPTER 6

Guy O. Williams

Detroit River Champion

The Detroit River is a thirty-two-mile, connecting river system that all the water from the upper Great Lakes—Superior, Michigan, and Huron—flows through on its descent to the lower Great Lakes—Erie and Ontario. It also forms the international border between the United States and Canada. Located on its banks are Detroit, Michigan, and Windsor, Ontario. Both cities have a long history of urban and industrial development. Detroit is the automobile capital of the United States, and Windsor is the automobile capital of Canada. However, the Detroit metropolitan area is much larger with a population of over 3.5 million, and the Windsor metropolitan area is only about 338,000. Detroit also had considerably more industrial development than Windsor.

Just like the long-held perception that Detroit and Windsor would always be automobile towns, the Detroit River was perceived as a working river that supported industry and commerce. Both cities became indifferent to water pollution, seeing it as a necessary by-product of industrial progress.

In the 1960s, the Federal Water Pollution Control Administration considered the Detroit River one of the most polluted rivers in the United States. Oil spills and pollution from poorly regulated industrial and municipal discharges were killing substantial numbers of waterfowl. No bald eagles, peregrine falcons, or osprey were reproducing anywhere in the watershed, and no beaver had been seen there since 1877 when the fur trade era ended. The sturgeon and whitefish were not spawning, and the invertebrates living on the river bottom were mostly pollution-tolerant species. Compounding the impact of the oil and industrial pollution, the wastewater treatment plants in the area only provided primary treatment that removed material that would either float or settle out by gravity, along with disinfection. On top of that, Detroit's regional combined storm and sanitary sewer system was pouring more than thirty-one billion gallons of untreated wastewater per year into the river. Perhaps it was not surprising when the Rouge River—a major tributary—caught on fire on October 9, 1969 (Hartig, Francoeur, Ciborowski, Gannon, Sanders, Galvao-Ferreira, Knauss, Gell, and Berk, 2020).

In the 1970s, growing public awareness and concern for pollution led to the enactment of many important environmental laws and a binational agreement, including the Canada Water Act of 1970, the U.S. National Environmental Policy Act of 1970, the Canada–U.S. Great Lakes Water Quality Agreement of 1972, the U.S. Clean Water Act of 1972, the U.S. Endangered Species Act of 1973, and the U.S. Toxic Substances Control Act of 1976. These laws and the agreement, as well as complementary state, provincial, and local programs like RAPs, which were initiated in 1985 to clean up Great Lakes AOCs, including the Detroit River, provided the framework and impetus for investing billions of dollars in pollution prevention and control over the next fifty years.

The Detroit River RAP addressed several major issues. Inadequate wastewater treatment and overflows from combined storm and sanitary sewer systems were major problems. The contaminated sediments were contributing to poisoning the fish, giving them cancer, and making them unsafe for humans to eat. This pollution was also threatening drinking water supplies. Ninety-seven percent of coastal wetlands had been lost to industrial and urban development, diminishing native fish and wildlife populations. But one other issue, for many decades, fell through the cracks: environmental justice—the fair treatment and meaningful involvement of all people regardless of race, color, national origin, or income in the development, implementation, and enforcement of environmental laws, regulations, and policies. Many people just didn't want to talk about how low-income people and communities of color suffered a greater burden from pollution and contamination.

Located on the banks of the Detroit River is an area called Southwest Detroit. It has long been notorious for poor air quality, particularly the zip code 48217, which remains among the most polluted in the state. It has the highest asthma hospitalization rates in Michigan. More than two dozen major industrial facilities surround the neighborhoods in 48217. This community is 82 percent Black and has a yearly median household income of $24,000, which is 35 percent lower than Michigan's average (Williams, 2020). Roughly 44 percent of the people in 48217 live below the poverty line according to current U.S. Census data, compared to 14 percent for the state as a whole.

When it launched in 1985, the Detroit River RAP did not make environmental justice a priority like it did for other environmental issues. Candidly, most people in Southwest Detroit felt that governments just didn't care. Then the National Wildlife Federation hired Guy O. Williams to head up a pollution prevention campaign trying to achieve zero discharge of persistent toxic substances. He was attracted to this issue and was passionate about making the environment healthy for all species and all people. Williams soon met people in Detroit working on environmental justice issues facing the area. He quickly fell in love with the city, and its people stole his heart—especially those with limited opportunities, those living in unsafe neighborhoods in the shadows of heavy industries, and those with little apparent influence on governmental and corporate policies that impact their lives.

The Early Years

Williams grew up in Lanham, Maryland—an unincorporated town of about 10,000 people approximately ten miles northeast of Washington, D.C. Despite being relatively close to the U.S. capital, Williams's hometown still had some open space and forestland that attracted a diversity of wildlife. Early on, he acquired a love of nature walking through these forests and meadows. Soon, science and math classes caught his attention, and he started questioning why society was not a better steward of natural resources and the environment. He went on to obtain his bachelor of science in education from Bucknell University, a liberal arts college in Lewisburg, Pennsylvania. His faith and life journey has not been easy as he had to struggle with and overcome drug and alcohol addiction. With

God's help, he went on to become nationally recognized as an advocate for environmental justice and a developer of community programming that values effective collaborations among business, government, and community interests.

An Awakening at Environmental Defense Fund

In 1989, Williams took his first job in the environmental movement with the Environmental Defense Fund (EDF) in Washington, D.C. A leading national nonprofit organization representing more than 2.5 million members, EDF is dedicated to preserving natural systems on which all life depends. Looking back, he feels that it was the hand of God that put him in the EDF office at that time. Williams first became aware of environmental justice working at EDF. Environmental justice is making sure everyone has a safe place to live, work, and play. "But unfortunately, there's also a world of great environmental injustice, and it's people of color who get the short end of the stick," he notes.

In 1990, several environmental justice leaders signed letters accusing ten of the largest and most influential environmental groups (then called the "Group of 10") of racism because of their policy development, hiring, and the composition of their boards. These were not just any nongovernmental organizations, but ones with national and international footprints, like the National Wildlife Federation (NWF), EDF, Sierra Club, Audubon Society, and more. The letters challenged these groups to address environmental issues experienced by people of color and the poor. The purpose of the letters was to get the nation's attention, which they did. They were featured on the national news as well as in the *New York Times*.

Table 3. Principles of Environmental Justice Adopted at the First National People of Color Environmental Leadership Summit, 1991

1. Environmental justice affirms the sacredness of Mother Earth, ecological unity and the interdependence of all species, and the right to be free from ecological destruction.

2. Environmental justice demands that public policy be based on mutual respect and justice for all peoples, free from any form of discrimination or bias.

3. Environmental justice mandates the right to ethical, balanced, and responsible uses of land and renewable resources in the interest of a sustainable planet for humans and other living things.

4. Environmental justice calls for universal protection from nuclear testing, extraction, production, and disposal of toxic/hazardous wastes and poisons and nuclear testing that threatens the fundamental right to clean air, land, water, and food.

5. Environmental justice affirms the fundamental right to political, economic, cultural, and environmental self-determination of all peoples.

6. Environmental justice demands the cessation of the production of all toxins, hazardous wastes, and radioactive materials, and that all past and current producers be held strictly accountable to the people for detoxification and the containment at the point of production.

7. Environmental justice demands the right to participate as equal partners at every level of decision-making, including needs assessment, planning, implementation, enforcement, and evaluation.

8. Environmental justice affirms the right of all workers to a safe and healthy work environment without being forced to choose between an unsafe livelihood and unemployment. It also affirms the right of those who work at home to be free from environmental hazards.

9. Environmental justice protects the right of victims of environmental injustice to receive full compensation and reparations for damages as well as quality health care.

10. Environmental justice considers governmental acts of environmental injustice a violation of international law, the Universal Declaration on Human Rights, and the United Nations Convention on Genocide.

11. Environmental justice must recognize a special legal and natural relationship of Native Peoples to the U.S. government through treaties, agreements, compacts, and covenants affirming sovereignty and self-determination.

12. Environmental justice affirms the need for urban and rural ecological policies to clean up and rebuild our cities and rural areas in balance with nature, honor the cultural integrity of all our communities, and provide fair access for all to the full range of resources.

13. Environmental justice calls for the strict enforcement of principles of informed consent, and a halt to the testing of experimental reproductive and medical procedures and vaccinations on people of color.

14. Environmental justice opposes the destructive operations of multinational corporations.

15. Environmental justice opposes military occupation, repression and exploitation of lands, peoples and cultures, and other life-forms.

16. Environmental justice calls for the education of present and future generations with emphasis on social and environmental issues based on our experience and an appreciation of our diverse cultural perspectives.

17. Environmental justice requires that we, as individuals, make personal and consumer choices to consume as little of Mother Earth's resources and to produce as little waste as possible and make the conscious decision to challenge and reprioritize our lifestyles to ensure the health of the natural world for present and future generations.

After looking into the allegations against EDF, his employer, Williams considered them to be true. "Rather than leaving EDF, I decided to stay and become part of the solution," he said. It was a watershed moment. You may have heard the phrase "first direction, then velocity." His decision to stay and fight racism set the direction of his career. He then channeled his intellect, street smarts, passion, and commitment into a thirty-year career of fighting for environmental justice for all. It put him on the front lines of engaging businesses that would typically be called the polluters and exploring how they could be more environmentally safe for all people and for all species.

Soon Williams became the EDF point person for planning the first National People of Color Environmental Leadership Summit on October 24–27, 1991, in Washington, D.C. The summit attracted more than five hundred delegates who ultimately drafted and adopted the seventeen Principles of Environmental Justice (table 3). These principles have gone on to guide and nurture the growing grassroots movement for environmental justice.

Next Stop: National Wildlife Federation, Ann Arbor, Michigan

During his four years at EDF, Williams encountered many outstanding people who expanded his horizons and inspired him, including EDF attorney Michael Bean, who was considered the "dean of Endangered Species Protection" in the United States. In 1994, Williams was recruited by Mark Van Putten, president and chief executive officer of the National Wildlife Federation's Great Lakes Resource Center, in Ann Arbor, Michigan. One of the country's leading legal experts on the Clean Water Act, Van Putten had established the center in 1982. Williams had not only moved from one skilled organization making innovative, impactful changes that would alter the landscape of environmental policy to another but also was working with a man who would mentor, encourage, and inspire him to follow his passion and believe in his vision.

NWF had been working to eliminate pollution from persistent, bioaccumulative toxic substances, like mercury, PCBs, dioxin, and DDT, since its Ann Arbor office opened in 1982. As these toxic substances move up the food web, they become more concentrated in the tissues of aquatic organisms and humans through a process called biomagnification. Their accumulation becomes problematic because they are linked to neurological and reproductive abnormalities in humans and wildlife. NWF and others were pursuing the goal of "virtual elimination of the discharge of persistent toxic substances" with a philosophy of "zero discharge," as called for in the 1978 U.S.–Canada Great Lakes Water Quality Agreement.

But it was his work on a lawsuit focused on improving water quality in the Great Lakes and reducing discharges from the Detroit Wastewater Treatment Plant (now called the Detroit Water Resource Recovery Facility) that put Williams on the map as an environmental innovator and collaborator to prevent pollution at its source. He and his team first documented that Detroit's regional sewer system was releasing high levels of mercury into the Detroit River and then recommended methods for controlling it while the lawsuit was argued over several years.

Among the data and information presented as part of the litigation, Williams and his colleagues showed that in 1995 the treatment plant was discharging four pounds of mercury into the Detroit River each week. Yes, that is per week. Health advisories were in effect warning people against eating the mercury-contaminated fish, especially women of childbearing age and children. "We figured that if we could clean up that one major source of mercury to the Great Lakes, it would be a great victory and model for others to follow," Williams said.

The lawsuit provided a unique opportunity to offer collaborative pollution prevention strategies as a creative means of encouraging a settlement. Williams's critical thinking and skills in team building led to a major victory in preventing the release of mercury. By the time the lawsuit was settled in 2002, the defendants agreed to implement the changes sought by Williams and his colleagues at NWF. Eventually, many cities around the country replicated the same mercury-pollution prevention approach, resulting in some of the strictest environmental protections in the United States.

As part of this pollution prevention initiative, Williams and his colleagues worked with hospitals and dental offices to identify and implement practical and economical ways of reducing mercury use in the healthcare industry. They encouraged medical organizations to inventory the sources of mercury in their facilities and then made recommendations to their hazardous waste and safety committees, as well as the administration, to lessen or eliminate these sources. They also called on healthcare businesses both to reduce immediate mercury use and to set goals for stopping the use of this toxic metal altogether.

Their seminal work was heralded as one of the most effective, collaborative approaches to preventing mercury pollution in the country and even helped catalyze a new organization called Health Care without Harm, now a group with international impact. The results in Detroit speak for themselves: hundreds of pounds of mercury stopped being released from dental offices each year to the municipal sewer system. The pollution prevention toolbox of Williams and his team included alternative disposal methods and incentives for using mercury-free amalgams. Early results showed that fourteen Michigan hospitals had agreed to limit the use of mercury, two of them by 80 percent (Williams, 1997). Industries such as battery makers complied with efforts to reduce the use of the substance as well. In fact, standard practices in the healthcare field and the design of many commonly used products were soon transformed to include mercury-free formulas.

This pollution prevention effort directly contributed to the cleanup of the Detroit River AOC through the RAP. Williams served on its Public Advisory Committee and many others. Among the beneficial uses that the RAP seeks to restore is the ability of people to safely consume fish and wildlife. Mercury is one of the major pollutants contributing to health advisories against eating fish caught locally. Thanks to Williams and his team, the amount of mercury flowing into the river fell, thus reducing the amount found in the fish, making them safer to eat.

Detroiters Working for Environmental Justice (DWEJ)

The same year Williams came to Ann Arbor and took the job with NWF, he met likeminded people in Detroit working to achieve environmental justice for all. The connections Williams made helped shape how he would apply his spiritual mission in Detroit. He and likeminded Detroiters organized the city's first environmental justice gathering in the spring of 1994 to explore what they could do together. They did not want to simply redistribute environmental harms but to abolish them. Out of that gathering came DWEJ—a nonprofit organization that provides all Detroit residents with tools they need to address environmental concerns in their own neighborhoods. "The people who formed the nucleus of DWEJ were already there and working," notes Williams (Shine, 2015). "They were a source of inspiration to me and welcomed me into their body of work. For that, I am forever grateful." As a founding member of DWEJ, he has maintained an active presence in the organization and was named president and chief executive officer in 2010.

Williams's work has been grassroots and on the ground. Over the years, he has battled on behalf of Detroit and its people, arguing for solutions to deal with the effects of steel mill emissions, dust from heavy truck traffic, the nation's largest municipal waste incinerator, thousands of parcels of contaminated land, and now inoperable lead smelters. These smelters were contributing to high lead levels in the blood of the city's children, producing lead-related illnesses and neurological and behavioral impairments. The collective impact of these sources of pollution on Detroit and its people is demonstrated by an unusually high number of low birthweight babies, cancer hotspots, high asthma rates, and a higher-than-average rate of death.

He brought a unique skill set to bear on addressing environmental justice issues in Detroit. In his own words:

> I have been blessed with a wide range of life experiences that help me communicate well with basically anyone. This is one of my strengths. I feel I can connect with people at any stage of life. I can hang with company presidents and chief executive officers or be on the street with addicts and have no fear. I have a knack for seeing across different points of view. You won't get movement on an issue if you can't see all points of view.

Under his leadership and with the support of many, DWEJ has grown from a grassroots volunteer organization to a major voice recognized locally, statewide, and nationally for its innovative programs and projects that create sustainable, livable communities. As the first environmental justice organization in Michigan, its work is woven into the fabric of every Detroit neighborhood.

For decades DWEJ has been promoting environmental justice through education, building relationships, and shaping policy. A good example of DWEJ activities and leadership include the city's first climate action plan, published in 2017 after the organization spent many years of working with representatives from nonprofit, educational, business, and governmental organizations, as well as people in all Detroit neighborhoods. In the same year, DWEJ's advocacy, in partnership with other groups, led the city to establish an Office of Sustainability. Williams's organization provided key leadership for, and participated in, the development of the Detroit Sustainability Action Agenda in 2019. And it has established the Future Build Construction Group to help break the cycle of poverty by giving Detroit residents the skills to work in living-wage jobs with a focus on repairing and protecting the environment. Two initiatives are especially worth expanding upon.

Human Health Impacts from Air Pollution in Detroit

As noted earlier, Southwest Detroit, particularly the zip code 48217, remains among the most polluted in the state. The major sources of its poisoned air are industry and transportation, and one of the major pollutants is particulates. Per the U.S. Environmental Protection Agency, particulate matter is a complex mixture of extremely small particles and liquid droplets. The particles can be made up of a number of components, including acids (from nitrates and sulfates), organic chemicals, metals, and soil or dust particles. When people breathe them in, these small particles can accumulate in the lungs and undermine heart and lung health. Exposure to particulate matter can trigger asthma attacks, result in abnormal births, reduce lung function, weaken the heart, cause cancer, and lead to death. Children, teenagers, and the elderly are particularly vulnerable to high particulate matter exposure. Although there has been about a 90 percent improvement in particulate air pollution since 1971, concern remains for long-term exposure and cumulative health burdens, particularly for vulnerable populations.

The American Lung Association (2019) reported that despite improvements in air quality, the metropolitan Detroit region is still ranked the twelfth most polluted city in the United States based on year-round particle pollution. The region also experienced more days than the national average with dangerous spikes in short-term particle pollution. Particulate air pollution is undoubtedly worse in Southwest Detroit than in the city as a whole.

Why haven't clear air rules made more of a difference in Southwest Detroit? Federal and state regulations fail communities of color like those living in zip code 48217 because they weren't designed to account for multiple pollutant exposures (Williams, 2020). Simply put, the pollutant-by-pollutant regulatory approach does not adequately address the unique issues of having a cluster of major sources of pollution in a highly concentrated area like 48217. Neither the U.S. Environmental Protection Agency nor Michigan's Department of Environment, Great Lakes, and Energy require cumulative assessment of exposures. DWEJ has long advocated for this approach.

As part of other efforts to ensure that community organizations and people benefit from research, Williams, on behalf of DWEJ, has long been involved in academic partnerships. Founded in 1995, the University of Michigan School of Public Health's Detroit Urban Research Center (URC) fosters health equity through community-based participatory research. Williams and DWEJ played a formative role in establishing one of its research partnerships, Community Action to Protect Healthy Environments, which developed and implemented a public health action plan to improve air quality and health in Detroit. Wayne State University's Center for Urban Responses to Environmental Stressors is one of a few dozen select environmental health sciences core centers in the nation funded by the National Institute of Environmental Health Sciences. As DWEJ's president and CEO, Williams was one of the inaugural community-engagement advisees when the center was launched in 2014, and he has continued to help shape its ongoing exploration of how stressors affect people.

One notable project coming out of these collaborations is worth mentioning. In 2017, partnering with the University of Michigan's School of Public Health, Williams co-authored a study of human health impacts on residents in Southwest Detroit resulting from exposure to air pollution. This study examined the diseases and health disparities attributable to air pollutants for the Detroit urban area. Based on current levels, exposures to fine particulate matter, ozone, sulfur dioxide, and nitrogen dioxide are responsible for more than 10,000 disability-adjusted life years per year—or the number of years lost due to ill-health, disability, or early death per year, causing an annual monetized health impact of $6.5 billion (Martenies et al., 2017). This burden is mainly driven by the fine particulate and ozone exposures, which cause 660 premature deaths each year among the 945,000 individuals in the study area. Nitrogen dioxide exposures, largely from traffic, cause significant respiratory problems among older adults and children with asthma. In total, 46 percent of air pollution–related asthma hospitalizations are due to this substance. Based on quantitative inequality metrics, the greatest inequality of health burdens results from industrial and traffic emissions. In other words, white and well-to-do people suffer least from these kinds of pollution, whereas people of color and low-income individuals suffer most. These metrics also show disproportionate burdens among Hispanic/Latino populations due to industrial emissions, and among low-income populations due to traffic emissions. People's poor health depends on what pollutants they are exposed to, how often, and in what concentrations, as well as their own health status, susceptibility, and vulnerability.

Climate Change Action Plan

Working collaboratively with business, educational, nonprofit, and governmental organizations, Williams was, as mentioned above, the primary author of one of the country's first community initiated and generated Climate Action Plans. It was written from the streets up, not from the government down. DWEJ convened many stakeholders through its Detroit Climate Action Collaborative and commissioned city-specific studies on greenhouse gas emissions, vulnerability, climatology, and economic impacts. They then talked and listened through town halls; neighborhood meetings; and business, health, and youth summits, and revised their findings and recommendations in an iterative process to get them right. The Detroit Climate Action Plan was truly the result of deep collaboration, including thousands of hours of research, brainstorming, and meetings.

Detroit Mayor Mike Duggan has this to say about the plan: "The Detroit Climate Action Plan, Detroit's first, is the result of the tireless work of a wide spectrum of Detroit organizations—business, governmental, academic, nonprofits—with input from residents from every community in the city. The plan reflects the collaborative and cooperative nature of many looking to become one—one city with a clear commitment to its growth and greening" (Detroiters Working for Environmental Justice, 2017).

The Detroit Climate Action Plan includes goals and near- and long-term action steps. It is not just a report and collection of ideas. The plan lays out specific actions and attainable goals, with benchmarks. It contains over one hundred action steps focused on solid waste disposal; public health; business and institutions; parks, public spaces, and water infrastructure; and homes and neighborhoods. The intent is to accelerate the pace of positive transformation of Detroit's built environment, energy use practices, and energy generation options. The combined impact of these changes will reduce more than Detroit's fair share of the worldwide releases of greenhouse gases.

Williams's Lessons and Advice to Others

People of color frequently have limited experience with legal and policy-making tools to address environmental concerns affecting their lives and neighborhoods. Williams says, "We need to make sure that people of color are at the table where decisions are being made that affect their health and neighborhoods and that their voices and concerns are being heard."

Over his more than thirty-year career, Williams has learned that success in his line of work is plodding. He feels that it takes a minimum of three years to get traction on an issue. In his view, "Regardless of victory or defeat, you need to be prepared to take on issues for the long haul to succeed at positive transformation. History has taught me that the best outcomes feel like they take forever. You must be committed to the long-term or don't take on the issue."

Williams also feels that the next generation must be well grounded in civics. Civics is important because it helps people to understand how government works and it provides citizens with knowledge about how to influence government. Williams's advice is: "Learn as much as you can about the systems of regulatory policy making and commit yourself to making a difference."

Finally, Williams identified the importance of developing and mentoring the next generation of activists working on environmental justice. Over the years, he has worked with many Detroiters and Michiganders on their way up. Ritchie H. Harrison, a member of the Board of Directors of DWEJ and co-director of the Great Lakes Leadership Academy, had this to say about his colleague and friend:

> I have tremendous appreciation for Guy Williams and his work through Detroiters Working for Environmental Justice. As a team member and collaborator, I have come to appreciate Guy as a leader and innovator in the space of environmentalism, environmental advocacy, and justice. He has supported impactful projects that have improved the health and well-being of Detroiters and beyond. Moreover, early in my career, Guy took the initiative to reach out to me while we were on a project committee together. He expressed an appreciation for my skills as an emerging leader, which gave me a huge boost in confidence. He backed his words by becoming my mentor, supported my growth, and encouraged me to pursue opportunities that helped to further my development. I have a deep appreciation for Guy and his impact. He has shown the vision to support Detroit's communities, invest in future leaders, and build a legacy regarding the role of environmental justice for the city's future.

Williams recognizes that we need to connect and commit, that each of us makes a difference. He calls on all of us to recognize that "as a society, we need to invest in young people, lift them up, and open doors for them. We need to mentor them to carry on this important work."

Next Challenges and Opportunities

A water crisis started in Detroit in 2014 when, during the city's bankruptcy proceedings, its water department abruptly shut off water service to tens of thousands of Detroit residents for nonpayment. Simply put, many Detroiters could not afford escalating water rates. And low-income households were disproportionately affected. Shutting off water service was a contravention of United Nations' human rights standards. Williams feels strongly that the city of Detroit needs an affordable water plan. It is well known that the Great Lakes Water Authority, which provides water and sewer services to southeast Michigan communities, will need to invest $500 million over the next five years to upgrade its water infrastructure. We also know that at the federal level there is the new Infrastructure Investment and Jobs Act signed in 2021. Williams states, "Our elected officials should be seeking opportunities and investment to provide affordable water to all."

For Williams, another challenge in Detroit's environmental justice arena is the new Gordie Howe International Bridge crossing between the United States and Canada, projected to open in 2024. The U.S. footing of this new bridge is in Southwest Detroit. What will the area within a three-mile radius of the new bridge look like? Will it have enough green infrastructure? What is being done upstream from the river to prevent pollution and control contaminants at their source? How is the city going to handle traffic flow on and off the bridge? How can we mitigate air pollution from trucks? It must be remembered that idling trucks put out more air pollution. What quality of life do we want for residents and businesses in the area, and how will we assure the best possible outcome?

Williams feels that the Gordie Howe International Bridge, still under construction, affords a unique opportunity for responsible planning and action. The U.S. footing of the bridge is in the Delray neighborhood, known for its cohesive multicultural spirit and tenacious residents. Over the years pollution and disinvestment have robbed the area of much of its earlier vitality. It is also home to Zug Island, known as the industrial heartland of Detroit and a pollution behemoth. Williams is one of the consultants engaging with people in Delray to find out how to mitigate the harm done while helping to revitalize and stabilize the community. He believes that the building of the new bridge is an opportunity to think more broadly and holistically, to move beyond doing the minimum, and to strive for revitalization and sustainable redevelopment. This process should include cleanup of brownfields using bioremediation—using plants and microorganisms to reduce the concentrations or toxic effects of contaminants, greenways, blueways, parks, revitalizing historic Fort Wayne, green infrastructure, and more. This holistic mitigation of past and future harms could then serve as a model all along the river. As he points out:

> Look at what Ford Motor Company did years ago under William Mc-Donough, world-class architect and proponent of sustainable design, at its Rouge Plant to clean up brownfields using bioremediation, rehabilitate habitats, and build green infrastructure. That now needs to be done in Southwest Detroit. There is a ripple effect of change up and down the river, and this is an opportunity to rethink how things are happening. Here, again, we must leapfrog traditional practices of abandonment of brownfield sites and demonstrate new technologies to clean up and restore contaminated sites for sustainable redevelopment. It can be done.

Williams also sees the new Ralph C. Wilson Jr. Centennial Park, which is being built as part of the Detroit RiverWalk in Southwest Detroit, as another unique opportunity to showcase sustainable development. "What a great project to showcase brownfield cleanup, habitat restoration,

Zug Island in Southwest Detroit along the Detroit River
THE CENTER FOR LAND USE INTERPRETATION

green infrastructure, and benefits for all. It also is a unique opportunity to showcase pollution prevention and new technologies in addressing upstream combined sewer overflows."

Williams's Proudest Project

The project he is most proud of is the mercury-pollution prevention campaign he led because of the impact it had. When he showed up in Ann Arbor, the charge was to lead a team in finding solutions to mercury pollution. Keenly aware that they were not the first to be faced with this challenge, he set out to determine who else was working to that end and what they were doing. The strategies he and his team adopted were precedent setting and enabled them to apply best practices from great distances. Their work accelerated change very quickly. Sure, there were

Guy O. Williams, environmental justice champion in Detroit, Michigan

DAVID LEWINSKY, COURTESY OF *BUCKNELL ALUMNI MAGAZINE*

many obstacles, a lawsuit, and nobody wanted to move. But Williams and his team found a way forward that set better standards for cleaner water, provided guidance on how to achieve them, and put into effect an educational campaign. He says proudly, "We even found middle ground and practical solutions with hospitals." The partnership between NWF and the Michigan Hospital Association was groundbreaking. The Henry Ford Hospital incinerator closed because of community action to address emissions, including mercury and other chemicals from the burning of plastics. Even mercury thermometers were banned. Williams concluded: "This gave confidence to step out of our comfort zone and take other risks—like climate change. It was a model for others to follow and has guided every other step and significant initiative along my path. There's such power in recognizing where the turn occurs. So much is possible then."

Concluding Thoughts

Williams has been a shining light for environmental justice in Detroit for twenty-five years. He has worked both in the trenches and at the negotiating table and been involved with most of the significant green initiatives in the city. He continues to stand at the crossroads of energy, water, jobs, safety, air quality, green technology, recycling, land use, community, and more—all the while mentoring the next generation of environmental justice champions.

His impact has been as broad as his knowledge. He serves as chair emeritus of the Great Lakes Leadership Academy Board of Governors. He also serves on the Board of Directors of the Rails-to-Trails Conservancy (chairperson in 2013) and has served on the boards of the Center for Urban Responses to Environmental Stressors, the Detroit Urban Research Center, and the Great Lakes Integrated Sciences and Assessment Center.

In recognition of his many accomplishments, Williams was named a Michigan Green Leader by the *Detroit Free Press* in 2014. In 2016, he received the Bucknell University Alumni Association Award for Service to Humanity, followed by the William Milliken Leadership for the Common Good Award in 2017. He is known locally and nationally for his environmental justice advocacy and for innovative community programming that values effective collaborations among business, government, and community interests.

Humbly, Williams notes: "My dream is to see a city that is vibrant across all aspects of the society—a place where the current disparities of power, wealth, and education are greatly reduced, and where the voices of the 'people-at-large' are always heard and respected by decision-makers. I try to do my part toward this end, day in and day out" (Shine, 2015).

In 2020, he stepped down as president and chief executive officer of DWEJ. But his retirement is only the beginning of the next chapter of his faith and life journey. He feels called to spend more time with his family and new grandchildren as he remains open to finding new ways to stay engaged for the good of the community. And we know that he will continue to be a shining light!

CHAPTER 7

Jim Murray

Rouge River Champion

Early Native Americans traveled the Rouge River by canoe, fished it and hunted game in its watershed, buried their ancestors next to it, and gathered at the water's edge for cultural ceremonies and celebrations. They called it "mishqua sibe" or "minosagoink," both terms meaning "singeing skin river"—referring to the place where game was dressed. Then fur trappers and traders arrived in the late 1600s in search of beaver to meet European demand for hats made from the pelts. They found plenty and trappers, like Native Americans, benefited from this water route to the interior. Today, the Rouge River flows 126 miles through the most densely populated and urbanized area of Michigan— metropolitan Detroit. It has four branches—including the main, upper, middle, and lower—and empties into the Detroit River at Zug Island. Its watershed spans approximately 466 square miles and is home to approximately 1.5 million people living in forty-eight communities and portions of three counties.

Like most urban rivers, this one has experienced more than a century of human exploitation and neglect. Heavy industry dominates the lower end of the river near its confluence with the Detroit River. As a result, these waters have long had a reputation of being a working river that supported industry and commerce. Pollution was just considered part of the cost of doing business. Industries discharged oil and other petroleum products, heavy metals, and organic compounds like PCBs that killed organisms living on the river bottom, caused cancer in bottom-feeding fish, made game fish unsafe to eat, and created other water pollution problems in the Detroit River. These were the circumstances in which the river caught on fire on October 9, 1969. On that infamous day, a welder's torch ignited oil and oil-soaked debris in the lower river. Flames climbed fifty feet into the air and the U.S. Coast Guard had to halt traffic on the river. The Detroit Fire Department contained the fire and let it burn out.

But it was not just the lower river that was polluted. The middle and upper portions of the watershed were also being impacted by urban sprawl. Like many major metropolitan areas throughout the United States, people in southeast Michigan began moving away from Detroit beginning in the 1950s, seeking suburban areas with more space and within driving distance to their workplace. Personal automobiles and cheap fuel made this sprawl possible. In addition, federal tax subsidies for home mortgage interest and property taxes, as well as infrastructure financing policies and racial tensions, fueled this new growth outside the central city. This outward migration trend accelerated during the 1960s with more people fleeing the central city for outer-ring suburbs, including the Rouge River watershed.

But this urban sprawl had unintended consequences. Much of the watershed was developed with combined storm and sanitary sewers, a practice that is no longer followed. When there is excessive rainfall, the carrying capacity of the combined sewer system is exceeded and stormwater runoff and untreated municipal sewage are discharged into the Rouge River. By 1985, there were 168 CSO points in the watershed that were contributing raw sewage and other wastes that were overwhelming the river. As the municipal sewage decomposed, it used up the oxygen in the water of many parts of the Rouge River, making the river uninhabitable for many fish and invertebrates. In total, 23 percent of the watershed had become roads, parking lots, rooftops, and other impervious surfaces, which increased urban runoff and brought sediment, trash, fertilizers, pesticides, and other pollutants into the river, further degrading it. To put this situation in perspective, ecologists recommend that the impervious surface of a healthy watershed should be less than 10 percent. Everyone was contributing to the water pollution problems of the Rouge River.

The magnitude of the water pollution problems became manifest in the October 21, 1965, headline of the local newspaper called *Dearborn Guide*: "Rouge Called State's Most Polluted River" (Gnau, 1975). The article identified three major sources of pollution: industrial waste, primarily from the Rouge Auto Plant, stormwater and raw sewage from overflows of the combined storm and sanitary sewer system, and garbage and trash thrown into the river. But most people didn't notice or care. Most people accepted this pollution as part of the cost of doing business and suburban living. Industrial jobs, technological progress, and homes in suburbia were the priorities, not environmental protection.

An aquatic study of the Rouge River in the early 1970s reported that approximately forty of its miles had very poor water quality, as evidenced by the fact that the dominant life was pollution tolerant insects, worms, and fish (Jackson, 1975). The principal contaminants at that time were

The concrete channel of the
Rouge River in the mid-
1980s, with decomposing
raw sewage and dead carp,
Melvindale, Michigan
LARRY CARUSO

raw sewage and inorganic sediment entering the river from CSOs and
stormwater runoff. The 1972 Clean Water Act called for watershed-wide
planning throughout the United States so that all waters would be "fishable and swimmable" within twenty years. Under section 208 of this law,
municipalities were encouraged to experiment with best management
practices to address stormwater challenges, but no broad-based funding
for implementation was provided.

Then in 1983 a "tipping point" occurred: residents of Melvindale and
Dearborn could not keep their windows open at night because of the
putrid smell of rotten eggs was wafting into their bedrooms. At the time,
people thought that the source was air emissions from nearby industries.
However, after scientific investigations residents learned that the Rouge

River was so polluted with raw sewage that all the oxygen was being used up and, in its absence, hydrogen sulfide was forming and being released from the water. This gas smells like rotten eggs. The raw sewage was coming from the sanitary sewer overflows, CSOs, and illegal discharges. Even the most pollution tolerant fish, like carp, were dying in the river because they had no oxygen to breathe. Locals were finally starting to realize that the Rouge River was a public health threat.

Concerned citizens from Melvindale and Dearborn started a petition drive in 1984 and gathered nearly 1,000 signatures. They sent this petition to the regional administrator of U.S. Environmental Protection Agency (EPA), the Michigan Department of Natural Resources, and the Michigan Water Resources Commission. Residents demanded that something be done immediately to stop the illegal raw sewage discharges to the Rouge River and to eliminate the water quality standards violations occurring in the river. Public awareness of the pollution was growing, and state and federal agencies were forced to take notice.

Then in 1985 a tragic accident occurred. A twenty-three-year-old man fell into the Rouge River and, after swallowing some water, died of a rare waterborne parasitic disease called leptospirosis or rat fever. Even though the local health department news release stated that there was no evidence that the man's illness and death were directly linked to the polluted water, most people realized that the probable cause of death was his exposure to raw sewage in the river. Governments have always said "show us the smoking gun" or "show us the human health impact." There was now compelling evidence that the polluted Rouge River was the source of the waterborne pathogen that caused one man's death and that it was a public health risk to 1.5 million watershed residents. The health departments had no choice but to warn the public to avoid contact with the river. Yes, you heard that correctly, the health departments banned human contact with the Rouge River. After that, the Michigan Department of Natural Resources and its Michigan Water Resources Commission had no choice but to comprehensively address this public health problem.

At the time, these problems seemed overwhelming. But not to one person who grew up in the watershed and was driven to make a difference. His name was Jim Murray.

A Champion Rises

Murray grew up along one of four branches of the Rouge River called the Lower Rouge in what is now Westland, Michigan. Back then these waters were grossly polluted. Mothers always know best, and his mother regularly told him to "stay away from that nasty river." Despite his mother's plea, Murray was drawn to the waterway and has fond memories of playing "Tarzan in the jungle" in the Lower Rouge behind Westland's Jefferson Elementary School. He would swing on a rope tied to a large willow tree hanging over the water's edge and, just as he reached the peak of his swing, let go and free fall into the water. Obviously, he did not share those stories with his mother. Those early childhood experiences stayed with him, and he vowed to one day clean up his beloved river.

Murray went on to become an activist and then a key government official who would forge the partnerships required to clean up the Rouge River. His career has been defined by water and always at the center has been this urban waterway. In the 1980s, he served as the Washtenaw County drain commissioner, with responsibility for the Huron River and a small portion of the Rouge River watershed that flowed through his county. Murray was appointed in 1983, by then Michigan Governor James Blanchard, to the Michigan Water Resources Commission, which is charged with protecting the waters of the state. He would soon rise to become its chairperson. Under his leadership, the commission developed an action plan in 1985 to spur cleanup the Rouge River. He also helped establish the Rouge River Basin Committee, made up of all forty-eight mayors in the watershed.

Murray believed strongly in thinking regionally but acting locally. He fostered regional thinking by chairing the Areawide Water Quality Board of the Southeast Michigan Council of Governments. He practiced local stewardship by helping establish Friends of the Rouge, a nonprofit organization dedicated to raising awareness and involvement in cleaning up the river, serving as its first president for five years. In the 1990s, Murray moved on to become the director of Wayne County Department of the Environment, where he helped establish the Rouge River National Wet Weather Demonstration Project, which brought in over $350 million from the federal government for river cleanup, with the help of Congressman John D. Dingell.

In 2006, he helped establish the Alliance of Rouge Communities, which represented thirty-six watershed communities, to promote watershed cleanup. Not only did Murray help get the alliance off the ground, but he strategically gave them half of the money it needed from the Rouge River National Wet Weather Demonstration grant to do watershed planning, implement controls over nonpoint source pollution (contaminants that could not be traced to a single pipe or point), restore habitats, and more. The other half came from the watershed communities, so that they would have "skin in the game" and would understand their long-term responsibility for caring for the Rouge River as their home.

From the Wayne County Department of the Environment, Murray went on to become director of Dearborn Department of Public Works, one of the watershed communities, where he oversaw implementation of stormwater and CSO controls that were completed in 2021. As you can see, he has used his unique gifts and talents to raise awareness of the major pollution problems in the Rouge River watershed and get all involved in solving them.

Watershed Cleanup

In 1985, the Michigan Water Resources Commission (the state agency responsible at that time for protecting waters of the state, establishing rules, and issuing permits), under Murray's leadership, passed a resolution implementing the Rouge River Basin strategy, which included an action plan and a public participation process. This plan would culminate in the development of the Rouge River RAP designed to restore all impaired beneficial uses throughout the watershed.

As chairman of the commission, Murray would give tours of the Rouge River. But these were not your standard river tours. His purpose was to shock, generate outrage, and propel action to clean up Michigan's most polluted river. One technique he regularly employed was to take reporters, elected officials, and community leaders down to the river and ask them, "What are those floating objects in the river?" The answer was human feces, and you imagine the response. Condoms and sanitary napkins were also floating in the river. All the visitors were aghast. As they got close, the smell became offensively malodorous and overwhelming. Over a decade had passed since the 1972 U.S. Clean Water Act and yet raw sewage was still overwhelming the Rouge River.

Solving these water pollution problems would require the state and county governments, all forty-eight communities, and other stakeholders working together. It may sound easy, but it was not. Indeed, the Rouge River initiative became a leader in the efforts to clean up the forty-three Great Lakes AOCs through the U.S.–Canada Great Lakes Water Quality Agreement. Its international designation as a Great Lakes AOC also raised the priority for cleanup and gave legitimacy the Rouge River RAP.

Clearly, no one community's actions could restore the Rouge River. A study of the quantity and quality of CSOs throughout the entire watershed was completed in 1980. It showed definitively that if the City of Detroit alone implemented necessary CSO control measures, the quality of the Rouge River would not be improved one iota. It would take all forty-eight communities each doing its part to restore the river. The plan was to build on the strengths of the Michigan Department of Natural Resources, the U.S. Environmental Protection Agency, Southeast Michigan Council of Governments, and others, yet also to achieve local ownership among all the communities within the watershed.

Everyone recognized that the river could be studied for decades with little improvement. That's why the RAP process was envisioned with two parallel tracks, with the necessary studies and cleanup actions happening concurrently. To facilitate public participation, a Rouge River Basin Committee was established with representatives from all forty-eight watershed communities, and all major stakeholder groups and an Executive Steering Committee that included representatives from both state and federal agencies.

The Basin and Executive Committees focused on governmental and watershed coordination. What was missing was a mechanism to engage citizens. In 1986, under Murray's leadership, the nonprofit Friends of the Rouge was set up to help coordinate grassroots engagement, foster environmental education, and encourage citizen stewardship. Its signature projects included the annual Rouge Rescue, which involves citizens in cleaning up debris and removing log jams, and the Rouge River Education Project. The education project was a partnership with University of Michigan professor William Stapp and students from most of the high schools across the watershed, who tested water quality, compared results with each other, and recommended corrective action projects. This effort earned the Friends of the Rouge the 1986 Take Pride in America Award—one of ten projects nationwide to be so honored. Ford Motor Company became the first major sponsor of Friends of the Rouge with a donation of $50,000. With the success of the first Rouge Rescue event, Ford donated an additional $50,000.

In 1988, the Rouge River RAP was completed and submitted to the Michigan Water Resources Commission, which adopted it in 1989 with a twenty-year goal of restoring impaired uses. All wanted an aggressive, "move-ahead" attitude toward cleanup. The initial plan focused heavily on sanitary sewer overflows and CSOs because approximately 7.8 billion gallons of combined stormwater and sewage were being discharged into the Rouge River during rain events annually. It is important to note that the 1988 RAP recommendations focused on sanitary sewer capacity and CSO controls. However, it also recognized polluted stormwater from separated sewers as a significant problem across the entire watershed. In the spirit of continuous improvement, the Rouge River RAP was updated in 1994, 1998, 2004, and 2008.

In 1992, the representatives of the Rouge River Basin Committee were reorganized into the Rouge RAP Advisory Council, and in 1993 the Rouge River National Wet Weather Demonstration Project (Rouge Project for short) was created under Murray's leadership with federal funding. Over time and with the help of Congressman John D. Dingell, the project obtained $350 million in federal grants to help implement the CSO controls and innovative stormwater management techniques called for in the plan (Murray, 1994). This essential funding came from the EPA and was funneled through to Wayne County's Department of Environment for a demonstration project to implement cost-effective, control programs in a collaborative fashion with local governments.

Solving pollution problems in a cost-effective manner required a level of collaboration among varied partners that had never been seen before in southeastern Michigan, let alone the entire Great Lakes Basin. It also required flexibility across regulatory programs. Because the Rouge River watershed is so large, it was divided into seven subwatersheds with distinct watershed advisory groups and subwatershed management plans. Seventy-five communities and agencies have implemented more than 380 cleanup, restoration, and preservation projects under the umbrella of the Rouge Project. Other major accomplishments include the State of Michigan's Watershed-Based Stormwater Permit—the first of its kind in the nation. This new permit voluntarily addressed CSOs and stormwater within seven subwatersheds. In addition, the project oversaw the passage of the Watershed Alliance legislation Public Act 517 of 2004, the establishment of the Alliance of Rouge Communities in 2003, and the implementation of a comprehensive monitoring plan for the Rouge River watershed. The Alliance of Rouge Communities has been particularly effective in facilitating communication among watershed stakeholders and in coordinating subwatershed planning to implement stormwater plans mandated under the Michigan Stormwater

General Permit. The alliance has an annual budget of over $600,000 to support watershed monitoring, data analysis, and report writing, and coordination of public education and involvement activities under the Watershed-Based Stormwater Permit.

Rouge River Revival

Environment laws, like the federal Clean Water Act of 1972, helped regulate and control water pollution from identifiable sources or discharge pipes of industries and municipal wastewater treatment plants. The Rouge River RAP placed a priority on something else: CSOs, urban stormwater runoff, contaminated sediment remediation, and habitat restoration. For example, since 1985, over $1 billion has been spent on sewer improvement projects and eliminating many CSOs and controlling the remaining ones (Ridgway et al., 2018). Approximately 518,000 cubic yards of contaminated sediment have been remediated at a cost of $62.8 million, and more than $7 million has been used to implement habitat rehabilitation and enhancement projects in the watershed, including restoring an oxbow in the lower river and constructing a fishway at the Henry Ford Estate Dam to allow fish access to the upper watershed. These cleanup and rehabilitation efforts have resulted in considerable river improvements.

In 1969, when the Rouge River caught on fire, oil slicks were common on the lower river; hydrogen sulfide—the smell of rotten eggs—was off-gassing from the river. County health departments had to ban human contact with the river because there was so much raw sewage being discharged into it, and even pollution-tolerant carp were dying in the lower river because it lacked oxygen. Today, there's more oxygen in the water; pollution-sensitive stoneflies are appearing again. Northern pike and steelhead can now be found in the lower river. Peregrine falcons have returned at the river mouth. Beaver have come back to the reach near the University of Michigan–Dearborn and the headwaters, and the river is being rediscovered as a recreational resource.

The improvement in oxygen levels is a good example of how much the project has achieved. When dissolved oxygen concentrations fall below 4 mg/L, few aquatic organisms can survive. To protect aquatic life, State of Michigan water quality standards specify that dissolved oxygen must always be greater than 7 mg/L for streams designated as cold-water fisheries and 5 mg/L for streams designated as warm-water fisheries. All the Rouge River and its tributaries are designated as warm-water streams, except for Johnson Creek.

A 1973 study of the Rouge River, performed by the Michigan Department of Natural Resources, found the 5 mg/L standard was only met approximately 20 percent of the time (Jackson, 1975). In the 1980s and early 1990s, dissolved oxygen concentrations in the lower Rouge River were routinely zero. Today, it rarely goes below 5 mg/L. While the 1973 study showed that only 24 percent of the samples taken from the main branch of the Rouge exceeded the State of Michigan's water quality standard of 5 mg/L (Jackson, 1975), by the 1990s, the average percent compliance was 67 percent. And progress has not stopped since then: 89 percent of samples met the state standard in the 2000s and 97 percent in the 2010s (DeMaria and Mullett, 2020).

The bottom-dwelling, small aquatic invertebrates that scientists call "benthic macroinvertebrates" are widely used as indicators of the biological health of rivers. The Michigan Department of Natural Resources surveyed these creatures in the Rouge River from 1973 to 1994. Most of these early studies found "very poor" to "poor" benthic communities in the downstream portions of the main, upper, and middle branches, as well as the Evans branch on the main, Bell Creek on the upper, and all of the lower branch. "Fair" communities that included sensitive families like mayflies and caddisflies were found in the upstream sections of the main, upper, and middle branches and in Tonquish Creek, a middle branch tributary. The only "good" rating in the watershed was for Johnson Creek, a cold-water tributary to the middle branch, and the middle branch downstream of the confluence with Johnson Creek all the way to Newburgh Lake.

In 2001, Friends of the Rouge began collecting benthic macroinvertebrates every spring and fall using a protocol developed by the state of Michigan Department of Environmental Quality and updated by the Michigan Clean Water Corps. They used these samples to calculate stream quality index scores that categorize sites from "poor" to "excellent." Wayne County partnered with Friends of the Rouge to use the same protocol to sample downstream sites. Between 2001 and 2019, data were collected from 108 sites. Sites were sampled each season for three years, then put on a rotation to be sampled every other year.

In comparison to the 1973–1994 Michigan Department of Natural Resources data, the Friends of the Rouge data showed an overall improvement in benthic macroinvertebrate communities in the downstream sections of all of the major branches, with most sites achieving a "fair" rating. Exceptions to that included continued "poor" communities in Evans Creek and the middle Rouge downstream of the confluence with Tonquish Creek, as well as one site on Tonquish Creek. The main branch near Eight Mile had several sites with "good" communities, including pollution-sensitive species like dobsonflies. In short, the data show that the Rouge River project has greatly improved the water quality and habitat—and that much remains to be done.

Murray's Proudest Achievement

Of all his efforts, Murray is most proud of his success in helping organize a Rouge River monitoring program for high school students. While working as Washtenaw County drain commissioner, he recruited Professor Stapp of the University of Michigan, who is considered a pioneer in the field of environmental education, to engage students in monitoring water quality of the Huron River, which runs through Ann Arbor. Murray gave $10,000 from Washtenaw County to the university to get Stapp's program off the ground. It was an enormous success with thousands of students engaged and water quality data shared with elected officials. Murray then got Professor Stapp to bring his program over to the Rouge River watershed.

In 1987, Stapp and his university students worked with Friends of the Rouge to organize the Rouge River Interactive Water Quality Monitoring Program for high school students. The University of Michigan provided technical support in the form of a team of university students and facilitated data sharing via a computer network. High school classes throughout the watershed would sample the river water, analyze nine different water quality parameters (dissolved oxygen, fecal coliform bacteria, pH, biochemical oxygen demand, temperature, total phosphorus, nitrate, turbidity, and total solids), calculate a water quality index developed by the National Science Foundation, share the data among high schools in the watershed, and participate in the Water Quality Congress at which the students would inform community leaders about river health.

Can you imagine the power of bringing all the elected officials and community leaders together in a room and making them the audience for students to share their data on health of the Rouge River? Murray remembers vividly one Water Quality Congress where the high school students brought glass jars of water from each of their sampling stations and lined them up from downstream to upstream. It was a dramatic moment: the color of the water ranged from chocolate brown in the lower end of the watershed to pale blue in the upper watershed. It was a powerful moment and received considerable media attention. But most importantly, the program helped reconnect young people to the river, raise awareness of pollution problems, increase environmental literacy, and expand civic mindedness. It started out with just science teachers, but grew to include music, art, and history. From just a few teachers at a handful of schools, it eventually spread to over one hundred schools.

Professor Stapp went on to establish the Global Rivers Environmental Education Network (GREEN) to cultivate youth as watershed stewards in 1989. This program is distinct from other water-monitoring programs because it emphasizes action-oriented and problem-solving approaches based on interdisciplinary education and extensive networking with others traveling down a similar path. Before long communities around the Great Lakes in the United States and Canada, and eventually across the world, adopted GREEN. And it all started in the Huron and Rouge River watersheds.

Murray feels strongly that public involvement is critical to watershed protection and river revival. An uninformed, unaware public is one of the greatest environmental threats in the Rouge River watershed. When he talks about the GREEN program and how it has raised environmental awareness and literacy and expanded civic mindedness, it brings a big smile to his face. He notes: "After thirty-five years of cleaning up the Rouge River, the public is engaged; the educational community is involved at the elementary, secondary, and university levels; and the regulatory agencies and local governments have entered a new era of collaboration, replacing top-down, throw money at the problem, and 'Big Brother will save us' syndrome."

He goes on to say: "People support having clean water and a healthy watershed—give them a workable program and they will support it. If you have the public engaged and speaking out, you will get the attention of politicians and the necessary political support."

The Next Challenges

Murray has seen firsthand how the major water quality problems in the Rouge River have changed over time. In the 1960s, oil pollution from industry was viewed as the major problem. In the 1970s and 1980s, CSOs were the focus of attention. Today, Murray says that stormwater is the Rouge River's biggest problem. More than 50 percent of the Rouge River watershed is urbanized, and 23 percent of it is still impervious surfaces like roads, parking lots, and rooftops. This increases land runoff to the river and degrades habitat. The long-term goal is to have a watershed with less than 10 percent impervious surface so that fish, invertebrates, and other biological organisms can live and play their important roles in a healthy ecosystem. Clearly, more needs to be done to restore wet-lands, rehabilitate habitats, build green infrastructure, and create more sustainable communities.

The chances that more will be done have been enhanced by the work the Rouge Project has already done. A cleaner Rouge River is providing an opportunity to redefine human relationship with it and the Great Lakes Basin Ecosystem, alongside watershed residents' responsibility for stewardship of their water resources. Murray says, "As water quality of the Rouge River has improved in recent years, that debate has shifted to how we are going to use the river. For many years we used it as a sewer. Our opportunity now is to reconnect more people to the river."

A cleaner Rouge River is now attracting residents who for generations shunned it as unsafe for both people and wildlife. One good example is the Rouge River Gateway Partnership, which is an alliance of leaders from municipalities, cultural institutions, and businesses. Long term, this partnership wants to attract investment, but in the short term it is already improving recreational opportunities, celebrating history, and preserving and enhancing habitats. The partnership has developed a Rouge Gateway master plan that is creating connections where barriers long existed. One business, Roush Industries that provides engineering services to the transportation sector, has oriented the front door of its $37.5 million research park toward the river, showcasing a cleaner river and returning wildlife.

In another good example, Friends of the Rouge and many partners have created the Lower Rouge River Water Trail—a twenty-seven-mile kayak and canoe trail connecting people to the river's natural environment and its history. Under construction in 2020–2021 is the Fort Street Bridge Interpretive Park, located at the foot of the Fort Street Bridge in Southwest Detroit. The park will include a sculpture, kayak launch, boardwalk, rain garden, and a walking path symbolizing the renewed health and viability of the Rouge River and the regional commitment to the environment. Additional greenways and a water taxi are in the planning stages. Murray feels strongly that "reconnecting people to the

Rouge River in ways that get them to feel that they belong to the watershed will ultimately help develop a stewardship ethic."

Concluding Remarks

The Rouge River project has been a leader in use of an ecosystem approach on a watershed scale. It is the first watershed in the United States in which all forty-eight watershed communities have a stormwater permit to control CSOs and manage stormwater. We must remember that all the people who live in this watershed are part of the Rouge River ecosystem and what they do to their ecosystem they do to themselves. Further, all must do their part and be stewards of the place they call home. As Murray notes: "It's been a community-wide effort. People now recognize that restoring the Rouge River is a long-term effort, and they are committed to the long haul. People are taking pride in restoring their watershed."

It is indeed amazing to think that the Rouge River was once the most polluted river in Michigan and even the United States. The Rouge River has risen like the phoenix from the ashes of a burning river to overcome enormous obstacles and achieve surprising environmental improvement and ecological revival. This success not only gives the people living in its watershed much to be proud of but also offers a shining example of urban river revival that serves as a beacon of hope throughout the world. Murray put this achievement into perspective this way: "The Rouge is the connective tissue not only for the 1.5 million people who live in the basin, but the tissue that connects one generation to the next."

For over four decades, Murray has worked tirelessly to clean up the Rouge River. Indeed, thanks to his leadership and the partnerships he forged, the EPA is now heralding the Rouge River cleanup effort as a

Jim Murray on the banks of the Rouge River at Henry Ford Estate in Dearborn, Michigan
ASSOCIATED PRESS/CARLOS OSORIO

national model and a blueprint for success on a watershed scale. Looking back, Murray is so pleased that Friends of the Rouge has continued to grow in influence and impact thirty-five years after its creation, and that people now think of the Rouge River less in terms of Rust Belt pollution and more as a healthy ecosystem that provides many benefits and enhances their quality of life. Evidence of people taking pride in their river can now be seen throughout the watershed. And this brings a smile to Jim Murray's face.

CHAPTER 8

Richard Micka

River Raisin Champion

Native people called it "Nummasepee" (River of Sturgeon) because of the large number of sturgeon that came up the river to spawn. When the French colonized the area in the late 1600s, they called it "La Rivière au Raisin" (River of Grapes) because the trees along the river were draped in vines heavy with wild grapes. Today, the river is called River Raisin.

This waterway is in the southeastern portion of Michigan's Lower Peninsula with the watershed extending into five counties and even dipping into a small portion of northern Ohio. The river flows into western Lake Erie in Monroe, Michigan, the county seat for its namesake county. The town was established in 1817 as one of the first steps in the organization of the Michigan Territory following the War of 1812 and was named for then President James Monroe.

Not too long after pioneers settled alongside or near the River Raisin, they dammed it and built grist mills across it. These buildings were water-powered mills that ground grains. The word "grist" meant cereal grains that have been separated from their chaff and then ground into flour. In 1834, the first paper company was located on the south bank of the river several miles from Monroe. At least twelve paper companies followed, producing cardboard boxes, newsprint, wrapping paper, binder cardboard, liner board, fiber board, cereal cartons, recycled fiber, and more.

The town, strategically located on Lake Erie and at the mouth of the River Raisin, provided a natural harbor. Water helped provide early competitive advantage for many industries. In 1916, an automotive equipment company was established in Monroe. In 1927, a furniture-making business that would soon grow into Lay-Z-Boy Inc., with retail stores and manufacturing facilities in North America, Europe, and Asia, set up shop here. Then in 1929, a steel plant opened. This industrial growth required energy, and in 1971 the fourth largest coal-fired power plant in the United States came online at the mouth of the river. A roofing shingles company and wind turbine manufacturing company would follow in more recent years.

This long history of industrial development eventually took its toll on the River Raisin, leaving behind a legacy of pollution, primarily from paper mills and automotive manufacturing. This legacy pollution earned the River Raisin designation as a Great Lakes AOC from the International Joint Commission in 1985. The Michigan Department of Natural Resources, in cooperation with U.S. EPA, responded by committing to develop and implement a RAP to restore the river's impaired beneficial uses. The environmental problems included heavy metals and polychlorinated biphenyl (PCB) contamination of the sediments and the water column (pollutants that contributed to reproductive failure of bald eagles), excess sediment runoff from sources outside of the AOC, and PCB contamination of fish, making them unhealthy for people to eat.

One person stood out during this massive cleanup effort for his commitment and tenacity—Richard Micka. But he was no newcomer to protection of natural resources. By the time the RAP started, Micka already had over twenty years of conservation and environmental advocacy work under his belt.

From Outdoorsman to Conservationist to Environmentalist

Micka was born in 1938 in Monroe, which in addition to its industrial history, was the site of the Battle of River Raisin, the largest battle ever fought on Michigan soil, during the War of 1812. Monroe was also the childhood home of General George Armstrong Custer, who distinguished himself in the Civil War, but led his men to death in the Battle of the Little Big Horn, also known as Custer's Last Stand, where the combined forces of the Lakota, Northern Cheyenne, and Arapaho defeated the U.S. Calvary in 1876.

From a young age Micka worked in his father's butcher shop in downtown Monroe, washing what seemed to be an endless supply of meat pans, pots, and cutlery used to dress meat and prepare it in a fashion appealing to all that walked in the door. He was befriended by a French butcher named Robert Duvall, who was an amazing outdoor storyteller and helped inspire Micka's love for the great outdoors. Duvall's stories were so captivating that they motivated Micka to jump on his bicycle, any chance he got, to explore the amazing natural resources surrounding his home. These included the River Raisin, the marshes that formed its delta, numerous creeks that fed Lake Erie, and the amazing wetlands that dominated the lake's western shoreline. The Monroe marshes were a nationally famous duck hunting mecca, totaling over 5,000 acres of wild celery, wild rice, and American lotus beds. Wild celery is a submerged aquatic plant whose underground stem, called a tuber, is a favorite food of diving ducks, along with wild celery seeds that are produced each fall.

Back then boys had the freedom to ride bikes and hike anywhere they wanted to. Micka fondly remembers riding his bike two miles to Stoney Creek in the summer and catching his first fish, an eighteen-inch northern pike—a monster catch by any boy's standard. In the winter, when ice formed on the creeks, he would ride his bike on the creeks, his rubber bicycle tires slipping and sliding while he heard the unsettling sounds of ice cracking, all the way down to Lake Erie to explore and look for waterfowl. As a young boy, he was always outside.

One day at the age of ten, he walked out of the butcher shop with his father and was surprised with how dark it was outside, especially considering the sun had not gone down. To Micka it was like a grayish black veil had just been pulled over the sky. But as they looked up and to their astonishment, they realized that the sky was blackened with millions of waterfowl migrating south. What an amazing, awe-inspiring moment. Micka notes that "this single breathtaking experience gave him a sense of wonder that lives within him to this day."

Micka attended Monroe Catholic Central High School and went on to graduate from the University of Detroit. Attending university near his home provided him the opportunity to regularly get out into the woods and marshes and feed his need to recharge in nature. He feels strongly that people today do not go outside enough, nor pay attention to what is happening outdoors.

According to Micka, no single moment or event propelled him to become a conservationist, but rather a series of outdoor experiences and relationships with people who loved the outdoors. Other compelling outdoor memories from his youth include lantern fishing for bullhead in Sterling State Park and night fishing for blue pike (now extirpated) off the pier at Pelee Island, both in western Lake Erie, and visiting his Uncle George, who was a farmer who took impeccable care of his land and believed in stewardship through best management practices.

Soon Micka was exposed to waterfowl hunting and learned the art of punting. Punting involves using a long pole to propel and deftly maneuver a flat-bottomed boat through marshes and other shallow waters. To him, punting gives you the opportunity to look and listen to the beauty of nature. It develops your outdoor senses, and you see and learn something new all the time. Waterfowl hunting soon became a life-long passion, and it soon brought him in contact with a local Michigan Department of Natural Resources biologist named Jim Foote.

At an early age Foote began carving duck decoys as part of his love of hunting. After enlisting in the Navy at the age of seventeen and serving in World War II, he returned home and earned bachelor and master degrees in wildlife management from the University of Michigan. He then took a job with the Michigan Department of Natural Resources, working as a biologist at the Pointe Mouillee (moo-YAY) State Game Area—one of Micka's favorite hunting areas—for twenty-seven years. In those same years, he grew into a self-trained, world-class bird carving artist. Foote won many decoy competitions in the 1970s, including two from the Ward

World Championship Competitions in 1973 and 1975 in the Decorative Decoy Pairs competition, and went on to become an outdoor legend.

The friendship between Foote and Micka blossomed because of their mutual love of natural resources and a passion for hunting and fishing. Foote was instrumental in teaching Micka about conservation and helping him grow into a fierce champion for protecting the beloved wetlands, creeks, river, and lake that he explored during his youth. Soon Micka grew into an avid conservationist and environmentalist who worked with local duck hunters in a seventeen-year battle to protect and restore Pointe Mouillee. This initiative would become one of the world's largest marsh restoration efforts in the 1970s.

Saving Pointe Mouillee

Indigenous peoples long marveled at the western Lake Erie delta and wetlands near the mouths of the Huron and Detroit rivers for their diverse and abundant populations of wildlife and fish. The Potawatomi and the Wyandot both occupied the area long before French explorers and colonists came in the seventeenth century in search of beaver pelts. The early French settlers called it Pointe Mouillee, meaning "wet point."

Scientifically, the area can best be described as a continentally significant stopover habitat on the migratory bird flyway for vast numbers of waterfowl, raptors, and songbirds. Early reports from Pointe Mouillee note that on a quiet day during waterfowl migration, you could hear tens of thousands of ducks and geese quacking and cackling from a mile away. Wetlands and wild rice beds were so thick that men in waders had to remove the plants by hand so that hunters could pass in their boats. Just as Micka and his father were amazed at the migrating birds darkening the sky, local hunters told stories of seeing rafts of ducks so extensive that when they lifted off the wetlands they turned the sky grayish black. But today Pointe Mouillee bears little resemblance to the natural marshland that Native Americans, early French settlers, early hunters, and Micka marveled at—for it has gone through major changes.

Today it is known locally as the "Big Banana"—a banana-shaped, 3.5-mile set of armored dikes that function like a long, narrow barrier island to protect the marshland. In total, 97 percent of the coastal wetlands along the Detroit River and 90 percent of the coastal wetlands along western Lake Erie have been lost to human development. It should be no surprise that this remaining marshland contributes substantially to continentally significant biodiversity in western Lake Erie, heralded in the North American Waterfowl Management Plan, the United Nations Convention on Biological Diversity, the Western Hemispheric Shorebird Reserve Network, and the Important Bird Area Program of Michigan Audubon. From an airplane it looks like an ecological jewel sandwiched between the major metropolitan areas of Toledo, Ohio, and Detroit, Michigan.

In the early nineteenth century, descendants of those French settlers lived in cabins on the islands and beaches, making a living by market hunting for waterfowl and other game for money, and serving as guides for those who, in the middle of the nineteenth century, came into this region to hunt recreationally. Pointe Mouillee was first purchased in 1872 by William O. Hall for duck hunting. In 1875, Hall partnered with E. H. Gilman to amass 1,200 acres in the area and formed the Big Eight Shooting Club. This club was then expanded in 1879 to include ten wealthy businessmen from Michigan, New York, and Ohio, and renamed the Pointe Mouillee Shooting Club. As an exclusive hunting and shooting society, it even employed punters and cooks to ensure world-class hunting and memorable culinary experiences. The wealthy hunters came to the area during the spring and fall, when they used decoys to attract migrating waterfowl. There were no bag limits in nineteenth and early twentieth centuries, and they used punt guns with bore diameters as large as two inches that could fire over one pound of shot at a time to shoot large numbers of waterfowl. These weapons were eventually outlawed in 1918. More land was acquired over time, to help solidify the club's reputation as one of the most prestigious in North America. Indeed, it often was referred to as the world center of market hunting, supplying even the White House and Buckingham Palace with canvasback ducks.

It remained a private shooting club from 1875 to 1945 during what is considered the golden age of waterfowl hunting. In 1945, the State of Michigan bought 2,608 acres from the Pointe Mouillee Shooting Club and established the Pointe Mouillee State Game Area. Sixty-nine percent of the funds came from Michigan Department of Conservation's Game Division, 18 percent from the Federal Aid to the Preservation of Wildlife Act, and 13 percent from State of Michigan fishery programs for public recreation and trust (Fine, 2012). Managed waterfowl hunting started that year under the direction of the Michigan Department of Conservation, now called the Michigan Department of Natural Resources. Soon after, in 1947, avid hunters created the Michigan Duck Hunters' Tournament and the Pointe Mouillee Waterfowl Festival, which became nationally recognized and continues today, passing on a passion for waterfowl hunting and its traditions.

However, the quality of the hunting experience at Pointe Mouillee declined in the 1950s as high water levels in western Lake Erie eroded the natural protective barrier beaches through wind and wave action. It was generally agreed during that time that a combination of record high water levels in western Lake Erie and dams on the Huron River caused the erosion of large sections of the barrier beaches that led to loss of marsh habitat. Henry Ford and others had begun to build dams on the Huron River in the 1930s, altering the flow and sedimentation patterns in western Lake Erie. Over time, less sediment was entering western Lake Erie to replenish the barrier beaches that allowed the marsh vegetation to flourish. Then in 1952, several large storms breached the barrier beaches and diminished the marshes.

In the 1950s, the Port of Detroit tried to develop the land around Pointe Mouillee but was unsuccessful. Sportsmen's groups strongly opposed the port's planned development because the area had been purchased with public funds designated for hunting and other recreational benefits for all people. Sportsmen's advocacy for the preservation of Pointe Mouillee for public outdoor recreation culminated in 1960 with the founding of the Pointe Mouillee Waterfowlers' Association, affiliated with the Michigan United Conservation Clubs and the National Wildlife Federation. It was dedicated to the restoration of this marshland. Founding members included Micka, Hy Dahlka, Leonard Manaassa, Dick Whitwam, Ron Gorski, Jerry Ansman, and Don Girard.

By the early 1960s, these sportsmen were lobbying U.S. Secretary of Interior Stewart Udall, Michigan Governor G. Mennen Williams, and U.S. Congressman John D. Dingell to restore the Pointe Mouillee marshland by building a barrier dike. In response, the first artificial dikes were constructed at Pointe Mouillee in 1963, reestablishing 365 acres of marshland in one unit (Hartig, 2014). Water levels within this area could now be managed independently of Lake Erie by pumps and dewatering practices.

Then in 1966, in response to public outrage over the disposal of contaminated, dredged sediment in the open waters of the Great Lakes, President Lyndon Johnson signed an executive order banning such practices. Governments had no choice but to find places to confine contaminated sediment. Their solution was to construct confined disposal facilities that would isolate contaminated sediment, much like the efforts to curtail the spread of infectious diseases by quarantining the sick. The unique confluence of strong hunter advocacy to restore Pointe Mouillee marshland and governmental need to confine contaminated sediments led to one of the largest marsh restoration projects in the world. The solution to both problems was to construct seven hundred acres of diked disposal areas consisting of five cells that would eventually contain 18 million cubic yards of contaminated dredged material from the Rouge and Detroit rivers.

With the support of U.S. Senator Robert Griffin, the Pointe Mouillee Confined Disposal Facility was authorized by the River and Harbor Act of 1970 and constructed by the U.S. Army Corps of Engineers. The 3.5 miles of diked disposal cells were constructed during 1976–1981 at a cost of $45.5 million (Hartig, 2014). As part of a win-win solution, these cells would double as a wave barrier, enabling the re-establishment of marshland at Pointe Mouillee State Game Area in support of sustaining a world-class hunting heritage. The perimeter and cross dikes were constructed of clay and various sized limestone, along with filter fabric, to prevent the contaminated material from leaking and to resist wave action.

In 1974, Micka was honored as Conservationist of the Year by Michigan United Conservation Clubs for his tenacious and longstanding advocacy for preserving Pointe Mouillee. Today, the area continues to provide world-class, close-to-home hunting opportunities to nearly seven million people within a forty-five-minute driving distance. Indeed, this area was designated by Ducks Unlimited in 2011 as one of the top ten urban waterfowl hunting areas in the United States. The annual tradition of the Pointe Mouillee Waterfowl Festival has been sustained for over seventy years, still attracting 7,000 to 8,000 people each year.

Cleanup of the River Raisin

Like many North American cities, Micka's hometown of Monroe went on to lose many steel, paper, and automotive industries, and the jobs they provided, in the 1970s and 1980s. When the paper mills and automotive plants eventually closed, they left behind a legacy of pollution. Micka stepped up and became the compelling voice for cleanup and restoration. In the early 1980s, he got involved in the Shorelands Advisory Council to the State of Michigan, working on setbacks to protect shorelands. He has been involved from the very beginning of the River Raisin RAP, first giving testimony on beneficial use impairments in 1986 and then joining the River Raisin Public Advisory Council.

The initial RAP for the river was completed in 1987 and has been updated periodically. The AOC is located entirely within the city of Monroe. Its boundaries are the lower 2.6 miles of the River Raisin, downstream from Dam No. 6 at Winchester Bridge in the city of Monroe, and extending one-half mile out into Lake Erie following the Federal Navigation Channel and along the nearshore zone of Lake Erie one mile north and south.

Today, all cleanup and restoration work called for in the RAP has now been completed. They included $45 million of upgrades at the Monroe

Contaminated sediment remediation in the lower River Raisin, 2016
MICHIGAN DEPARTMENT OF ENVIRONMENT, GREAT LAKES, AND ENERGY

Metropolitan Wastewater Treatment Plant, $43.1 million of contaminated sediment remediation, and $7 million of habitat restoration and dam removal to open the river to an additional twenty-three miles for Great Lakes fish migration and spawning (Foose et al., 2019).

The remediation of contaminated sediment alone was a massive effort that took three decades to complete. It required the Ford Motor Company to remove 26,200 cubic yards of PCB-contaminated sediment at a cost of $6 million in 1997, and then fifteen years later, the U.S. Army Corps of Engineers had to perform a strategic dredging project that removed 69,000 more cubic yards of PCB-contaminated sediment at a cost of $800,000. Unfortunately, these efforts did not eliminate the problem, and the federal and state governments, in a partnership with Ford, remediated another 125,000 cubic yards at a cost of $36.3 million in from 2012 to 2016.

The fish passage project was particularly significant. Andrew Mc-Dowell, a landscape architect and conservationist who worked on the fish passage project, had this to say about its significance:

> Providing fish passage over, around, and through eight dams is an important and defining moment for the River Raisin and the Great Lakes. By reconnecting the lower twenty-three river miles of the River Raisin, the state-threatened lake sturgeon can reclaim part of their former spawning territory, as well as numerous other fish, wildlife, plant communities, and people will benefit from this project. This is an impressive and strategic process to restore natural systems that have been severely disturbed. This project is a compelling story of healing, humility, and hope: healing through providing fish passage and creating the conditions to restore natural systems critically disturbed by unsustainable development practices for the lower twenty-three miles of the River Raisin; humility to accept that despite the many innovations produced by our Western culture, we have not done enough to support natural systems; and hope that the future will only continue to strengthen the relationship between humans and nature.

In total, more than $43 million in Great Lakes Restoration Initiative funding alone was provided to accelerate remediation and restoration. Micka notes that "this federal investment of money was essential to catalyze cleanup partnerships and move from planning to implementation." Today, much to his pleasure, bald eagles have returned to Monroe County after an absence of more than twenty-five years and are now fledging over fifteen young per year (Foose et al., 2019). Both new and long-absent fish species can now be found in the river. Gar pike and crappie are just two of the species that have returned following the cleanup. Remember that Native Americans called the River Raisin *Nummaseppe* (River of Sturgeon). Micka's hope is that one day he will see once again sturgeon running his beloved river. He notes: "Maybe one day the woods will sing once again with the music of the sturgeon! When spawning in the early days, the sturgeon was so thick, the Potawatomi and Wyandot could hear them rubbing against each other making a sound that reverberated through the woods."

River Cleanup Leads to Reconnecting People to the River Raisin and Waterfront Revitalization

However, Micka was still not done. Like many other North American cities, for decades Monroe turned its back on the river. More recently, the city has been developing greenways like the River Raisin Heritage Trail to help improve public access to the waterfront and to strategically link community, business, historical, and recreational assets.

After much of the industry left town, the city came to realize that it had many unique assets that could serve as the foundation for revitalization efforts. Among these assets are ones near and dear to Micka's heart—the creeks, river, and lake, the city's history, which he and his wife Jeanne cherish, and exceptional, outdoor recreation right in their backyard. Monroe's master plan now guides development with the goal of making the city a vibrant community that preserves its natural resources and history, while welcoming new development. For example, Monroe has nine properties listed on the National Register of Historic Places, including three historic districts and six historic sites. General

George Custer in memorialized in a prominent downtown statue. It also has significant water resources, including River Raisin, its 1,072-square-mile watershed, and Lake Erie.

The cleanup of the river has been an essential and integral part of this revitalization strategy. Monroe's master plan has championed improved recreational access to the River Raisin in the downtown so that people can enjoy riverfront gathering places. To increase recreational opportunities, the Downtown Development Authority is looking into ways to extend, increase use, and improve safety and aesthetics of the downtown riverwalk. According to the latest Parks Master Plan, the city is also planning to invest more than $3.5 million in two of its riverside parks—St. Mary's Park in downtown Monroe and Mill Race Park on the city's west side—within the next ten years. Plans include the installation of nature paths, boardwalks, and a kayak and canoe launch.

The City of Monroe also reports an increase in small business owners and developers inquiring about property for residential, dining, and retail development opportunities along the riverfront. A new restaurant has recently opened with an outdoor dining patio overlooking the river. Another dining establishment is relocating one block north to be closer to the river, again with an outdoor patio on its banks. Further, existing building owners have made riverfront improvements to their buildings to help strengthen connections to the river and help create a riverfront sense of place.

As part of its revitalization efforts, Monroe championed the establishment of the River Raisin National Battlefield Park in 2009 to celebrate the history of this battle. Richard and Jeanne Micka have been key local champions from the beginning. The city and Monroe County

Historical Society developed a heritage master plan to complement and reinforce the city's development master plan. Thanks to the Mickas' encouragement, both plans view the cleanup and restoration of the River Raisin as an integral part of a vibrant community with a sustainable economy.

Both Mickas are history buffs and reenactment aficionados. Richard has served as a member of the Michigan Historical Commission, and Jeanne has served on the Monroe Historical Commission. Today, the River Raisin National Battlefield Park is the only national park that is adjacent to an international wildlife refuge—the Detroit River International Wildlife Refuge—and a state park—Sterling State Park. Annual attendance at the national park has steadily increased from 36,206 people in 2011 to 238,813 in 2017 (Bentley et al., 2019). In total, 75.5 percent of the 2016 visitors were from outside of Monroe County, including forty-nine states (all but North Dakota) and twenty foreign nations. Much to the pleasure of the Mickas, by 2018 the National Battlefield Park was in the middle of a $100-million redevelopment effort aimed at enhancing the appeal of this historical site to tourists. It was kicked off with the purchase of twenty houses that will be demolished to make room for re-creation of historic Frenchtown and a $20-million educational center.

Economic benefits of River Raisin National Battlefield Park, based on a 2017 National Park Service model, have been estimated at $16.4 million in 2016. Michigan State University, in partnership with the park, projected in 2019 that annual attendance will eventually reach approximately 635,000. At this visitation rate, state and local economic impacts are projected at $31.6 million and $21.9 million, respectively (Bentley et al., 2019).

Richard Micka, who has dedicated his life to restoration of the River Raisin and surrounding areas
DOUG COOMBE PHOTOGRAPHY

Concluding Thoughts

Micka has been the single constant in saving Pointe Mouillee in the 1960s and 1970s, cleaning up the River Raisin from the 1980s to the 2010s, and now reconnecting people to these waterways and celebrating history and community in recent years. Clearly, an integrated approach to protecting the environment, celebrating history, enhancing the community, and furthering the economy is helping transform Monroe. The cleanup of the River Raisin was an integral and essential part of this revitalization strategy. As Mark Cochran, assistant city manager of Monroe, has said, "We are redefining Monroe from a Rust Belt city with a polluted river to a desirable urban community with outstanding natural resources, significant historical assets, and a growing, diverse economy."

Advocating every step of this journey has been Micka—the champion of the River Raisin. Today, he proudly stands guard on his beloved natural resources by continuing to serve as a member of the River Raisin Public Advisory Council and as a founding member and current chairman of the International Wildlife Refuge Alliance. He is truly a visionary and inspiration to others, showing how the determination, persistence, and advocacy of one person can make a difference in a river and community. His advice to the next generation of river champions is simple and to the point: "Provide compelling outdoor experiences for children at an early age and create programs and places that give compelling outdoor experiences and inspire a sense of wonder in children."

CHAPTER 9

Jane Goodman

Cuyahoga River Fighter

or thousands of years Native Americans have hunted, fished, and farmed in northeast Ohio. Attracted by the natural resources and water transportation, they lived in relative harmony with the land. The Haudenosaunee gave the river that winds its way through this region its name—Cuyahoga (Crooked River)—for its meandering ways. The waterway is a u-shaped, one-hundred-mile, low gradient river with a watershed of over eight hundred square miles. The river begins its journey as two branches near the Lake Erie plain, thirty miles east of its mouth at Cleveland. These two branches merge to form the mainstem, which heads south, away from Lake Erie. At Akron, the river is then forced north by the high ridge left by historical glaciers. It continues its journey through the Cuyahoga Valley National Park and into Cuyahoga County before pouring into Lake Erie.

In the 1700s, the Cuyahoga marked the American colonies' western border. The area around Cleveland was part of the colony of Connecticut's

Western Reserve, which encompassed approximately 3.3 million acres of land in what is now northeast Ohio. Toward the end of the eighteenth century, Connecticut sold the Western Reserve to the Connecticut Land Company. These speculators sent Moses Cleaveland to survey and divide the land into townships, laying the groundwork for the region's settlement and development.

The city of Cleveland was founded in 1796. It was named after Moses Cleaveland, but the original "a" was removed, it is said, by a printer, to save space. The city of Akron was established in 1825 along the Little Cuyahoga River, a strategic position at the point where the Cuyahoga would meet the new canal systems then being developed to open overland trade via the Ohio River. The opening of the Erie Canal in 1825 connected Lake Erie to the Atlantic Ocean. The opening of the Ohio and Erie Canal in 1832 connected Cleveland to the Ohio River. The Cuyahoga River provided the water for this canal between Akron and Cleveland. To handle the goods flowing into and out of Cleveland via the canal system, city residents created a maritime district near the mouth of the Cuyahoga River called the Flats. This name is a reference to the original state of the river mouth—a shallow, marshy area at the base of the valley.

The Flats surround the Cuyahoga River along its last few miles before it enters Lake Erie. The river was the original border between the city of Ohio, an independent municipality on the west bank, and the city of Cleveland on the east bank. These two cities competed fiercely over maritime and mercantile business until Ohio City was annexed to Cleveland in 1854. During the 1820s, the Flats became the center of industry and commerce. The original river mouth was nearly a mile west of its current location. However, the river was too winding to provide optimal access for large ships, so in 1827 a new, straight shipping channel was dug, bypassing what is now known as the Old River Channel. This improved channel helped attract shipping companies, docks, warehouses, and bars for sailors, and helped develop the city into a shipping powerhouse. Soon Cleveland became the most important city between Buffalo, New York, and Detroit, Michigan.

During the mid-1800s, Cleveland became one of the leading wooden shipbuilding centers on the Great Lakes, rivaling Buffalo and Detroit. While water transportation on both Lake Erie and the Ohio & Erie Canal did much to facilitate the early development of Cleveland, it took the appearance of the railroad, and later the synergy between rail and maritime shipping, to fully develop Cleveland's industrial base. For an entire century beginning in the 1860s, railroads served as the principal mode of transportation for goods and people to and from the city. Strategically located on Lake Erie, it became the inevitable meeting place of coal brought in by the railroads from mines in Pennsylvania, Ohio, Virginia, and Kentucky and the ores brought down by ship from the Lake Superior region. People came, settled, worked, prospered, and developed Cleveland into an industrial powerhouse, with the Cuyahoga River, where rail and water met, at its center.

From 1860 to 1930, the city and its riverbanks were dominated by heavy industry, most notably steel, petroleum, chemical products, paint, and automobiles. Ironworks and steel mills had a major presence in the Flats. In 1863, John D. Rockefeller and his business partners entered the oil refining business in Cleveland. Demand for oil was rapidly increasing, particularly kerosene as an inexpensive fuel for household lighting in a period prior to electrification. In 1870, Rockefeller and his partners organized the Standard Oil Company and developed its refinery on the banks of the Cuyahoga. By 1884, Cleveland was considered the oil capital of the world, with eighty-eight oil refineries. Sherwin-Williams set up its paint production facility on the Cuyahoga's east bank in 1870. However, Cleveland's prosperity and wealth were facilitated, in large part, by the ability to dispose of waste into the river at no financial cost or consequence—at least not for the businesses doing the dumping.

Affluence Begets Effluents

As Cleveland grew into an industrial powerhouse, the shipping channel and the Flats became grossly polluted with industrial waste. The lower Cuyahoga River, sitting at the bottom of a valley, was not readily visible to most of the population. For those who did witness the pollution, they felt that it was just part of the cost of doing business. Growing public awareness of water pollution in Lake Erie and the Cuyahoga River during the 1960s led to substantial public outcry. During the mid-1960s, the Federal Water Pollution Control Administration—the predecessor of the U.S. Environmental Protection Agency—characterized the Cuyahoga River as one of the most polluted rivers in the United States. Then on June 22, 1969, the Cuyahoga River caught on fire for the thirteenth and last time.

Yes, the Cuyahoga River caught on fire thirteen times in the previous century. But the 1969 fire was different from the others in that it ignited national outrage over water pollution. What probably happened is that oil and oil-soaked, wooden debris caught on fire from a spark from a passing train. Flames climbed five stories high before a fireboat brought the conflagration under control. The sight of a river on fire must have been incredible, but so must have been the smell. The aroma of burning oil is unmistakable, like that of an asphalt parking lot being resurfaced or roofing tar being spread on a hot day, but stronger. The blaze lasted just

Picture taken shortly after the Cuyahoga River fire on June 22, 1969
CLEVELAND PUBLIC LIBRARY, PHOTOGRAPH COLLECTION

thirty minutes, but it did approximately $50,000 of damage, principally to two railroad bridges crossing the river.

The 1969 Cuyahoga River fire was a catalyst for change because of a perfect storm of circumstances that drew national attention to the fire and the city (Adler, 2002). The August 1, 1969, issue of *Time Magazine* rolled out a new environment section that featured the river's pollution. The story read: "No Visible Life. Some river! Chocolate-brown, oily, bubbling with subsurface gases, it oozes rather than flows. *Anyone who falls into the Cuyahoga does not drown*, Cleveland's citizens joke grimly. *He decays*. The Federal Water Pollution Control Administration dryly notes: *The lower Cuyahoga has no visible life, not even low forms such as leeches and sludge worms that usually thrive on wastes.* It is also—literally—a fire hazard." This issue was one of the most widely read at a time because it also featured the return of Apollo 11 from the moon and Senator Ted Kennedy's car accident in Chappaquidick, which resulted in the death of twenty-eight-year-old female passenger.

The 1969 fire helped awaken the nation to widespread environmental degradation. Indeed, this disaster became a national symbol of industrial indifference and the weakness of public regulation. It should be noted that in November 1968, the year before, Cleveland residents passed a $100 million bond issue to finance river protection and cleanup efforts, including sewer improvements, stormwater controls, harbor improvement facilities, and debris removal (Adler, 2002). The fire then catalyzed the passage of the National Environmental Policy Act in 1970, the Clean Water Act and the U.S.–Canada Great Lakes Water Quality Agreement in 1972, and the Endangered Species Act in 1973. The environmental movement needed a poster child and the burning Cuyahoga River became it.

Public Outcry Leads to River Cleanup

During the 1960s, Cleveland was referred to as the "Mistake on the Lake" because it was a city of many misfortunes, most notably the 1969 fire. But its misfortune had some positive results. During the 1970s and early 1980s much effort was placed on regulating and controlling discharges from industries and municipal wastewater treatment plants. Governments soon recognized, however, that a much broader effort would be needed to clean up the river. In 1985, as a result of a recommendation from the International Joint Commission's Great Lakes Water Quality Board, the State of Ohio committed to developing a RAP to clean up the Cuyahoga River AOC and three others under the auspices of the U.S.–Canada Great Lakes Water Quality Agreement. The parties to the agreement

Table 4. Beneficial Use Impairments Identified in the Cuyahoga River RAP
Restrictions on fish and wildlife consumption
Degradation of fish populations
Fish tumors or other deformities
Degradation of benthos—invertebrate animals that live on the river bottom
Restrictions on dredging activities
Eutrophication or undesirable algae
Beach closings (recreational contact) and public access and recreation
Degradation of aesthetics
Loss of fish habitat

emphasized developing a RAP that local stakeholders, who were the very ones who would be implementing it, would accept yet that would also win the support of state and federal governments.

In 1988, the Ohio Environmental Protection Agency (Ohio EPA) appointed a thirty-three-member planning group called the Cuyahoga River RAP Coordinating Committee (CCC) to help develop the plan. This body had a balanced representation of stakeholders to foster local ownership, ensure the coordination and integration called for by an ecosystem approach, and build support for implementation. In 1989, the nonprofit Cuyahoga River Community Planning Organization (later renamed Cuyahoga River Restoration) was created to support the RAP's activities.

As with all RAPs, the goal of this one was to restore all impaired beneficial uses (table 4), prevent further pollution and degradation, and protect the resource for future generations. The CCC completed an initial Stage 1 RAP that identified use impairments and causes in 1992 and updated it in 1996. A Stage 2 RAP that identified necessary cleanup and restoration actions was completed in 2013 and updated in 2015.

A Fighter Steps Forward

Many people have played key roles in the cleanup of the Cuyahoga River, but one stands out—Jane Goodman. Goodman is an unabashed workaholic. Her proof, she says, is that it has only been twenty seconds since she last checked her email. By day she works as the executive director of Cuyahoga River Restoration, a nonprofit organization working to restore, protect, and revitalize the Cuyahoga River watershed. By night and on weekends, she serves as a councilperson for South Euclid, Ohio, an inner-ring suburb of Cleveland. She has held these two positions since 2006. Her unique skill set as an experienced executive director, a seasoned environmental educator, and a skilled politician make her an ideal person to bring people, businesses, and organizations together to sustain cleanup efforts and promote stewardship of the river that has and always will define Cleveland.

Goodman views her path toward environmentalism as a collection of beads added, one by one, to a string, each bead a learning experience. "I'd always been somewhat of a tomboy, and some of my fondest childhood memories involve catching tadpoles in wetlands near my home in Beachwood before suburbanization there took hold," she remembers. That was her wetland bead. "My father and I had a Sunday morning ritual of driving out to 'the country' through the densely forested areas east of Cleveland, and these experiences with my father led me to love trees." That was her tree bead. By 1970, she was in college at Northwestern University participating in the first Earth Day, and that event started her seeing the world through a green lens—her planet Earth bead. A few years later she was back in Cleveland when her mother called her to her parents' apartment, which overlooked a beautiful wetland. Her mother cried out, "They're bulldozing it!" and worried about what would happen to the geese and other wildlife that lived there. That wetland is now the Beachwood Place mall, and its loss added Goodman's conservation bead. In later years, rafting the Colorado, she added a water conservation bead on the string. By 1990, she had returned to Cleveland for good and became involved in organizing the twentieth Earth Day celebration. "Since then, with the last bead in place, you could say I've converted to environmentalism as my religion," she concludes.

Although Goodman cannot identify a single turning point that instantly made her a Cuyahoga River fighter, two experiences with 1976 elections nudged her along her journey to environmental activism. She worked on both U.S. Senator Howard Metzenbaum's (Ohio) campaign staff and Congressman Mo Udall's (Arizona) presidential campaign team. Both were vocal environmentalists, and each had urged her to adopt a cause and fight for it. Because Goodman was from Cleveland, the most obvious environmental problem was the Cuyahoga River. That same year, also in the context of the elections, she met Virginia Aveni, an Ohio state representative and environmental advocate from Cleveland. Goodman was drawn to Aveni's advocacy on behalf of the river. The first thing that Goodman did when she was offered a job with the river organization thirty years later was to call Aveni, who also happened to be one of the original founders of the cleanup effort called the Cuyahoga River RAP. Aveni said "do it," and Goodman accepted the job.

To some, it may sound easy to clean up a river known nationally for its water pollution, but it is not. There is no quick fix, considering the time it takes to build trust among stakeholders, reach agreement on problems, identify and select remedial and preventive actions, and secure funding for implementation, especially given all the competing interests for funding. Goodman describes the process this way: "Restoring, revitalizing, and protecting a river is like peeling an onion. As soon as you get a layer off, there could be something else underneath."

She readily acknowledges that she cannot take credit for the cleanup of the Cuyahoga. Indeed, she feels that she stands on the shoulders of many people who have come before her. By the time she joined the Cuyahoga River Community Planning Organization as outreach and education director in 2006, the river was already well on the way to recovery thanks to the contributions of many. The organization was beginning to identify specific things that needed to be done to reach the federal and state restoration targets, and it needed to develop programs and actions to meet those targets and improve the general state of health of the Cuyahoga watershed. She had previously developed urban forestry outreach and education programs at Clean-Land and Ohio/ParkWorks, and those skills were important to improving riparian, stream health. Goodman's major contribution has been to further watershed restoration and raise awareness among the public.

Cuyahoga River Restoration has effectively involved stakeholders, established local ownership, fostered a spirit of cooperation, and laid the foundation for implementation of necessary cleanup and restoration actions. Goodman's role as executive director of the organization is to educate and involve watershed stakeholders, support and facilitate the work of the Advisory Committee and tributary groups, raise funds, and manage programs and projects on behalf of the river. She notes: "By cleaning up the river and no longer contributing to the degradation, it's allowing our river and lake to recover. If you stop poisoning it, the river can recover."

Working Together

Under the leadership of Cuyahoga River Restoration, Ohio Environmental Protection Agency, and many other partners, much pollution prevention and control has been accomplished. For example, the Northeast Ohio Regional Sewer District has spent over $2 billion on wastewater treatment facilities and collection system improvements since 1972 (Goodman and Gigante, 2019). In addition, the district has spent over $850 million reducing CSOs by nearly 50 percent. These overflows occur in sewerage systems that carry both sanitary sewage and stormwater runoff and are the portion of the flow which goes untreated to receiving streams or lakes when heavy rain overloads the system's capacity. The district is now implementing its Combined Sewer Overflow Long Term Control Plan over a twenty-five-year period at a cost of $3 billion. The City of Akron is also implementing a similar plan at a cost of $890 million.

River sediments have been another problem. The lower six miles of the Cuyahoga River are designated as a federal navigational channel and require a minimum water depth of twenty-three feet to support transportation for industry and commerce. The upper portions of the river annually deposit considerable amounts of sediment into the federal navigational channel, requiring the U.S. Army Corps of Engineers to dredge approximately 225,000 cubic yards each year to maintain the necessary twenty-three-foot depth for freighters (Goodman and Gigante, 2019). From 1979 to 1999, these sediments were deemed contaminated and had to be placed in an eighty-eight-acre confined disposal facility along the Cuyahoga River. From 1999 to 2011, they had been taken to another confined disposal facility near Cleveland's Burke Lakefront

Airport. In 2011, the Ohio Environmental Protection Agency determined that the dredged sediment was clean enough to be used on industrial and commercial sites. In one case, approximately 300,000 cubic yards of dredged sediment was used to remediate a brownfield site at the Cuyahoga Valley Industrial Center. At least 20 percent of the dredged sediment still does not meet standards for open lake disposal.

The Great Lakes Restoration Initiative has funded over $7.5 million of habitat restoration and enhancement within the Cuyahoga River AOC, including the restoration of five acres of coastal wetlands (living filters and nurseries of life) and 1,500 feet of shoreline habitat for native plants and animals on lower Euclid Creek and the rehabilitation of nine hundred feet of shoreline habitat in headwaters (so important in protecting downstream portions of the watershed) of two Euclid Creek tributaries and 2,400 feet along Euclid Creek. Other successes include stream restoration for native fish in the Tinker's Creek watershed, enhancement of fish habitat along the Cuyahoga River Ship Canal, restoration of wetlands along Mill Creek, and control of invasive species and enhancement of riparian habitat in Cuyahoga Valley National Park (Goodman and Gigante, 2019).

Restoring the last few miles of the Cuyahoga River is even more challenging than the upstream areas, because they flow through Cleveland's industrial corridor, and the shoreline is dominated by steel and concrete bulkheads to hold back and stabilize the riverbanks and ensure clear passage for seven-hundred-foot-long lake carriers. These bulkheads provide no habitat for fish or other organisms. Cuyahoga River Restoration and its partners have implemented an innovative Habitat for Hard Places Program that enhances habitat in bulkheads to increase the survival of fish migrating through the area, as well as resident species. Think of these as truck stops or nurseries for fish. Essentially, Cuyahoga River Restoration is experimenting with creating small habitats for young fishes in the corrugations of bulkheads that will provide food for young fishes, places to hide from predator fishes, and places to rest on their long journey through the shipping channel.

The one project that Goodman is most proud of is Scranton Flats, where a former marina and some adjacent industrial land along the river channel were turned into fish spawning and nursery ground habitat. Previously a fenced off brownfield, the site is now an urban oasis complete with wildflowers and habitat for fish, frogs, and turtles along 3,000 feet of shoreline. The restoration of almost five acres of shoreline created a buffer zone that minimizes runoff and enhances fish and wildlife habitat. Here, urban stormwater sinks into the ground rather than pouring pollutants into the river.

In addition to creating a welcoming haven for wildlife, the Scranton Flats project also provided recreational benefits to humans, including access to birding and fishing, and it educates the public about local history, industry, and the environment through interpretive signage and displays. And there's more, because the inspiration for this habitat restoration project was not the river, but the Towpath Trail. A simple conversation between Cuyahoga River Restoration's former executive director and the director of the Towpath Trail, a shared recreational trail that generally follows the path of the 1832 Ohio & Erie Canal, led to forming a large coalition to build an urban greenway for bicycling, jogging, and walking, and for picnicking and just sitting along the river. The trail connects bicyclists and pedestrians in downtown Cleveland with neighborhoods south of downtown, and by 2025, all the communities along its more than one-hundred-mile length.

It is popular with walkers, joggers, and bicyclists, and in some sections, even horse riders.

Evidence of River Revival

"Fish are our benchmark, our canary in the coal mine," said Goodman. "If the fish are abundant, healthy and diverse, then that is a good sign." In 1969, when the Cuyahoga River last caught fire, there were few if any fish in the lower river. Fish monitoring in the natural river and the ship channel by Ohio Environmental Protection Agency and the Northeast Ohio Regional Sewer District has documented dramatic improvements both in numbers and in species. Today you can find seventy species of fish, including many pollution sensitive species like smallmouth bass (Goodman and Gigante, 2019). Recent fish surveys have found golden redhorse, greenside darter, and walleye—all considered pollution intolerant species—ten miles south of Cleveland. Pollution-sensitive small, bottom-dwelling creatures are now present in most reaches and now meet Ohio EPA's criteria for stream protection in many river segments. Peregrine falcons, bald eagles, and osprey have returned to the banks. Even the industrial Flats now has increased fish populations, resident blue and gray herons and cormorants, and seasonal visits from migrating birds and waterfowl. Fish have become so abundant toward the southern, upriver end of the AOC that park personnel enforce limits on net fishing in order to help sustain the recovery of the fishery. The dam in Cuyahoga Valley National Park, soon to be removed, has become a popular spot for steelhead fishing during the spawning season.

As of 2020, three of the original ten beneficial use impairments—degradation of aesthetics, restrictions on fish and wildlife consumption, and public access—were deemed no longer impaired and removed from the list. This means that the Cuyahoga River no longer has smelly sludge deposits or colorful oil sheens, and the contamination of fish and other wildlife has declined so that the health advisories are the same here as for the open lake. Now that the water is no longer repellant and dangerous, public access and recreation have improved through development of trails, rowing clubs, fishing areas, boating and paddle sports, and dining and entertainment facilities. However, much remains to be done to restore the remaining seven impaired beneficial uses. The target for removing those is 2024.

From Cleanup to Reconnecting People to the Cuyahoga to Waterfront Revitalization

Many American Rust Belt cities have risen high, fallen hard, and come back to life, but few rose so high or fell quite so far as Cleveland, Ohio. The fortunes of this city on the shores of Lake Erie have ebbed and flowed with its iconic river, the Cuyahoga. During much of the 1800s and the early 1900s, the Flats was ground zero for the second industrial revolution, with heavy industry, manufacturing, transportation, and warehousing. However, with the industrial decline after World War II, the Flats became a symbol of the aging Rust Belt, complete with massive environmental degradation. The burning of the Cuyahoga River in 1969 was a harsh symbol of Cleveland's decline. However, the river that was once a source of embarrassment is now a cause for celebration. As the river was cleaned up, people started calling for improved public access to it. Between the 1970s and 1990s, the Flats underwent a dramatic transformation from a manufacturing and distribution center to a district that combined restaurants, entertainment, and some housing with industrial and transportation activity. This redevelopment first peaked in the 1990s when the Flats were recognized as the region's entertainment mecca. Then in the early 2000s, the recession hit the area hard. Properties were neglected and crime moved in. Now, however, the Flats are experiencing another wave of transformation, with warehouses that once stored goods from the river's heyday as a maritime transportation center being converted into residential lofts and condos, restaurants, and event spaces. Investors are building major new developments along the channel, notably the Flats East Bank development and the Nautical Entertainment Complex at the mouth of the river.

Today, the area is a unique urban neighborhood where nature, commerce, and industry live together. Leading the current transformation is Flats Forward, a neighborhood organization dedicated to enhancing the quality of life and economic well-being of all Flats stakeholders. Established in 2012, this group has been building upon earlier community and economic development efforts, advocating for residents and businesses, and fostering strong neighborhood connections. It has documented that the area has experienced $750 million in economic development since 2012, including Flats East Bank, The Foundry, Settler's Point, Scranton Flats Towpath Trail, and Cleveland Foundation Centennial Trail (Goodman and Gigante, 2019). In addition, $270 million of new projects are in the planning phase.

This waterfront revitalization has attracted people who want to live, work, and play in the Flats. Visitation in 2016 was approximately 577,000 (Goodman and Gigante, 2019). In addition to the music venues and entertainment options, both banks of the Flats now host unique festivals year-round. Take-a-Hike walking tours afford visitors the opportunity to learn about the area's history. Other attractions include a

5,000-seat amphitheater called Jacobs Pavilion at Nautica, a repurposed power plant that houses the Greater Cleveland Aquarium and a party and conference center, the Nautica Queen cruise ship, the landing for Cleveland Metroparks' new water taxi, and a watersports rental facility (Flats Forward, 2018). Across the river, the Flats East Bank boardwalk offers pedestrians sweeping views of the Cuyahoga River and Cleveland's iconic bridges and provides dock space for transient boats.

Farther up the channel, Columbus Peninsula has become an outdoor recreational hub, including home to the Cleveland Rowing Foundation and The Foundry, which offers competitive rowing. The latter has the unique mission of reconnecting children to the Cuyahoga River and Lake Erie through rowing and sailing, inspiring a sense of wonder in them, helping develop a stewardship ethic, and literally changing lives. Columbus Peninsula is also where the foundation's annual Head of the Cuyahoga Regatta attracts rowing teams from across the country to compete each fall. The peninsula's Columbus Bridge area features Cleveland Metroparks' Rivergate Park and Merwin's Wharf restaurant, Hart Crane Park, Crooked River Skate Park, and the Ohio City Bicycle Coop. Connecting it all is a network of trails taking people to and through pocket parks and greenspaces. Eventually, trails will connect to the lakefront at Wendy Park.

A new consortium led by the city of Cleveland has begun the Vision for the Valley initiative to develop a master plan that integrates land and water all along the ship channel, recognizing that the perception of the Cuyahoga River has also changed in response to this revival and revitalization. People no longer see it as a polluted Rust Belt river, but an asset that helps sustain the economy, enhance the community and quality of life, and provide numerous ecosystem services and benefits to all. An important sign of this change in perception was the designation

Jane Goodman on the banks of the Cuyahoga River
PAUL SOBOTA

of the Cuyahoga River as one of fourteen American Heritage Rivers by presidential executive order.

"The comeback of the river has been a key contributor to the comeback of Cleveland," Goodman says proudly. You can see it from the headwaters, down the class V whitewater to the Gorge in Akron and Cuyahoga Falls, through the Summit Metro Parks, Cuyahoga Valley National Park, and Cleveland Metroparks reservations, and along the Ohio & Erie Canal Towpath Trail and the Cuyahoga Valley Scenic Railroad—all the waters that lead to Cleveland and Lake Erie.

Lessons Learned, the Next Challenge, and Advice to Others

Goodman believes that patience is not only a virtue, it's a requirement. Partners aren't just people who come to meetings; they're the people and organizations who help carry out cleanup and restoration efforts and programs. An important lesson she offers to activists is, "First, stop making it worse—enforce clean water laws. Then, do what you can to help nature and natural processes work as they're supposed to."

For Goodman, the next challenge for the Cuyahoga River is to think and act in terms of the whole watershed. "Scientists have shown that the health of the river is the result of the health of the watershed. New challenges will come up all the time. For example, climate change is here and affecting plants, animals, and humans. We need to encourage all watershed communities to do their part. One message we need to stress is that streams and forests are infrastructure and need to be treated as capital assets to be improved and maintained." Goodman's advice to the next generation of people who care about the Cuyahoga River and the Great Lakes is that they should: "Pay attention, and use your skills, whatever they are, to promote and carry out restoration and conservation. You don't have to have a degree in environmental science or even have taken a course. Get out there and participate in cleanups. If you like working with numbers, nongovernmental organizations and initiatives need people to do the books. If you write well, we need people to write grants, and articles, and outreach materials. Become an ambassador in your world." In terms of what people working to restore and protect other areas of the Great Lakes and other watersheds can learn from the Cuyahoga River, she says, "It helps to have a notorious event like a river fire to get attention. It helped us identify and make known the problem, which was the first step from which all the recovery flowed. So, let people know there's a problem, then give them mostly free rein to do what they do in service to the recovery."

CHAPTER 10

Jill Spisiak Jedlicka

Buffalo River Champion

During the 1800s, the city of Buffalo, New York, and its namesake river were well known as the terminus of the Erie Canal, the grain storage capital of the world, and the fourth largest port globally, giving it the title of "Queen City of the Lakes." Soon railroads would follow and flourish because of Buffalo's strategic location on the canal and between two Great Lakes—Erie and Ontario, its critical role in moving people and goods, and early advantages from hydropower provided by Niagara Falls. By the 1900s, the city would attract numerous industries, including automotive, steel, chemical, and oil, and became a thriving hub for retail and wholesale distribution. These industries would soon take a toll on the Buffalo River.

First, it must be recognized that this waterway is only about eight miles long. It has three tributaries: Cayuga, Buffalo, and Cazenovia Creeks. The river begins at the confluence of the Cayuga and Buffalo Creeks and flows through primarily industrial and residential areas to its mouth at Lake Erie. The watershed is only about 445 square miles, draining portions of Buffalo and Wyoming Counties in western New York. Like the Cuyahoga and the Rouge, the Buffalo's final 6.2 miles are a federal navigational channel, meaning it must be dredged to twenty-three feet to handle large vessels. The average annual flow of the Buffalo River is relatively low—approximately 525 cubic feet per second, with minimum annual flow of ten to twenty cubic feet per second. This small volume reflects that fact that it receives water from only three small tributaries. To put it into perspective, the flow of the Buffalo River is only 0.3 percent of that of the Niagara River.

History of Pollution

By the 1940s, both industrial and municipal waste was overwhelming this modest waterway. It may be an understatement to say that from the 1940s to 1960s, environmental issues did not have the same priority as economic development and technological progress. Jobs and bread on the table were the priorities and people ignored the pollution, except for a very few activists. The 1960s were the decade when the Buffalo River reached the apex of industrial pollution. Dr. Barry Boyer, former University of Buffalo law professor and long-time advocate for the river's restoration, commented that: "It had taken almost 150 years of abuse to make the Buffalo River 'normally' anoxic, toxic, and flammable" (Boyer, 2002). During the 1960s, the International Joint Commission reported that "the Buffalo River exhibited significant, objectionable pollution." Oil was the major pollutant during this time: "The Buffalo River is always coated with oil. The principal known sources of these oils are the

Pennsylvania Railroad shops, Mobil Oil Refinery, Donner-Hanna Coke plant, and Republic Steel Corporation" (International Joint Commission, 1967).

Because of these grossly polluted conditions, the Buffalo Stream Improvement Project was initiated in 1967. Its purpose was to draw water from Lake Erie to meet the manufacturing needs of five industries that, in turn, would discharge their increased volumes of wastewater to the river to maintain a minimum river flow of 160 cubic feet per second. This enhanced flow would help flush out pollutants. The prevailing wisdom, at that time, was that the solution to pollution was dilution. Despite these efforts, pollution continued and climaxed in January 1968 when, just like the Cuyahoga and Rouge Rivers would the following year, the Buffalo River caught on fire. This 1968 fire caused the South Park Avenue lift bridge to be closed for several days as officials investigated the damage. But the fire was no big deal in Buffalo; the local newspaper only gave it a three-inch column on the back page. Again, most people viewed the Buffalo River as a working river and pollution was just a by-product of industrialization. Oil spills were hardly news here. The regional engineer of the State Health Department echoed this sentiment: "It could have been just the normal oil load that happened to collect in that spot" (*Buffalo Courier-Express*, 1968).

The federal agency responsible for protecting water quality, the Federal Water Pollution Control Administration (FWPCA), had this to say about sorry state of the river during this time: "The Buffalo River is a repulsive holding basin for industrial and municipal wastes. It is devoid of oxygen and almost sterile. Oil, phenols, color, oxygen-demanding materials, iron, acid, sewage, and exotic organic compounds are present in large amount. . . . In places the river's surface is a boundless mosaic of color and patterns resulting from the mixture of organic dyes, steel mill and oil refinery wastes, raw sewage, and garbage" (U.S. Department of the Interior, 1968). To no one's surprise, the river at its worst was considered one of the most polluted waterways in the Great Lakes. People who lived near it complained angrily and loudly about the pollution, as the FWPCA acknowledged: "Residents who live along its backwaters have vociferously complained of the odors emanating from the river and of the heavy oil films" (U.S. Department of the Interior, 1968). Pressure was building to do something about a river that for decades had been a sacrificial lamb for economic progress.

The national awakening that brought so many groundbreaking federal environmental laws began reshaping politics in Buffalo as well. Demands to clean up the city's polluted waterway increased. Then in the 1980s, a recession weakened its economy and led to the closure of many industries, lessening the amount of waste going into the Buffalo River. It was at this point that the community began to envision a post-industrial future with a cleaner and more natural river. Soon a leader with a conservation and environmental pedigree would emerge to champion the cleanup effort and become a key player in the revitalization of Buffalo—Jill Spisiak Jedlicka.

Born to Lead

As a little girl, Jedlicka loved playing in the woods and along streams near her home in Lancaster, New York, part of the greater Buffalo area. She used to catch tadpoles and toads, take them home, and build little houses for them. Growing up, her parents often joked that her childhood interest in the environment and nature was simply because "ya know, it's in her blood . . . she's just like Uncle Stan."

Her Uncle Stan or Stanley Spisiak was an activist and legendary in this part of New York for his groundbreaking environmental activism ranging five decades—from the 1930s to the 1980s. He was even given the moniker "Mr. Buffalo River" for his crusading advocacy. During the 1950s and early 1960s, the city had no strong environmental watchdog groups, but Spisiak helped raise awareness of pollution and put pressure on governments and industries to stop it. He was born in 1916, the fifteenth of sixteen children born to Polish immigrants, and orphaned by the time he was sixteen years old. He credits one of his teachers in Folsomdale, New York—Mary Coyle—with mentoring him about conservation and inspiring him to become an advocate for the environment.

Following his graduation from Burgard Vocational High School, he enrolled at Millard Fillmore College at State University of New York. After taking a course in mineralogy and gaining some experience at the Buffalo Museum of Science, he went into the jewelry business with the sum of $1.96 (Sanders, 2012). Although selling jewelry was his occupation, environmental protection was his calling, including cleaning up the Buffalo and Niagara Rivers and Lake Erie. During those years, few people were concerned about the environment, and even fewer people were outspoken advocates for the environment and conservation.

For over fifty years, Spisiak filled that role, and his environmental activism is credited with attracting President Lyndon Johnson to witness the pollution of the Buffalo River on August 19, 1966. Spisiak got President Johnson aboard the U.S. Coast Guard cutter *Ojibwa*, along with First

Lady "Lady Bird" Johnson, New York Governor Nelson Rockefeller, and other key leaders, and had water and sediments hauled on board in a galvanized pail so that his guests could see firsthand how polluted they were. He dipped a wooden spoon into the pail of sediments and water and then pulled it out to show oil dripping from the spoon. Mrs. Johnson memorably described the Buffalo River sediments as a "bucket of slop" in response to this display. Spisiak told the party that this "bucket of slop" contained the type of material that was annually dredged from the Buffalo River and disposed in the open waters of Lake Erie. After that visit, President Johnson was so moved that when he went back to Washington, D.C., he signed a presidential executive order banning the open-water disposal of polluted sediments in Lake Erie. A jeweler from Buffalo, New York, had changed national environmental policy.

Despite being ambushed with filthy water and mud, the president and first lady appreciated Spisiak's advocacy. In 1966, Johnson honored him with a presidential "Water Saver of the Nation" award. Lady Bird Johnson had also bestowed on him the National Wildlife Foundation's "Water Conservationist of the Year" award. Spisiak expanded his environmental advocacy work by serving as chairman of the Water Resources Committee of the New York State Conservation Council. His grassroots advocacy, along with that of others across the nation, led to an environmental awakening that catapulted across the country and climaxed with the first Earth Day in 1970 and with the enactment of many environmental laws and the signing of an international agreement between the United States and Canada to protect the Great Lakes.

Jill Spisiak Jedlicka is Stanley's grandniece. What he was to his generation, Jill Spisiak Jedlicka is to hers—a leading force in the cleanup and stewardship of the Buffalo River. But it wasn't until high school that her love of the natural world morphed into something resembling a vocation. In fact, in her sophomore year, her public high school chose her to participate in a leadership conference in Seattle and Portland, Oregon. She was awestruck at the beauty and grandeur of the Pacific Northwest. This experience was an epiphany, when she realized that you must speak up for things you believe in. She went home to Buffalo determined to fight for the woods, waters, toads, and tadpoles that she so loved as a child.

Jedlicka went on to receive a bachelor of science in environmental studies and a master in business administration, both from the State University of New York at Buffalo. She continues to live in the Buffalo area, along with her husband and two children. Her professional work on the Buffalo River began in the late 1990s as an environmental education specialist with the Erie County Department of Environment and Planning. Her first project was community engagement and habitat restoration along the Buffalo River. In doing this work, she first encountered a small volunteer based nonprofit organization called the Friends of the Buffalo River. She went on to become a board member and spent many years learning from dedicated volunteers about the science and sociology of managing and restoring a polluted waterway. After five years with the county and her first maternity leave, she initially worked part-time as a project consultant for the Friends. Interestingly, her first project was coordinating the Buffalo River RAP—the blueprint for cleaning up the waterway. She would soon go on to lead this nonprofit organization and build it into an international model of river restoration and sustainability.

Remedial Action Plan

In 1985, the International Joint Commission's Great Lakes Water Quality Board reported that, despite implementation of regulatory pollution control programs, progress had stalled on the cleanup of forty-two Great Lakes AOCs, including the Buffalo River. In response, the state and federal governments committed to developing and implementing a RAP using an ecosystem approach. The combined Stage 1 and 2 Buffalo River RAP, which identified problems and causes, necessary remedial actions, and responsible parties, was completed in 1989. That same year, a group of concerned citizens came together and formed the Friends of the Buffalo River. The Stage 2 RAP addendum was completed in 2011 and has been updated periodically thereafter. These two plans identified several ecosystem problems or beneficial use impairments, all of which will be familiar by now. The fish and wildlife caught in or near the river tasted bad and restrictions on eating them were in force. Having lost much of their habitat, populations of wild creatures had fallen, and they suffered from tumors, deformities, and reproductive problems. The invertebrates living at the bottom of the river were in a similarly poor state. Aesthetically, the river was not appealing, and its sediments were so toxic that dredging had to be limited.

In the late 1980s, 1990s, and early 2000s, the New York State Department of Environmental Conservation served as the RAP coordinator, with public participation and input from a Remedial Advisory Committee. In 2003, the Friends of the Buffalo River, now called the Buffalo Niagara Waterkeeper, was the first nonprofit organization in the Great Lakes selected to re-energize the RAP process, coordinate implementation, and catalyze further progress—a leadership role that was normally carried by a government entity. That same year, Jedlicka became one of the first staff members of the organization and has been standing at the helm ever since. Today, the Buffalo Niagara Waterkeeper still fulfills this coordination role, but Jedlicka had to turn over the role of RAP coordinator to one of her colleagues when she stepped up to become the executive director in 2012.

Over a ten-year year period, including some bold and risky decisions, the Buffalo Niagara Waterkeeper helped form the Buffalo River Restoration Partnership. This unique public-private-nonprofit partnership was formalized by a cost-share agreement among Waterkeeper, the U.S. Environmental Protection Agency, the New York State Department of Environmental Conservation, the U.S. Army Corps of Engineers, and Honeywell. Waterkeeper brought citizens' voices to the table when key decisions needed to be made and helped find common ground among the partners when the whole effort was at risk of falling apart. The result was a decades-long project that secured $100 million in local, state, federal, and private corporation resources for contaminated sediment dredging, habitat restoration, and waterfront revitalization.

A good example of collaboration is in the mid-2000s when the U.S. Army Corps of Engineers signed a $2 million cost-share agreement with the Friends of the Buffalo River to study contaminated river sediments. This jump-started the remediation process, built trust, and proved that the nonprofit organization could deliver. Looking back, Jedlicka admits, "I laugh because at the time we didn't have two nickels to rub together." But she and her colleagues, frustrated by the slow pace of progress up to that time, wanted to make a public statement that a nonprofit organization could do this. They even convinced the New York State Department of Environmental Conservation to cover the local share for this study.

Top: Buffalo River before cleanup and restoration in 2013
BUFFALO NIAGARA WATERKEEPER

Bottom: After cleanup and revitalization in 2015
JOE CASCIO PHOTOGRAPHY

Indeed, the river revival has been dramatic. In 1968, when the Buffalo River caught on fire, there were no fish in the lower river. Today, you can find twenty-five to thirty species of fish, including the prized largemouth bass, a substantially improved invertebrate community with more pollution intolerant species like mayflies, and peregrine falcons that are reproducing after an over thirty-year absence. In addition, the recreational use and commercial redevelopment of its shorelines has brought hundreds of thousands of people to a riverfront that was once a dead zone.

Despite these improvements, two outstanding issues remain in the cleanup of the Buffalo River—combined sewer overflows (CSOs) and nonpoint source pollution, such as road runoff, pesticides, animal waste, and litter—what Jedlicka calls "all the stuff you cannot grasp." The Buffalo Sewer Authority has committed $500 million under a consent decree to stop the overflows through a combination of gray infrastructure (holding tanks) and green infrastructure (bioswales, rain gardens, porous surfaces). However, Jedlicka worries about complacency. If citizens get complacent, they will once again become apathetic and repeat past mistakes. No one wants to go through another $100 million cleanup. That's why it's important to develop a stewardship ethic and make sure that every person knows that they have a civic responsibility to care for the place they call home.

Lessons Learned

As the Buffalo Niagara Waterkeeper grew and evolved, the organization learned many things that can best be summarized as four strategies to guide community action for the greatest impact:

- Carry a Bold vision: "Things didn't always have to be the way they have always been on our waterfront," notes Jedlicka.
- Consistent communication and messaging: She says, "We have learned through trial and error how to communicate a bold vision to many different audiences. One of the best pieces of advice I had ever received from a former board member was to learn how to 'speak human' about our environmental challenges."
- Educate and engage the entire community: Jedlicka offers the following advice, "Engagement doesn't start and stop with the average citizen—it was also critical to get elected officials and business and civic leaders out of their offices and onto the water. You want to show them the great beauty or even the disgusting conditions. They have to see it, smell it, and experience it for themselves. Get them talking about their own memories. Make it personal."
- Advocacy is not a bad word: According to Jedlicka, "The most challenging part of guiding community action is focusing that energy and sustaining it for the long term. We have learned that people not only have to show up but speak up—frequently. Not necessarily to always fight against something, but to come to the table with possible solutions. Advocates raise awareness of an issue, and often times build the case for action or funding."

Jedlicka's advice to the next generation is clear and to the point: "If the community has the courage to lead, the leaders will follow. You don't have to be a professional environmentalist to improve the environment. We, as water advocates, do not champion our cause simply because it is our job or someone else has asked us to do it, but because we are driven by our own inspirations, our own stories, and our love of community.

Find your inspiration. Tell your story. Make positive change in your community."

From the outset, RAPs called for use of an ecosystem approach to solving aquatic ecosystem problems. That mandate, through the U.S.-Canada Great Lakes Water Quality Agreement, gave the Buffalo Niagara Waterkeeper the freedom to experiment and it crafted multidisciplinary teams and approaches to just about every problem. Team members had skills ranging from environmental law, business, Great Lakes policy, landscape architecture, water quality analytics, natural resource planning, and all the "-ologies" you can imagine—hydrology, ecology, biology, limnology, etc. This mix of expertise was essential to solve problems. But the experts aren't enough on their own. As Jedlicka insists, one should never underestimate the importance of public testimony and advocacy by a concerned citizen or group.

> Fish don't vote, and our waterways don't have a Lorax. I know through personal experience, public speaking and testimony can be very intimidating. There is often a stigma attached to environmentalists—that they are just special interests and even worse obstructionists. However, we have learned that you can be an advocate, and a problem-solver, and a partner all at the same time. The story of the Buffalo River's remarkable recovery is shared around the world as evidence that this approach can work. Plain and simple, consistent advocacy led to the restoration of our dead river.

Concluding Remarks

The cleanup of the Buffalo River has led to a substantial ecological revival. Public-private-nonprofit partnerships have been essential. Recently, federal funding from the Great Lakes Restoration Initiative and the Great

Jill Spisiak Jedlicka, executive director of Buffalo Niagara Waterkeeper

BUFFALO NIAGARA WATERKEEPER

Lakes Legacy Act has accelerated river cleanup and led to improving public access to the river and now waterfront revitalization. Buffalo Mayor Byron W. Brown reports:

> The Buffalo River has gone from a severely damaged waterway to one of our City's greatest assets, with more than $400 million in investment since 2012. The healthy, rediscovered Buffalo River is now attracting residential, entertainment, and recreational development, and its waters are an increasingly popular destination for kayaking, rowing, and fishing, while cyclists, runners, walkers, and birders, are drawn to its shoreline. The Buffalo River is now an economic engine, which hand-in-hand with our reimagined waterfront, is playing a critical role in Buffalo's rebirth as the Queen City of the Great Lakes. (Hartig et al., 2019)

Clearly, Jedlicka has played a key role; she has spent nearly two decades cleaning up the Buffalo River and served as the executive director of Buffalo Niagara Waterkeeper for nearly a decade. In addition, in 2013, she was appointed by the governor and legislature to serve on the New York State Great Lakes Basin Advisory Council. Three years later, she was appointed to the regional Great Lakes Protection Fund Board. In 2018, she was honored as a Woman in Leadership by the Buffalo Niagara Chapter of New York State Women Inc. In 2019, she was named one of Waterkeeper Alliance's top twenty "Waterkeeper Warriors." Further, the significance of the work of the Buffalo Niagara Waterkeeper was recognized in 2015 with the North American Riverprize and in 2016 with the Thiess International Riverprize—a global award for river basin management.

However, Jedlicka is a humble and generous person. Good leaders often practice generous leadership, giving credit away readily because they understand the value of creating a sense of shared success and community. She exemplifies this approach, and she is most proud of the collaboration and partnerships, which broke down a generation of barriers, that she and her team have spearheaded to get the job done. Today, the river physically looks different. The people of western New York are enjoying their waterfront again. People are genuinely proud of their river and the international attention its restoration has received, and this, in turn, is leading to a sense of stewardship that will hopefully ensure long-term protection of our Buffalo River.

There is no doubt that if Stanley Spisiak were here today, he would be so proud of his grandniece's leadership and advocacy and pleased with the revival of their beloved Buffalo River and a growing stewardship ethic.

CHAPTER 11

John Hall

Hamilton Harbour Champion

Hamilton Harbour is a 5,313-acre embayment located at the western end of Lake Ontario, connected to the lake by a ship canal across a barrier sandbar that forms the bay. Situated on its banks is the city that bears its name—Hamilton, Ontario. The city has a population of approximately 540,000, with about 770,000 living in the metropolitan region. It lies in a region known as the Golden Horseshoe that stretches from Lake Erie in the south to Lake Simcoe in the north, cradling the western end of Lake Ontario. This area is the most densely populated and industrialized area of Canada and earned its name because of its historical prosperity and wealth, serving as an economic growth engine for the entire nation. Hamilton is a mere forty-three miles from Toronto, Canada's largest city.

In the middle of the nineteenth century, the Great Western Railway was founded in Hamilton, making this city the center of Canadian industry. Its over one-hundred-year history of steel-making gave rise to the much-deserved monikers of "Steel Capital of Canada" and "Steeltown."

It also resulted in substantial environmental degradation of the harbor and surrounding ecosystems.

In Canada, as in the United States, prior to the passage of environmental laws starting in the 1970s, industries dumped waste into the harbor unabated and without recourse. Over the past century, metals, polynuclear aromatic hydrocarbons (PAHs), PCBs, and other hazardous chemicals were released into the environment, contaminating fish, wildlife, and sediments. While that era of unregulated pollution has come to an end, legacy contaminants continue to threaten public health, contaminate fish and wildlife, and restrict the use of the waterfront.

A second fundamental factor in the polluting of Hamilton Harbour was the decision in the city's early history to take its drinking water from Lake Ontario and discharge municipal sewage to the harbor. This situation continues today, although now the city has had to upgrade its two major wastewater treatment plants to protect the harbor and meet water quality standards. But in the 1960s, the harbor was infamous for its pollution. A member of parliament Colin D. Gibson said in a 1969 parliamentary debate: "The situation which exists at Hamilton Harbour with respect to pollution is extremely serious. The bay area, once a magnificent natural resource, is now a stinking, rotten quagmire of filth and poisonous waste" (*Canada House of Commons Debates*, 1969). Something had to be done.

Laying the Foundation for Conservation Ethic

Despite being given the nickname of "Steeltown," Hamilton has a long history of working to establish a green oasis in the middle of the city.

Thomas Baker McQuesten was first elected to the Hamilton City Council in 1913 and soon after became a member of the Board of Park Management. He was inspired by his mother, Mary Baker McQuesten, and the City Beautiful movement that flourished during the 1890s to the 1920s. Its advocates believed that city design could not be separated from social issues and should encourage civic pride and engagement. McQuesten became a great champion of parks and green space in the city and cleverly used a small tax levied on industry to buy and develop several parks and nature preserves. By the time he moved on to become a member of the Legislative Assembly of Ontario, Hamilton had more parks per inhabitant than any other city in Canada. His legacy also includes preservation of Cootes Paradise wetlands and part of the Niagara Escarpment, the Royal Botanical Gardens, scenic entrances to the city, and many park lands along the Niagara River.

Not only did the City Beautiful movement leave a legacy of parks and green space in Hamilton, but it left a conservation ethic that can still be seen today. Hamilton citizens and harbor users have a long history of advocacy for harbor cleanup. Another legacy is a very substantial and sophisticated network of scientists living and working within the community, including professors from McMaster University, scientists from the Royal Botanical Gardens, and aquatic research scientists from the Canada Centre for Inland Waters. This informed and socially conscious community resulted in a community anxious to engage and embrace a comprehensive harbor cleanup effort. Consequently, the Hamilton Harbour cleanup effort got off to a well-organized, running start and today is well recognized as a leader in stakeholder engagement, ecosystem-based management, and clean up and restoration.

Hamilton Harbour Becomes a Leader in Use of an Ecosystem Approach

Despite its many parks, all was not well in Hamilton. The Harbour Commission had for years been infilling the harbor to expand its port operations. In fact, during the 1980s, the Hamilton Conservation Authority unsuccessfully attempted to prosecute the commission for its actions. This failure led to many groups joining forces to demand harbor cleanup.

Then in 1985 the International Joint Commission's Great Lakes Water Quality Board shined a spotlight on Hamilton Harbour, identifying it as one of forty-two Great Lakes AOCs. As it did for all AOCs, the board recommended developing a comprehensive RAP to restore all impaired uses, using an ecosystem approach. It was a watershed moment. The federal and provincial governments committed to the RAP process and the Hamilton Harbour community quickly recognized the opportunity and embraced it as well. At that time, scientists had already recognized that the harbor was one of the most polluted areas in the Canadian portion of the Great Lakes. National media portrayed it as a "polluted city with a toxic harbor." Hamilton stakeholders became leaders in use of an ecosystem approach and the requisite collaborative decision-making and financing.

Soon after the 1985 commitment to develop the RAP, a Hamilton Harbour Stakeholder Group was established to ensure public participation and use of an ecosystem approach. A scientific writing team prepared RAP reports. The two organizations worked by consensus. It is fair to say the Hamilton Harbour RAP is steeped in a collaborative approach to decision-making and project implementation. Prerequisites for achieving an ecosystem approach include participation by all stakeholders; development of a mutually agreed upon decision-making process; and legitimacy demonstrated through political support, public participation, and funding. The stakeholder group was formalized as the Hamilton Harbour Stakeholder Forum in 1998 and made fifty recommendations to encourage partnerships and guide cleanup efforts.

The Stage 1 RAP, completed in 1989, ensured stakeholder agreement on the problems and impaired uses. In total, it identified eight beneficial use impairments: restrictions on fish consumption; degradation of fish populations; degradation of wildlife populations; degradation of invertebrates living on the bottom of the harbor; eutrophication or undesirable algae; beach closings and restrictions of sports involving contact with the water; degradation of aesthetics; and loss of fish and wildlife habitat.

In 1992, the Stage 2 RAP identified remedial and preventive actions to restore the impaired uses. At this point, the stakeholder group disbanded and established two groups to take its place: the Bay Area Implementation Team (BAIT) and the Bay Area Restoration Council (BARC). BAIT includes all the agencies and organizations that accepted implementation responsibilities. BARC is an independent, incorporated citizens' group responsible for monitoring remedial progress and charged with education and advocacy. BAIT and BARC are equal partners in restoring of Hamilton Harbour to a thriving, healthy, and accessible Great Lakes ecosystem. A revised Stage 2 RAP, released in 2003, included fifty-seven recommendations and 159 tasks for the parties to undertake (Hamilton Harbour Stakeholder Forum, 2003).

John Hall Takes the Helm as RAP Coordinator

From the onset of the RAP in 1985 through 1999, Environment Canada provided the RAP coordinator. When the federal RAP coordinator left the position in 2000, Environment Canada needed a replacement to take the RAP to another level. The agency found someone who had grown up in the region, had gained street credibility by rising through the ranks in conservation and environmental planning, and was well respected by all stakeholders—John Hall.

Hall grew up in Brantford, Ontario, within walking distance of the Grand River. This waterway meanders some 175 miles from Lake Huron's Bruce Peninsula through fertile farm fields of south-central Ontario and empties into Lake Erie at Port Maitland. It drops approximately 1,154 feet along the way. When Hall was a boy the Brantford stretch was so badly polluted that he and his childhood friends were forbidden from going down to it. That, along with a railway line he had to cross, was just enough of a reason for the youngster to spend time hiking its banks, much to the consternation of his parents.

A very fortunate kid, he never spent a summer in the city because he had parents, grandparents, and teachers who offered him opportunities to connect with and learn about nature. His grandparents owned a cottage on Lake Erie. Growing up he spent most spring and fall weekends exploring the lake's shores. His youth spanned the 1950s and 1960s, when algal blooms were a regular occurrence, caused by over-fertilizing with nutrients like phosphorus. Most algae are normally not visible to people because of their small size and low density. However, when we pour phosphorus and other nutrients into the water through agricultural runoff, these plant plankton keep multiplying until they become massive floating mats called algal blooms. One of Hall's vivid memories from swimming in Lake Erie during his youth was that he and his friends would cover themselves in mats of algae just for fun. Just as Superman donned his cape, they put on their capes of algae. It was probably not the healthiest thing to do, but kids will be kids.

Hall also spent summers at the Hamilton YMCA camp on a lake in northern Ontario. At this camp, he met a teacher who brought the forest alive with his knowledge and storytelling. This experience inspired a sense of wonder in Hall that he has carried throughout his life. During high school, he had a compelling geography teacher who instilled in him an interest in Earth processes, stimulated debates, and encouraged the students to get involved in local community planning. He went on to study geography at the University of Waterloo and become a professional planner. To Hall, it was just a natural progression.

He started his career in 1976 at Conservation Halton, a nonprofit organization that works to protect, restore, and manage natural resources in a watershed that encompasses 386 square miles of land, seventeen creeks, approximately sixteen miles of Lake Ontario, and fifty miles of the Niagara Escarpment. He ended his career forty-one years later in 2016 at the very place he started—Conservation Halton. In the middle of his career in the mid-1980s, he initiated a collaboration to create a new park plan for the Halton waterfront. In a little over two years, a team of staff from Halton Region, the City of Burlington, and the Town of Oakville developed a plan for parklands along the Lake Ontario shoreline. Then Hall worked on its implementation while running the Planning Department of Conservation Halton. This work, along with an early job as the project manager of Hamilton Harbour's Fish and Wildlife Restoration Program, brought him into contact with the Hamilton Harbour RAP, and he represented Conservation Halton in the Hamilton Harbour Stakeholder Group.

When the RAP coordinator left in 1999, Environment Canada approached Conservation Halton about temporarily transferring Hall into this position. Knowing the RAP's potential, Hall jumped at the chance. Conservation Halton generously allowed this second temporary assignment but included his RAP coordinator position in the senior management team of Conservation Halton. In essence, he had one foot in each camp, maximizing his ability to bring about change and ensure benefits to both sides.

Soon after taking the job, Hall took a cross-Canada automobile trip with his wife. During their travels, they would chat with people they met, and frequently he would be asked what he did for a living. When he explained that he was the Hamilton Harbour RAP coordinator and worked on cleaning up this body of water, they often responded: "Well, that's an impossible task." Absolutely everyone had an opinion.

The RAP coordinator leads the process and reports to the BAIT—the implementation team—as a board of directors, and these directors and their organizations are responsible for the implementation of remedial projects and programs. This structure allowed him to speak on behalf of the RAP, while being cognizant that he did not speak for any individual partner. For Hall, the integrity and independence of the RAP coordinator was extremely important. He reported to the BAIT. He could speak truth to power by just presenting the facts based on science. As a professional planner, he had a legal and ethical responsibility to consider all members of the community, whether they were present or not. This independence and professional responsibility had to be used wisely and could not be used politically. He was not a provincial or federal employee, but someone on assignment from a local conservation authority to a position of public trust. Politicians knew he was not speaking a party line but was their independent advisor. Hall believed that this independence elevated his position and allowed him to speak on equal terms with senior management and all levels of staff.

The first task for him and his colleagues was to update the Stage 2 RAP. Once again, they used a multi-stakeholder process to complete a work plan in 2002 that included requirements for necessary funding from the federal and provincial governments and local sources. Hamilton Harbour was the focus of many scientific studies, but many in the community were unaware of the findings and research, and they were not optimally coordinated for cleanup. Hall and his team initiated annual research and monitoring days that quickly grew to include a day for the harbor, a day for Cootes Paradise, and a day for the watershed. At each event, researchers were asked to describe what they proposed to do and to summarize preliminary results without preparing a report, so that they could publish research papers in the future. These workshops were well received and continue to this day. Clearly, the Hamilton Harbour RAP benefits from close proximity to researchers from the Canada Centre for Inland Waters, McMaster University, and Royal Botanical Gardens who not only studied the harbor but also lived in the area and wanted to make a difference. As a result, two of the strengths of the RAP have been science-based decision-making and strengthening the science–policy linkage.

In order to gain necessary support from federal, provincial, and local politicians for RAP projects, Hall and his team worked with BAIT and BARC (the citizens' group) to hold occasional breakfast meetings with senior politicians to inform them of progress and advise them of necessary support for upcoming projects. BARC hosted these meetings and invited BAIT members speaking directly to politicians about the severity of the problems, the nature of remedial projects, and the benefits to the community. These events were important because they gave the civil servants of BAIT an opportunity to speak candidly with elected officials. These meetings were always well attended and much appreciated. At one memorable breakfast meeting, Hall remembers asking senior managers at McMaster University, Dofasco Steel, and Hamilton Health Care about the city's image and how it affected recruiting the best and the brightest. They all had the same answer that Hamilton is considered a polluted city with a toxic harbor, and this holds back Hamilton. This was a stark revelation to the local politicians and, more than any other single event, yielded essential funding for big projects like contaminated sediment remediation and upgrading wastewater treatment plants.

Also attracting support for cleanup was the construction of much parkland and many trails from 1993 to 2000. Once the public could get down to the harbor's edge, they demanded improvements to water quality and embraced more parklands and extensions to the trail network. Before the construction of these amenities, the harbor had been accessible to only those able to join private boat clubs.

Hall Leads Habitat Restoration

Loss of fish and wildlife habitat in Hamilton Harbour was a major problem, well recognized by many within the community. By the mid-1980s, 60 percent of the wetlands, nurseries of life that can support hundreds, if not thousands, of plants and animals in the food web, had been filled by industries and the Port Authority. The wetlands that still existed in

Cootes Paradise, the mouth of the Grindstone Creek, and the nearshore of Hamilton Harbour were severely degraded. Most of the underwater fish spawning reefs and shoals, and essential nursery habitats, had been lost to dredging, development, and pollution. Colonial waterbirds were nesting on contaminated port lands that were slated for development.

The stakeholders called for a major fish and wildlife habitat restoration effort that would be precedent setting throughout the Great Lakes. They did not want a project manager who had a vested interest or potential bias, like an engineer or biologist. Rather, they wanted a neutral and objective person with a track record of bringing people together and making projects happen. They immediately thought of Hall because of his background, his expertise on the Halton waterfront, and his reputation as a facilitator. Prior to becoming the RAP coordinator, Fisheries and Oceans Canada entered into an agreement that allowed Hall to work on this project exclusively while he continued his employment with Conservation Halton.

He managed the entire project from 1992 to 2000 with guidance and support from a steering committee made up of government landowners, scientists, civil servants, and citizen representatives from nongovernmental groups like the Hamilton Naturalists Club. This position involved securing funding for his salary and office, raising funds for the various projects, developing project plans through collaborative working groups, securing all necessary permits and environmental approvals, letting contracts for construction, and overseeing construction—"none of which I had ever done at this scale before," Hall admitted. He's quick to point out that while he was central to this Fish and Wildlife Habitat Restoration Program, the landowner partners, including the Royal Botanical Gardens, Hamilton Port Authority, Hamilton Waterfront

Trust, and the cities of Hamilton and Burlington, did the contracting and day-to-day work.

The results were nothing less than amazing, considering where the project started. Key accomplishments included enlisting the Royal Botanical Gardens to oversee the restoration of the 618-acre Cootes Paradise Marsh and the ninety-nine-acre mouth of the Grindstone Creek, a project that continues today; constructing a fishway/carp barrier that would keep destructive carp out of Cootes Paradise Marsh, yet allow desirable native fish to enter; and restoring a pike spawning marsh, again with the help of the Royal Botanical Gardens. Equally important were the construction of small islands in the harbor for nesting of colonial waterbirds and underwater reefs as fish spawning and nursery habitat, and the enhancement and naturalization of shorelines to provide habitat for a variety of species.

As part of these projects, the partners also built trails to reconnect citizens to Hamilton Harbour and provide teachable moments. The result was that public access to Hamilton Harbour increased from less than 3 percent to over 25 percent, enabling more citizens to have firsthand experiences with the water and hopefully develop a stewardship ethic.

Cootes to Escarpment EcoPark System

The Cootes to Escarpment EcoPark System is the project the Hall is most proud of. It was a collaborative effort to protect, restore, and connect more than 9,637 acres of natural lands from the Niagara Escarpment to Hamilton Harbour. One of Canada's most biologically rich areas, it is home to nearly a quarter of the country's wild plants and more than fifty species at risk of extinction, including mammals, birds, reptiles,

amphibians, fishes, mollusks, vascular plants, and more. While technically not a RAP project, the effort to restore it was born from the RAP
process.

In 2007, Hall and two colleagues came together with an idea to
recognize the importance of an ecological corridor as a World Biosphere
Reserve. Dr. David Galbraith of the Royal Botanical Gardens pulled
together botanical information and Leo DeLoyd, director of planning
for the City of Burlington, took steps to connect the municipalities, local
environmental agencies, and provincial and federal interests. Hall pulled
together stakeholders and helped define a community planning process.
The Royal Botanical Gardens wrote a successful grant application to the
Green Belt Foundation for planning and initial community participation.
Hall's RAP office acted as the secretariat for the oversight committees.
The multi-stakeholder approach championed by the RAP was essential
to realizing the EcoPark System vision. In 2013, all municipalities and
agencies holding public lands signed a memorandum of understanding
to make the park system a reality.

This park system is very personal to Hall. He raised his family in
Watertown and hiked the EcoPark lands owned by the local conservation
authority. As more and more people started to mountain bike and hike
these lands, he feared they would be damaged by the very people who
loved to play in them. In addition, Hall and his colleagues feared that
the natural lands belonging to the Royal Botanical Gardens could be
divested as part of a review of the organization's mandate. His frequent
complaints about the potential loss of these significant lands started to
irritate his wife. On one hike, she told him: "Do something to protect
these lands or stop whining, as you are ruining our hiking trip." He got
the message and his marching orders.

The engineered containment facility being filled with contaminated sediments from Randle Reef, Hamilton Harbour, 2021
RIGGS ENGINEERING LTD.

Hall worked with his colleagues to successfully educate the Royal Botanical Gardens and others in the community about the nationally significant biodiversity right in their backyard. Today, the Royal Botanical Gardens is a leading member of the EcoPark initiative. Sadly, Hall lost his wife to cancer in 2009, and her loss invested the park system with even more personal meaning for him.

Randle Reef Contaminated Sediment Remediation

One of the legacies of Hamilton's century of industrial production was considerable contamination of harbor sediments, the worst concentration being near Randle Reef. This area is approximately 148 acres in size and contains approximately 2.45 million cubic feet of contaminated sediment, a volume that would fill a major hockey arena three times over. This kind of pollution was making the fish unsafe to eat and degrading habitats for fish and wildlife; and it is toxic to the invertebrates living in the bottom of the harbor.

The RAP took this issue on, and today Randle Reef is the largest contaminated sediment remediation project in the Canadian Great Lakes, at a cost of CAD 139 million (O'Connor and McGlaughlin, 2019). The Government of Canada and the Province of Ontario have each committed $46.3 million, with the final third coming from the City of Hamilton, City of Burlington, Regional Municipality of Halton, Hamilton Port Authority, and Stelco (formerly U.S. Steel Canada).

Located along the south shore of the harbor in the vicinity of piers 14, 15, and 16, the project involves constructing an engineered containment facility (ECF). This specially designed, double, steel-walled and sealed "box" is approximately 15.3 acres in size and designed to contain the most heavily contaminated sediment.

The project, led by Environment and Climate Change Canada, has three stages. Stage 1 involves reconstructing an adjacent harbor pier wall and constructing the facility. It began in 2015 with the pier wall reconstruction, which will allow sediment to be dredged from this area in the second stage of the project. The in-water construction of the facility began in 2016 and was effectively completed in 2017. Stage 2, completed in 2020, involved dredging contaminated sediment from the surrounding areas and placing them in the facility via an underwater pipeline. Stage 3 involved removing the water from the ECF, compacting the contained sediment, and then constructing an impermeable cap on the facility by 2022. This "new land" will then be turned over to the Port Authority, giving it the room to expand its operations without filling in more wetlands.

And this isn't the only positive outcome for business that the RAP partners anticipate. As in other places where RAPs have significantly reduced pollution and restored wildlife habitat, Hamilton Harbour's supporters hope that business development will accelerate as contamination is reduced and the harbor loses its stigma. New public spaces and amenities, along with new residential and commercial waterfront development in the piers 5–8 area, are also expected to encourage more tourism in the area. Economists have projected that the Randle Reef remediation will realize estimated economic benefits (by 2032) of Can$96 million to local property owners, Can$38 million to local businesses, and Can$29 million to municipal governments (Institute for Research and Innovation in Sustainability and Schulich School of Business, 2006). The economic benefits of completing all sediment remediation, wastewater treatment, and habitat projects for Hamilton Harbour are projected to be (by 2032) Can$592 million for local businesses, Can$496 million for recreational users, and Can$338 million for the federal government (Institute for Research and Innovation in Sustainability and Schulich School of Business, 2006).

Restoration Progress

Since 1985, considerable progress has been made in implementing the RAP and restoring impaired beneficial uses. The investment in the cleanup has been and continues to be significant. Prior to 1990, industry and government spent Can$600 million on remedial and preventive actions (Hamilton Harbour Remedial Action Plan, 2014). Between 1990 and 2010, the spending rose to a total of Can$610 million, with 77 percent coming from local government and private sources, 11 percent from the provincial government, and 11 percent from the federal government (Hamilton Harbour Remedial Action Plan, 2014). In addition, between

2006 and 2017, the contributing organizations committed another Can$622 million and began work on three major projects: Randle Reef sediment remediation (Can$139 million), Skyway Wastewater Treatment Plant (Can$153 million), and Woodward Wastewater Treatment Plant (Can$330 million). Managers predict that by the time Hamilton Harbour is ready for delisting, nearly Can$2 billion will have been invested in controlling contaminants at their source, upgrading wastewater treatment plants, controlling combined sewer overflows, managing urban stormwater, assessing and remediating contaminated sediment, restoring fish and wildlife habitat, restoring and protecting wetlands, and more.

Though Hall and his partners and colleagues have achieved a great deal, more remains to be done. Fish consumption advisories remain in effect, mainly because of PCBs, and work continues to prevent the release of contaminants at their source. Fish populations are still degraded, though the biotic integrity values (a scientific measure) have risen from twenty-four in 1990 to thirty-six in 2016. To be delisted, the harbor will need a value of fifty-five to sixty. Efforts to reintroduce the walleye, a top native predator, are ongoing. The picture looks a little better for the birds; the RAP partners have largely met their targets for improving the populations of black-crowned night herons, Caspian terns, common terns, and herring gulls. Continued management is needed to maintain reductions in double-crested cormorants and ring-billed gulls. The tiny invertebrates that call the bottom of the harbor home are not doing well, though the Randle Reef sediment remediation work is expected to make a big difference. Eutrophication (those overgrown algal mats that Hall used to drape over his shoulders) is still a problem, but 50 percent less phosphorus is being poured into the harbor now than in the 1980s, reducing the key nutrient that stimulates algal growth. Two large wastewater treatment plants have been upgraded, which will also help reduce accelerated aging of the harbor. Hamilton Harbour's two human-made beaches aren't ready for prime time yet. Significant challenges remain from *E. coli* and toxins from cyanobacteria that make the water unsafe for human contact. Whether the area is at least more pleasant to walk around and look at—the aesthetic qualities—is under evaluation. Certainly, improvements have been made in aquatic vegetation, shoreline zone, and wildlife habitat, but more remains to be done in the Cootes Paradise coastal wetland.

Lessons Learned

Experience in Hamilton Harbour, as in many of the Great Lakes AOCs, has shown that sustained funding for restoration requires many voices and that cooperation is essential to foster the use of an ecosystem approach. Public involvement and local leadership, as evidenced through the early work of the Hamilton Harbour Stakeholder Group and now through BAIT and BARC, have been critical to success. Such stakeholder involvement has not only brought diverse interests together to share different gifts but also built understanding and trust and fostered an ethical and sustainable perspective, systems thinking, and a spirit of collaboration.

Other key lessons learned from thirty-five years of restoration under the Hamilton Harbour RAP include the importance of connecting people personally with remedial projects. For funders and politicians, making the connection requires finding out what resonates with them. The remedial projects should be designed and ready to go once the stakeholders have agreed to them, and structured work plans make it possible to hold all the partners accountable. At the same time, the work of building partnerships and collaboration must be continuous. To that end, it helps to communicate and celebrate successes and to track cleanup investments and benefits. Perhaps the most fundamental lesson of all is that the RAP must foster and constantly improve collaborative governance.

Next Challenges

By necessity, most of the RAP effort early on was focused on restoring the harbor and Cootes Paradise Marsh. Nutrients from the wastewater treatment plants and toxic substances from past industrial discharges had vastly overwhelmed watershed inputs, and they had to be ameliorated before anything else could be done. As upgrades to the wastewater treatment plants and measures to remediate contaminated sediments in Randle Reef and the Dofasco Boat Slip are completed, the watershed will, for the first time in perhaps one hundred years, become the dominant source of pollution in the harbor. From Hall's perspective, the next major push needs to be on improving watershed water quality, particularly with respect to stormwater and control of sediment from construction sites.

Another challenge is to figure out how to integrate all the scientific research done on the harbor to measure how far the cleanup has come and how far it must go to meet the targets for restoring beneficial uses. Hall feels that realistically, even after the partners have completed all the remedial actions they identified as necessary, it is likely to take generations before the harbor fully responds. Climate change will make

John Hall by the banks of the Grand River
MARGOT NEILL

meeting the RAP's goals even be more challenging. Eternal vigilance will always be needed.

In Hall's view, perhaps the greatest challenge will be keeping the partnerships and collaborations going. The Hamilton Harbour model of stakeholder and intergovernmental collaboration has been very effective but must be sustained. If individual partners recognize each other's value and continue to trust each other, then the RAP will continue to generate positive change well after all the remedial actions have been completed. This is particularly necessary in the case for restoring Cootes Paradise Marsh, which the dedicated staff of the Royal Botanical Gardens have led and are stewards of. Continued RAP community support and constant monitoring will be needed for upgrading the Dundas Wastewater Treatment Plant and controlling urban stormwater runoff and CSOs. The restoration of the Cootes Paradise Marsh, what Hall calls the heart and lungs of the harbor, is the real test of the RAP delisting of Hamilton Harbour as an AOC.

Advice to the Next Generation

Echoing the words of many of the Great Lakes champions, Hall's advice is simple and direct. First, don't lose what you already have. For example, we need to protect existing natural areas as a priority and then expand and connect them to meet long-term goals. Second, we can always make things better. For example, Grindstone Creek, which drains into Hamilton Harbour, was nearly denuded of vegetation by 1900. Restoring the watershed and protecting all tributaries will realistically take a long time and will be an incremental process. The third piece of advice Hall has is again to practice eternal vigilance. It is so easy to backslide after making environmental improvements. Science and remedial practice are always improving our knowledge, and new knowledge can be applied to old solutions in a continuous improvement process called adaptive management—assessing, setting priorities, and taking action in an iterative fashion for continuous improvement.

Concluding Remarks

The Hamilton Harbour RAP pioneered the use of a multi-stakeholder process that today is a model throughout the Great Lakes Basin Ecosystem. All successful initiatives have leaders step forward at the right time with the right skills. Hall was a key leader for the cleanup and restoration in this case. He spent forty-one years honing his planning skills and applying them for betterment of the area.

In 2005, Hall was presented a lifetime achievement award for his work as Hamilton Harbour RAP coordinator and for being the backbone of ecological restoration efforts since the early 1990s. Upon accepting this award, Hall deflected credit for harbor cleanup to many partners, but his humility was identified as one of the key factors in mobilizing diverse stakeholders to work together so effectively.

In 2017, Hall received a Bay Area Restoration Council Award for twenty-five years of outstanding leadership of the implementation of the Hamilton Harbour RAP. In the award ceremony, he was singled out for his significant, positive influence on almost every aspect of the restoration of the harbor, using his deep knowledge, diplomatic skills, and personal integrity to align stakeholders, overcome obstacles, and move projects forward.

He is always quick to point out that he was supported by a great team known as the RAP office, including his administrative assistant of twenty-five years, Kathy Trotter, and Kristin O'Connor, who joined the team in 2000 and now serves as RAP coordinator.

Hall is now retired, serves on the Brant Waterways Foundation, and lives with his wife, Margot Neill, in Brantford just a few blocks from where he grew up as a kid. The Grand River is changed, cleaner and with more fish and wildlife—just the kind of place to spend time again. And the old rail line he used to cross to get to the Grand is now a community trail.

CHAPTER 12

Gord MacPherson

Toronto Harbour Champion

For thousands of years, First Nations people were attracted to the area known today as Toronto because of its rivers and Lake Ontario, exceptional hunting and fishing opportunities, and the fertile soil suitable for planting corn and other crops. These Indigenous people lived in relative harmony with their lands and waters until European fur traders came in search of beaver. Little did they know that this region known as "tkaronto"—meaning where there are trees standing in the water—would grow into Canada's largest city and a world leader in business, finance, technology, entertainment, and culture.

As Toronto and its region urbanized to provide for its expanding population, environmental pollution increased. There is probably no better example of historical water pollution in the region than the Don River. This twenty-four-mile river stretches from its headwaters on the Oak Ridges Moraine to the Keating Channel, where it empties into Lake Ontario. At one time, the river's mouth had one of the largest marshes on the lake. Over time Toronto residents straightened the Don River for their convenience; channelized, paved, and built over it; and befouled it with all kinds of municipal and industrial waste and land runoff to the point that it twice caught on fire—a familiar story by now. Heavy oil pollution caused the river to catch on fire in 1931, which destroyed a bridge crossing the Don River at Keating Street. In 1943, the same problem sparked a fire fronting the British American Oil Company's property. To no one's surprise, on July 30, 1958, the *Toronto Globe and Mail* editorialized that the Don River has "waters heavily polluted and laden with scum, its banks littered with all varieties of filth, and the whole sending up foul odours." Little wonder that in the fall of 1969, Pollution Probe—a leading environmental group—organized a funeral for the river, commemorating its death. On that November day, several hundred mourners paraded a casket from the University of Toronto campus to the banks of the river. The cortege included a hearse, a band playing a dirge, a weeping widow in black, and a top-hatted student portraying a greedy capitalist.

Clearly, for many decades environmental protection was not a priority. As everywhere around the Great Lakes, people prioritized commerce and industry and considered pollution part of the cost of doing business. By 1985, Toronto was suffering from extensive impacts of several centuries of agricultural land runoff, industrialization, and extensive urbanization—including poor water quality, contaminated sediments, fish that were unsafe to eat, loss of wildlife habitat as well as native plant and animal species, and beaches that were often closed due to high levels of bacteria.

Loss and degradation of habitats was particularly striking. Wetlands like Ashbridges Bay Marsh had been drained and filled; the forests and riverbank vegetation had been removed. Creeks had been buried and channelized, and their natural beds sometimes replaced with concrete. Hardened shorelines provided no habitat for animals and plants, and dams and weirs prevented fish from moving through the water. The water quality in the river and along the waterfront was predictably poor because of urban runoff and the discharge of industrial and municipal wastewater. Poisoned by industrial spills, road runoff, and historically unregulated dumping of chemicals into the sewers, Toronto's aquatic ecosystem was severely degraded.

A Watershed Moment and RAP Development

As citizens awoke to the visible damages and invisible dangers of polluted water and toxic residues, stifling local economies and degrading the quality of life for all living near these waters, they began to speak out. Then in 1985 the International Joint Commission's Great Lakes Water Quality Board identified Toronto and its surroundings as one of the forty-two Great Lakes AOCs because of all the problems listed above. The AOC extends from Etobicoke Creek in the west to the Rouge River (Ontario) in the east. It includes six major watersheds that drain into Lake Ontario, including Etobicoke Creek, Mimico Creek, the Humber River, the Don River, Highland Creek, and the Rouge River. In total, these watersheds drain an area of 772 square miles and include twenty-six miles of waterfront, eleven municipal jurisdictions, and over four million people. In response to being designated an AOC, Environment Canada (now called Environment and Climate Change Canada or ECCC) and the Ontario Ministry of the Environment (now called Ontario Ministry of the Environment, Conservation, and Parks or Ontario MECP) committed to developing and implementing a RAP to clean up the harbor and restore all impaired beneficial uses using an ecosystem approach.

Identifying the Toronto region as a Great Lakes AOC elevated the priority for cleanup within the federal and provincial governments and provided a focus for stakeholders and partners to work together to restore the health of their ecosystem and its beneficial uses. A partnership of federal, provincial, and local stakeholders first came together to develop a Stage 1 RAP that identified eight use impairments in 1989 and three others that required further study. These were exactly what you'd expect: restrictions on fish consumption, degradation of the invertebrates living on the river and lake bottom, limits on dredging because of sediment contamination, eutrophication or overgrowth of algae, beach closings, unappealing aesthetics, and degradation and loss of fish and wildlife habitats and populations. Whether fish, birds, and animals also suffered from tumors and reproductive problems, and whether plant or animal plankton populations had declined, as they had elsewhere, required further study. Recent studies have now confirmed that animal tumors and reproductive problems are not impaired, and that plankton populations still require monitoring. A Stage 2 RAP, identifying actions to restore the uses and remove impairments, was completed in 1994.

A collaboration among ECCC, the Ontario MECP, the Ontario Ministry of Natural Resources and Forestry (MNRF), Toronto Water, and the Toronto and Region Conservation Authority (TRCA), managed the Toronto-area RAP. Since 2002, TRCA has taken the lead under an agreement with ECCC and the MECP.

But it wasn't always that way. Not too many years ago, agencies, and organizations lived in separate silos, infrequently communicating with each other or coordinating and integrating their programs. When governments, communities, universities, nongovernmental organizations, businesses, and concerned citizens joined forces to clean up the place they called home, it changed the nature of the game. No one could solve these problems alone, and they all had to learn to work together to solve otherwise intractable environmental degradation.

Toronto and Region RAP partners have set a goal of completing all necessary remedial actions by 2025 so that the area can be removed from the infamous AOC list. This goal will be challenging to meet, but the team feels that it is indeed within reach. Continuous and vigorous oversight will be needed to achieve this restoration target date, protect ecosystem gains, and ensure long-term sustainability.

Cleanup and Restoration Progress

Working together to implement remedial and restorative actions over the past thirty-five years has led to substantial improvements in the quality of water and sediment, the amount and condition of terrestrial and aquatic habitats, and the health of aquatic species. Since 2007, assessments of three of the eight original impairments have shown that they are no longer impaired. The bottom-dwelling invertebrates are no longer degraded, dredging no longer has to be restricted, and aesthetic conditions are no longer considered a problem. Springtime total phosphorus concentrations in Inner and Outer Harbour have fallen to moderate levels, and overall levels of this nutrient in the watershed continue to decrease. Bacterial pollution on Toronto's beaches has significantly declined; eight beaches now have high water quality, although three beaches adjacent to watercourses still do not meet the RAP target (Kidd, 2015).

In the area's watersheds, levels of metals are no longer a problem at most sites, and some decreases in copper and lead concentrations in tributaries have occurred since 1999. PCB and PAH levels are similar to those found in urban streams that scientists use as reference sites to assess pollution; these levels are strongly related to the amount of urbanization in the watershed and tend to be higher in wet weather. Troublingly, however, chloride levels continue to increase in the watersheds and Lake Ontario; elevated concentrations are becoming a year-round issue in some places.

In the Inner Harbour and Humber Bay, the concentrations of metals and organic compounds in the sediments continue to decrease, though elevated concentrations of some metals are still found in some Central Waterfront slips. Projects designed to control CSOs and urban stormwater runoff will ameliorate this problem. Reflecting improved sediment conditions along the waterfront, the diversity of bottom-dwelling invertebrate organisms has increased overall.

Above the water, the waterfront and watersheds look a lot nicer, but unfortunately, the improved aesthetics don't always mean better habitat. The amount of natural habitat cover is relatively stable; however, quality has declined over time, and the continued loss of wetlands to development has only been partially offset by the creation of new ones. Restoration initiatives and floodplain regulations seem to have slightly increased the amount of riparian habitat. Things look better along the waterfront, where the extent and quality of aquatic habitat has improved through habitat creation and restoration projects.

Fish and wildlife populations show a similarly mixed picture. Native fish species have declined, while pollution-tolerant species have increased in watersheds. Particularly along the waterfront, pollution-tolerant species are most common, and the index of biotic integrity for the harbor is only "fair," though at least the proportion of piscivores reflects a "healthy" state (Kidd, 2015). Levels of PCBs and mercury in fish have declined substantially over last thirty years and consumption of many resident species is no longer restricted. However, restrictions are still in place for most migratory fish species, as well as common carp and white sucker, at certain sizes (bigger, older fish will have higher levels of these persistent toxic substances). On the banks, too, animal populations are rebounding; wildlife targets are being met and are within the normal range of variability in scientific reference sites.

As this list of achievements and continuing problems shows, and as scientific research has confirmed, although much has been accomplished, much remains to be done to restore Toronto Harbour and its watersheds, and achieve the long-term goal of ecosystem health and integrity as called for in the Canada–U.S. Great Lakes Water Quality Agreement.

In environmental work, the old adage of "an ounce of prevention is worth a pound of cure" holds true. The top priority for the cleanup of Toronto Harbour is preventing pollution and controlling contaminants at their source through legislation, regulations, and voluntary initiatives. In addition, the City of Toronto has made significant progress in implementing the city's Wet Weather Flow Master Plan. This plan addresses the familiar problem of CSOs pouring raw sewage into waterways during rainstorms. Since the city council adopted the plan in 2003, it has invested approximately Can$485 million in projects to improve water quality in Toronto's watercourses and the shoreline along Lake Ontario, build resilience to reduce basement flooding risks associated with extreme storms, and carry out projects to restore and protect watercourses from future erosion, which supports ecosystem health (Francella, 2019). Toronto

Water's Ten- Year Capital Plan (2016–2025) identifies almost Can$2.8 billion for the implementation of plan projects over the next ten years.

The city also completed an environmental assessment study for the Don River and Central Waterfront in 2012 to address the release of raw sewage during CSOs. This study produced a project designed to capture and treat stormwater discharges and CSOs from the lower Don River, the tributary Taylor-Massey Creek, and Toronto's Inner Harbour. This project consists of three massive tunnels spanning a total of fourteen miles that are connected to twelve underground vertical storage shafts, twenty-seven connections to outfalls, seven off-line storage tanks, an integrated pumping station at the Ashbridges Bay Wastewater Treatment Plant, and a new facility south of Ashbridges Bay. It is also designed to accommodate future growth.

This Can$2 billion project is being implemented in stages over twenty-five years, and once fully constructed, it will virtually eliminate CSO discharges into these bodies of water, as well as reduce polluted stormwater discharges (Francella, 2019). Discharges of nutrients, suspended solids, and heavy metals will also decline. The resulting improvements in water quality will, in turn, improve fish habitat. Project design was completed in 2015, and construction of the Coxwell Bypass Tunnel is underway and expected to be finished in 2025.

Gord MacPherson Becomes a Leader of Habitat for All

Many people and organizations had to pull together to undertake integrated planning, research, and management necessary to clean up Toronto Harbour, but a young biologist named Gord MacPherson would rise from performing fishery surveys to leading a multidisciplinary team that today is a model of urban habitat restoration in North America. I will still never forget the first time I met him. It was an early spring day, and we were standing on a human-made peninsula in Toronto called the Leslie Street Spit that extends a little over three miles into Lake Ontario. The air temperatures were still biting cold, reflecting the long time it takes Lake Ontario to warm up.

All of us participating in the Leslie Street Spit tour were thinking how nice it would be to cut the tour short and get out of the cold, with the exception of MacPherson, who was our tour guide. He was a large and striking figure who could have easily been mistaken for a professional football player. But what was most memorable was his knowledge of the region and science, and his passion to restore habitats. His enthusiasm was so contagious that by the end of our site visit, despite the cold temperatures, all of us were inspired to believe that urban habitat restoration was possible if you had the proper knowledge, the right players, and a clear understanding of potential natural resource outcomes and benefits. This knowledge, passion, and enthusiasm would be strengths that would serve him well in the future.

MacPherson spent his early years camping with his family throughout Ontario, including many provincial parks. As a result of these formative camping experiences and considerable hunting, fishing, and trapping in the northern parts of the province, he quickly became infatuated with the outdoors. As a young man, he often wondered how wonderful it would be to have a career in natural resources. He has a vivid memory from the year between grade school and high school, when he took an exciting trip to an outdoor educational center run by Toronto and Region

Conservation Authority (TRCA). Little did he know that this visit would be a prelude to a thirty-seven-year career with this very agency.

At the age of seventeen, MacPherson was selected by the Ontario Ministry of Natural Resources to be part of its Junior Ranger Program, which was designed to inspire young people to enter the conservation field through compelling summer education, outdoor work, and recreation. Every junior ranger cleared trails, planted trees, maintained canoe routes, restored fish and wildlife habitats, collaborated with First Nations and Indigenous people, and worked in the camp kitchen and on camp maintenance. As any good angler will tell you, he got hooked. MacPherson's strong and growing passion for the outdoors led him to complete a fish and wildlife conservation program at the Natural Resources Campus of Sir Sanford Fleming College in Lindsay, Ontario.

MacPherson started working with the TRCA in the fall of 1982—three years before the RAP got started. He had previous experience with electrofishing—a scientific fish survey technique in which a direct electric current is used to attract and temporarily immobilize fish for easy identification, counting, and assessment of health—in northern Ontario, which helped him design and carry out fish surveys in and along the Toronto Harbour. Incidentally, these fish community survey techniques are being used nearly four decades later. They are essential to assess fish community health and track ecosystem trends and are the foundation for designing habitat restoration projects.

Habitat rehabilitation and enhancement have been longstanding priorities of the Toronto and Region RAP. At the helm, every step of the way, has been MacPherson collecting data, performing assessments, designing projects with partners, overcoming obstacles, helping secure funding, overseeing construction, and measuring effectiveness. Indeed,

MacPherson has been one constant in the RAP since its initiation in 1985 through his retirement in 2019. Throughout his thirty-seven-year career, he demonstrated the centrality of habitat restoration in a RAP.

As we've seen in all the champion profiles here, in urban environmental protection and conservation work, partnerships are critical because of the number of people and stakeholders involved and impacted, and the complexity of problems and solutions. The biggest lesson MacPherson learned through the Toronto and Region RAP is the power of getting people to work together to achieve consensus on what restoration efforts are needed and then to speak in one voice. He notes that the most significant reason why he came to focus on improving the Toronto waterfront was the regulatory hurdles TRCA faced getting approval for the capping of Cell 1 in a confined disposal facility for contaminated sediments within Tommy Thompson Park. MacPherson reflects: "it took over fourteen years to get approval for this project, and I was struck by the contrast between federal and provincial agencies' desires to improve Great Lakes habitat versus their absolute inability to embrace new or innovative management techniques." This long approval process compelled him to work to forge the development and delivery of transformational habitat restoration projects that made such a difference to the Toronto Harbour.

He was particularly adept at getting all the agencies to work together on habitat projects. Initially, agencies and other partners were overly protective of their own turf and wanted to stay in their silos. But over time, MacPherson and his partners were able to pull them out and get them to believe that cooperative, urban, habitat restoration was possible. Isolated and individual work rarely produced the same results or progress as cooperative, ecosystem-based management. In this way and through MacPherson's leadership, more than Can$80 million has been spent on habitat rehabilitation since 1987. In the last ten years alone, the partners have created or restored over 2,030 acres of habitat and thirty-six miles of shoreline in the AOC.

Following this approach, the federal, provincial, and municipal governments announced in 2000 that they would provide Can$1.5 billion to revitalize the Toronto waterfront under the guidance of the Toronto Waterfront Revitalization Corporation (now called Waterfront Toronto). It was immediately evident this project needed an aquatic habitat restoration strategy to ensure sustainable redevelopment in a cost-effective manner that met the needs of the developers, while achieving the mandates and objectives of the many resource management agencies.

In 2003, a Toronto Waterfront Aquatic Habitat Strategy was developed to guide aquatic habitat restoration efforts in support of waterfront revitalization. Once again, MacPherson was in the middle of the negotiations, guiding and steering the Aquatic Habitat Toronto committee to achieve common goals, including restoring coastal wetlands and sheltered embayments for warm and cool water fishes, open coast habitat for populations of cold-water fishes, and river mouths and freshwater estuaries for resident and migratory fishes.

Aquatic Habitat Toronto works with developers on waterfront projects to incorporate aquatic habitat that will support healthy waterfronts and sustainable aquatic ecosystems. Experience has shown that if habitat experts like MacPherson are not at the table with developers when critical decisions get made, there is virtually no possibility of adding habitat and green infrastructure after the fact. When he and his peers are involved, such elements can be built in before the buildings go up.

Using this approach, Aquatic Habitat Toronto has overseen the creation of seventy-four acres of wetland and coastal habitat and nearly four miles of shoreline habitat. The coastal wetlands include almost fifty-nine acres in Tommy Thompson Park, Embayment D, and the Toronto Island areas. The Port Union Shoreline Restoration Project and the Mimico Linear Waterfront Park Project restored nearly three miles of shoreline. Many acres of sheltered embayments and river mouths are now much healthier for their inhabitants, and the project also created new fish habitat along the Central Waterfront.

Canada's First Urban National Park

The great author and naturalist Henry David Thoreau, while watching civilization expand into the countryside during his lifetime (1817–1862), recommended that every town should have a forest of 500 to 1,000 acres to be used for conservation instruction and outdoor recreation (Malnor and Malnor, 2009). MacPherson agrees that we need to make nature experiences part of everyday urban life and was a key early advisor to the governments on this matter.

In response to this need to bring conservation to cities, the Canadian federal government announced in 2011 the establishment of Canada's first national urban park—Rouge Park. This protected area is rich in natural, cultural, and agricultural features, including 1,700 species of plants and animals; traces of over 10,000 years of human history; and some of the rarest and best remaining wetlands, forests, and agricultural lands in the Greater Toronto Area. It contains working farms, Carolinian forests—found in eastern North America and characterized by deciduous trees—one of the region's largest wetlands, unspoiled beaches, kilometers of hiking trails, and the city's only campground.

Not far from Toronto's skyscrapers, the park is a unique wilderness in the midst of Ontario's capital. Once completed, Rouge National Urban Park will be 30.5 square miles in size—some twenty-two times bigger than New York's Central Park—making it one of the largest and best protected urban parks of its kind in the world. In 2015, the federal government announced it was committed to expanding the park by over 36 percent with the addition of 8.1 square miles of lands. Federal investment in Rouge National Park is projected to be Can$100 million (Francella, 2019).

Restoring the Don

The pollution of the Don River was one of the primary reasons that the International Joint Commission designated it a Great Lakes AOC. At that time, this waterway clearly was one of the most polluted rivers in the Great Lakes—and that was saying a lot, given the degraded state of the Rouge and Cuyahoga rivers. Nearly all of the historical wetlands in the Don had been lost to urban development. Who would have thought that it could be brought back from near death?

MacPherson and his TRCA colleagues were at the table from the outset of planning for restoring the Don. After years of planning, the federal, provincial, and municipal governments announced in 2017 a Can$1.25 billion project to bring back the Don and restore the eastern waterfront (Francella, 2019). In the early twentieth century, Toronto's Ashbridges Bay Marsh had been filled to create land for the port, and the mouth of the river had been straightened to form the Keating Channel. The loss of

Don River Mouth Naturalization and Port Lands Flood Protection Project under construction, 2019
TORONTO REGION CONSERVATION AUTHORITY

this 1,058-acre coastal marsh made flooding worse, degraded the aquatic habitat, and reduced fish and wildlife diversity and abundance.

The Port Lands Flood Protection and Don River Mouth Naturalization Project will undo much of the damage done a century ago by constructing a new naturalized river mouth through the Port Lands and creating a new urban island neighborhood called Villiers Island. The river valley will add forty acres of new parkland, promenades, and riverfront open space, and create thirty-five acres of new aquatic habitat and wetlands to improve biodiversity and water quality and to naturally moderate the effects of flooding and erosion.

In addition to the environmental benefits, an economic impact study (urbanMetrics, 2013) estimated that spending on construction would generate considerable economic benefits: Can$1.1 billion in value to the Canadian economy, 10,829 person years of employment, and Can$ 373 million in tax revenues to all levels of government.

Tommy Thompson Park

Out of former disposal sites for dredged sediments have come wild-flowers. Located on the Toronto waterfront, Tommy Thompson Park is an urban wilderness just minutes from downtown. As noted earlier, it was created from a human-made peninsula known as the Leslie Street Spit that extends 3.1 miles into Lake Ontario. This 1,236-acre park now represents some of the largest existing natural habitats on the Toronto waterfront and includes wildflower meadows, cottonwood forests, coastal marshes, cobble beaches, and sand dunes. Birds are attracted to the stopover habitats created in the park, making it one of the best nature-watching areas in the Greater Toronto Area.

Tommy Thompson Park contains three confined disposal facilities that were created to hold contaminated sediments dredged from the Keating Channel and Toronto Harbour. Cells 1 and 2 were filled to capacity in 1985 and 1997, respectively. Capping and restoration of Cell 1 was completed in 2007 (and catalyzed MacPherson's commitment to building partnerships on behalf of waterfront restoration), converting it to a 17.3-acre coastal wetland. In 2016, Cell 2 was capped with 1.6 feet of clay and additional clean topsoil to physically and biologically isolate contaminated sediments, improving water and sediment quality and creating a twenty-three-acre deep-water wetland characterized by a mix of different habitats for fish and wildlife. Deep-water pockets offer shelter for overwintering fish and amphibians, while in-water shoals and other submerged structures serve as fish breeding grounds. Amphibians were given an area suited for their reproduction as well. Nursery and foraging habitats support young fish, and there are emergent and floating vegetation areas as well. Two small islands offer nesting sites for common terns and turtles. A riparian area combines meadow and shrubs. And a fish and water control structure is designed to prevent large common carp from getting into the wetland and damaging it.

Much like a caterpillar metamorphosizes into a butterfly, this confined disposal area was transformed into a wetland treasure in 2018. Creating this park was a strategic move to help make nature part of everyday urban life and showcase Toronto as a city where humans can flourish as part of nature's beauty and diversity.

MacPherson's Proudest Achievement

Imagine waking up one summer weekend morning and going down, not to the beach, but to a wetland. Why would you ever want to visit a bog, a swamp, a marsh, or any of the many names for a wetland? Not many people understand the importance of these places. They *are* transitional zones between land and water, and are valuable resources ecologically, recreationally, and aesthetically. Scientists refer to them as "nurseries of life" because they provide habitat for thousands of species of plants and animals. During extreme floods and storm surges, they serve as living sponges, soaking up water and protecting adjacent lands from flooding. They are well known for minimizing bank and shoreline erosion along rivers and lakes and filtering out nutrients and sediments from upland runoff. Some even help to recharge groundwater, replenishing and purifying the water in aquifers that supply local wells. Many provide recreational opportunities, such as hunting, fishing, birding, and hiking.

But in Toronto, more than 90 percent of the original wetlands have been lost to human development. MacPherson saw this need and rose to the challenge. Indeed, he is most proud of is his work with wetlands. The rehabilitation, restoration, and creation of wetlands have reaped some of the greatest conservation successes in this metropolitan area. At the beginning of his career, the TRCA did not undertake any wetland restoration work, and now it is a national leader. Cells 1 and 2 at Tommy Thompson Park are the largest wetland creation projects on Lake Ontario. MacPherson and his partners have restored hundreds of wetlands within the watershed that contribute daily to Toronto's urban resiliency and water quantity and quality. His favorite wetland rehabilitation project is Corner Marsh at Duffins Creek. This marsh was restored ten years ago, and after decades of decline, wetland vegetation, nesting birds, and amphibians are flourishing there. It has the highest population density of muskrats on the northern shore of Lake Ontario, which inevitably attracted river otters into the area because muskrat is an important part of their diet. Then otters spread out from Duffins Creek and now occupy the entire Toronto waterfront. It has been over a hundred years since these pollution-intolerant animals freely inhabited these waterways.

Building a New Waterfront Porch Reaps Economic Benefits

When the federal and provincial governments and the City of Toronto established what is now called Waterfront Toronto in 2001, its task was to redefine its waterfront as a public asset for everyone. Working with public and private partners, the organization creates complete neighborhoods anchored by parks and public spaces, and diverse, sustainable, mixed-use communities that offer a high quality-of-life for residents and visitors alike. Joining other proponents of sustainable development in calling for recreating front porches on city homes to encourage a sense of community, Toronto and its neighboring municipalities are recreating lakefront gathering places for both people and wildlife.

Waterfront Toronto has worked with the RAP team to restore and sustain a vibrant ecosystem that provides environmental, social, and economic benefits to local communities and visitors. As part of an effort to measure the economic effectiveness of their work, Waterfront Toronto commissioned studies of the financial benefits stimulated by its investments. Between 2001 and 2017, developers invested a total of Can$1.6 billion in projects aimed at establishing attractive gathering places that foster a sense of authentic human attachment. Economists have estimated that this investment, adjusted for inflation, will generate approximately 14,100 full-time years of employment (of which approximately 88.5 percent will be in the city of Toronto), stimulate Can$4.1 billion in total economic output to the Canadian economy (the majority in Toronto), and yield total government revenues of approximately Can$848 million (urbanMetrics, 2013). Although Toronto Waterfront's expenditures are significant, they are relatively small compared to the recurring benefits, like permanent jobs, property taxes, income taxes, and tourism spending, that result from continued development of new office, residential, retail/service, cultural, and entertainment uses along the waterfront. Without the initial Waterfront Toronto investments, these new buildings and services wouldn't have happened.

In addition to direct spending on planning and infrastructure, economists have also quantified benefits accruing to private- and public-sector real estate projects both on lands controlled by Waterfront Toronto and other privately-owned land on the waterfront. For example, the combined development on East Bayfront and West Don lands and the adjoining neighborhoods will generate nearly 207,900 years of employment, add Can$13.8 billion to the Canadian economy, and provide Can$7.5 billion in tax revenues to the three levels of government (urbanMetrics, 2013).

Clearly, Toronto has become a North American leader in harbor cleanup—revitalizing its waterfront and reaping economic benefits— and creating a waterfront destination that is accessible and welcoming to all. The cornerstone of this effort was the cleanup and restoration of Toronto Harbour. Without it, the revitalization would not have been possible.

The Next Challenge

MacPherson believes that the biggest challenge facing the Toronto and Region RAP is how to fight public apathy toward the environment. Concern has now shifted to the climate change crisis but has not yet become a catalyst for local solutions. Torontonians need to think globally but act locally. In his view, the conservation community now needs to channel the public concern for climate change into concrete actions that both adapt to changing weather patterns and achieve huge conservation benefits, like restoring wetlands, building green infrastructure, naturalizing shorelines, planting trees, and more.

MacPherson's advice for the next generation of people who care about Toronto Harbour and the Great Lakes in simple—be bold! He is adamant that right now the environmental movement, the Great Lakes, and the planet need bold leaders. Improving habitat is a simple and effective method of engaging people and educating them on the economic, social, and environmental benefits of looking after our communities as our home. He has always been struck at how people universally accept the need to improve our environment, how easy it is to explain habitat restoration projects, and how involvement in restoration can foster a stewardship ethic and lead to advocacy. "We need to be bold and aggressively show the significance, importance, and function of restoring our waterfront to a greater percentage of the population," he argues.

MacPherson feels that the integration of habitat restoration components into traditional shoreline engineering designs is the biggest lesson learned from the Toronto and Region RAP for other areas of the Great Lakes. These universal ecological concepts are outlined in the Toronto Waterfront Aquatic Habitat Restoration Strategy and championed by Aquatic Habitat Toronto. TRCA made these techniques and designs the cornerstone of its habitat restoration projects, and they are applicable and beneficial throughout the Great Lakes and beyond.

Concluding Remarks

Today, 80 percent of all Canadians and Americans live in urban areas. Where will the next generation of conservationists come from? It will have to be predominantly from the cities, which also face some of the greatest environmental and ecological challenges. TRCA's vision is of a new kind of community—a living city—where human settlement can flourish forever as part of nature's beauty and diversity. To realize this goal, the organization's mission is to protect, conserve, and restore

Gord MacPherson with a walleye caught at Tommy Thompson Park, 2017
TORONTO REGION CONSERVATION AUTHORITY

natural resources and develop resilient communities through education, the application of science, community engagement, service excellence, and collaboration with partners.

McPherson has made conservation his life's work. His commitment to conservation defines him, guides him, and gives him purpose, and his passion has been an inspiration to countless people. He understands clearly that habitat restoration is about people management and that he and his partners are playing a critical role in city building.

His legacy includes one of the longest running fishery monitoring programs on the northern shore of Lake Ontario; many wetland restoration projects; and a greener, healthier, and more sustainable city. Every day throughout his career, MacPherson worked to open the minds of all who he met to the amazing natural wonders of Toronto and its surroundings and to pass on his knowledge and practical experiences. In 2016, he was awarded the Latorness Leadership Award for demonstrated, life-long, outstanding contributions to the field of conservation.

CHAPTER 13

Henry Lickers

St. Lawrence River Champion

T he St. Lawrence River, known to the Haudenosaunee as the Katarakwi, and its entire watershed have always been sacred to Indigenous people. Before the Europeans came to this area, traditional knowledge ensured that Mother Earth was respected and revered. But non-native society lost its respect for these waters, abused them, and even lost its connection to them.

Massena, New York, is nestled along the southern shore of the river between two of its tributaries, the Grasse and the Raquette. The Mohawk called this place Nikentsiake, which means "where the fish live." In 1792, Anable Faucher leased land here from Indigenous people living in Canada and named it after André Massena, a French general under Napoleon Bonaparte. The first European settlers came to the area from the neighboring state of Vermont.

Indigenous people long recognized the curative powers of sulfur mineral springs along the Raquette River and described them as a place where many moose, deer, and sick individuals of these species would come to drink the healing waters. In the 1800s, these springs provided a booming economy for the area, which became a health retreat known as Massena Springs. People flocked here to enjoy the medicinal benefits of bathing in the sulfur mineral springs, including President Theodore Roosevelt. Many grand homes and hotels were built to accommodate large numbers of visitors. For those who could not travel to Massena Springs, the curative waters were locally bottled and shipped far and wide.

These sulfur mineral springs were the primary community industry until the turn of the twentieth century, when Henry H. Warren built the first hydroelectric facility, connecting the Grasse River with the mighty St. Lawrence by a 1.8-mile canal. In that distance, the water dropped forty-five feet, allowing for the harnessing of 200,000 horsepower.

This source of inexpensive, reliable hydropower enticed the Pittsburgh Reduction Company, later named the Aluminum Company of America or Alcoa, to establish a facility in the community. The influx of workers at this new industrial plant was so great that it created a housing shortage, requiring many workers to stay at the grand hotels formerly filled with those who sought the healing powers of the sulfur mineral springs.

The next phase of industrial development occurred in the 1950s, when a new hydropower facility was constructed and the St. Lawrence Seaway opened. Located between Massena and Cornwall, Ontario, the Robert Moses–Robert H. Saunders Power Dam on the St. Lawrence River was completed in 1958, straddling the border between the United States and Canada. The dam supplies water to two adjacent hydroelectric power generating stations, the St. Lawrence–Franklin D. Roosevelt Power

Project in the United States and the R. H. Saunders Generating Station in Canada. It also provides safe passage for large ships—a necessary feature because of the St. Lawrence Seaway. This international system of locks, canals, and channels permits oceangoing vessels to travel from the Atlantic Ocean to the Great Lakes.

With the completion of the seaway and the two power generating stations, the Alcoa plant—now recognized as the oldest continuously operating aluminum production and fabricating facility in the western hemisphere—expanded significantly. Massena also became home to Reynolds Metals (now part of Alcoa), eventually providing employment to more than 2,200 people and adding over $200 million to the regional economy in payroll, taxes, and local purchases. Also opening in 1959 was a General Motors' foundry that produced aluminum cylinder heads for Chevrolet automobiles. This plant closed in 2008.

This industrial expansion, not surprisingly, would come at great environmental cost. The Alcoa, Reynolds, and General Motors facilities released toxic substances into the St. Lawrence River and the surrounding area, making fish unsafe to eat; water unsafe to drink; and contaminating sediments that then poisoned invertebrates, fish, mammals, reptiles, and amphibians. Contaminants included PCBs, PAHs, cyanide, fluoride, and dioxins. Eventually, all three industrial locations—Alcoa, Reynolds, and General Motors—would become listed as Superfund sites that required major, long-term clean up.

Across the St. Lawrence River, Cornwall was first settled in 1784 by United Empire Loyalists—people who supported the British during the American Revolution. Canal and lock construction in the late 1800s and the early 1900s would bring work and expand commerce. But it was the combination of water transportation, hydropower, and burgeoning

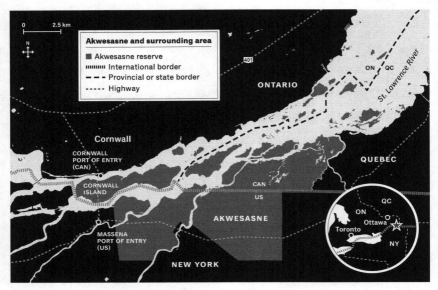

The Akwesasne territory and surrounding area

MEREDITH HOLIGROSKI/THE WALRUS; DATA FROM THE MOHAWK COUNCIL OF AKWESASNE

railroads that eventually attracted major industries to the area. It soon grew into an important industrial center in eastern Ontario. Major industries included Domtar Fine Papers, which operated for nearly one hundred years and closed in 2006; Cortaulds Limited, a cotton processing company that operated from 1924 to 1992; and Canadian Industries Limited (later called Imperial Chemical Industries and then bought out by AkzoNobel), a chemical plant that has operated since 1935. These industries released mercury, PCBs, and other contaminants into the river with all the effects you'd expect: they were toxic for the fish, wildlife, and invertebrates in and along the river and made fish unsafe to eat.

This contamination became internationally recognized in 1985 when the International Joint Commission's Great Lakes Water Quality Board identified the St. Lawrence River as one of forty-two Great Lakes AOCs.

What's unique about this AOC is that its waters are a shared resource among Canada, the United States, and the Mohawk Council of Awkesasne, the Saint Regis Mohawk Tribal Council, and the Mohawk Nation Council of Chiefs. The AOC includes twenty-five miles of river shoreline in present-day Canada, twelve miles of shoreline in present-day United States, and nearly three miles in Akwesasne territory. In addition to the political complexities, the AOC is also geographically and hydrologically complex, including four rivers, three dams, dikes, and canals.

A Champion Emerges

The Mohawk Territory of Akwesasne is jurisdictionally unique in that it includes portions that are in Ontario and Quebec within present-day Canada and portions within New York State in present-day United States. The Canada–United States border runs along the St. Lawrence River through Akwesasne, where the Mohawks have lived, hunted, and fished for many hundreds of years. Excluding waters and disputed territories, the Mohawk Council of Akwesasne governs about 13,000 acres, with 11,720 in Canada and the remainder in New York. No other First Nation community in Canada has these unique jurisdictional and geographical features. Approximately 17,000 people are registered with the Mohawks of Akwesasne; however, this number is likely an underestimate of the population size because many Traditional people don't register with Canada or the United States.

First Nations have long championed the protection of Mother Earth. However, one person stands out in the St. Lawrence River AOC over the last nearly four decades—Henry Lickers.

Lickers is a Haudenosaunee citizen of the Seneca Nation, Turtle Clan. He lives and works in Akwesasne. The community's name is a Mohawk word meaning "where the partridge drums"—the drumming being the beat of the bird's wings against a hollow log as it calls its mate. He is very proud of his Haudenosaunee heritage and has lived his life fulfilling his calling by the Creator to care for all things. It is the basic tenet of the Haudenosaunee way of life. They do this by thanking all things in creation every day and every evening with the Ohen:ton Karihwatehkwen (the Word that comes before all else). This thanksgiving address keeps them focused on what is important.

The Haudenosaunee use the Great Law of Peace or the Way to maintain their responsibility to all of their relationships with people, nation, communities, and families. The Mother Earth is one component of the thanksgiving address. It starts with the People, the Mother Earth, and the Waters; goes through the animals and plants; moves on the four winds; rises higher through thunders to the sun, moon, and stars; and on into the spiritual world, concluding with the Creator. The Way is based on three principles: respect, equity, and empowerment.

Haudenosaunee believe that in every deliberation they must consider the impact of their decisions on seven generations. Their duty is to protect the world for the seven closest generations, including their great-grandmother, grandmother, mother, themselves, daughter, granddaughter, and great-granddaughter. Lickers views his commitment to his family as important as his commitment to life. He has been married for fifty years to his wife Bev—a relationship he proudly states is his greatest accomplishment. He also has three grown children, Kimberley, a teacher in Halifax, Nova Scotia; David, a media events manager; and Donald, who is in the Canadian Armed Forces. He also has two granddaughters whom he dotes on.

For Lickers, cultural heritage is very, very important. Haudenosaunee people are forever looking at the world around them, seeing the animals and plants that live in their ecosystem. And each of those animals and plants has a significant place in the history and culture of Akwesasne. They are indeed inextricably linked—you can't separate culture from the animals, plants, and the ecosystem. Everything the Mohawks do has to address responsibility. He says:

> The non-native society around us looks always to laws and rights, and they talk about fulfilling their rights or fulfilling their laws. Within the Mohawks, you'll hear always the talk that the responsibility is the most important thing for us—our responsibility to the world, our responsibility to the animals, our responsibilities to all of the things that surround us. And culture is one of those lessons that you learn because that shows our responsibility to each other—not only from Mohawk to Mohawk, but from Mohawks to Senecas, and from Senecas to Cree, from Senecas to any of the other peoples of North America. And so that culture was a way in which we could store our information and knowledge. Now, unlike non-native peoples and the non-native culture of here, that wrote everything down, our people did it with stories. And we passed that information—I always like to say that we saved our cultural understandings of the world in our heads and in our stories. And so those stories we could pass from person to person to person, to our neighbors, and to our friends. And they would keep those stories for us. So that if some time in the future the Haudenosaunee forgot, for example, why the turtle was important to us, we could go to our

neighbors and say, "Tell me about the turtles." And when they would do that, that story would come back to us, and with that story would come all of the complexity of that turtle and how it lived in this world. And that would fill in that place and that bit of culture that we needed.

Lickers is a trained biologist and to a biologist those stories about the natural are wonderful because they describe how things were, not only as they are today, but the way they were long ago—10,000 years ago. The Haudenosaunee, for example, were here when global climate change—before the last Ice Age—was important. As a biologist, he can interpret those stories and share a picture or an image of what it looked like at that time.

Cultural understanding and heritage also show the Haudenosaunee how to act together. The Great Law of Peace or the Way enables them to build partnerships and understanding between people and to have good relationships with them. Therefore, many of the projects undertaken by the Akwesasne include many different partners and are guided by the Great Law of Peace. A good example is how they open and close all their meetings. These openings and closings set the stage by giving people about fourteen to fifteen things that they think are important in the world. They send greetings and thank-yous to all present. They remind people of their responsibility and acknowledge instructions given to them by the Creator.

If you ask Lickers, as a biologist and scientist, "What is the importance of that opening?" he would respond:

Well, it becomes an environmental framework by which the Mohawks look at every project that we do within our community to make sure that we fulfil our responsibilities to the Creator. Our environmental assessment process is established on that as a guideline and framework. So, when we talk about culture and heritage, sometimes we think that that is in the past, but to the Mohawks and to the Senecas and the Haudenosaunee, it's living in the present, but also extends to the future. So, we end up using those good words that our grandfathers and our grandmothers gave to us to work in the world today, but then also see how we can make the future better for seven generations to come.

For Lickers, that is why heritage and culture are so important to the Mohawks and Haudenosaunee. It gives them the way to live their daily lives. And that is why he became a champion of the St. Lawrence River.

Cleanup of St. Lawrence River AOC

Once the area was designated an AOC, the relevant governments committed to developing plans to restore ecosystem health and integrity. Although the parties agreed to a common vision statement to guide efforts in the spirit of ecosystem-based management, they developed two separate RAPs, starting in 1986, for the U.S. and Canadian portions of the St. Lawrence River. The Akwesasne had long been concerned about contamination by fluoride, PCBs, and other toxic substances, and had been instrumental in many scientific and environmental initiatives on the river. The Mohawk Council at Akwesasne became a key leader and voice for cleanup. Seven BUIs were identified in the Cornwall/Akwesasne RAP, while the Massena/Akwesasne plan named two known and five likely impairments (table 5).

Over the last thirty years, the U.S. Environmental Protection Agency and New York State Department of Environmental Conservation have cleaned up a considerable number of hazardous waste sites and

TABLE 5. A COMPARISON OF BENEFICIAL USE IMPAIRMENTS (BUI) IN THE CORNWALL/AKWESASNE AND MASSENA/AKWESASNE AOCS

BUI	CORNWALL/AKWESASNE	MASSENA/AKWESASNE
Restrictions on fish and wildlife consumption	Impaired	Impaired
Degradation of fish and wildlife populations	Impaired	Likely impaired
Degradation of benthos	Impaired	Likely impaired
Restrictions on dredging activities	Impaired	Not impaired
Fish tumors or other deformities	Not impaired	Likely impaired
Bird or animal deformities or reproductive problems	Not impaired	Likely impaired
Degradation of phytoplankton and zooplankton populations	Not impaired	Likely impaired (removed in 2015)
Eutrophication of undesirable algae	Impaired	Not impaired
Beach closings/ no water contact sports	Impaired	Not impaired
Loss of fish and wildlife habitat	Impaired	Impaired

contaminated sediment hotspots through the Superfund program; legal settlements with Alcoa Corporation, General Motors, and Reynolds Metals Company; and a natural resources damage assessment—a legal process of identifying ecosystem damages and the amount and kinds of restoration needed to offset impacts on fisheries, wildlife, habitats, and human uses. This assessment led to a lot of dredging to remove contaminated sediments, with General Motors starting the work in 1995 and Alcoa in 2001, culminating in 2009 with the capping of the Alcoa East site. In total, the parties spent $460 million on hazardous waste site remediation and $75 million on contaminated sediment remediation

(Hartig, Krantzberg, and Alsip, 2020). In addition, $74.2 million went toward habitat restoration and $1 million toward controlling agricultural nonpoint source pollution during the same time frame.

Hazardous waste site and contaminated sediment remediation has been a slow and lengthy process because of the nature of regulatory enforcement programs. Advocating every step of the way to protect Mother Earth, the water, plants, and animals have been the Mohawk people of Akwesasne, including speaking out at community meetings and public hearings, and writing letters to governments.

In the early 1990s, the Stage 1 Cornwall/Akwesasne RAP identified that sediments along much of the city's waterfront were contaminated by mercury and other metals, with organic contaminants such as PCBs, PAHs, and petroleum hydrocarbons present but less extensive. Additional sediment studies over the past thirty years have determined the extent of the contamination and established that the sediments are not acutely toxic to invertebrates living in the river bottom.

A science advisory working group has recommended monitored natural recovery, meaning that monitoring would track sediment contamination over time and special procedures and practices would be implemented to prevent disturbance of contaminated river sediments along the Cornwall waterfront by any future waterfront development. Managers will allow naturally occurring processes to contain, destroy, and/or reduce the contaminants. These natural processes will slowly diminish the degree to which invertebrates, fish, and wildlife can absorb a contaminant and how toxic these legacy contaminants are to them. Between 1985 and 2019, Can$3.4 million was also spent on habitat rehabilitation projects and Can$2.1 million on agricultural nonpoint source pollution controls (Hartig, Krantzberg, and Alsip, 2020). All identified management actions to restore impaired uses have now been implemented, and monitoring is underway to confirm that they worked.

For the Cornwall/Akwesasne RAP, the implementation of federal and provincial pulp and paper regulations and the provincial Municipal Industrial Strategy for Abatement regulations in the mid-1990s led to process changes and upgrades to local wastewater treatment at pulp and paper mills. These efforts significantly improved water quality in the area, including the elimination of dioxins and furans in pulp mill discharges. All industrial discharges containing mercury have also been eliminated along the Cornwall waterfront, and there are no longer any active sources of other heavy metals here.

In addition, the Government of Canada, the Province of Ontario, and the City of Cornwall funded an upgrade of the municipality's wastewater treatment plant, which reduced nutrient loading to the St. Lawrence River. As part of the Cornwall Pollution Prevention and Control Program, the retrofit of the city's Fly Creek stormwater pond reduced the number of combined sewers and CSO events. In total, Can$107.7 million has been spent on upgrading the wastewater treatment plant and controlling CSOs between 1985 and 2019 (Hartig, Krantzberg, and Alsip, 2020). And in all of this work, Lickers and the Akwesasne were provocateurs for action.

Henry Lickers's Calling

Lickers's whole life has been shaped by the St. Lawrence River and his calling by the Creator to care for all things. He holds a bachelor of science in biology and geography from Trent University and undertook graduate studies at the University of Waikato in New Zealand. In 1976, when he returned to Canada, he found a job as a biologist with the Mohawk Council of Akwesasne, working on the St. Lawrence River and the environment. The council had established the Environment Division to maintain and enhance the natural environment of Akwesasne and the Akwesasne community. Lickers has served as a director of the Mohawk Council for thirty-two years and has been the environmental science officer for the past six years. Throughout his career, he has been a strong voice for caring for all of creation and has been instrumental in incorporating First Nations people and knowledge into environmental planning and decision-making.

In 1979, after carrying out many studies on the health of animals, humans, and plants, the council issued a recommendation to the people of Akwesasne that women of childbearing age, pregnant women, and children under the age of sixteen should consume no fish species from the St. Lawrence River because they were contaminated by toxic substances. The council then began the fight to carry out a human health study to gauge the effects of these contaminants. At the same time, Lickers and other Elders knew the impact this finding would have on their people. Fishermen stopped fishing, trappers stop trapping, farmers were only able to sell limited amounts of meat from their cattle, and their whole way of life changed. Since he was at the center of the scientific work, he could do nothing less than dedicate his life to the cleanup of the river. He said: "This was my responsibility to my people, my family, and the world!"

The Akwesasne had long been concerned about ecosystem contamination by fluoride, PCBs, and other toxic substances, and had undertaken many environmental investigations. When the RAPs started in 1986, the Mohawk of Akwesasne immediately got involved. In fact, both the Mohawk Council at Akwesasne and Lickers were at the table as key stakeholders from the very beginning, helping identify and reach agreement on the problems and use impairments, figuring out what remedial and preventive actions would be necessary, determining who was responsible for the cleanup and when the actions would be taken, and monitoring progress, all to increase accountability. Lickers acknowledges, "At first, no one knew how to work together, and many missteps and misunderstandings took place, but some work was getting done."

One example is that some funding was obtained from the U.S. and Canadian governments for the council to take part in the RAP processes and to continue monitoring of the St. Lawrence River. Soon the Mohawk Council of Akwesasne became dissatisfied with the progress and launched a court action against Reynolds Metals and Alcoa for the fluoride contamination of the farmlands on Cornwall Island. This ultimately led to a $19.4 million settlement in 2013 with Alcoa and the former Reynolds Metals Company to help heal past wounds to this rich ecological and cultural ecosystem with many restoration projects.

The Mohawk had long witnessed sick and dying livestock on their land. A Cornell University study showed that the livestock were suffering from fluorosis—a crippling disease resulting from the accumulation of fluorides in hard and soft tissues that disfigures teeth, affects bones, and impairs joints—because of being downwind from Reynolds. The Mohawk Council also was able to procure major funding from the Canadian federal government to carry out a human health study on PCBs, fluoride, mirex, and mercury. In total, a team of doctors from Mount Sinai Hospital in New York City, headed by Dr. Iving J Selikoff, examined some 2,500 Mohawk people. This study found elevated fluoride levels in their blood and voiced concern for long-term human health impacts, including marked disability.

In the 1990s, the council approached the International Joint Commission's International Air Quality Advisory Board with their concerns about fluoride contamination of Akwesasne cattle and lands from the gases coming from the Reynolds Metals aluminum plant in Massena. At the same time, the commission was looking for a scientist who could work on an advisory board to study water levels and flows of the St. Lawrence River. It asked the council if Lickers could join their study board, and they agreed, but only if Lickers could serve in his professional and personal capacity and not as a representative of the council. This appointment enabled him to become even more involved with the Great Lakes and the St. Lawrence River work.

In 1992, the Mohawk Council of Akwesasne helped establish the St. Lawrence Institute of Environmental Science to build research capacity, strengthen science–policy–management linkages, and bolster community engagement. To no one's surprise, Lickers was appointed a director and later vice president. Six years later, the St. Lawrence River Restoration Council was formed to oversee and address restoration of BUIs in Cornwall and Akwesasne. It was designed as a forum for information sharing among the involved parties, which included members from the federal and provincial governments, the Mohawk Council of Akwesasne, Saint Regis Mohawk Tribe, the Raisin Region Conservation Authority, the municipalities of Cornwall and South Glengarry, the River Institute, other environmental groups, and industry. Its oversees the implementation of the sixty-four recommended Canadian remedial actions to ensure that the river water is drinkable, swimmable, fishable, and sustainable, and it holds the cleanup partners accountable.

Lessons Learned

Lickers has been one of the constants in the cleanup and restoration of the St. Lawrence River, and his work has opened doors for other Indigenous environmental advocates. Today, there is a growing awareness of the rich but untapped depth of knowledge and experience across Indigenous cultures in the restoration and sustainability of the Great Lakes. Strengthened connections to nature are essential to managing and restoring these freshwater seas. Indigenous-led initiatives and commitments to partnerships and collaboration can enrich collective efforts in realizing a shared vision for the future of the Great Lakes.

The lessons Lickers learned from more than forty years as an Indigenous biologist from Akwesasne are direct and straight to the point. First, the Earth is our Mother. We must care for and protect the Earth, which includes the St. Lawrence River. From this principle flows the other lessons: Cooperation is the way to survive. You need courage to work with people. It is the only way to survive and succeed. No one can do this alone. Knowledge is powerful only if it is shared. Share your knowledge and experiences with others. Innovation grows from sharing. Responsibility is the best practice. Laws and rights will not protect you and the environment since they are based on the minimum level of protection. Your responsibilities will dictate your actions. Everything is connected to everything. A single word or action can profoundly affect a person or the world. Place is important. Where you live and learn is what you know best and often better than anyone else. The spiritual world is not distant from the Earth. Care for your spiritual and physical self. And don't forget that help is always within reach. Don't be afraid!

Finally, he advises his counterparts in other areas of the Great Lakes to never to give up. "The cleanup is never done regardless of the general head nodding, and we must continuously work to improve and sustain our ecosystems. You will need everyone to do this and learn how to work together. There are many different models of collaboration—choose one and be inspired."

The Next Challenge for the St. Lawrence River

Lickers identifies two kinds of challenges—challenges as threats and challenges as opportunities. He sees climate change, including the increasing frequency and intensity of storms, associated threats to property and people, changes in plants and animals, and more, as a major threat. Others include contaminants and microplastics, invasive species, loss of and threats to species at risk, and loss of coastal wetlands and all the ecosystem benefits they provide. But there are also many opportunities. Engaging youth and providing activities and educational experiences that make meaning in their lives is a big one. So too are ensuring information freedom and improved communication, seeking out the wise and wisdom of elders, and learning to work in and through networks.

For the next generation of scientists, resource managers, and activists aspiring to care for the St. Lawrence River and the Great Lakes, he has some advice. Indigenous people have thrived on the lands and waters now known as Canada and the United States for thousands of years. They have developed an intrinsic understanding of the land, water, and all living things, including the interrelationships among them. This

Henry Lickers, environmental science officer at the Mohawk Council of Akwesasne and Canadian commissioner of the International Joint Commission

INTERNATIONAL JOINT COMMISSION

understanding is often referred to as Traditional Knowledge or Indigenous Knowledge. Lickers willingly shares his Traditional Knowledge and provides wise counsel to all who will listen. He says, "All my experiences have led me to this truth—that science and Traditional Knowledge need each other to be a whole knowledge system."

Many organizations and environmental advocates regularly seek his input and advice. Many years ago, the International Joint Commission tapped him to serve on its International Air Quality Advisory and Great Lakes Science Advisory Boards. Then in 2019, the Government of Canada appointed him to serve as one of only six members of the International Joint Commission—three from the United States and three from Canada. This body is the transboundary institutional mechanism that oversees and evaluates progress under the U.S.–Canada Great Lakes Water Quality Agreement. It was the entity that identified AOCs in 1985.

Lickers is the first Indigenous person ever appointed to the International Joint Commission. This speaks volumes to how much his colleagues respect his knowledge, advocacy, and effectiveness. As a commissioner, he is well positioned to help put Traditional Knowledge into environmental planning and decision-making practice, and to promote better care of the Great Lakes. He brings a long overdue Indigenous perspective on collective responsibility to building collaborative and trusting relationships for sustainable water governance. In recognition of his past and present commitment to the Great Lakes, he was awarded an honorary doctor of science degree from the State University of New York at Syracuse, and he has also served as a Trent University PhD Elder Council member.

His advice to the next generation is clear and compelling: Be courageous—if you think something is wrong or it feels wrong, it probably is, so work to change it! Question everything—authority and science depend on questioning. Care for everything—even the smallest thing is important. And not least, have fun and learn to play—include it in your group's constitution. We must have fun!

Concluding Thoughts

Lickers, by nature, is a humble person and is quick to give and share credit. But he has made a huge difference in the St. Lawrence River and Great Lakes. The effort he is most proud of is educating and "lifting up" the next generation:

When I started the Department of the Environment in 1976, I was one of ten or twenty Indigenous biologists in North America. We started the department to study the natural environment using science and Traditional Knowledge to show our children that they could hunt, fish, garden, and harvest while making a good living and being well paid for their efforts. Today we have hundreds of our young people who have obtained diplomas and undergraduate and graduate degrees, and I like to believe we helped our people move down this path. I also feel and hope that my great-grandmother, grandmother, and mother would be proud of my efforts, but I know I still have a lot of work ahead.

CHAPTER 14

Traits of a Champion and a Call to Action

The Laurentian Great Lakes are awe-inspiring "sweet-water" seas that make up nearly one-fifth the standing fresh water on the Earth's surface. Perhaps it is easiest to visualize this chain of lakes as a gigantic staircase, where the top step is Lake Superior and water descends down a series of lake steps—Michigan, Huron, Erie, and Ontario—to the Atlantic Ocean. These inland seas display a tapestry of biodiversity that is unique throughout the world. And these water resources provide many ecosystem services or benefits that are the very foundation of the economy in Great Lakes Basin Ecosystem.

But what attracts us to the Great Lakes beyond their natural features? I think it is memories. So many of us, including the champions profiled here, love them because of childhood memories of visiting their shores while vacationing with loved ones and friends, catching your first fish, kayaking or canoeing down winding tributaries, or being inspired with a sense of wonder while birdwatching. Maybe you sang campfire songs and listened to scary stories while camping in parks near the lakes. Perhaps you scanned the horizon for tiny lake freighters and watched them loom into massiveness as they drew close. And surely many have watched the sun go down on the western horizon, an experience so beautiful and striking that words aren't enough to describe its magic.

These varied Great Lakes experiences often evoke a sense of authentic personal attachment or belonging. Today, urban planners and landscape architects are advocating practices, called placemaking, that create quality places that people want to live, work, and play in. Think of it as creating a sense of authentic personal attachment or belonging to a particular place. In the case of the Great Lakes, you do not need to create a sense of place because most people have one. These freshwater seas hold memories and stories that bond us to the Great Lakes for a lifetime. The personal connection that we feel to these waters keeps us longing to return, again and again, to their shores. And no matter how much time passes, we are always welcomed back.

Despite this sense of attachment, human use and abuse have threatened the lakes with pollution and loss of habitat and biodiversity. Some people's passion for these inland seas is so strong that they have become lifelong stewards, and I have told the stories of fourteen such people here. These champions have helped to clean up some of the most polluted areas of the Great Lakes and have catalyzed a sense of stewardship in many more people. These champions love the Great Lakes and have inspired others to follow, established and nurtured restoration partnerships, and persevered over decades and not given up in the face of adversity. They are well respected and trusted in their communities—a key factor enabling them to form coalitions of unlikely partners to improve the health and well-being of the Great Lakes. They are people not in it for acclamation or commendation. They simply and profoundly love the Great Lakes, show reverence for them, and work tirelessly to pass them on as a gift to future generations.

It has been my honor and privilege to get to know and work with each of these Great Lakes champions over the past thirty-five years. I truly admire them and respect all they have done for our Great Lakes and the denizens who live in the basin. Through telling their stories, I found nine traits that distinguish them as champions.

Passion for the Great Lakes and Their Restoration

Each of these outstanding stewards has passion for the Great Lakes and passing them on in a healthier state as a gift to future generations. The Great Lakes are deeply and personally meaningful to them. Through their energy, excitement, and enthusiasm, they inspire others to join and commit to the restoration effort. When you are in the presence of one of these passionate Great Lakes champions, you feel their excitement, know their commitment to the cause, and are stirred by their positive, contagious energy. They understand how their contributions can help their team succeed and work relentlessly to achieve their goals.

Big Dreams with Compelling Visions

Restoring the most polluted areas of the Great Lakes is no small task. It takes big thinking, big dreams, and a clear and compelling vision. Articulating such a vision is a critical step in any major undertaking, particularly when the number of stakeholders is large as is the case in Great Lakes AOCs. For example, contrast the vision, "we will be a leader in space exploration" with "we will put a man on the moon in ten years." The latter is much clearer and more compelling. A vision must be relevant, appealing, and engaging, and must offer a clear picture that all stakeholders can carry in their hearts and minds.

Collaborativeness and Good Ecosystem-Based Management Team-Building

There is an old African proverb that says, "If you want to go quickly, go alone. If you want to go far, go together." Forging partnerships among stakeholders and building relationships are essential to restoring Great Lakes AOCs. The champions know how to collaborate well and understand what it takes to build a good team. They are at the cutting edge of applying an ecosystem approach in the management of the Great Lakes. They know that effective collaboration requires trusting relationships, and they demonstrate it in everything they do. Great Lakes champions also know how to sustain collaboration over the long haul. This is critically important because cleanup of these pollution hotspots is now in its fourth decade and much remains to be done.

Eagerness to Learn and Share Knowledge with Others

Dealing with the Great Lakes AOCs has taught us that no one has all the answers on how to clean up and restore these highly polluted areas. Everyone needs to learn their way out of these problems together. Education is the key to long-term change in the way people understand and value the places they call home and the ecosystems within which they live. Great Lakes champions know and demonstrate with their actions that solutions to problems arise out of cooperative learning. This approach can be described as common learning that involves stakeholders working in teams to accomplish a common goal, under conditions that involve both positive interdependence (all stakeholders cooperate to complete a task) and individual and group accountability (each stakeholder is responsible for the outcome). Great Lakes champions are good facilitators of cooperative learning to achieve a common level of understanding that allows all stakeholders to move forward together.

Practical Problem-Solving to Overcome Obstacles and Inertia

Experience has shown that if you do not first agree to the problems and use impairments that make a place an "Area of Concern," you will never solve them. Agreement on problems and quantitative restoration goals are essential to focus the RAP process and get everyone "rowing in the same direction." Next, the partners have to review cleanup and restoration options and decide what to do. Each of these champions had to learn how to become good problem-solvers and how to overcome obstacles. Indeed, they had to create the framework and conditions for effective problem-solving. They also had a little entrepreneurial innovator in them. They were constantly on the lookout for new ways to solve problems, better ways to build bridges and form partnerships, and more creative and collaborative ways to finance a project. When you deal with a restoration process that already spans nearly four decades, stakeholders will undoubtedly encounter institutional inertia. Champions have had to learn when and how to step in to overcome inertia to keep the restoration process moving forward.

Action-Oriented and Committed to Continuous Improvement

Early on, the process of investigating and planning seemed to some to move at the speed of a glacier. It was slow because there were knowledge gaps to fill and because it took time to bring stakeholders together to develop their RAP. In the beginning, the advocates had no dedicated funding for implementing cleanup and restoration actions. Some feared that planning for planning's sake was leading to paralysis. The intent of RAPs was to increase accountability by identifying what remedial and preventive actions needed to be taken, by whom, and in what time frame. Great Lakes champions had to balance the need for proper research and studies to guide decision-making and planning with the desire to take action. As you have seen in the profiles above, these champions had to serve and satisfy many masters.

In general, the process they followed is called adaptive management, in which the participants make assessments, set priorities, and take actions in an iterative process for continuous improvement. Monitoring, research, and surveys are essential to practice adaptive management, and without them, management would be flying blind. Key questions that had to be addressed to ensure science-based continuous improvement included:

- Has there been a proper scientific assessment?
- Is there a scientific rationale for the proposed remedial and preventive action?
- Are the remedial and preventive actions being taken going in the right direction? (Is the trajectory correct—toward achieving long-term, measurable goals?)

- Will there be follow-up ecological assessment and monitoring?
- Is there a commitment to adaptive management and therefore a process in place to make additional improvements and mid-course corrections, as necessary?

Great Lakes champions had to ensure that there was a sound scientific foundation for remedial and preventive actions, translate the science to policy makers and community and industrial leaders, ensure proper science-based decision-making, help forge agreements among the stakeholders, and show remediation and rehabilitation progress. The best way to describe this is a dynamic tension between those investigating problems and planning for cleanup and those wanting to see action.

In It for the Long Haul

It has taken over thirty-six years to achieve the cleanup of nine of forty-three Great Lakes AOCs and the elimination of seventy-nine of 137 known use impairments in Canadian AOCs, and ninety of 255 on the U.S. side. Clearly, this effort is not for the faint of heart. These Great Lakes champions have demonstrated impressive perseverance and incredible commitment. The environmental and natural resource problems faced in most Great Lakes AOCs were not created in a few short years. Most often they were created over a century or more. Therefore, it is unrealistic to think that these environmental and natural resource problems could be solved in a relatively short period of time. Because restoring Great Lakes AOCs is such a long-term effort, these champions have also had to think about transition planning and how to bring along the next generation of champions. Each of them has mentored and inspired others to follow in their footsteps to become Great Lakes stewards. This has been their life work and mission, and all of us can be thankful for their service. Indeed, we all stand on their shoulders and benefit from these champions.

Honesty and Integrity

Science is the objective and verifiable search for the truth. We need to undertake sound science to solve the complex problems of restoring degraded areas of the Great Lakes and effectively translate and communicate the science to the public and decision-makers. Good science and good communication are even more important during these times of social media propaganda and misinformation. Today, science is increasingly under attack by special interests whose primary goals are short-term profits rather than long-term ecosystem and community sustainability. These Great Lakes champions bring honesty and integrity to the table every day, building trust and instilling confidence in multi-stakeholder decision-making.

Understanding the Importance of Celebrating Successes and Giving Credit

In any major environmental initiative, particularly when the population affected and number of stakeholder groups are large, it is important to build a record of success and celebrate it frequently in a very public fashion. Great Lakes champions understand this and have effectively used a variety of tools and techniques to celebrate successes in a way that builds momentum. Sometimes they've done it through annual or biennial reports that catalog environmental accomplishments to inform, educate, and inspire more community members to get involved. In other cases, they publicly celebrate the completion of a habitat rehabilitation or contaminated sediment remediation project. Experience has shown that recording these accomplishments and the ecosystem benefits they provide in a fashion that is meaningful to the public and resonates with them generates support for remediation. People always like to hear how an environmental action affects them directly.

Great Lakes champions also effectively cultivate the media and involve politicians, prominent community and business leaders, and school children in celebrating environmental accomplishments. Given that many people today are disconnected from the outdoors, the complexity of issues facing AOC communities, and the competing priorities within communities, the RAP team must routinely be out in front of the citizenry with messages and stories of positive actions.

In celebrating successes, these Great Lakes champions have consistently talked about and given credit to the important contributions of others. Indeed, they are generous servant-leaders who are quick to acknowledge and credit others for work well done. This generous sharing of credit enhances team cohesion and trust, promoting more and better collaboration.

Concluding Thoughts

One of the critical building blocks of the Great Lakes RAPs has been use of an ecosystem approach, as called for in the U.S.–Canada Great Lakes Water Quality Agreement. An ecosystem approach brings all the stakeholders together to plan and take action to clean up and protect the place they call home. The traditional governmental approach to environmental and natural resource management has been to have separate programs for air, water, land, fish, and wildlife. And each program existed in a "silo" with limited interaction with other programs. The ecosystem approach broke down barriers among the governmental programs and made governments equal partners with community and business stakeholders to restore and sustain ecosystem health and integrity.

The essence of an ecosystem approach is that it relates people to ecosystems that contain them, rather than to environments with which they interact. Think of it as a circle with three equal compartments representing social, economic, and environmental interests. The operating principle is that no compartment in the circle can be sacrificed and all are essential to maintain a functional and sustainable ecosystem. Therefore, to incorporate an ecosystem approach, we need to undertake integrated research, planning, and management. Another good way to think about it is that we need integrated knowledge; collaborative decision-making; and actions that are ecological, anticipatory, and ethical in respect to nature. Indeed, the AOC program has been a pioneer is use of an ecosystem approach at the watershed level.

If the state of ecosystem health is a barometer of the health of our home, then loss of wetlands and habitat, invasive species, climate change, runoff from agricultural and urban areas, and contaminated sediments and brownfields must become catalysts for further change. We need to continue to promote the use of an ecosystem approach, showcase its value and benefits over the long term, and incorporate it in all educational curricula. We need an enlightenment and ecosystem awakening where people understand that we are part of our ecosystem and what we do to our ecosystem we do to ourselves. Further, our ecosystems cannot be restored solely by regulations and policies but will require broad-based, civic awareness and knowledge that results in deep-seated concern and robust involvement in caring for our home.

The improvements in ecosystem health of the Great Lake AOCs.are clearly a sign of hope, but we are not finished. Much more needs to be done to achieve ecosystem integrity and sustainability. Simply put, if we want to continue to enjoy the Great Lakes and ensure that they are a gift to our children and grandchildren, we must develop a stewardship ethic in which we are trustees charged with protecting them for present and future generations.

These fourteen Great Lakes champions are also a sign of hope. They have shown by example that a new vision is possible, and how it can be achieved through cooperative learning and collaboration. They have shown how to overcome obstacles and realize cleanup and rehabilitation, sustain collective efforts over the long haul, and celebrate successes. They have shown what can be accomplished as generous servant leaders and have demonstrated the importance of developing a new generation of stewards to continue their work. These Great Lakes champions have so inspired me, and I hope that their stories read as a call to action, to care for the place you call home. The memories carried in the waters of the Great Lakes will only continue to grow as future generations discover their magic. May these champions inspire us to preserve and protect our inland seas. Perhaps you will become a Great Lakes champion.

Bibliography

Adler, J. H. 2002. "Fables of the Cuyahoga: Reconstructing a History of Environmental Protection." *Fordham Environmental Law Journal* 14, no. 1: 89–146.

Alexander, J. 2020. "Researchers Declare Fox River Clean-Up Project a Success." 2 First Alert (Green Bay, WI), September 1, 2020. https://www.wbay.com/2020/09/01/researchers-declare-fox-river-clean-up-project-a-success/.

Alexander, J. 2006. *The Muskegon: The Majesty and Tragedy of Michigan's Rarest River.* East Lansing: Michigan State University Press.

American Lung Association. 2019. State of the Air. https://www.lung.org/research/sota.

"America's Sewage System and the Price of Optimism." 1969. *Time Magazine*, August 1, 1969. https://content.time.com/time/magazine/article/0,9171,901182,00.html.

Angelos, L., G. Breidenbach, D. Desotelle, N. French, S. Galarneau, C. Hagen, S. Hanson, and N. Larson. 2013. "St. Louis River Area of Concern

Implementation Framework: Roadmap to Delisting." Duluth, MN: Limno Tech. https://www.pca.state.mn.us/sites/default/files/wq-ws4-02a.pdf.

Aquatic Habitat Toronto. 2013. "Toronto Waterfront Aquatic Habitat Restoration Strategy." Toronto and Region Conservation Authority. https://torontorap. ca/aquatic-habitat-toronto/strategy/.

Arnold, C. L., and C. J. Gibbons. 1996. "Impervious Surface Coverage: The Emergence of a Key Environmental Indicator." *Journal of the American Planning Association* 62, no. 2, 243–258.

Auer, M.T., A. Bradley, and N. A. Auer. 2015. "Growing the Seed for a Great Lakes Commons." *Journal of Great Lakes Research* 41: 667–668.

Bean, C. J., N. Mullett, and J. H. Hartig. 2003. "Watershed Planning and Management: The Rouge River Experience." Ed. J. H. Hartig, *Honoring Our Detroit River: Caring for Our Home*, pp. 185–198. Bloomfield Hills, MI: Cranbrook Institute of Science.

Bentley, S. J., M. Cochran,and J. Hartig. 2019. "From Cleanup of the River Raisin to Revitalization of Monroe, Michigan." Ed. J. H. Hartig, G. Krantzberg, J. C. Austin, and P. McIntyre, *Great Lakes Revival: How Restoring Polluted Waters Leads to Rebirth of Great Lakes Communities*, pp. 47–51. Ann Arbor, MI: International Association for Great Lakes Research.

Bonnell, J. L. 2015. *Reclaiming the Don: An Environmental History of Toronto's Don River Valley*. Toronto: University of Toronto Press.

Boyer, B. 2002. A Polluted River Comes Back. *Clearwaters* 32, no. 2: 10–12.

Boyer, B., and J. McMahon. 1992. "A 'Two Track Strategy' for the Buffalo River Remedial Action Plan." In J. H. Hartig and M. A. Zarull, *Under RAPs: Toward Grassroots Ecological Democracy in the Great Lakes Basin*, pp. 93–120. Ann Arbor: University of Michigan Press.

Buffalo (NY) Courier-Express. 1968. "Oil-Caused River Fire Still Probed." January 27, 1968.

Buffalo Niagara Riverkeeper. 2011. "Addendum to the Stage 2 Remedial Acton Plan for the Buffalo River Area of Concern." https://www.dec.ny.gov/docs/water_pdf/buffsg2rap11.pdf.

Canada House of Commons Debates, 28th parliament, 1st session, vol. 9 (May 29, 1969), p. 9262. https://parl.canadiana.ca.

Careless, J. M. S. 1984. *Toronto to 1918: An Illustrated History*. Toronto: James Lorimer.

Carson, R. L. 1962. *Silent Spring*. Boston: Houghton Mifflin.

Child, M., J. Read, J. Ridal, and M. Twiss. 2018. Symmetry and Solitude: Status and Lessons Learned from Binational Areas of Concern. *Aquatic Ecosystem Health & Management* 21, no. 4: 478–492.

Christie, W. J., M. Becker, J. W. Cowden, and J. R. Vallentyne. 1986. "Managing the Great Lakes Basin as a Home." *Journal of Great Lakes Research* 12, no. 1: 2–17.

City of Detroit. 2019. "Detroit Sustainability Action Agenda." https://detroitmi.gov/sites/detroitmi.localhost/files/2019-06/Detroit-Sustainability-Action-Agenda-Web.pdf.

City of Duluth. 2015a. "Riverside: Small Area Plan." https://duluthmn.gov/media/5742/riverside-small-area-plan_doc_approved.pdf.

City of Duluth. 2015b. "The St. Louis River Corridor: From Vision to Action."

City of Duluth. 2017. "Irving and Fairmount Brownfields Revitalization Plan." https://imagineduluth.com/media/8808/ifbrp-plan-document_final.pdf.

Collingwood Harbour RAP. 1994. "Planning for the Future: A Report to Collingwood Town Council." Coastline Development and Sustainability Subcommittee, Collingwood, Ontario.

Council of Great Lakes Industries and Great Lakes Commission. 2018. "Assessing the Investment: The Economic Impact of the Great Lakes Restoration Initiative; A Case Study of Duluth, Minnesota/Superior, Wisconsin." https://www.glc.org/wp-content/uploads/Duluth-092218.pdf.

Cuyahoga River Community Planning Organization. 2008. "Cuyahoga River Remedial Action Plan." Cleveland, OH.

Cuyahoga River Restoration. 2015. "Stage 2 Delisting Implementation Plan Update and Progress Report." Cleveland, OH. https://cuyahogaaoc.org/wp-content/uploads/2020/03/aoc-draft3_stage2-2015-08-30jg.pdf.

Dahmer, S. C., L. Matos, and A. Morley. 2018. Preface: Restoring Toronto's Waters; Progress toward Delisting the Toronto and Region Area of Concern." *Aquatic Ecosystem Health & Management* 21, no. 3: 229–233.

DeMaria, A., and N. Mullett. 2020. "Dissolved Oxygen Levels in the Rouge River." In J. H. Hartig et al., *Check Up: Assessing Ecosystem Health of the Detroit River and Western Lake Erie*. Windsor, ON: Great Lakes Institute for Environmental Research and the University of Windsor.

Detroiters Working for Environmental Justice. 2017. "Detroit Climate Action Plan."

Detroit Free Press. 1969. "The Burning Rivers," October 12, 1969.

Diebolt, J. 1985. "Bad Rouge Water May Have Killed Novi Man." *Detroit Free Press*, October 5, 1985.

Evans, K., P. Isely, and A. Steinman. 2019. "From Lumber to Foundries to Revitalization: The Muskegon Lake Story." In J. H. Hartig, G. Krantzberg, J. C. Austin, and P. McIntyre, *Great Lakes Revival: How Restoring Polluted Waters Leads to Rebirth of Great Lakes Communities*, pp. 39–46. Ann Arbor, MI: International Association for Great Lakes Research.

Fine, L. M. 2012. "*Workers and the Land in U.S. History: Pointe Mouillee and the Downriver Detroit Working Class in the Twentieth Century*." *Labor History* 53, no. 3: 409–434.

Flats Forward. 2018. "The Flats Neighborhood Guide." Cleveland, OH.

Foose, M., B. Laroy, and J. H. Hartig. 2019. "Restoration of the River Raisin Area of Concern. International Association for Great Lakes Research." *Case Study*

1: A New Day for the River Raisin. National Park Service History Electronic Library. http://npshistory.com/publications/rira/case-study-1.pdf.

Francella, V. 2019. "Cleanup of Toronto Harbour Leads to Waterfront Revitalization." In J. H. Hartig, G. Krantzberg, J. C. Austin, and P. McIntyre, *Great Lakes Revival: How Restoring Polluted Waters Leads to Rebirth of Great Lakes Communities*, pp. 67–77. Ann Arbor: International Association for Great Lakes Research.

Francis, G. R., J. J. Magnuson, H. A. Regier, and D. R. Talhelm. 1979. *Rehabilitating Great Lakes Ecosystems*, technical report 37. Ann Arbor, MI: Great Lakes Fishery Commission.

French, N. T., T. Dekker, and J. H. Hartig. 2018. "Use of Collaborative Funding to Implement the Remedial Action Plan for the St. Louis River Area of Concern, Minnesota, USA." *Aquatic Ecosystem Health & Management* 2, no. 14: 409–420.

Giffels/Black and Veatch. 1980. *Quantity and Quality of Combined Sewer Overflows.* Detroit, MI.

Globe and Mail (Toronto, ON). 1958. "Potemkin Rides Again," July 30.

Gnau, T. B. 1975. "Indian Mounds to Dumping Grounds: A History of the Rouge River." *The Dearborn Historian* 15, no. 2: 57–75.

Goodman, J. 2019. "How the Last Fire on the Cuyahoga River Kick-Started the Clean Water Movement." National League of Cities. https://www.nlc.org/article/2019/06/21/how-the-last-fire-on-the-cuyahoga-river-kick-started-the-clean-water-movement/.

Goodman, J., and M. Gigante. 2019. "Cleveland Flats' Revitalization Linked to Recovery of the Cuyahoga River." In J. H. Hartig, G. Krantzberg, J. C. Austin, and P. McIntyre, *Great Lakes Revival: How Restoring Polluted Waters Leads to Rebirth of Great Lakes Communities*, pp. 17–26. Ann Arbor: International Association for Great Lakes Research.

Great Lakes Commission and the Council of Great Lakes Communities. 2018.
"Assessing the Investment: The Economic Impact of the Great Lakes
Restoration Initiative; a Case Study of Muskegon, Michigan, September
2018." https://www.glc.org/wp-content/uploads/Muskegon-092218.pdf.

Hall, J. D., K. O'Connor, and J. Ranieri. 2006. "Progress towards Delisting a Great
Lakes Area of Concern: The Role of Integrated Research and Monitoring in
the Hamilton Harbour Remedial Action Plan." *Environmental Monitoring
and Assessment* 113: 227–243.

Hall, J. D., and K. O'Connor. 2012. "Remedial Action Plan Case Study: Participatory
Governance Used in Hamilton Harbour." In V. I. Gover and G. Krantzberg,
Great Lakes: Lessons in Participatory Governance, pp. 268–292. New York:
CRC Press.

Hall, J. D., and K. O'Connor. 2016. "Hamilton Harbour Remedial Action Plan
Process: Connecting Science to Management Decisions." *Aquatic Ecosystem
Health & Management* 19: 107–113.

Hamilton Harbour Remedial Action Plan. 2014. "2006–2010 Stakeholder
Investments." Bay Area Restoration Council, Hamilton, ON.

Hamilton Harbour Stakeholder Forum. 2003. "Remedial Action Plan for Hamilton
Harbour: Stage 2 Update." Hamilton, ON.

Hamilton Harbour Stakeholder Group and Remedial Action Plan Technical
Team. 1989. "Remedial Action Plan for Hamilton Harbour: Environmental
Conditions and Problem Definition." Bay Area Restoration Council,
Hamilton, ON.

Hamilton Harbour Stakeholder Group and Remedial Action Plan Technical Team.
1992. "Remedial Action Plan for Hamilton Harbour: Goals, Options, and
Recommendations." Bay Area Restoration Council, Hamilton, ON.

Harris, H. J. 1990. "State of the Bay: A Capsule View." University of Wisconsin–
Green Bay: Institute for Land and Water Studies.

Harris, H. J. 1994. "The State of the Bay: A Watershed Perspective." University of Wisconsin–Green Bay: Institute for Land and Water Studies.

Harris, H. J., D. R. Talhelm, J. J. Magnuson, and A. Forbe. 1982. "Green Bay in the Future: A Rehabilitative Prospective," technical report 38. Ann Arbor, MI: Great Lakes Fishery Commission.

Harris, H. J., R. B. Wenger, P. E. Sager, and J. V. Klump. 2018. "The Green Bay Saga: Environmental Change, Scientific Investigation, and Watershed Management." *Journal of Great Lakes Research* 44, no. 5: 829–836.

Harris, V. A., 1998. "Waterfowl Use of Lower Green Bay before (1977–78) and after (1994–97) Zebra Mussel Invasion." Master's thesis, University of Wisconsin–Green Bay.

Hartig, J. H. 2010. *Burning Rivers: Revival of Four Urban-Industrial Rivers That Caught on Fire.* Burlington, ON: Aquatic Ecosystem Health and Management Society.

Hartig, J. H. 2011. "Jack Vallentyne's Ecosystemic Legacy." *Aquatic Ecosystem Health & Management* 14, no. 2: 147–148.

Hartig, J. H. 2014. *Bringing Conservation to Cities: Lessons from Building the Detroit River International Wildlife Refuge.* Burlington, ON: Aquatic Ecosystem Health and Management Society.

Hartig, J. H., S. F. Francoeur, J. J. H. Ciborowski, J. E. Gannon, C. Sanders, P. Galvao-Ferreira, C. R. Knauss, G. Gell, and K. Berk, eds. 2020. *Checkup: Assessing Ecosystem Health of the Detroit River and Western Lake Erie.* Windsor, ON: Great Lakes Institute for Environmental Research and the University of Windsor

Hartig, J. H., G. Krantzberg, and P. Alsip. 2020. "Thirty-Five Years of Restoring Great Lakes Areas of Concern: Gradual Progress, Hopeful Future." *Journal of Great Lakes Research* 46, no. 3: 429–442.

Hartig, J. H., G. Krantzberg, J. C. Austin, and P. McIntyre. 2019. *Great Lakes Revival:*

How Restoring Polluted Waters Leads to Rebirth of Great Lakes Communities. Ann Arbor, MI: International Association for Great Lakes Research.

Hartig, J. H., and R. L. Thomas. 1988. "Development of Plans to Restore Degraded Areas in the Great Lakes." *Environmental Management* 12: 327–347.

Hartig, J. H., and J. R. Vallentyne. 1989. Use of an Ecosystem Approach to Restore Degraded Areas of the Great Lakes. *AMBIO* 18, no. 8: 423–428.

Hatcher, H. 1945. *Lake Erie.* New York: Bobbs Merrill.

Helal, L. 2014. Duluth Voted *Outside* Magazine's Best Outdoors Town. https://blogs.mprnews.org/statewide/2014/06/duluth-voted-outside-magazines-best-outdoors-town/.

International Joint Commission. 1967. "Summary Report on Pollution of the Niagara River."

International Joint Commission's Great Lakes Water Quality Board. 1985. "Report on Great Lakes Water Quality."

Institute for Research and Innovation in Sustainability and Schulich School of Business, York University. 2006. *Benefits Assessment: Randle Reef Sediment Remediation.* Environment Canada. https://www.documentcloud.org/documents/3227973-Benefits-Assessment-Randle-Reef-Sediment.html.

Isely, P., E. S. Isely, C. Hause, and A. D. Steinman. 2018. "A Socioeconomic Analysis of Habitat Restoration in the Muskegon Lake Area of Concern." *Journal of Great Lakes Research* 44: 330–339.

Jackson, G. 1975. "A Biological Investigation of the Rouge River, Wayne and Oakland Counties, May 17 to October 19, 1973." Lansing, MI: Michigan Department of Natural Resources, Bureau of Water Management.

Jedlicka, J., and J. H. Hartig. 2019. "Buffalo River Cleanup Improves Ecological Health, Economy, and Public Spaces." In J. H. Hartig, G. Krantzberg, J. C. Austin, and P. McIntyre, *Great Lakes Revival: How Restoring Polluted Waters Leads to Rebirth of Great Lakes Communities*, pp. 3–10. Ann Arbor:

International Association for Great Lakes Research.

Johnson, B. 2017. "Endi Development Opens Its Doors on London Road." *Duluth News Tribune*, January 26, 2017. http://www.duluthnewstribune.com/business/4206607-endi-development-opens-its-doors-london-road.

Kidd, J. 2015. "Within Reach: Toronto and Region Remedial Action Plan Progress Report." Toronto Region Conservation Authority.

Klump, J. V., J. Bratton, K. Fermanich, P. Forsythe, H. J. Harris, R. W. Howe, J. L. Kaster. 2018. "Green Bay, Lake Michigan: A Proving Ground for Great Lakes Restoration." Journal of great Lakes Research 44, no. 5: 825–828.

Kraft, C. E. 1984. "Origins of the French and English Names for the Bay of Green Bay, Wisconsin." *Voyageur* 1, no. 1: 9–14.

Krantzberg, G. 2006. "Sustaining the Gains Made in Ecological Restoration: Case Study Collingwood Harbour, Ontario." *Environment, Development and Sustainability* 8, no. 3: 413–424.

Krantzberg, G. 2020. "Examining Governance Principles That Enable Rap Implementation and Sustainable Outcomes." In J. H. Hartig and M. Munawar, *Ecosystem-Based Management of Laurentian Great Lakes Areas of Concern: Three Decades of U.S.-Canadian Cleanup and Recovery*. Burlington, ON: Aquatic Ecosystem Health and Management Society.

Krantzberg, G., and N. Farrer. 2019. "From Shipbuilding Center to Great Lakes Pollution Hot Spot to Waterfront Revitalization: The Collingwood Harbour Story." In J. H. Hartig, G. Krantzberg, J. C. Austin, and P. McIntyre, *Great Lakes Revival: How Restoring Polluted Waters Leads to Rebirth of Great Lakes Communities*, pp. 11–16. Ann Arbor: International Association for Great Lakes Research.

Krantzberg, G., and M. Rich. 2018. "Life after Delisting: The Collingwood Harbour Story." *Ecosystem Health & Management* 21, no. 4: 378–386.

La Violette, N. 1993. "A Comparison of Great Lakes Remedial Action Plans and St.

Lawrence River Restoration Plans." *Journal of Great Lakes Research* 19, no. 2: 389–399.

Lorenz, K. 1980. *King Solomon's Ring: New Light on Animal Ways.* New York: Time-Life.

Malnor, B., and C. L. Malnor. 2009. *Earth Heroes: Champions of the Wilderness.* Nevada City, CA: Dawn.

Marsh, J., and B. Marsh. 2015. *Pte. Mouillee Shooting Club, History & Decoys, Nate Quillin, Punt Guns, Spring Hunting, Live Pigeon Shooting & Live Decoys.* Monroe, MI: Marshduck.

Martenies, S. E., C. W. Milando, G. O. Williams, and S. A. Batterman. 2017. "Disease and Health Inequalities Attributable to Air Pollutant Exposure in Detroit, Michigan." *International Journal of Environmental Research and Public Health* 14: 1243–1266.

Martin Associates. 2018. "Economic Impacts of the Port of Duluth-Superior." https://duluthport.com/wp-content/uploads/2020/11/Duluth-Superior-Port-Econ-dnr

Michigan Department of Environmental Quality. 2011. "Stage 2 Remedial Action Plan: Muskegon Lake Area of Concern." https://muskegonlake.org/wp-content/uploads/2020/02/muskegon-lake-stage-ii-remedial-action-plan-2011.pdf.

Michigan Department of Natural Resources. 1987. *Remedial Action Plan for Muskegon Lake Area of Concern.* Lansing, MI: Surface Water Quality Division, Great Lakes and Environmental Assessment Section. https://muskegonlake.org/wp-content/uploads/2020/02/1987_Muskegon-Lake_RAP.pdf.

Minnesota Pollution Control Agency and Wisconsin Department of Natural Resources. 1992. "Stage I St. Louis River System Remedial Action Plan."

Minnesota Pollution Control Agency and Wisconsin Department of Natural Resources. 1995. "Stage II St. Louis River System Remedial Action Plan."

Murray, J. 1994. "Rouge River Watershed Management: Implementing a Remedial Action Plan (RAP)." *Proceedings of the Water Environment Federation 67th Annual Conference & Exposition, Chicago, Illinois, U.S.A., October 15–19, 1994.* Alexandria, VA: Water Environment Federation.

Muskegon Lake Watershed Partnership. 2018. "Muskegon Lake Ecosystem Action Plan." https://muskegonlake.org/documents/4-2019_Action-Plan-Muskegon.pdf.

New York State Department of Environmental Conservation. 1989. *Buffalo River Remedial Action Plan.* https://www.epa.gov/sites/default/files/2015-08/documents/buffalorap198911.pdf.

O'Connor, K., and C. McGlaughlin. 2019. "Economic Benefits of Remediating Contaminated Sediments at Hamilton Harbour's Randle Reef." In J. H. Hartig, G. Krantzberg, J. C. Austin, and P. McIntyre, *Great Lakes Revival: How Restoring Polluted Waters Leads to Rebirth of Great Lakes Communities*, pp. 33–38. Ann Arbor: International Association for Great Lakes Research.

Ontario Ministry of the Environment. 1989. "Metro Toronto Stage 1 Remedial Action Plan: Environmental Conditions and Problem Definition." Toronto, ON.

Ontario Ministry of the Environment. 1994. "Metro Toronto Stage 2 Remedial Action Plan." Toronto, ON.

Patrella, S., T. J. Macguire, S. Thompson. 2020. "Benthic Macroinvertebrates in the Rouge River Watershed." In J. H. Hartig et al., *Check Up: Assessing Ecosystem Health of the Detroit River and Western Lake Erie.* Windsor, ON: Great Lakes Institute for Environmental Research and the University of Windsor.

Qualls, T., H. J. Harris, and V. Harris. 2013. *State of the Bay: The Condition of the Bay of Green Bay and Lake Michigan.* Green Bay: University of Wisconsin Sea Grant Institute.

Rayno, A. 2017. "How Duluth Became the Outdoor Capital of the Midwest." *Star*

Tribune (Duluth, MN), April 30, 2017. http://www.startribune.com/how-duluth-became-the-outdoor-capital-of-the-midwest/420664303/.

Renalls, C. 2016. "Pier B Resort in Duluth Aims to Open by Grandma's Marathon." *Duluth News Tribune*, May 15, 2016. http://www.duluthnewstribune.com/business/4033223-pier-b-resort-duluth-aims-open-grandmas-marathon.

Ridgway, J. 2010. "The Rouge River National Wet Weather Demonstration Project: Eighteen Years of Documented Success." *Proceedings of the Water Environment Federation: Cities of the Future/Urban River Restoration Conference* 2: 337–354. https://doi-org.proxy2.cl.msu.edu/10.2175/193864710798285642.

Ridgway, J., K. Cave, A. DeMaria, J. O'Meara, and J. H. Hartig. 2018. "The Rouge River Area of Concern: A Multi-Year, Multi-Level Successful Approach to Restoration of Impaired Beneficial Uses." *Aquatic Ecosystem Health & Management* 21, no. 4: 398–408.

Ross, T. 2014. "The Town That Cycling Saved." *Bicycling*, November 24, 2014. https://www.bicycling.com/news/a20038587/don-ness-interview/.

Sanders, B. I. 2012. "A Retrospective on Stanley Spisiak: A Man with a Mission." U.S. Army, October 25, 2012. https://www.army.mil/article/89945/a_retrospective_on_stanley_spisiak_a_man_with_a_mission.

Schrameck, R., M. Fields, and M. Synk. 1992. "Restoring the Rouge." In J. H. Hartig and M. A. Zarull, *Under RAPs: Toward Grassroots Ecological Democracy in the Great Lakes Basin*, pp. 73–91. Ann Arbor: University of Michigan Press.

Senge, P. M. 1990. *The Fifth Discipline: The Art and Practice of a Learning Organization*. New York: Currency Doubleday.

Sherman, K. 2019. "Economic Benefits Helped Provide the Rationale for Cleaning Up Severn Sound." In J. H. Hartig, G. Krantzberg, J. C. Austin, and P. McIntyre, *Great Lakes Revival: How Restoring Polluted Waters Leads to Rebirth of Great Lakes Communities*, pp. 53–59. Ann Arbor: International Association for

Great Lakes Research.

Sherman, K. 2017. "Economic Benefits Help Drive Cleanup of Severn Sound." International Association for Great Lakes Research. https://iaglr.org/aocdocs/CS3-SevernSound.pdf.

Sherman, K. R., R. Whittam, and J. Cayley, 2018. "Severn Sound Remedial Action Plan: The Friendly Little Monster." *Aquatic Ecosystem Health & Management* 21, no. 4, 387–397.

Shine, K. N. 2015. *City of Hope.* Lewisburg, PA: Bucknell University.

Snodgrass, W. J., R. Dewey, M. D'Andrea, R. Bishop, J. Lei. 2018. "Forecasting Receiving Water Response to Alternative Control Levels for Combined Sewer Overflows Discharging to Toronto's Inner Harbour." *Aquatic Ecosystem Health & Management* 21, no. 3: 245–254.

Soderstrom, M. 2006. *Green City: People, Nature & Urban Places.* Montreal: Vehicule Press.

Steinman, A. D., M. Ogdahl, R. Rediske, C. R. Ruetz, B. A. Biddanda, and L. Nemeth. 2008. "Current Status and Trends in Muskegon Lake, Michigan." *Journal of Great Lakes Research* 34: 169–188.

Tejani, R., and T. Muir. 2004. "Economic Benefits of the Severn Sound Remedial Action Plan (1990–2002): Cost Savings and Environmental Benefits." Burlington, ON: Environment Canada Great Lakes Sustainability Fund. https://www.severnsound.ca/Shared%20Documents/Reports/SS_ECONOMICS_STUDY_Tijani_Muir_2004.pdf

Thomas, S. 2000. "The Cuyahoga Revisited." *The Freeman* (May 2000): 37–38. https://fee.org/articles/the-cuyahoga-revisited/.

Thorp, J. H., G. A. Lamberti, and A. F. Casper. 2005. *St. Lawrence River.* In A. Benke and C. Cushing, *Rivers of North America*, pp. 983–1028. Cambridge, MA: Academic Press.

U.S. Army Corps of Engineers. 2015. "Port Stats and Facts at a Glance." https://

duluthport.com/about-us/port-statistics/.

U.S. Census Bureau. 2017. "2012–2016 American Community Survey 5-Year Estimates for Duluth, MN." Washington, DC.

U.S. Department of the Interior. 1968. Lake Erie Report: A Plan for Pollution Control. Washington, DC: Federal Water Pollution Control Administration. https://nepis.epa.gov/.

U.S. Environmental Protection Agency. 2012. "Brownfields Area–Wide Planning Program," Fact Sheet, EPA-560-F-12-182. https://www.epa.gov/sites/production/files/2015-09/documents/awp-factsheet-july-2012_0.pdf.

U.S. Environmental Protection Agency. 2017. "What Is Particulate Matter?" Region 1: EPA New England. https://www3.epa.gov/region1/eco/uep/particulatematter.html.

U.S.–U.K. 2016. The Boundary Waters Treaty. January 11, 1909. https://www.ijc.org/sites/default/files/2018-07/Boundary%20Water-ENGFR.pdf.

urbanMetrics. 2013. *Economic Impact Analysis (2001–2013): Toronto, Ontario.* Toronto: Waterfront Toronto. https://waterfrontoronto.ca.

Vallentyne, J. R., and A. M. Beeton. 1986. "The Ecosystem Approach to Managing Human Uses and Abuses of Natural Resources in the Great Lakes Basin." *Environmental Conservation* 15, no. 1: 58–62.

Vaughan, R. D., and G. L. Harlow. 1965. *Report on Pollution of the Detroit River, Michigan Waters of Lake Erie, and Their Tributaries.* Washington, DC: U.S. Department of Health, Education, Welfare, and Public Health.

Waterfront Toronto, 2017. "Corporate Social Responsibility and Sustainability Report: 2015–2017." https://www.waterfrontoronto.ca/.

West Michigan Shoreline Regional Development Commission. 2016. Muskegon Lake Vision 2020. https://wmsrdc.org/?s=Muskegon+Lake+2020.

Williams, G. O. 1997. "Mercury Pollution Prevention in Healthcare: A Prescription for Success." Ann Arbor, MI: National Wildlife Federation. https://archive.

epa.gov/greatlakes/p2/web/pdf/p2healthcarerpt.pdf.

Williams, G. O. 2020. "Air Pollution and Environmental Justice in Southwest
Detroit, Michigan." In J. H. Hartig et al., *Check Up: Assessing Ecosystem Health
of the Detroit River and Western Lake Erie*. Windsor, ON: Great Lakes Institute
for Environmental Research and the University of Windsor.

Williams, K., J. Hoffman, and N. T. French. 2019. "From Remediation to
Restoration and Revitalization: The St. Louis River Story." In J. H. Hartig, G.
Krantzberg, J. C. Austin, and P. McIntyre, *Great Lakes Revival: How Restoring
Polluted Waters Leads to Rebirth of Great Lakes Communities*, pp. 61–66. Ann
Arbor: International Association for Great Lakes Research.

Williams, K. C. 2015. "Relationships, Knowledge, and Resilience: A Comparative
Case Study of Stakeholder Participation in Great Lakes Areas of Concern."
PhD diss., University of Wisconsin–Milwaukee. Theses and Dissertations
(936). https://dc.uwm.edu/etd/936.

Williams, K. C., D. W. Bolgrien, J. C. Hoffman, T. R. Angradi, J. Carlson, R. Clarke, A.
Fulton, M. MacGregor, H. Timm-Bijold, A. Trebitz, and S. Witherspoon. 2018.
"How the Community Value of Ecosystem Goods and Services Empowers
Communities to Impact the Outcomes of Remediation, Restoration,
and Revitalization Projects," EPA/600/R-17/292. Washington, DC: U.S.
Environmental Protection Agency.

Index

Wolf River, 38

Woman in Leadership honor, 193

World Biosphere Reserve, 207

WREN. *See* West Michigan Region
 Environmental Network

Wye Marsh Wildlife Center, 74, 76

Zero Discharge campaigns, 51, 100, 104

Zug Island, 116, *117*, 121